FLYING HIGH

C0-GCK-849

THE WORLD

FLYING HIGH

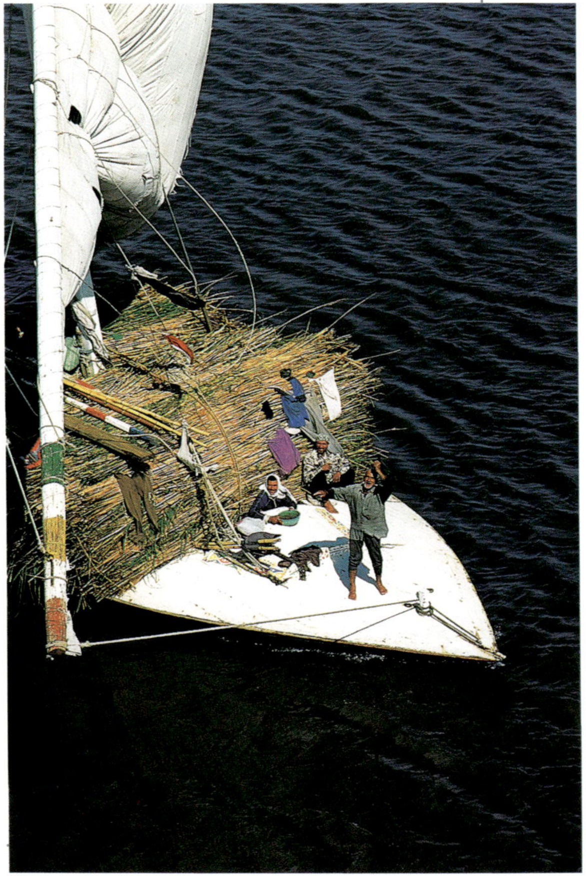

WHITE STAR
PUBLISHERS

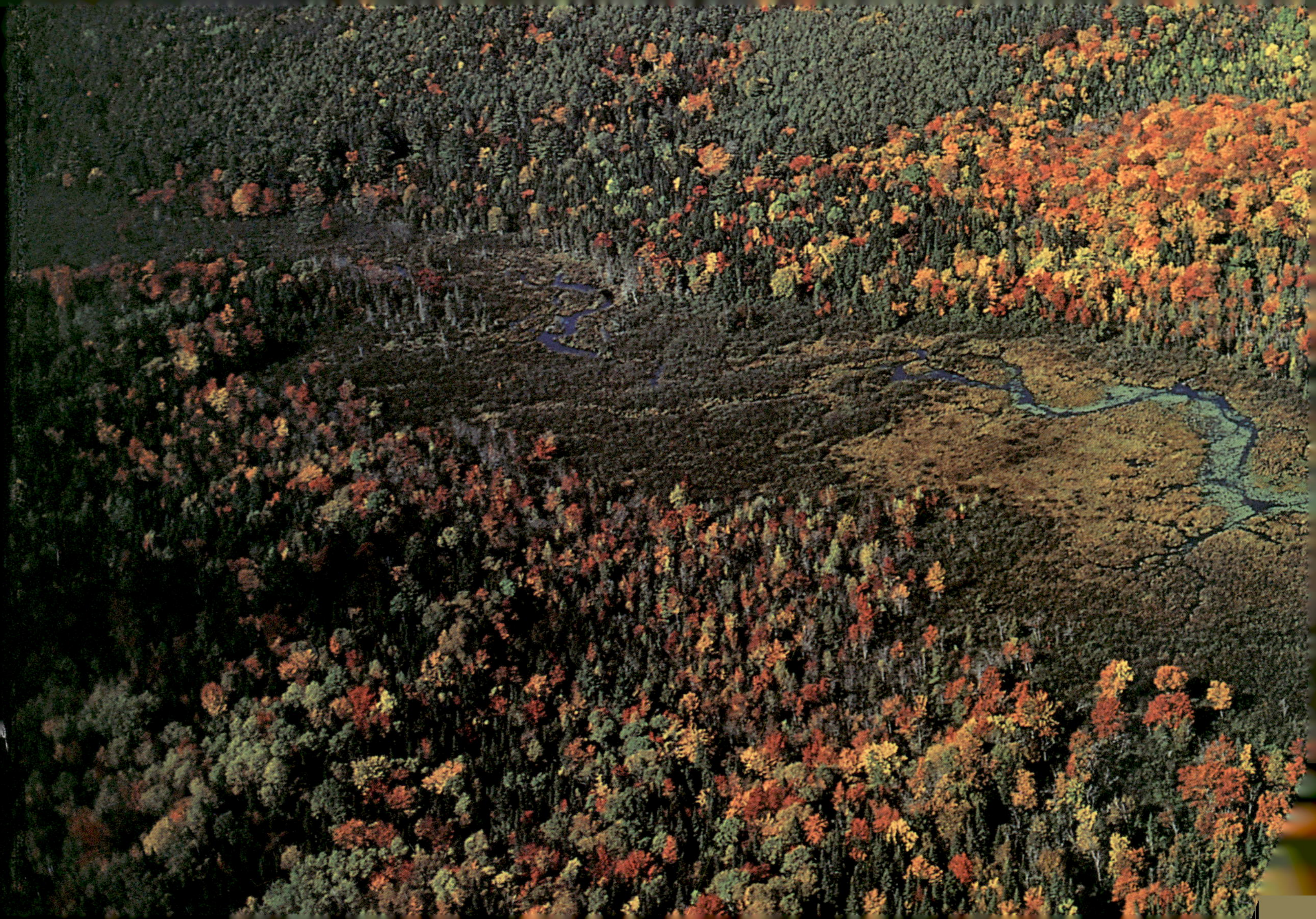

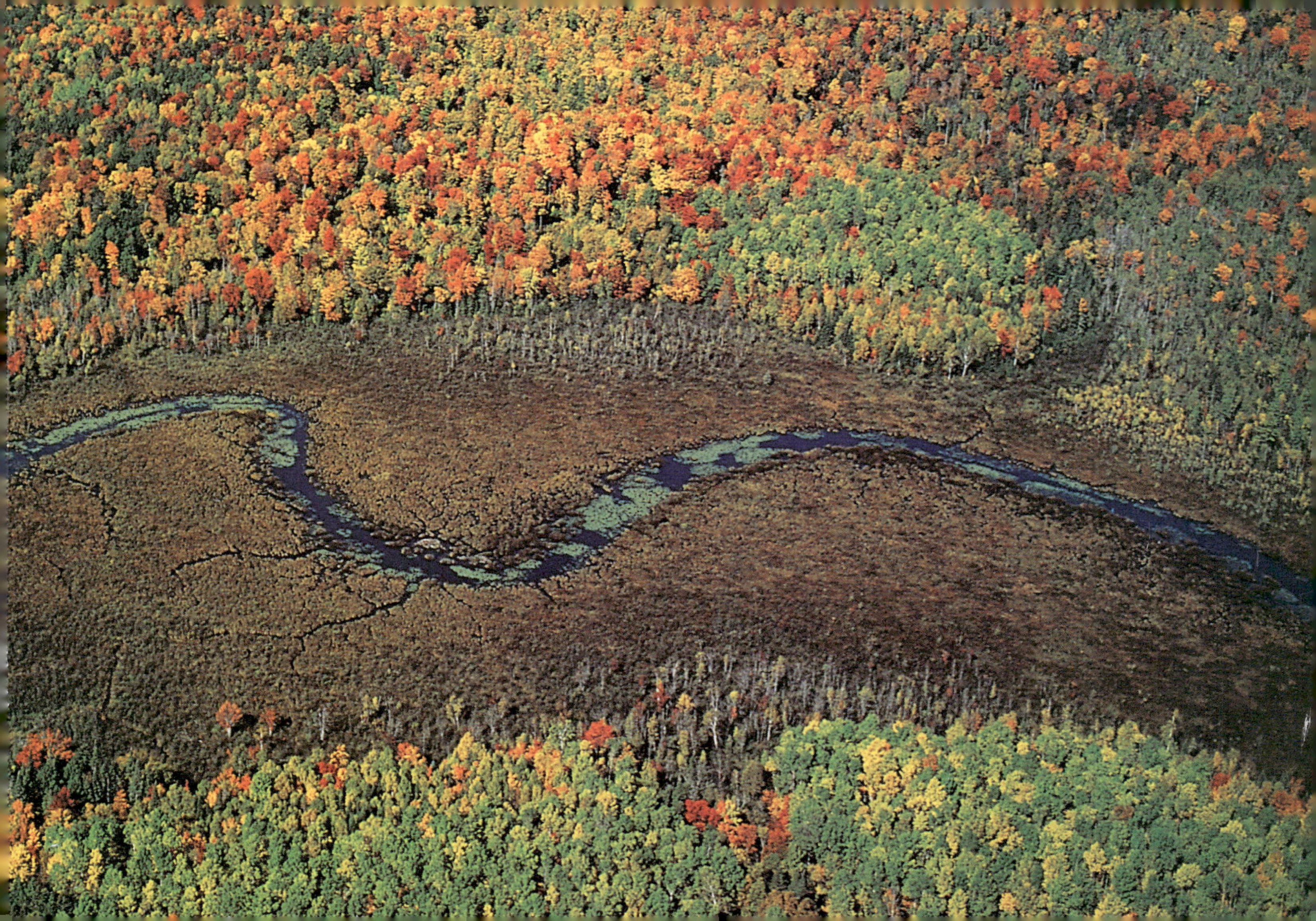

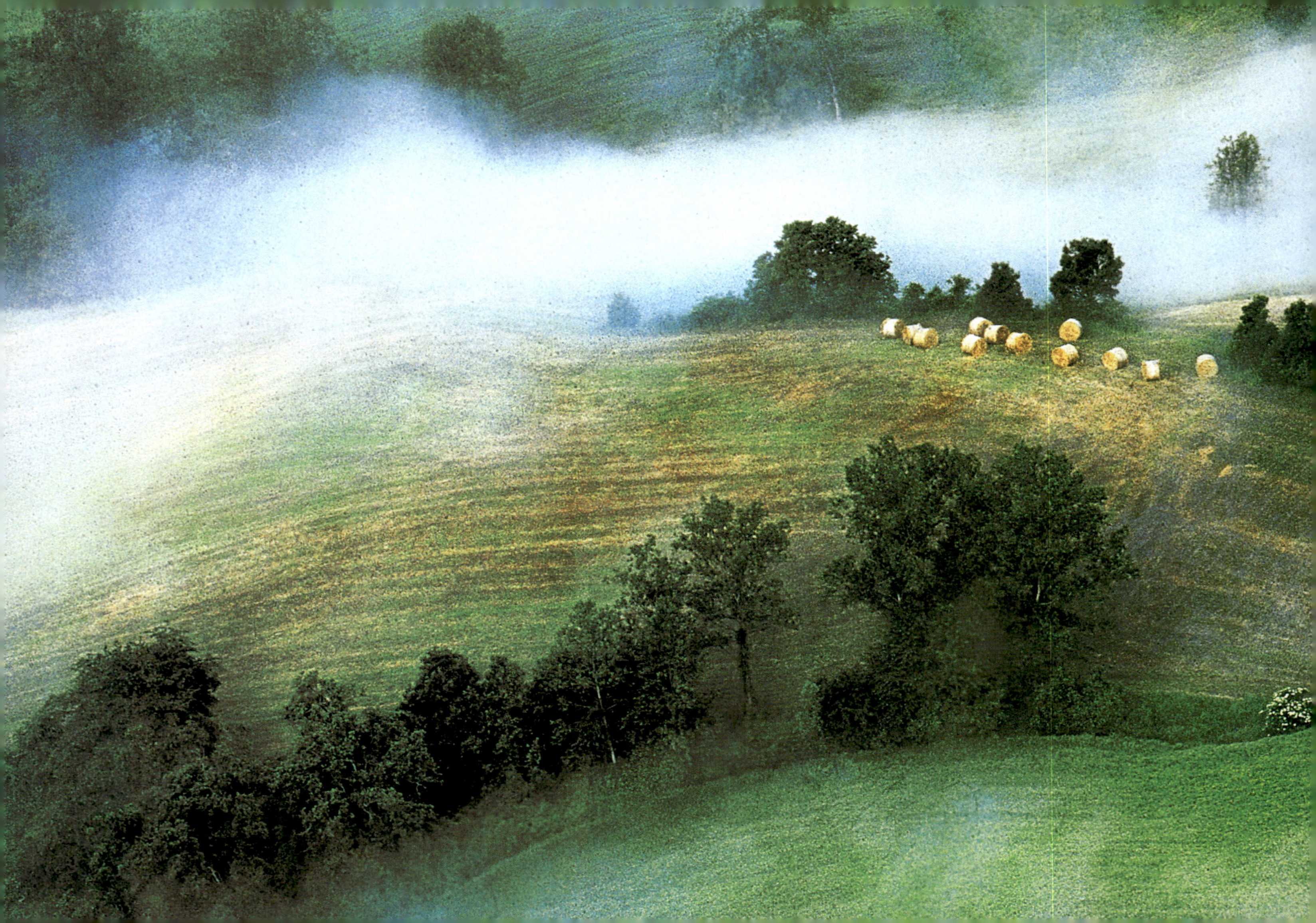

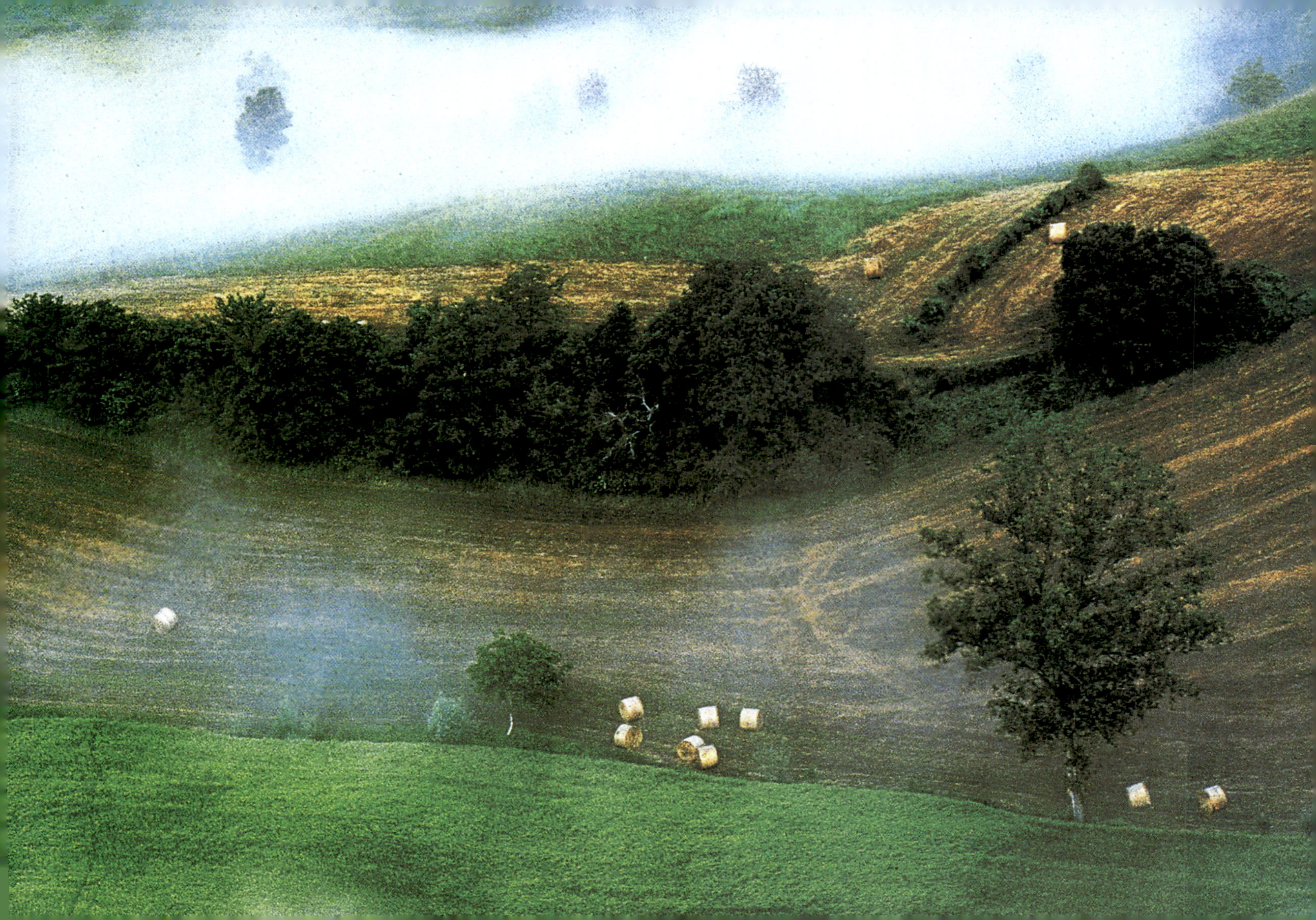

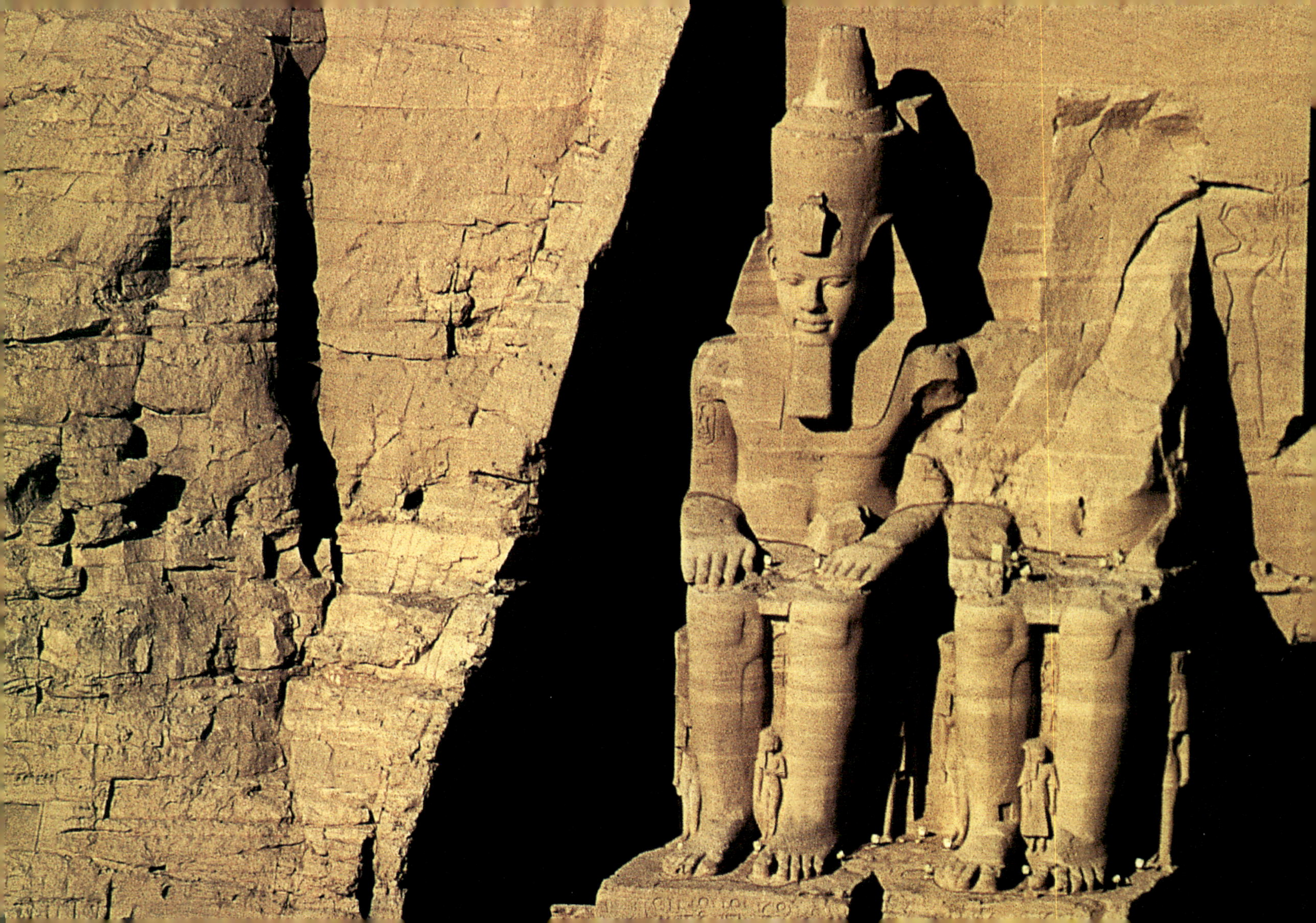

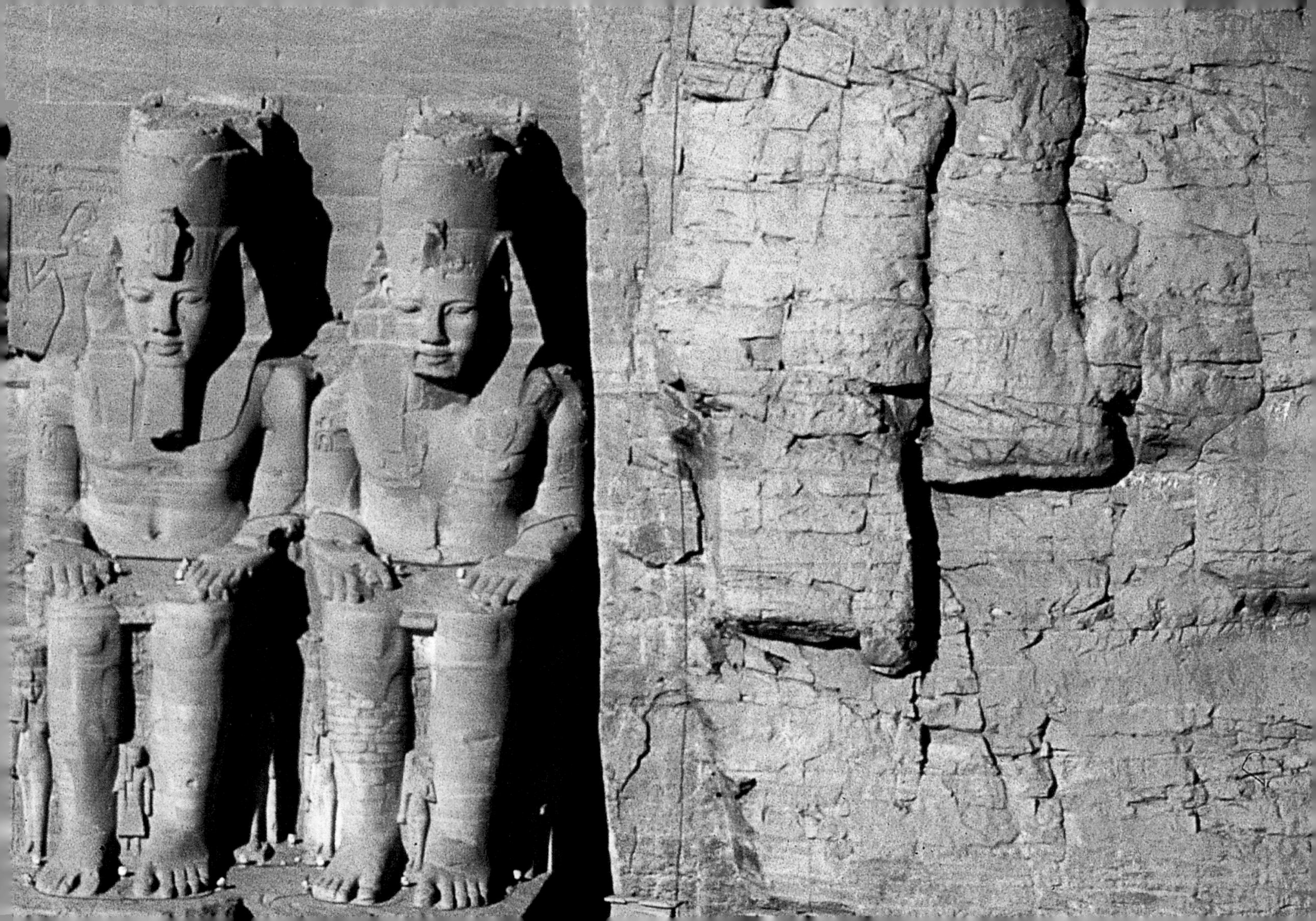

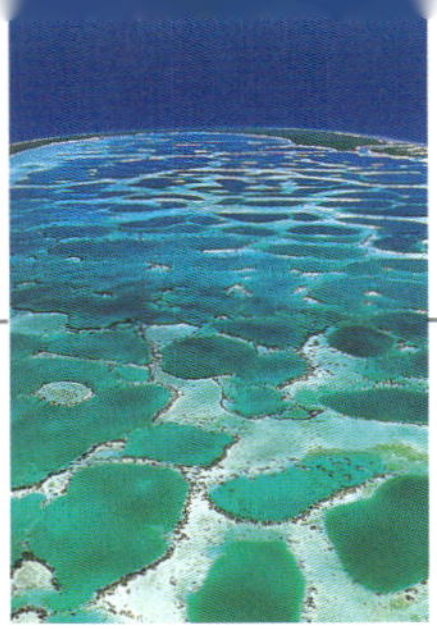

TEXT

Enrico Lavagno

PROJECT EDITOR

Valeria Manferto De Fabianis

EDITORIAL COORDINATION

Giada Francia
Laura Accomazzo
Marcello Libra

GRAPHIC DESIGN

Paola Piacco

© 2005 WHITE STAR S.P.A.
Via Candido Sassone, 22-24
13100 Vercelli - Italy
WWW.WHITESTAR.IT

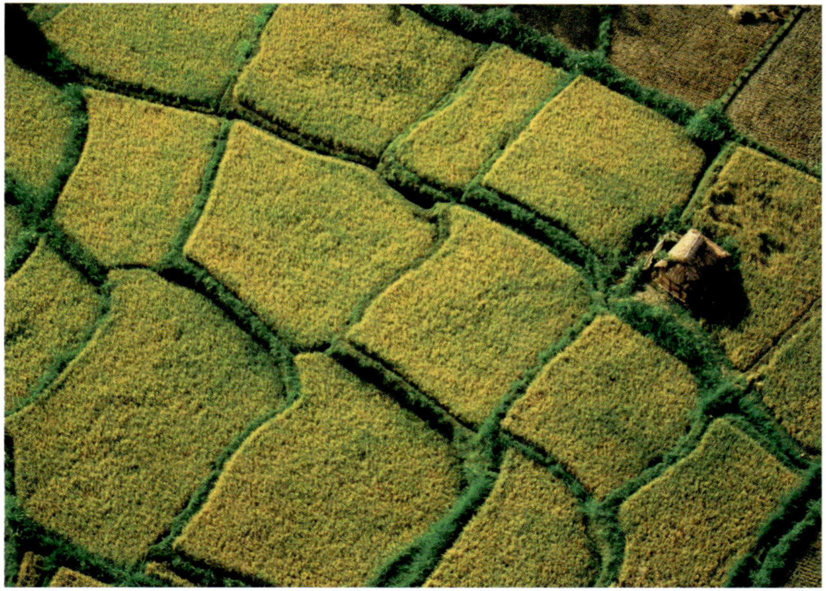

TRANSLATION: AMY CHRISTINE EZRIN

All rights reserved. No part of this publication may be reproduced, stored in a retrieval system or transmitted in any form or by any means, electronic, mechanical, photocopying, recording or otherwise, without written permission from the publisher. Flying High® and White Star Publishers® are registered trademarks property of Edizioni White Star.

ISBN 88-544-0077-7

REPRINTS: 1 2 3 4 5 6 09 08 07 06 05

Printed in China

1
A raft on Lake Manzala, in Egypt.

2-3
The meanders of a river form a huge expanse of wetlands in Franklin County, in Maine (USA).

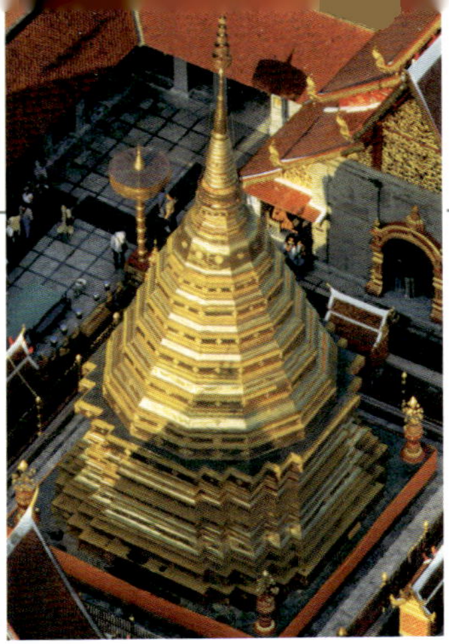

FLYING HIGH THE WORLD

Contents

4-5
A bucolic view of the Tuscan countryside in Italy.

6-7
The colossi at the entrance to the temple of Ramesses II at Abu Simbel, in Egypt.

8
The reticular bay of Mataiva in Polynesia.

9
Fields planted with rice in Bali, in Indonesia.

10
A dome in the temple of Wat Phra That Doi Suthep, in Chiang Mai in Thailand.

11
San Marco Square, the symbol of Venice, Italy.

12-13
Chiaroscuro designs on the Sahara dunes, in Libyan territory.

14-15
Cima Tosa, part of the Dolomite chain, in Italy.

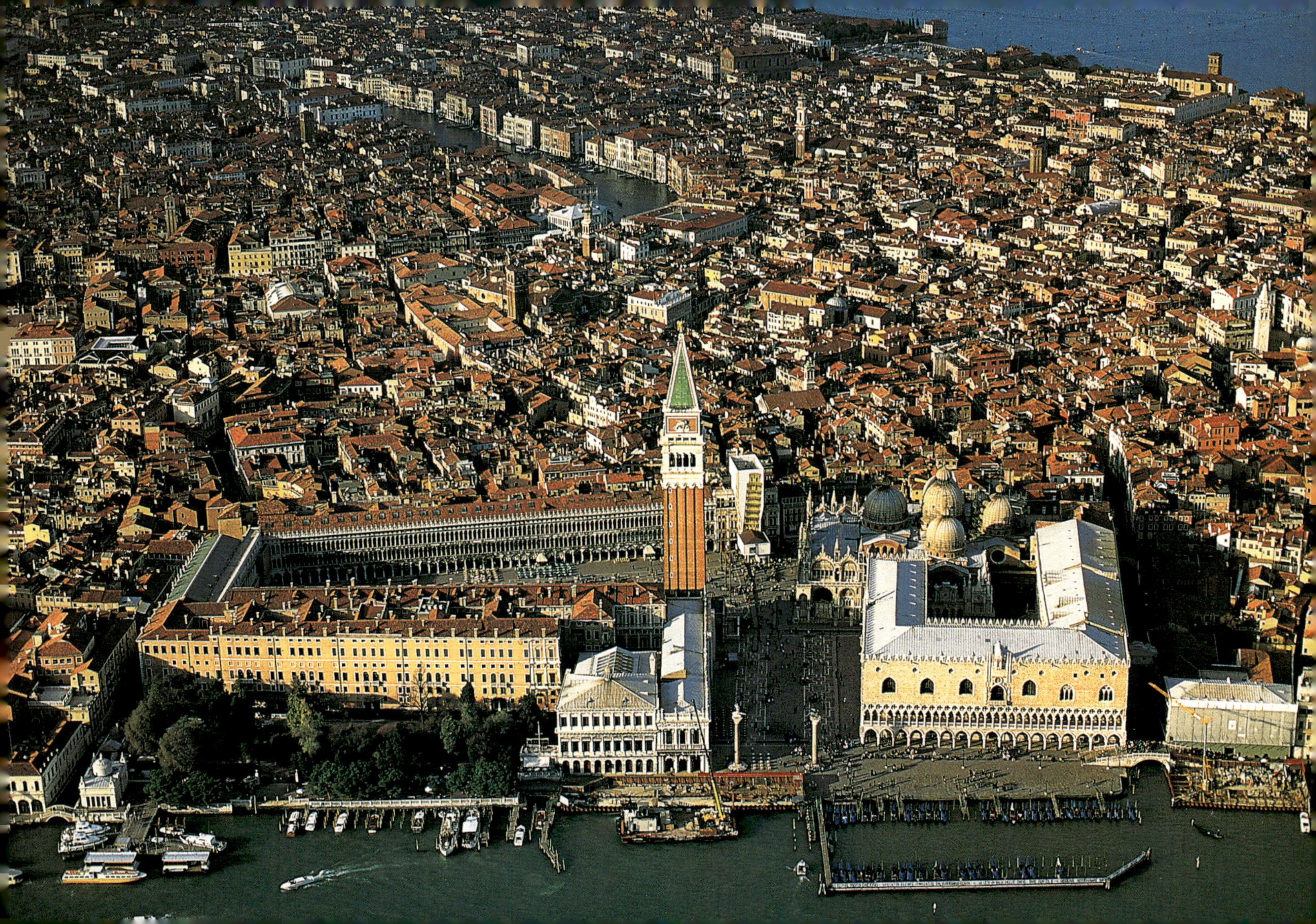

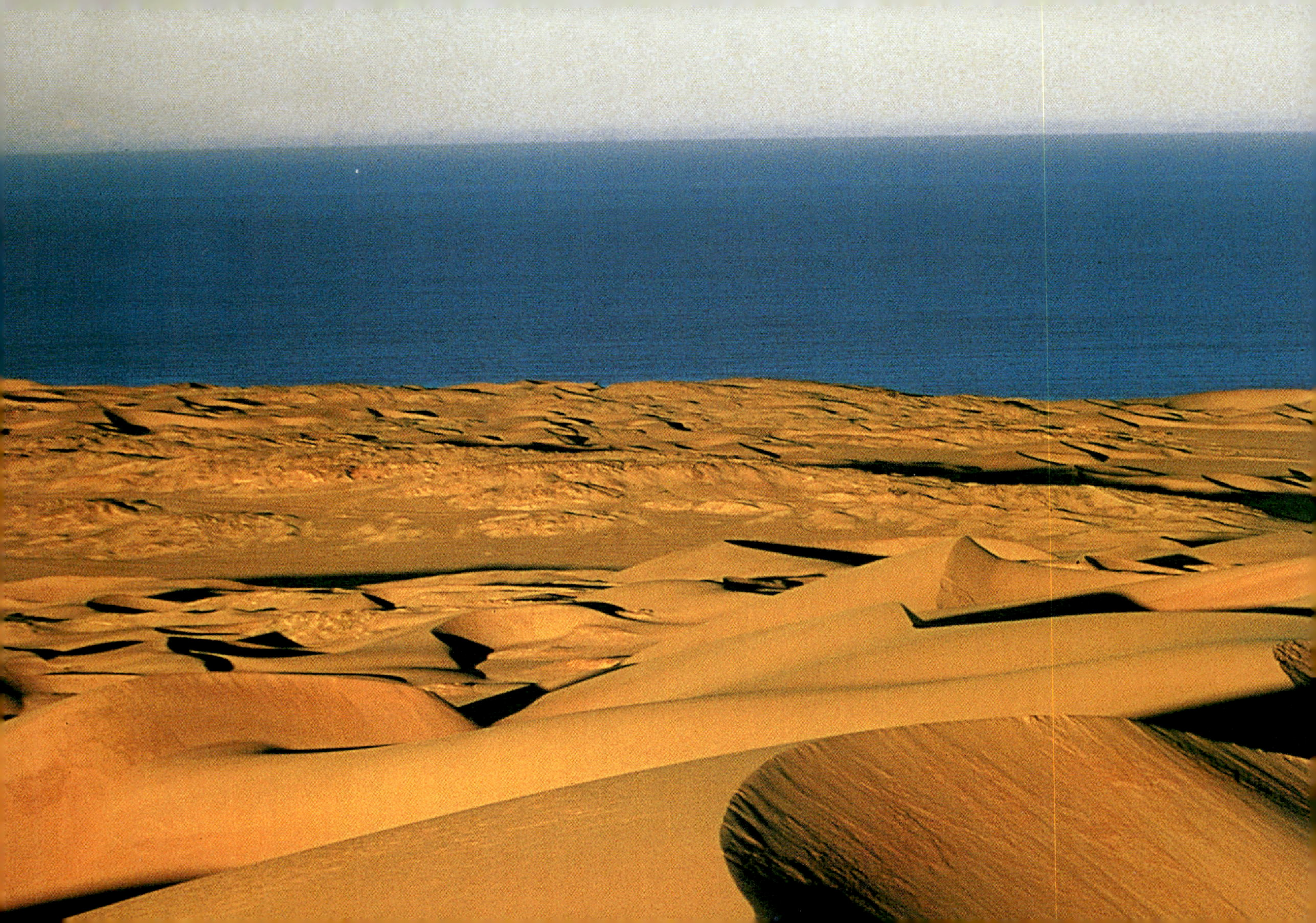

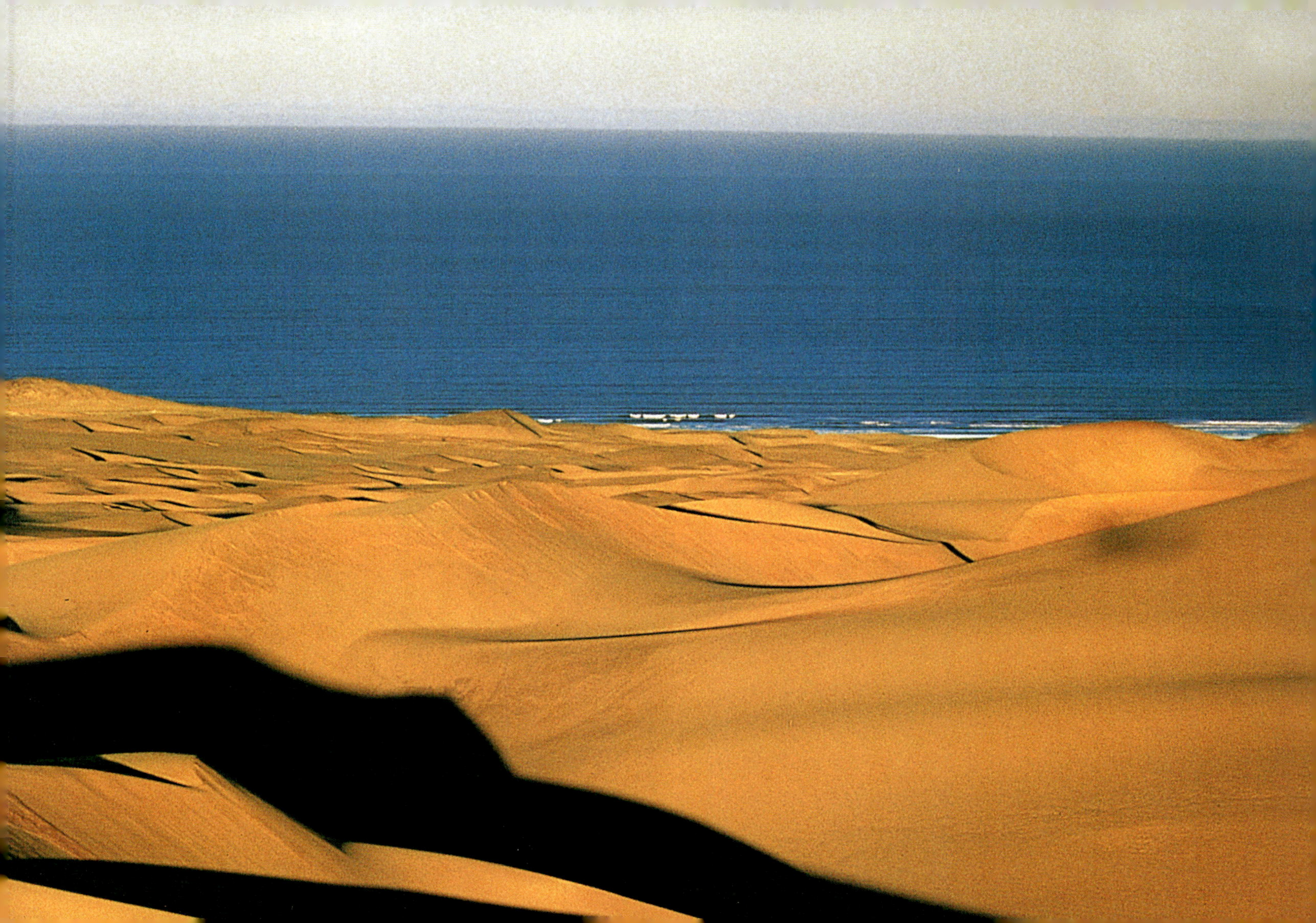

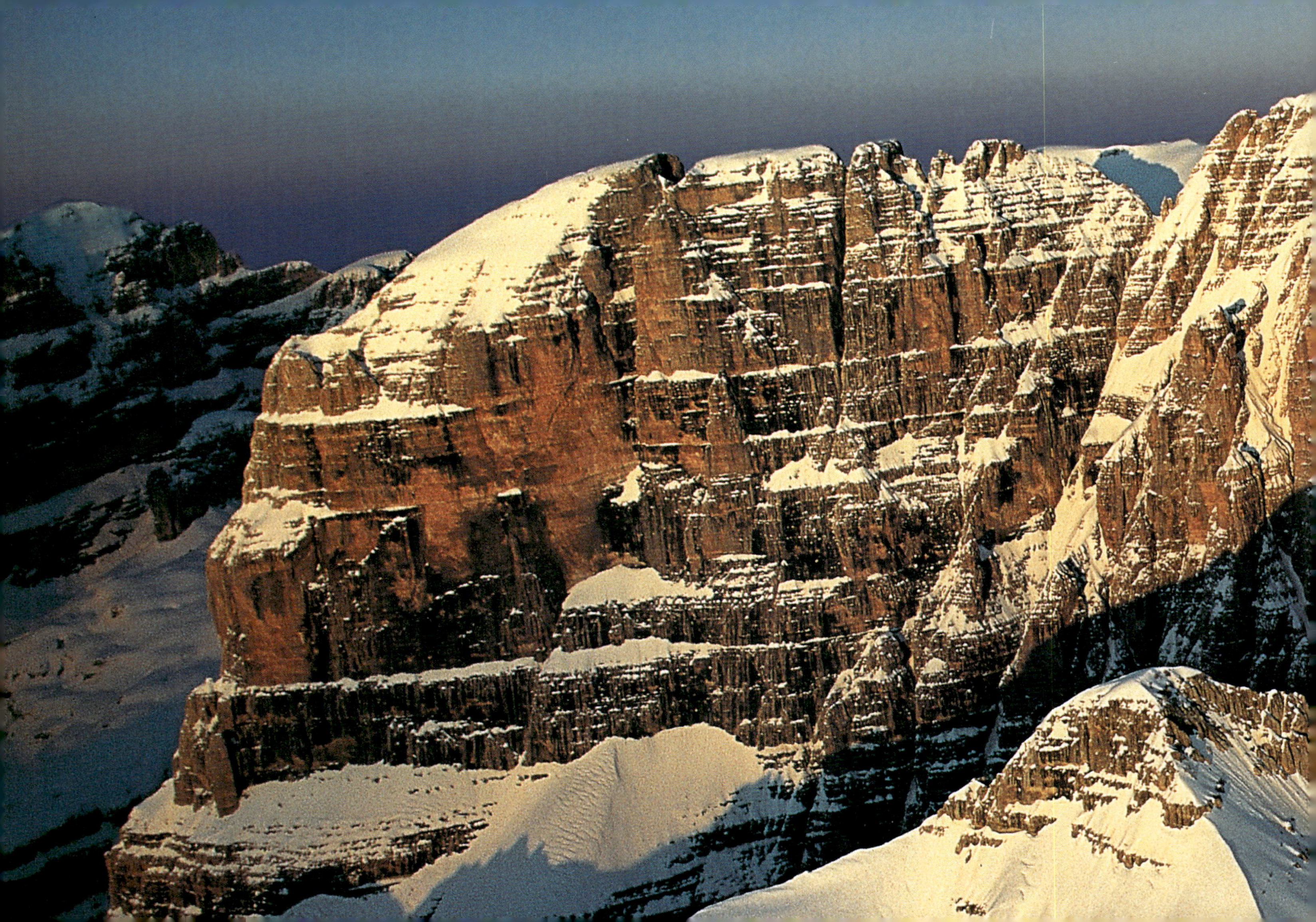

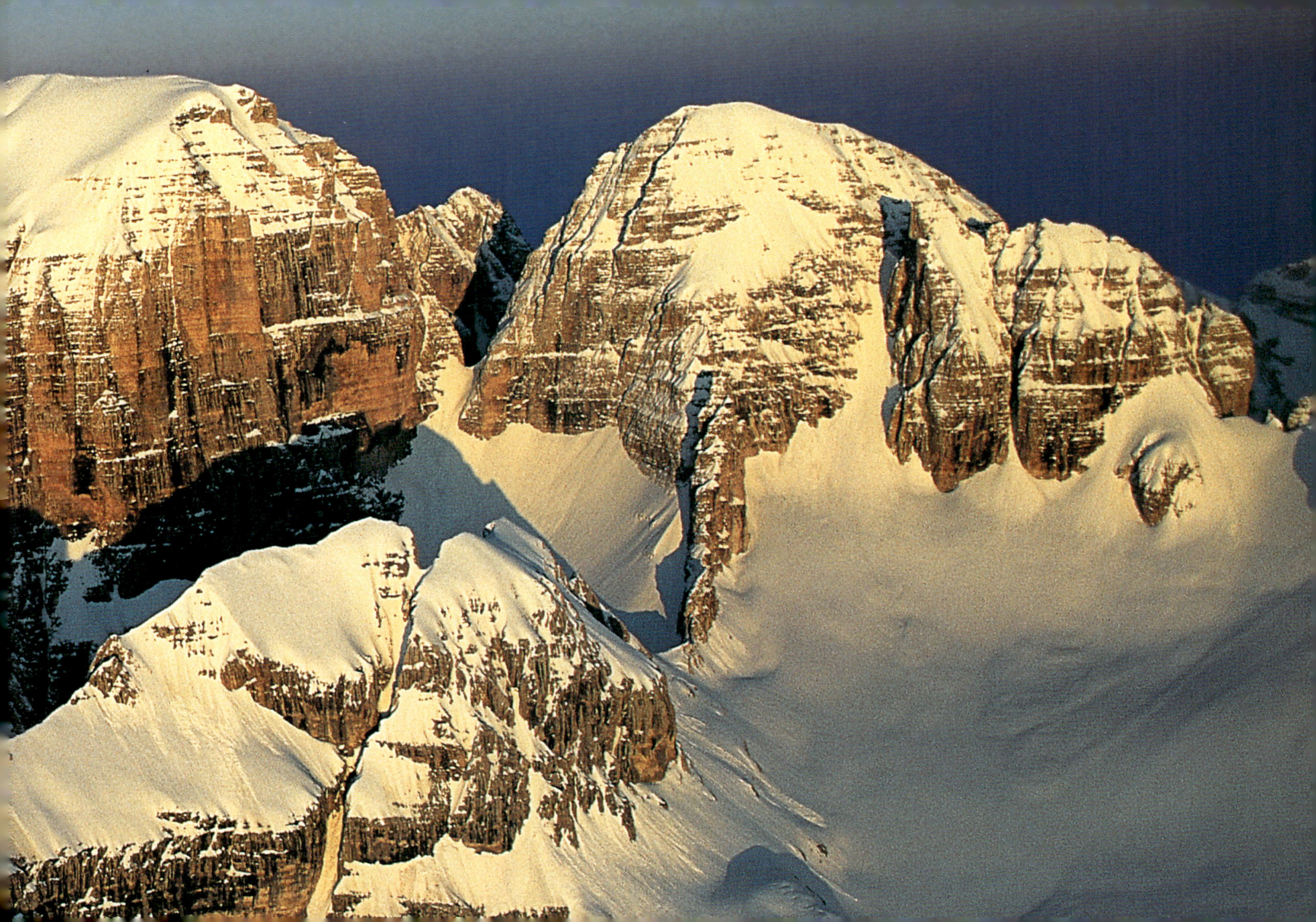

FLYING HIGH THE WORLD

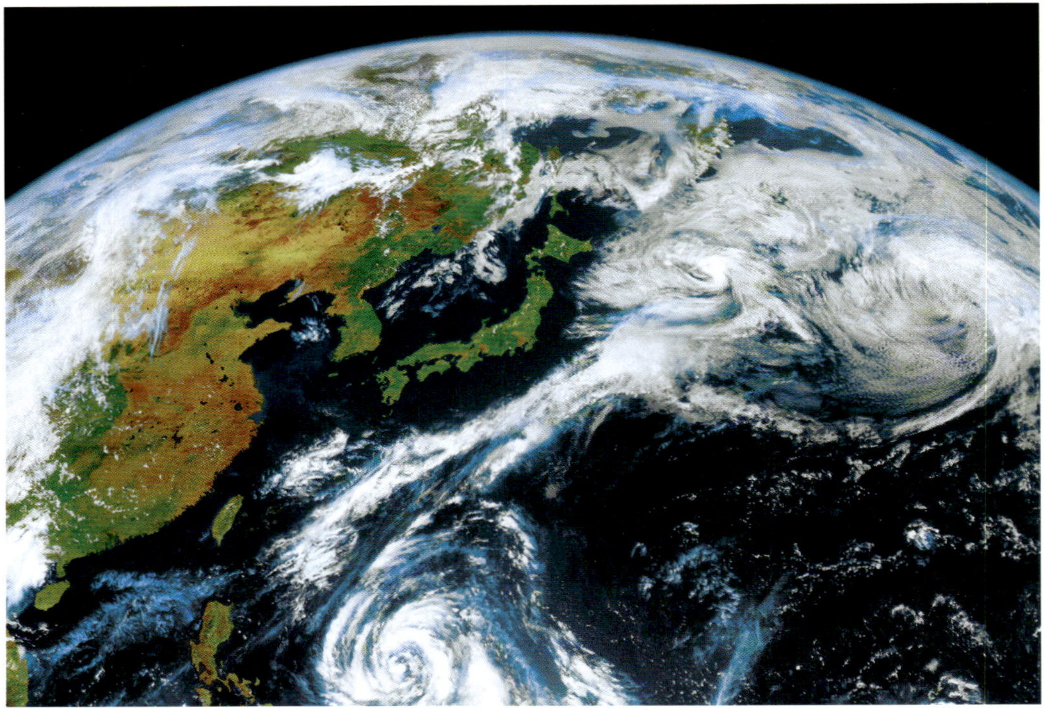

Introduction

UNDERSTANDING THE WORLD PRESUMES KNOWING THE DEFINITION OF TWO DISTINCT FORCES: NATURAL AND HUMAN. IN FACT, THE VERY WORD *MUNDUS*, WHICH FOLLOWED THE GREEK *KOSMOS*, MEANING "ORDER," INDICATES NOT ONLY THE EARTH BUT THE RESULT OF MAN'S INTERACTION WITH THE ENVIRONMENT. IN OTHER WORDS, THE OBJECT AND SUBJECT ARE THE TERMS OF THE QUESTION. OUR PLANET IS WHAT WE FEEL IT TO BE THROUGH OUR PERCEPTIONS, EXPERIENCES, AND, EVEN, FANTASIES. THEREFORE, THE WORLD CAN ALSO BE WHAT WE WOULD LIKE IT TO BE. WHEN THE OFFSPRING OF MANY MORE HIGHLY EVOLVED LIVING SPECIES CONTEMPLATE THE FACE OF THEIR MOTHER, A SUBTLE RELATIONSHIP IS ESTABLISHED BETWEEN THEM, A SPECIAL KIND OF COMMU-

16
The Far East and the Pacific Ocean seen from space.

Introduction

NICATION IN WHICH THE TERMS COME FROM AFAR, FROM THE UNKNOWN SCHEMES THAT NATURE USES TO TRANSPOSE THE UNIVERSE OVER THE EXISTENCE WE KNOW. ACCORDING TO ONE OF THE SEVERAL CHINESE COSMOGONIES, MAN WAS BORN OF THE UNION OF THE SKY, THE MASCULINE ARCHETYPE, AND THE EARTH, FEMALE. THE FERTILIZING VEHICLE OR CATALYST WAS WATER, RAINWATER BEING STERILE ON ITS OWN. THE RESULT OF THIS INTERACTION IS MUD, AS SO MANY TRADITIONS MAINTAIN. WE MUST THEREFORE BE CHILDREN OF THE EARTH IN FULL AND WITH FULL RESPONSIBILITY. WE, CHILDREN OF CLAY, HAD DREAMED ABOUT FLYING FOR THOUSANDS OF YEARS AND FINALLY TOOK AN INCREDIBLY BIG LEAP THE DAY WE GAVE OURSELVES WINGS, OPENING THE WAY TO CLIMB UP TO THE SHOULDERS OF THE SKY. GAINING THIS POINT OF OBSERVATION, FINALLY GAVE US THE OPPORTUNITY TO ADMIRE THE FACE OF OUR CREATOR, TO RECOGNIZE IT, STUDY IT, AND UNDERSTAND ITS EXPRESSIONS AND, ABOVE ALL, ITS MOODS.

Introduction

THE EXPLORERS WHO DESCRIBED THE "THINGS NEVER SEEN" OF OUR PLANET EARTH WERE LACKING (THEY KNEW IT AND SUFFERED BECAUSE OF IT) AN AERIAL PERSPECTIVE. HOW DIFFERENT, HOW MUCH VASTER AND YET SMALLER, APPEARS THE EARTH FROM ABOVE. IT DEPENDS ON THE ALTITUDE, BUT USUALLY AN AERIAL VIEW PERCEIVES VARIOUS CHARACTERISTICS THAT BEAR GREAT WEIGHT ON LIFE "WITH ITS FEET ON THE GROUND." THE LATTER SIMPLY DISAPPEAR, PAINLESSLY. ARTIFICIAL CONFINES GIVE WAY TO GEOPHYSICAL AND ENVIRONMENTAL ONES, WHICH HAVE THE PECULIARITY OF BEING INCREDIBLY SEDUCTIVE IN THEIR BEING DETERMINED SOLELY BY THE TWISTED COURSE OF RIVERS OR MOUNTAINS CRESTS, BY THE EXTENSION AND INTERACTION OF FOREST AREAS AND ARID ZONES, BY THE UNSTOPPABLE LOGIC OF THE OCEAN CURRENTS AND THE MOVEMENT OF DUNES. THE LINES OF EVERY BORDER ARE ERASED: FROM THE SKY, ANY JOURNEY SEEMS POSSIBLE, ANY DISTANCE REACHABLE. IF TRAVELERS OF THE PAST HAD BEEN ABLE TO

Introduction

SURVEY CERTAIN DIFFICULT TRACTS – OFTEN A BIT FOOLISH – ALONG THEIR EXPEDITIONS, THEY WOULD HAVE PROFITED IN TERMS OF HEALTH AND KNOWLEDGE, DISCOVERING HIDDEN WONDERS LIKE THE "THUNDERING SMOKE" OF VICTORIA FALLS AND PUTTING TO REST ILL-FATED UTOPIAS LIKE ELDORADO.

DRASTICALLY CHANGING THE PROPORTIONS, OUR OWN PERCEPTION OF SPACE AND OUR EMOTIONAL RESPONSE TO THIS OR THAT FEATURE EXPANDS, SUBSTITUTED BY FEELINGS THAT ARE SOMETIMES DISCONCERTING. THE SEAS AND THE OCEANS MAKE THEMSELVES KNOWN IN THOUSANDS OF WAYS THAT COULD ONLY BE IMAGINED FROM THE COAST OR, EVEN LESS, FROM THE CRESTS OF THE WAVES. THE COLORS OF TIDAL LAGOONS AND WATERS AROUND CORAL REEFS ARE OFTEN SO LOADED WITH NATURAL ENERGY AS TO IMPEDE LENGTHY OBSERVATION: THE INTENSITY OF THE "TURQUOISE" OF MANY SEAS – PRAISED TO THE POINT OF EXTINGUISHING ITSELF IN THE FACE OF REALITY – IS INDESCRIBABLE

Introduction

FROM THE SKIES. THE PRESENCE OF SMALL OR LARGE BOATS IS A PREDICTABLE SURPRISE THAT, HOWEVER, AROUSES ASTONISHMENT WHEN THEIR SIZE IS COMPARED TO THE DIMENSIONS OF THE INVISIBLE DEEP. RIVERS LIKE THE AMAZON, NILE, AND COLORADO TRANSFORM. FROM INSCRUTABLE AND MYSTERIOUS, AS THEY ARE WHEN TRAVELED BY BOAT, THEY BECOME GIANT HORIZONTALLY GROWING TREES, THEIR BRANCHES TRIBUTARIES OF DIFFERENT COLORS, OUTSTANDING AGAINST THE BACKGROUND OF THE FOREST OR DESERT, OR LOOKING LIKE TRACKS LEFT BY GIANT SNAKES BETWEEN ARID MOUNTAINS AND FERTILE PLAINS. CONTRARILY, THE GREAT MOUNTAINS LIKE THE K2 LOOK INCOMPARABLY MORE IMPOSING THAN WHEN SEEN FROM OUR MODEST PHYSICAL SIZE. FROM THE BASE OF ANNAPURNA, FOR EXAMPLE, THE WHOLE THING CAN BE SEEN EXCEPT FOR THE MOUNTAIN ITSELF, WHICH IS TOO TALL AND DISTANT. THE VILLAGE OF TATOPANI, IN THE VALLEY WEST OF THE PEAK, IS FOUND IN THE DEEPEST VALLEY IN THE WORLD (OVER 22,000 FEET),

Introduction

BUT IT IS IMPOSSIBLE TO COMPREHEND: SIGHT DOES NOT EVEN COVER A THIRD OF THE SLOPE. ON THE OTHER HAND, AT THESE ALTITUDES THE EYE FLIES AS FAR AS THE CURVE OF THE HORIZON, ACROSS THE DELICATE CONTOURS OF THE EARTH'S FACE, CARESSED BY A BLUE AND GREY VEIL OF DISTANT DUSTS. THE VALLEYS SWALLOW ONE'S GAZE; THEY ARE STREAM CHANNELS ALONG WHICH THE VIEW SLIPS LIKE RUNNING WATER TOWARDS THE DEEP BLUE, WHERE HUMAN BEINGS LIVE, PRACTICALLY INVISIBLE.

AGRICULTURE, THE GENEROUS GOVERNESS OF THE WORLD'S HILLS AND PLAINS, OFTEN IMPOSES ITS OWN LIMITS, SHOWING OFF A PRACTICAL APPLICATION OF GEOMETRY SO ESTHETICALLY PLEASING AS TO LEAVE ONE SPEECHLESS. TO COMPREHEND THIS, JUST FLY OVER THE CROPS OF TRADITIONAL FARMS ON THE TERRACE-COVERED HILLS OF ASIA AND SOUTH AMERICA, OR INTENSIVE CULTIVATIONS PLANTED IN THE VOID OF FARAWAY PLAINS IN ARID REGIONS OF THE GLOBE, BUT ALSO IN FERTILE PLAINS LIKE THOSE OF THE CENTRAL UNITED STATES, OR THE VAST PAS-

Introduction

TURE LANDS OF ARGENTINA AND MONGOLIA, ALMOST DEVOID OF HUMANS, AND YET IN SOME WAY SUBJECT TO THEIR NEEDS.

CITIES, THE GREAT DWELLINGS OF MAN, ALSO APPEAR MUCH DIFFERENT FROM ABOVE, AND IN A CERTAIN SENSE, EVEN MORE ALIVE. ANY MEGALOPOLIS, SEEN FROM ABOVE, IS MUCH MORE THAN A PLACE OF INSUPPORTABLE CHAOS OR AN OVERLY INTRICATE ANTHILL. WHEN THEY ARE VISITED BY WAY OF THE "HIGH ROAD," IT SEEMS TO SPREAD OUT LIKE A LIVING ORGANISM, MUCH MORE HOMOGENOUS AND IDENTIFIABLE, UNDERSTANDABLE, AND EVEN MORE LIVABLE IN CERTAIN CASES. IT HAS HIGHWAY OR CANAL ARTERIES, SHOWS SURPRISING MUSCULAR STRIPS PLACED VERTICALLY WHERE TOWERS, MONUMENTS, AND SKYSCRAPERS – THE TALLEST WORKS OF MAN – GROW, IS ENDOWED WITH LUNGS SPREAD AROUND THE PARKS AND GARDENS, AND HAS BIG BLUE-GREEN EYES OF ARTIFICIAL LAKES AND RESERVOIRS. IT IS IMPOSSIBLE TO NOT FEEL EXCITED BY THE SKYLINE OF A GROWING NUMBER OF CITIES AROUND THE

Introduction

WORLD, ALL COMPETING TO HAVE THE TALLEST BUILDING. SHANGHAI AND NEW YORK CAN BOTH BOAST AN EQUAL NUMBER OF STRUCTURES THAT ARE MASTERPIECES OF THE UNION BETWEEN PURE ESTHETICS AND PURE INGENUITY, NOT TO MENTION AN ESSENTIAL FUNCTIONALITY.

THE NEW AND THE OLD ARE LAYERED EVERYWHERE IN THE CITIES, FROM THE BIGGEST ONE TO THE SMALLEST. IN FLIGHT, OBSERVING THE SASSI (STONES) OF MATERA PRESENTS AN EXCELLENT EXAMPLE OF HOW AN URBAN ENVIRONMENT CAN INTEGRATE DIFFERENT AREAS AND TYPES OF HOUSING – FAR DIFFERENT FROM EACH OTHER DUE TO AN EVOLUTIONARY PROCESS SPANNING THOUSANDS OF YEARS BUT FOR PRACTICAL PURPOSES SEPARATED BY ONLY A FEW DECADES – INTO A SINGLE ORGANIC ENTITY. EVERY BIT OF EVIDENCE LEFT BY PAST HUMAN ACTIVITY REVEALS UNAPPARENT TRACES OF ITS MEANING: THE ARC DE TRIOMPHE STANDS WITH ITS PORTENTOUS MONUMENTALITY (IT IS THE LARGEST BUILDING OF ITS KIND IN THE WORLD) WITHIN A BUSY CIRCLE THAT HAS MORE

Introduction

THAN JUST AN ESTHETIC-ARCHITECTURAL-PROPAGANDISTIC SIGNIFICANCE. IT IS A PECULIAR FACT THAT THE BEAUTIFUL THINGS SEEN FROM THE SKY ARE VERY OFTEN INVOLUNTARY, CREATED BY NATURE WITH GENEROUS INDIFFERENCE OR BY MAN WITH UNINTENDED GOOD WILL. TO FLY AND SEE THE EARTH FROM ABOVE MAKE IT POSSIBLE TO ACQUIRE A FREE, OPEN HORIZON. THE VIEW FROM THE SKY MAKES THE OBSERVER A GIANT, GIVING HIM THE FABULOUS "SEVEN-LEAGUE BOOTS," AND FINALLY OFFERING HIM A FACE TO RESPECT AND LOVE.

26-27
The *motu*, little islets surrounding Bora Bora, in Polynesia.

28-29
Artificial reservoirs of salt water in the French region of the Camargue.

30-31
The skyline of Manhattan with its major skyscrapers, the center of life in New York City.

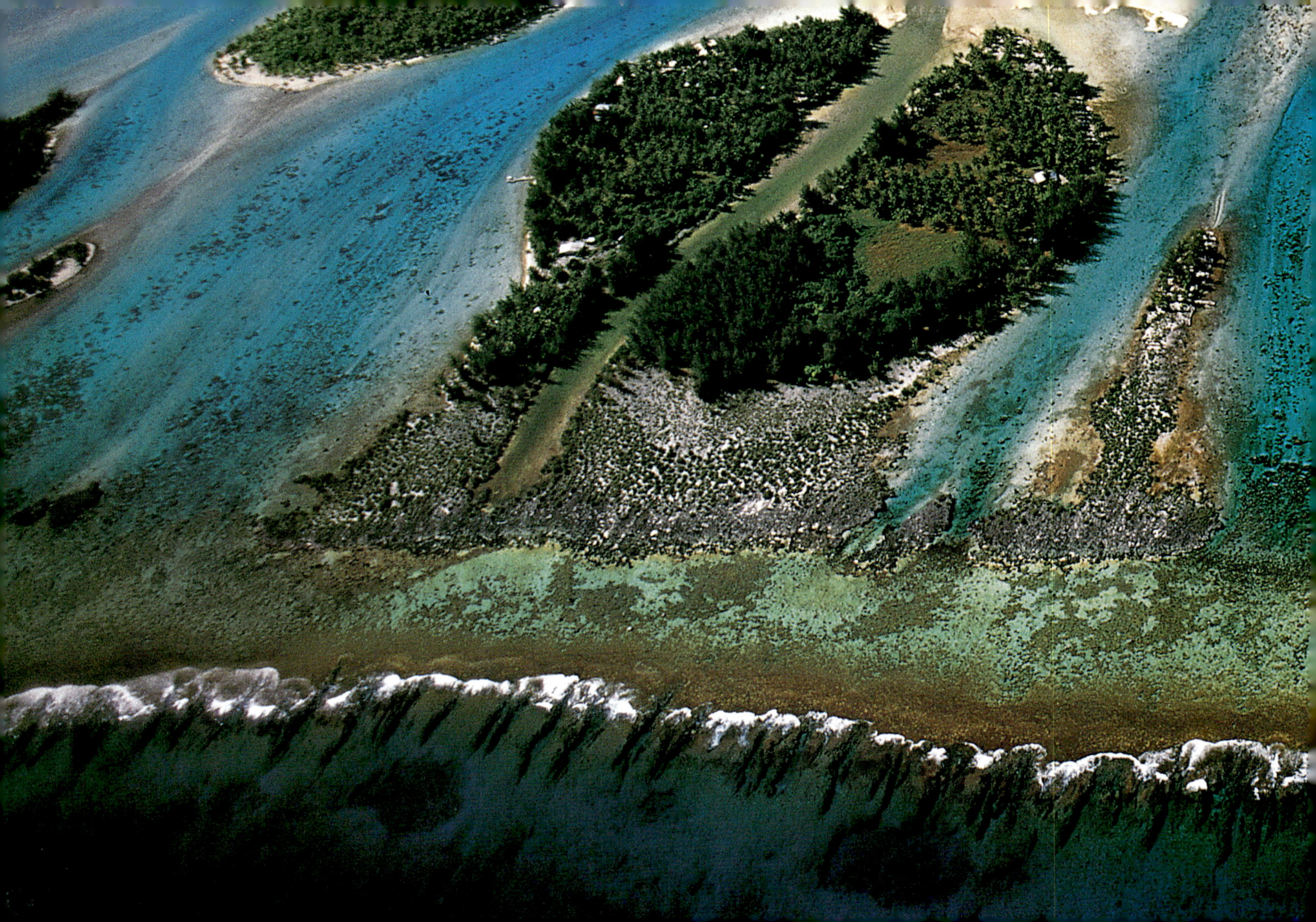

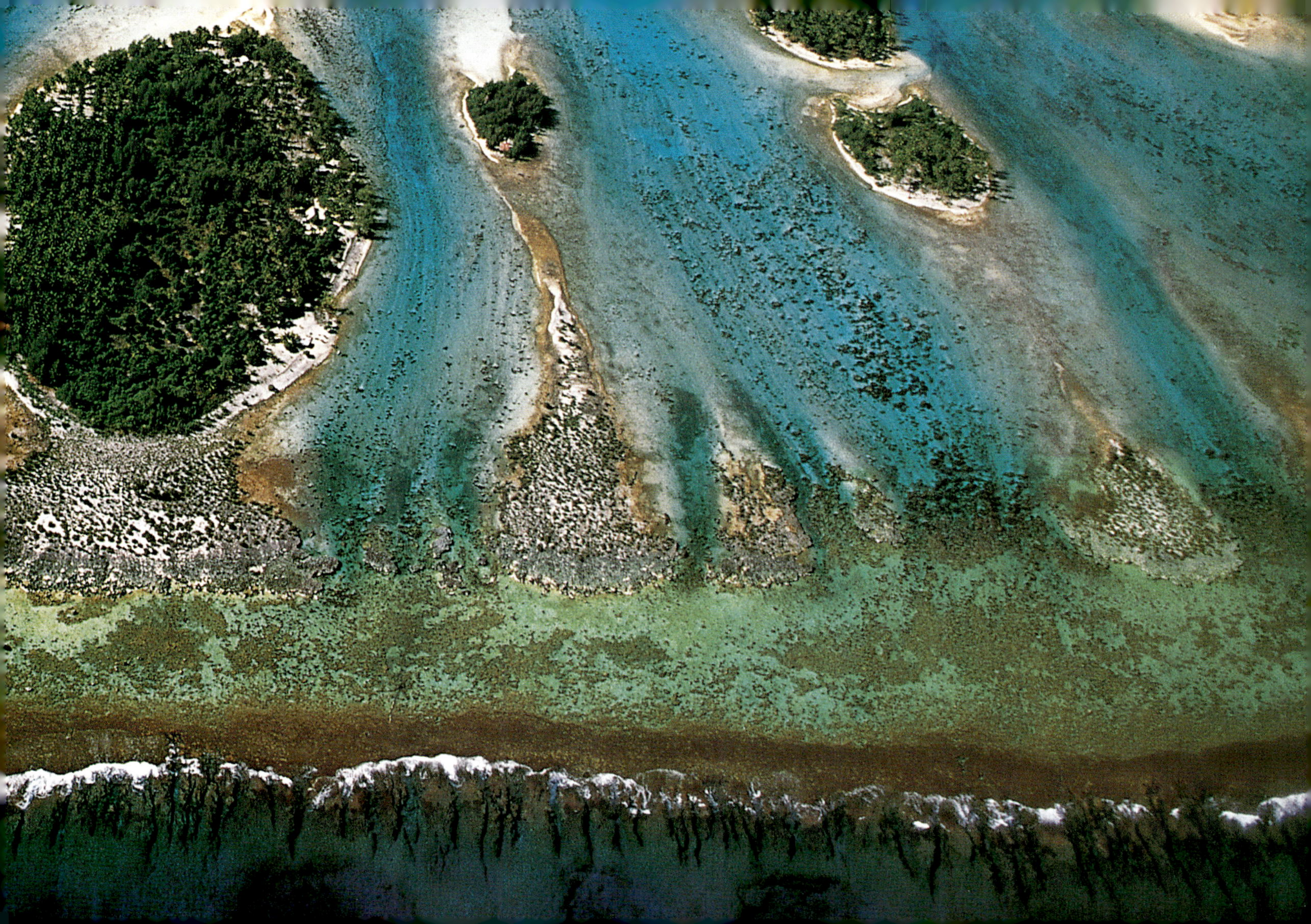

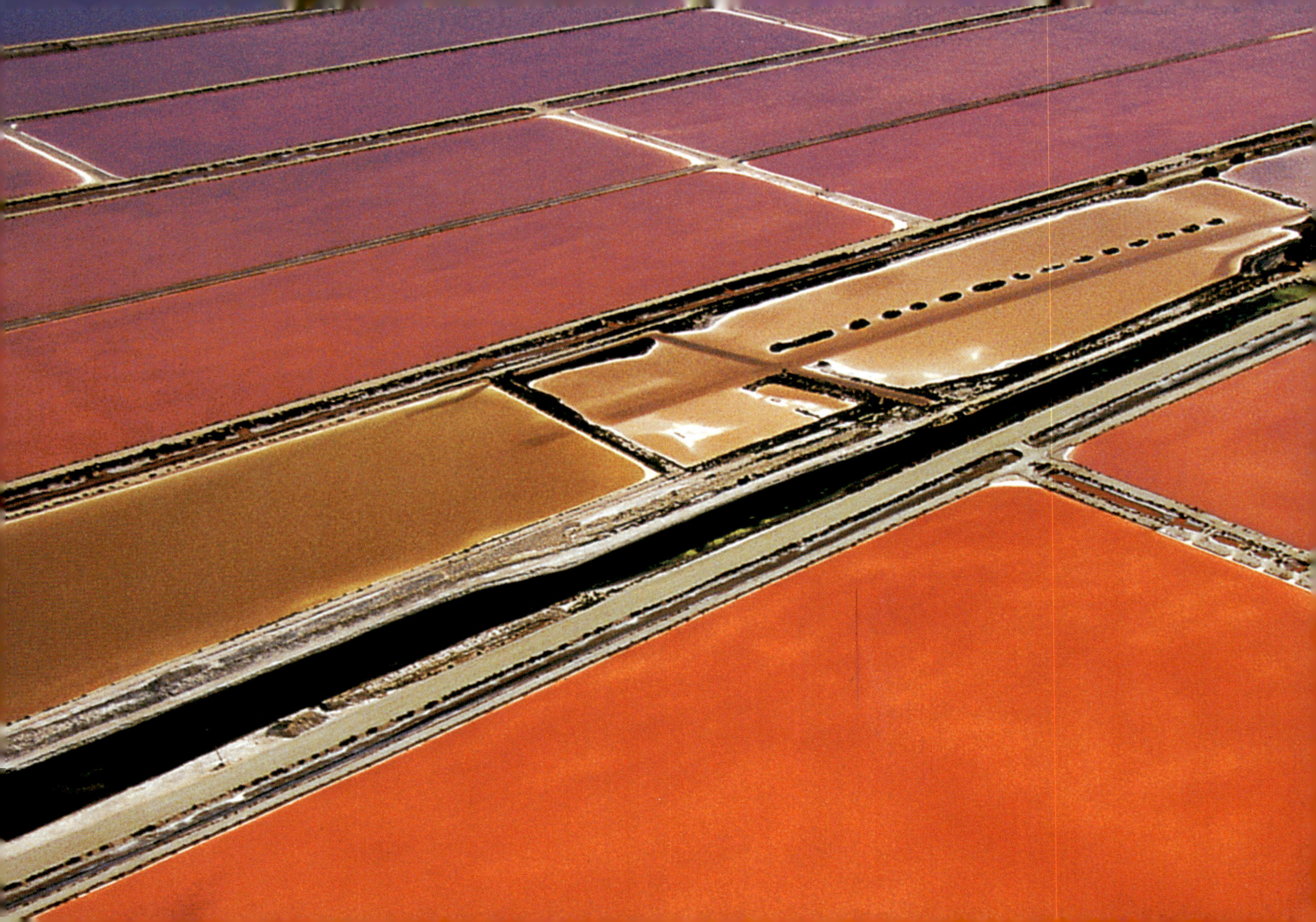

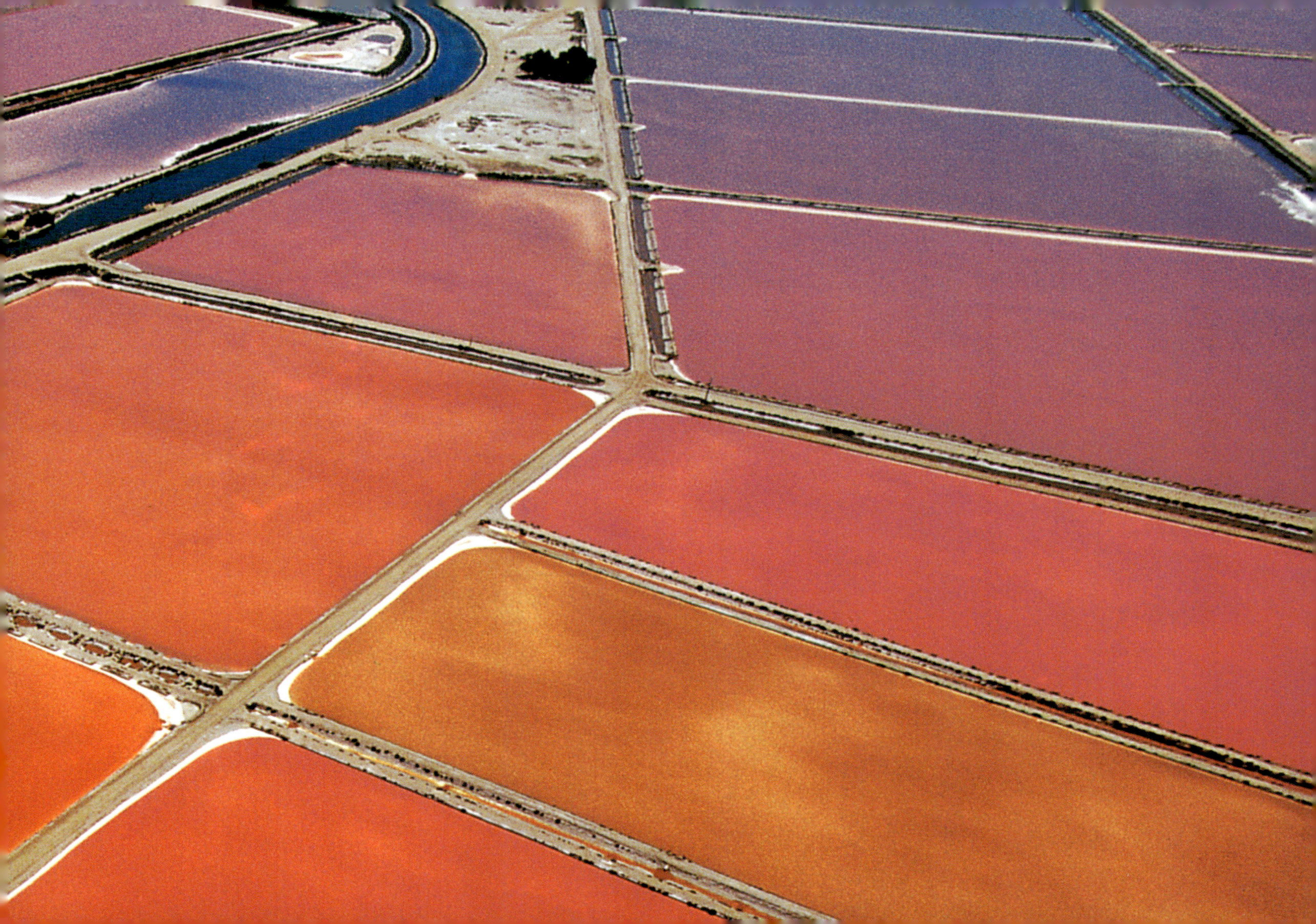

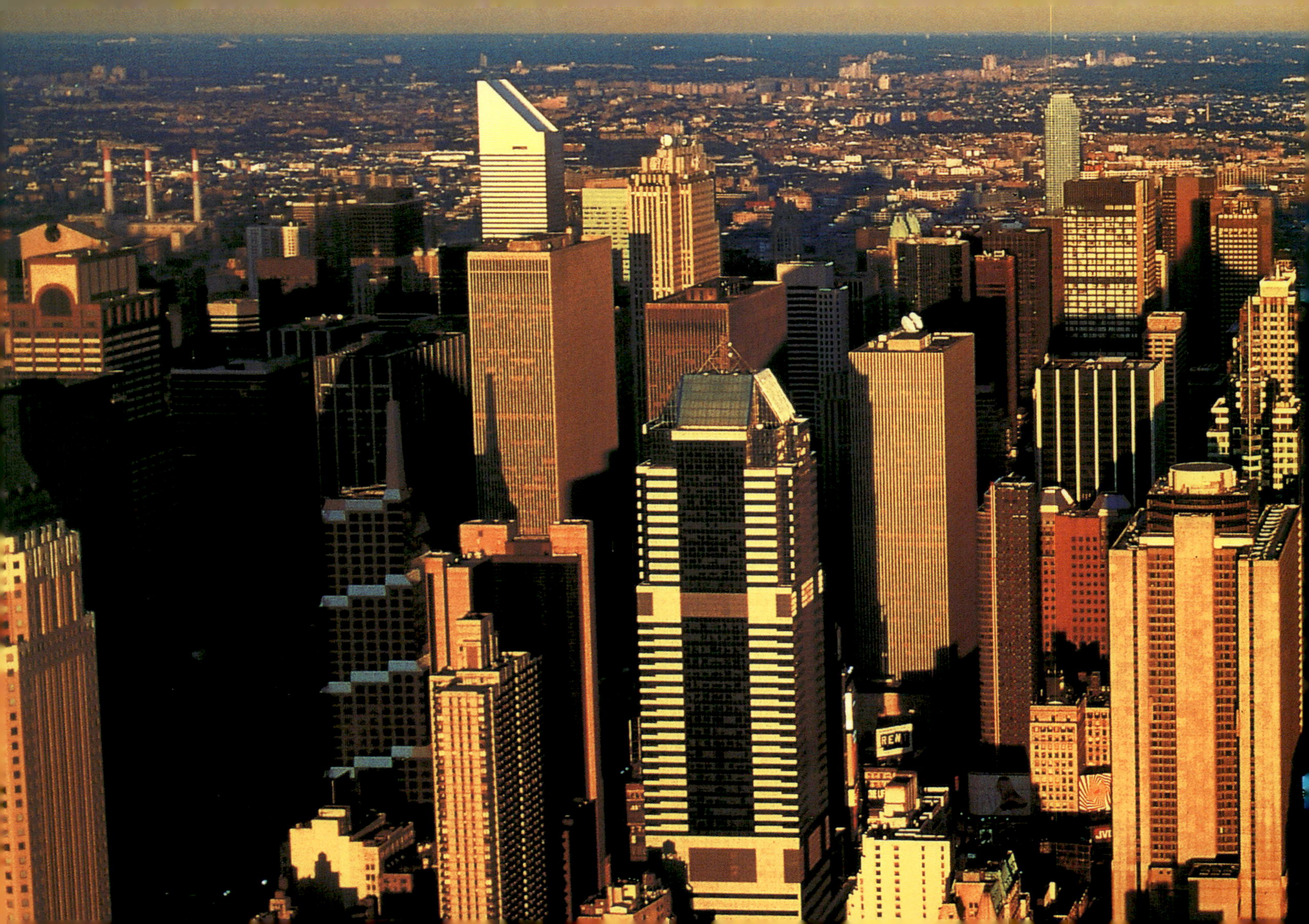

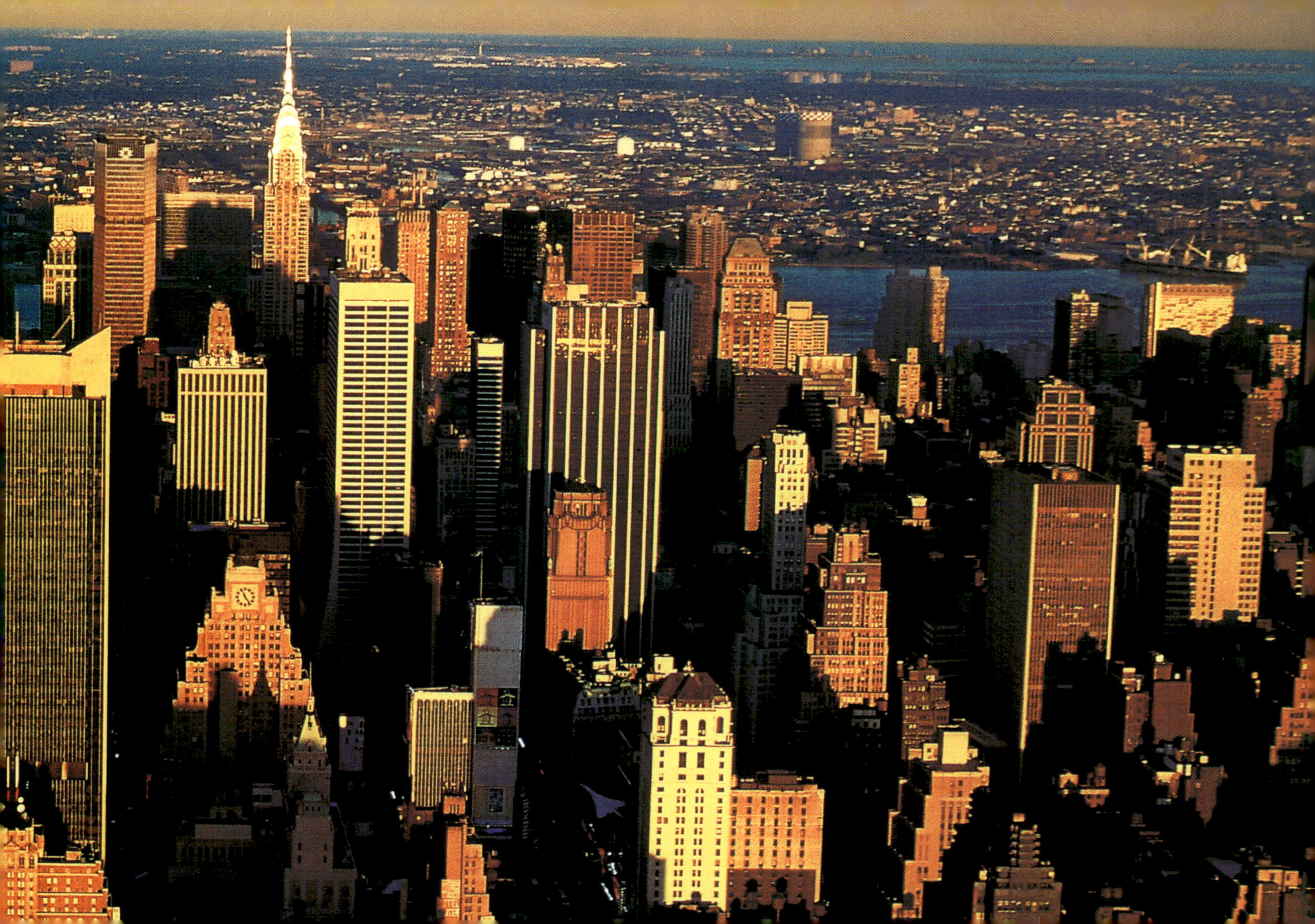

PLANET OF WATER

FLYING HIGH

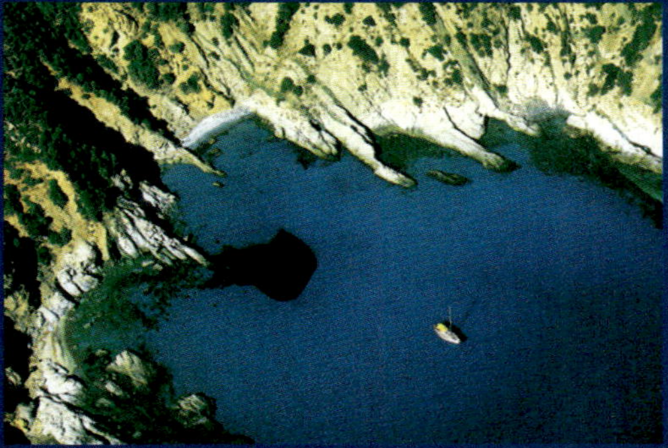
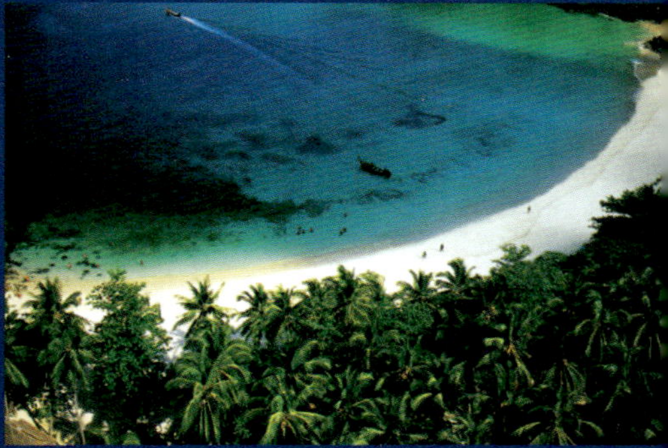

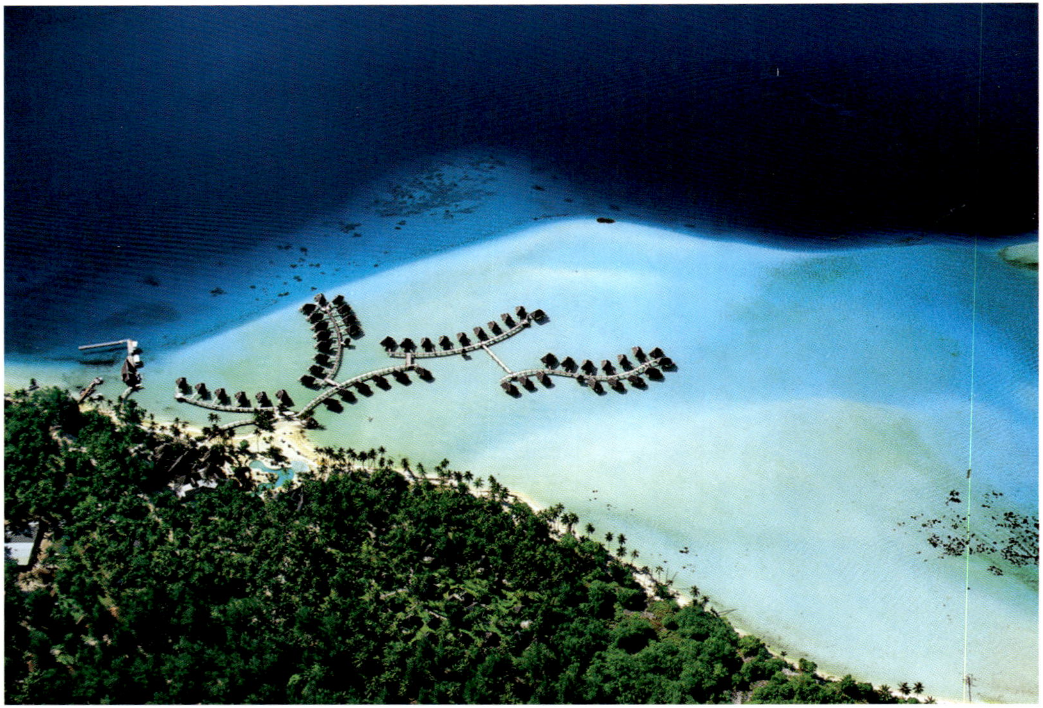

33
The Gulf of Quartu in Cagliari, in Italy (left); a beach on the island of Phuket, in Thailand (right).

Using the term "seas" is too limited. The sea is fundamentally one single entity: it is the element that separates the continental masses, making them what they are. It is the primary artifice of the earth's appearance. The Americas would not be the Americas without those two oceans isolating and characterizing them as a precise entity; oceans that for their part extend undivided across the entire surface of the globe. The oceans cover the world, both separating and uniting everything at the same time, forming the most voluminous inhabitable environment on the earth, with 12,000 feet of average depth covering three quarters of the planet's surface. Nonetheless, it is true that within this generic category, some differences can be defined.
Firstly, the open sea, composing the majority of the total mass of salt water enveloping the planet, can be set apart with its obvious preponderance. The Ocean-Sea of the ancients has dominated the earth's surface since primordial times. It was the first element to differentiate itself from the spheroid of slowly orbiting rock, progressively cooling that which was to become our world. Life probably originated in the sea, even though modern theories tend to transfer this paternity to the boiling newly emerged land or at least divide the origin between it and the sea.
The ocean was the source of a recent discovery, a revolutionary one, about the earth's biological evolution. Not even the 10,000- to 16,000-foot depth of the Mid-Atlantic Ridge can prevent the possibility of life, or furthermore, reduce the underwater world to

34
Bora Bora, known as the "Pearl of the Pacific," is often considered the most beautiful island in French Polynesia.

Planet of Water

a nocturnal or even frozen desert as it was thought to be for a large part of the twentieth century. These forms of life can develop thanks to food chains not based on photosynthesis but sustained by the geo-thermal heat exiting along the ridge through hydrothermal vents of high temperatures.

All this proliferation is unimaginable when flying over it. The ocean floor is hidden by the extreme depth and the "mirror effect" of the surface: the sky looks blue and the sea reflects in large part the wavelength of this radiant light. On the other hand, this interaction of light, water, and marine floor creates some of the most extraordinary spectacles in the world. The colors of the sea near the coasts are extremely variable, evocative, and at times, even blinding. That special hue of blue, which is very appropriately called "ultramarine," dense and constant, varies according to the geomorphology in an assortment of greens, blues, and turquoises of an overwhelming intensity. It is striking that, usually, the liveliest colors are associated with the waters surrounding islands and coastlines like those of the tropical seas, the famous South Seas of the European-centric perspective. Just flying over the shores of Ireland, for example, is enough to realize that that same chromatic play of colors, from blue, to white, to green, also sparkles in a choppy ocean like the Atlantic. The North Seas are gray when the sky is gray.

The ocean is like a promise: leaving from its geographical center, you can fly for thousands of miles astonished to see almost nothing that is familiar. But, then, slowly, you notice that the curved limit of the horizon grows thicker. A coast begins to embrace the ocean beyond the windshield of the airplane. The ineffable haze between the sea and sky, which brings to mind ranks of poets, loses its enchanting ambiguity. From black it becomes brown, then it changes color according to the latitude. The triangle of southern Sinai shines in shades of opaque gold, standing out against the most crystal clear sea with the most misleading name in the

Planet of Water

world: the Red Sea, blue to the bottom beyond imagination, 2,600 feet below the shore. The tropical coasts are lush and vigorous to the point of exploding onto the surface of the water, as if they wished to expand indefinitely to the detriment of the sea. The polar coasts stick out from the icy fog, black and white, ever closer yet fleeting. Often, because of the solitude, the sea is compared to a desert, but this does not to justice to either of those environments. Taking a closer look, the play of sunlight on the blue surface is an inexhaustible source of landscapes, with endless stretches of waves expanding thousands of miles from one coast to another.

On the open sea, men and their nutshell-like boats are a sporadic presence relative to the vastness of the horizon. Whether it is a cruise ship or an oil tanker, an aircraft carrier or an enormous fleet of fishing boats, any boat appears in all its glory on the surface: it is a human construction that is winning an ancient challenge with the sea, insignificant and yet "floating," seen in that moment as if it were the only creature living in that vast area. The islands amplify this impression: they are made of solid rock, often of sedimentary or volcanic origin, but they are also big rafts on which live entire populations, transforming the environment. How could you not notice, flying over any island in the South Seas, the incredible lushness of that vegetation rising from the water, so dense and alive you imagine holding it in your hand like a precious stone. Just beyond, at its edges, super thin docking bridges clogged with rows of white boats, almost like bunches of white grapes born in a field of such bright turquoise you cannot look long at the same spot.

Then, there are the internal seas: the Mediterranean and the Black Sea on one hand and the Caspian, the Dead Sea, and Lake Baikal on the other represent two distinct types. The first of these was born of the irruption of ocean waters into deep valleys whereas the second was "forgotten" in the interior by the oceans as they withdrew over various ice ages. The Dead Sea is a unique sea: its harsh wa-

Planet of Water

ters are lethal to almost all life forms. Yet, trapped between two arid and indented shores, shaded red, white, and bright yellow, it lives through its colors, tormented and dynamic, to the extent of creating views unique throughout the world.

The Mediterranean gives life to one of the most extolled but also rarest ecosystems: its mild climate graces only a few areas on the globe, all located at latitudes above the two tropics. The Californian coast from Sacramento to Los Angeles, the Chilean shores south of the Atacama Desert, and a couple of places in southern Australia: all these areas are characterized by rather dry coastlines, though loaded with abundant and aromatic vegetation. A feature shared by these distant regions, besides their climate and environment, strikes observers from the sky. It is a minor detail: red roof tiles stand out against the light-colored land, dotted with big rosemary and laurel bushes, agaves, and tamarisks.

Finally, it is necessary to mention another kind of sea, the most elusive of all. The spherical confines of the world actually contain one that does not even seem as such. In fact, we have only recently learned that it is made of water and not ice patches on emerged ground or a big central archipelago. As discovered by Umberto Nobile in 1928, the Arctic Sea is a limitless flat polar cap, a sort of an illusion to the eyes of living beings, so convincing that land creatures like bears will in all effects live above the deep, highly salty water of high latitudes. Having adapted to this environment, this species has become white, large, fat, and shrewd. They present themselves on the planet's biological scene as the only land-borne creatures to have found a way to survive in a marine environment without the use of boats. As Nobile and other pioneers of Arctic exploration regretfully discovered, the Arctic Sea and the Antarctic Sea hold all the liveliness of more conspicuous seas – those that appear in the "official" form. Walking on the pack-ice thinking of going north or towards some other cardinal direction is foolish, because the cap moves constantly, brea-

Planet of Water

king into millions of floes that in turn move, rotating on their own vertical axis, within a crazy swirling puzzle. Large slabs of different sizes collide, rising up like giant knives of ice above the flat surface, creating fleeting chains of lethal mountains. Then, like true emerged land, tall, sheer, icebergs up to 300 feet long, and as flat as some land plateaus and high-altitude plains, detach and depart for warmer latitudes where they will melt back into the sea of whose vapor had condensed into the snow and ice that created these bergs millions of years ago.

Flying over the ocean is like sitting on the outermost layer of the atmosphere, which cloaks an alien world, in effect the function that it holds for its innumerable, and often unfamiliar, inhabitants. These beings can be observed from the air when a variety of necessities, from feeding to breathing, force them to see the light outside the watery canopy, the atmosphere they breathe.

Schools of fish move just below the surface of the seas, as big as islands and as such visible from above. Similarly, the largest creatures we know, the cetaceans, trace white tracks in the blue for thousands of miles along the coast and from archipelago to archipelago, from the Cape of Good Hope to the Strait of Magellan, from the Newfoundland Banks to the Antarctic Peninsula. Whales cross at higher latitudes and then travel down to the equator, following endless migratory routes relatively close to the coast, because the heart of the oceans is poor in plankton and is therefore a place of famine for the great whales, which survive by feeding on millions and millions of practically invisible creatures.

The sea produces life and attracts it, As the wide variety of different creatures living there makes us understand (some, like whales and seals, actually returned there after a long period on land). The sea has witnessed many of the world's epochs and will continue to do so even when this one has come to an end. In other words, it will carry on being the true home of life, unique and indivisible.

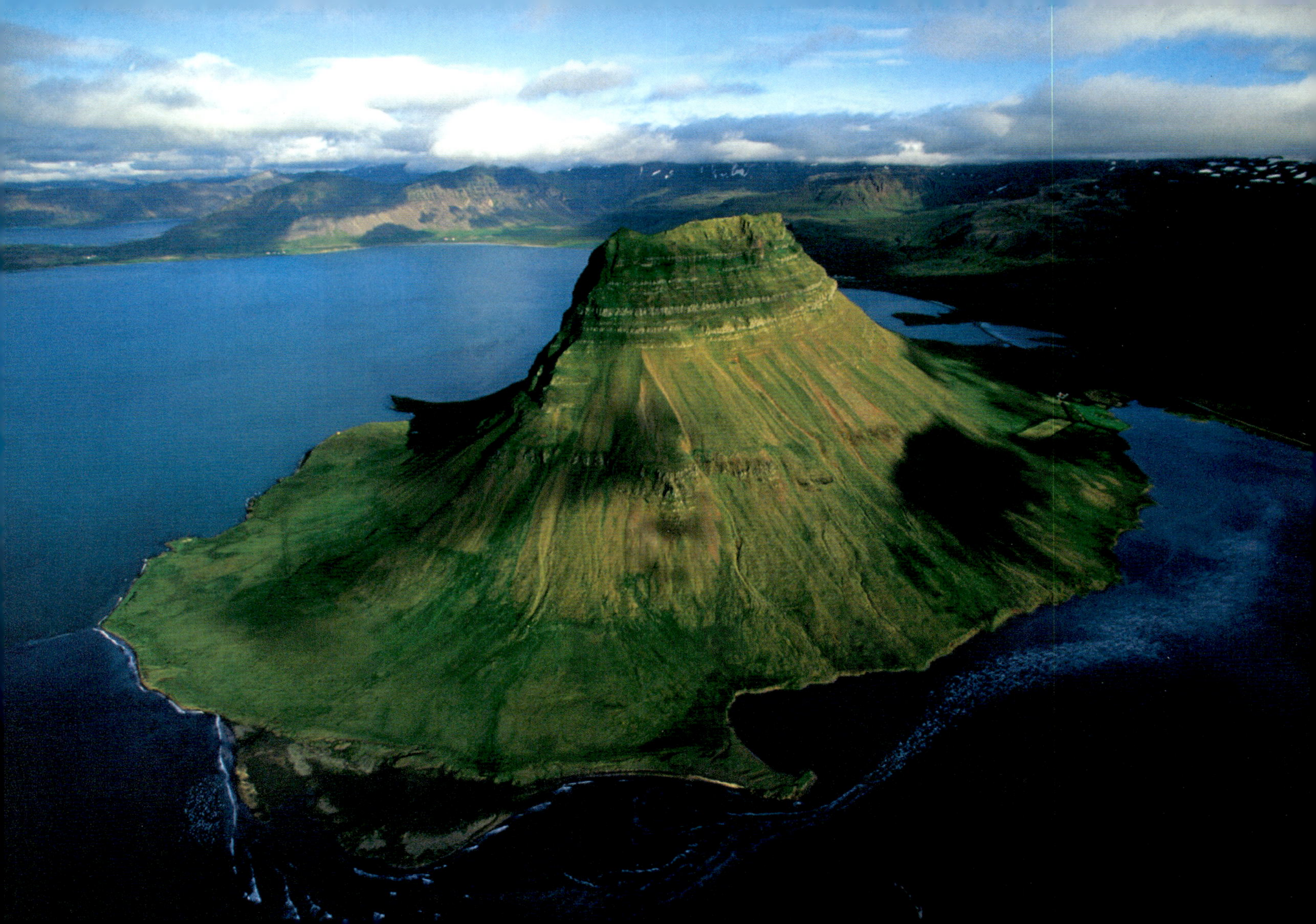

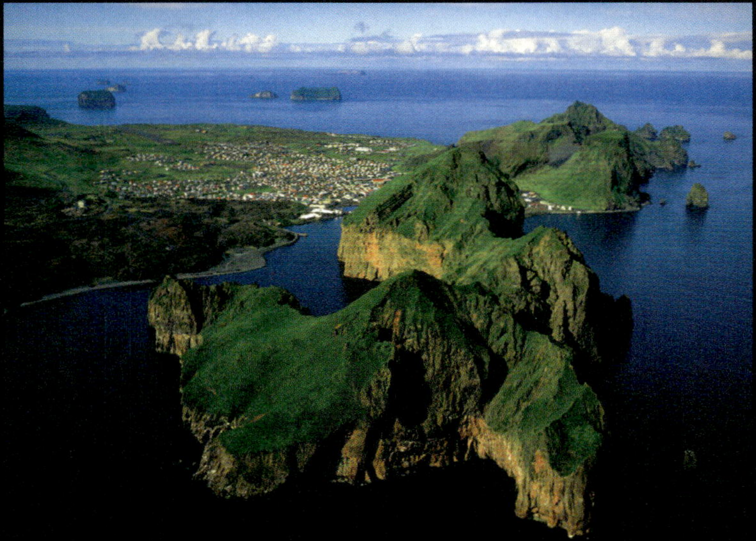

40
The seductive symmetry of Mount Kirkjufell in Iceland, 1,519 feet tall, originated at the end of the last Ice Age, when the glacial waters deeply scoured the coastal landscape.

41
Heimaey, in Iceland, hosts the biggest sea puffin colony in the world. The island was scarred by numerous eruptions. Its dizzying vertical appearance is due to explosions that occurred in rapid succession.

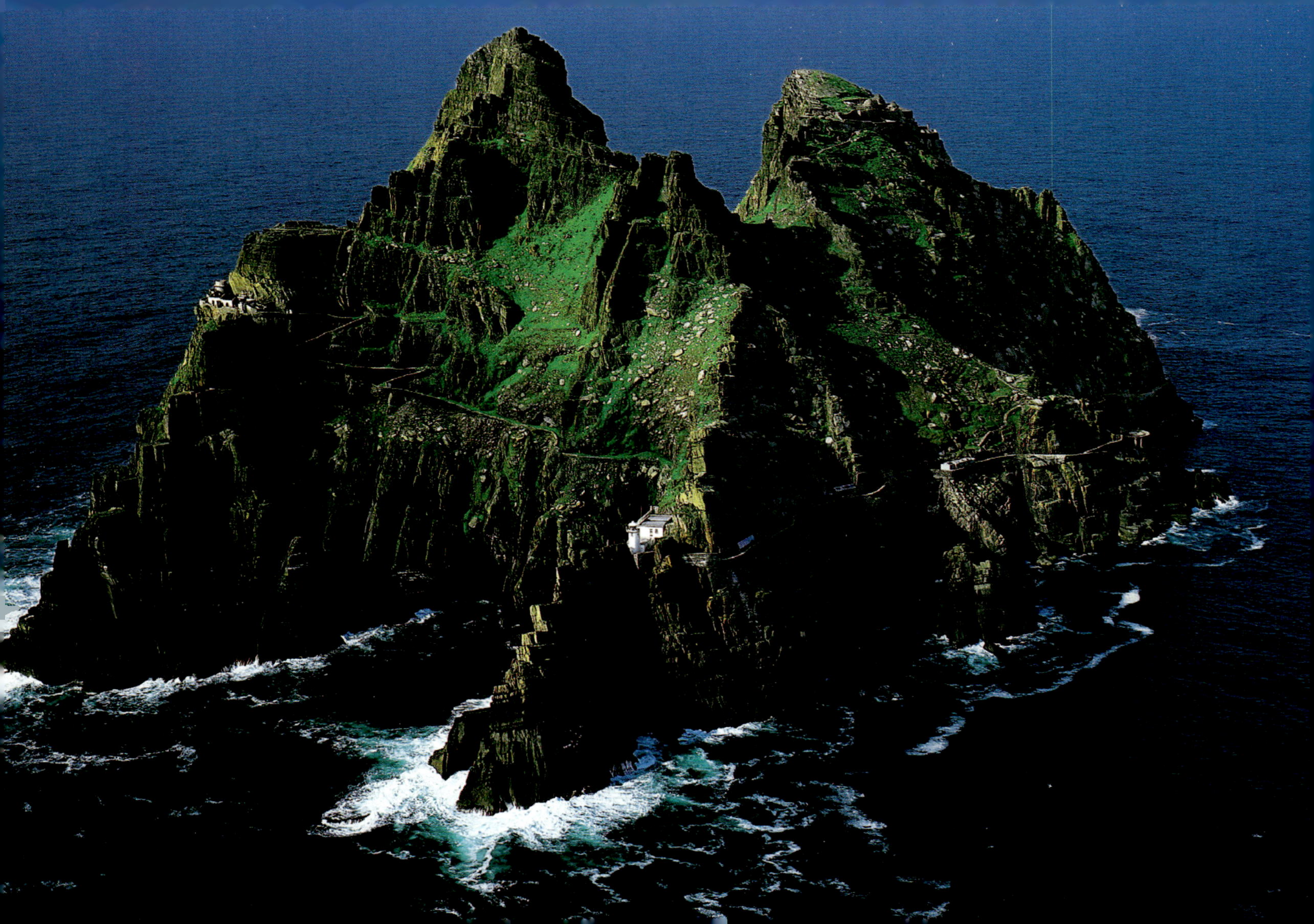

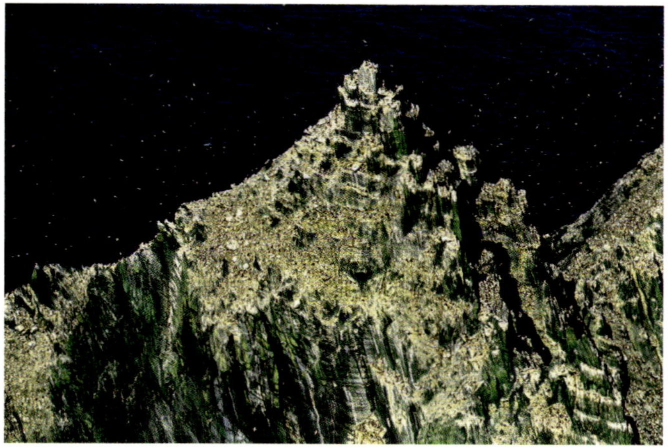

42 and 43
Skellig Rock, in Kerry County, Ireland, rises from the sea like a mountain peak. Its tallest point (on the right) brushes 715 feet.

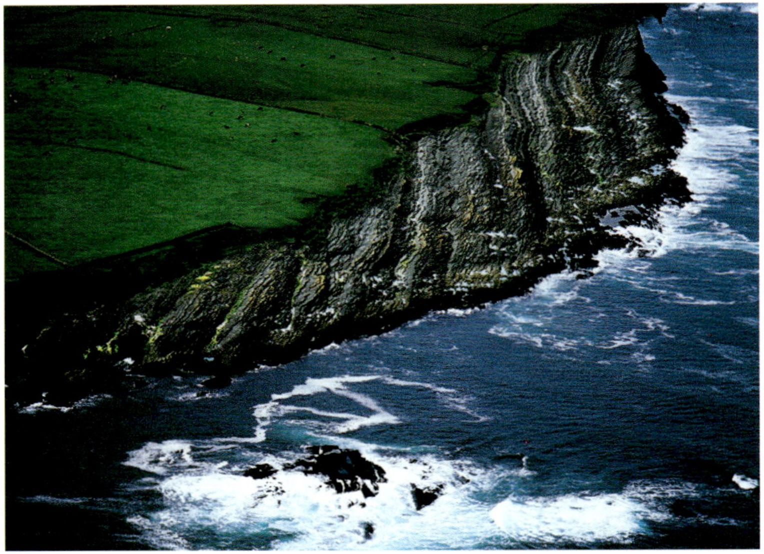

44

Foaming waves break onto a bay in Sligo County in Ireland. The incessant action of the sea on the sandy beaches of the shoreline is obvious in the geological stratifications, also similar to waves.

45

Galley Head Lighthouse, in Cork County, built around 1870, rises about 130 feet above sea level. These "sea sentinels" continue to be useful to sailing the treacherous waters lapping the Irish shores.

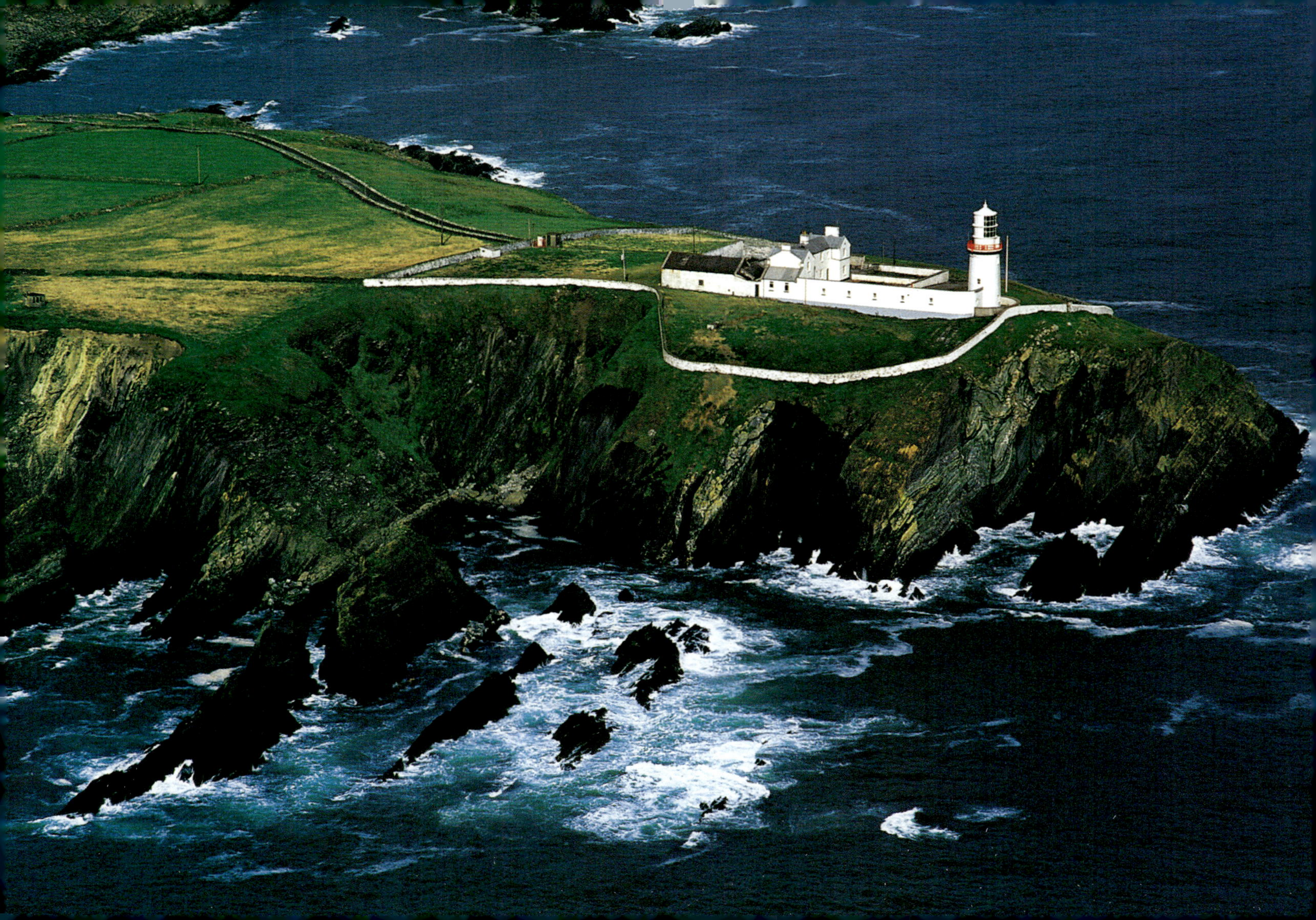

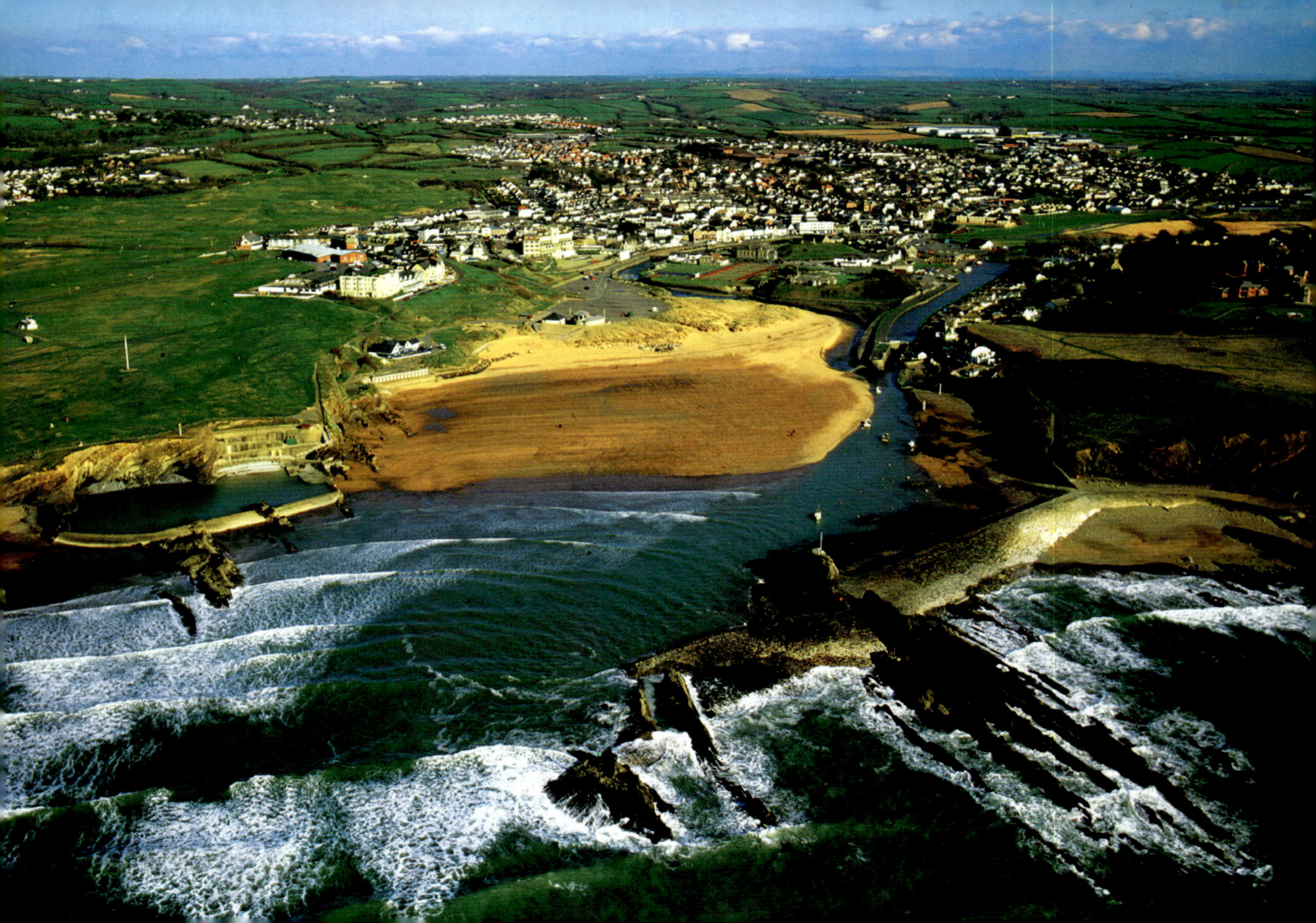

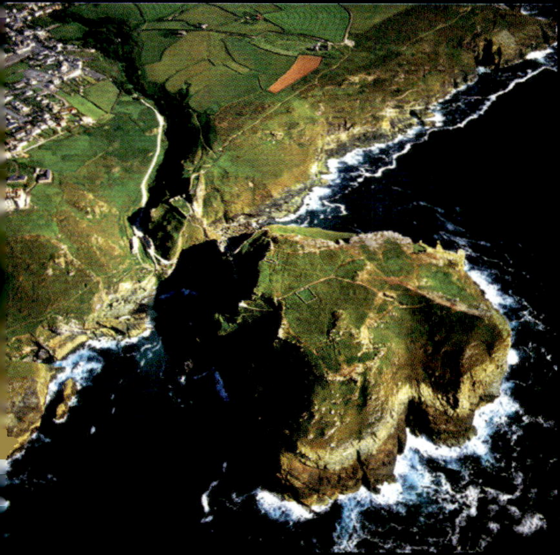

46 and 47

Cornwall County in England boasts impressive cliffs but also wide beaches of fine sand and little harbors for fishermen. On the right, Tintagel can be seen, where legend claims was the location of the castle in which King Arthur was born.

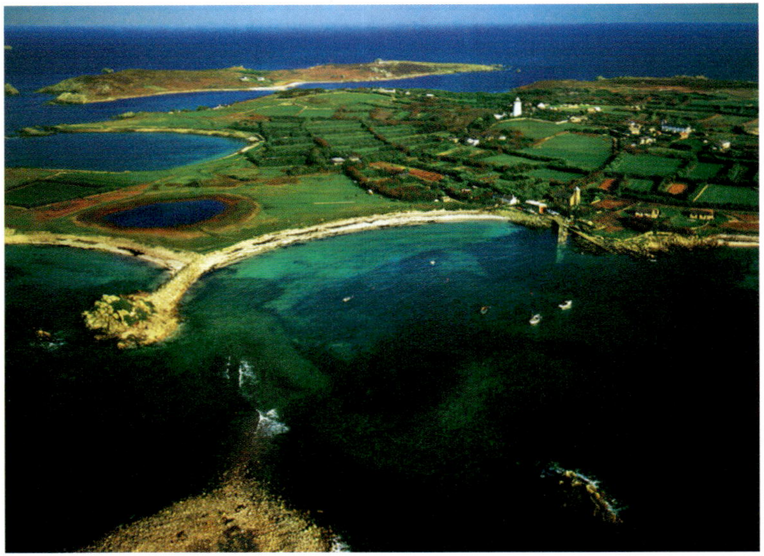

48
Sant'Agnese is one of the 140 islands of Scilly, in England. The sea of crystalline waters hides some shipwrecks.

49
Oxford Beach, in Suffolk County, submerges in an indented fashion into the calm seas of eastern England.

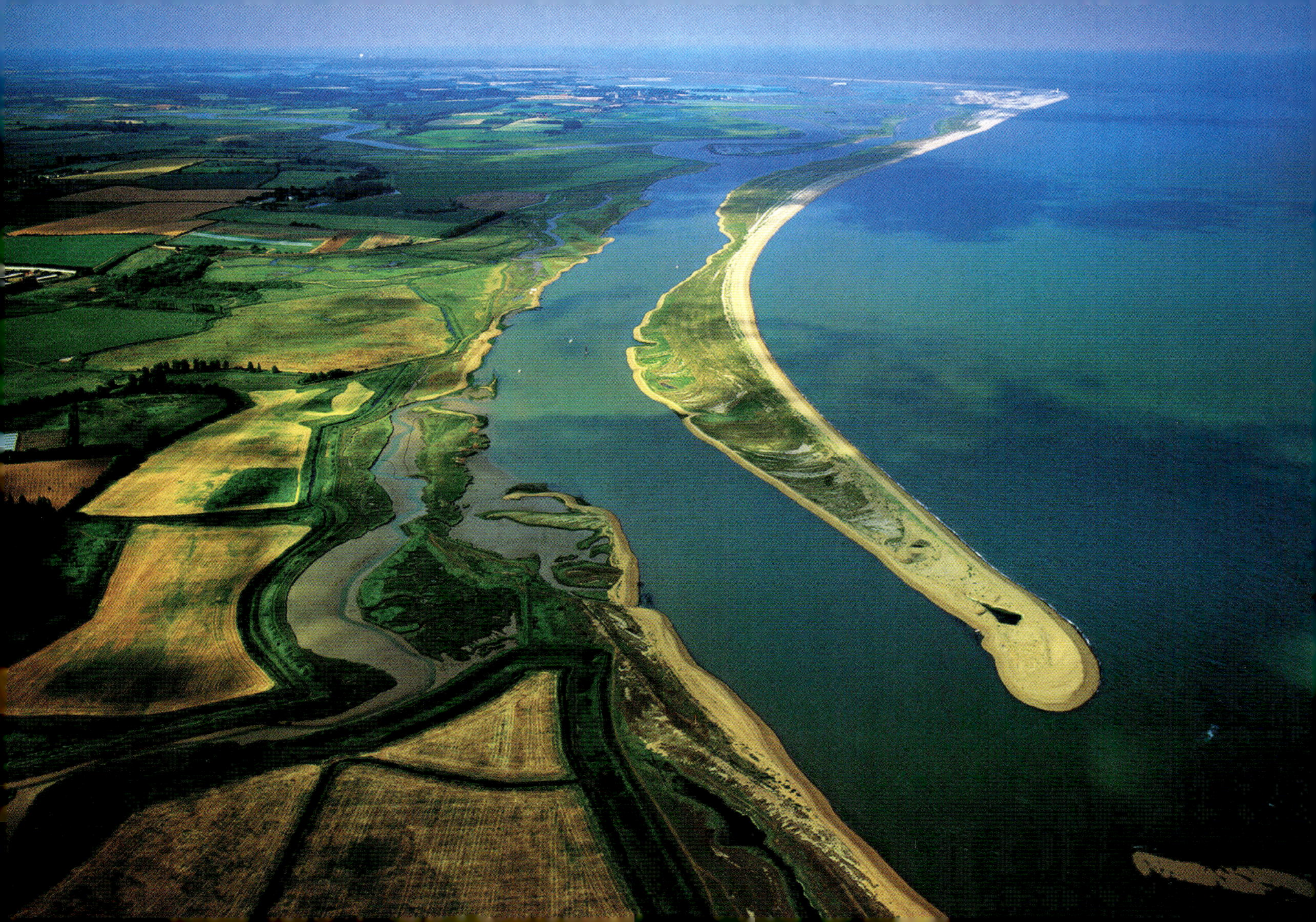

50
Few points of reference create views as "pure" as this one, where white cliffs near Beachy Head in Sussex, England, appear to stretch on infinitely.

51
The cliffs of Dorset in England have been declared part of the heritage of humanity by UNESCO for their abundance in fossils.

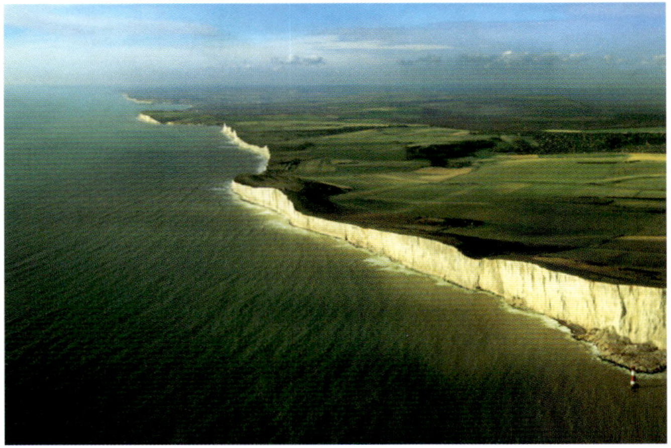

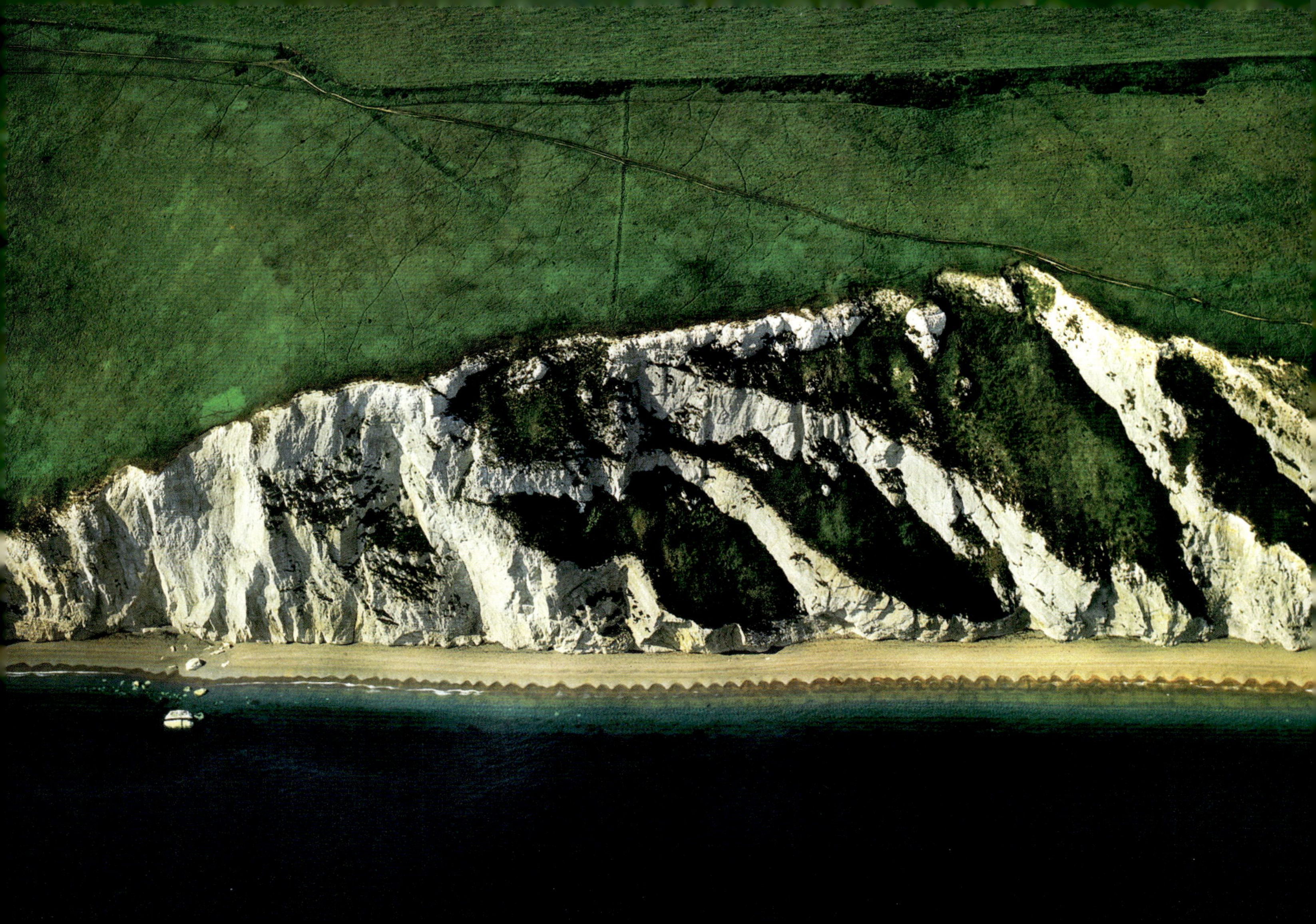

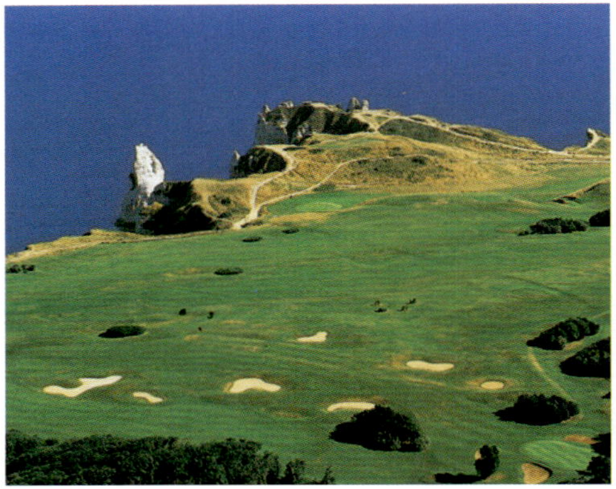

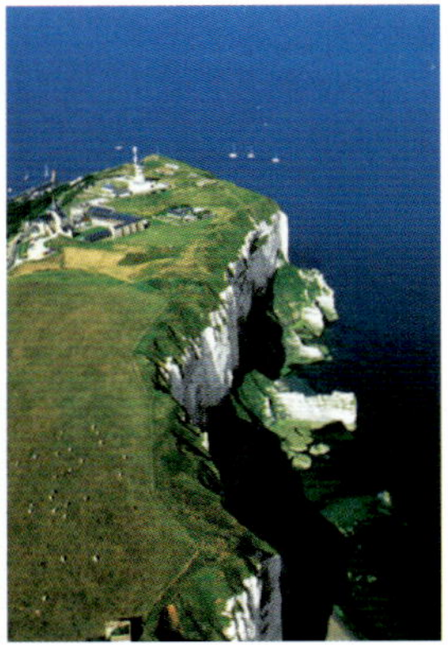

52
The prairies of Pays de Caux in France face brusquely onto the sea, about 230 feet below. The small column seen in the photo on the right commemorates the first flight across the English Channel, completed by Louis Blériot in 1909.

53
The Porte d'Aval (in the foreground) and the Manneporte, in France, are arches sculpted by the sea and wind, just like the Aiguille that surfaces just off the shore, 230 feet tall.

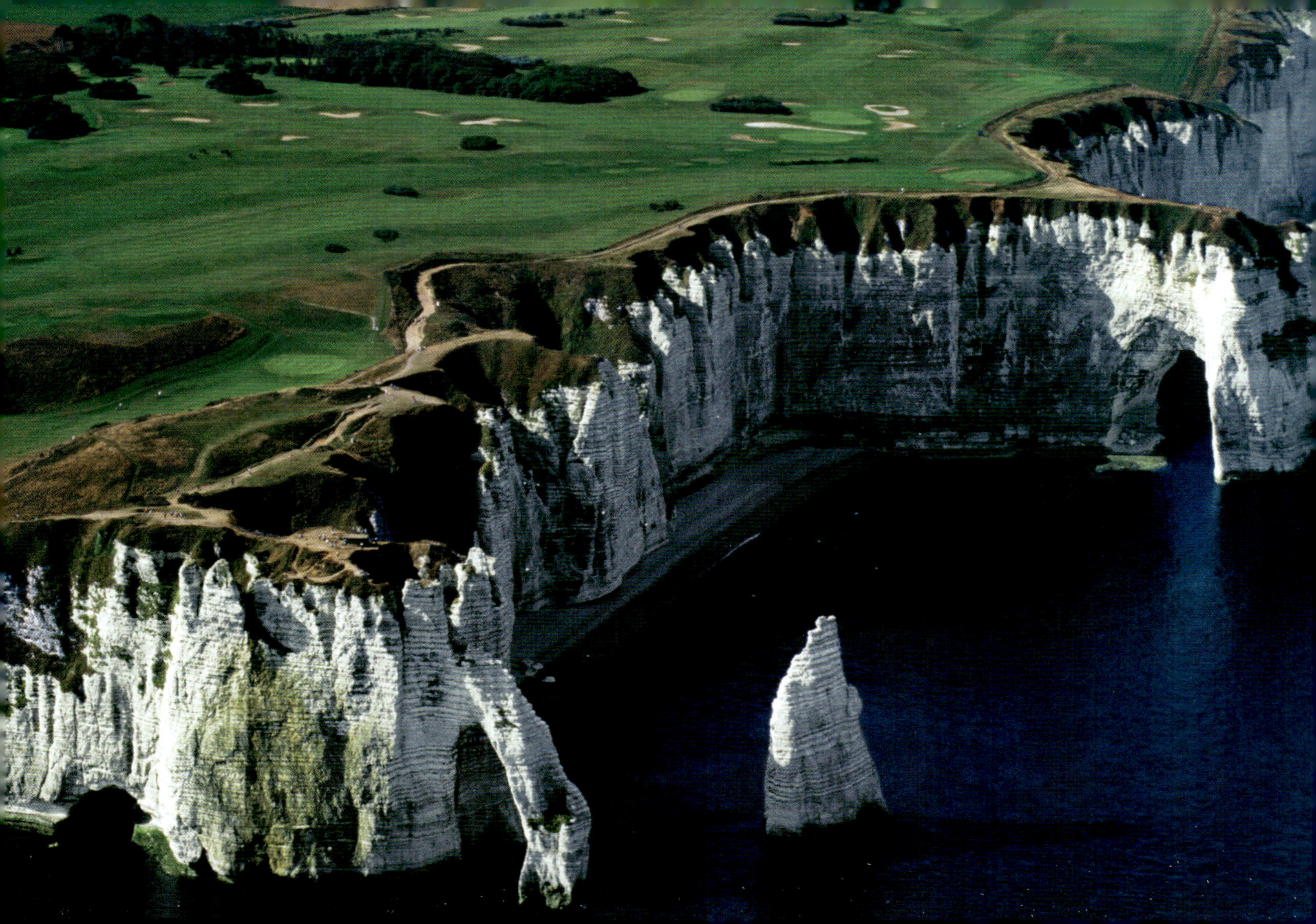

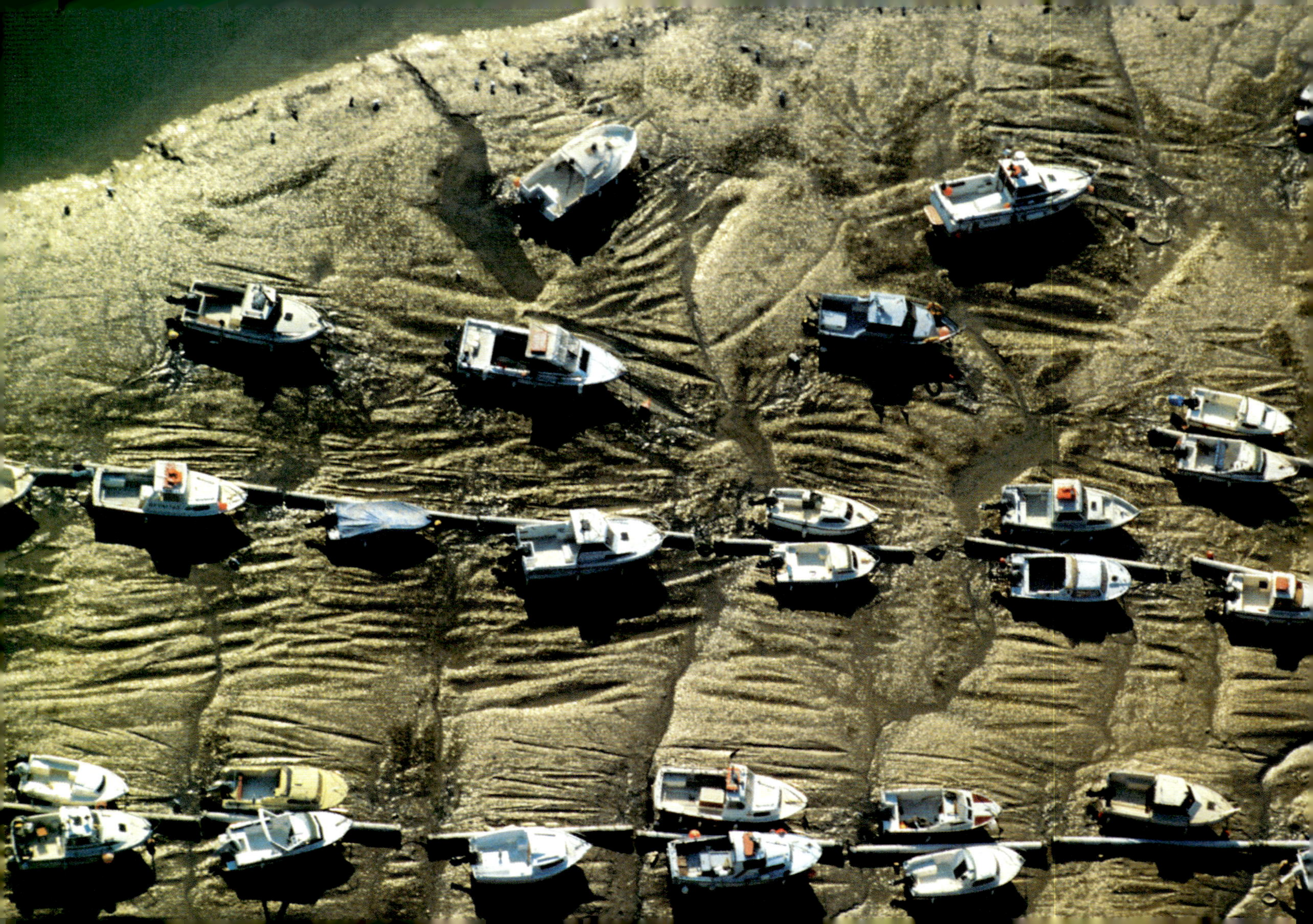

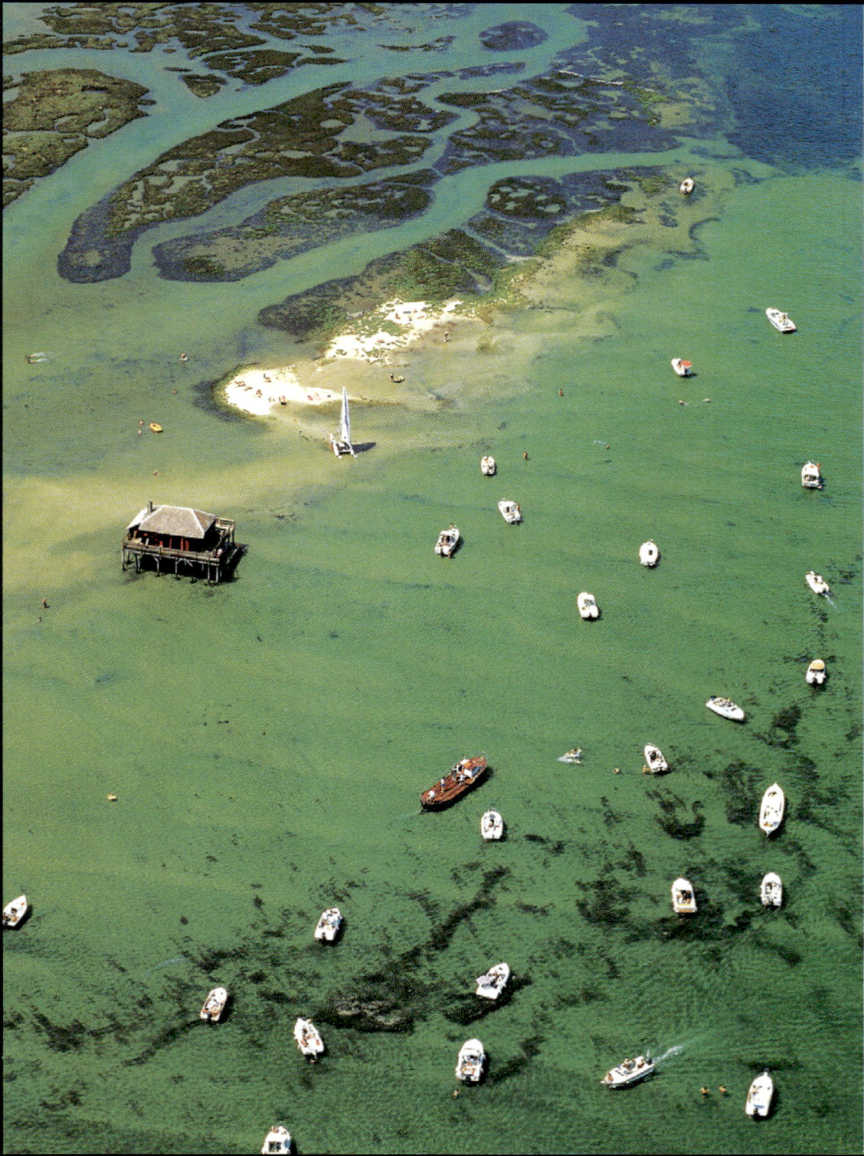

54 and 55
As often happens along the Breton coast, in northwest France, the small boats have to wait for high tide to be able to float again.

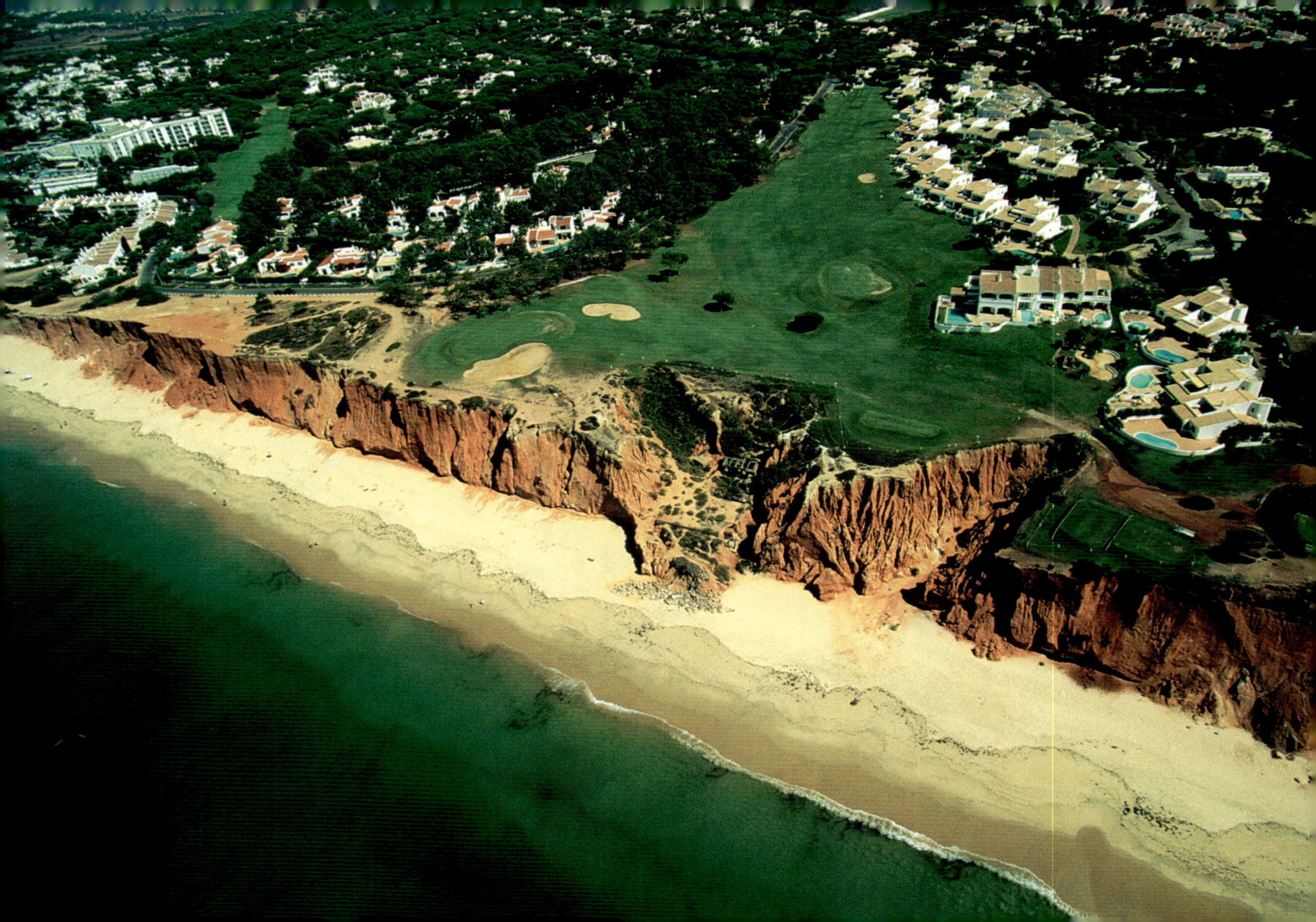

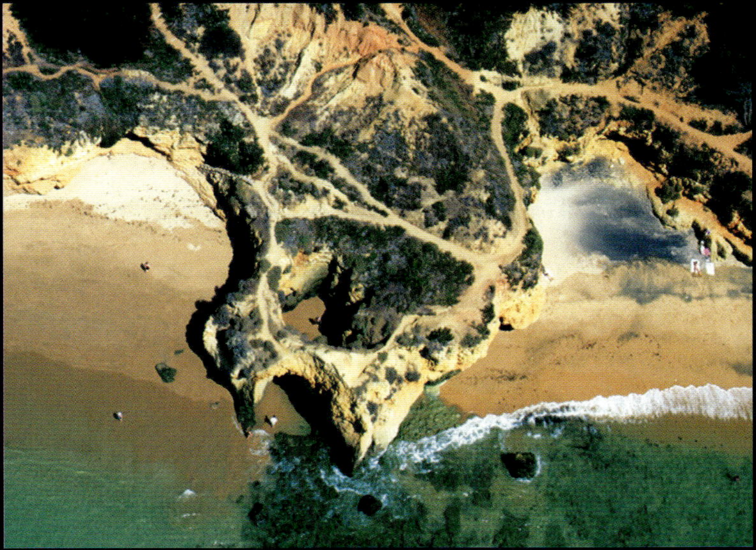

56

A golf course in Balaia, Portugal, faces directly onto the sea. Here, it is the Atlantic Ocean that dashes against the coastal rocks, pulverizing them to create long beaches.

57

Lapped by the Atlantic Ocean, Algarve in southern Portugal boasts spectacular bays with sheer cliffs dropping off into the sea.

58
The Rock of Gibraltar, a British holding located south of the Iberian Peninsula, rises dizzyingly in an otherwise serene landscape: after all, it is one of the Columns of Hercules.

59
Punta de Piedade, in Portugal, is surrounded by red stacks dropping precipitously into the ocean, which hides a labyrinth of rocks and caves.

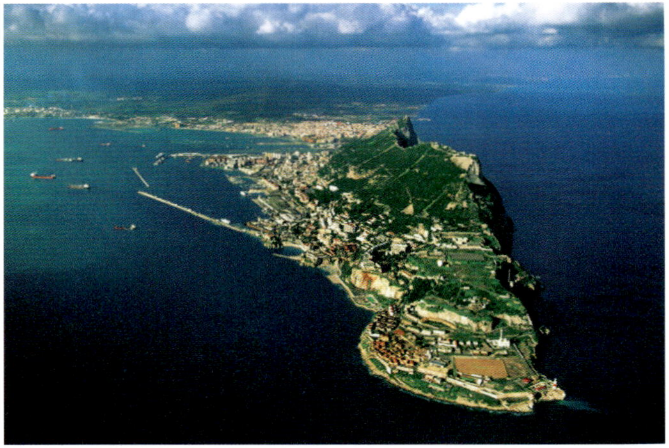

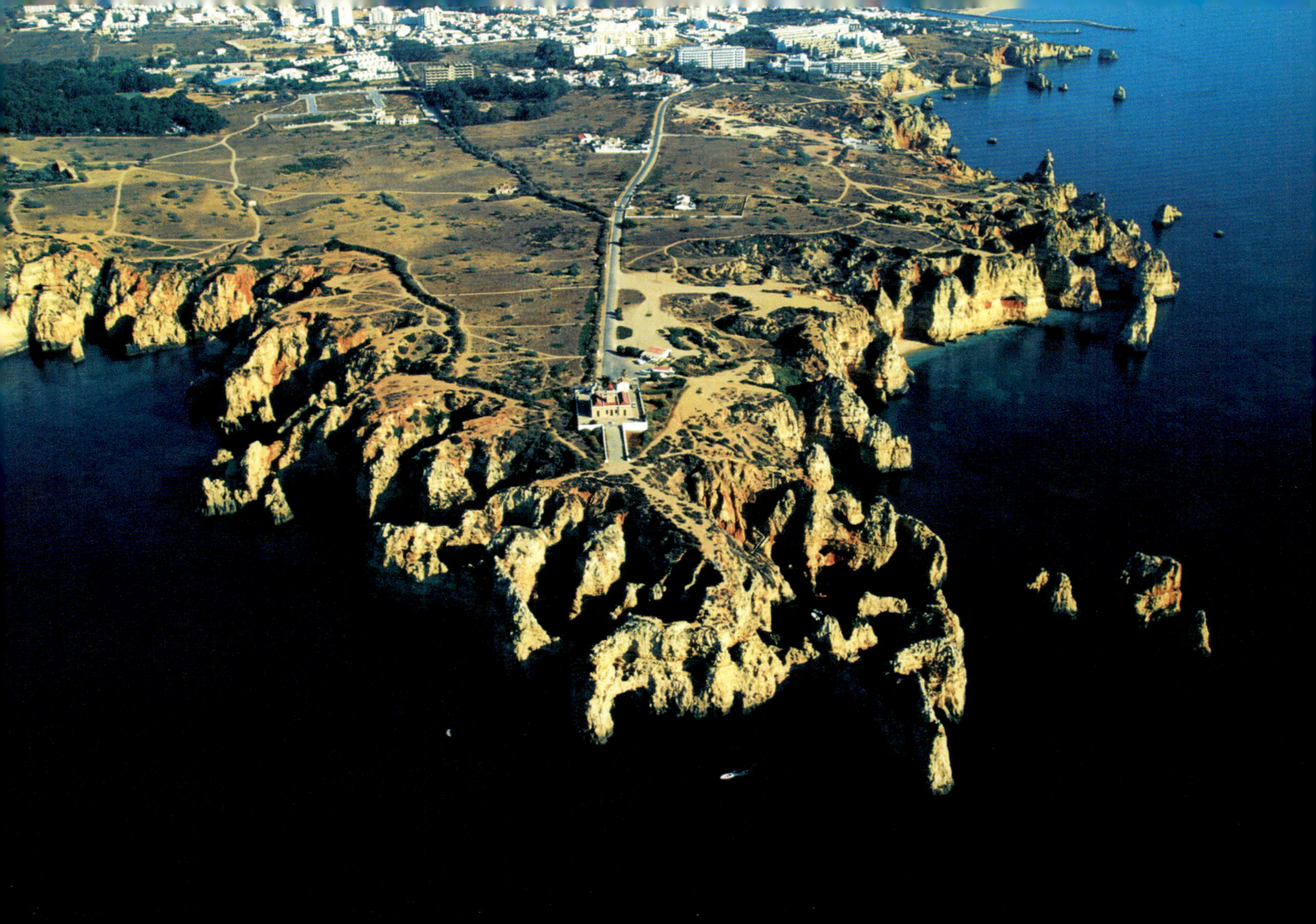

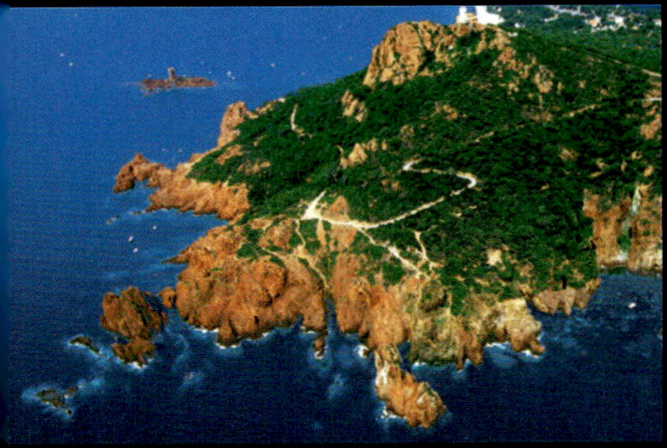

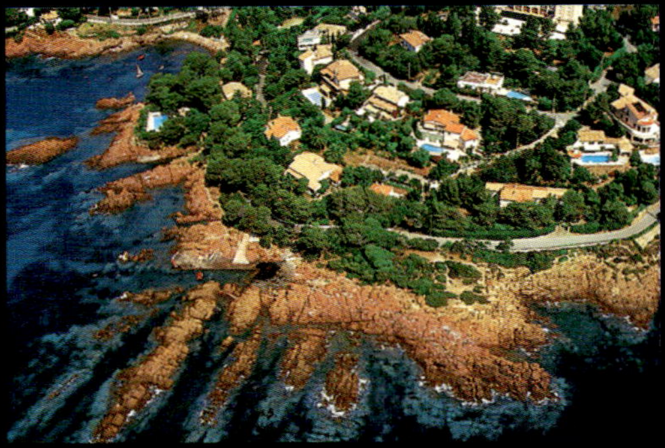

60
Between Saint-Raphaël and La Napoule, in France, the Estérel massif contains endless little inlets reachable only by boat, immersed in the Mediterranean. Red is the dominant color here.

61
Deep crevasses delimit the geological stratifications in one of the Iles de Lérins, just off Cannes in France. Movement of the earth's crust, over hundreds of thousands of years, has "vaulted" the surface in a vertical direction.

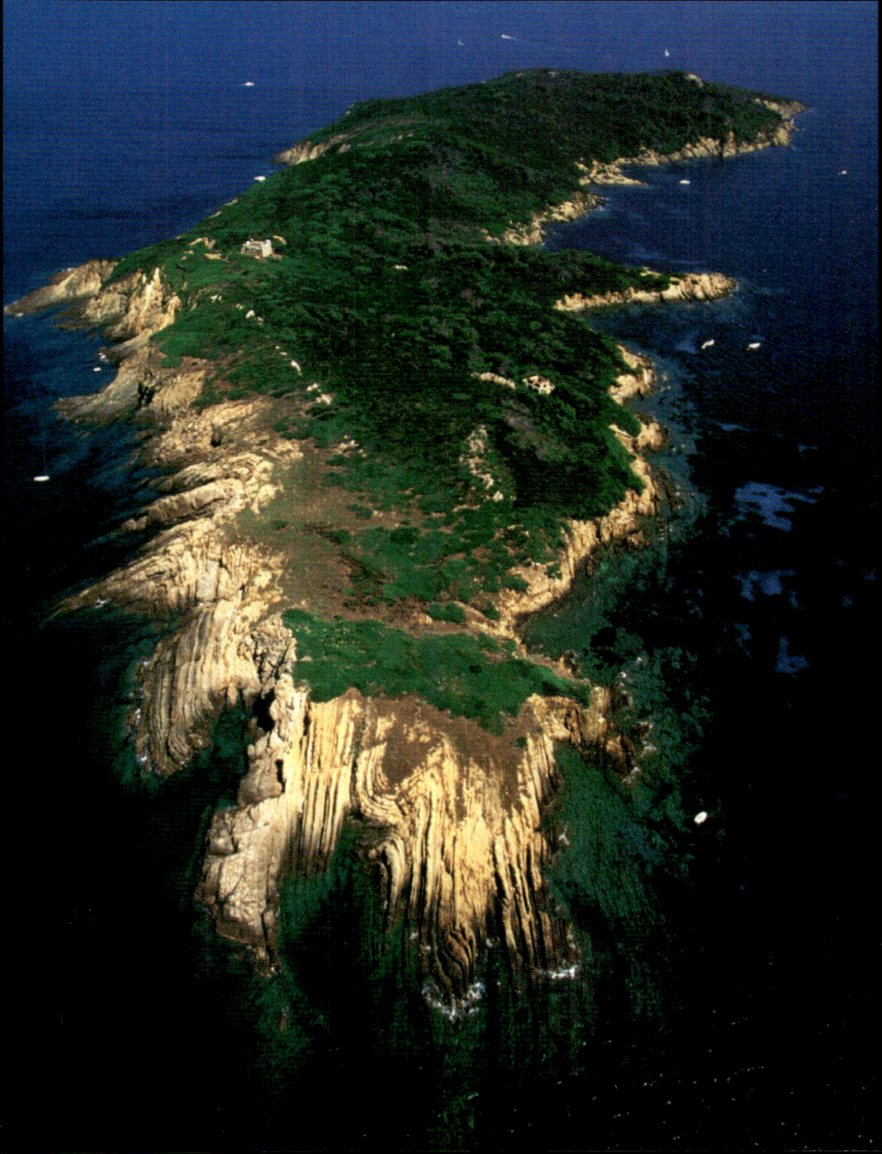

Mediterranean Sea

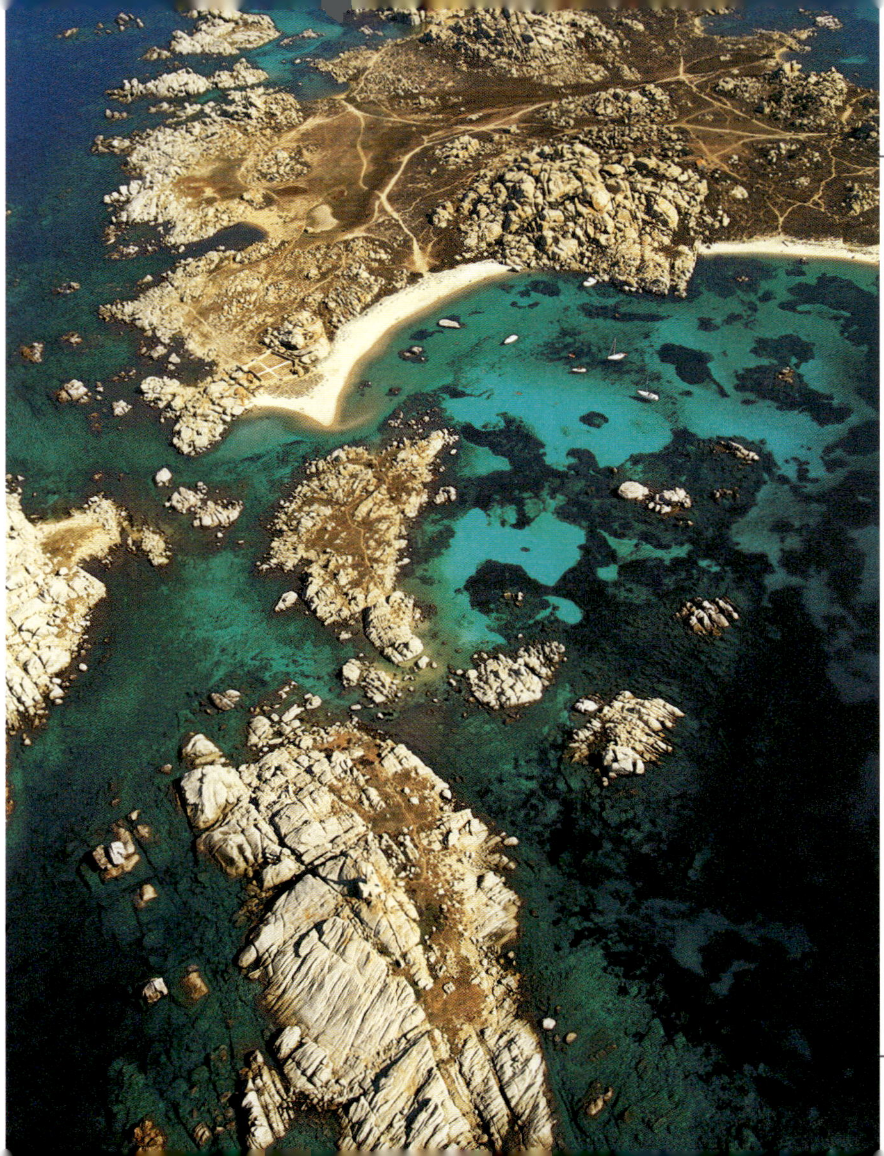

62
The tormented calcareous rock on the island of Cavallo, off Bonifacio in Corsica, creates magnificent natural vaults along the coast.

63
The warped calcareous rock on the island of Cavallo, off the coast of Bonifacio, in Corsica, creates magnificent natural vaults along the coast.

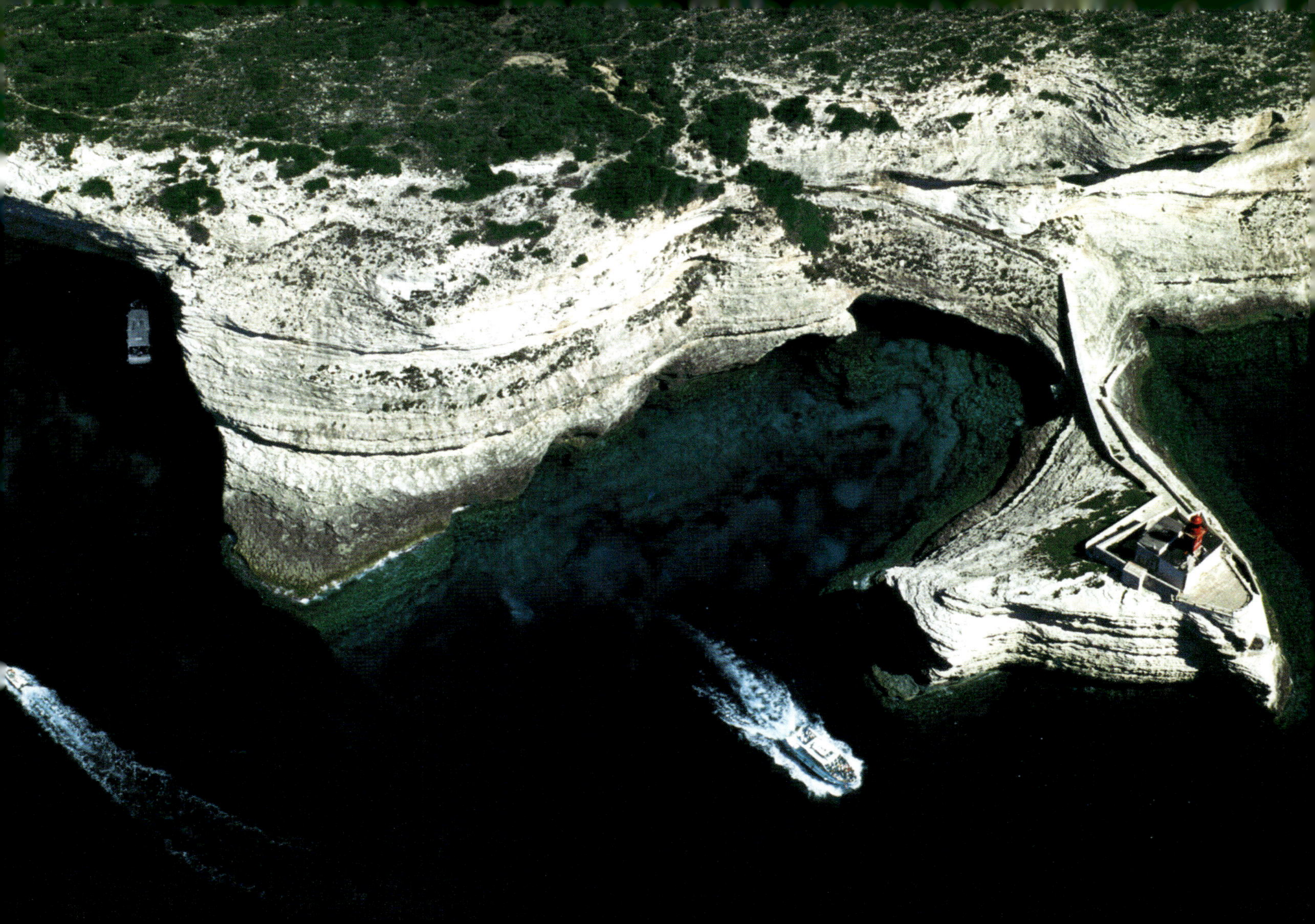

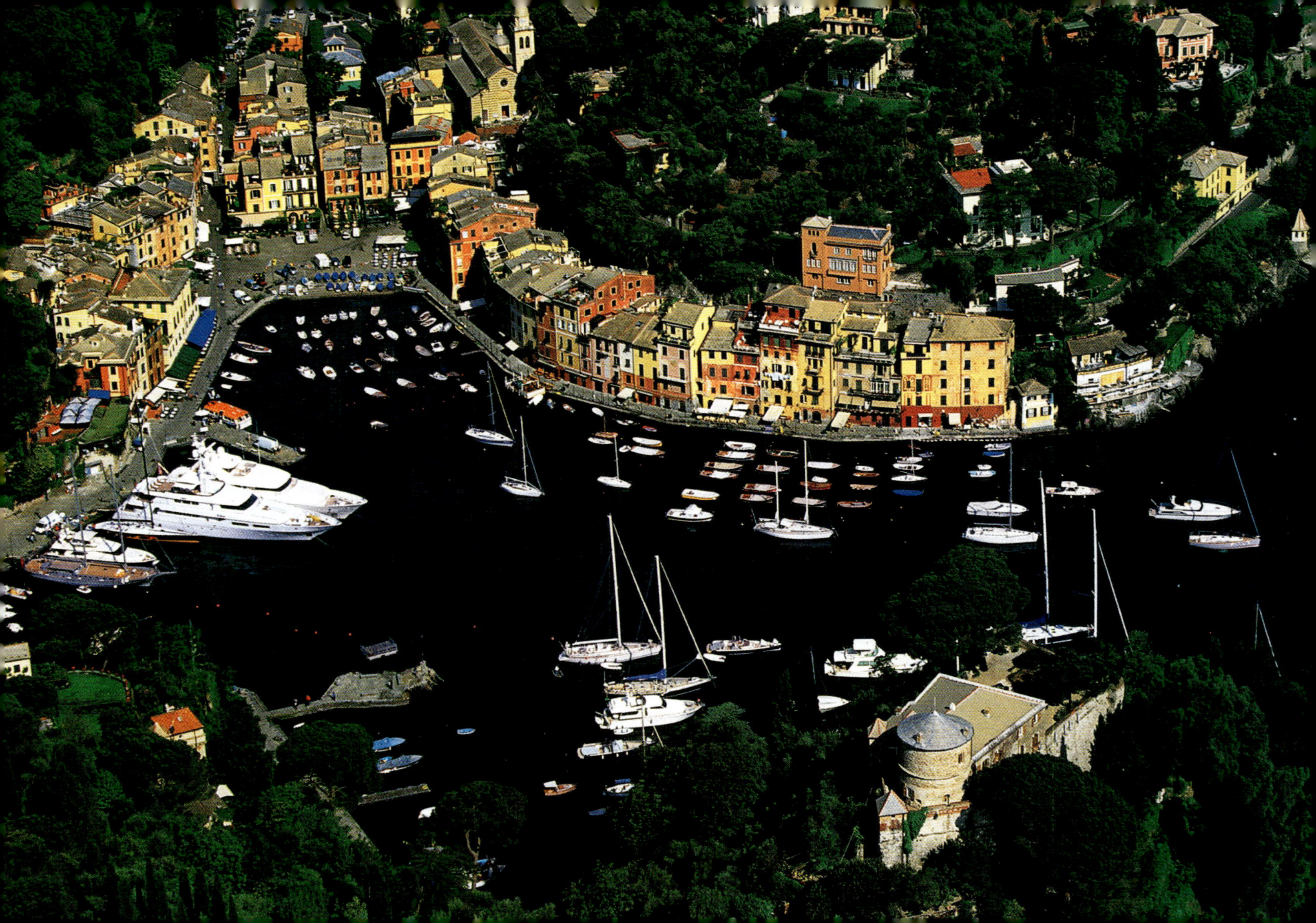

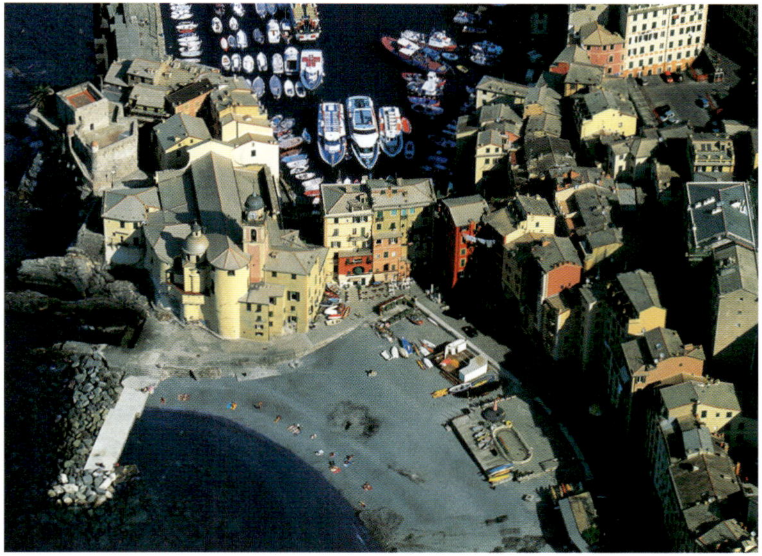

64 and 65

Given the inaccessible natural environment of the coast, the seaside villages on the Ligurian coastline in Italy (Portofino on the left, Camogli on the right) often feature an extremely concentrated appearance, with tightly packed houses often clinging to incredibly sheer cliffs.

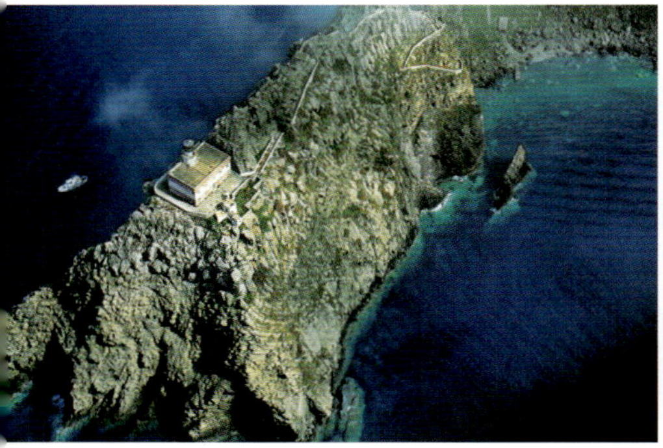

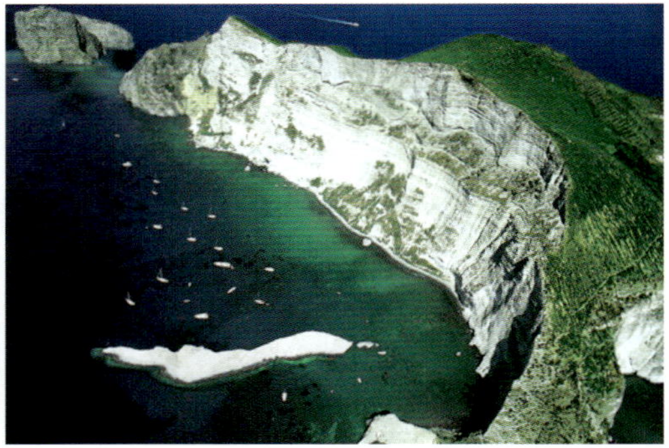

66 left
The island of Ponza in Italy is composed of material of volcanic origin that issued from below sea level and finally emerged on the surface.

66 right
Extraordinary combinations of color await those who fly over the island of Palmarola in Italy.

67
A smiling landscape characterizing the central area of Ponza, in Italy, between the lake of Cala Feola and the area of Mount Guardia. Fertility is a gift of the volcanoes, which really let themselves go wild here.

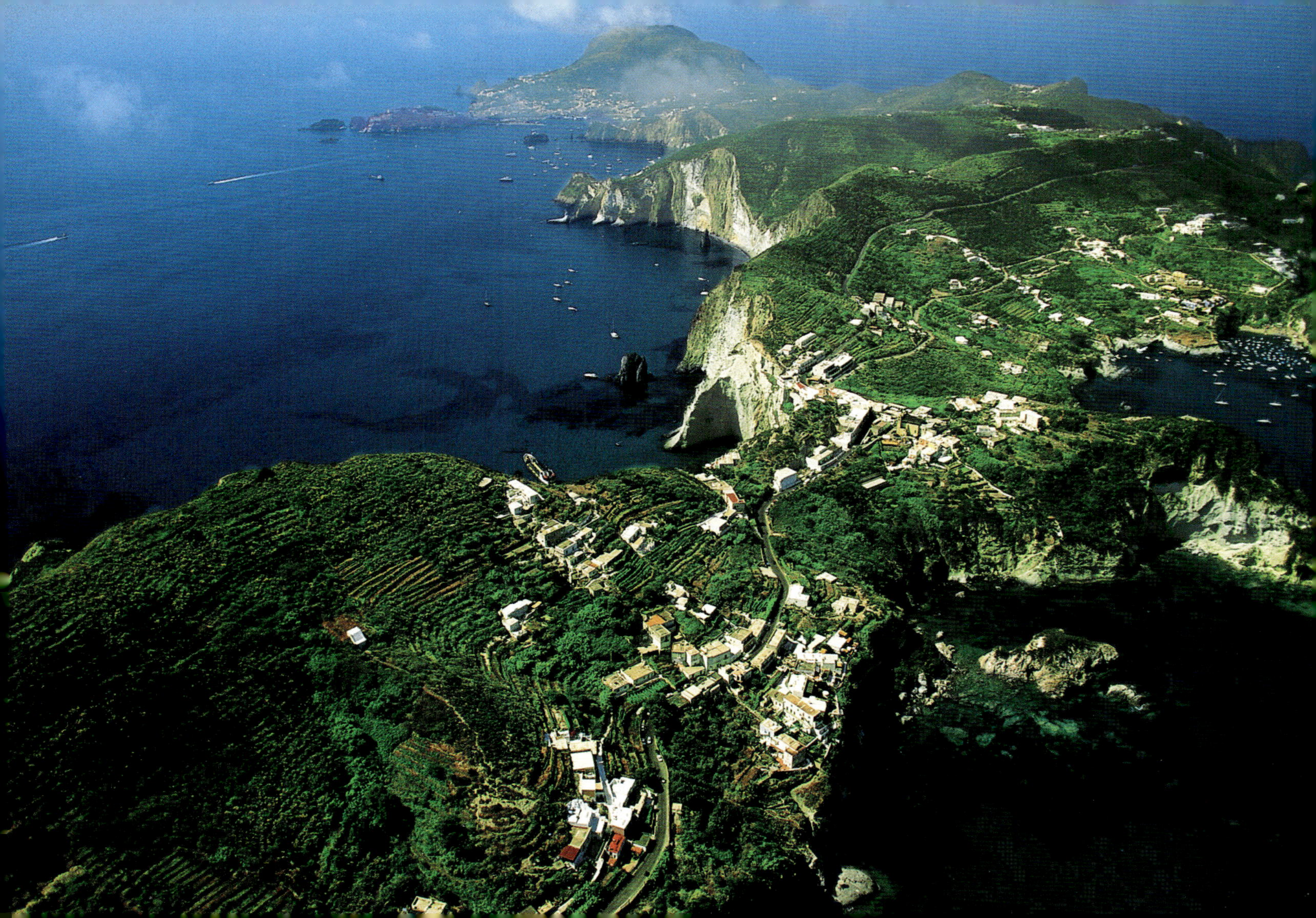

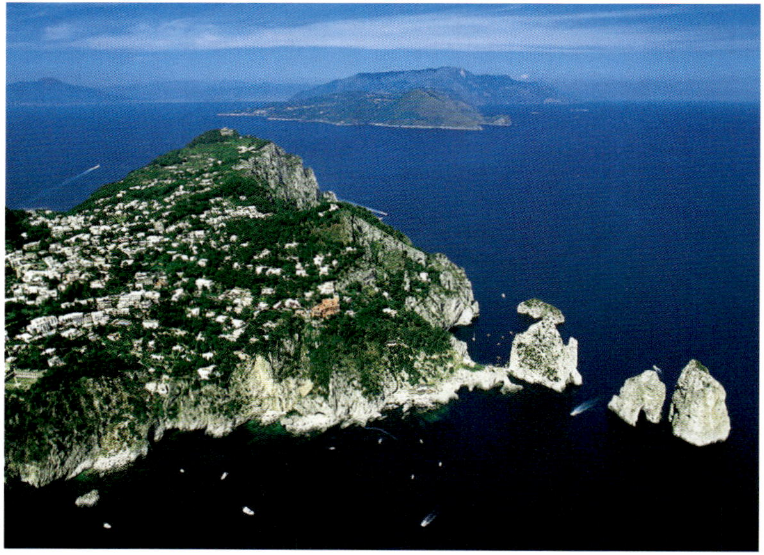

68

The stacks of Capri, in Italy, the island's main attraction, are Stella (358 feet), the Middle Stack (266 feet), crossed by a natural tunnel, and Scopolo (341 feet), the farthest from the coast.

69

The cliffs along the Amalfi Coast in Italy are truly precipitous, but this has not stopped human settlement, as proven by the village of Atrani, one of the gems of this area on the Italian Peninsula.

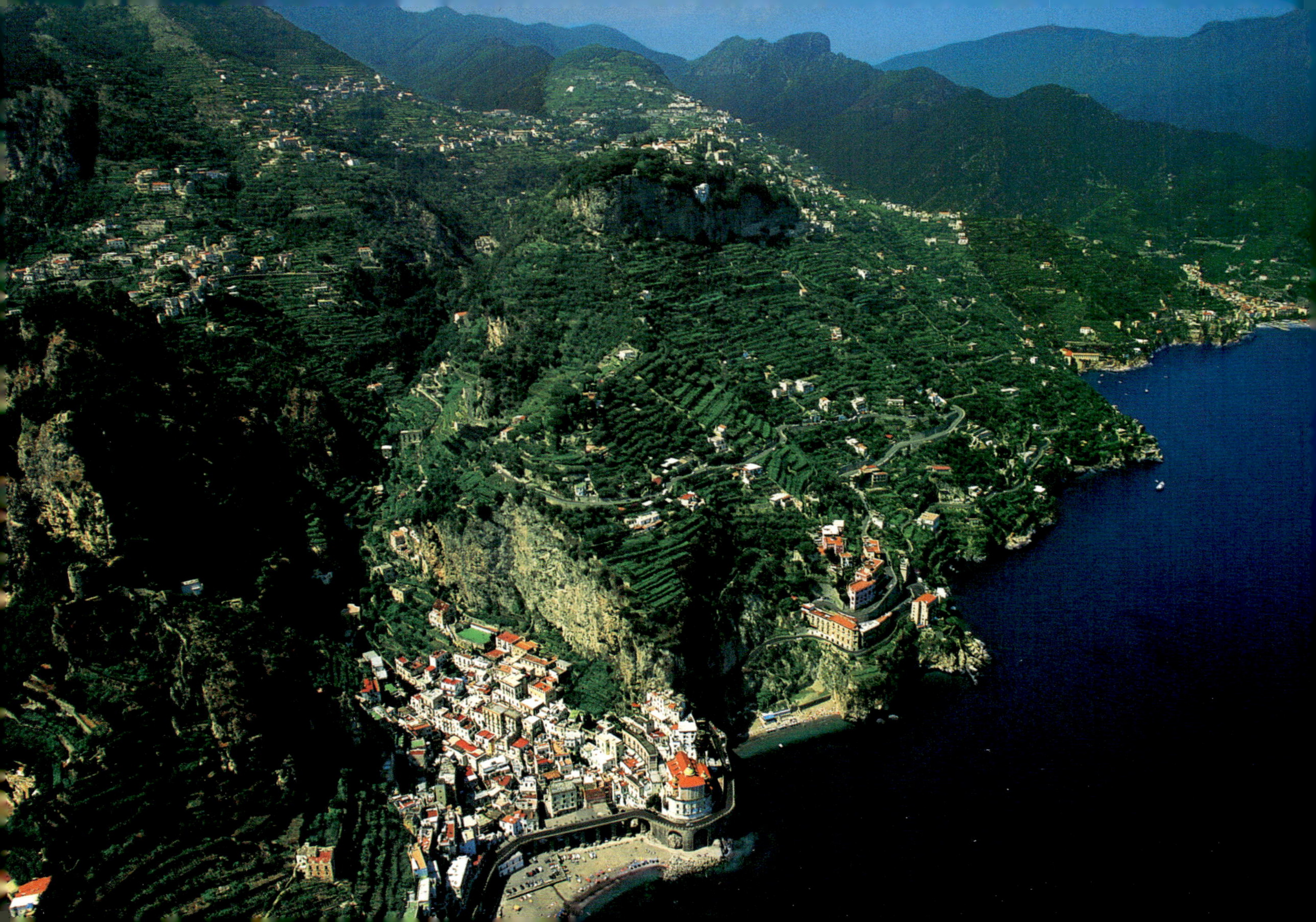

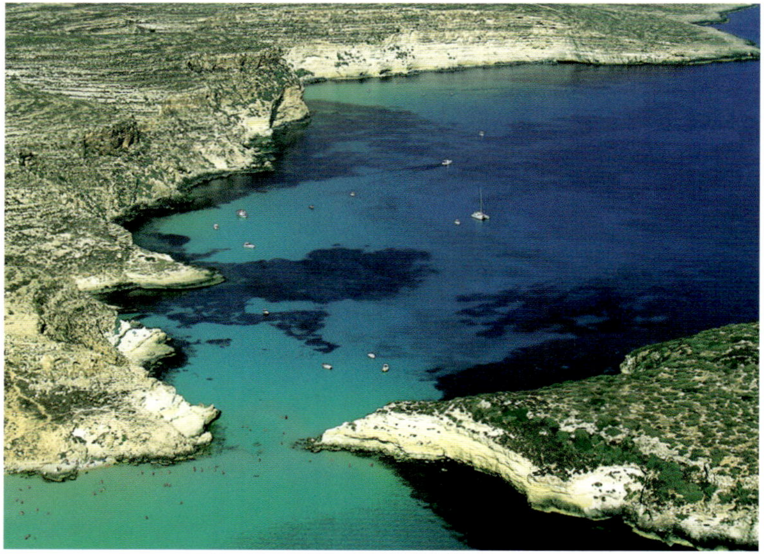

70

Lampedusa, along with Linosa, is the main island of the Pelagias, in Italy. Their name is derived from the Greek word *pelagos*, or sea, since they are composed of big volcanic rocks that surfaced from the sea floor.

71

The island of Budelli, in Italy, is famous above all for its gorgeous Pink Beach. This color is due to the presence of small fragments of red coral and the color of the island's granite.

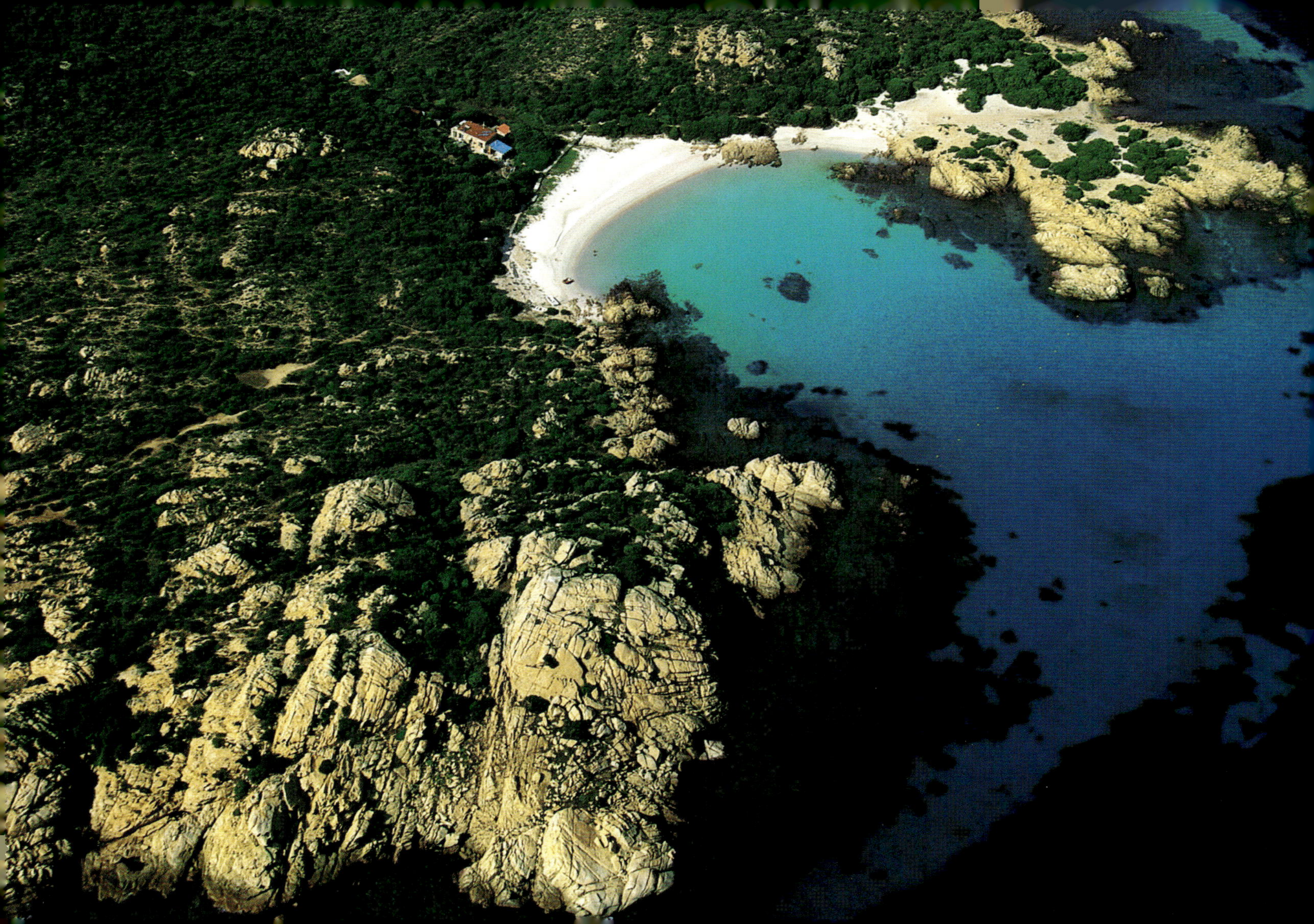

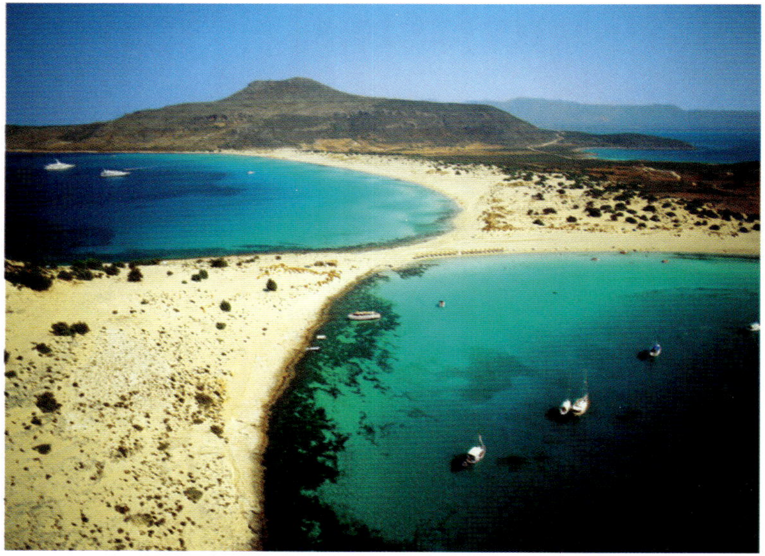

72

Twin bays trace the edges of a sandy isthmus on Elafonisos, in Greece, a small island in the Peloponnesus. The more rugged landscape changes appearance closer to the warm and luminous sea.

73

Calcareous gulfs border the Zante, or Zacinto, coast, the southernmost of the Ionian Islands in Greece. Zacinto has the biggest woods in the Greek Islands, but along the shore, the environment is amazingly harsh.

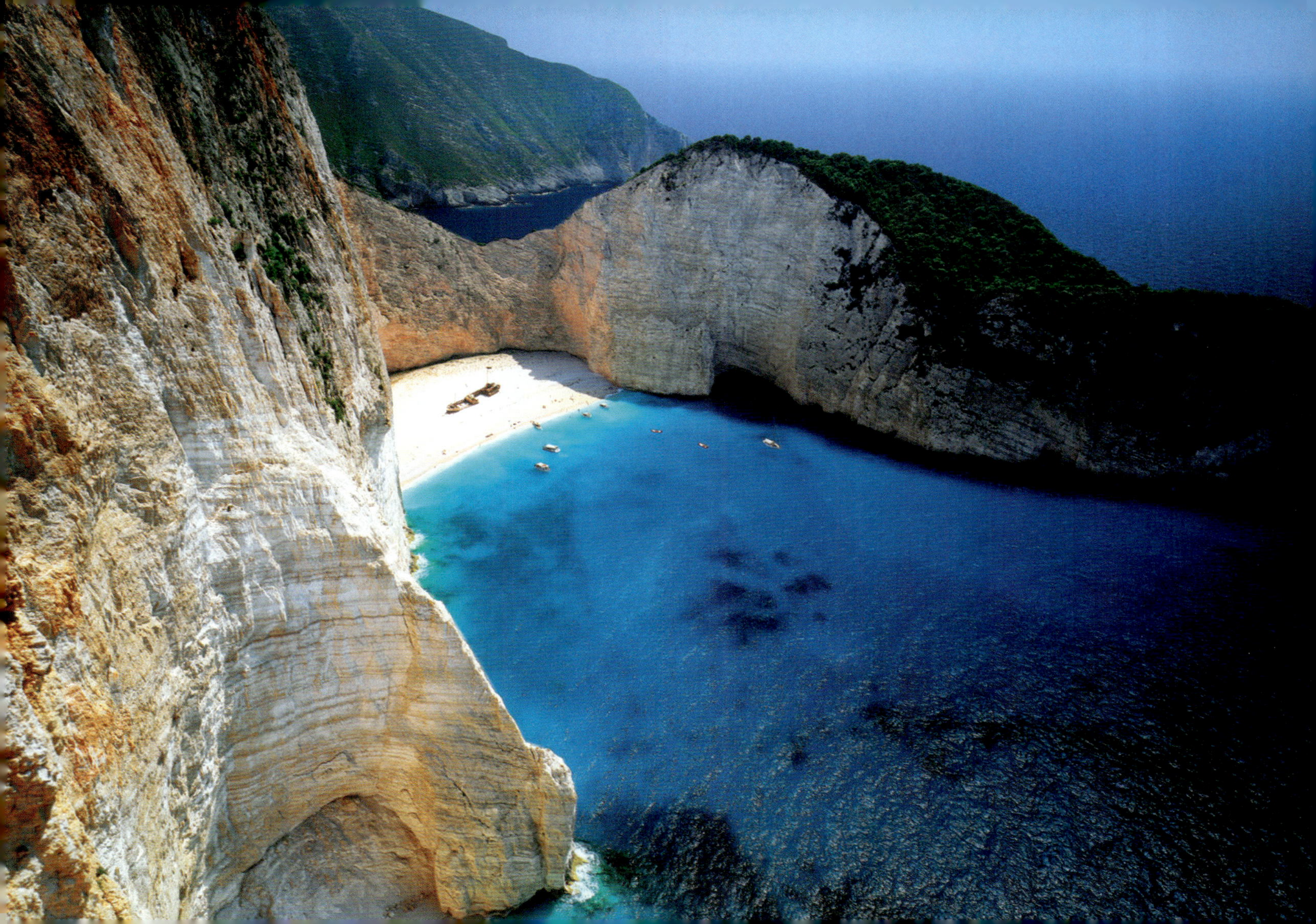

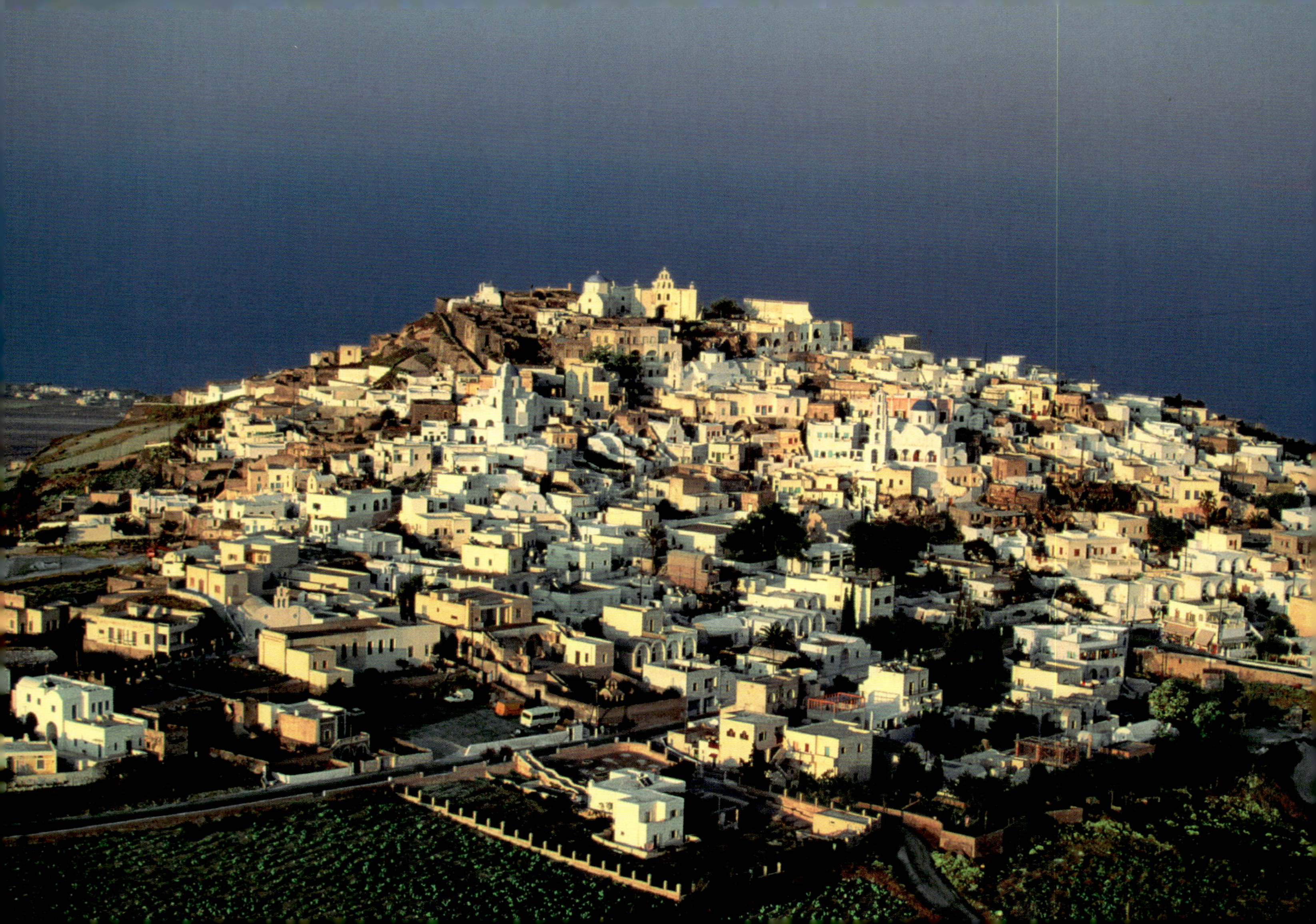

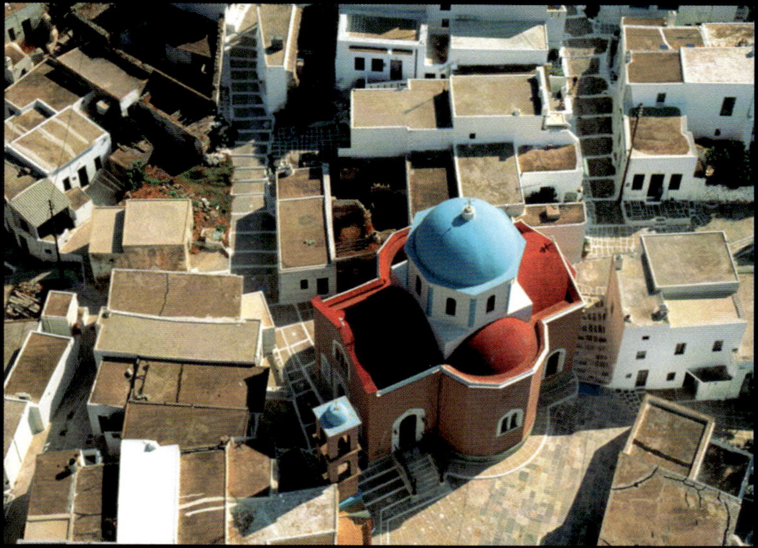

74
The village of Messaria, on Santorini Island in Greece, features the typical appearance of Cycladic towns: whitewashed houses, often perched on cliffs, originally chosen for defensive purposes. Pirates infested the Mediterranean for centuries.

75
Byzantine churches spread about the Cycladic Islands in Greece (in this case, Serifos) pop up like precious gems from little towns.

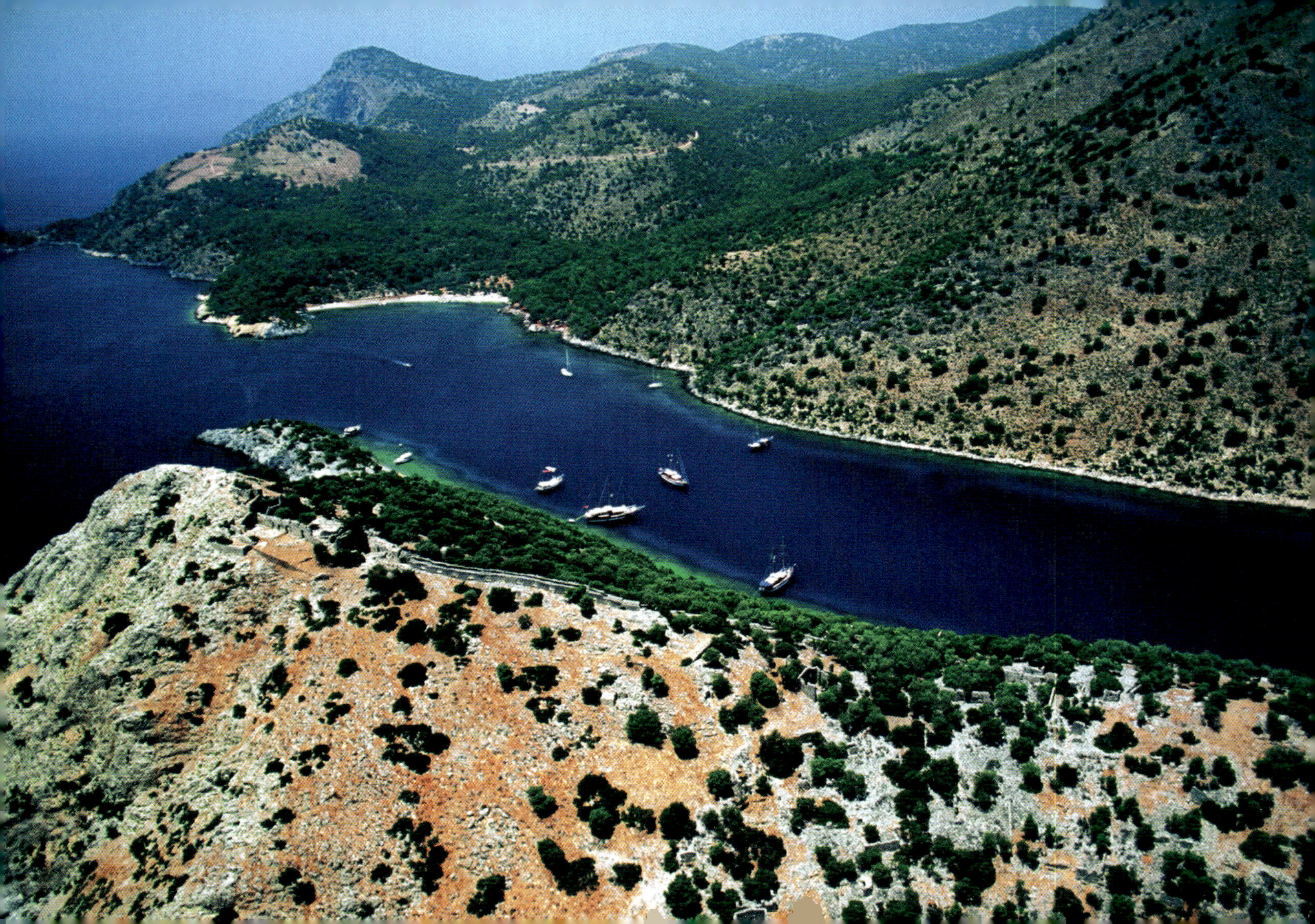

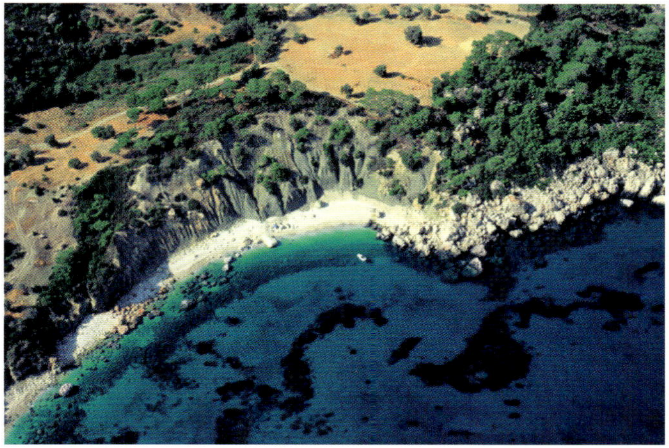

76 and 77
The southern coast of Turkey at Kas (left) and Fethiye (right) feature hidden inlets and harbors that often, because of the sparse population in the area and the relatively difficult access, can be completely deserted.

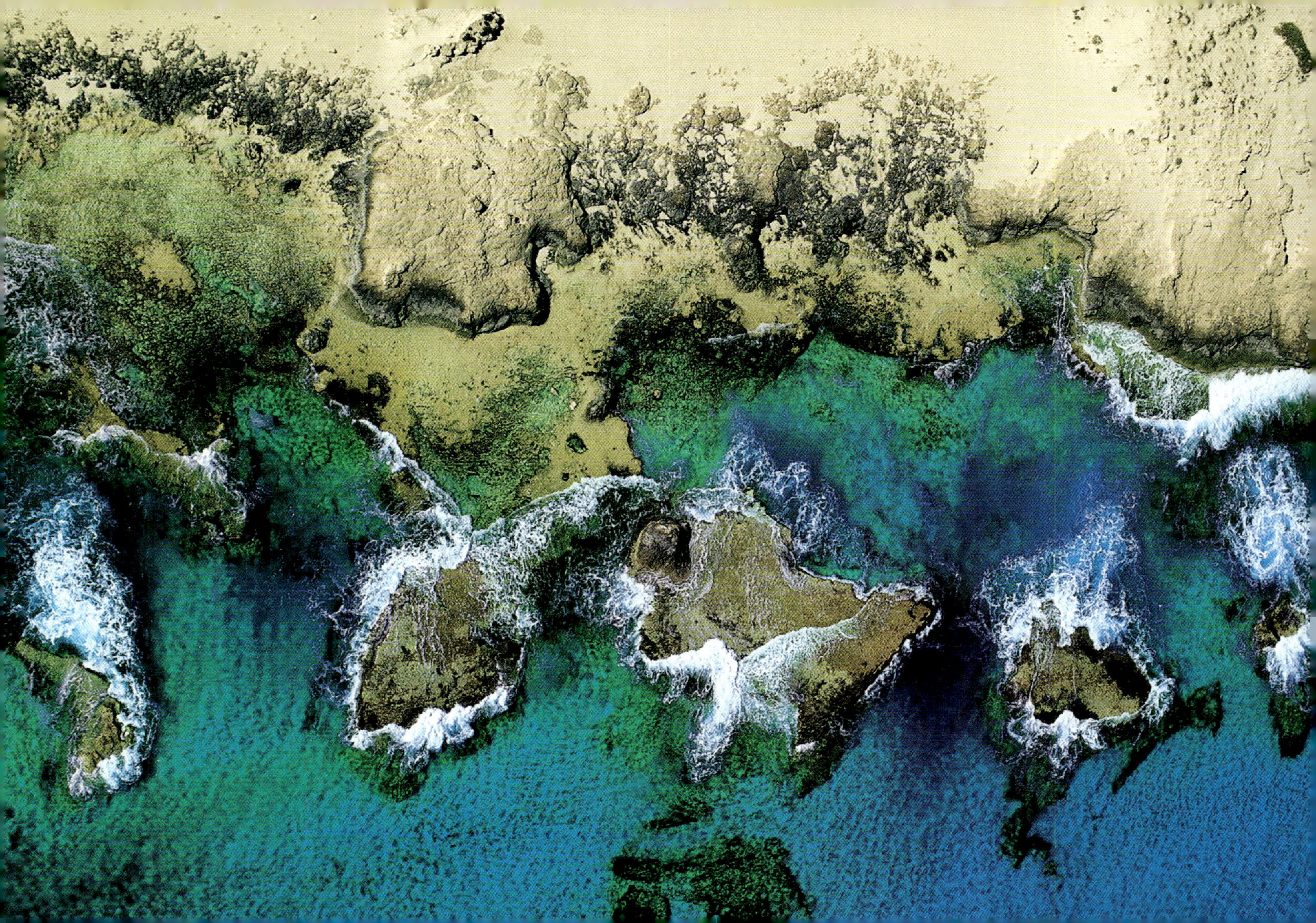

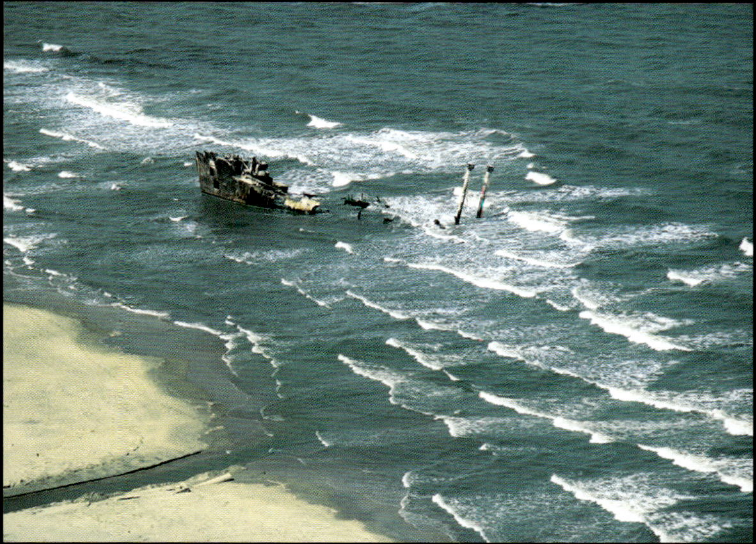

78 and 79

Colors of striking intensity sparkle along the Egyptian Mediterranean coast. It is not uncommon to see, in the shallow waters just off the coast, shipwrecks of old beached merchant vessels.

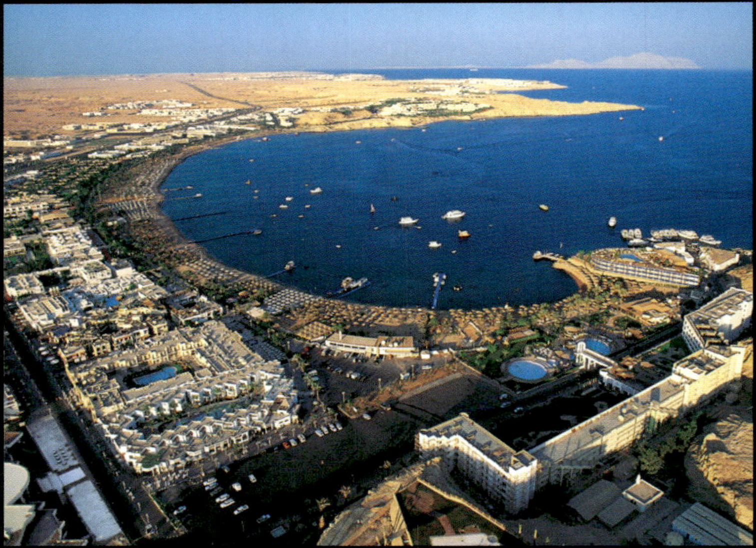

80
Sharm el-Sheik, in Egypt, is one of the most famous names to scuba-diving enthusiasts. An abundance of underwater life forms is proportionately opposite to the relative flatness of the landscape.

81
The turquoise realm seems to be found just under the surface of the water in the Strait of Tiran, in Egypt along the coast of the Red Sea.

Red Sea

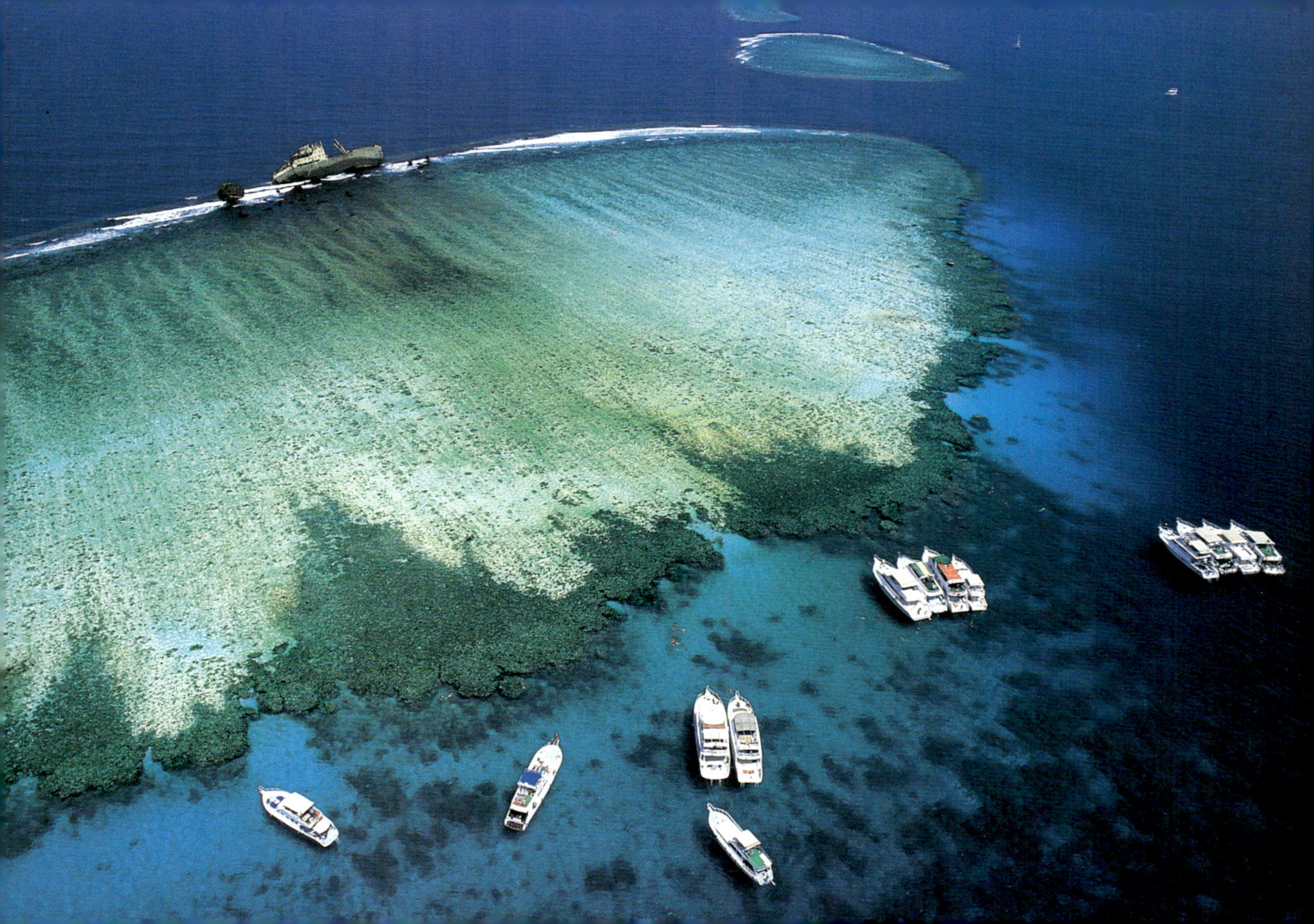

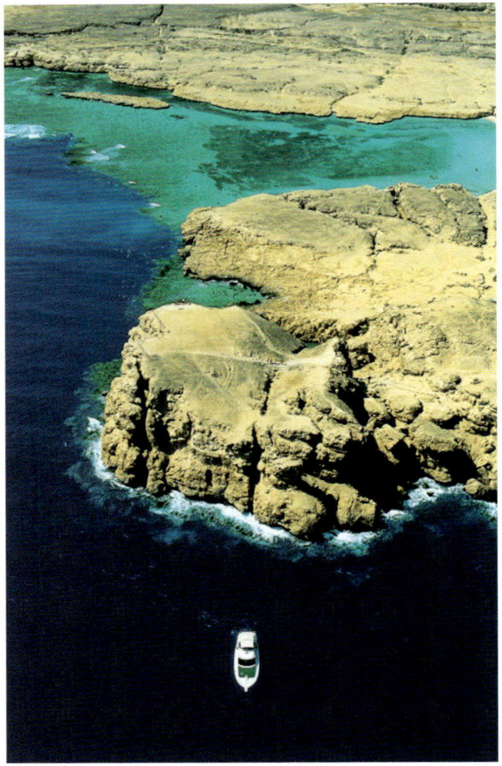

82 and 83

The Red Sea suddenly drops off 2,625 feet just off the peninsula of Ras Mohammed, formed by a fossil coral reef. The spot is found about 12 miles south of Sharm el-Sheikh, in Egypt.

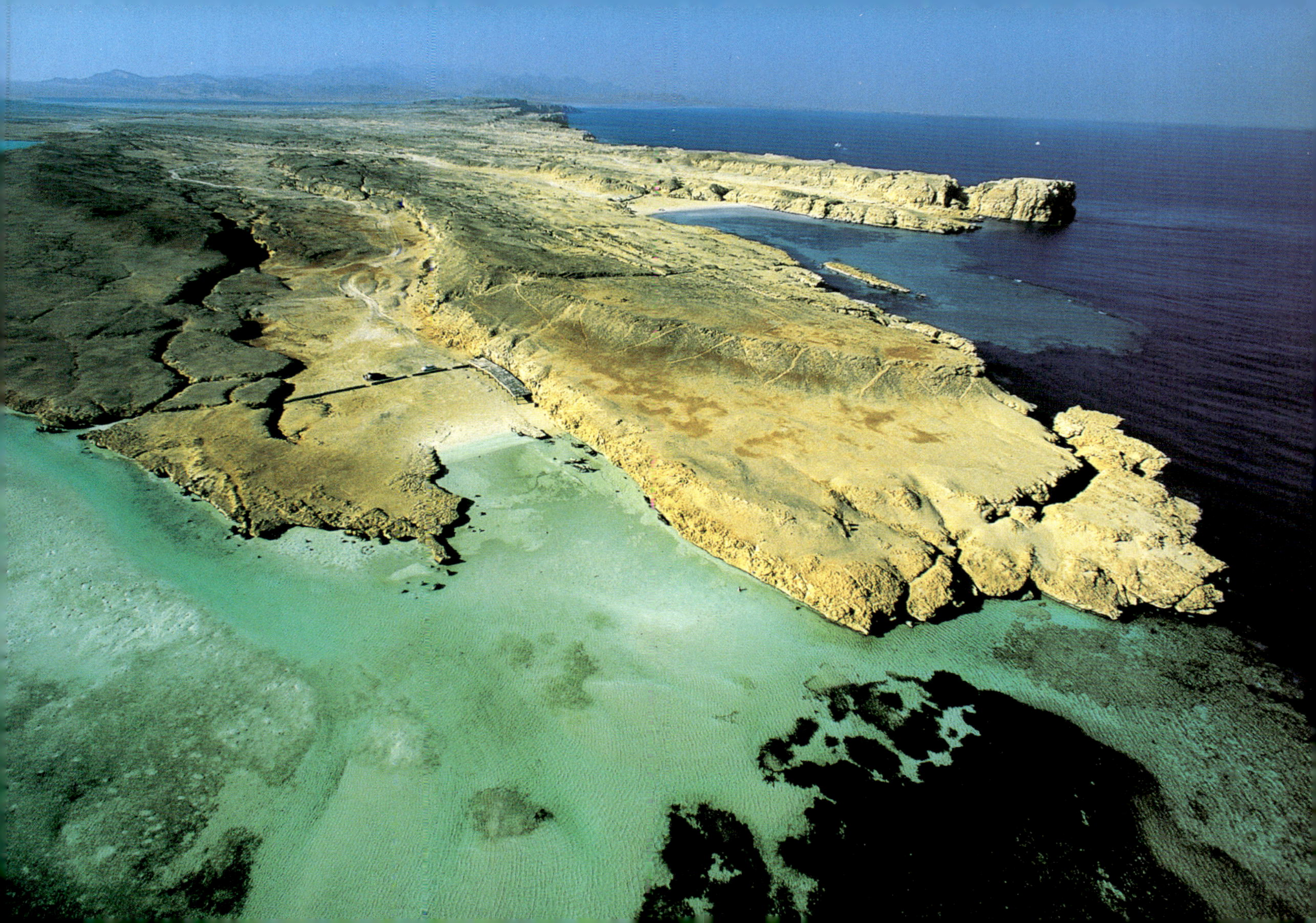

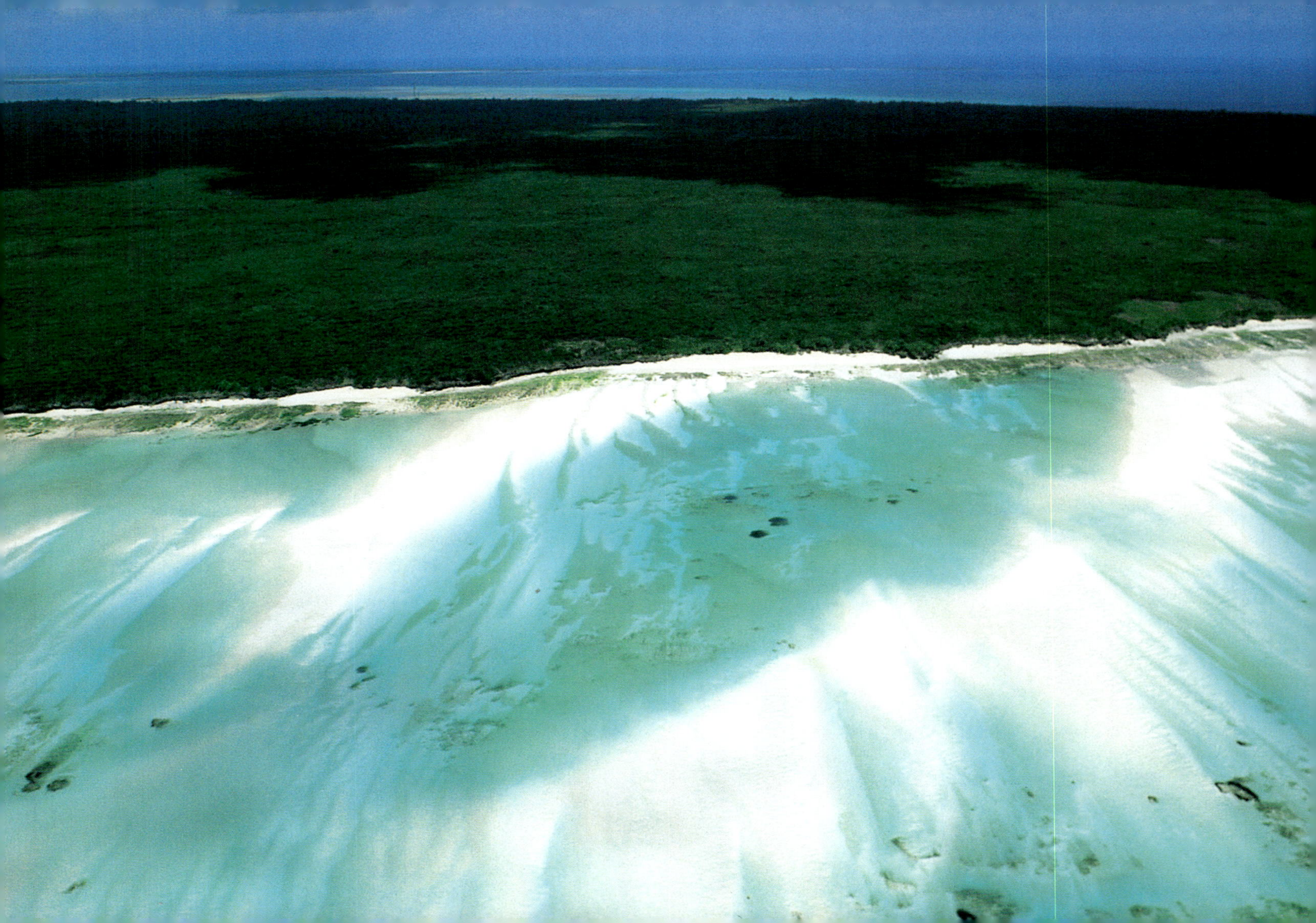

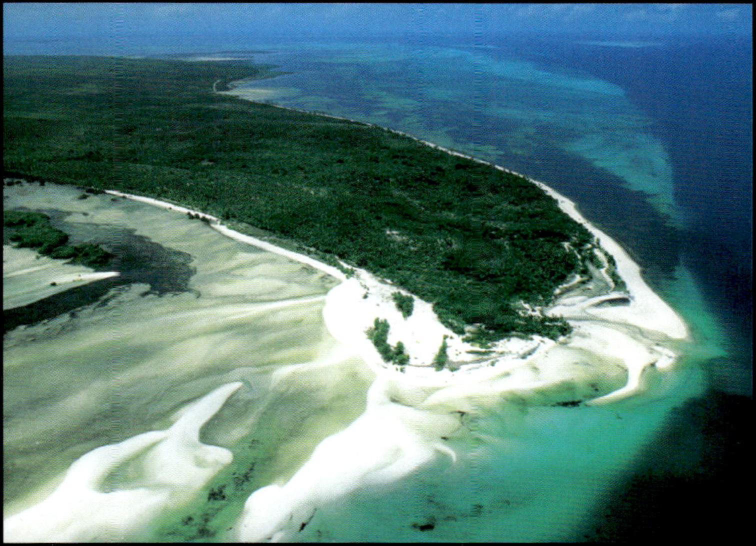

84 and 85
The eastern coast of the Tanzanian island of Zanzibar features beaches of fine sand and a transparent, shallow sea, in whose shallow waters marine algae are farmed.

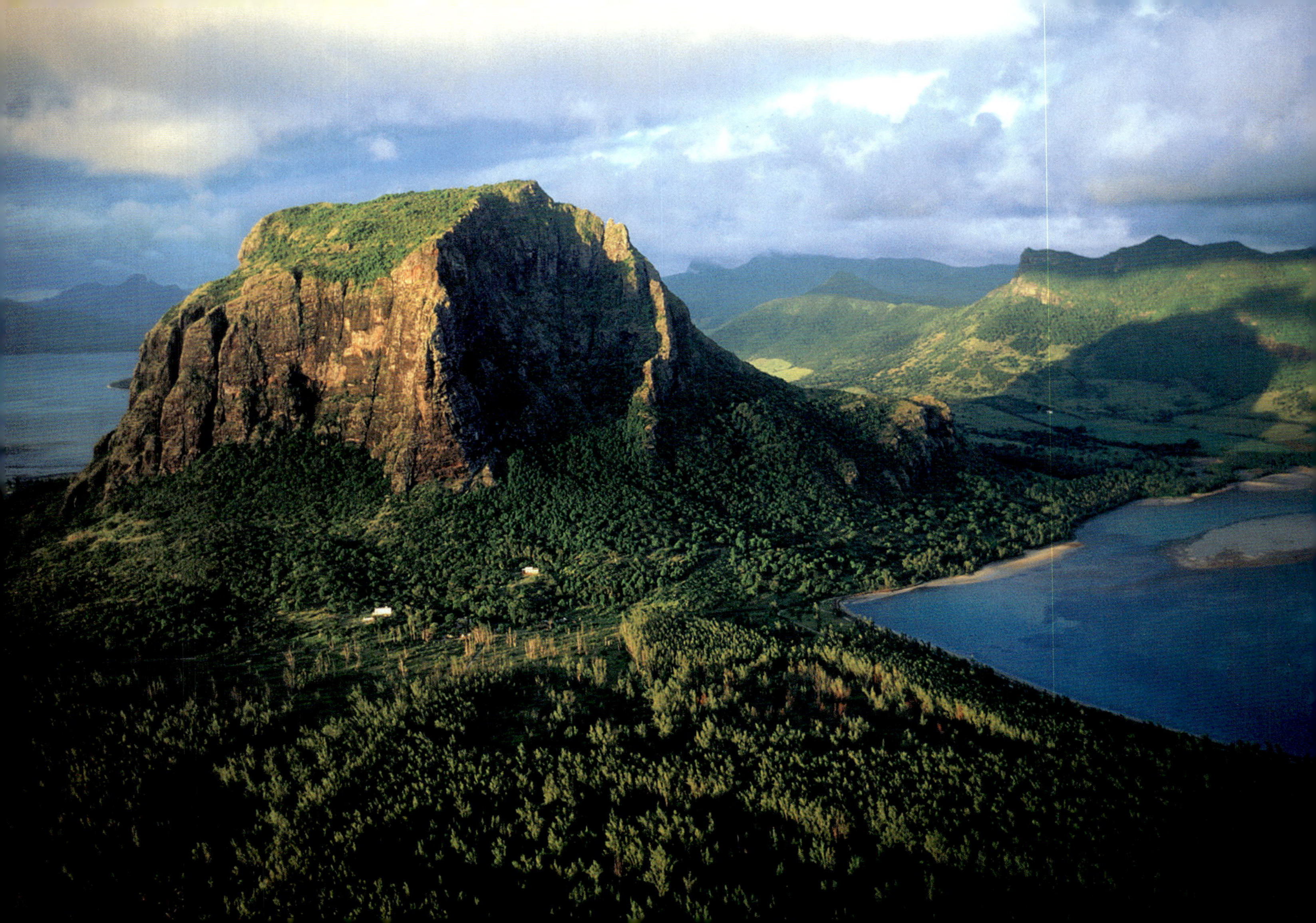

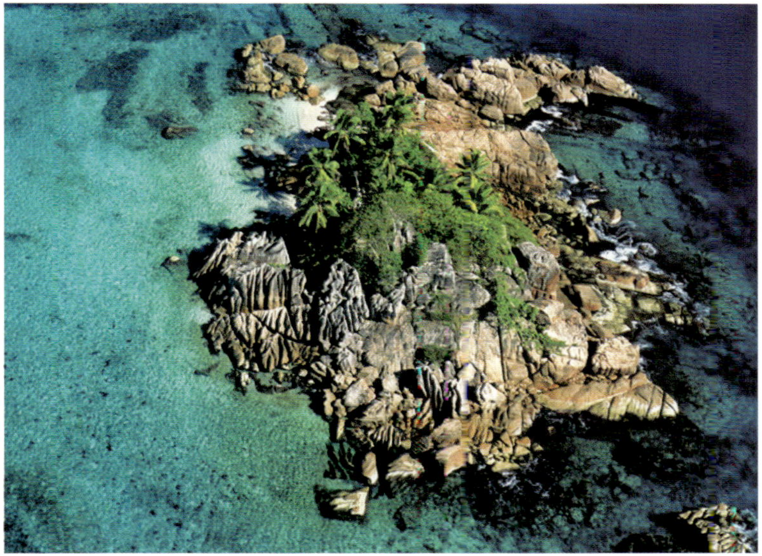

86

Morne Brabant rises suddenly from Mauritius Island, the county seat of the island state of the same name. The rise, friable and heavily eroded was supposedly a shelter to many fugitive slaves in the past.

87

In the tropics, there is no space too small to prevent the lush vegetation from prospering, as shown by this little island in the area of Ile de la Digue, in the island state of the Seychelles.

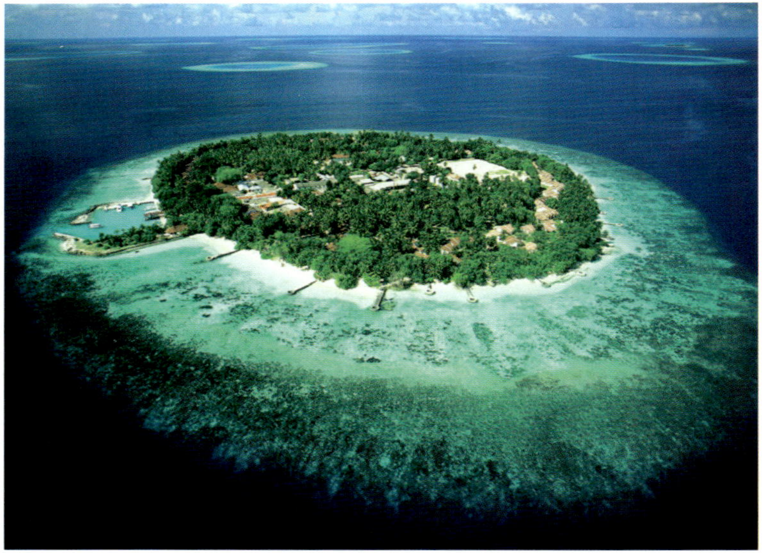

88

No less than 1,192 coral islands, big or small – and perfect like this one – compose the archipelago of the Maldive Islands, in the Indian Ocean.

89

The view of the atolls is probably the most spectacular that the ocean can offer. The Maldives contain 26 groups, placed in a strip running exactly from north to south.

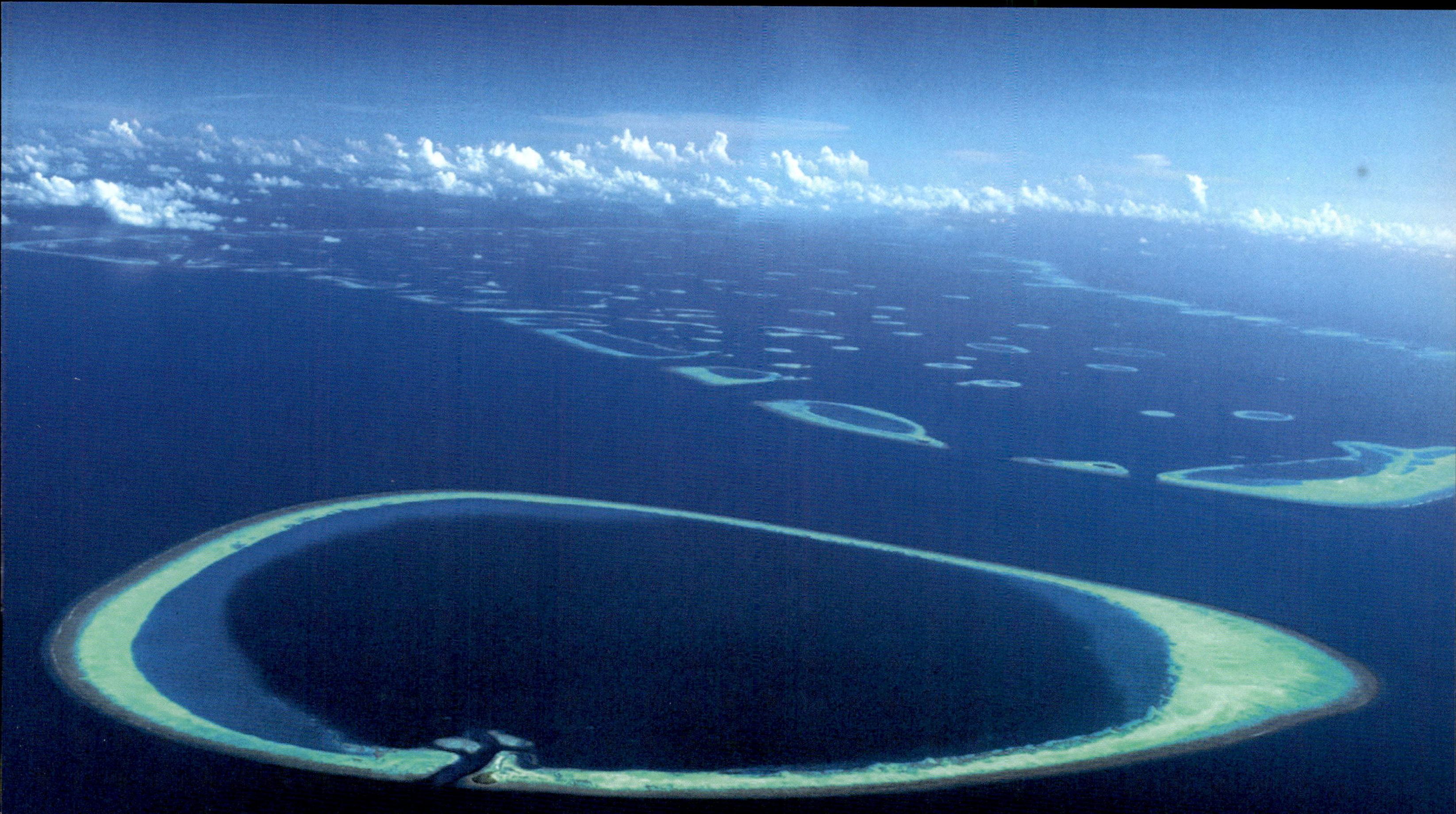

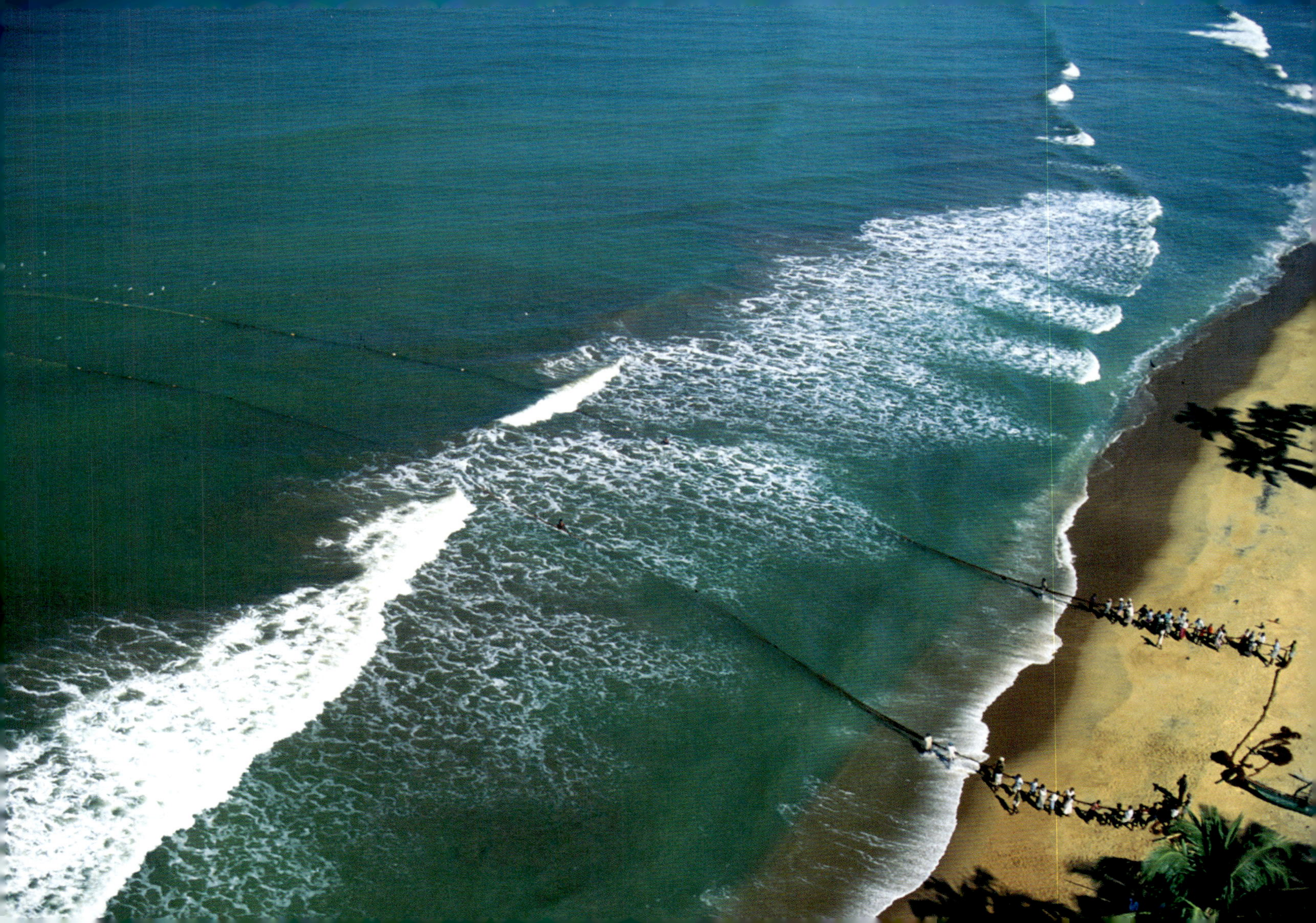

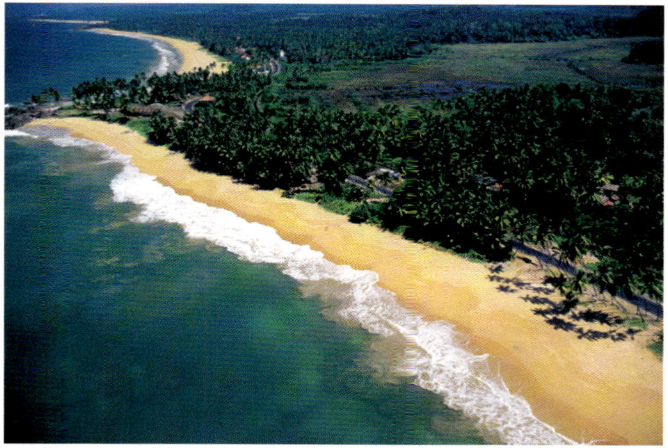

90 and 91
Along the beaches on the island of Sri Lanka (where at times it seems as if nothing has changed in 1,000 years), fishermen pulling nets from the low waters using the traditional method can still be seen.

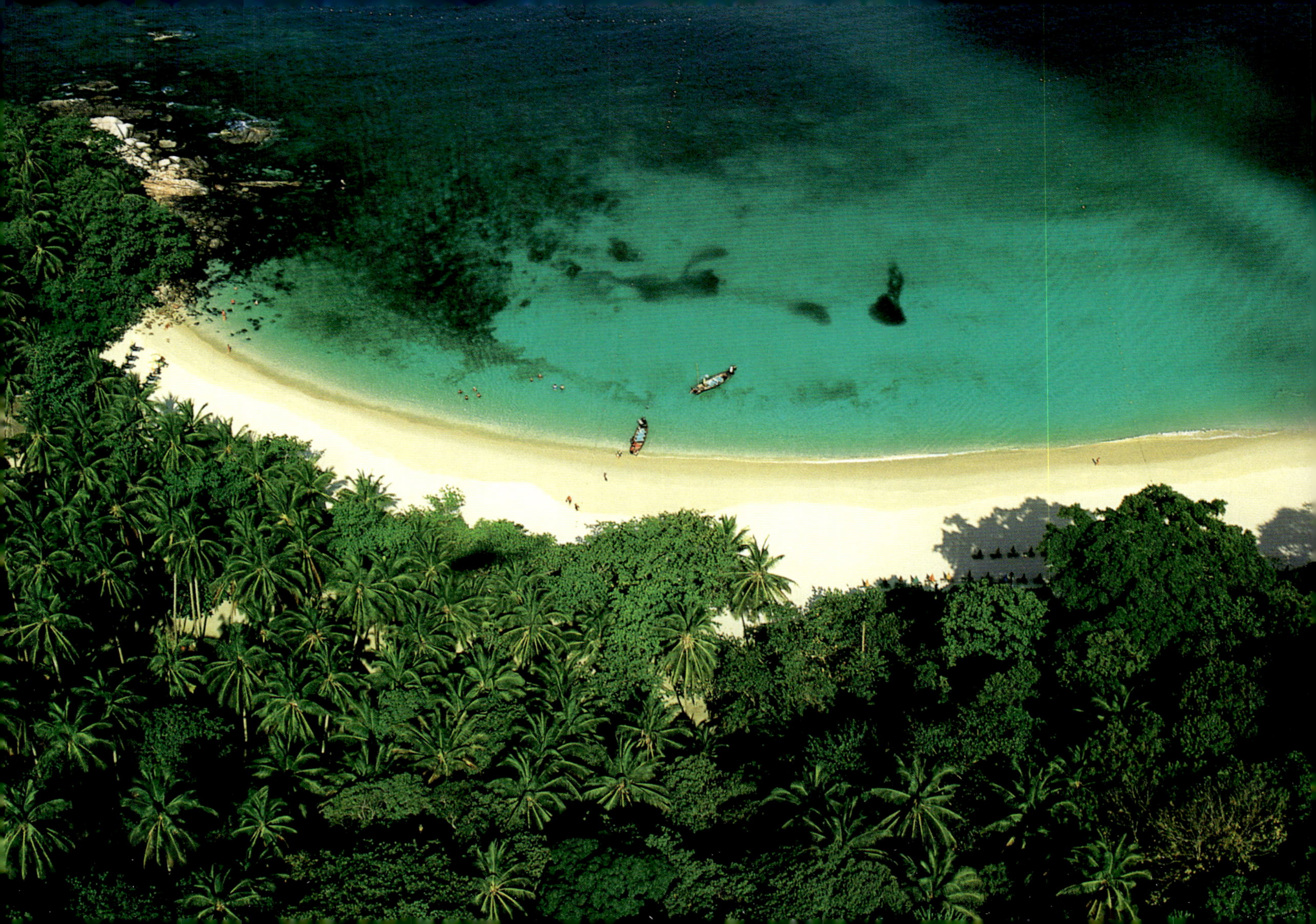

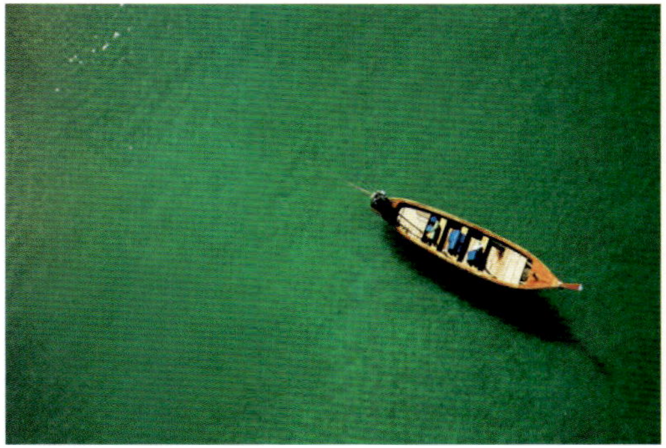

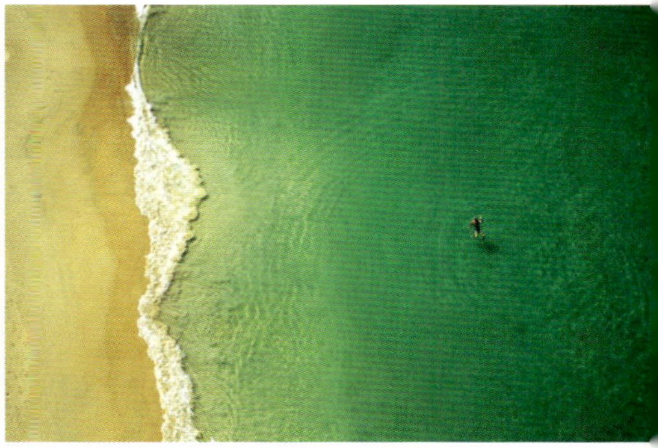

92 and 93

The island of Phuket, in Thailand, is deservedly famous for the purity of its colors. The sea is almost blinding in the dry months, between December and March, when monsoons do not churn up the waters.

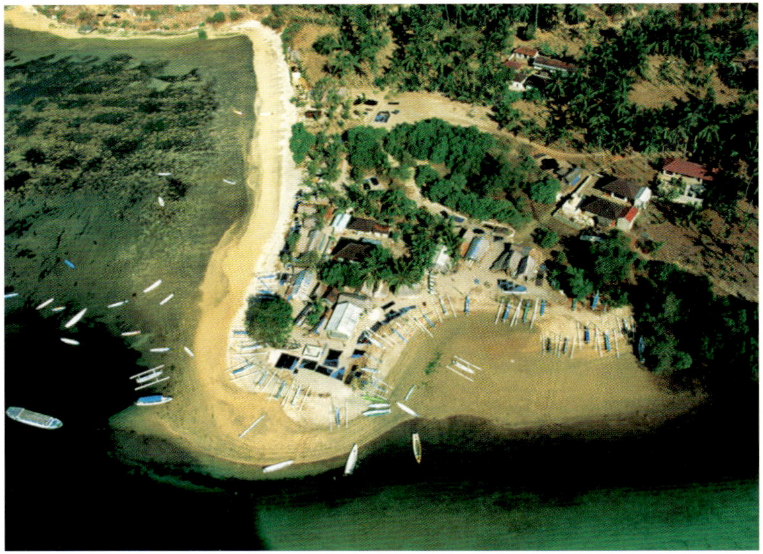

94 and 95

Thin, single-hull and catamaran boats stand out along these two beaches on the island of Bali, in Indonesia. Small fishing vessels of this type are generally painted with lively colors, making the view from the sky even more seductive.

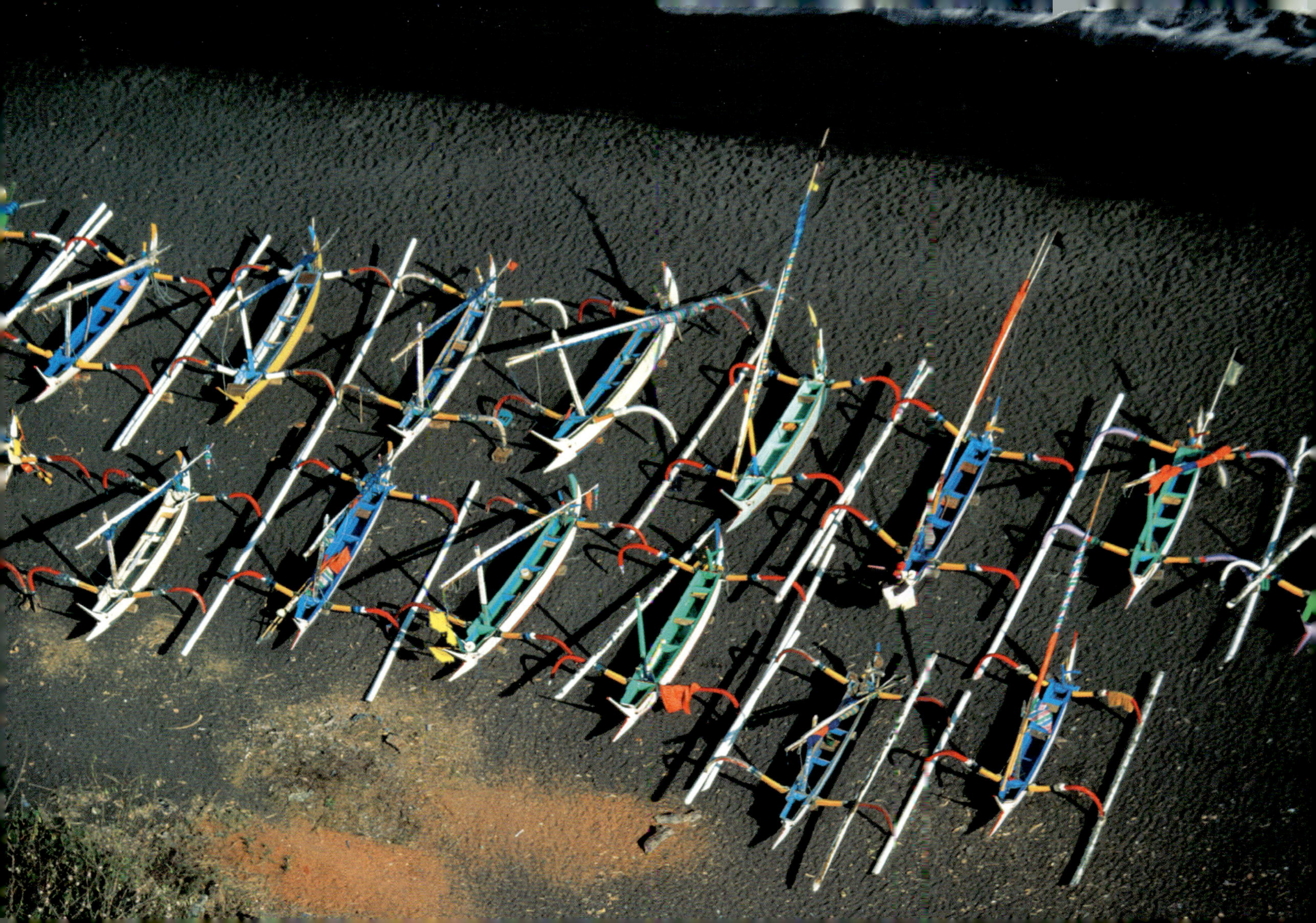

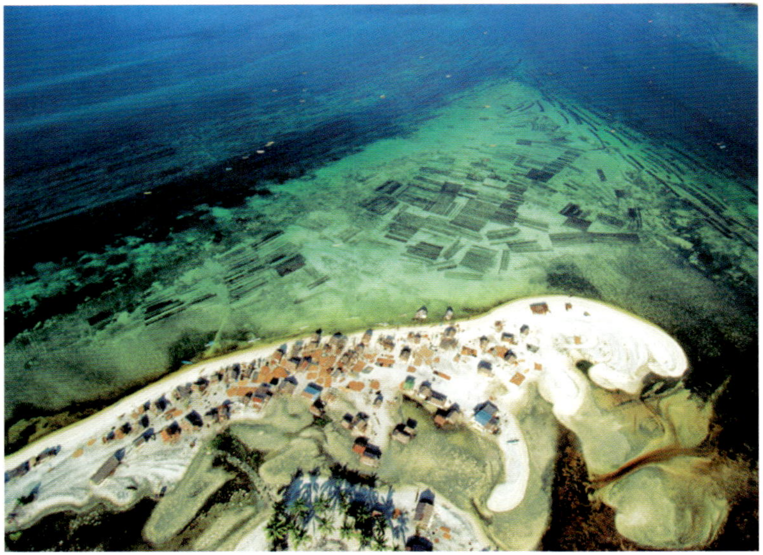

96
Fishermen's houses are spread about a little island in the archipelago of the Sulu Islands in the Philippines.

97
Unique color contrasts are created along the coast of the island of Panducan in the Philippines. Generally, the waters of colder, fresh-water streams poorer in nutrients give rise to these masterpieces.

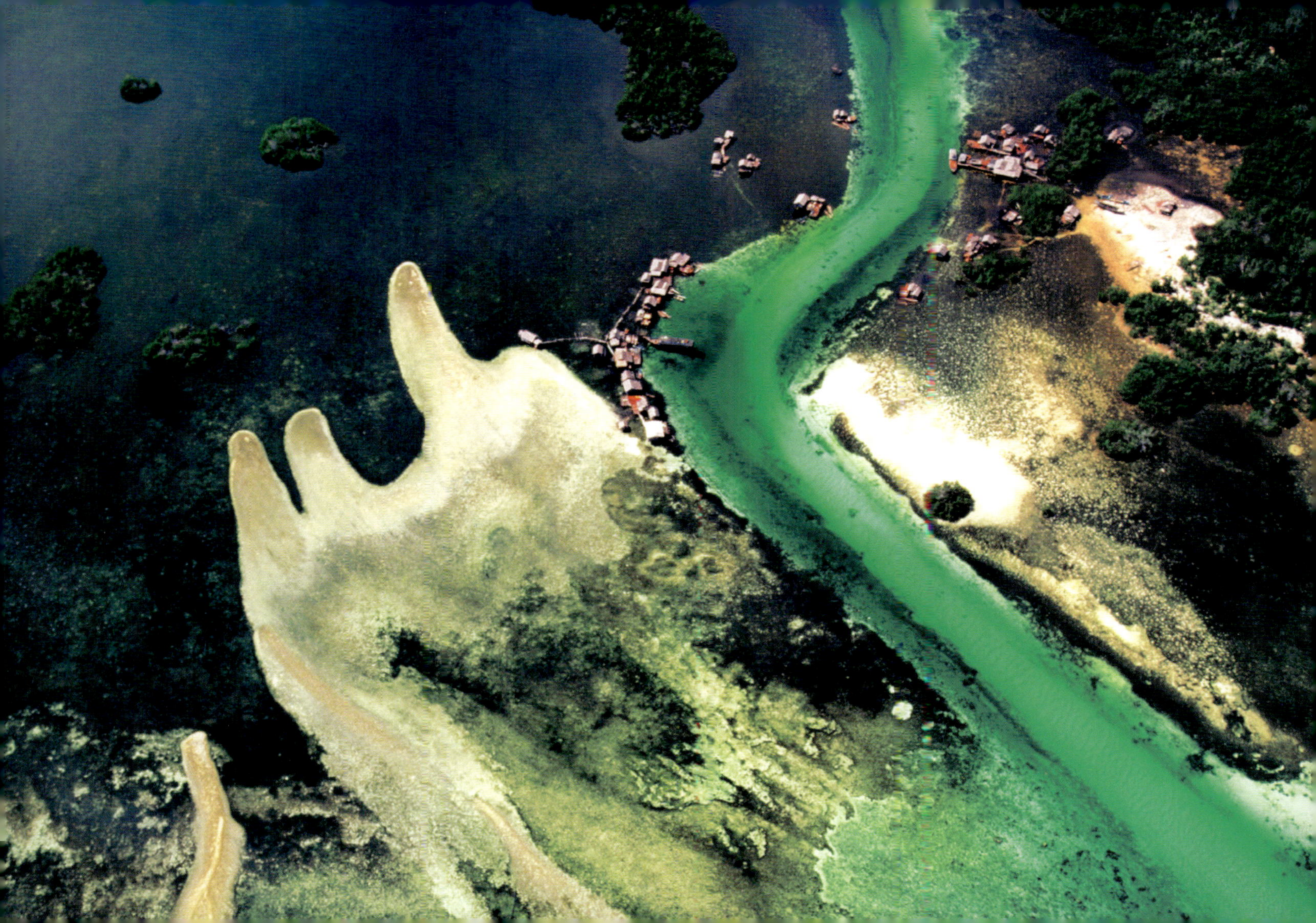

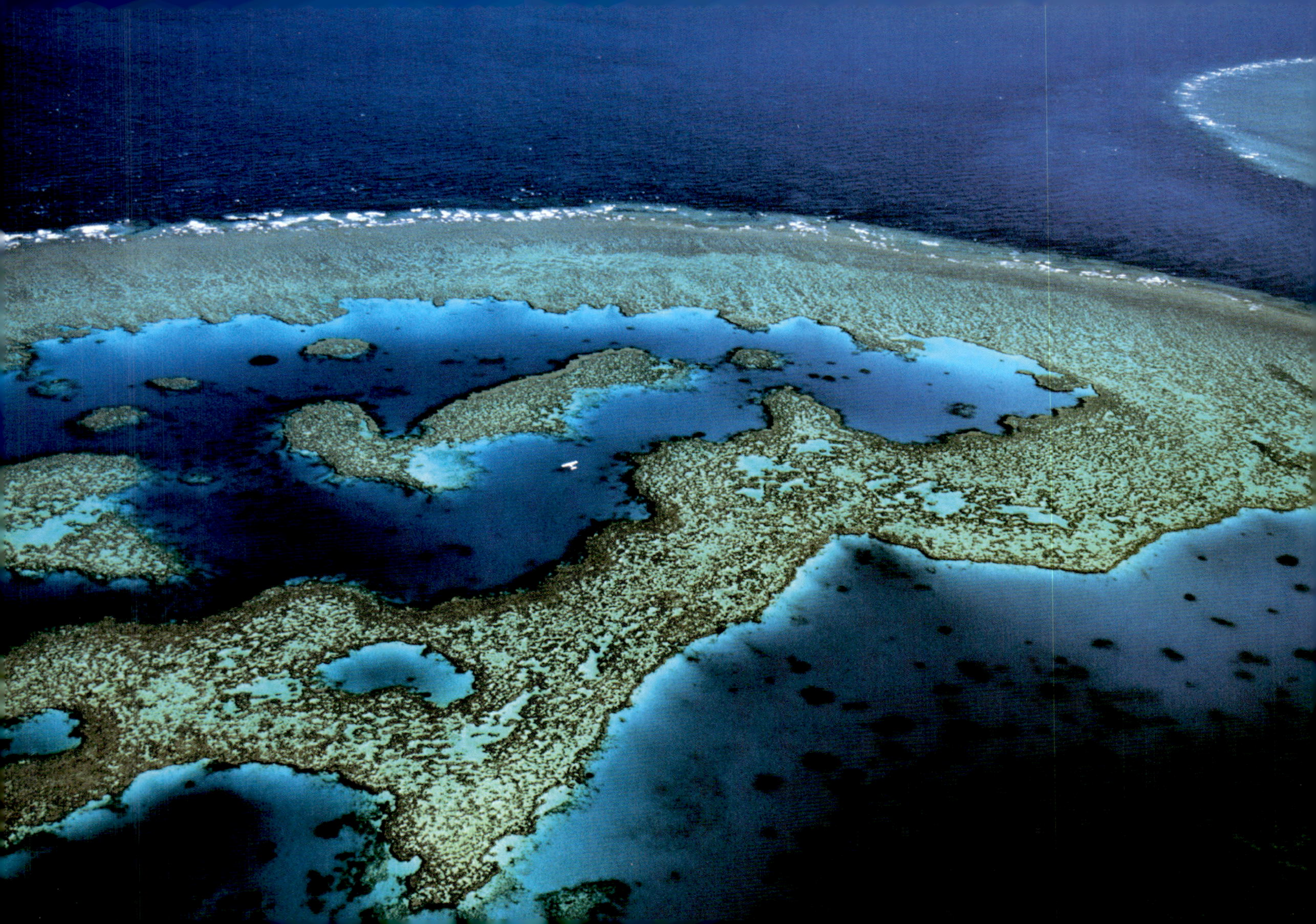

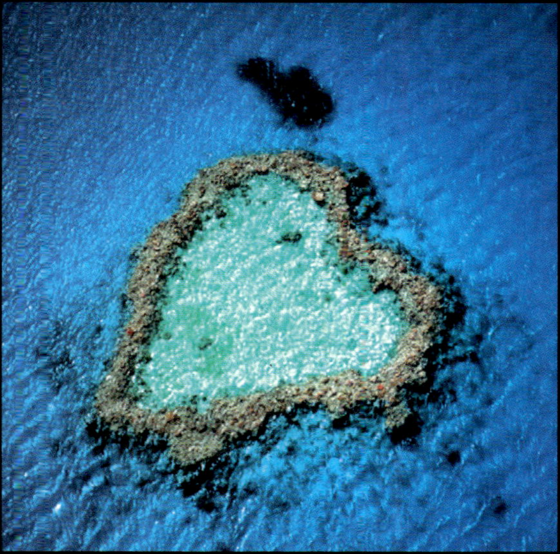

98
The Great Barrier Reef in Australia is the vastest ecosystem of its kind in the world: 1,246 miles of stony coral and countless millions of living creatures prosper in this fragile wonder of nature.

99
Stony coral, not uncommon, seem to enjoy themselves in producing evocative forms like this one, along the Great Barrier Reef.

Pacific Ocean

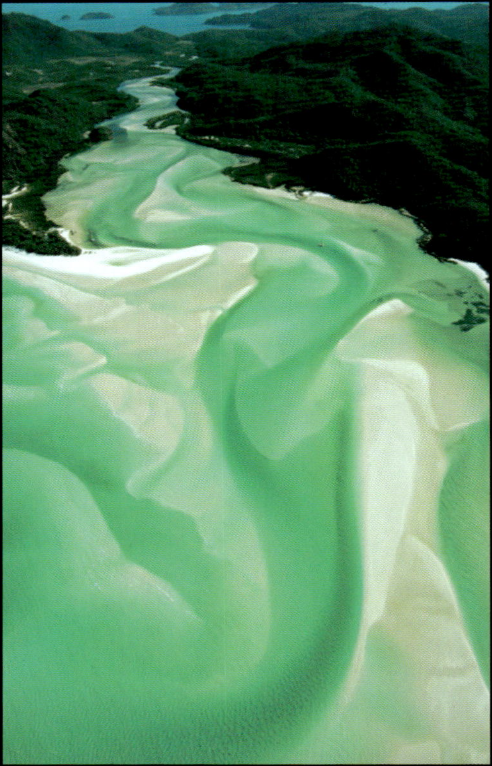

100 and 101
At low tide, sandbars off Whiteheaven Beach in Australia form white and blue trails with shades tending towards pink.

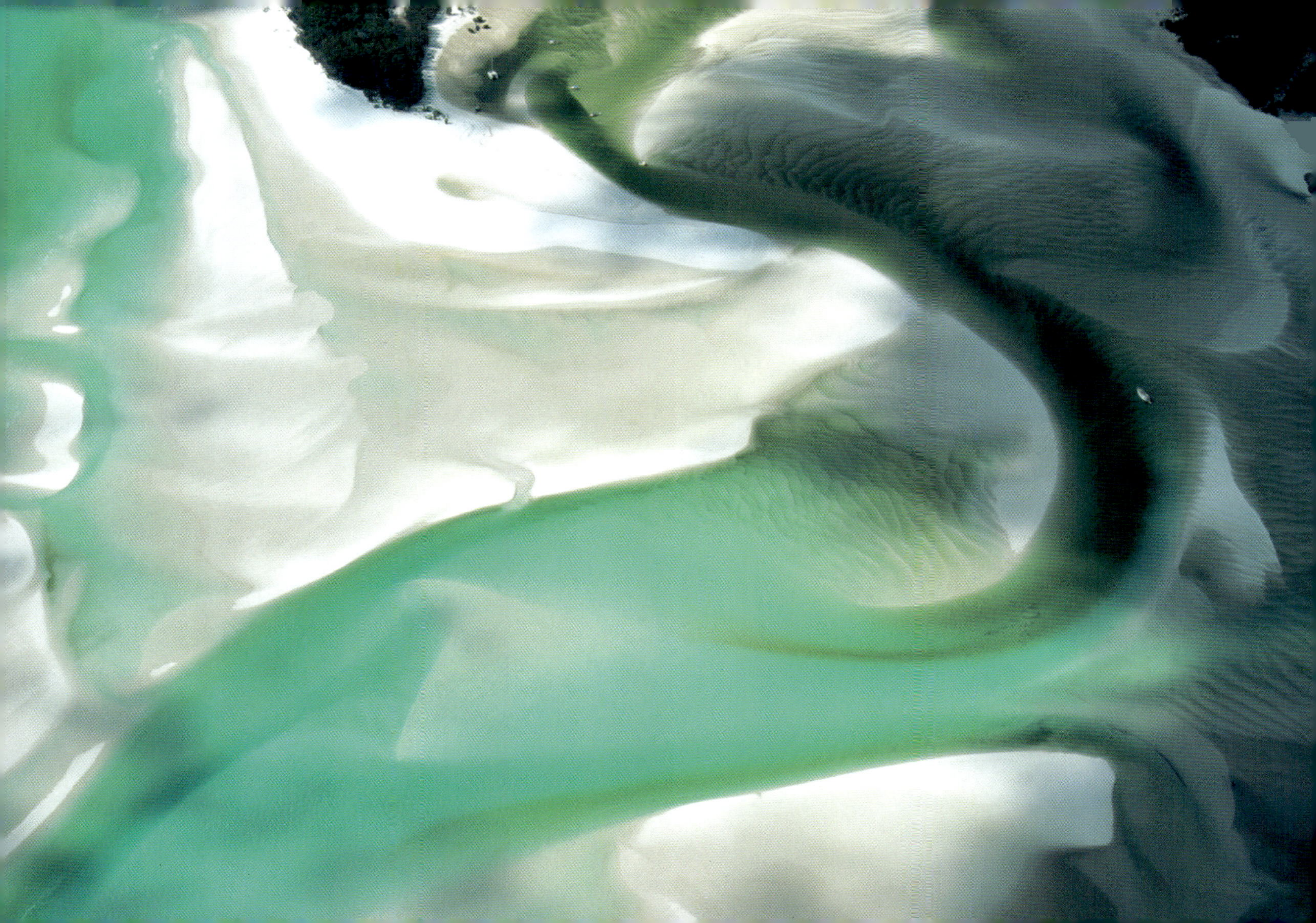

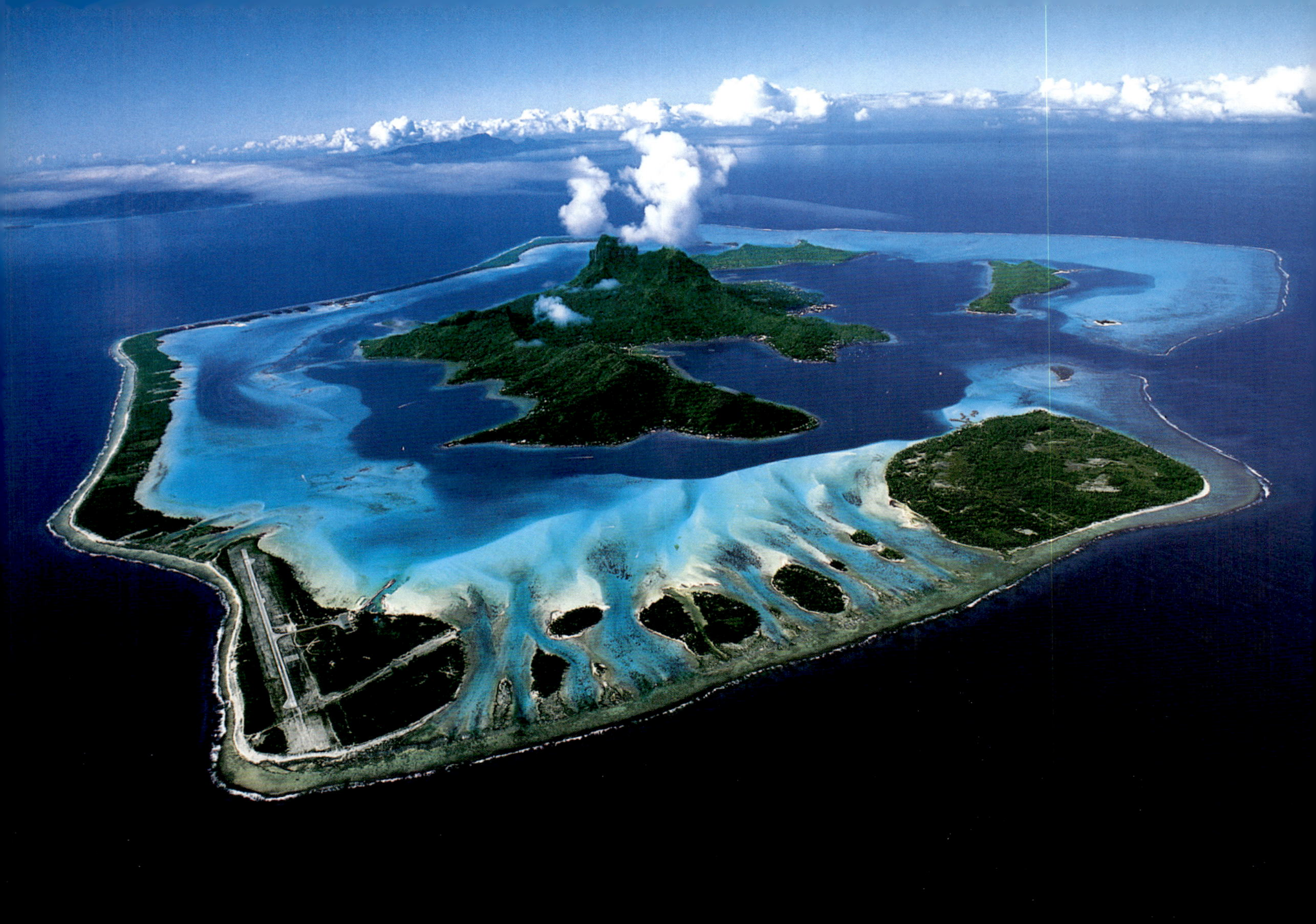

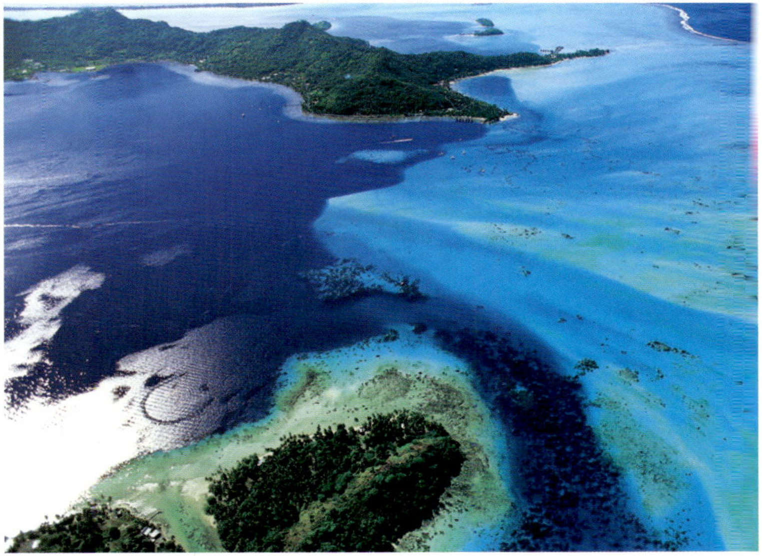

102 and 103

Polynesian Bora Bora, the main island of those known as Leeward, in the Society Islands, is surrounded by a coral reef and a lagoon dotted by little islets called *motu*.

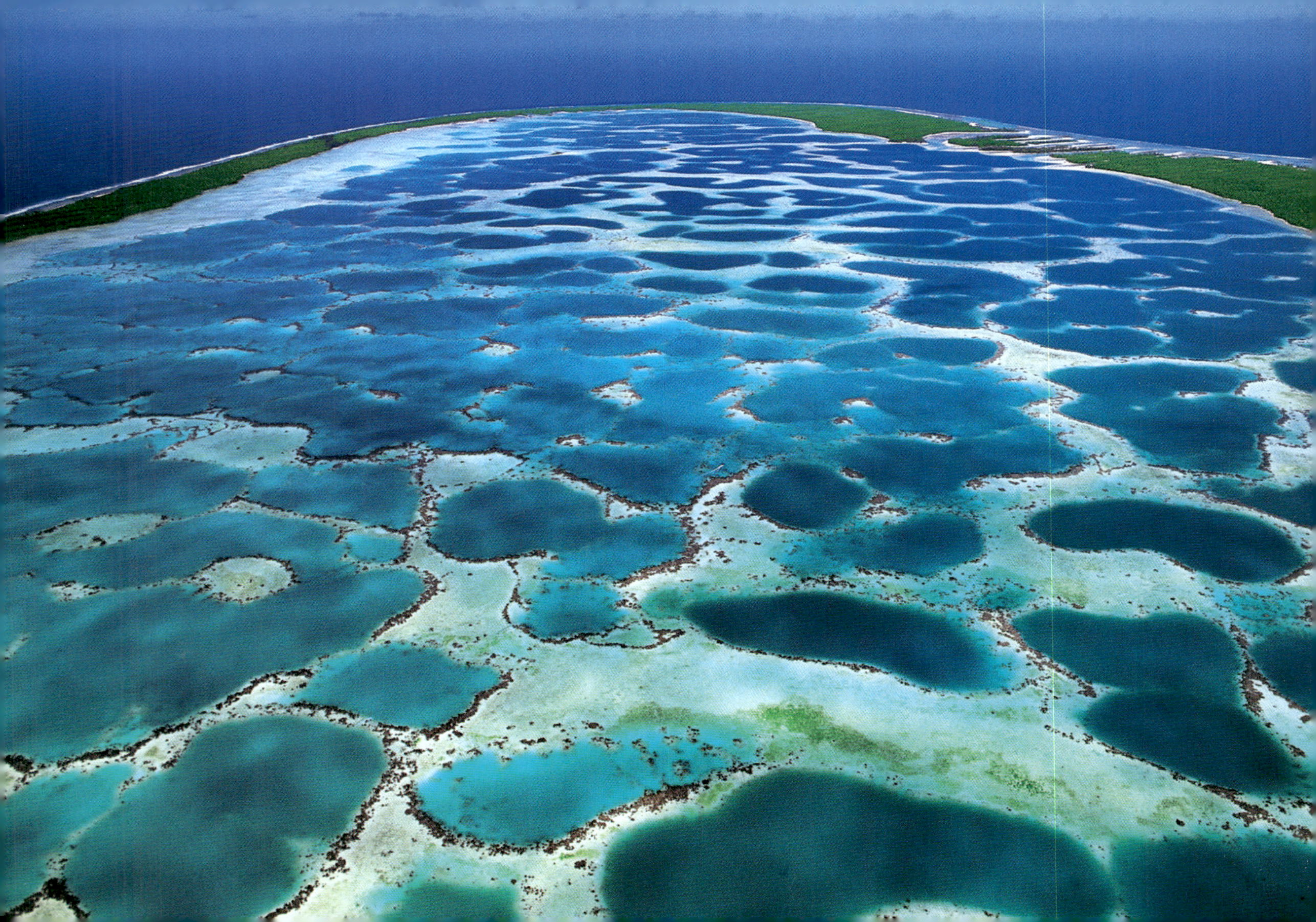

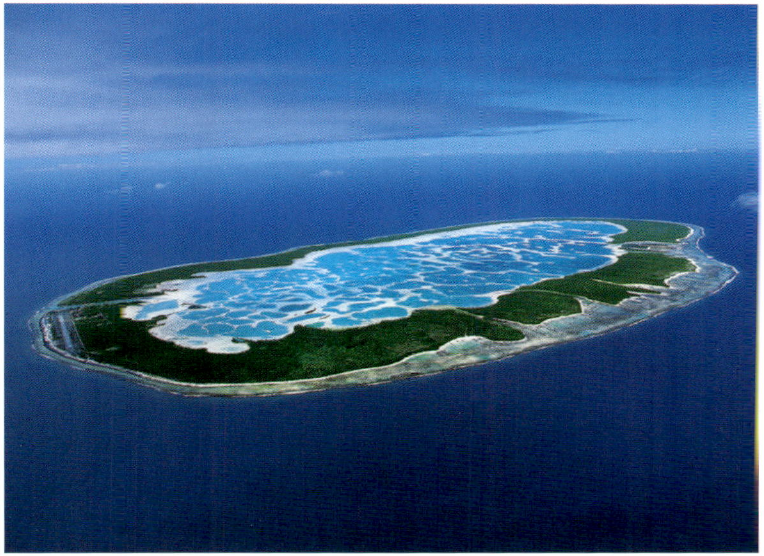

104 and 105

Centuries of telluric marine movement have shaped the lagoon of Mataiva, an atoll in the Tuamotu Islands, in Polynesia, giving it a reticular appearance. The lifting and lowering of the sea floor has, in fact, formed closed pools perfect for fishing.

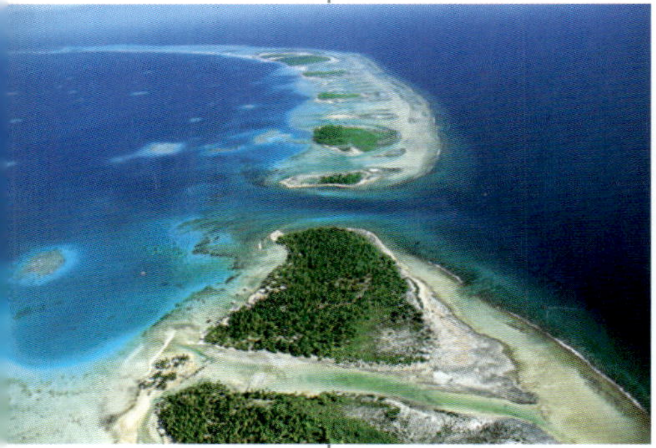

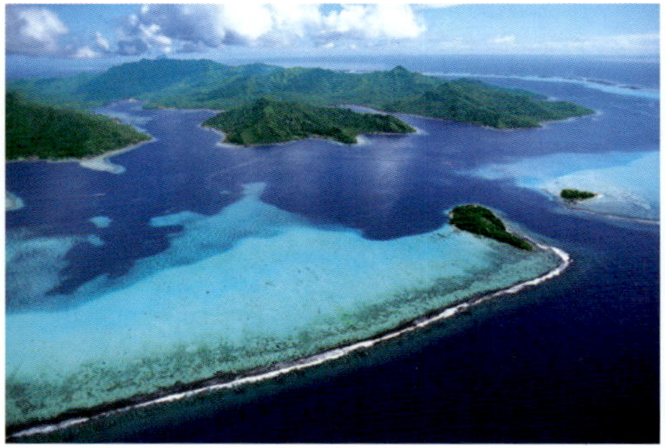

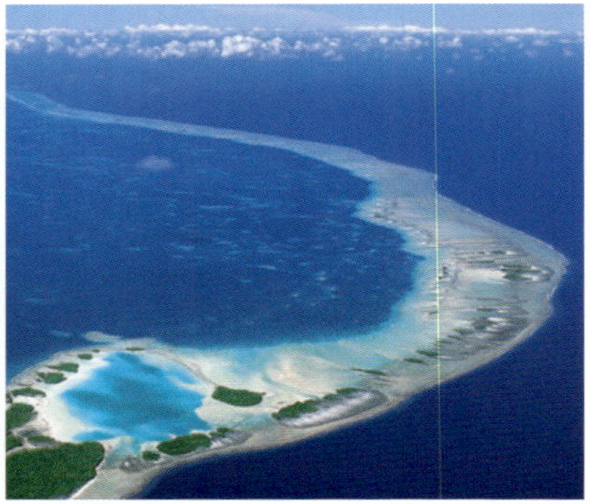

106 and 107
The Tuamotu Archipelago in Polynesia is formed by 78 sandy islands and atolls surrounded by a marine paradise composed of coral, anemones, sea stars, turtles, and fish of all kinds.

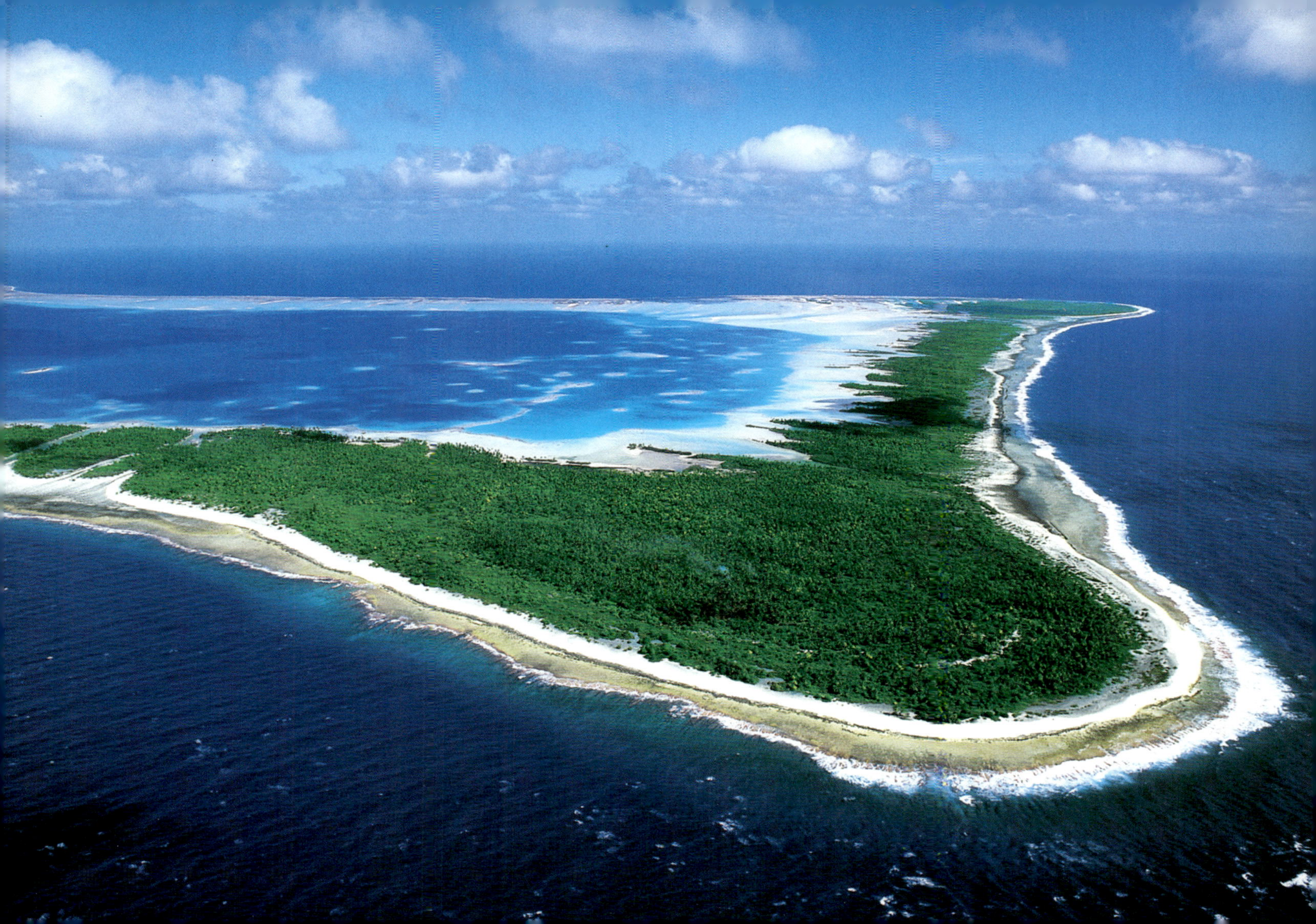

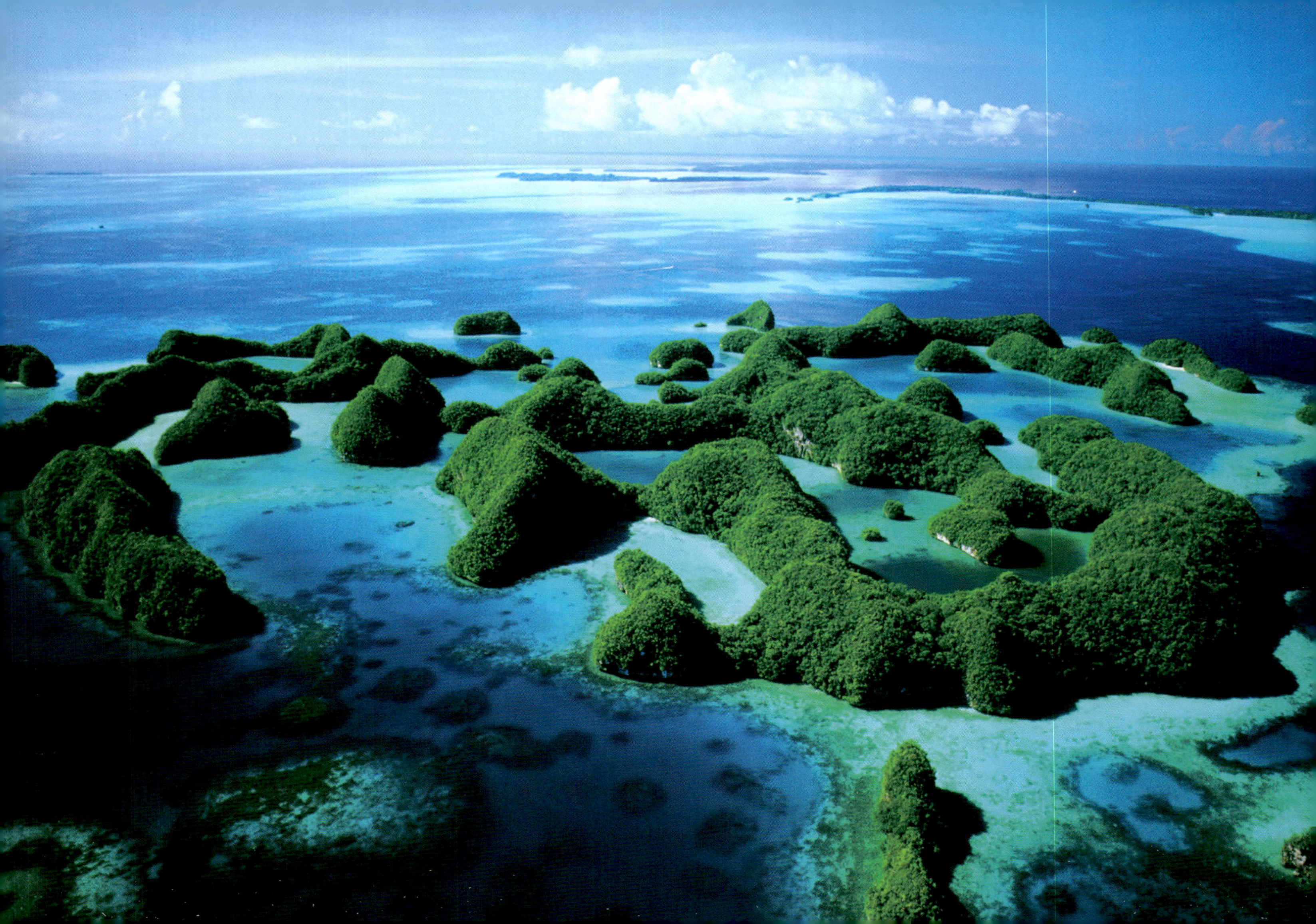

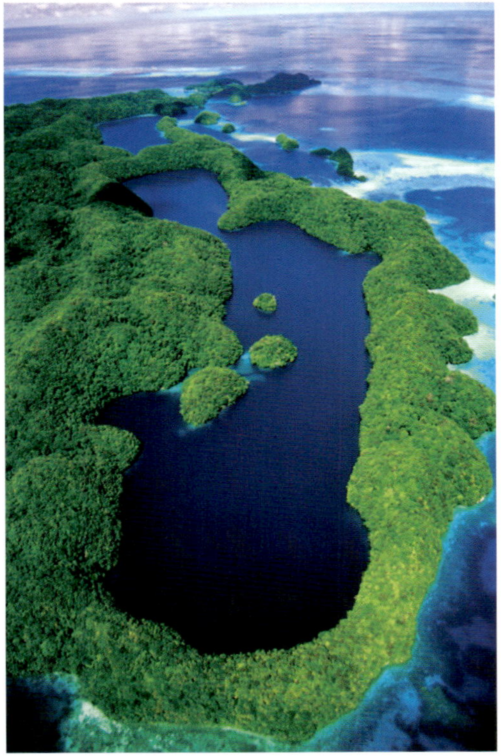

108 and 109
In the Micronesian archipelago of Palau, the sea is dotted by myriad little islands, covered by dense vegetation, known as the Rock Islands

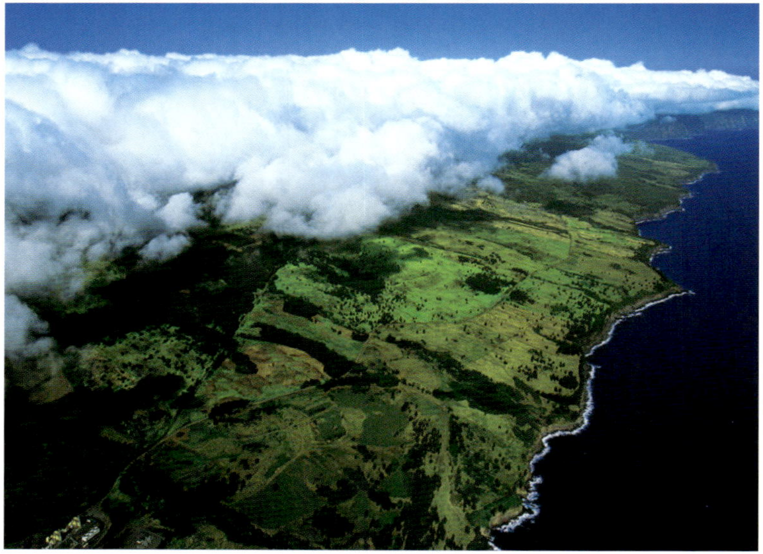

110
Sea, sky, and land meet along the coast of Onaka'a on Big Island, the largest island in Hawaii.

111
The coast of Na Pali, on the Hawaiian island of Kauai, is rendered inaccessible by its cliffs, about 1,900 feet tall, whose sheer walls face onto the Pacific Ocean.

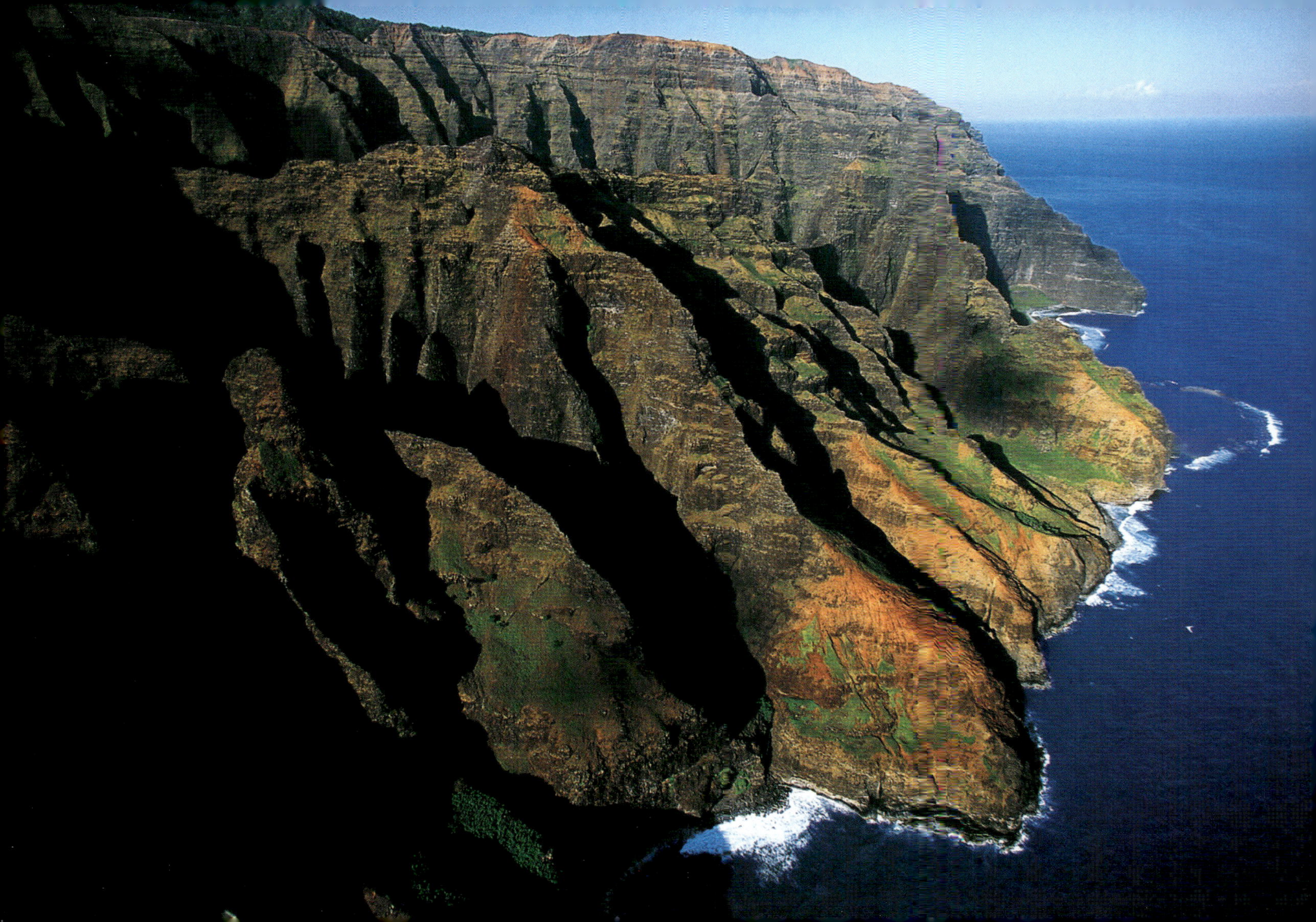

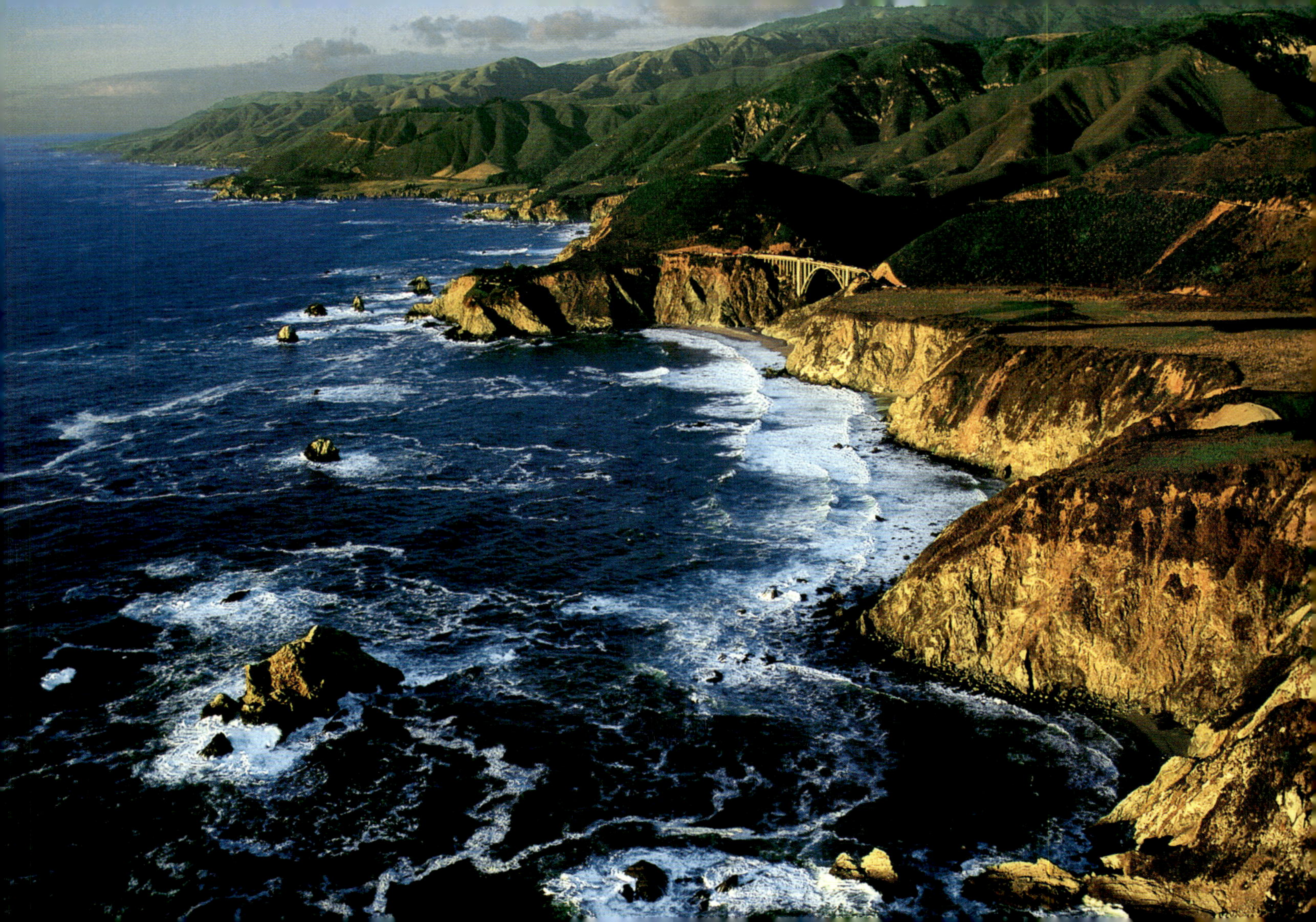

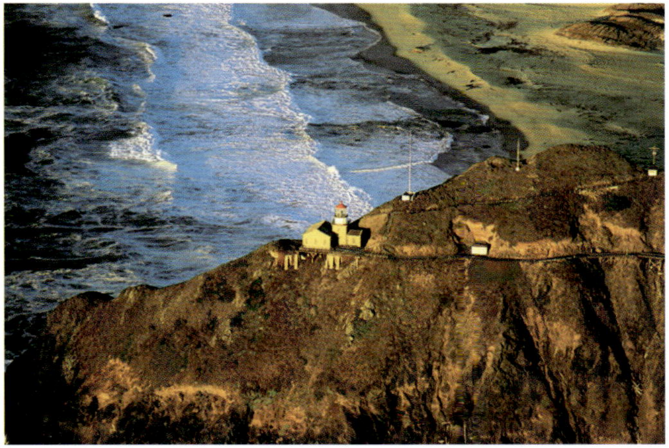

112 and 113

The indented Californian coastline of Big Sur, on whose inlets break the waves of the Pacific, extends from the San Francisco Bay to the Los Angeles area.

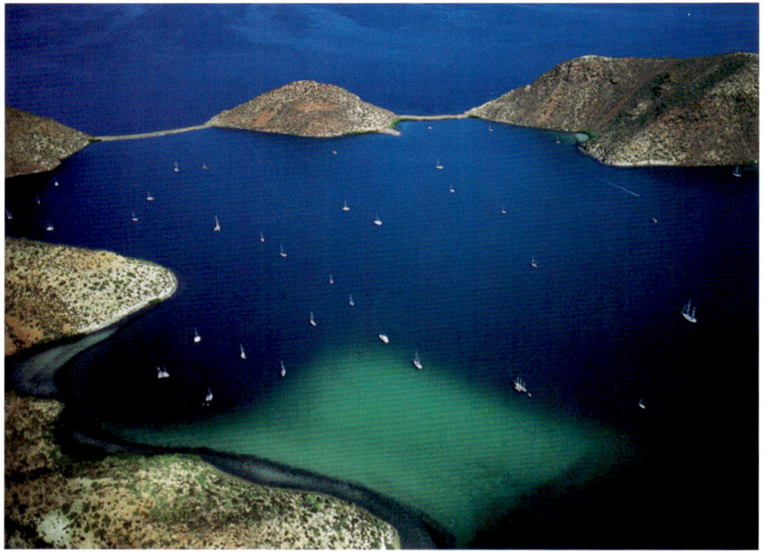

114 and 115

Long Baja California separates the western coast of Mexico from the Pacific Ocean with the Sea of Cortes, seen in these photos.

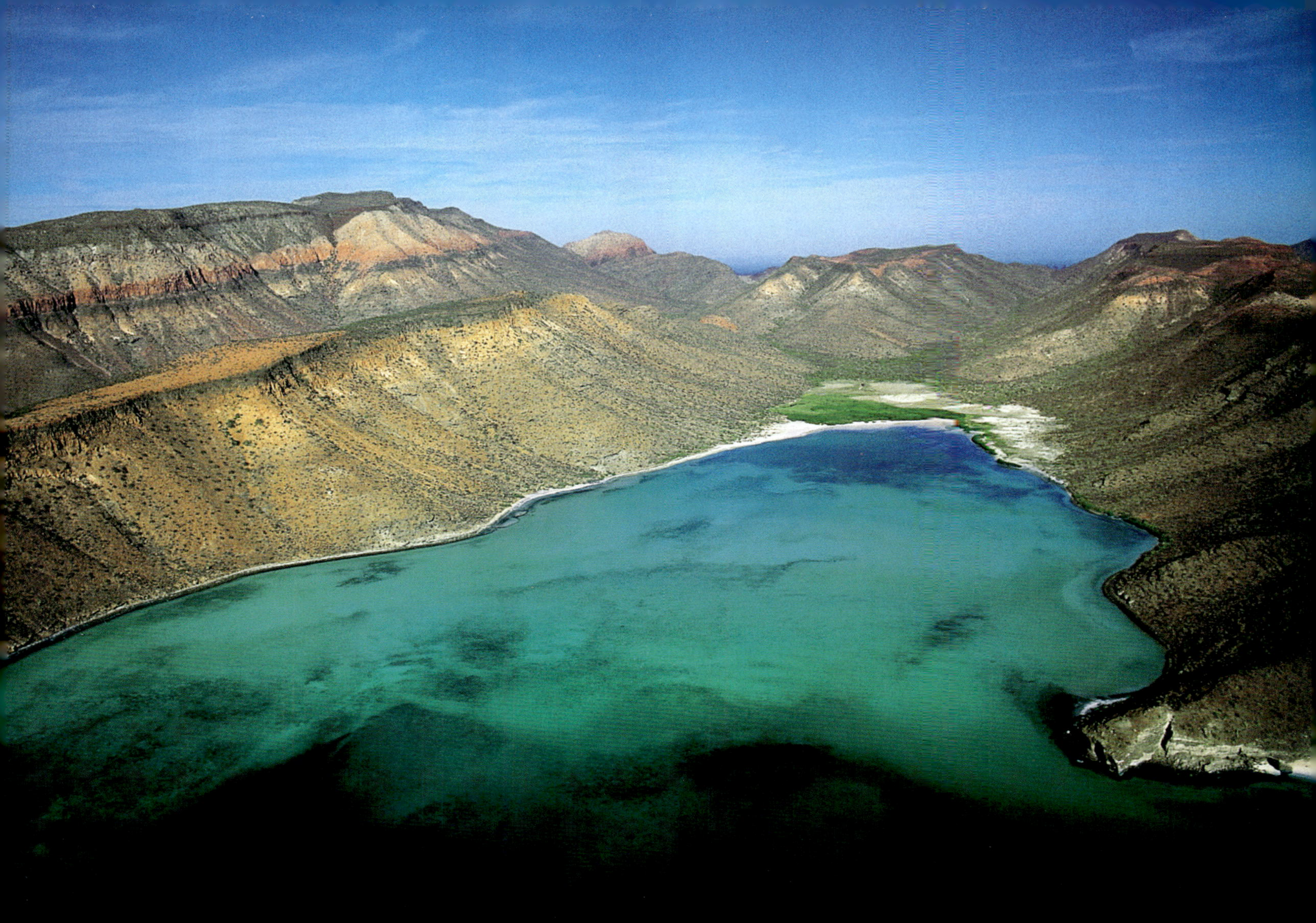

Atlantic
Ocean

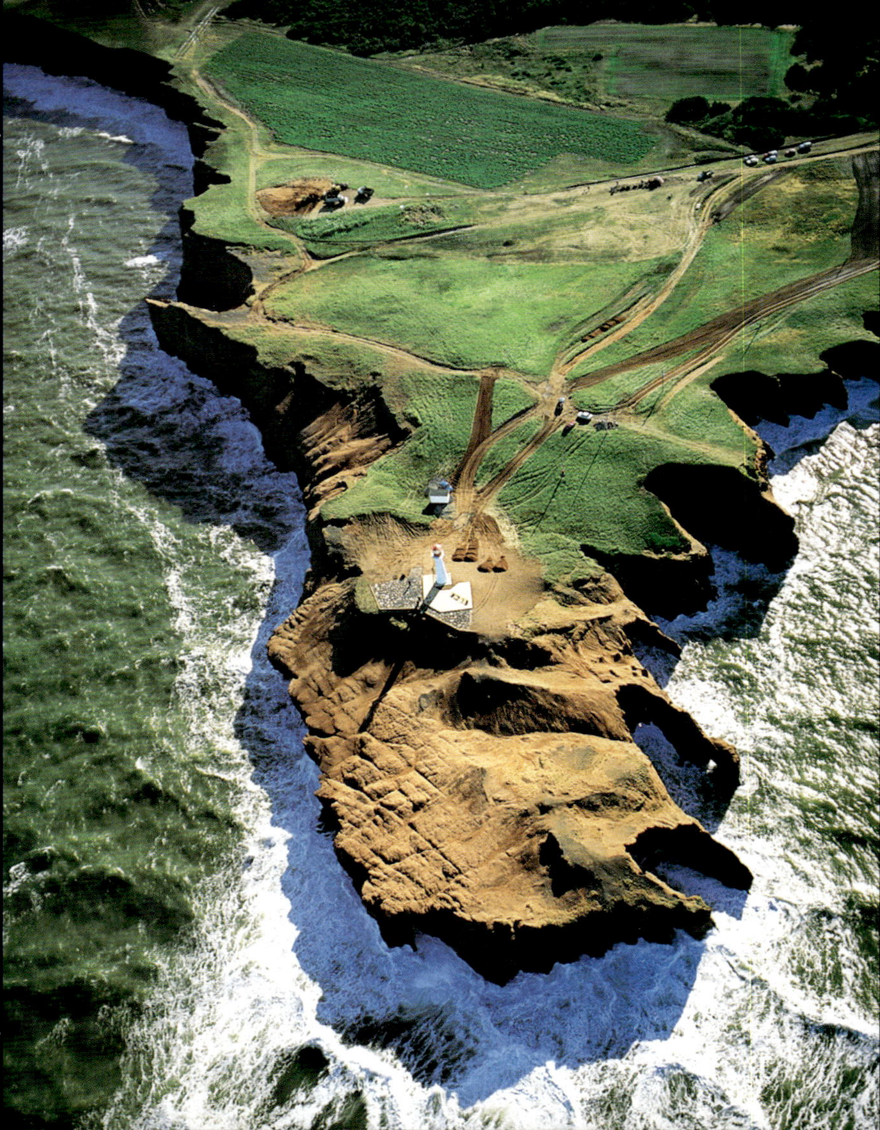

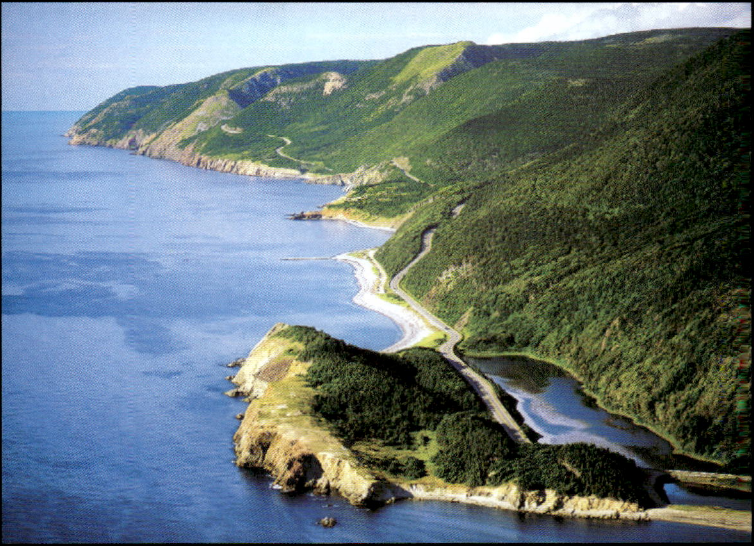

116

The lighthouse on one of the Canadian Magdalen Islands, in the San Lorenzo Gulf, aids boats in navigating in and out of the bay.

117

A peninsula with a double isthmus encloses a small internal lake along the coast of Cape Breton Island, in New Scotland, Canada.

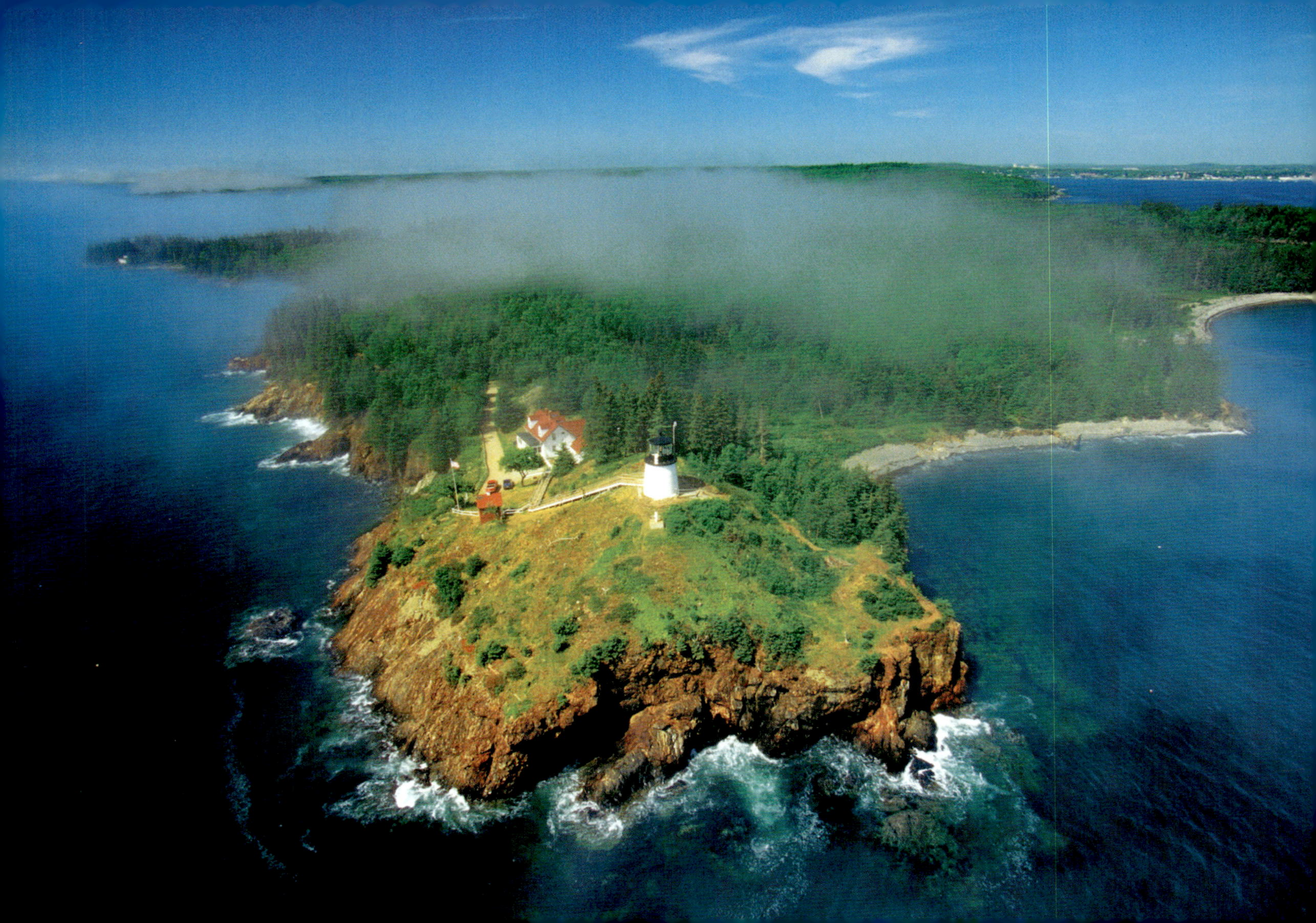

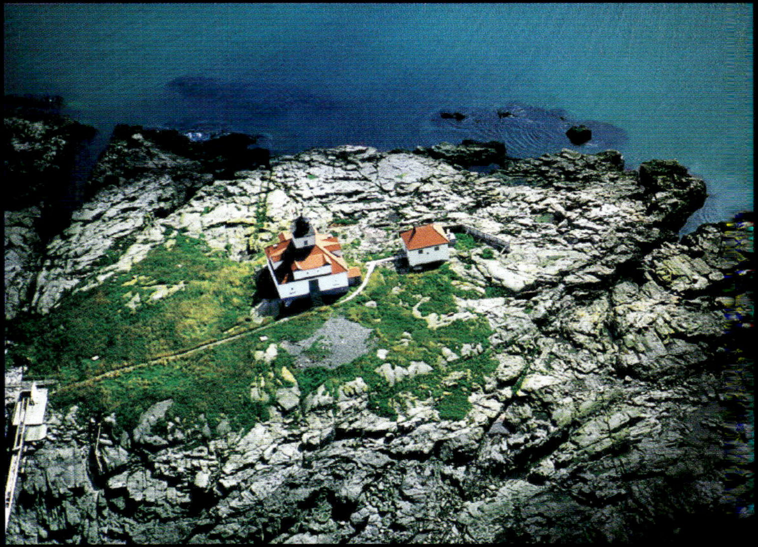

118 and 119
The rocky shores of Maine in the United States meet harshly with the Atlantic Ocean and are preceded by rocks surfacing above the waters. Lighthouses like the one at Owl's Head (photo on the left) and Rock Egg (photo on the right) help vessels from getting stuck on them.

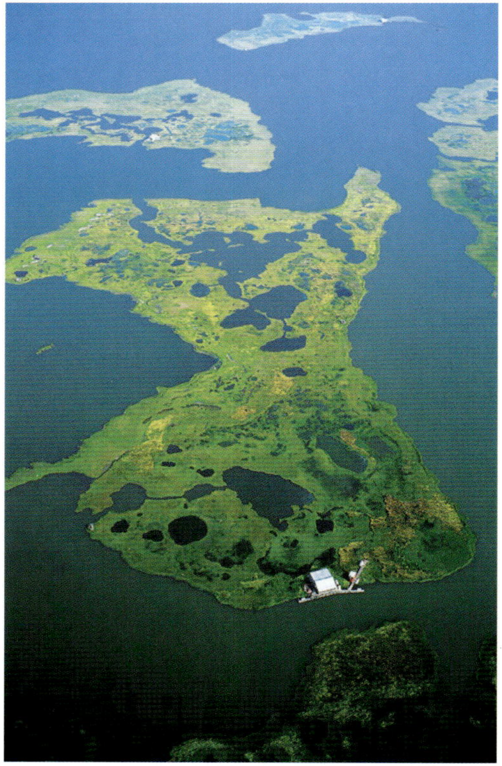

120 and 121
Chincoteague is a "barrier" island: thanks to its position, it protects a tract of coastline in Virginia from the powerful waves of the Atlantic Ocean. The waters surrounding it are known for the prized shellfish, like oysters, found there.

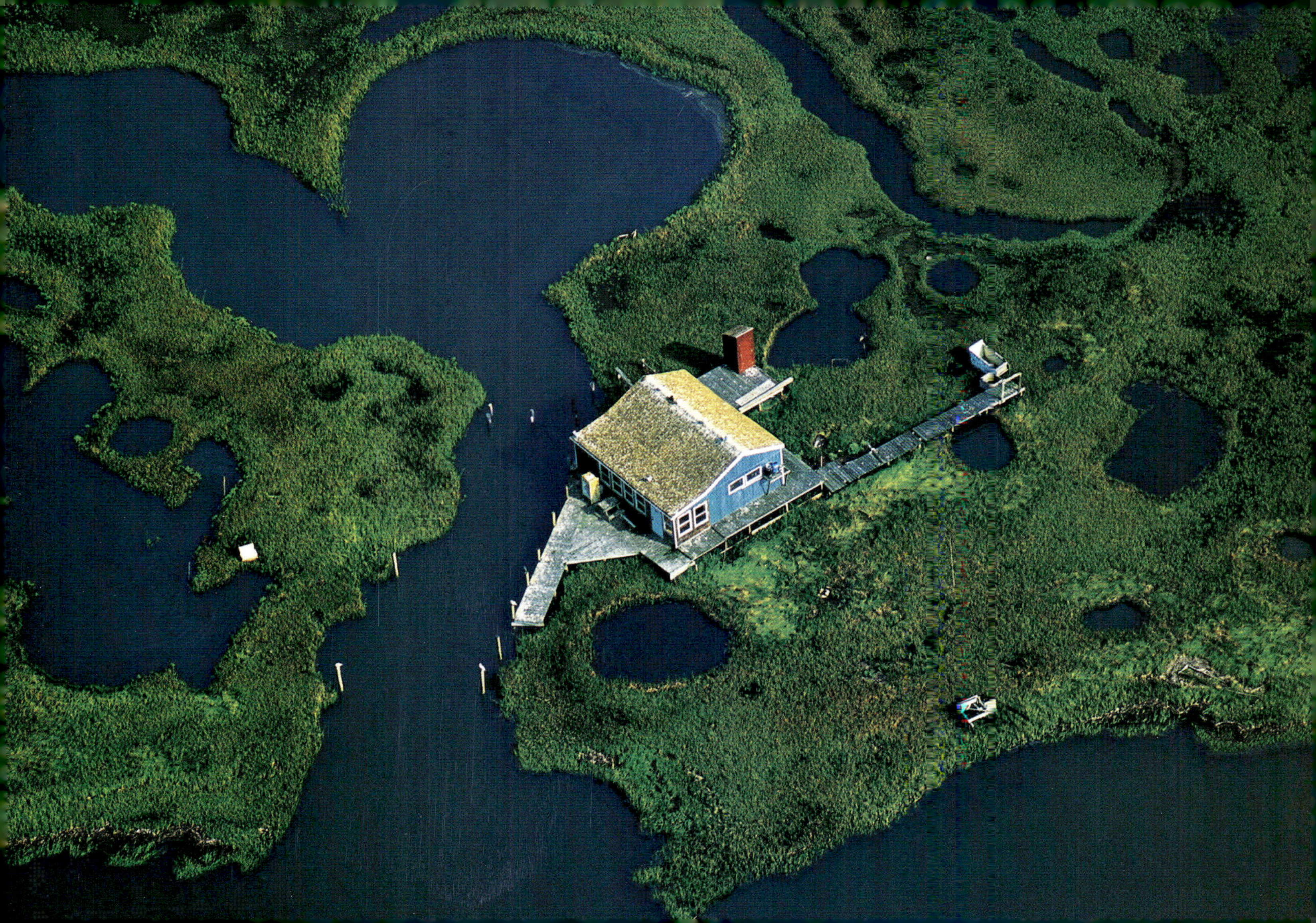

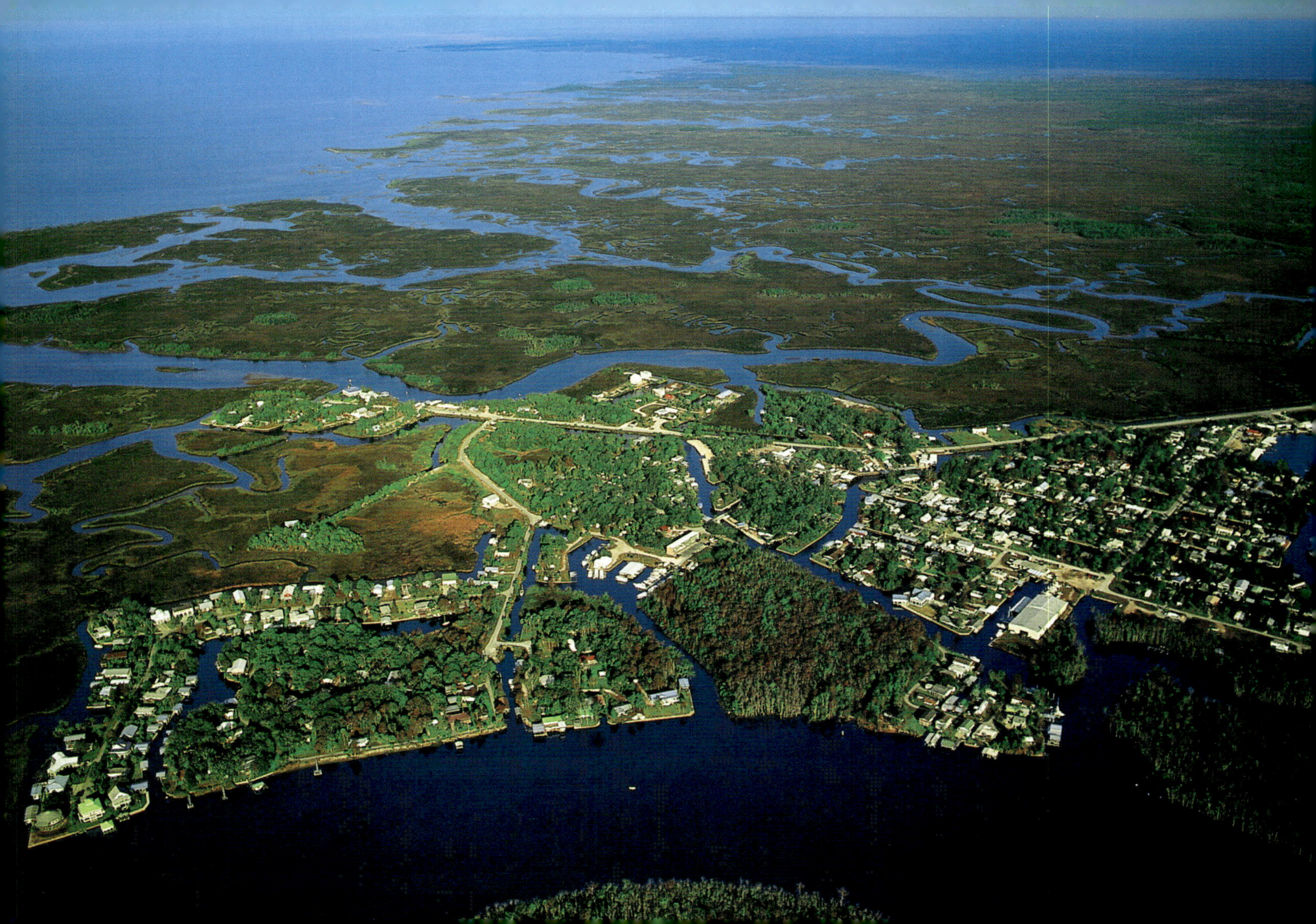

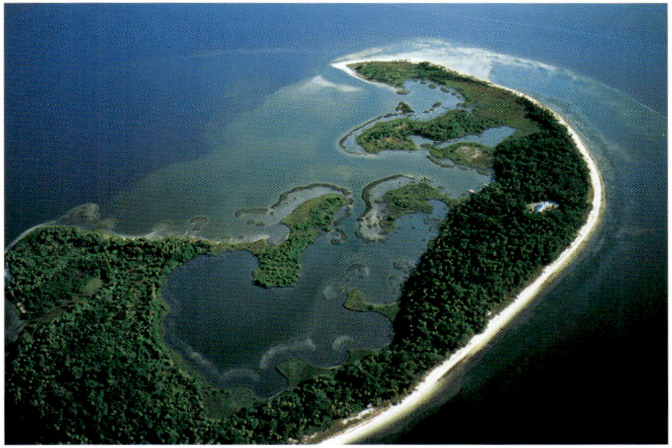

122 and 123
The coast of northwestern Florida, one of the southernmost offshoots of the United States, is a flat region characterized by the presence of lagoons and keys and coral islands scattered about the Gulf of Mexico and the Atlantic.

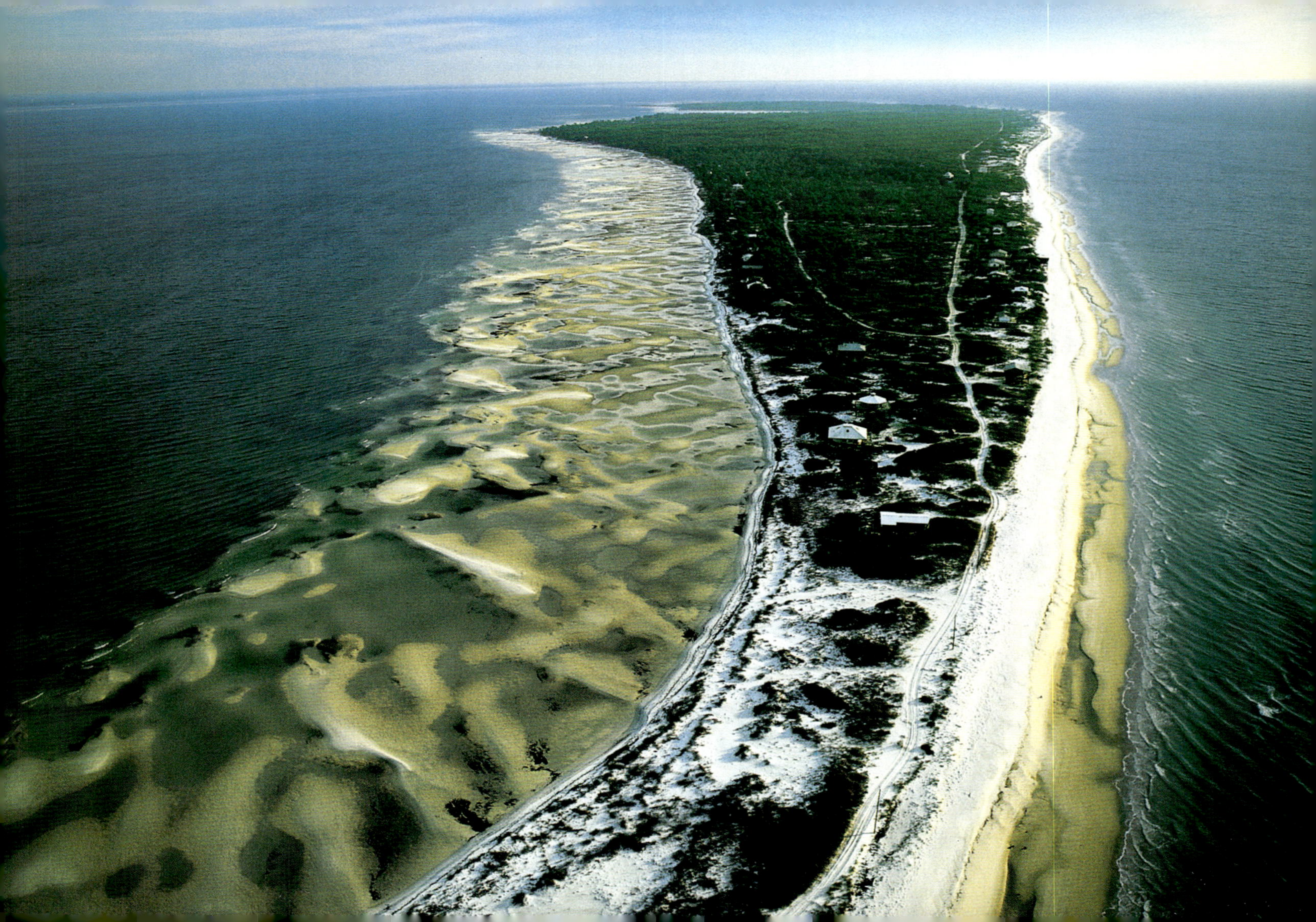

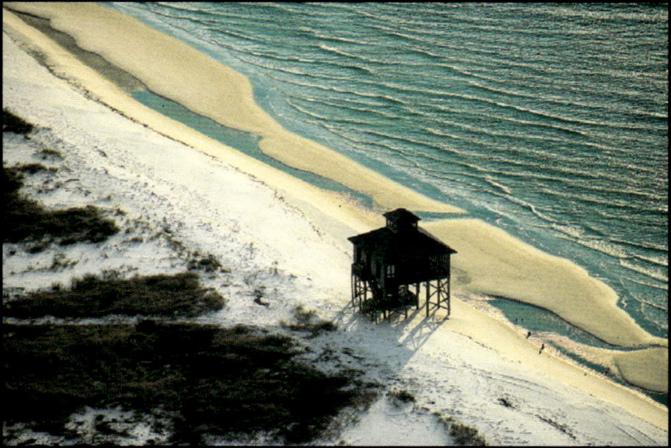

124 and 125
The shorelines of Florida's beaches facing onto the Gulf of Mexico are generally lined by low, shrub-covered dunes.

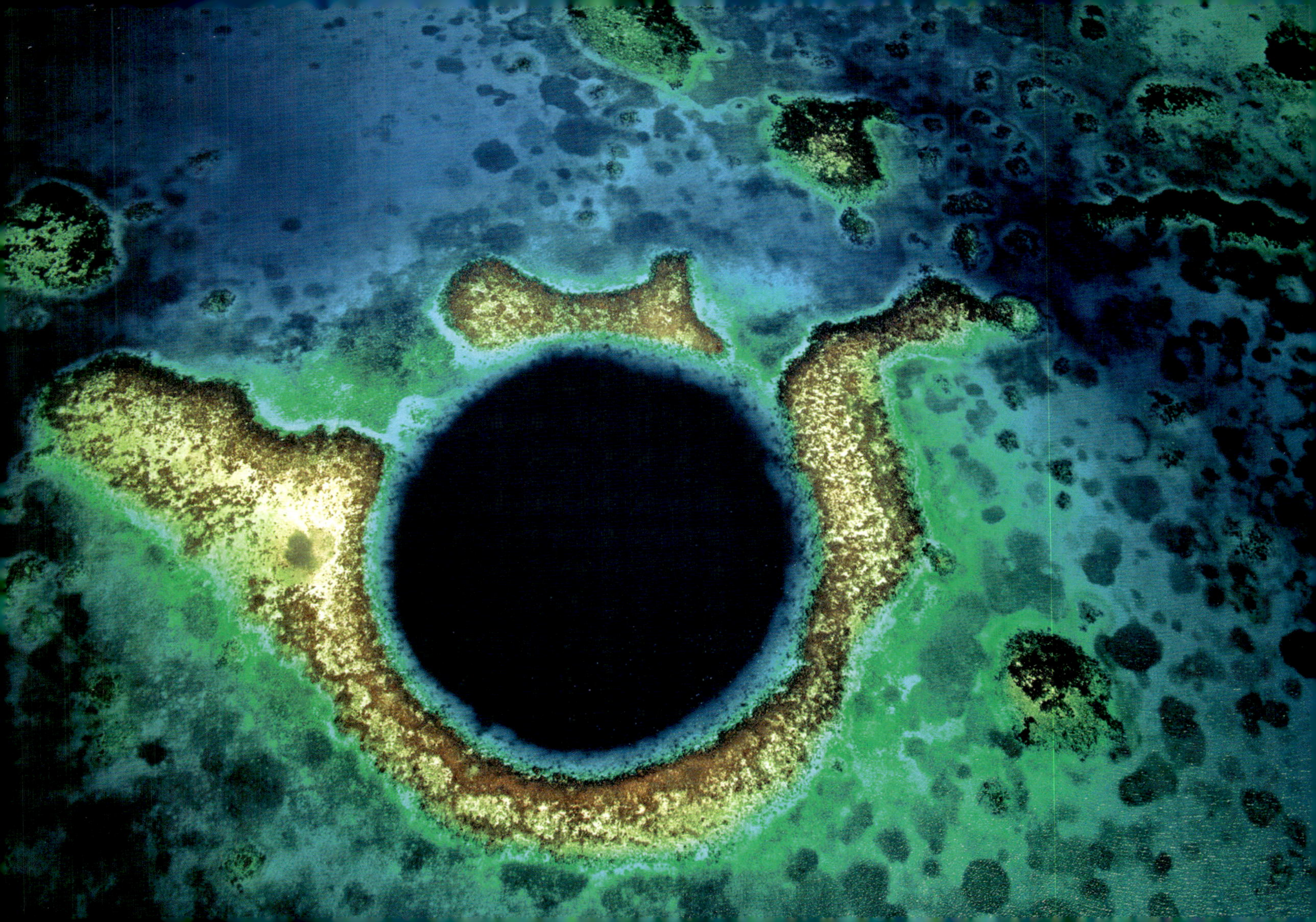

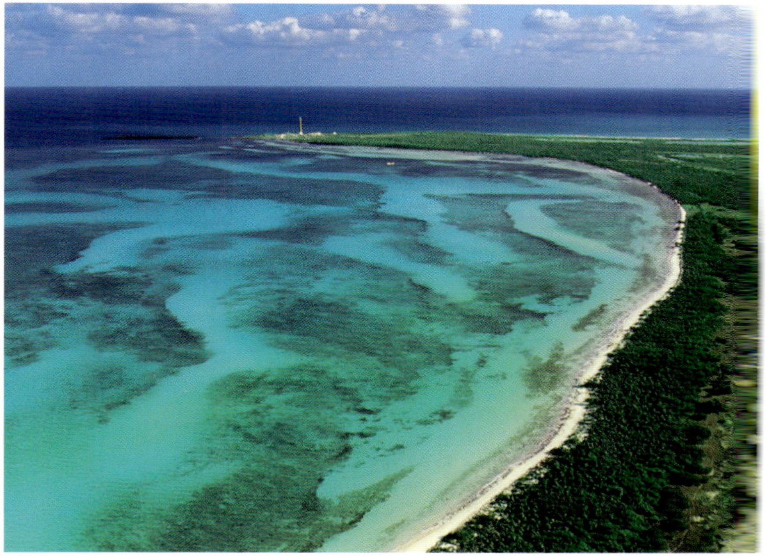

126
Off the coast of Belize are found the "blue holes": underwater atolls whose walls, often sheer drops, are lined by sponges, coral, and hydroids.

127
The white beaches of Cayo Coco, off the central eastern coast of Cuba, are lapped by a warm and shallow sea.

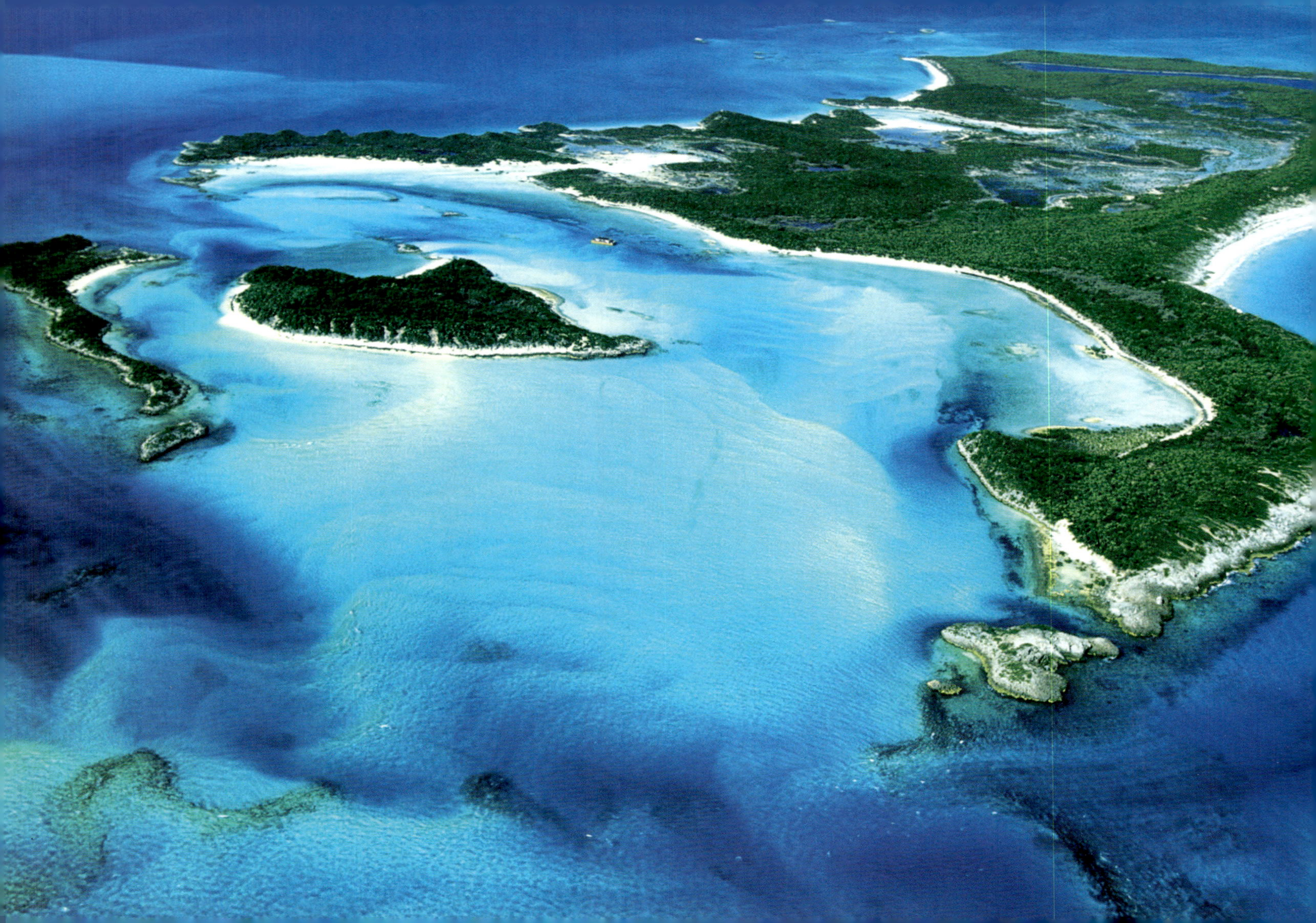

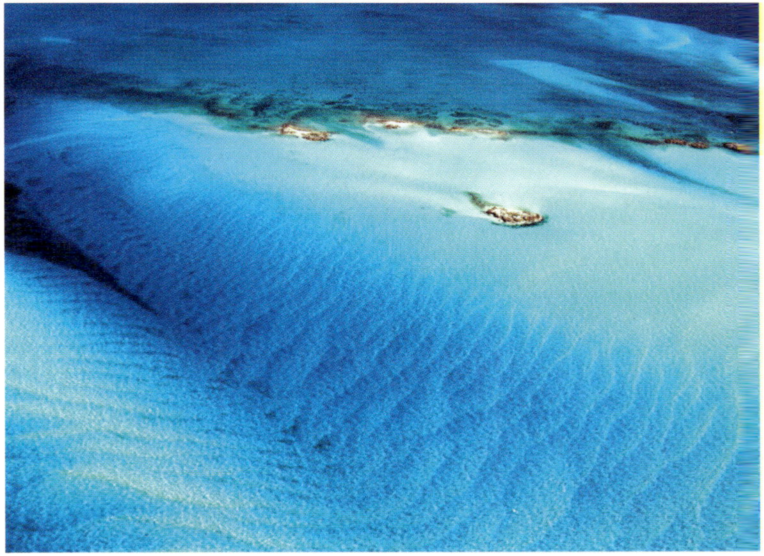

128 and 129
The archipelago of the Bahamas is composed of about 700 islands, each of which has its own geological and environmental peculiarities.

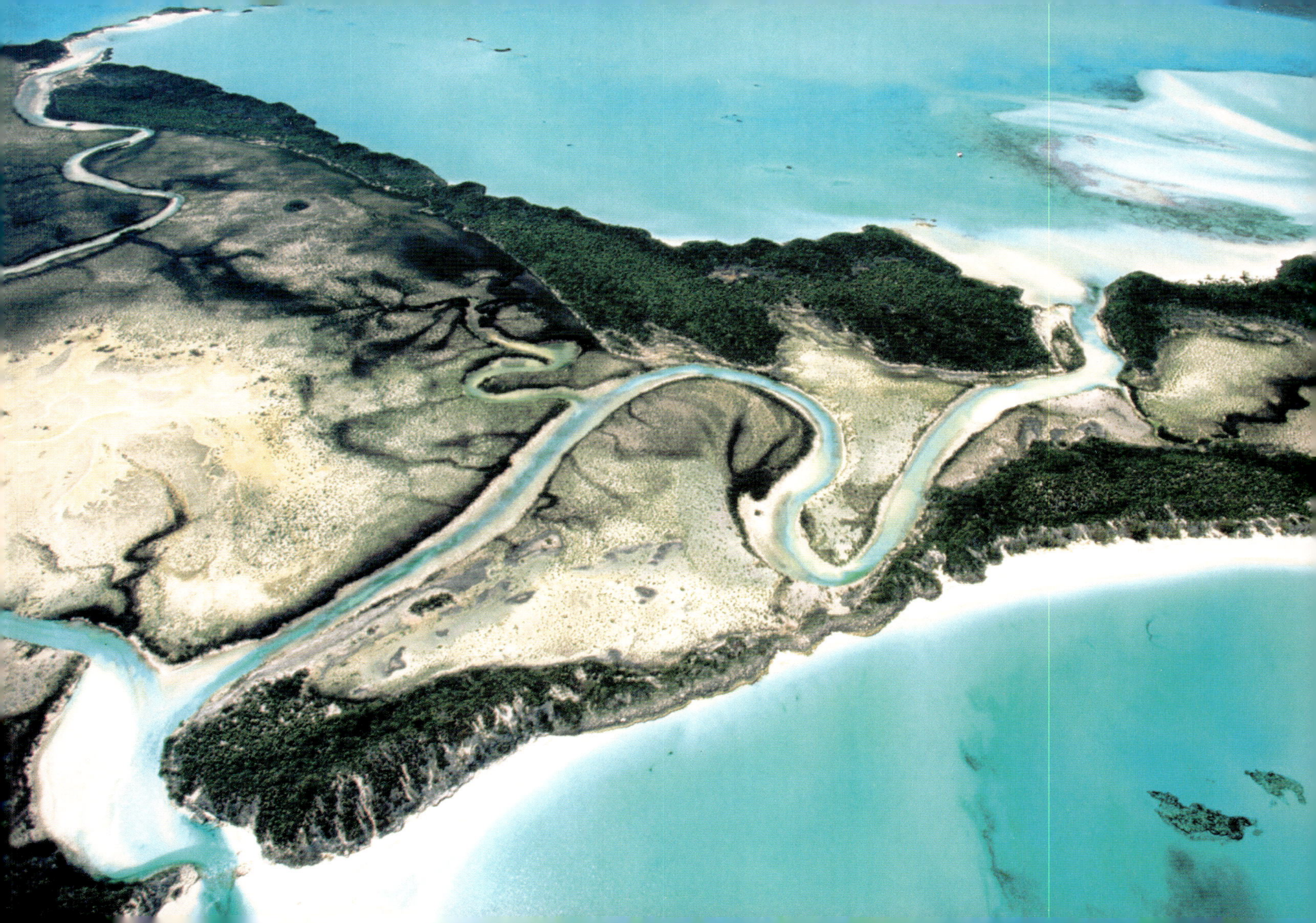

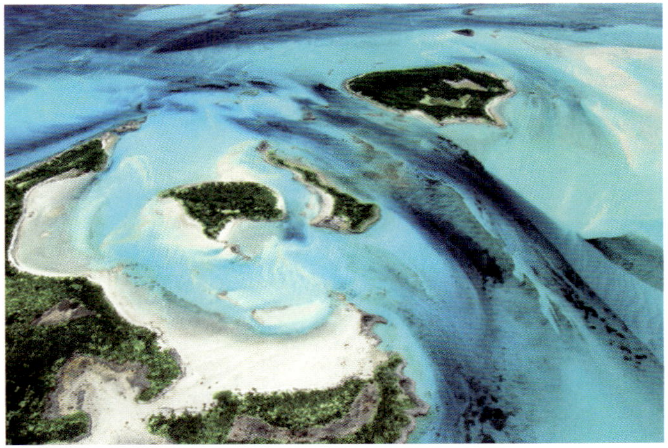

130 and 131
The islands of the Bahamas share the transparent waters that the Atlantic Ocean features in these areas.

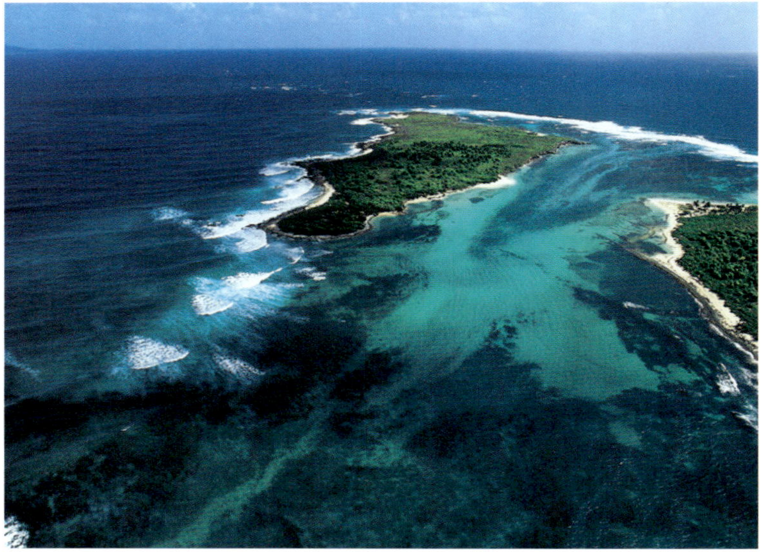

132
On Petit Terre Island, of volcanic origin like all of the archipelago of Guadalupe, dense forest grows right up to the shoreline.

133
The particular feature distinguishing the Los Roques Archipelago, off the Venezuelan coast, is the presence of little lakes surrounded by lush vegetation a few steps from the sea.

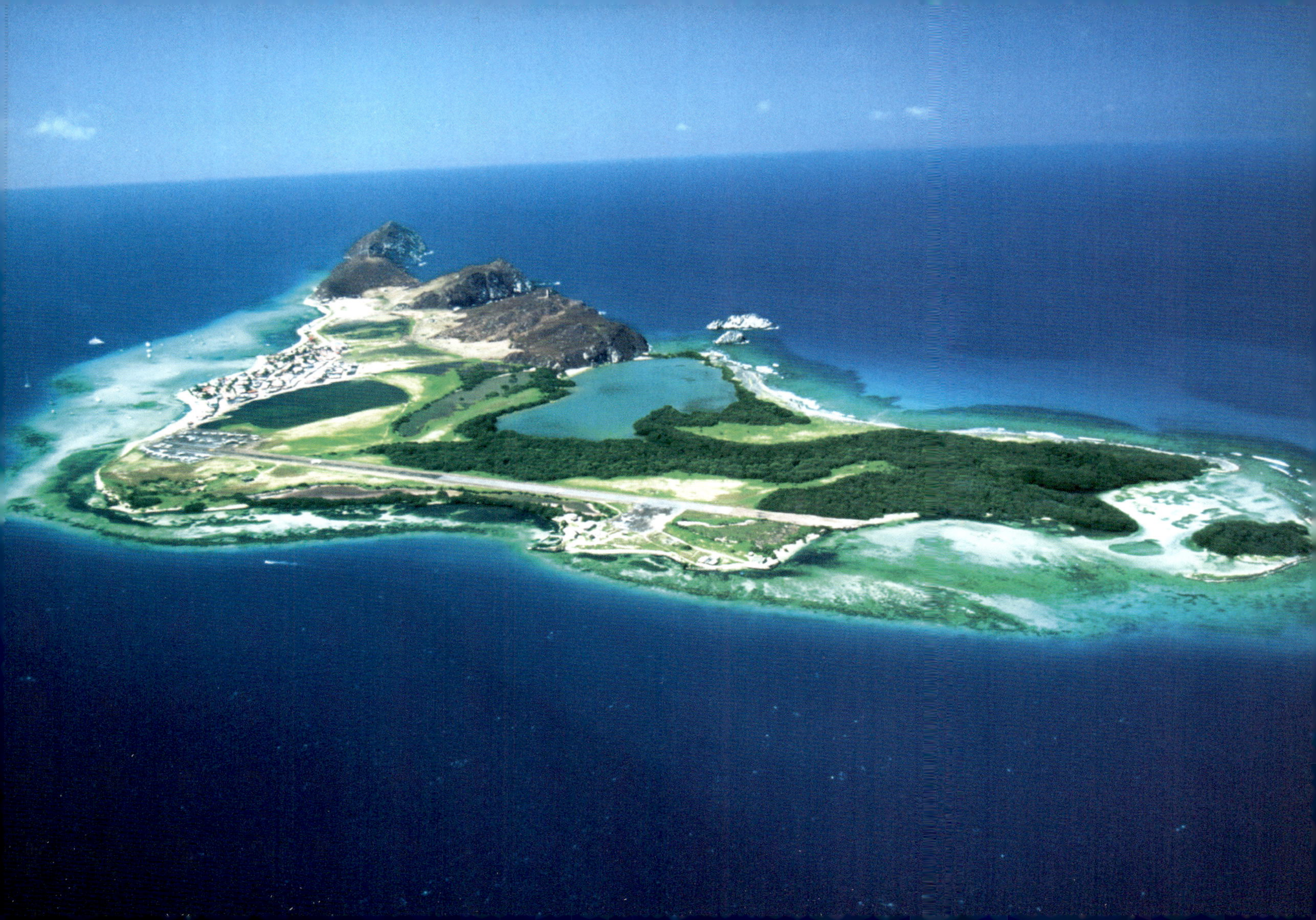

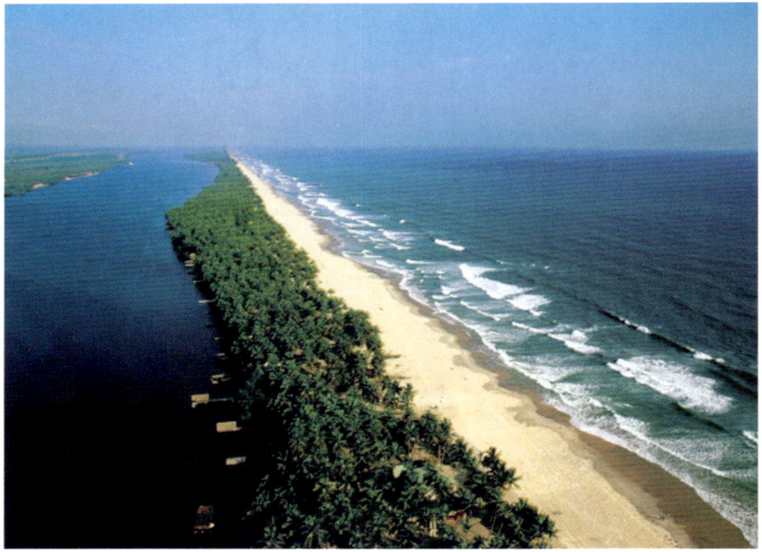

134
The eastern coastal area of the Ivory Coast is divided into two strips by a green lagoon 186 miles long.

135
A basic fishing boat, whose equipment consists of a simple net, rests on a beach in the Ivory Coast in the Abidjan area.

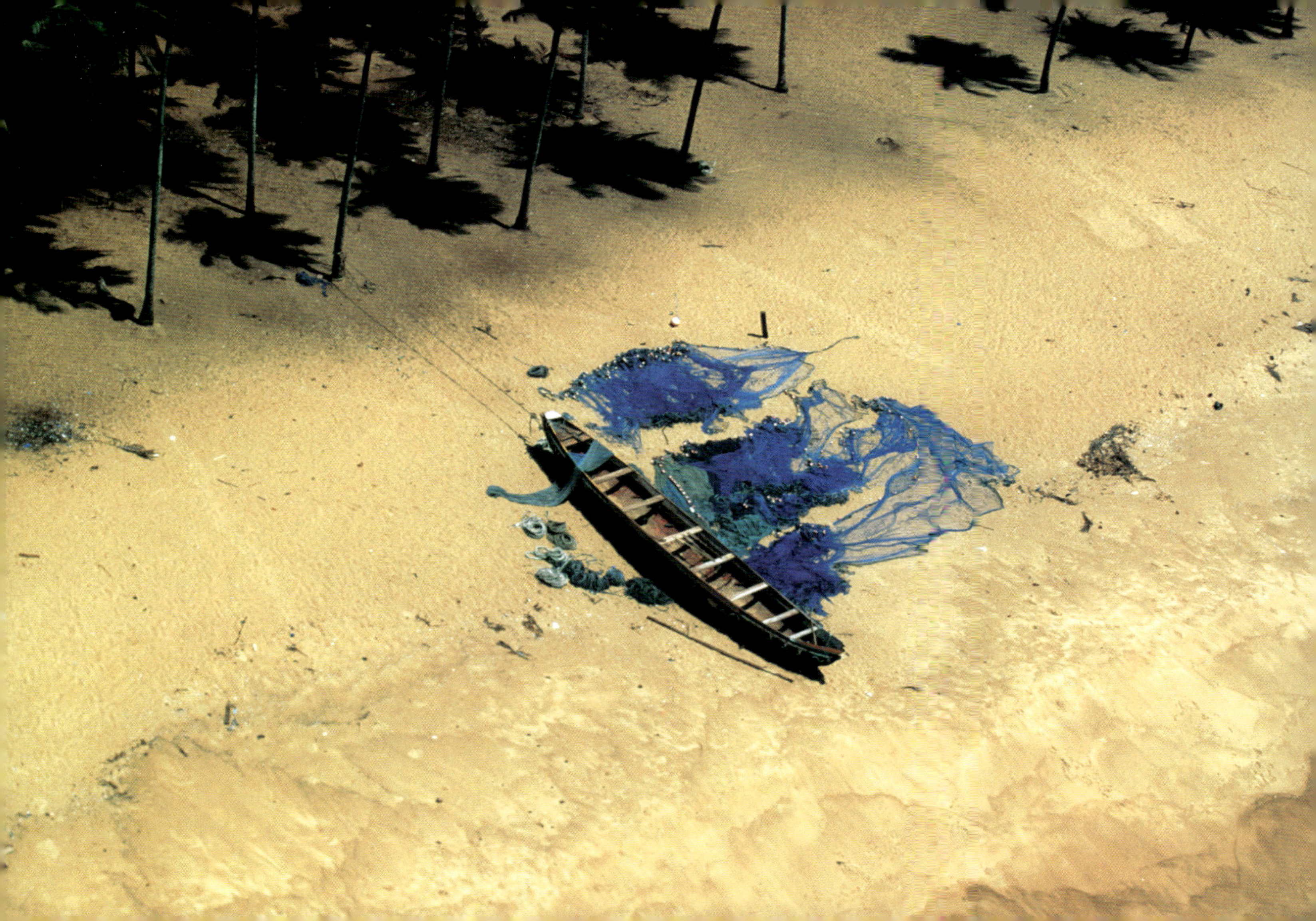

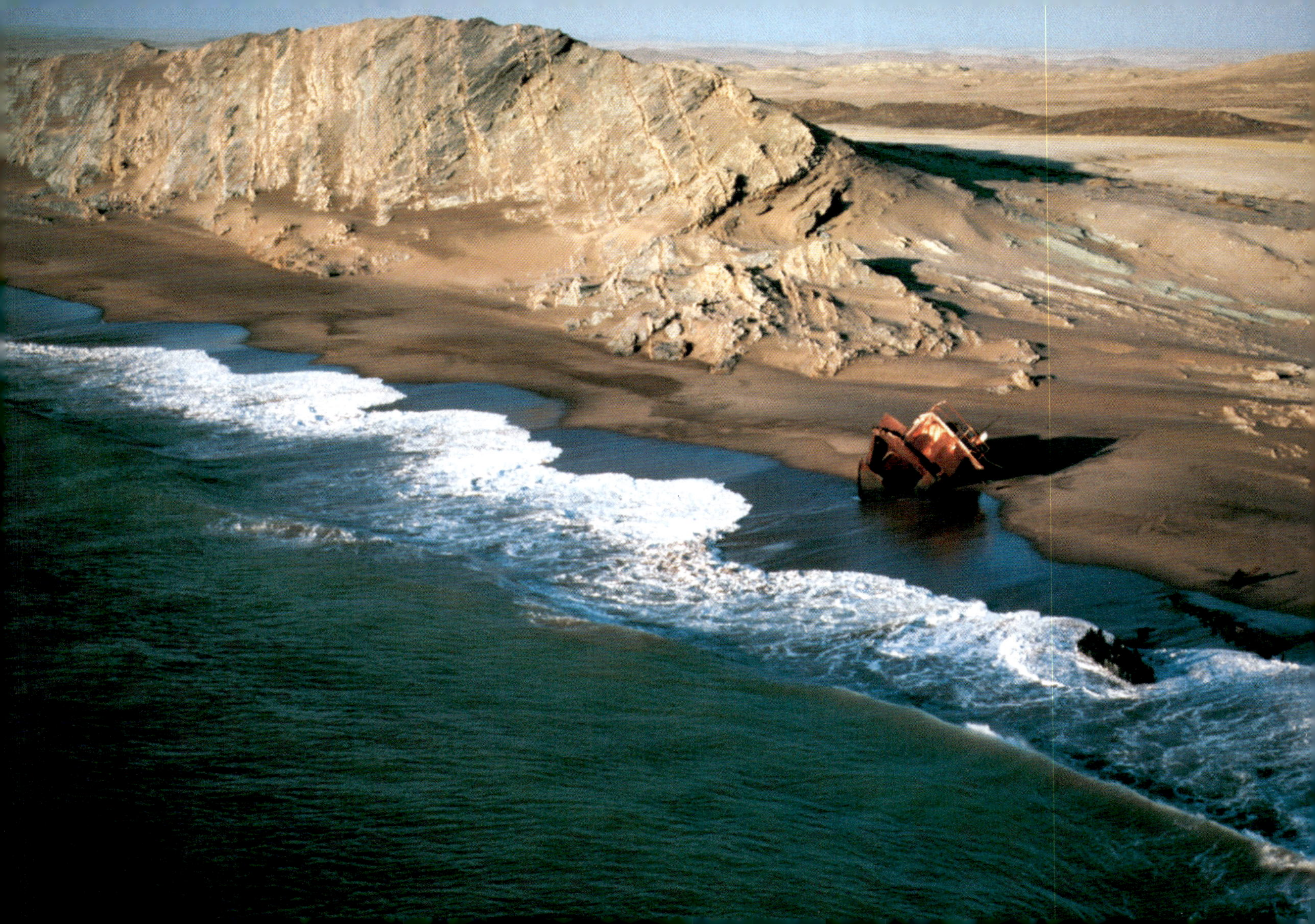

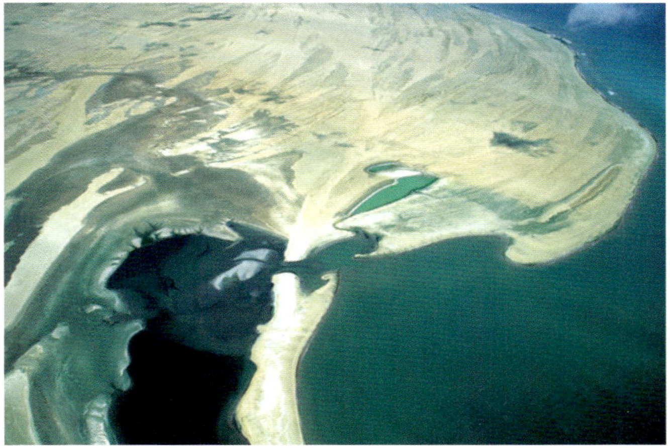

136
The wreck of a small craft is battered by the waves on a sandy beach along Skeleton Coast, in Namibia.

137
Surrounded by pristine dunes, the lagoon of Sandwich Harbour, in Namibia, is a paradise frequented by colonies of birds like pink flamingoes.

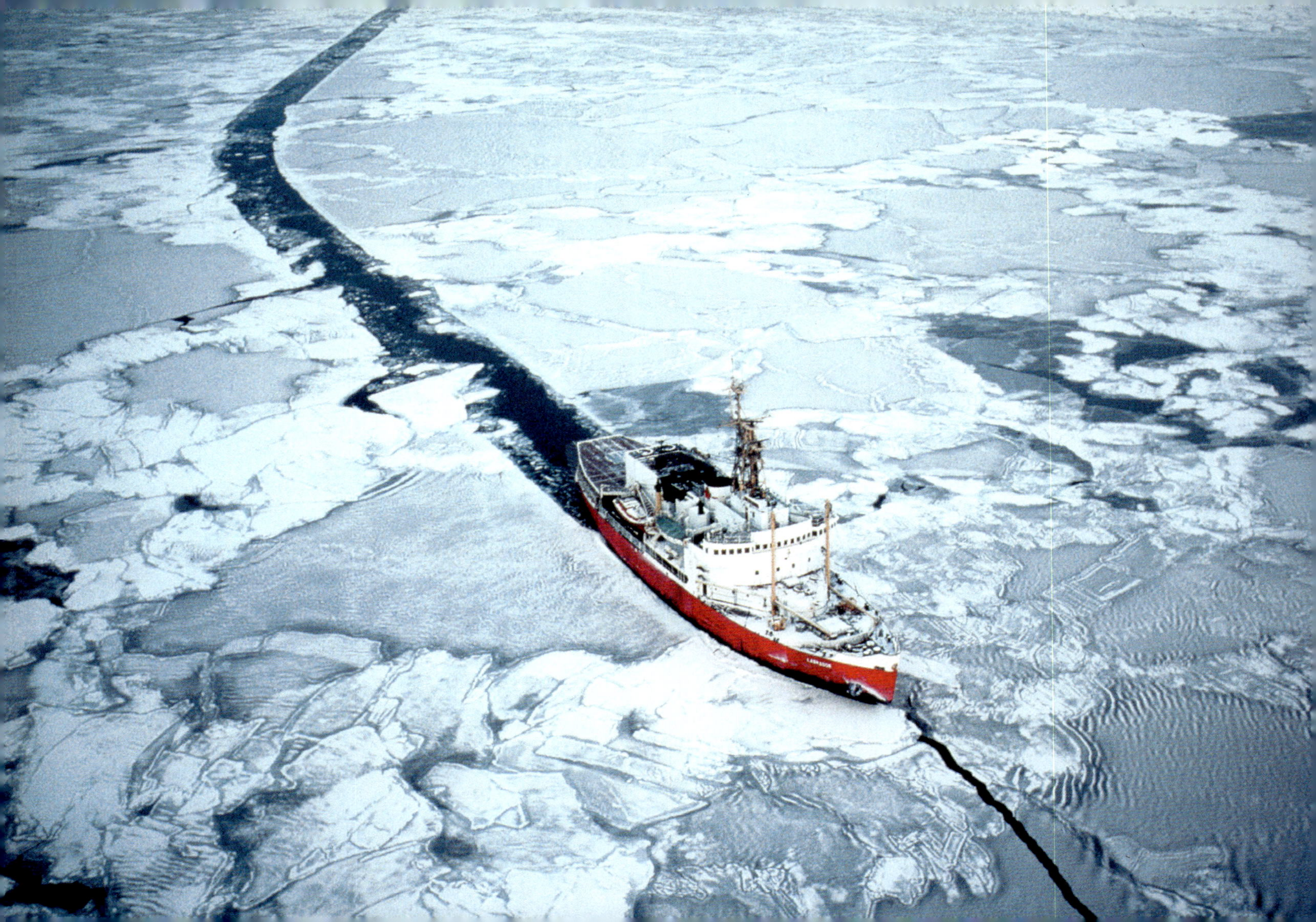

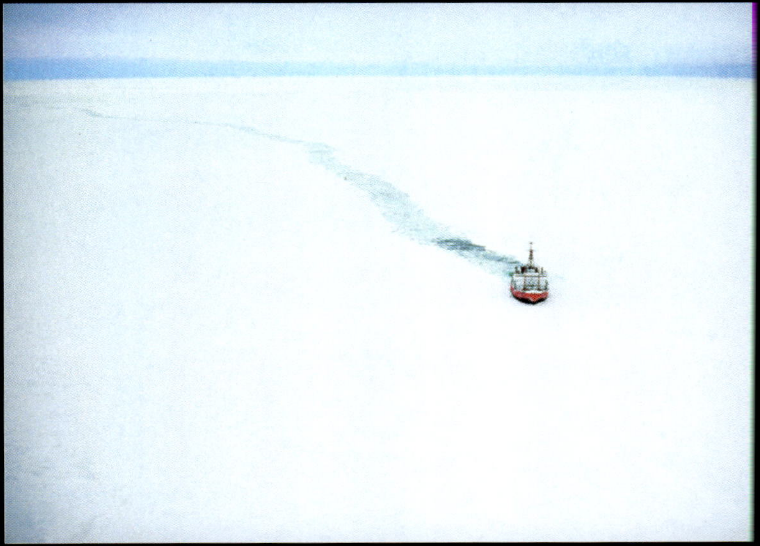

138 and 139
Two icebreakers cross the Northwestern Territory of Canada, where the icy temperatures create vast blocks of floating ice called "pack."

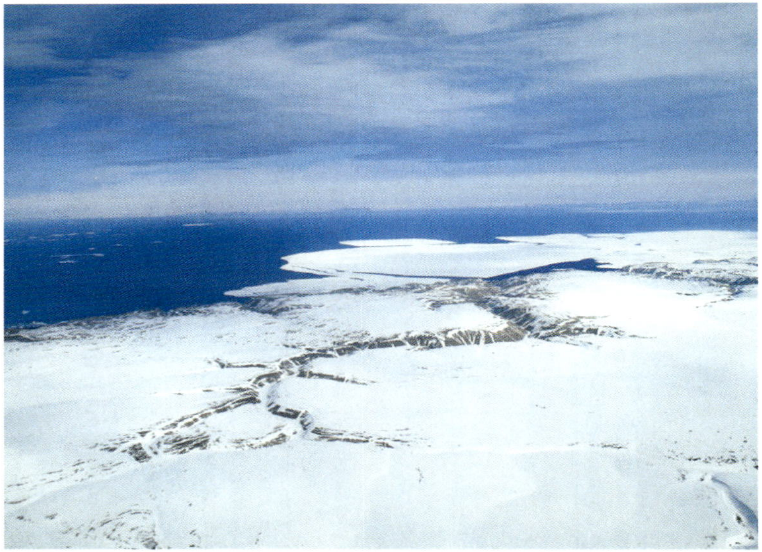

140 and 141
The Beaufort Sea, north of Alaska and Canada, is part of the Arctic Ocean and is always covered by pack ice. It was explored for the first time in 1914 by the Canadian Vilhjalmur Stefansson

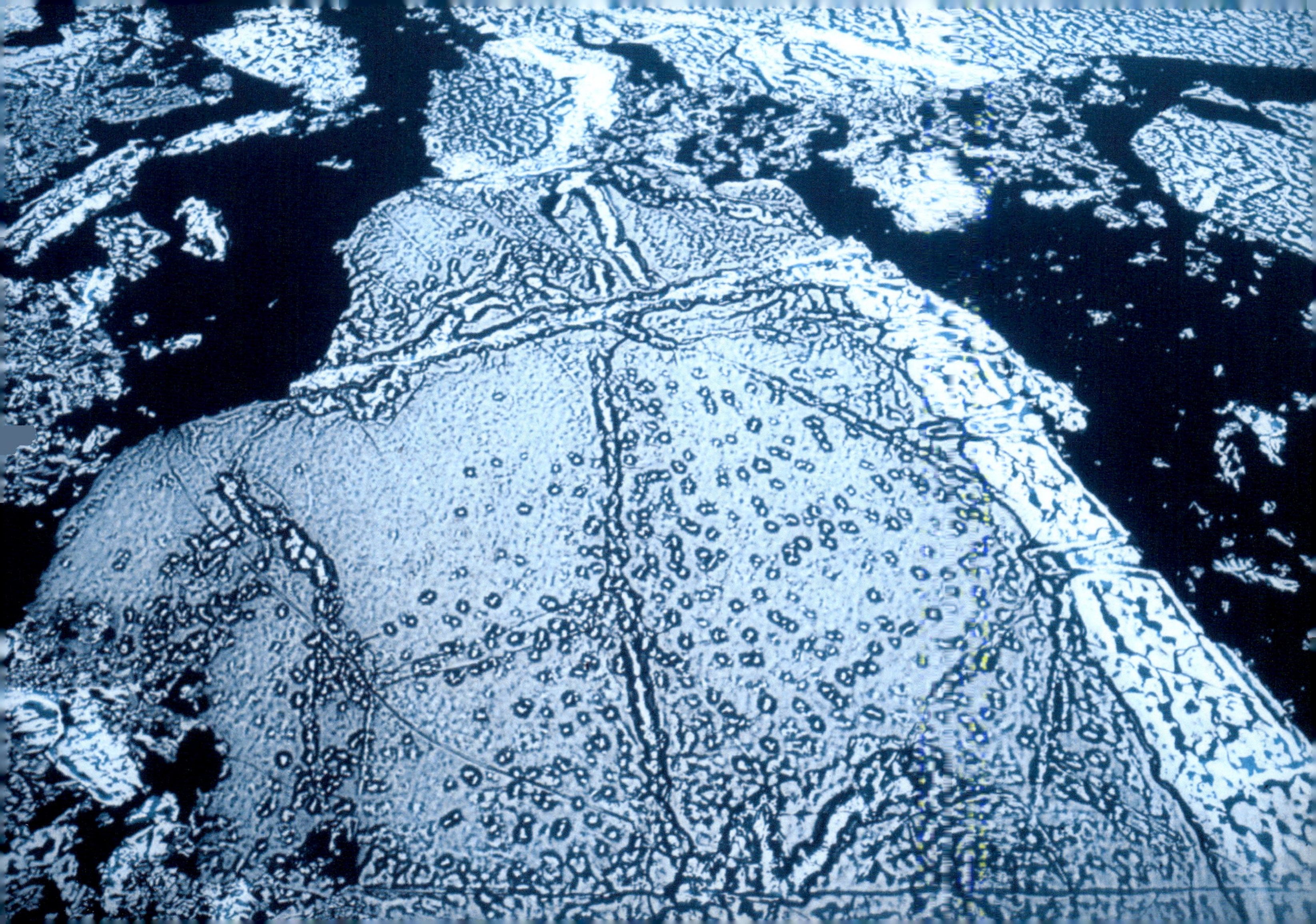

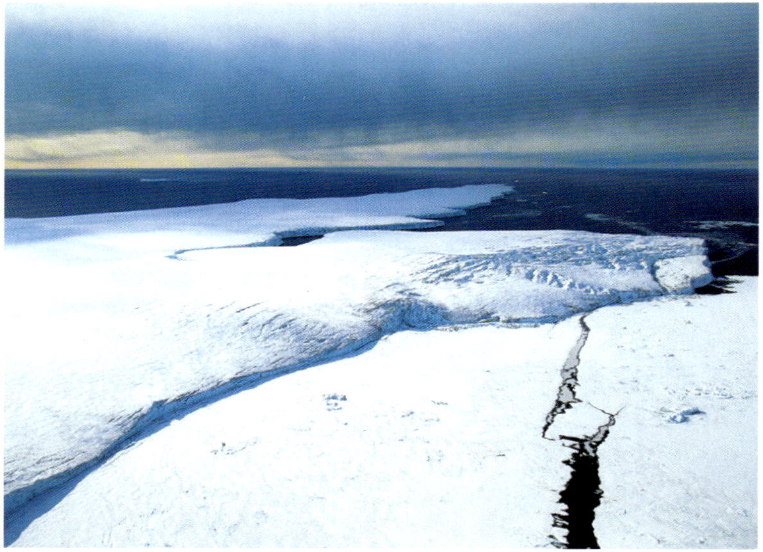

142
Floating blocks of ice in the Antarctic can vary from one to several feet thick, reaching up to a maximum of six miles across.

143
A close-up of the Dry Ice Tongue, a tongue of ice stretching for about 50 miles along the western coast of the Ross Sea in Antarctica.

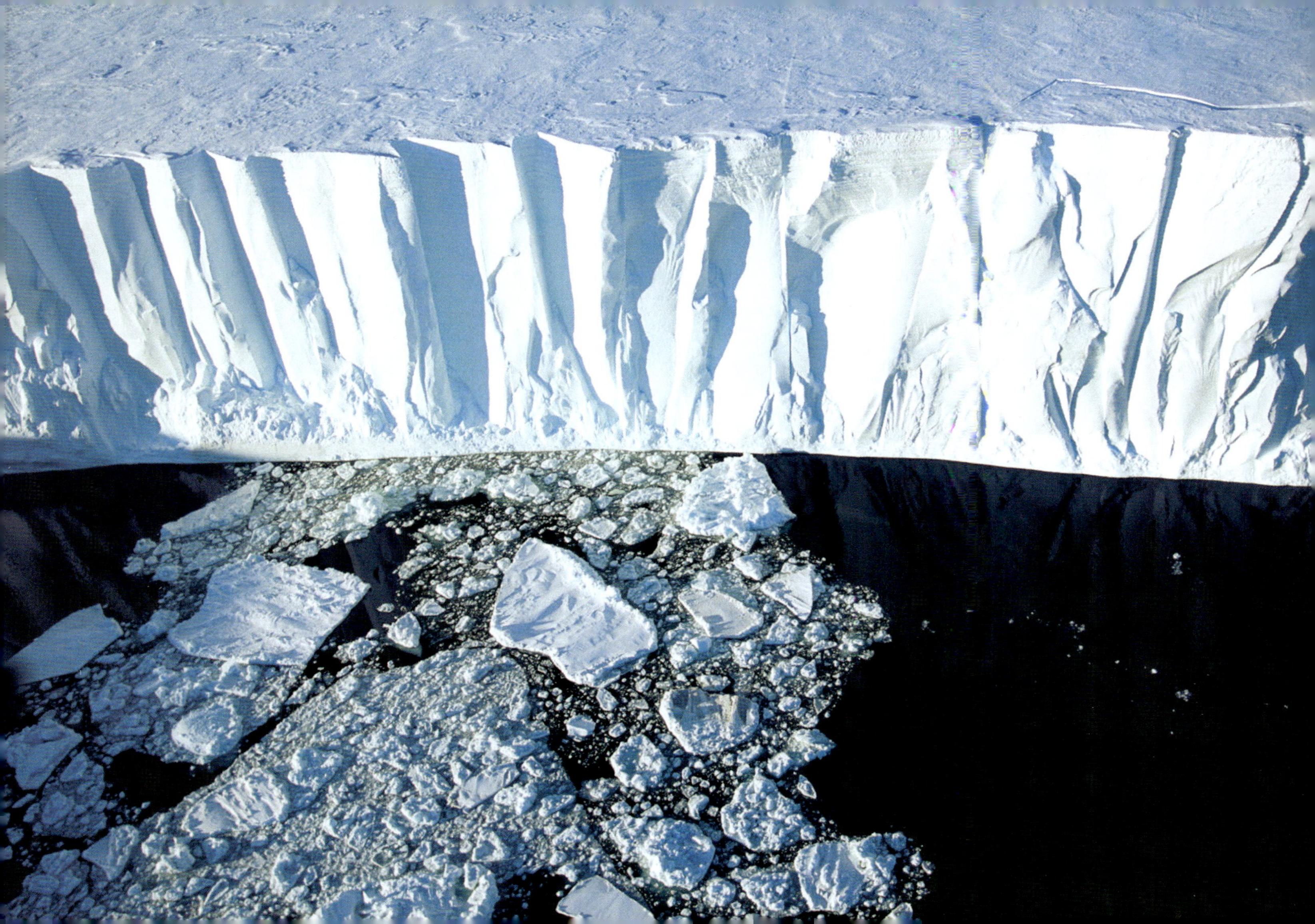

THE LOWLANDS

FLYING HIGH

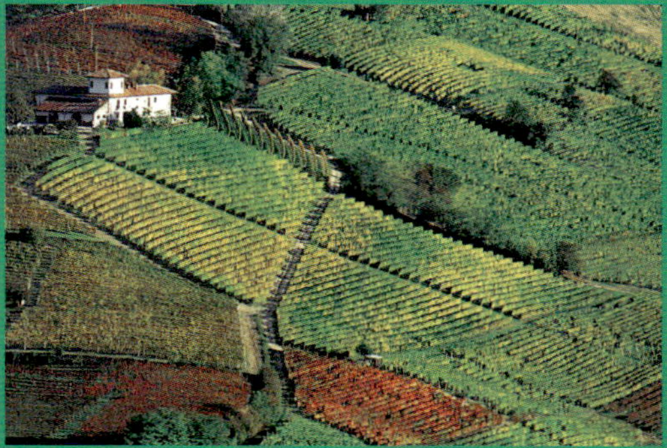
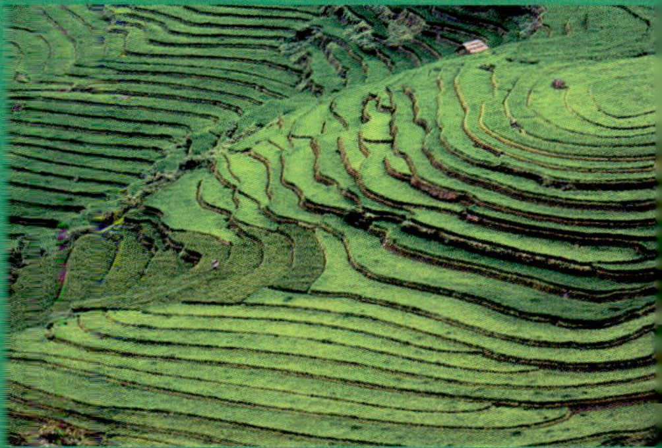

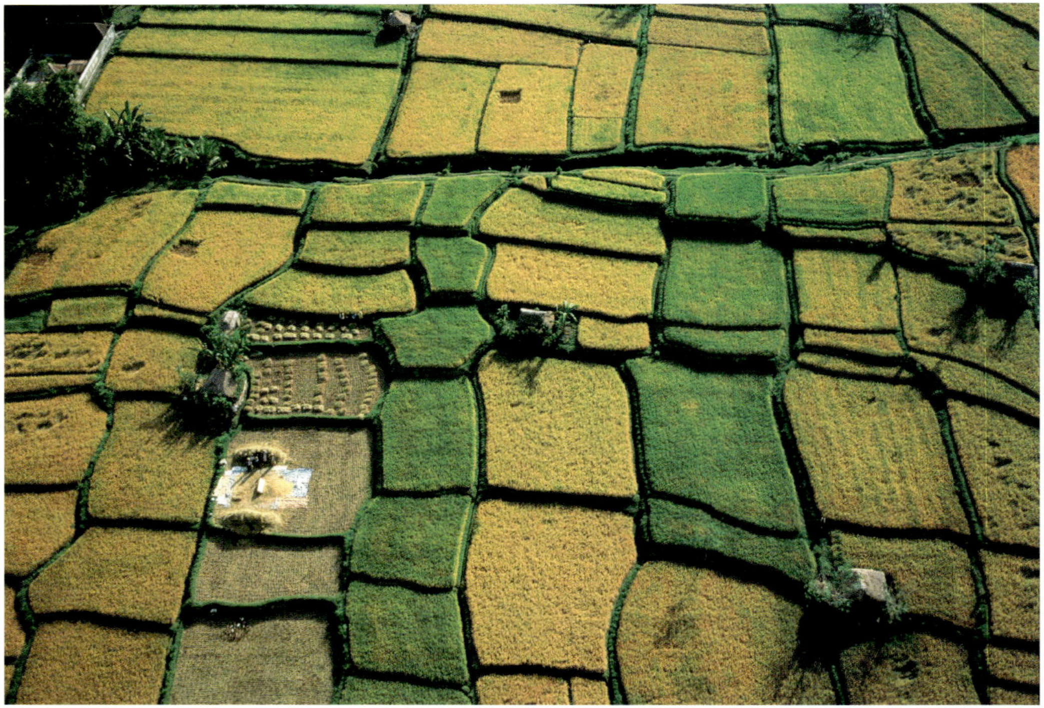

145
Vineyards in the La Morra area, in Italy (left); farming terraces planted with rice in north Thailand (right).

Every earthly environment has had its poets. The mountains, the seas, the forests, the cities, and even the eternal glaciers have found inspired voices to sing of their special beauty.

However, the places that have inspired the most passionate and nostalgic songs have probably been the world's hills, its plains, and its solid and controllable places, in the end very reassuring, even those never seen in person, where one was not born nor ever lived. Africa-sickness is one of the consequences of this natural need for interior tranquility.

The lower regions of the continent's tropical belts are infinite carpets of savannah, dotted here and there by the shadows of acacia and baobab trees. The grass bends beneath the sun and the step of elephants, which can be seen from above proceeding in loose lines from one tree to another, free to feed. Round warrior-shepherd villages pop up every now and then from the dust, the smoke of constantly burning fires, and in the reflection of river branches sleeping stagnantly in the plains' absence of any slope. Then not far away, rolling hills often marked by rammed terraces, in southern Ethiopia, Kenya, and Tanzania, give the human landscape order within a natural setting, among sparse forests and blinding-yellow prairies. It is just enough to

146
Irregularly shaped fields stretch across the volcanic-origin terrain of Bali. This type of soil is very fertile, so much so that it is not uncommon for it to yield two harvests a year.

The Lowlands

steal one's heart and rack it with regret when far away from those panoramas.
The steppes of Central Asia can rouse the same heartrending nostalgia. Flying over the boundless prairies of Mongolia immersed in the red light of sunset and creating long waves of wild graminaceous plants in the wind, is an experience that instills fear and excitement.
That which seems vacant comes to life from time to time: here the human presence seems more sporadic than ever because of the monotony of the surrounding landscape – for hundreds of miles in every direction – but at times a nomad family's tent sprouts up in the crystal-clear, icy-cold, and perfect air.
Not even a plume of smoke withstands the wind, but the herds and flocks in the distance cast long shadows on the flat ground, as do the wild horses – the last in the world – that stand out like white stars against the yellow-green of the prairies.
Even the tundra is part of this ensemble. It certainly cannot be considered welcoming, this last-to-be-abandoned land by the ice's retreat dozens of thousands of years ago. Yet, even its gray expanses, desperately flat and boggy, have their own form of beauty and riches.
During the fleeting Arctic summer, intensely colored flowers ignite their flameless fires on the wild fields, while herds of reindeer and caribou travel thousand-year-old routes in search of vegetation that every year, with the seasons, conquers territory and then loses it, only to conquer it again when the sun allows it.
Nonetheless, these are extreme environments. The hill areas able to stir emotions with their "colonized" look are many, consisting of rolling humps made verdant by farming activities like those on the island of Chiloe,

The Lowlands

so similar to the countryside of Western Europe or the northeast United States they seem erroneously located a few miles off the indented coasts of that realm of wind and solitude that is Patagonia.

In terms of countryside and hills, the epitome is expressed in the comparative words used above.

No places may exist in the world more welcoming in appearance than the rural areas of Britain, Ireland, France, or New England, with their cottages and pristine farms spread about the fields, at the base of undulating hills that rise like the backs of dragons from the dark woods of the valley floors, their meadow-covered summits crowned by giant elms, chestnut trees, and centuries-old oaks. Rivers and streams plow wide valleys, lacking any disturbing shadows or depths.

Everywhere is planted with crops, under control, cared for – one could almost say caressed – by thousands of years of the inhabitants' labor.

Immense plains occupy the heart of the United States, a giant raft of stone drifting between two oceans, closed to the east by the ancient eroded rises of the Appalachian Mountains, lush with deciduous woods and to the west by the spurs of the Rocky Mountains, heralded by highlands that always seem as far off as the Black Hills or the unbelievable Badlands of South Dakota, resembling a churning sea, petrified in an instant by some divine force irritated by that solidified chaos.

The ground of the great plains of the world is solid; one could even define them "gentle" as they never rise or fall. Here, the uniform disconcerting vastness of the plains' landscape is unexpectedly broken up by intensive crops using advanced methods.

Where nature has had a rest, depriving the prairies of any special personality because of

The Lowlands

their flatness, the hand of man has intervened. Dozens of perfectly circular fields stand out unnaturally from the driest plains of Jordan, expanding as far as the horizon. Functioning as compasses, drawing unique markings on this lean realm of nature, the arms of irrigation machines turn like dials to nourish that perfect space – it is a circle – rescued from the seeming chaos of a land consumed by sun and wind. A completely different chromatic impact is had from crops in more temperate environments, where fields of magenta-colored cranberries, 600 feet across, carve out impeccable rounded forms, often heart-shaped, in the dull brown of sand-covered bogs like those in Massachusetts, scattered along with dozens of others about the most rolling countryside of hills and woods imaginable.

What can be said about the rice paddies? Few spectacles are as overwhelming from the sky. They are like snake coils enveloping the hills of Asia, green almost beyond possibility, insistently clinging to them for up to two or three thousand years. They are sculptures that enliven the impossible mane of the hills as well as flat stretches of small square seas in perfect rows, all aligned like a checkerboard drawn by some mad genius, reflecting the sky in its entirety, all the clouds, and distant mountains, from the plains south of the Himalayas to the faraway Western countryside of northern Italy.

Remaining in flight over the peninsula, the wine-growing regions are lands of bright-green, delicate rows, which run parallel to each other for miles and miles, over vast hill systems with a surprisingly bleak appearance, given the abundance of their produce.

Under the burning sun, the ground seems perennially parched in the colors of its tuff rock, light and dark, often yellow like loess or in the color of "burnt sienna," perfectly ex-

The Lowlands

pressing the fragile but stubborn existence of the vines.

The Monferrato and the Langhe regions, in the northeast of the peninsula, the plains around Verona, the Chianti region in Tuscany, and the Salento region in Puglia are agricultural zones that seem created intentionally to please those who see them as much as those who appreciate their fruit.

They are borderlands, in climatic terms, generally stretching along the invisible frontier separating the colder zones of the Alps and Apennines from the warmer hilly or flat "lowlands." In fact, they owe their success to these transitory conditions. Vines are almost never found far from mountains. Beyond the hills, the Alps or the Apennines can be glimpsed, able to mitigate the harsh appearance of even remote snowy, ethereal, and blue landscapes like in Chinese paintings.

Terraces and agricultural enclosures, when taken together more titanic than any other work in the history of man, extend endlessly across the Andean slopes, as dry as any land can be, but also over the carpet-like meadows of Ireland, where water is never lacking. They are breathtaking sights, also because we can see the houses and villages of those who constructed them, and who did so without ever suspecting or thinking that all that hard work would produce such a magnificent result when seen from above.

All the hills and plains of the world, whatever kind they may be, contribute to creating landscapes that look like masterpieces.

An art unaware of itself, infinitely complex but so pure and obvious, it goes right to the heart of those who, over the millennia, have sung of the beauty of those "lowlands" and to those who have listened to those songs with nostalgia, even if they have never seen those lands.

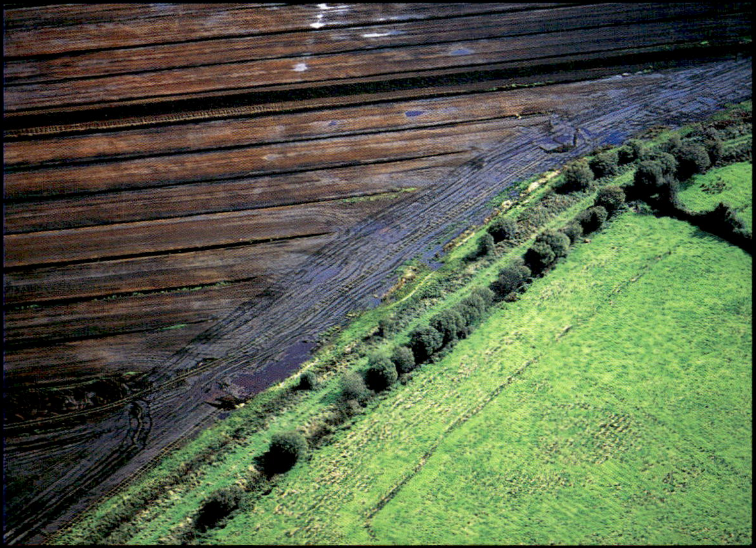

152
On generally low-altitude territories like that of Ireland (in this case in Westmeath County), farms often draw bizarre "chance" works of art.

153
A palette of shades of green is spread around Cork County, Ireland's southernmost county, not to mention the biggest.

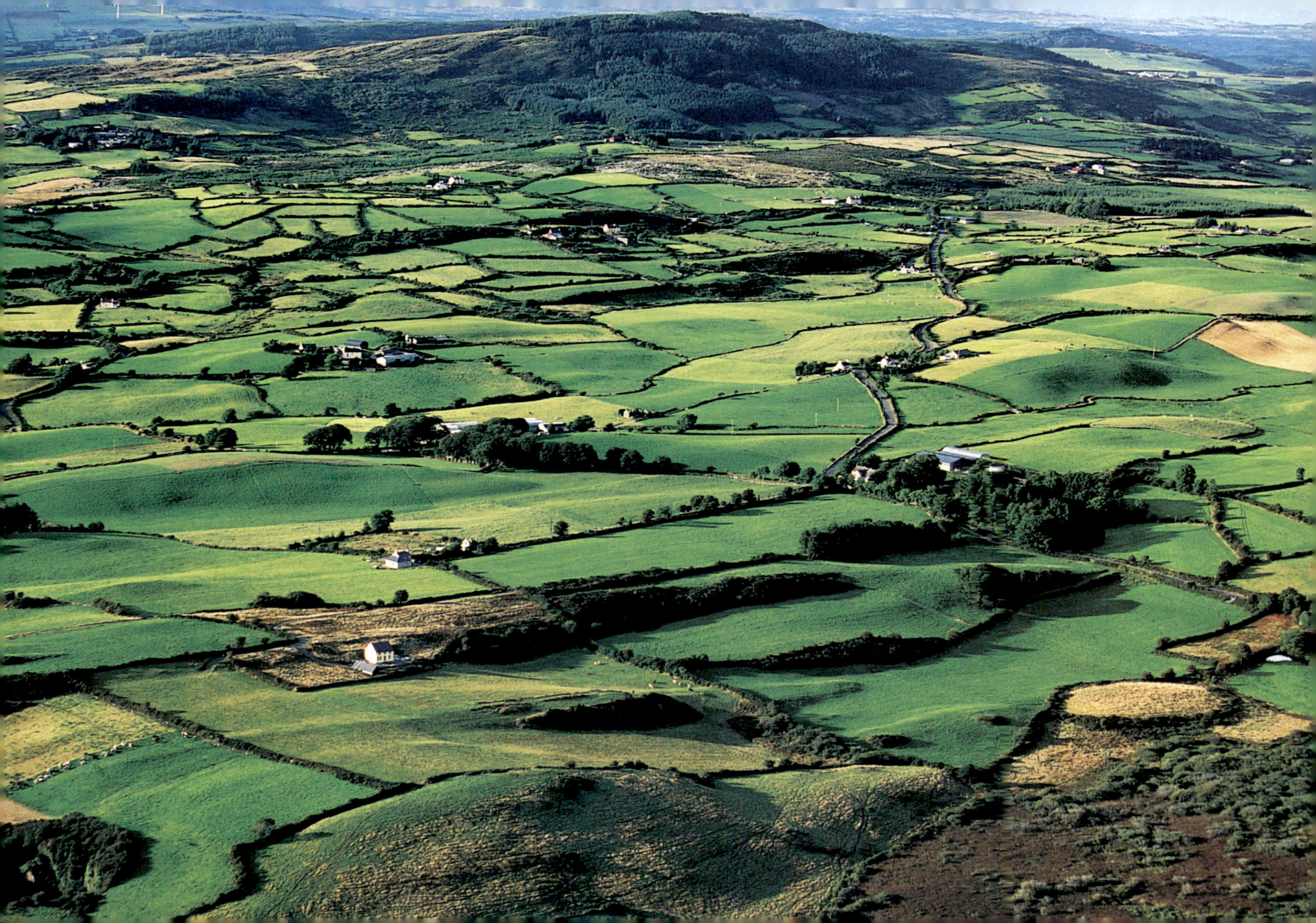

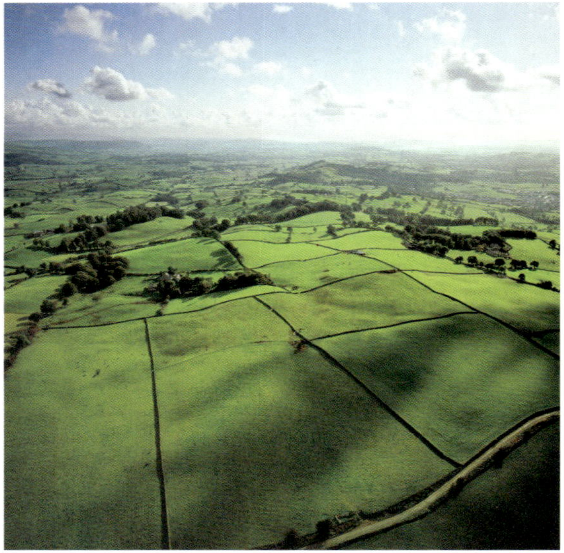

154

The green Lake District, near Kendal in Great Britain, combines valleys, mountains, and numerous lakes to compose panoramas among the most peaceful imaginable.

155

The charm of the even plains of Somerset Level, in Great Britain, is enhanced by the appearance of two tall rainbows.

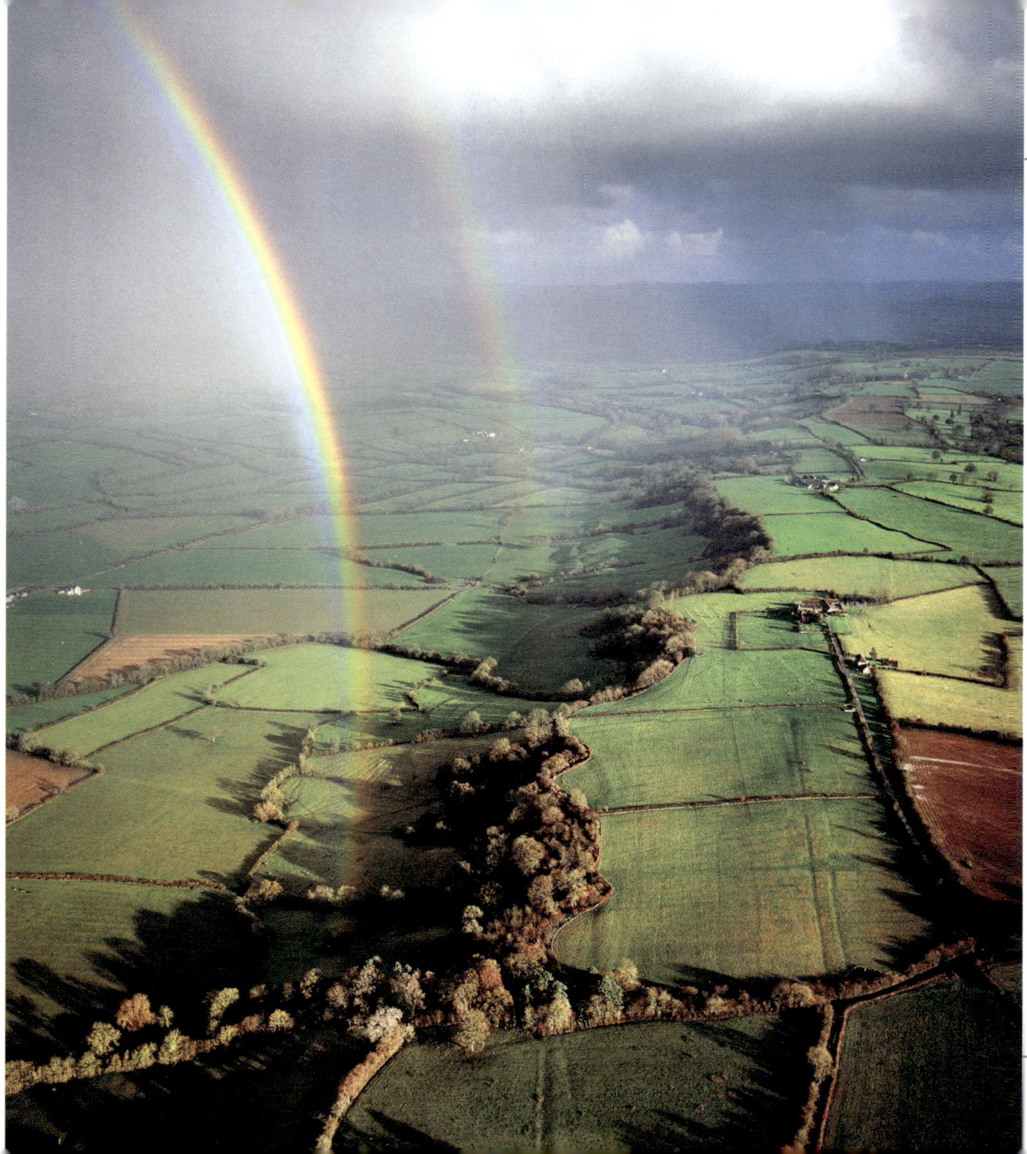

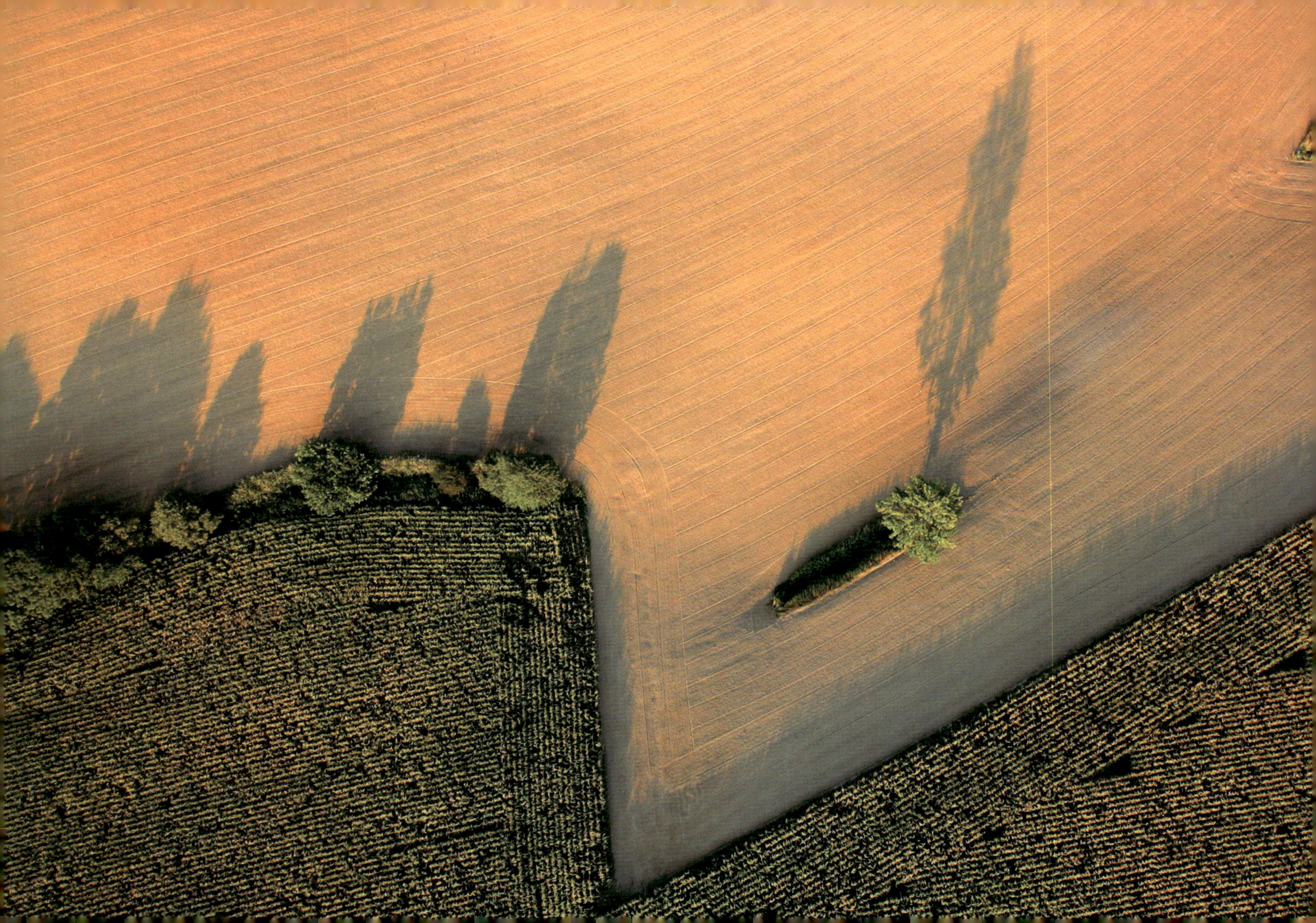

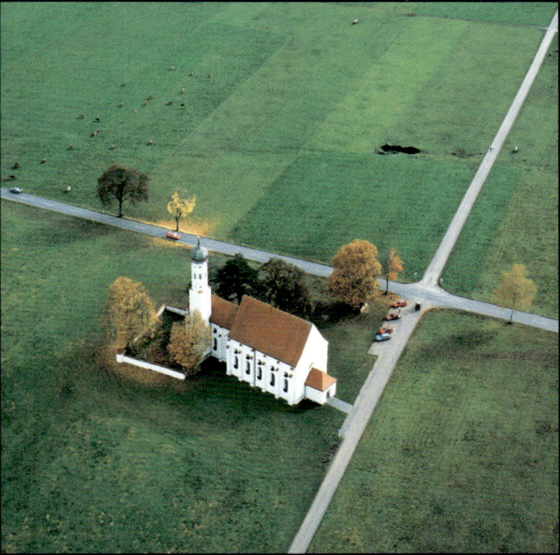

156

Plowed and sowed fields in Rottal, Germany, are delimited by extremely regular lines.

157

At the base of the Bavarian Alps, a lone white church stands near an intersection in the German valley: another almost symbolic composition, even if unintentional.

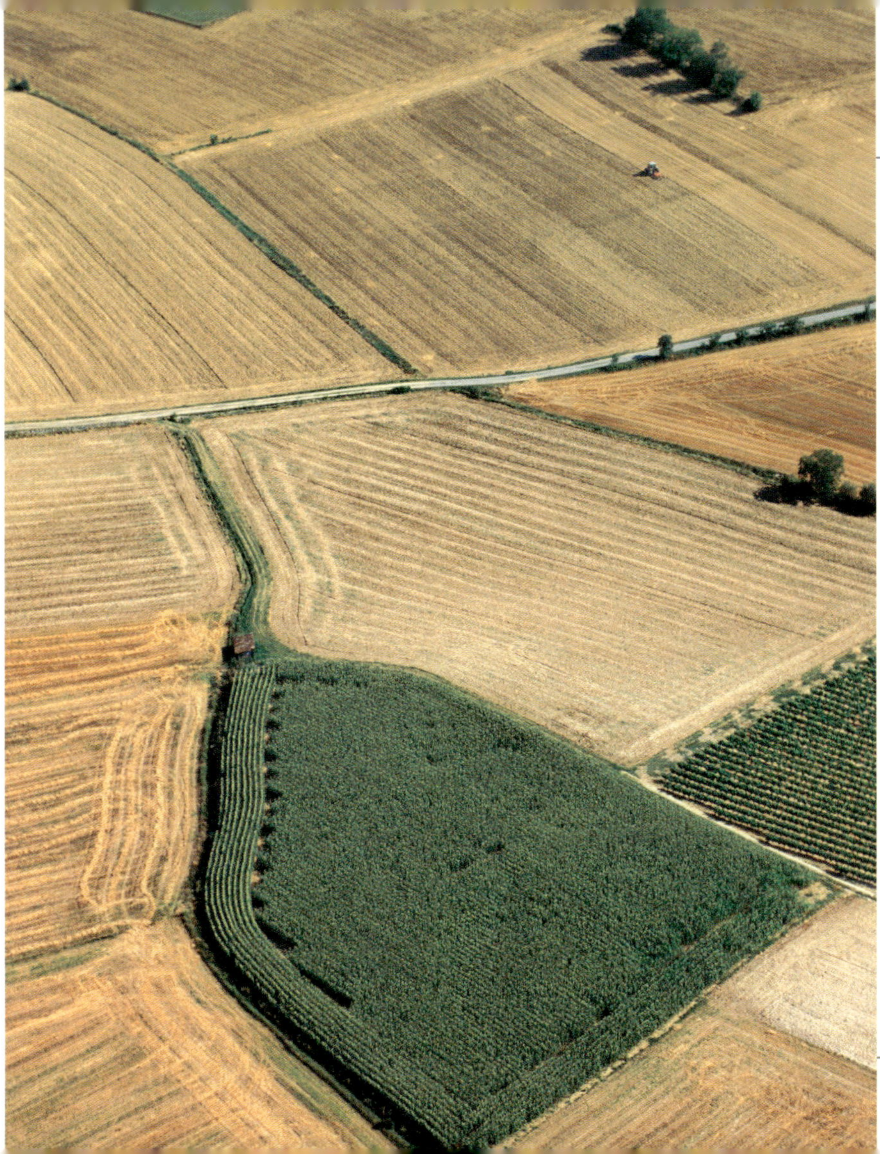

158
Summer floods the French countryside between Aude and the Garonne River with sun. Tiny from this perspective, a tractor works among the freshly plowed furrows.

159
A small village in the Beauce, in France, seems to squeeze in to give the most area possible to farmland.

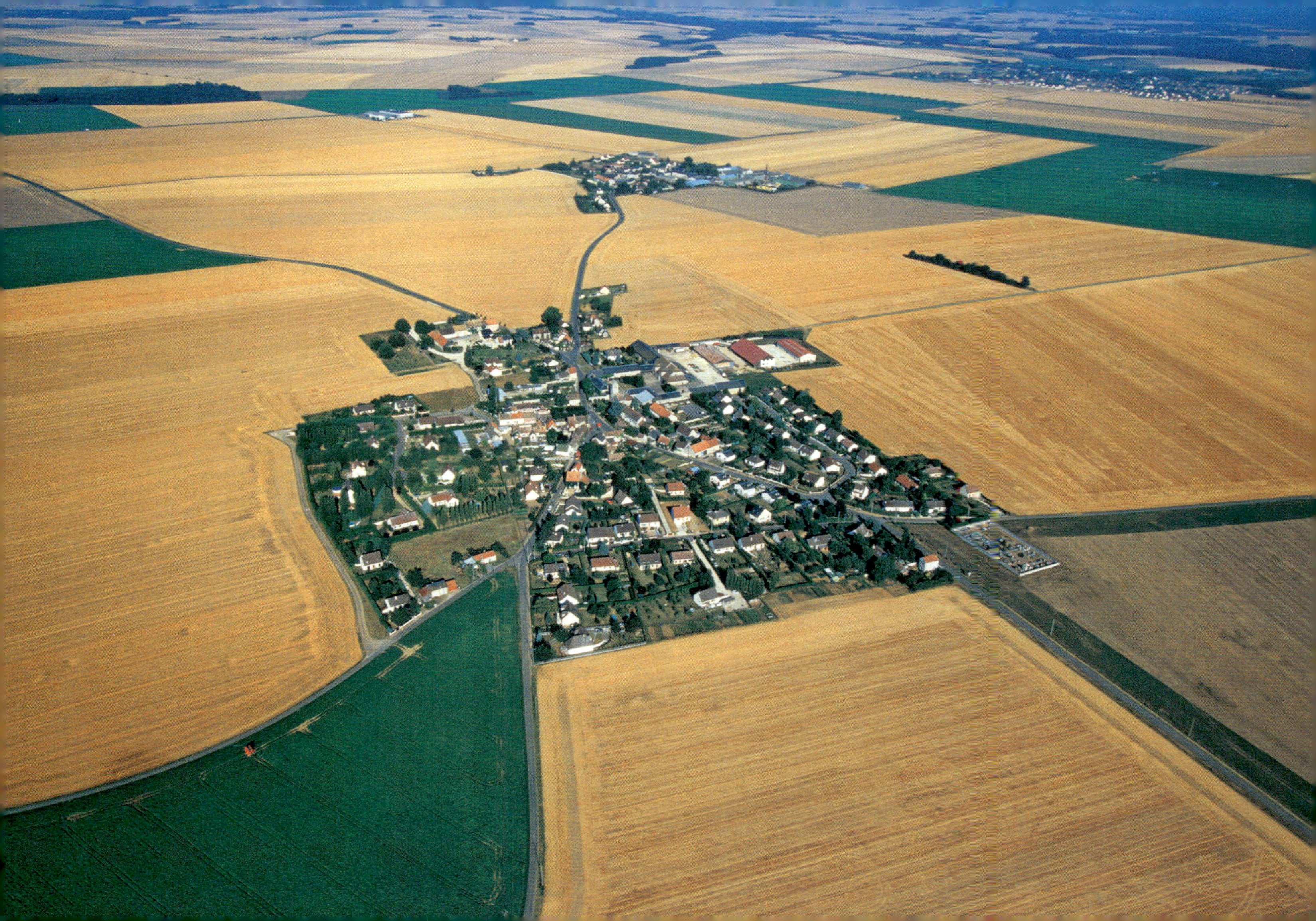

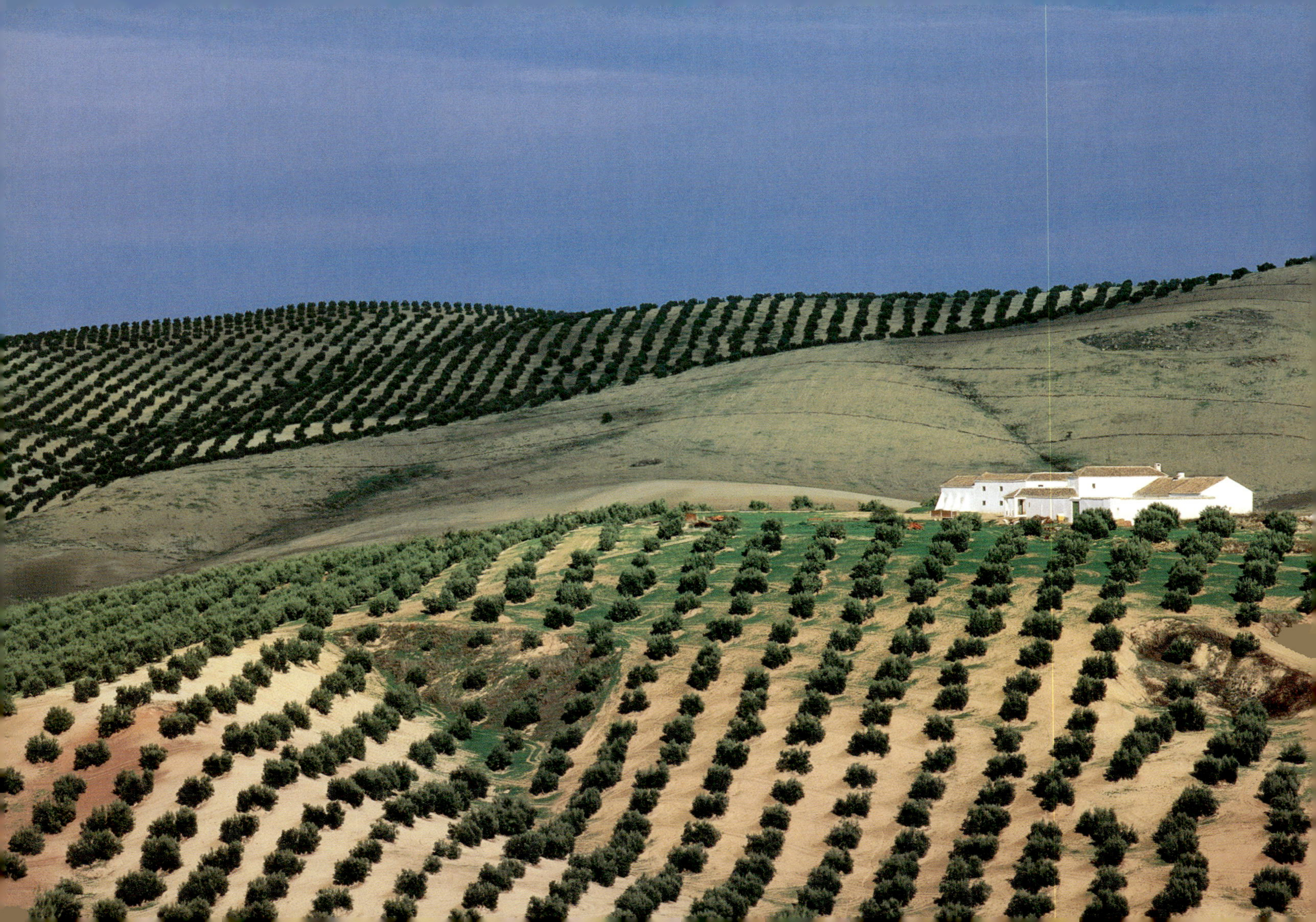

160
An impressionist painting forms in the province of Toledo, among orchards and waves of heat: this is the most widespread perception of Spain in the world.

161
A strange sort of puzzle appears near the Costa del Sol, in Spain: they are actually greenhouses for farming in special environments.

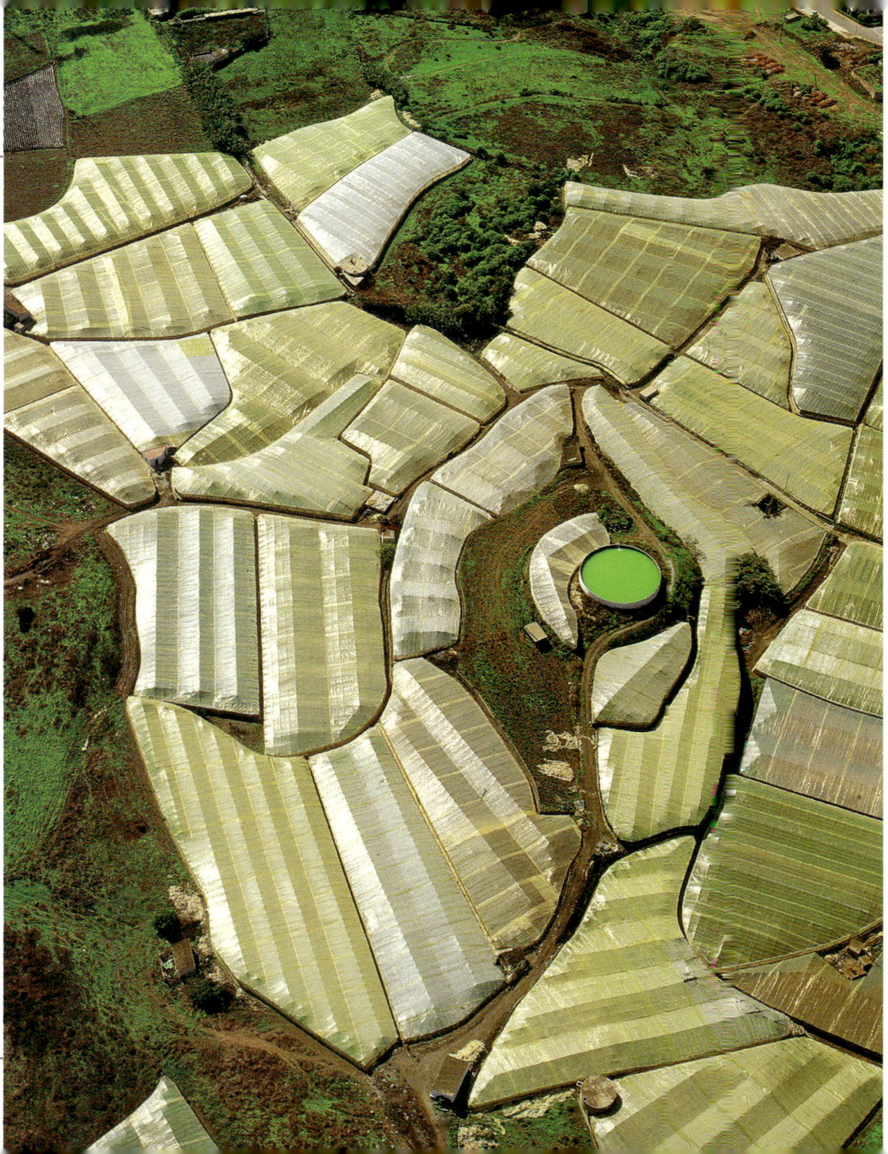

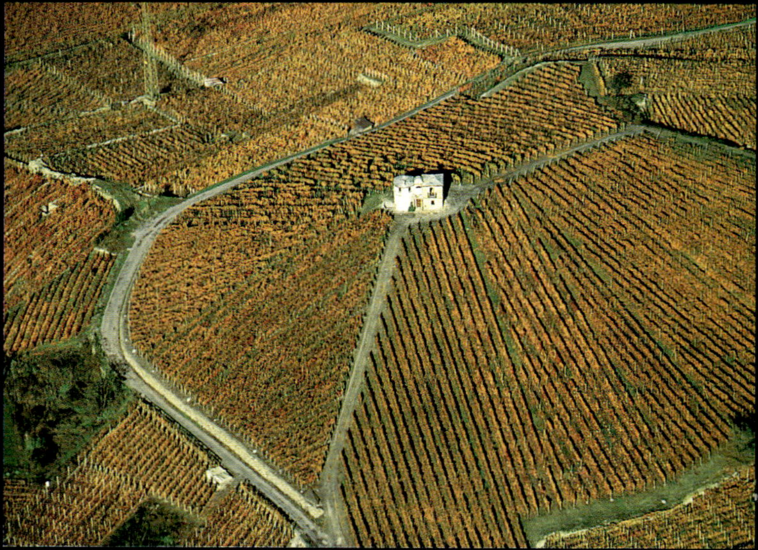

162
A stone house suddenly pops up from the "rust" of the rows of already harvested grapevines. The region is the Aosta Valley in Italy.

163
The hill regions of the Langhe, in Italy, can be considered synonymous with wine. The area boasts thousands of acres of vineyards, which color the landscape in the most surprising ways.

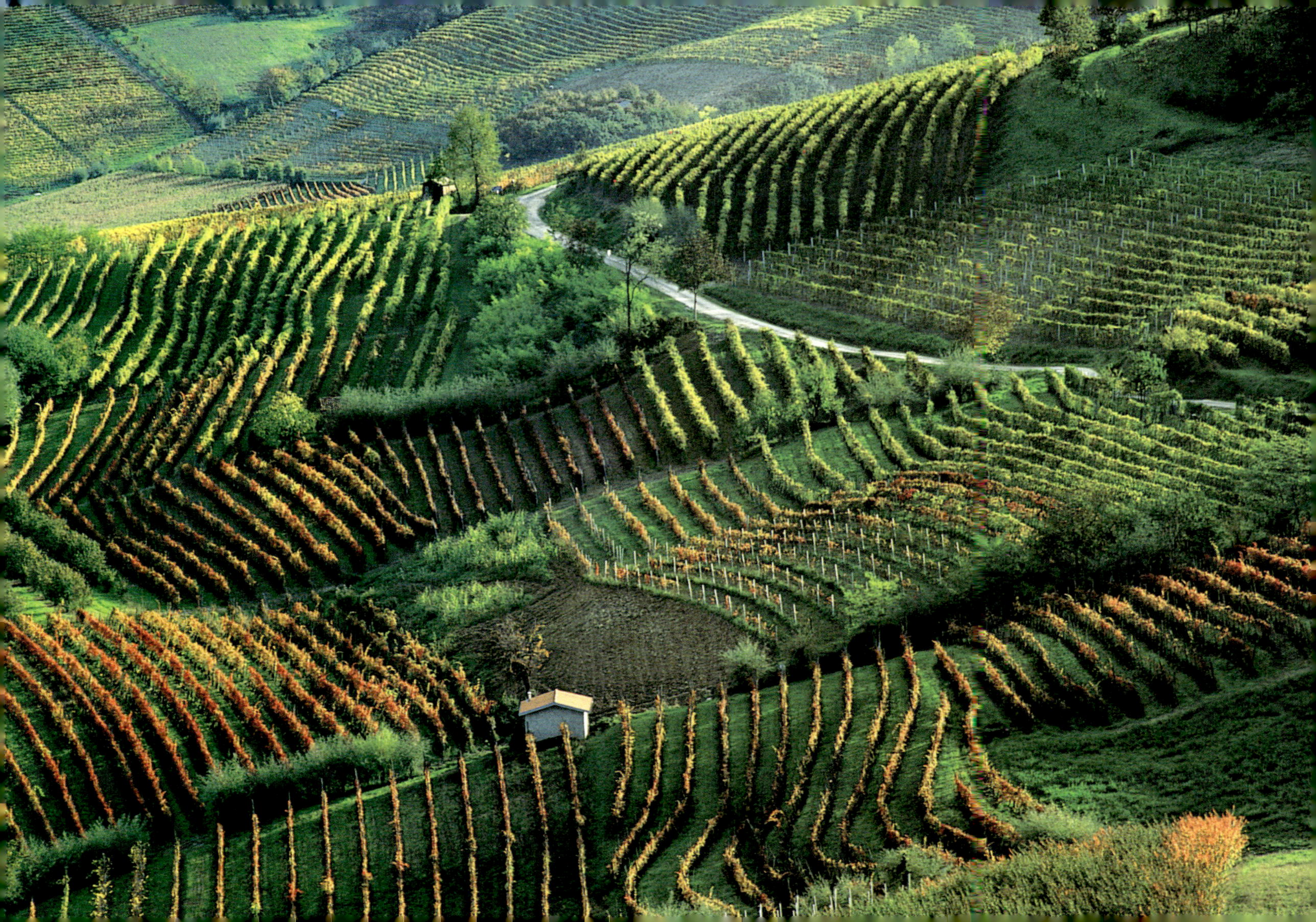

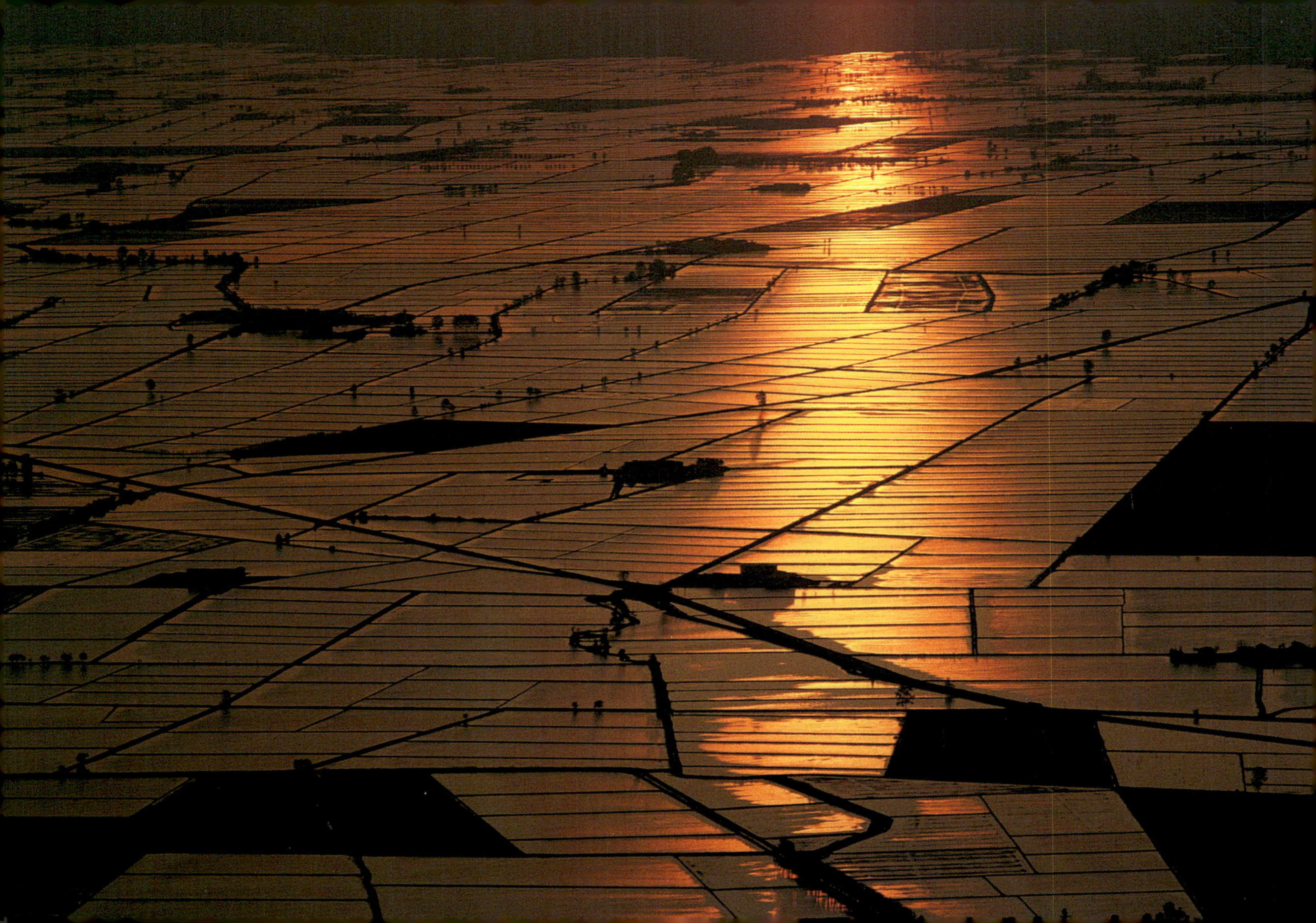

164

The countryside around Vercelli, in Italy, reaches the height of its beauty in spring, when the rice paddies are flooded, reflecting the sky in all its magnificence from dawn to dusk.

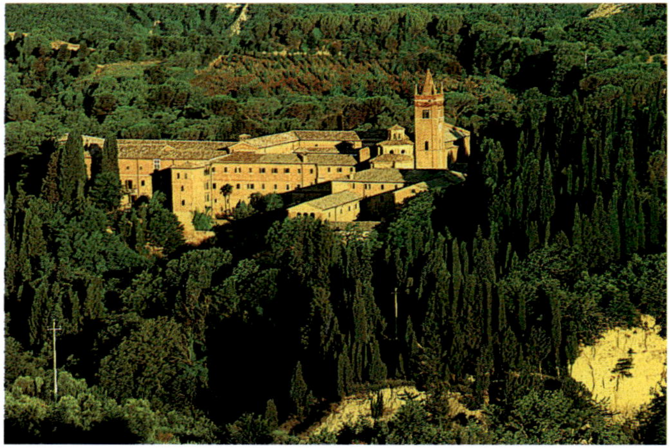

166
The Siena Crete in Italy, an area full of ancient villages, castles, and abbeys.

167
The hills are the domain of the mists, like here on the Apennine Mountains of the Emilia region in Italy.

168-169
The Tuscan countryside, in Italy, is deservedly famous for its variety and contrasts: smiling lands alternate with fertile hills.

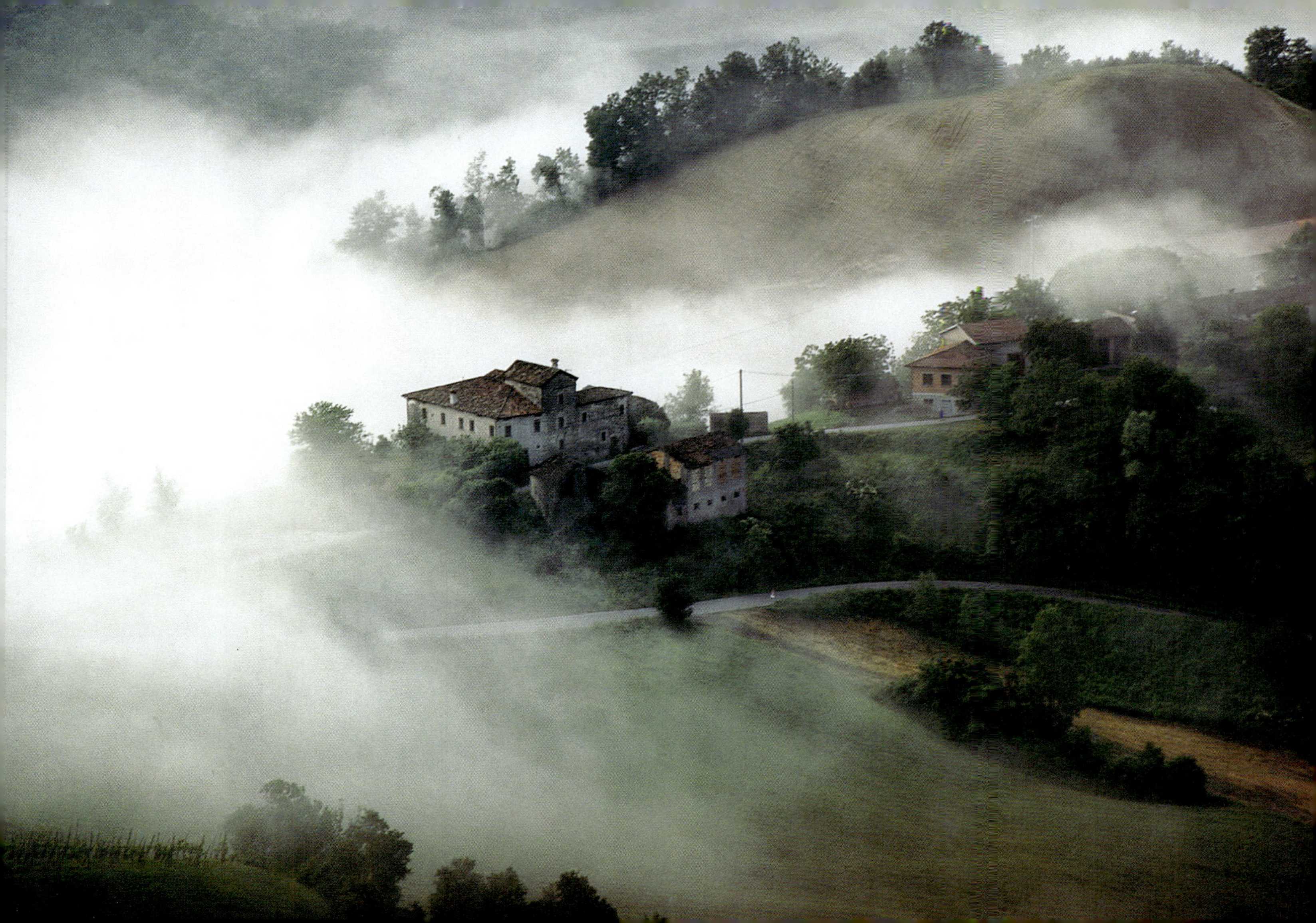

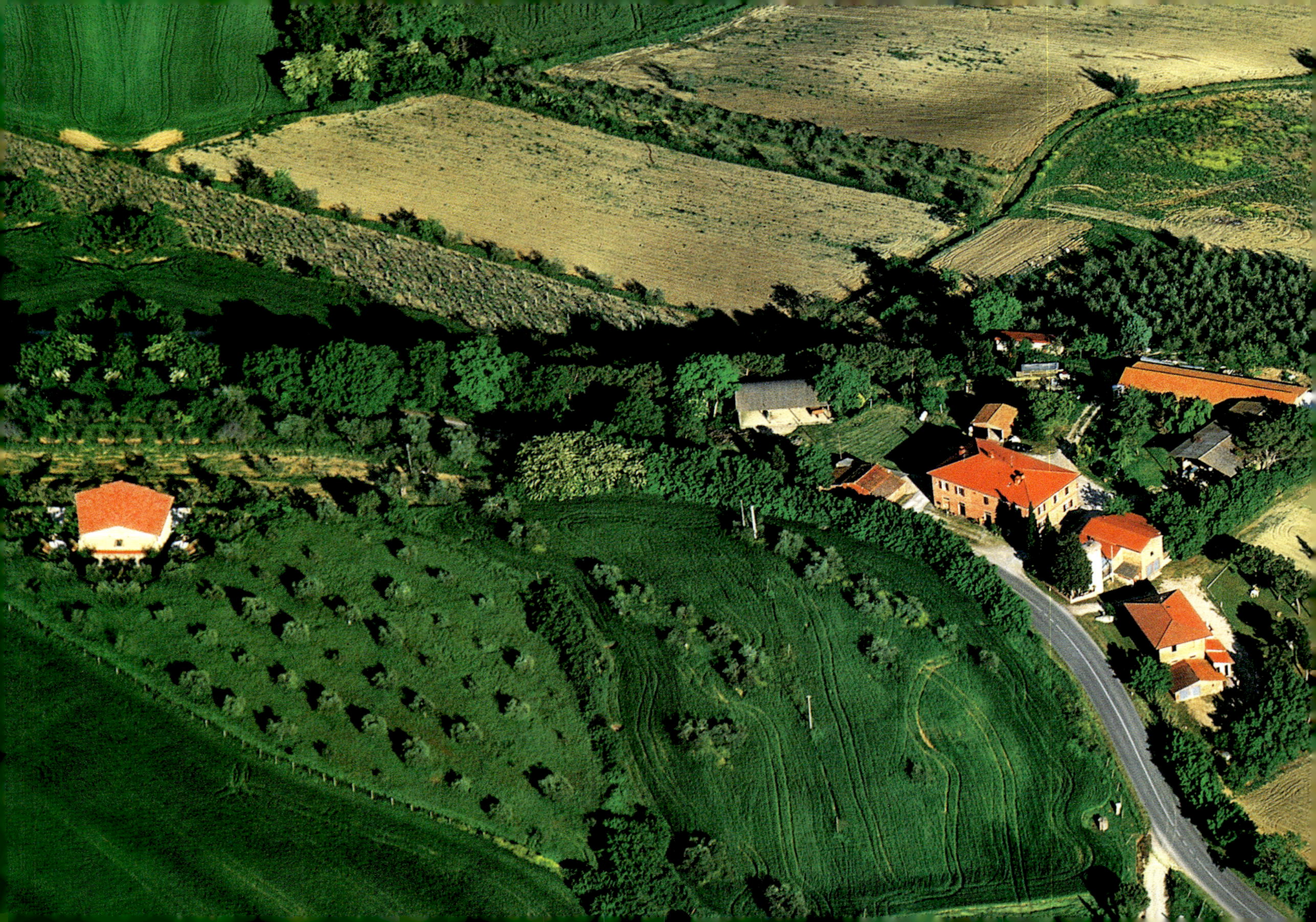

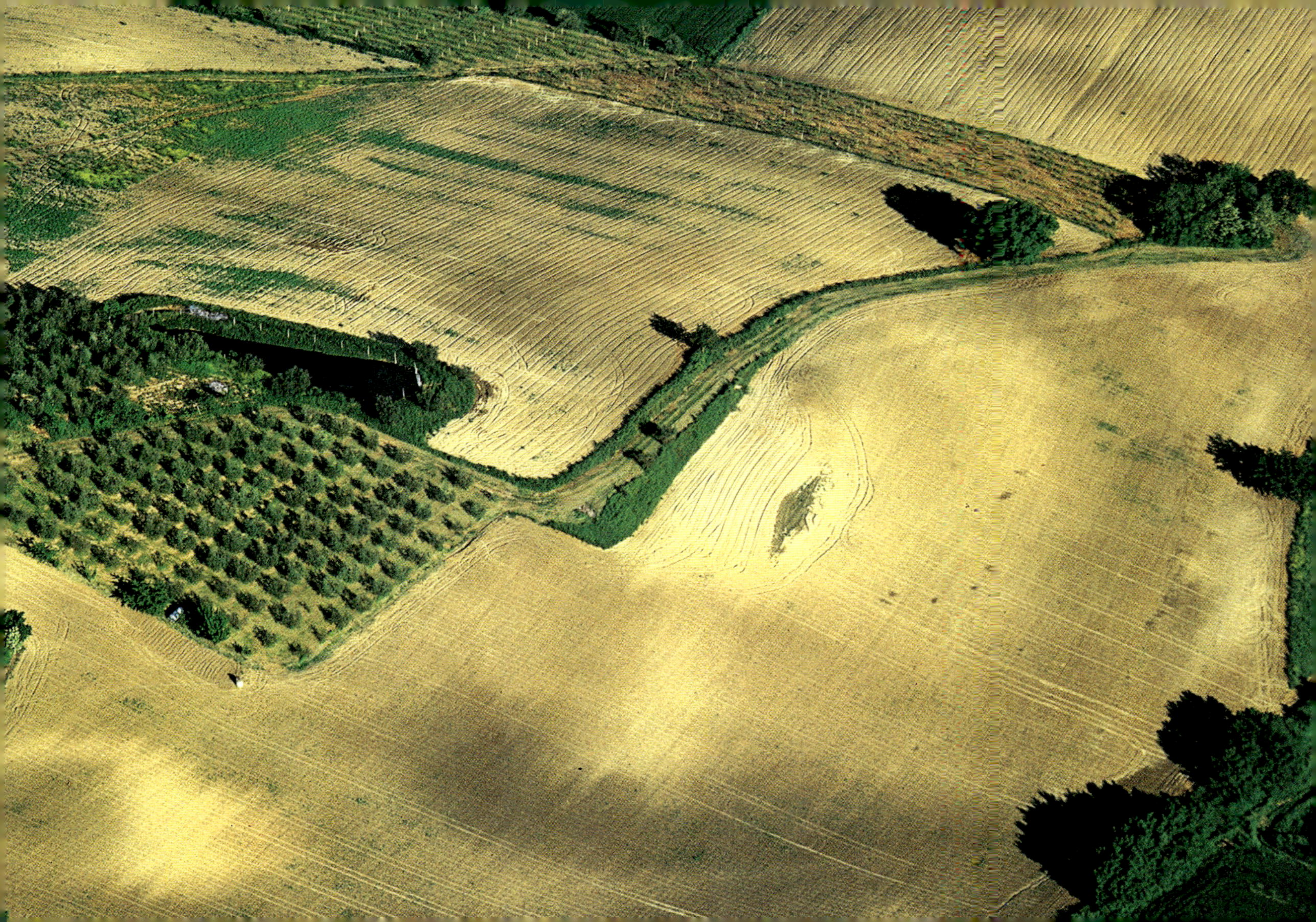

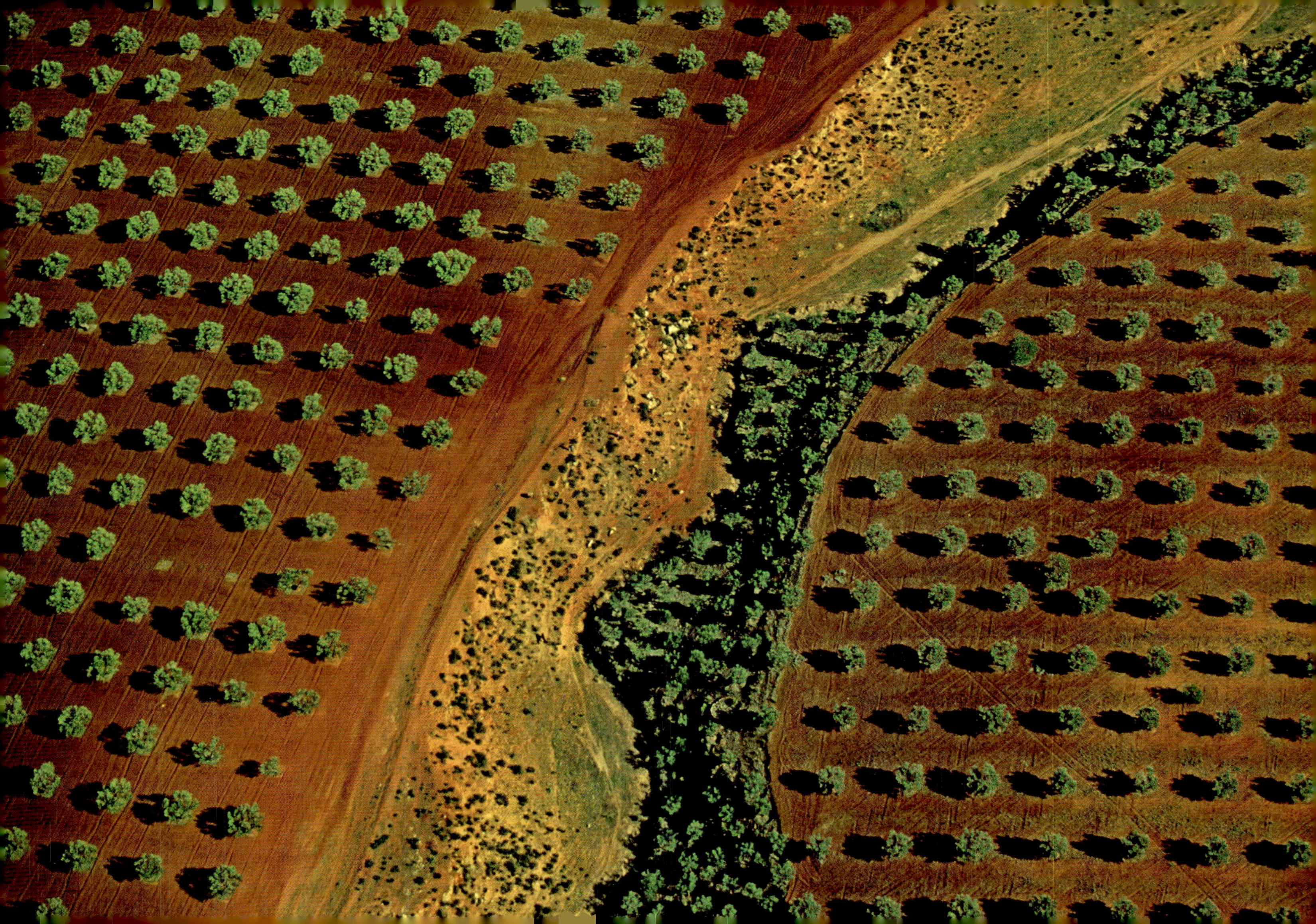

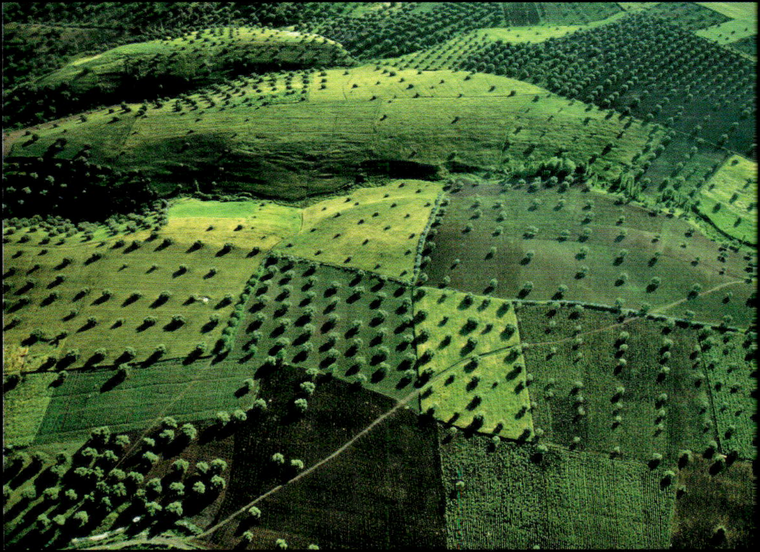

170

The geometric designs and the perfectly aligned trees at this Tunisian oasis, dedicated to olive trees, offer a unique landscape to observers in the sky.

171

Orchards in the area of Fez, in Morocco, dot the soft rolling hills of the countryside.

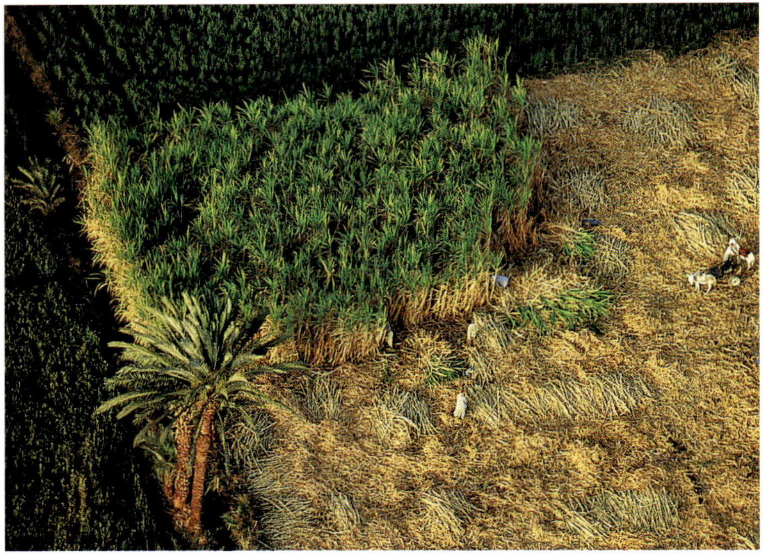

172

In the Luxor area in Egypt, once a group of farmers have reached their fields by donkey and cart, they proceed to reap the sugarcane.

173

Today like 4,000 years ago, small cultivated fields cluster around a farm in the countryside of Luxor, Egypt. Even the palms, of course, provide their own produce: dates, flour, and oil.

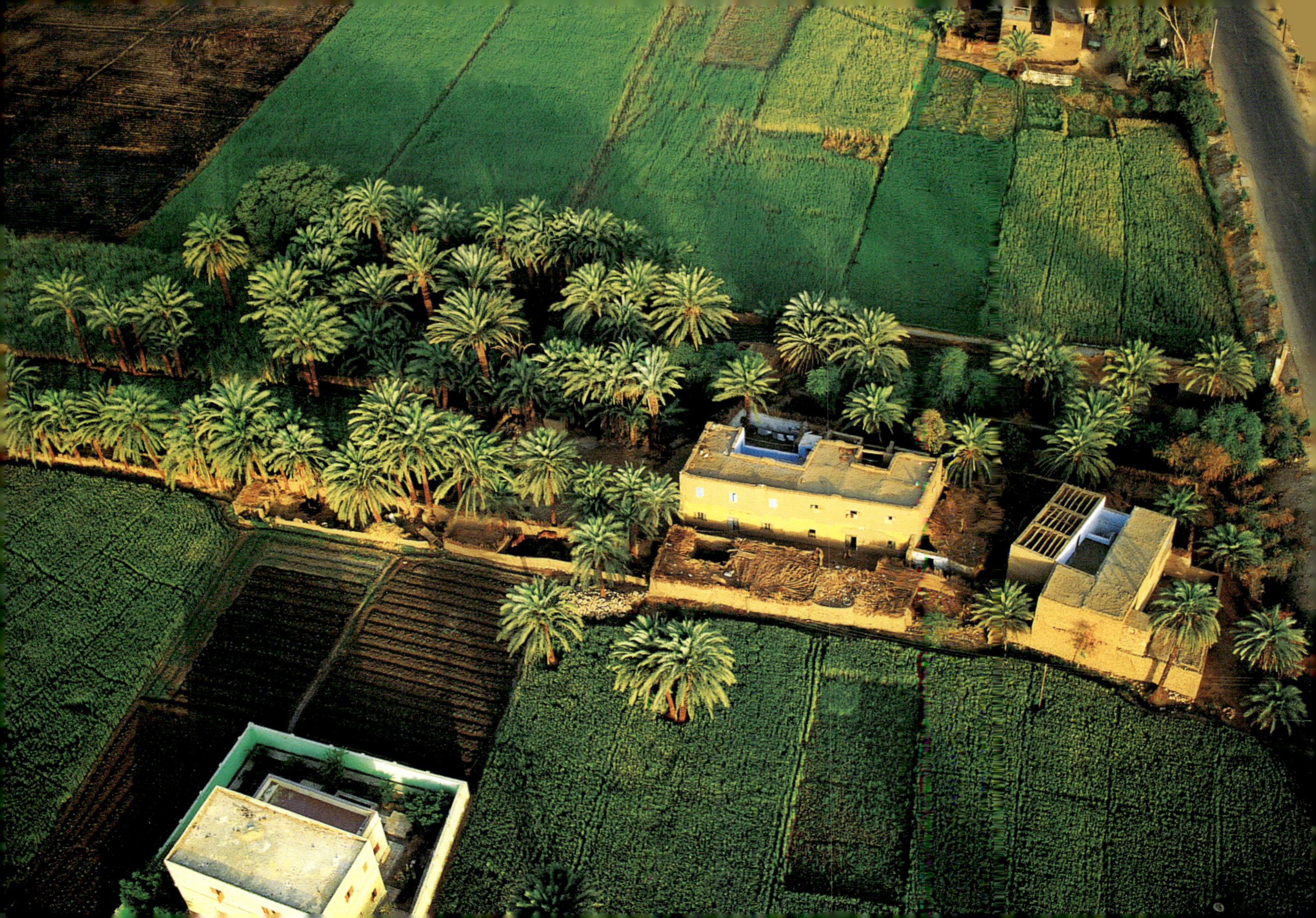

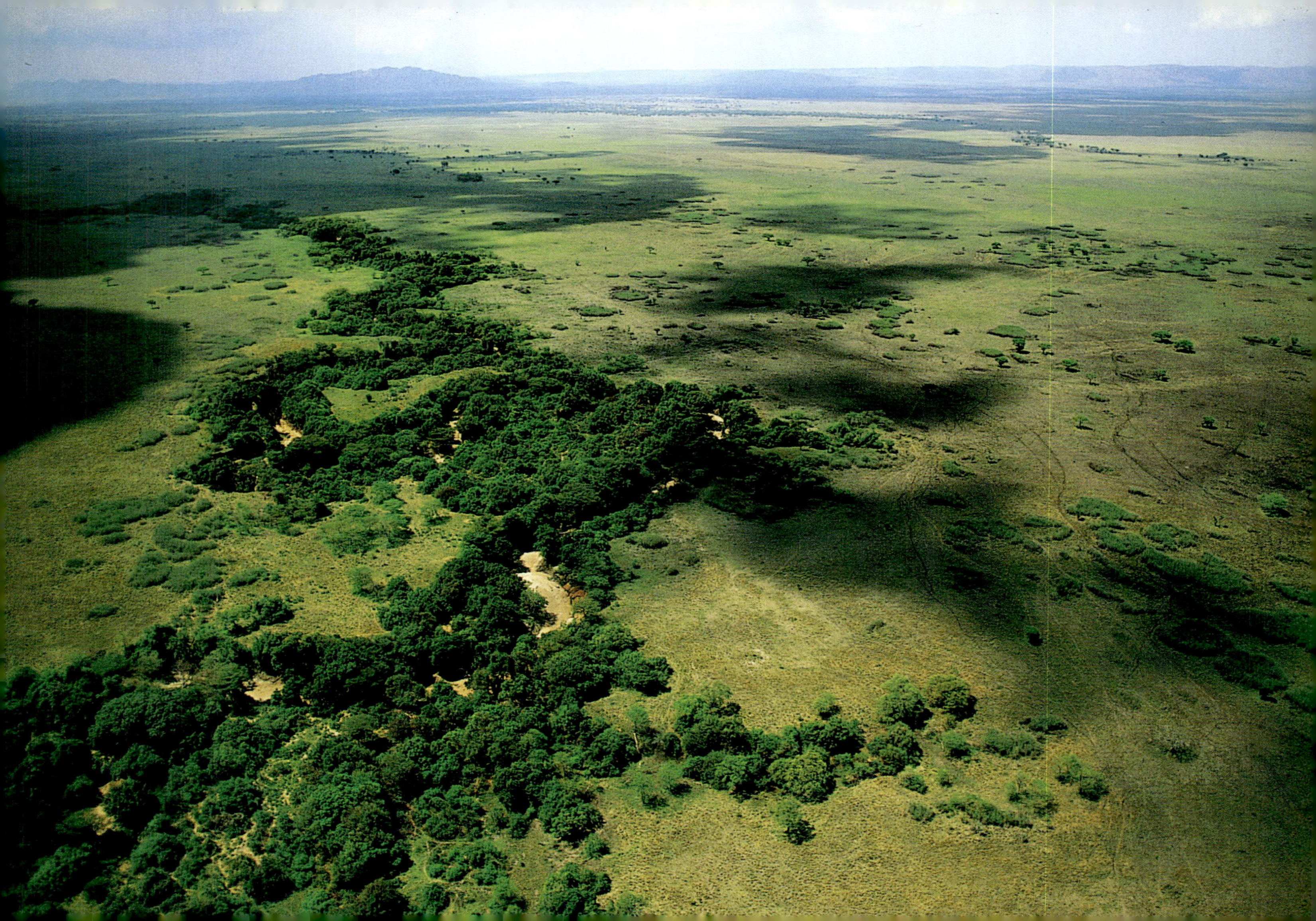

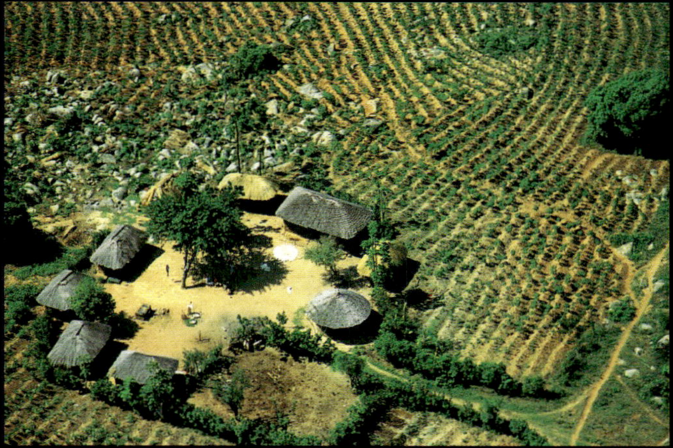

17[illegible]

The bed of a river opens a "road of vegetation" in the Tanzanian savannah. As inhospitable as it may be in its entirety, this ecosystem offers some of the most exciting views in the world.

17[illegible]

A tiny town functions as a sort of autonomous farming cooperative in the Tanzanian savannah. Farm produce is meager, though, and must be supplemented by livestock raising..

176

The sunburned crops leave the clayey terrain in the Tsavo zone, in Kenya, bare. This type of soil is not the most suitable for farming.

177

As if cut by enormous scissors, two cultivated areas east of Pretoria, in South Africa, enclose an uncultivated zone featuring low vegetation and shrubbery.

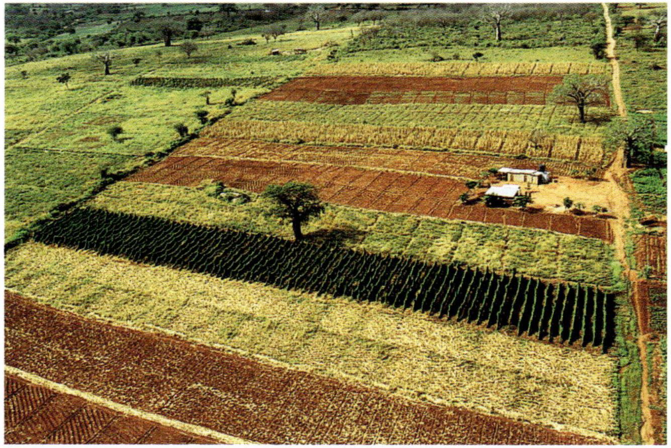

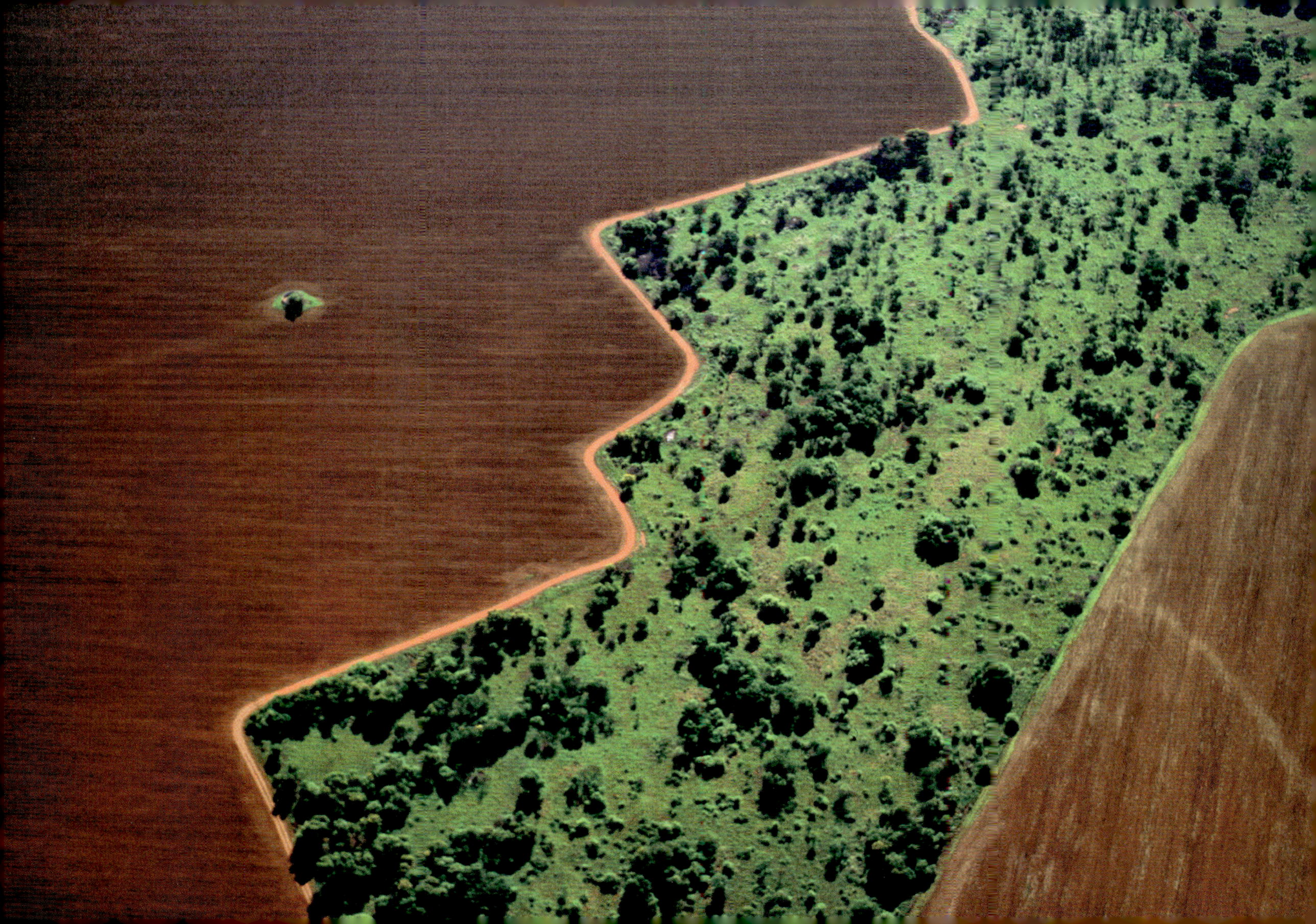

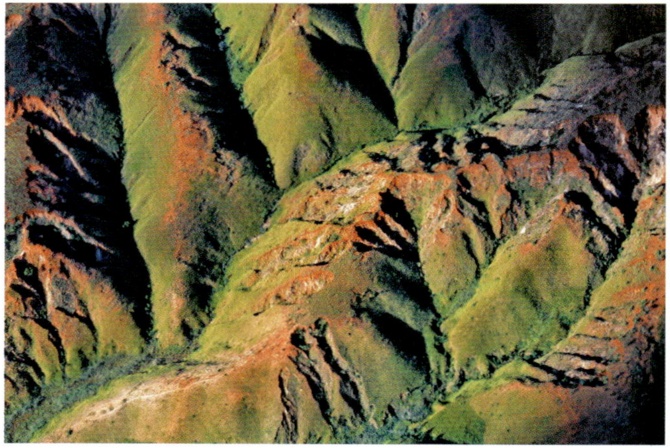

178
Intense rains leave deep marks on the hills north of Antanarivo, in Madagascar, flooding the thin soil layer and digging steep and short gorges.

179
At the bottom of the rounded hills, typical of the central Madagascar highlands, a mosaic is formed by the rice paddies.

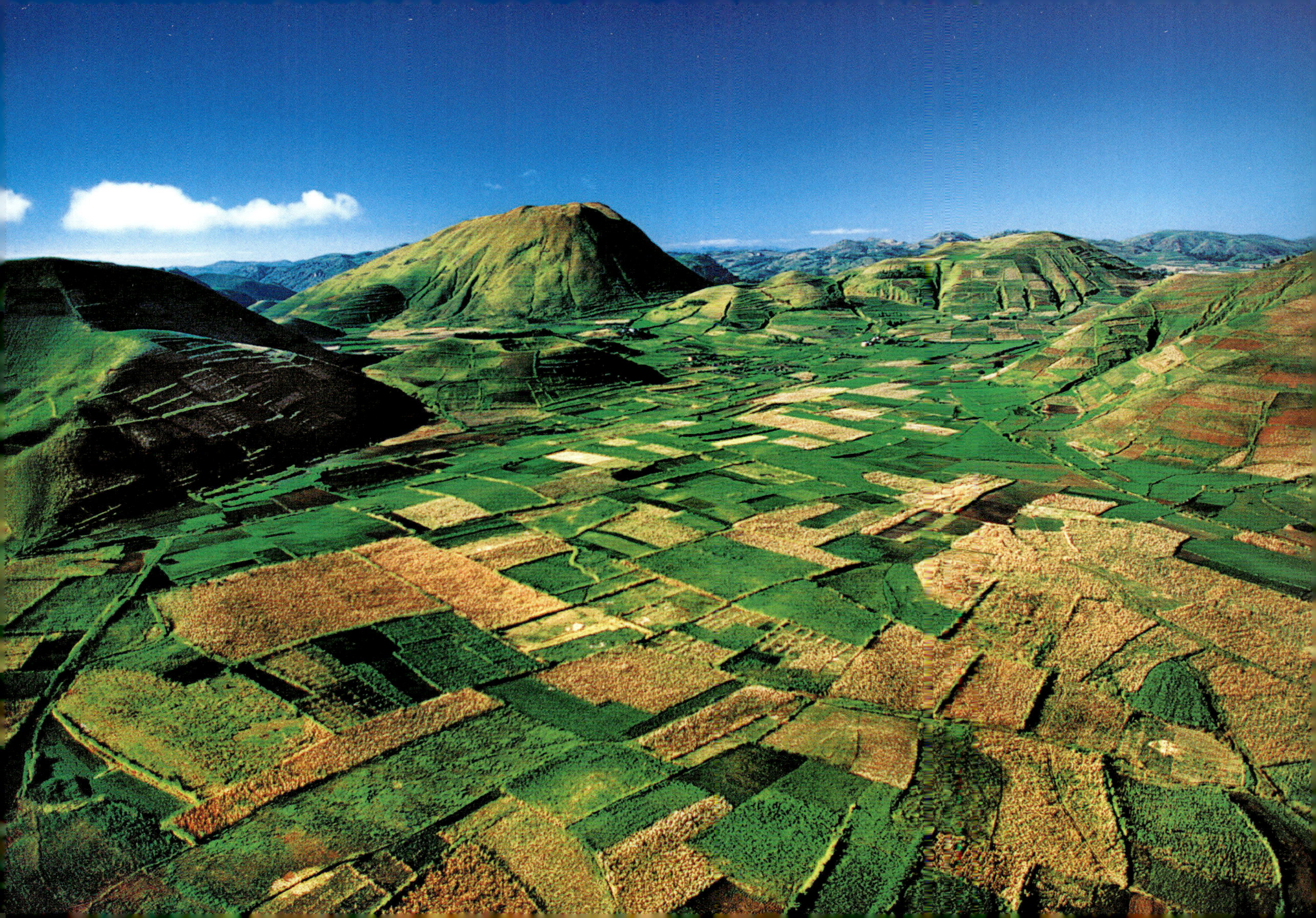

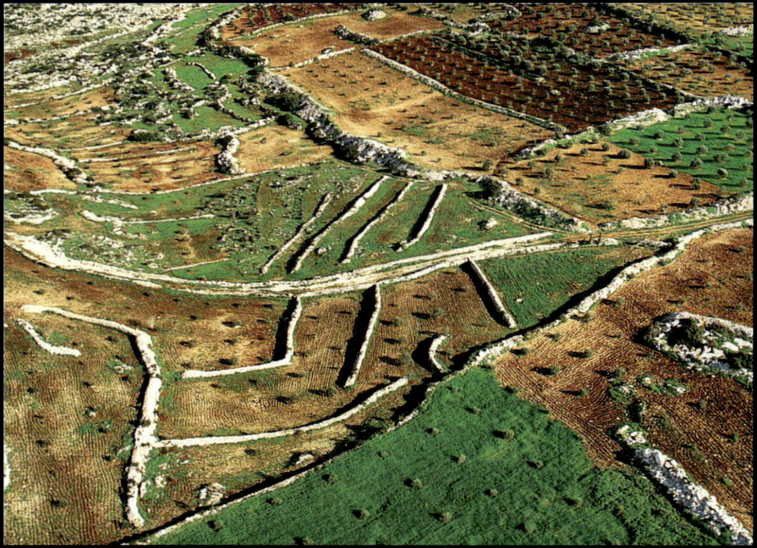

180

The so-called "Shepherds' Fields" near Bethlehem, in Israel, were once used only as pastureland for goats and sheep, hence its name. Today, cultivating olives has proved more lucrative.

181

Nahalal, in the Jezreel Valley in Israel, was founded in 1921 by pioneers dissatisfied with the kibbutz. In fact, they have been able to carve out private properties.

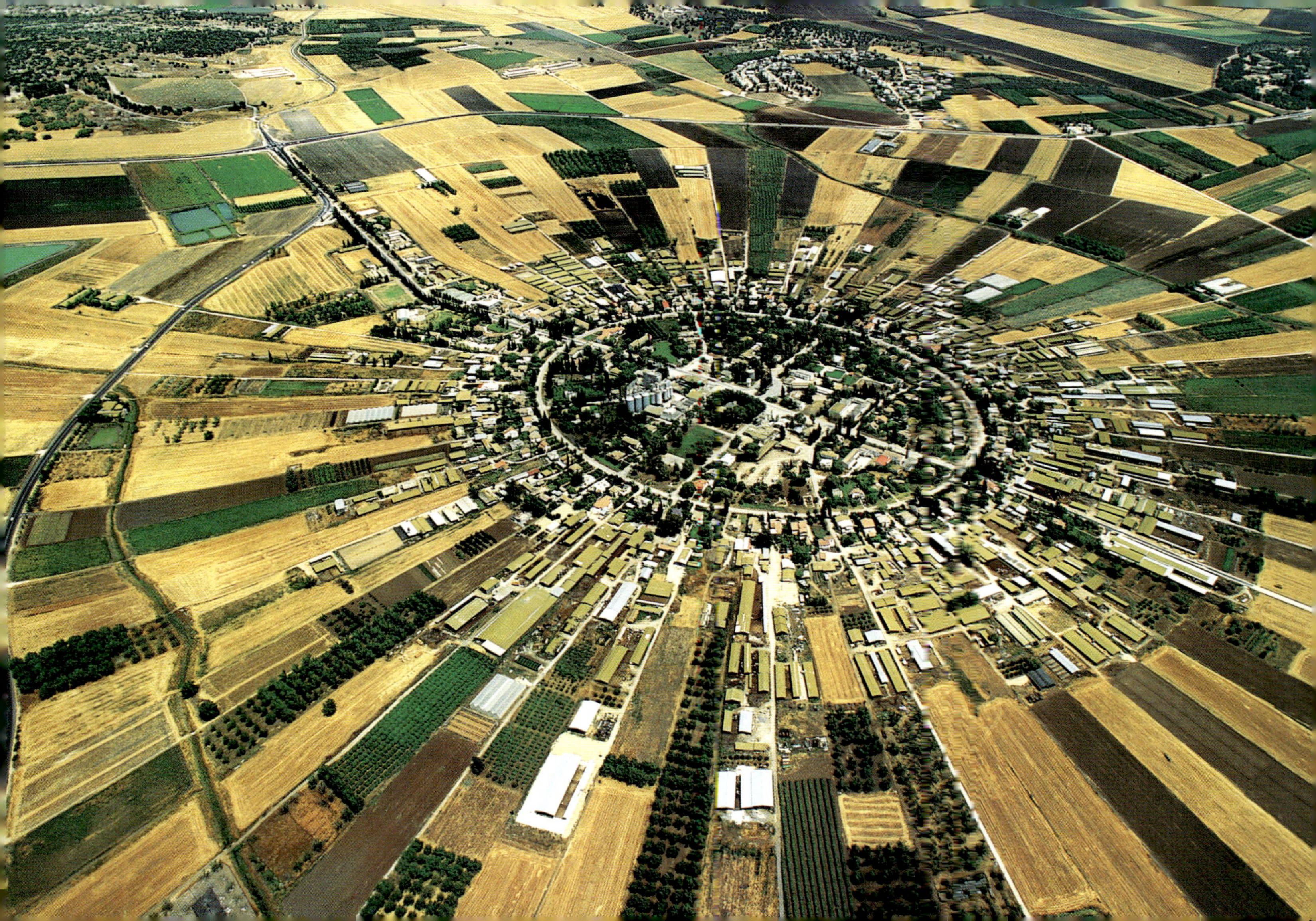

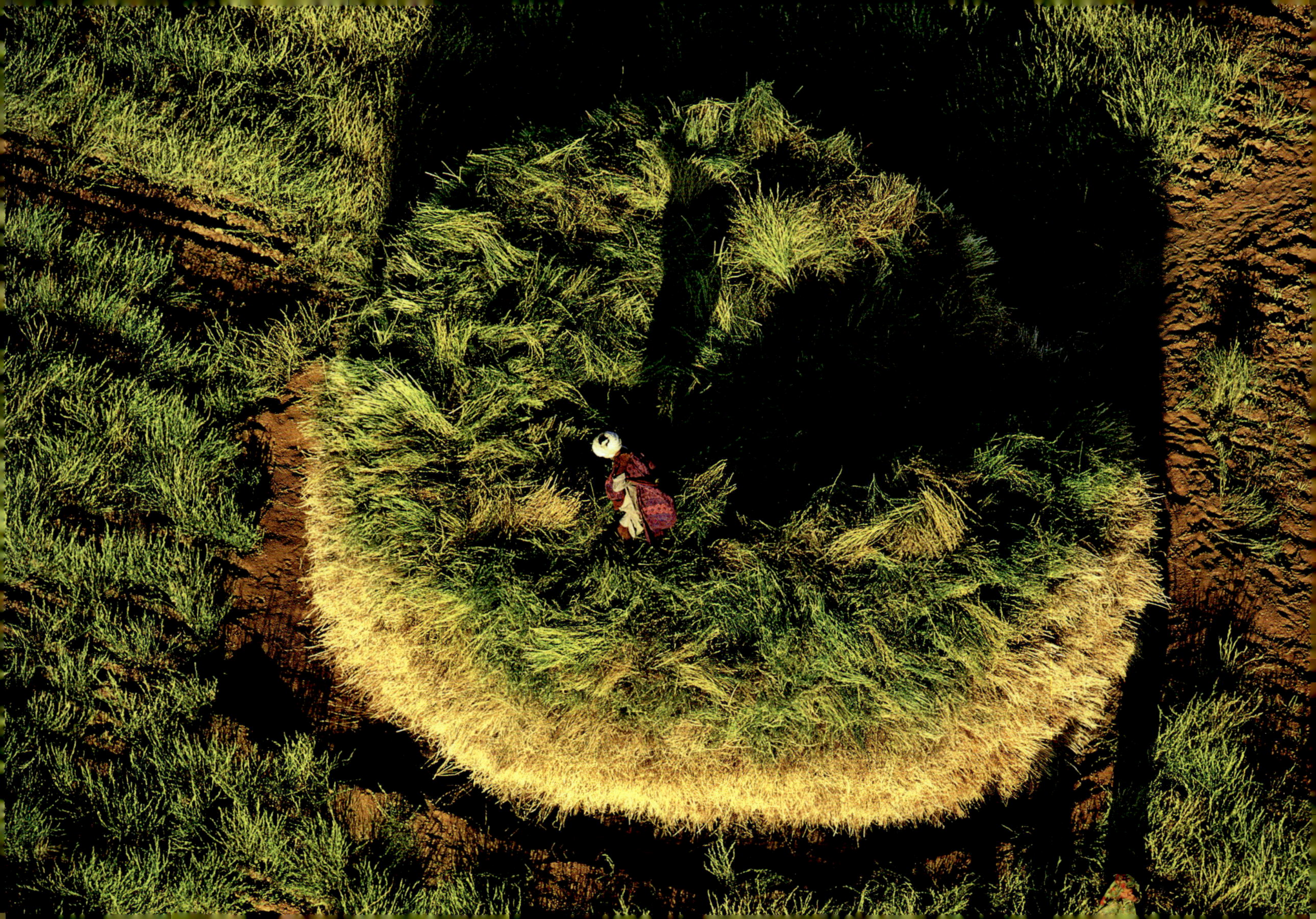

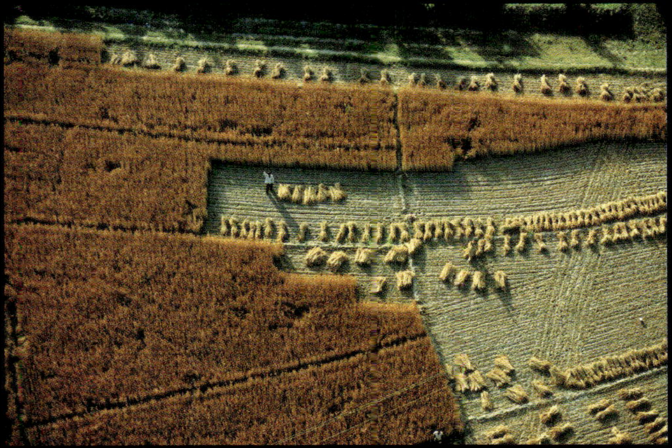

182

A lone farmer harvests wheat in a field in Rajasthan, India.

183

A group of farmers concentrate on harvesting wheat in a field in Fatehpur Sikri, India.

184-185

Rice paddies occupy every foot of the plains in this amazing landscape so typical of the Yunnan, in southwest China. The origin of these hills is karstic.

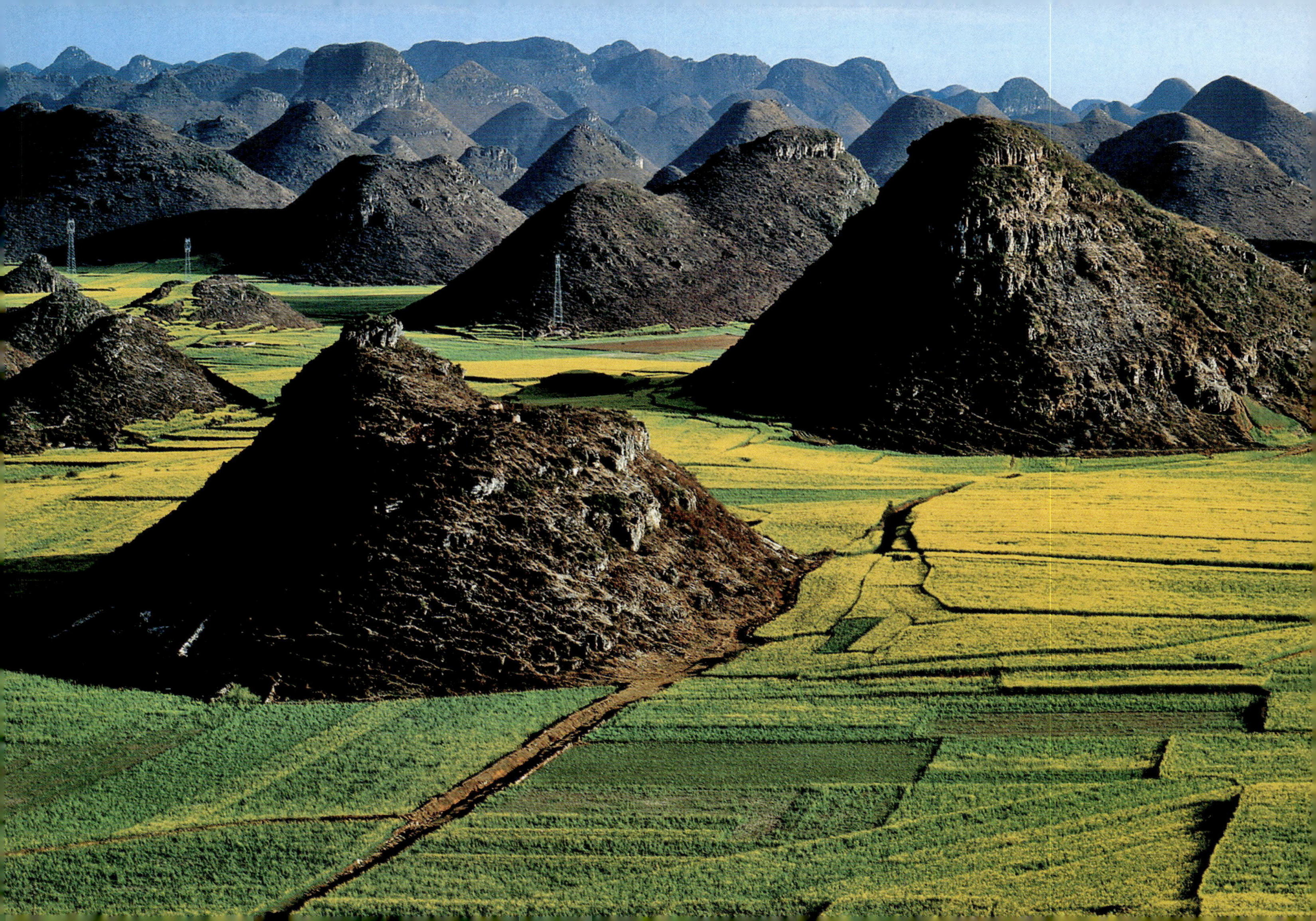

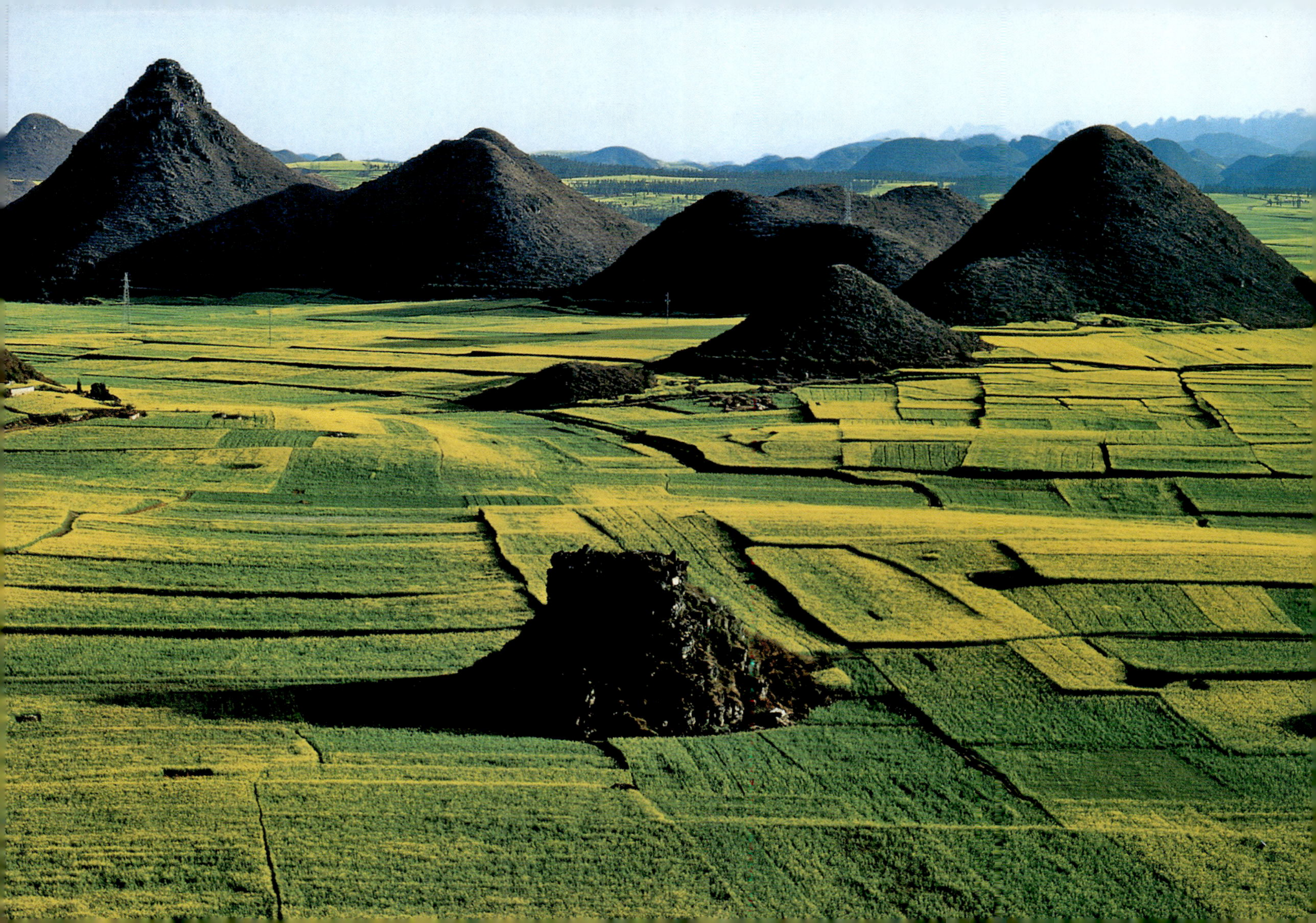

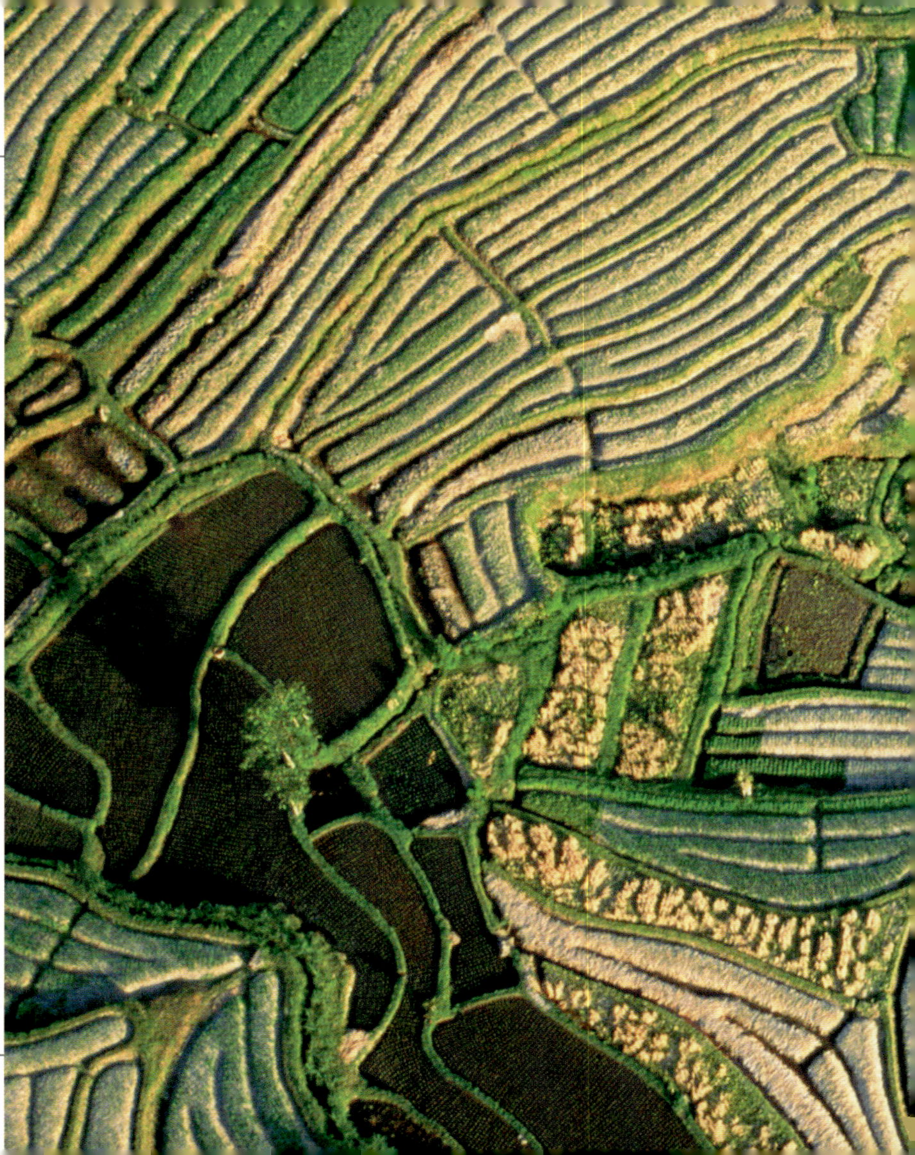

186-187
Cultivating rice on terraces creates some of the most spectacular views on the hills of several regions in the world and especially in Asia, like here in the Bali countryside, in Indonesia.

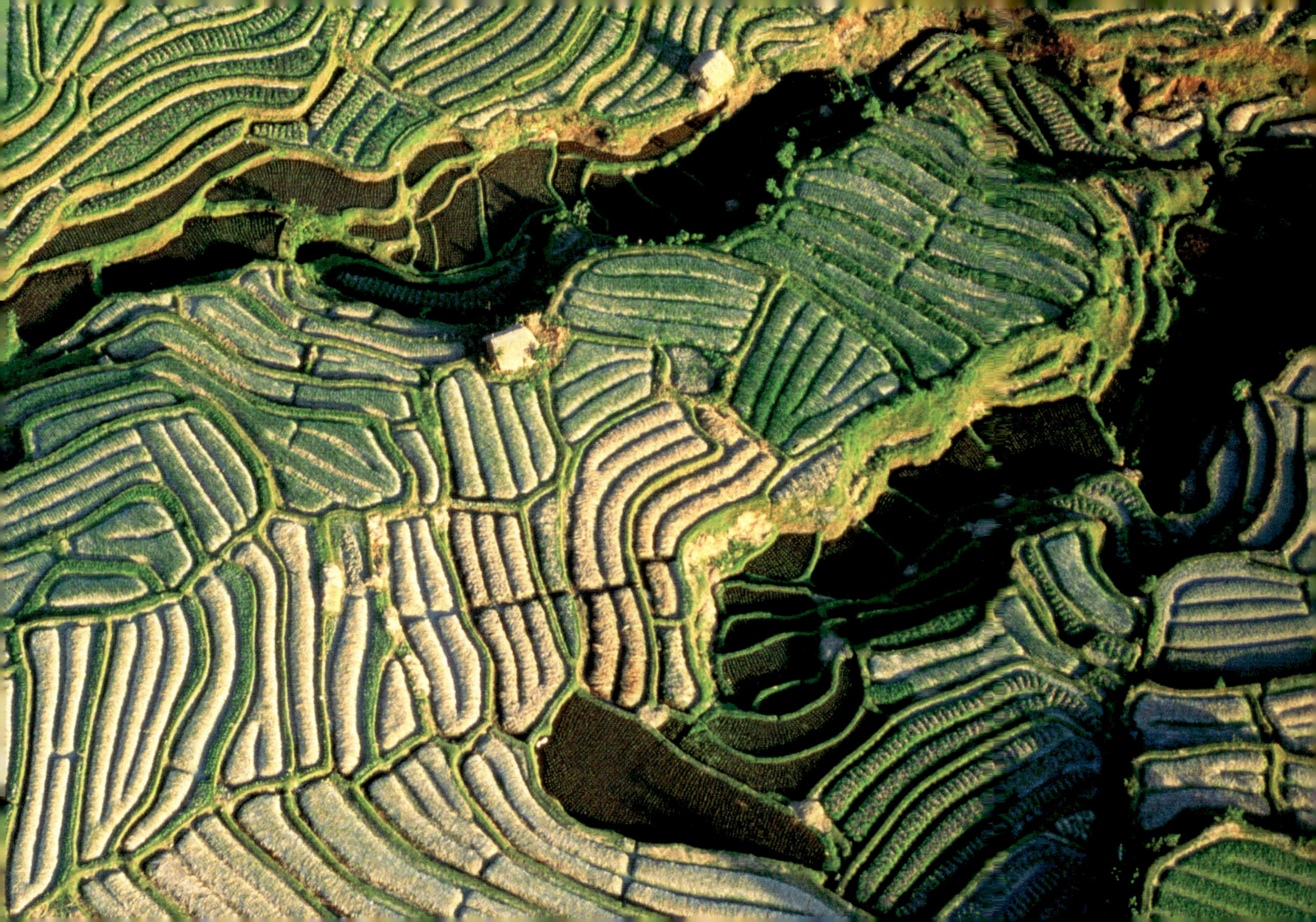

Oceania

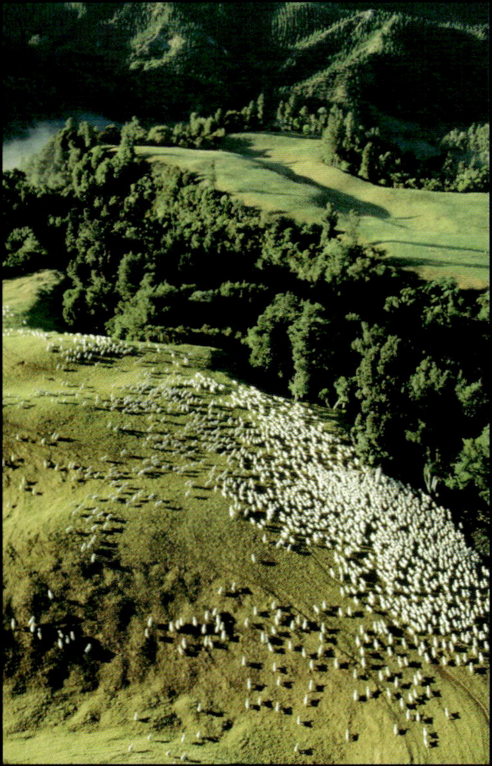

188
In autumn, ephemeral "clouds" form on the hillsides of New Zealand's North Island, when the flocks descend to the valley from the cold upper pastures.

189
Near Little Swansport in Tasmania, a bucolic setting characteristic of the Australian island opens up, featuring a fertile and open countryside, with seasonal woods, vast farms, and pasturelands.

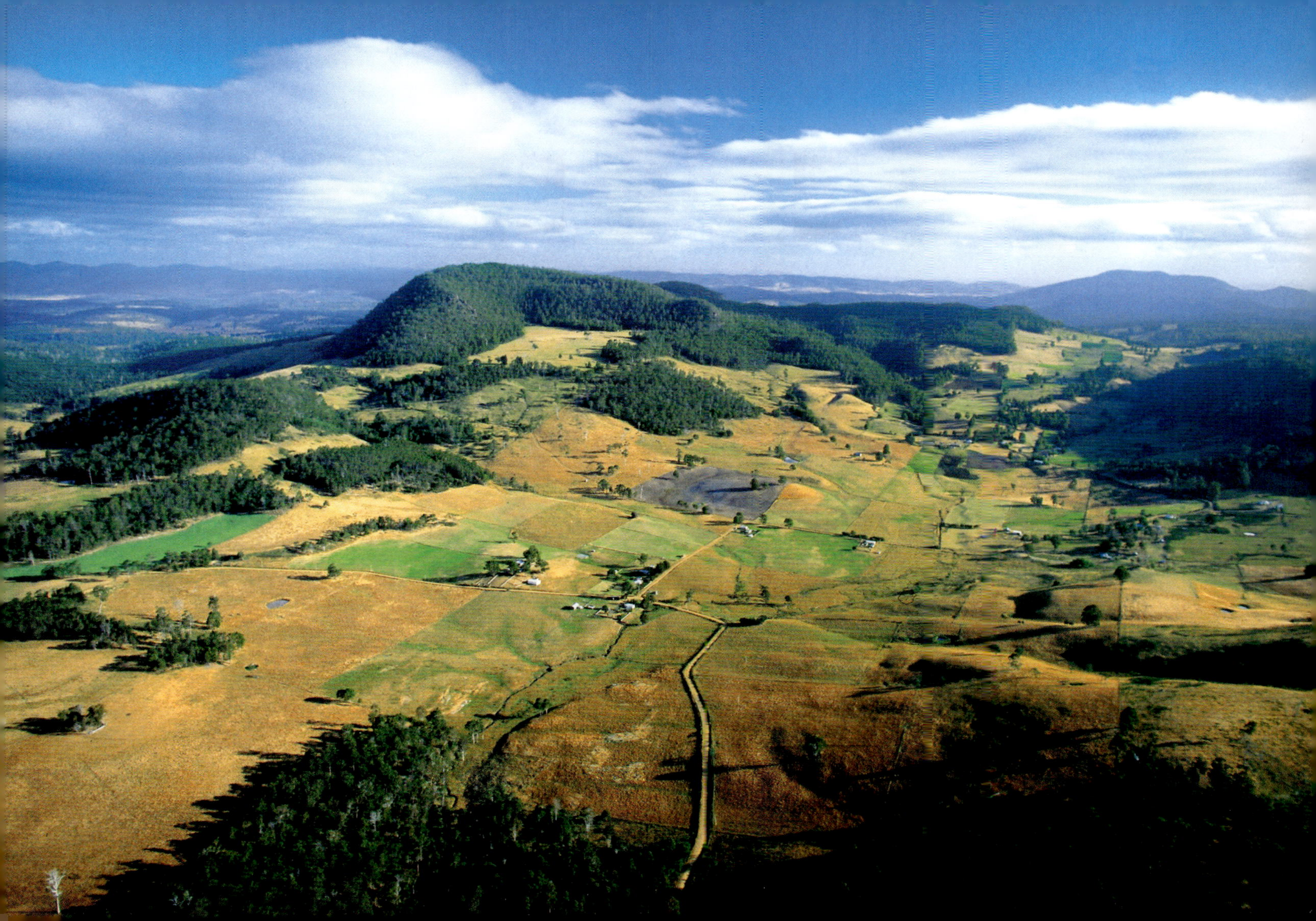

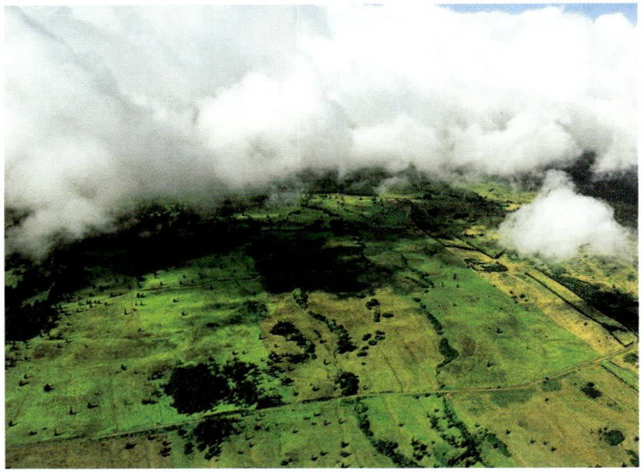

190

The fog, a very common phenomenon on the humid island of Hawaii, or the Big Island, hides the hills behind Honoka'a's cultivated fields from view. The zone is near the dormant volcano of Mauna Kea.

191

Taro fields at the mouth of the Hanalei Valley, on the Hawaiian Island of Kauai, are an undeniably beautiful sight. However, the valley system that stretches beyond the limits of the farms is partly closed to the public to protect the delicate environment.

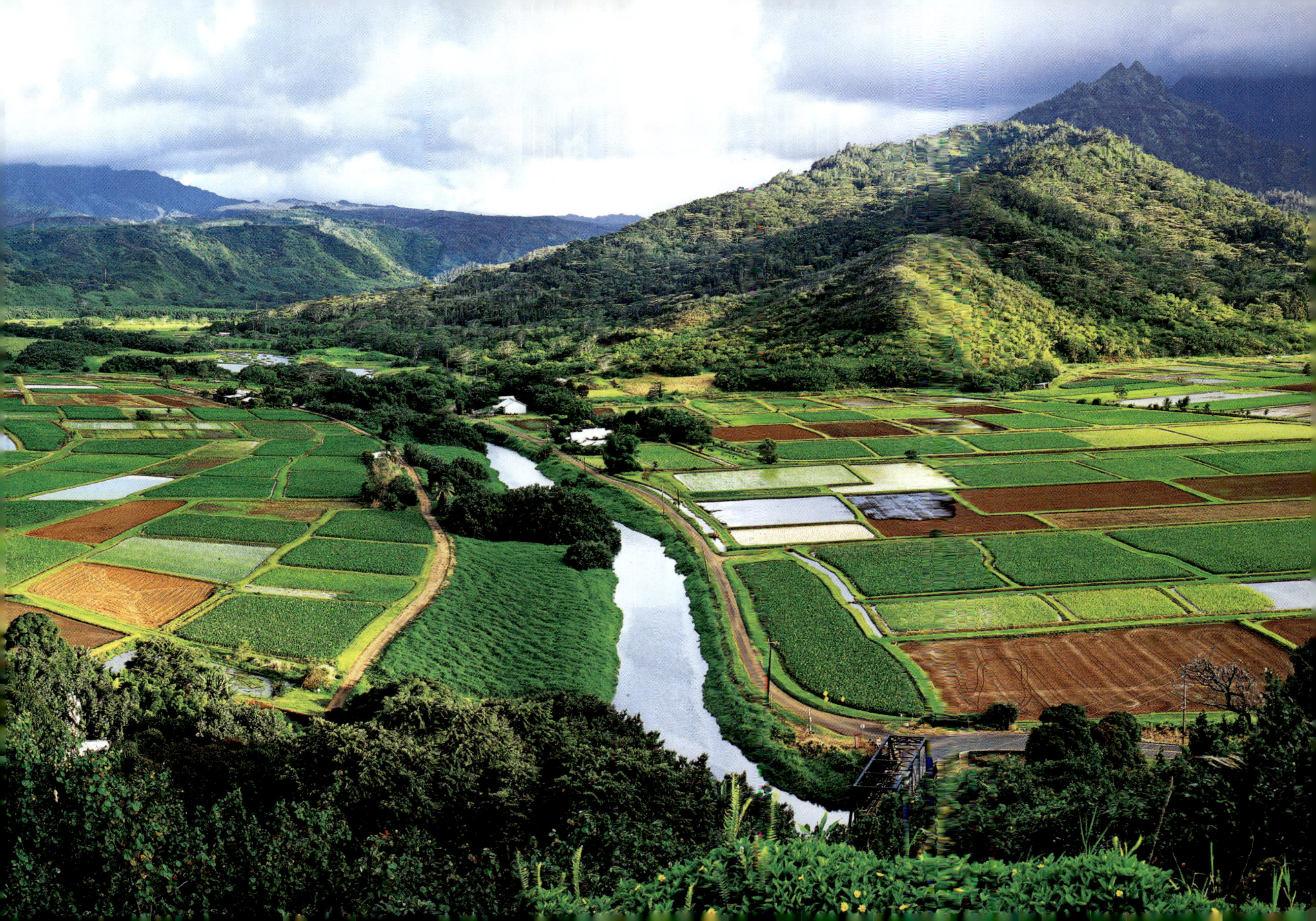

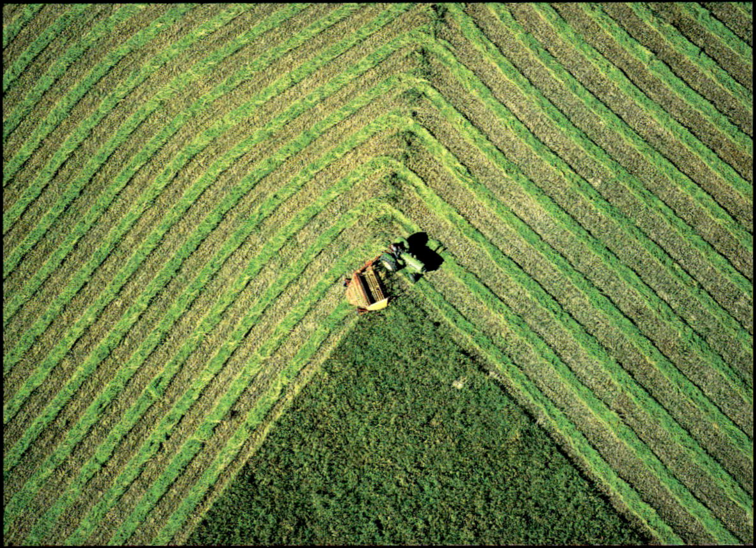

192

Rational use of the terrain and mechanized farming practices are at the origin of remarkable geometric designs like this one, near York-town, Canada.

193

The absence of hard angles, contrarily, creates a more rustic form of beauty in the plowed fields of southern Wisconsin.

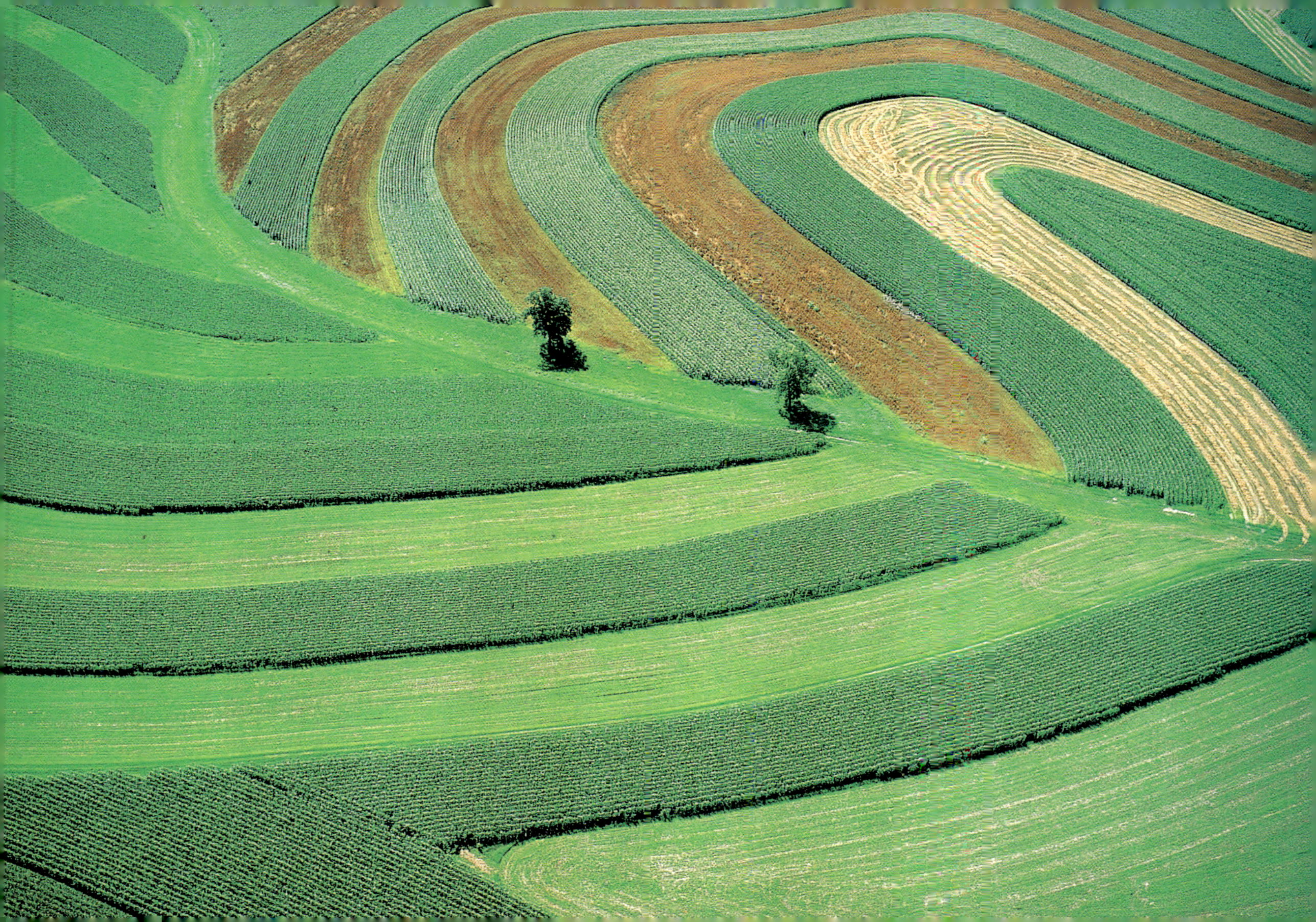

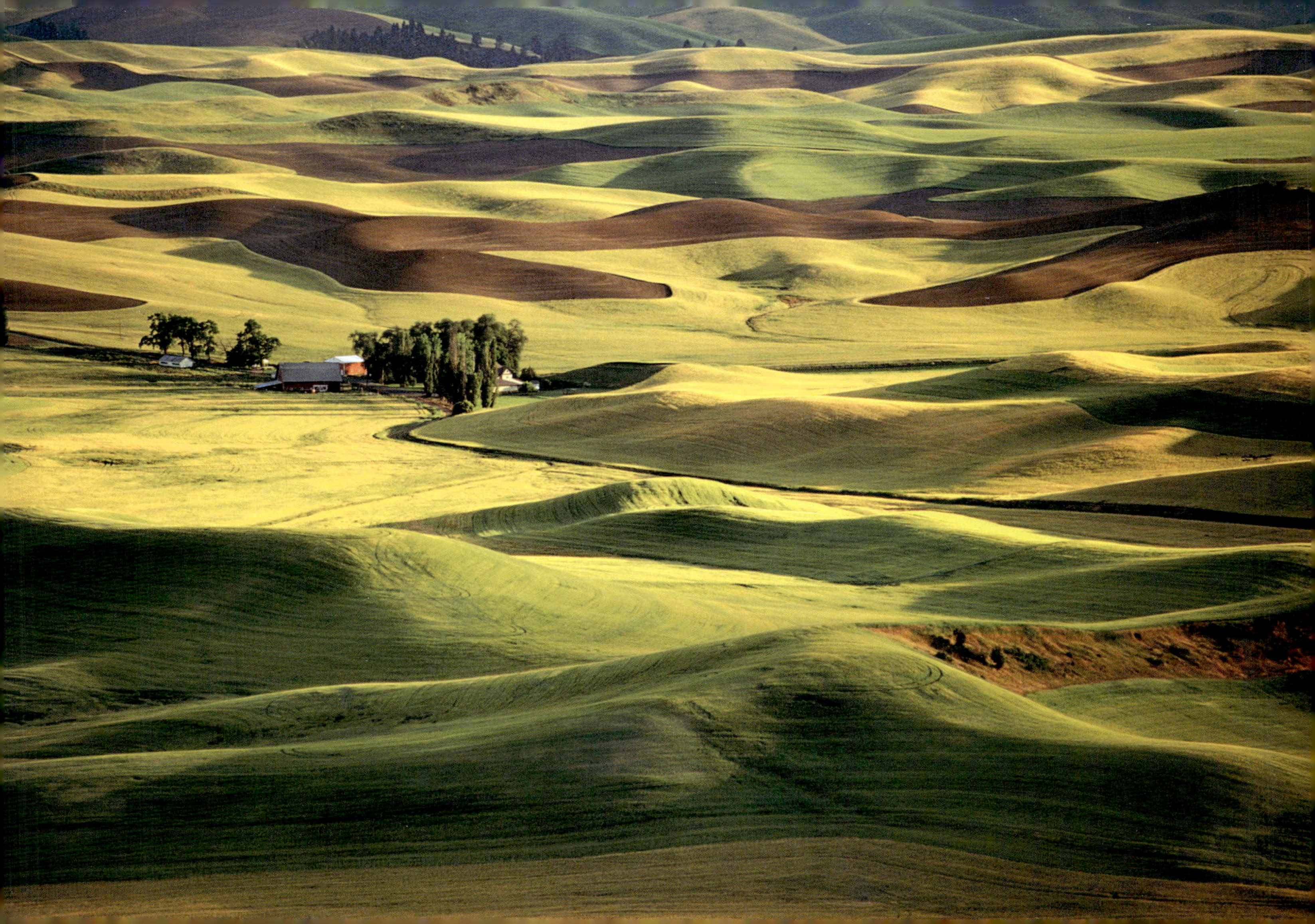

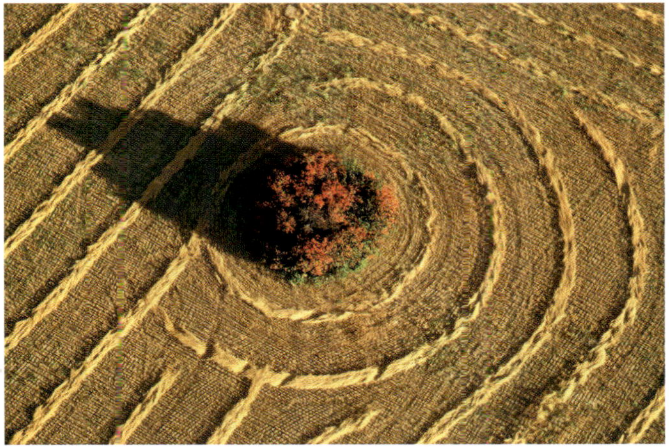

194

A sea of exceptionally fertile solid land enlivens the territory of Palouse, in Washington State.

195

Every phase of the agricultural cycle produces special effects: here, in the province of Saskatchewan, Canada, the harvest has drawn concentric circles around a cluster of trees.

196
The fields of wheat in Toole County, Montana, stretch as far as the Canadian border, in the distance.

197
Turbines used to store wind energy - clean and renewable - cast long shadows across the rolling terrain near Livermore, California.

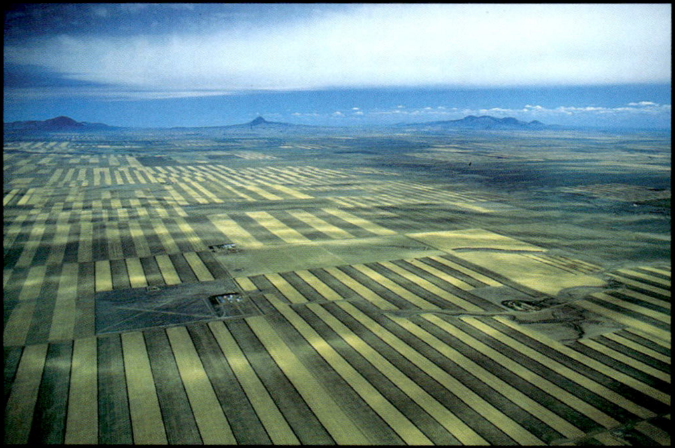

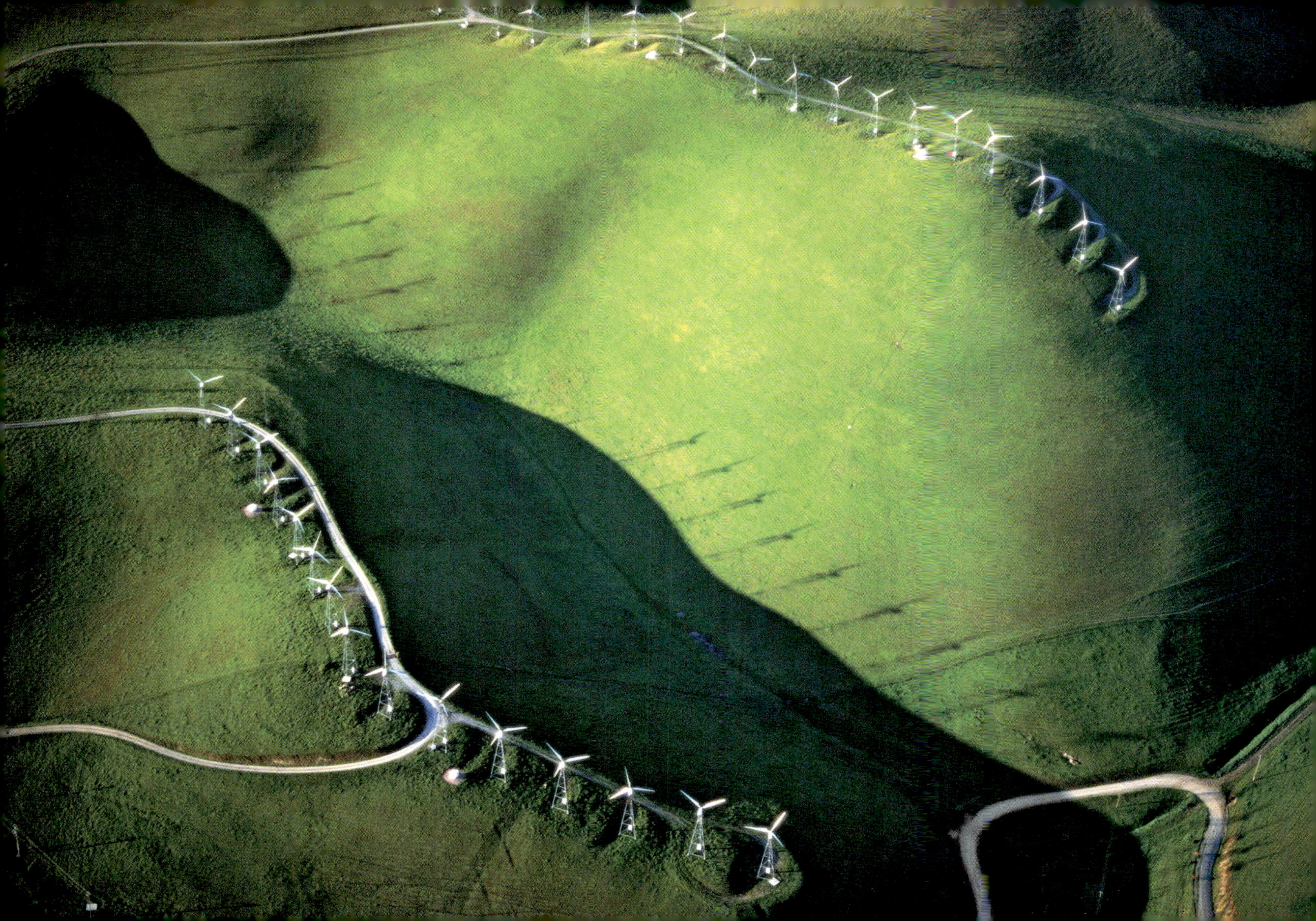

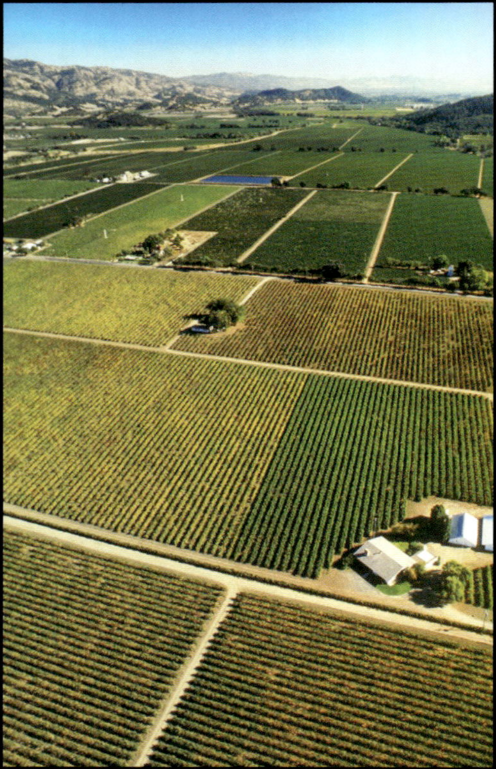

198 and 199

Vineyards were introduced to California around 1760. About a century later, more than 50 or so winemakers were counted in Napa Valley.

200-201

Sugarcane, the "gold of Cuba," constitutes the main crop in the Valley de los Ingenios, where, in the 1800s, several sugar refineries were operating.

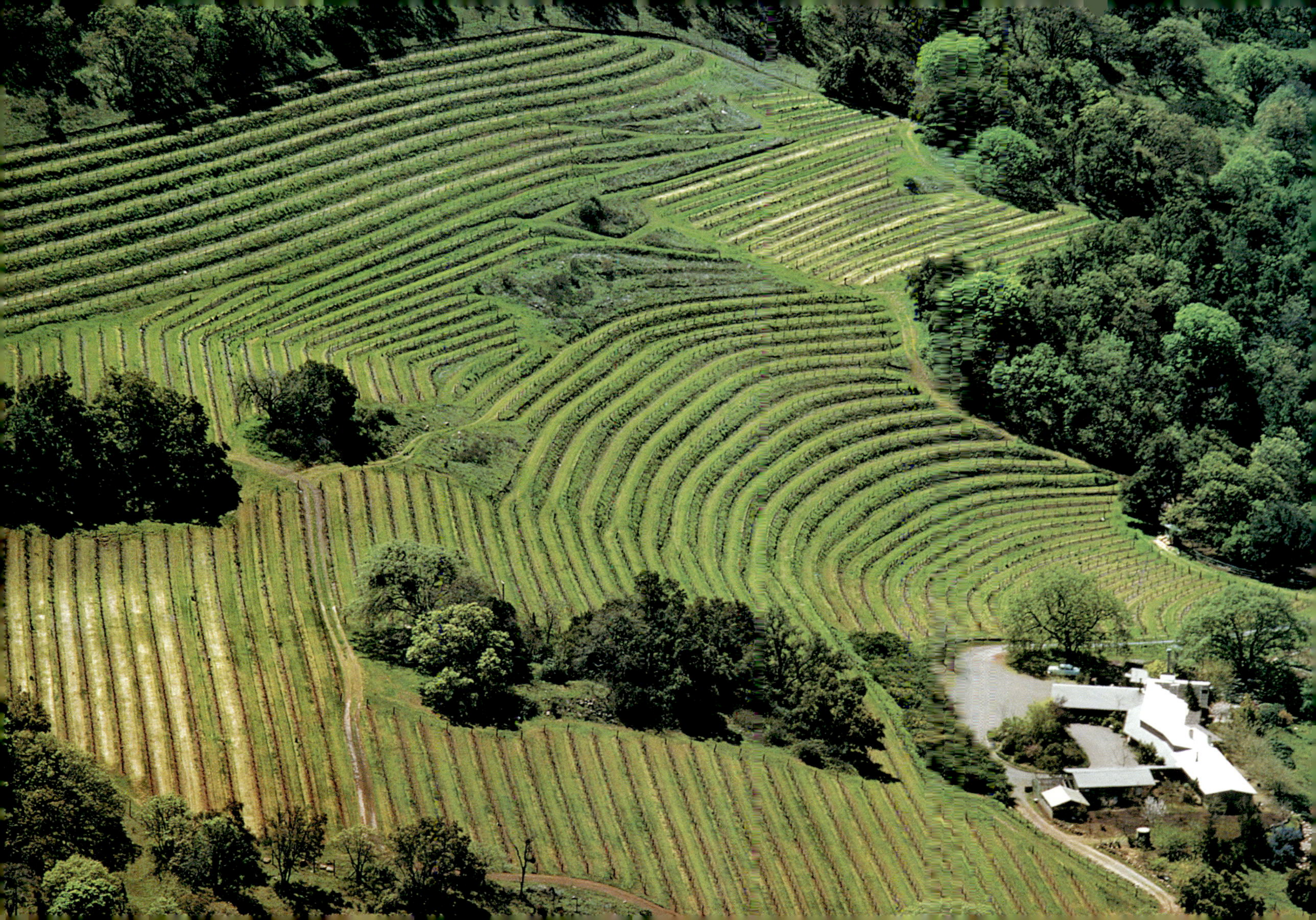

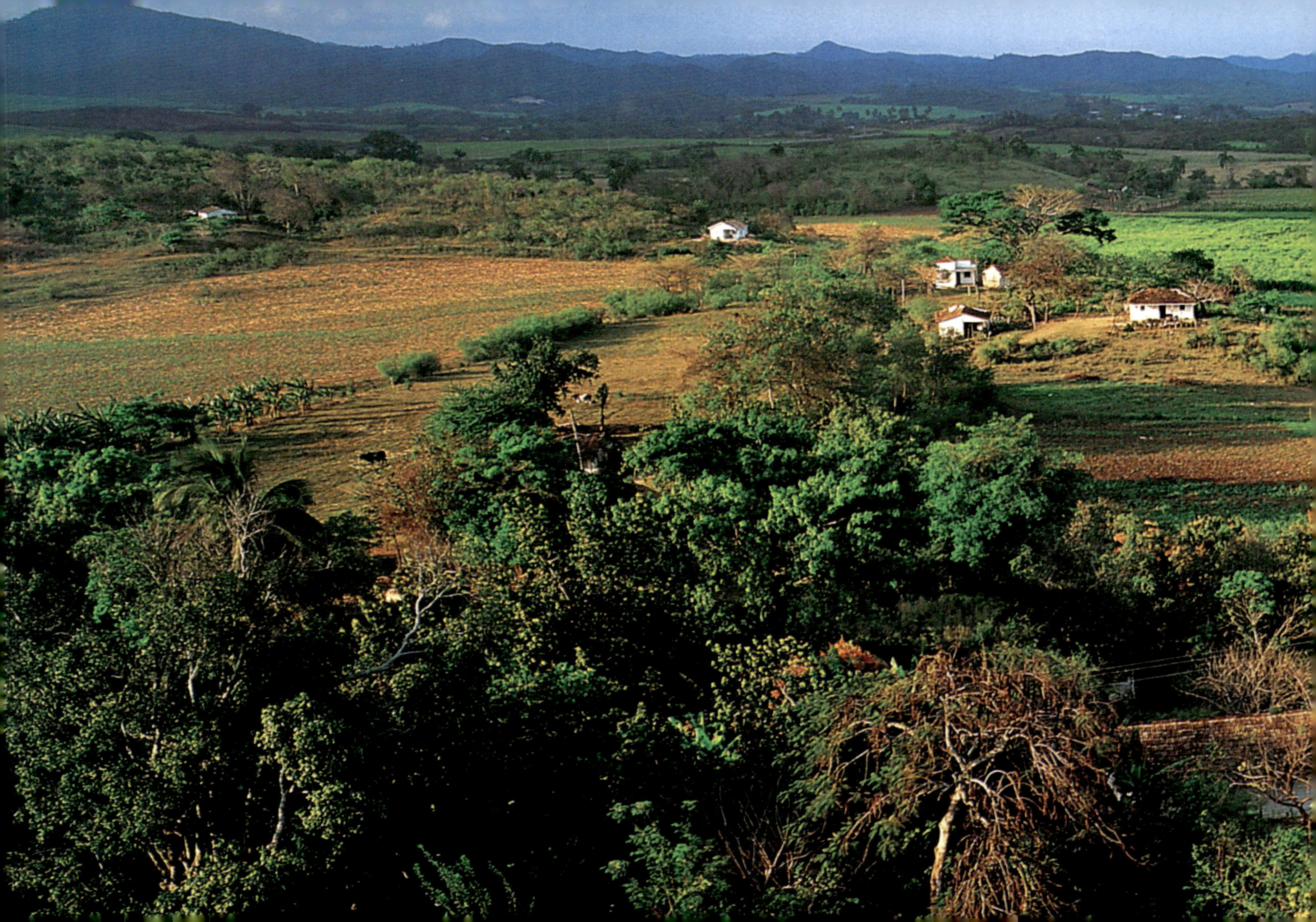

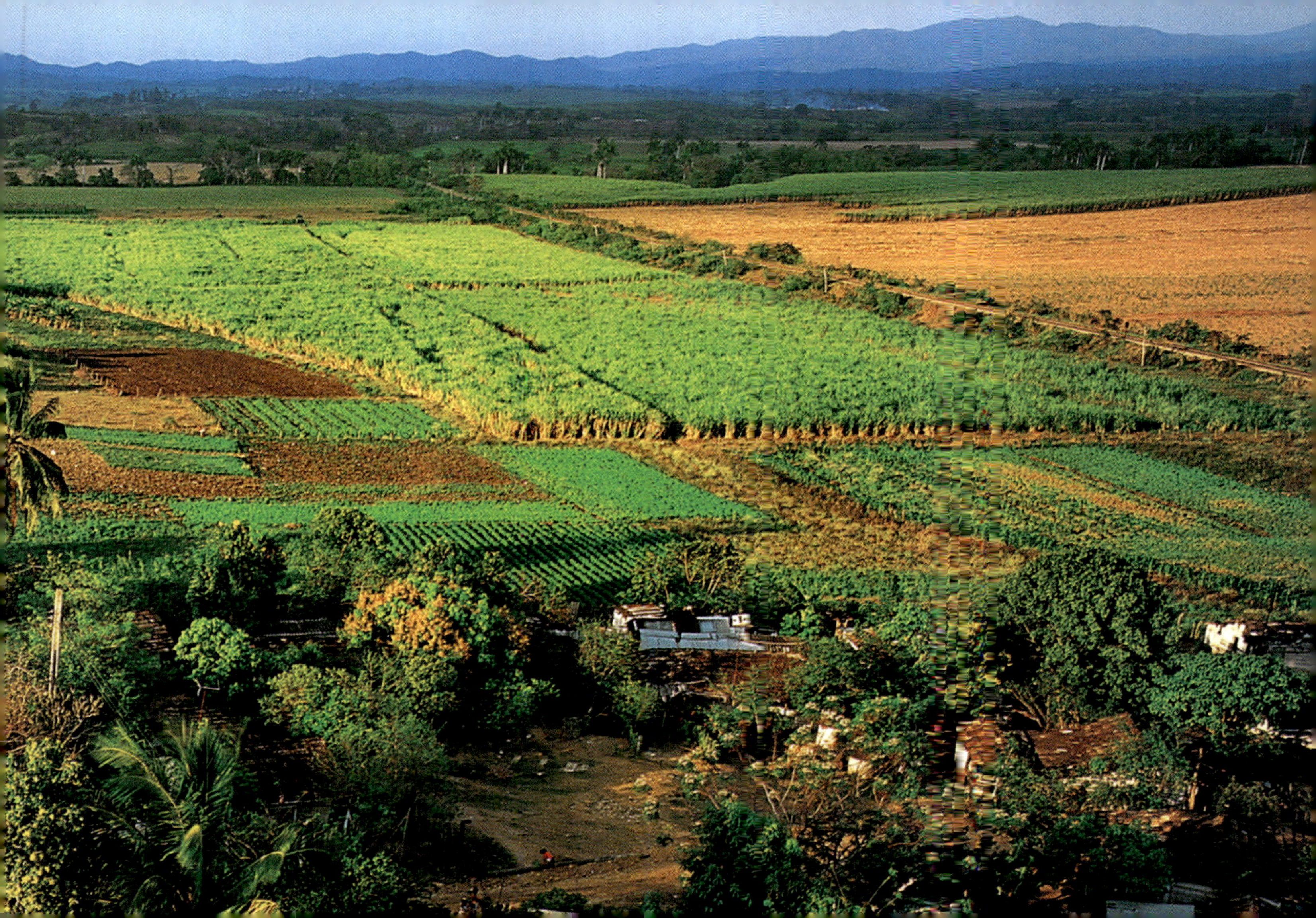

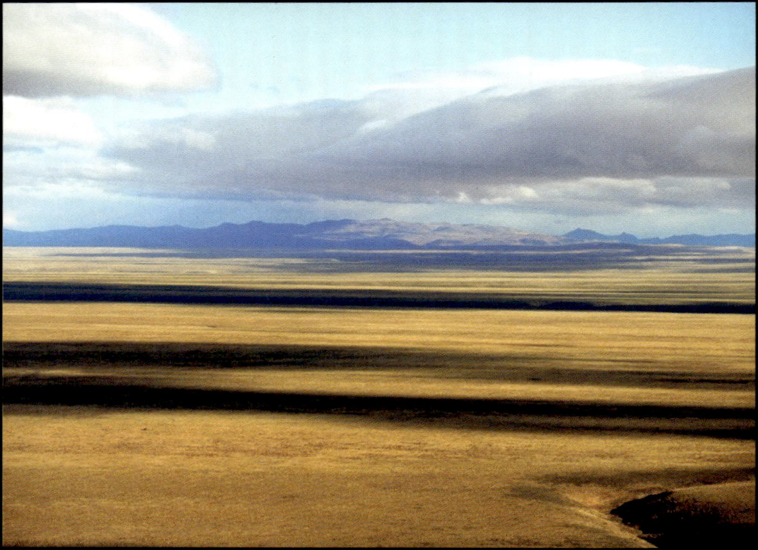

202

The region of Neuquen, in Argentina, stretches between the Pampas and Patagonia. Here, the wind dominates, not encountering any obstacles on this desolate plain.

203

Where nature does not provide, man intervenes: the orchards of Neuquen, in Argentina, are protected from the wind by barriers of tall and thin poplars.

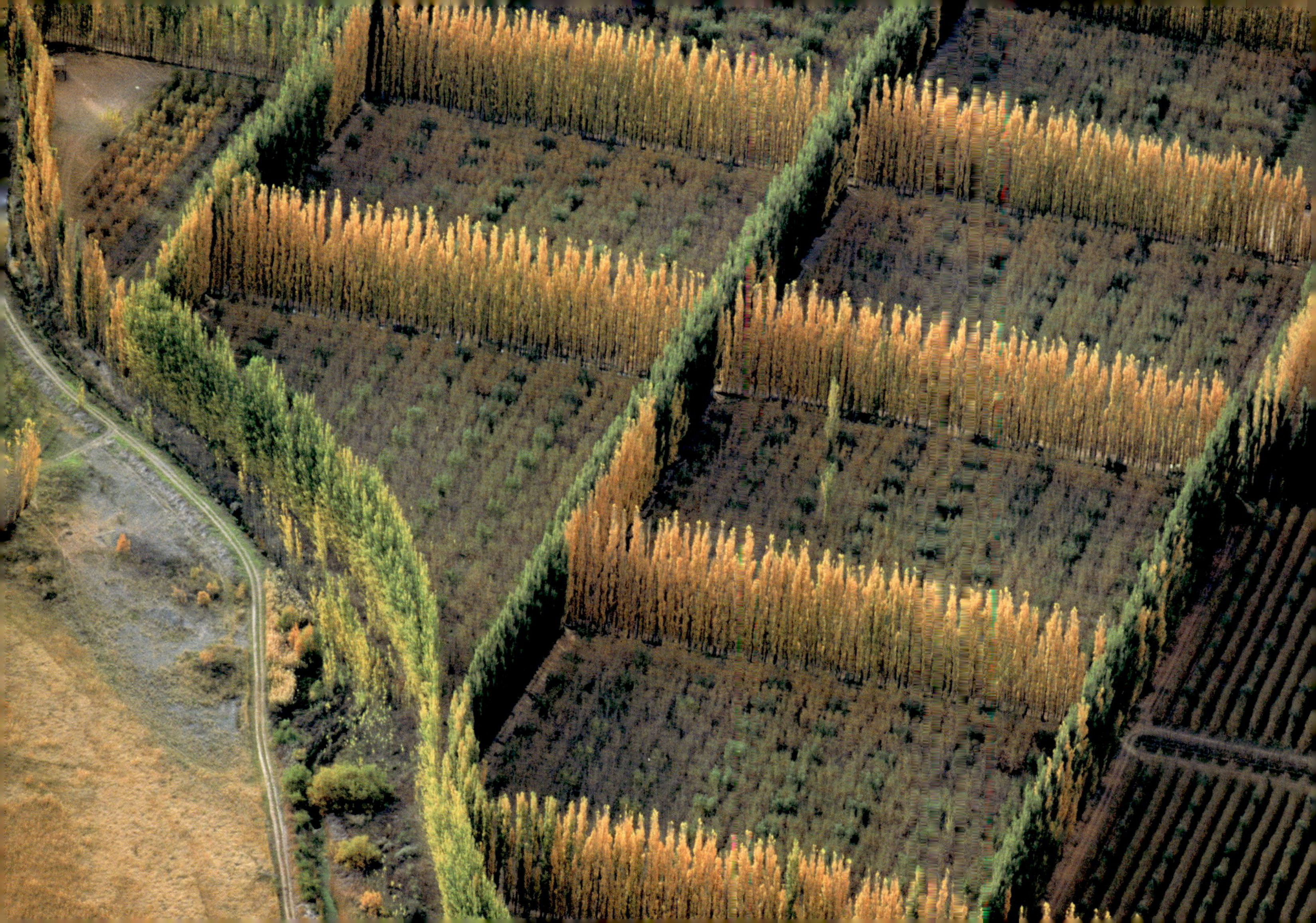

ROCK CATHEDRALS

FLYING HIGH

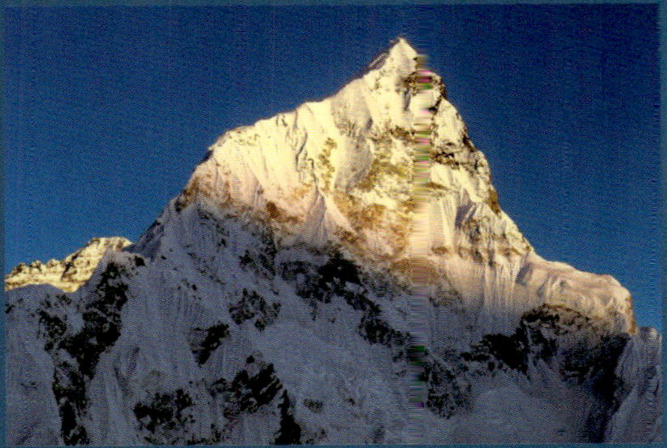

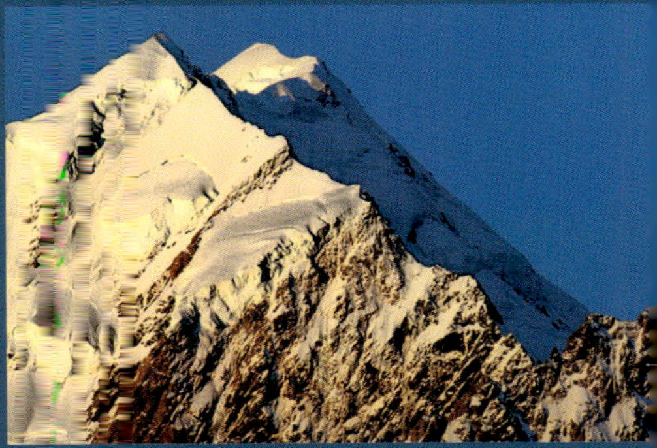

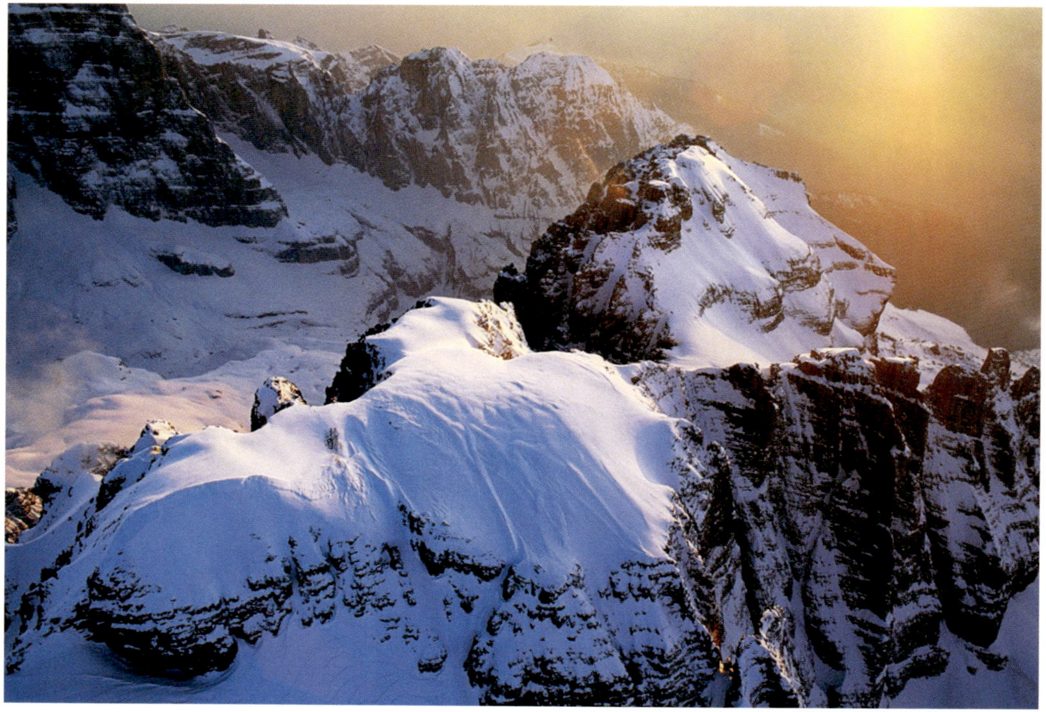

205
Nuptse in Nepal (left); Mount Cook
in New Zealand (right).

207

A subtle continuity exists between every ecosystem in human perception.
Naturally, the first places to be invaded by the ever growing crowd of the human species were low ones. Man came down from the trees and had to slowly regain the heights.
The plains and hill regions allowed all the earliest civilizations and cultures to prosper, which then pushed further on to fill every gap in length, width, and height.
If, during this long process of expansion, the sea was perceived as the sterile field of death, the mountains were the realms of terror, atop of which were housed the gods, a place where no human could ever enter. Slowly, however, those inviolable doors started to be opened by the urgency of demographic pressure, the primary engine of every artificial transformation on the face of the planet.
The Alpine and Himalayan slopes were reclaimed from nature over the course of thousands of years, as were the Andean highlands, by people who developed their own ways of life, beliefs, and wisdom that were very different from those that motivated the peoples of the lowlands.
Then, when conditions allowed it, the birth of alpinism, and above all the conquest of the skies, created a way to access the remote domains of the peaks for the purposes of

206
This sunset shows the rare beauty of the Brenta Dolomites
in Italy, which represent the southernmost portion of
the chain and were formed in more recent epochs than
the eastern groups.

Rock Cathedrals

study, trade, sports, challenge, or romantic hobby. In the highland setting, once shadowy and sparkling, several different types of main characters can be distinguished.
Above all, there are "positive" mountains, meaning those born of the lifting of the earth's crust, forced up by continental drift.
Mountain systems of different ages belong to this group.
The oldest are also the rarest and usually the lowest, leveled off by a greater period of erosion. The Caledonian orogeny left uncovered the hard soul of those ancient mountains in Scotland, the most venerable by far with their respectable 400,000,000 years, just as it did in Asia north of the Himalayas and the Tibetan Plateau, and in Africa from Ethiopia to Zimbabwe.
Around 230,000,000 years ago, it was the Hercynian orogeny's turn, which lifted the earth in eastern Australia and then in that true reserve of colossi that is Central Asia.
Finally, between 70 and 15 million years ago, the most recent orogeny, that of the Alps, gave the planet the deepest wrinkles furrowing its brow today.
The Alps and the Atlas Mountains, the Andes and the Rocky Mountains, the Himalayas the Abode of the Snows and all the connected chains, passing from Hindukush as far as the Zagros Mountains, are the result of these late periods of tumult in the planet's crust.
The tension between top and bottom and the titanic pressures that raised the earth's crust appear more evidently when one's sees how the hard granite soul of the mountain tops, raised high into the sky over the greatest mountain chains, is often covered by calcareous, sedimentary rock, which had been formed at the bottom of now vanished oceans.
Thus are the summits of the world, such as Everest, whose upper sides still bear the ho-

Rock Cathedrals

rizontal stratifications typical of sea cliffs.
Flying over the Dolomites, one can actually get the impression of swimming in a disproportionate aquarium, full of dips and peaks, or in a sea full of the purest water.
This impression is not a total fantasy: those spectacular rises are in all effects giant coral reefs pushed out of proportion toward the sky, submerged, and finally returned to the surface again. The Dolomites, however, appear as much "gentler" mountains than the others, given the scarcity of igneous rocks like granite and metamorphic rocks like gneiss. Thus the mountains, contrary to what superficial impressions may suggest, have always had much to do with the sea. It is not terribly rare to discover ammonites and fossilized coral at the highest points on earth.
The famous *saligram* that can be found in the Himalayas, used as amulets, are the shells of nautiluses that ended up buried in the ancient sea from which the chain lifted, 70,000,000 years ago. Then, from our point of view, there are "negative" mountains, or those dug out by erosion from a foundation of flat land, a bit like bas-reliefs in continental proportions.
For example, there is the plateau that is disappearing from the face of the earth, left behind Monument Valley, divided between Utah and Arizona, or Wadi Rum in Jordan.
These excavated mountains, as opposed to those that grew, often feature the most amazing rock stratifications, combining intense colors like red, yellow, white, and purple in folds contorted beyond imagination. In this case, the foundation is also the sea.
The sandstone that forms the American mesas, buttes, and unstable fingers is also the result of the layering of sand on ancient sea floors, abandoned by the water when the dinosaurs had yet to experience the greatest

Rock Cathedrals

glory their dominion would enjoy on the earth. Then, there are the active mountains, those that basically build themselves on their own: the volcanoes, which draw magma and lava from the depths of the earth and transfer them form onto their surface. And, how they transfer them!

No more shocking and brutal spectacle may exist than a volcanic eruption, and in a certain sense, no more "divine." In fact, volcanoes were gods to many civilizations: the Incas sacrificed to their benevolence young girls, often found intact by today's archaeologists on the frozen volcanic slopes.

Likewise, it is said that the Polynesians immolated virgins, throwing them into the belly of the Earth goddess with the intention of placating her. In A.D. 79, Pliny the Elder allowed himself be suffocated under the ashes of Vesuvius so as to not miss that monstrous and fascinating spectacle.

Watching a volcanic eruption from the sky is a frightening experience. On the other hand, seeing boiling plumes of smoke rise to the sky for dozens of miles and then bend on the horizon, following its curve, illuminated here and there by lightening and fountains of furious fire, does not inspire the terror it would if seen from the land. It only brings a sense of profound unease, a sort of unexplainable nausea, like a relentless ancestral fear.

Volcanic eruptions are so spectacular that they seem magnificent even from extraterrestrial surfaces like Io, a satellite of Jupiter.

Among the volcanoes on earth number some of the tallest mountains (if measured from their base to the top), which are also the youngest and often the most instable and ephemeral volcanos. Mauna Kea, on the island of Hawaii, from the point where its slopes begin up to its highly active peak is over 32,000 feet. It is interesting to note that Mauna Kea rises

Rock Cathedrals

near to the absolute limit of elevation possible for a mountain.

This is because of isostasy, a principle similar to that of floating, on the basis of which no mountain can exceed six miles high without sinking into the viscous layer on which the continents drift. Anak Krakata, the "son of Krakatoa," popped up like a deadly vow just after its father-volcano, which had wrought havoc on half the world with its rumbling and the ensuing tsunami in 1883, vanished into smoke and flames. Born small, like any child, today it is almost 1,500 feet tall and continues to grow.

Mountains are often compared to human ideals such as indestructibility and spiritual elevation, but in truth they are the exact opposite. They collapse constantly, are born, consume themselves, and vanish, descending suddenly into the dark abyss. The process is fully underway, heralded every now and then by more or less intense upheavals of the earth's crust. It is only question of speed: the Himalayas, the Alps and the Rocky Mountains will continue to grow slowly for millions of years more. They will thereafter begin to crumble like the Appalachians, destined to disappear into the plains. Many active volcanoes, on the other hand, will continue to offer great surprises.

Yet, once the myth of intransigence is wiped away, we will be able to continue to admire the highlands from the sky in all their living beauty, finding new similarities between them and our human qualities. The world changes incessantly at every level of greatness, upon which we can reflect positively in a time like ours, which has witnessed an ever greater number of certainties now in question. The important thing, as the world teaches, is that changes take place in a natural fashion, as much as they may be upsetting: as happens to the mountains.

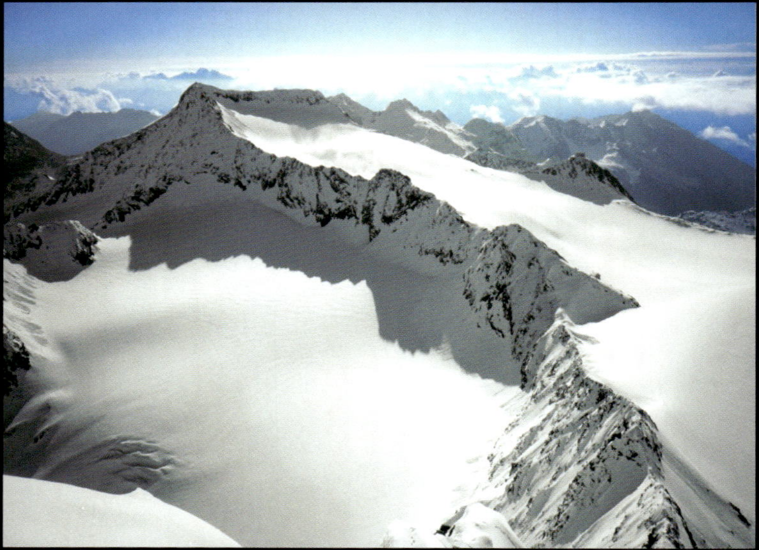

212
The peak of the magnificent Wilder Freiger Glacier, in the Stubai Alps in Austria, reaches up to 11,214 feet high.

213
The Matterhorn, or Mount Cervino, is one of the best known mountains in the Alps. Its peak, which reaches 14,692 feet high, can be reached both from the Swiss as well as the Italian sides.

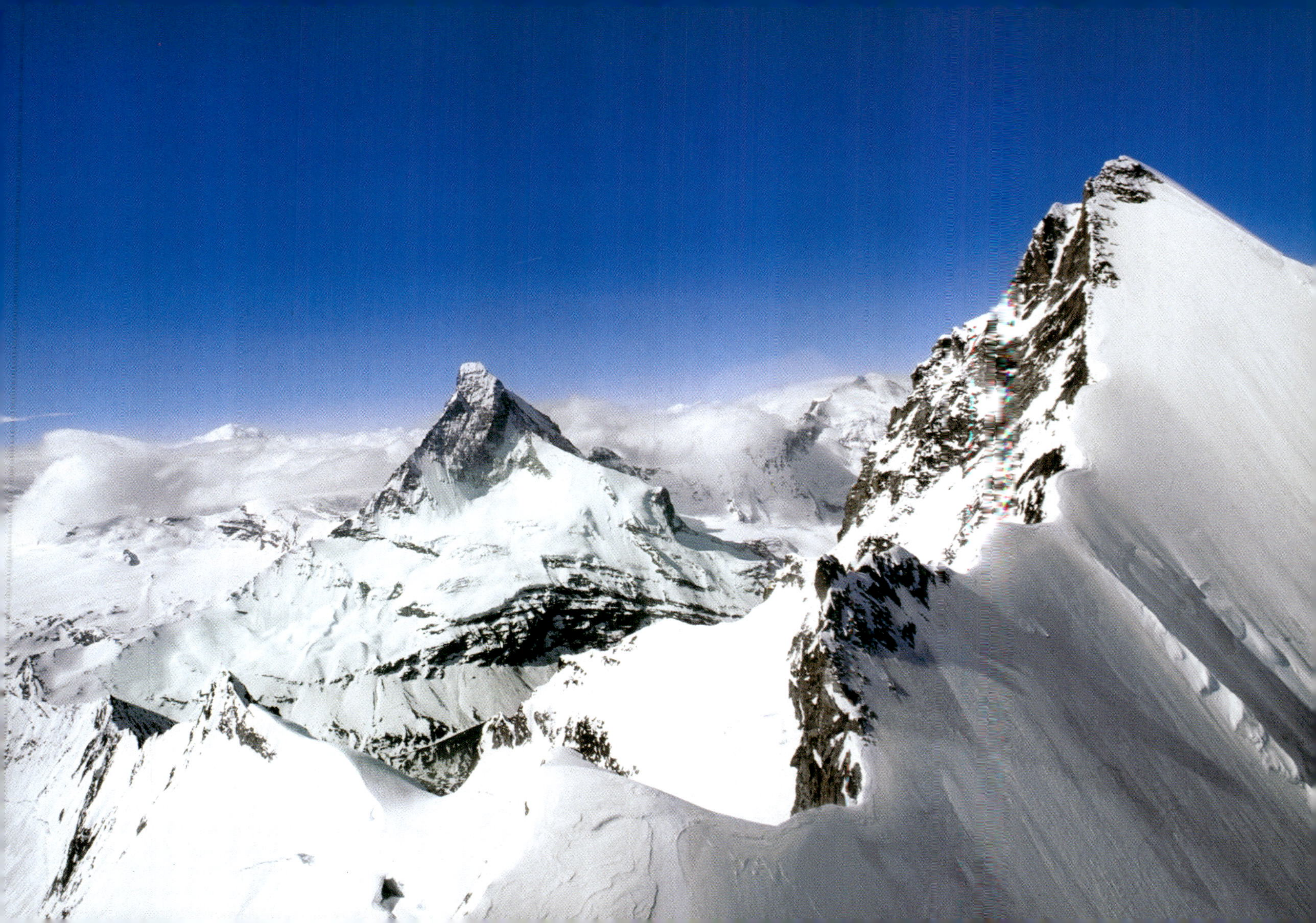

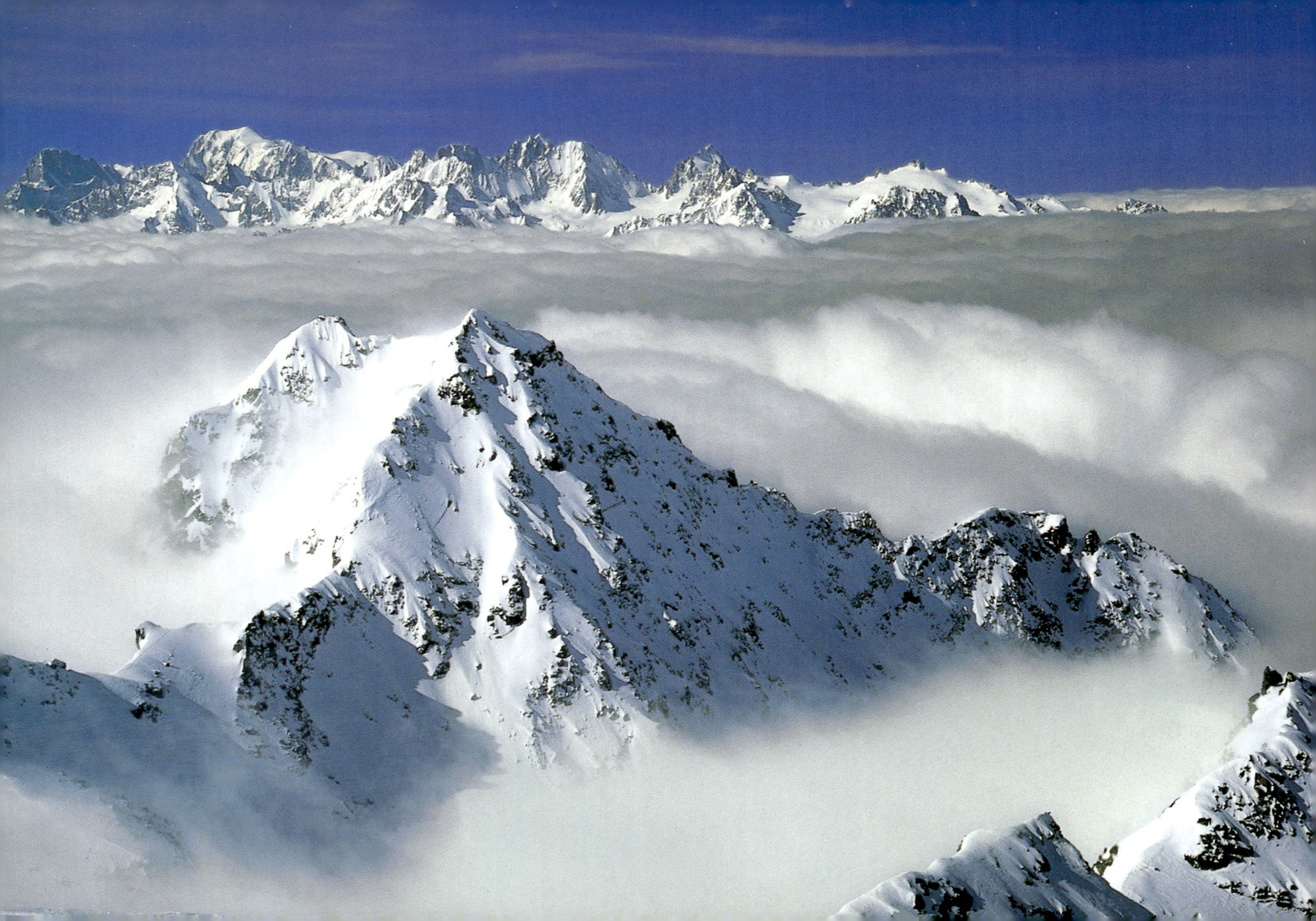

214 and 215

These two views of Mount Eiger, in the Swiss Alps, enveloped by the clouds (photo on the left) and with the famous wall on its north face (photo on the right), show its majesty

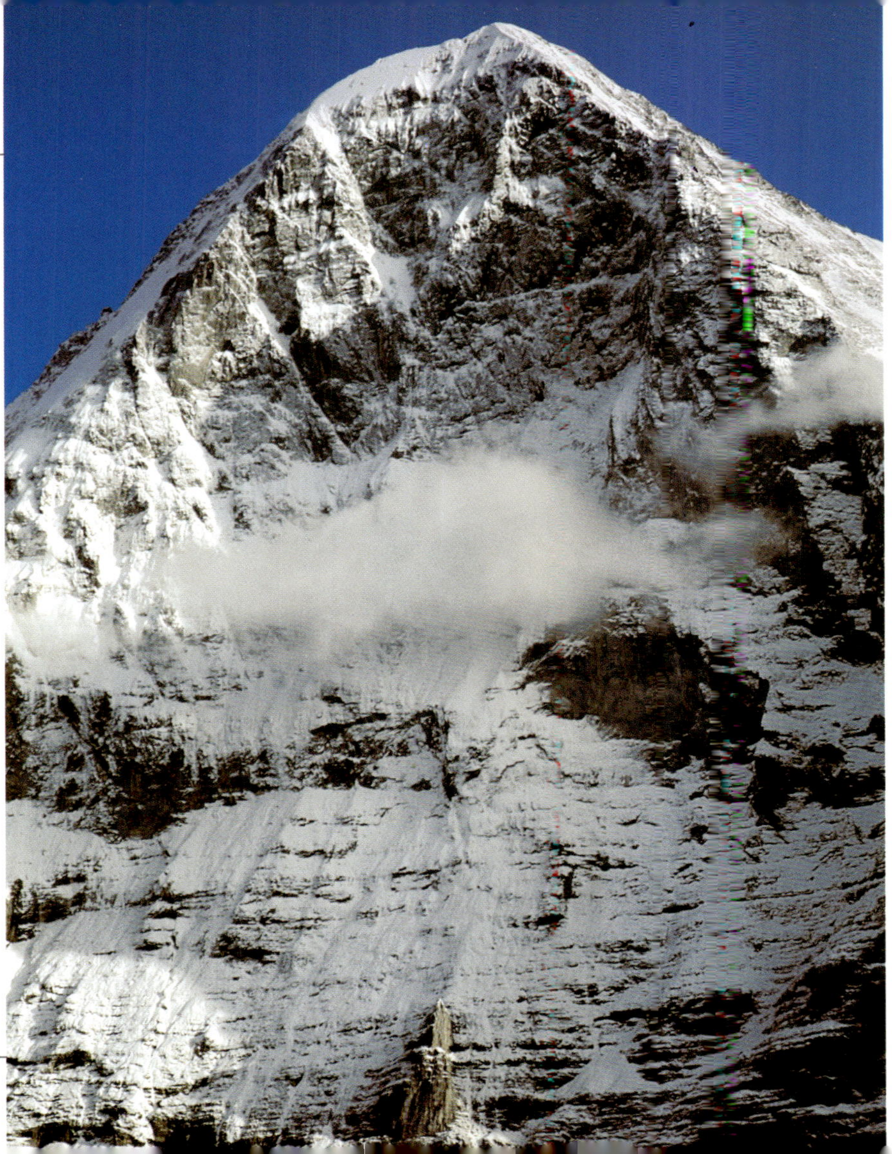

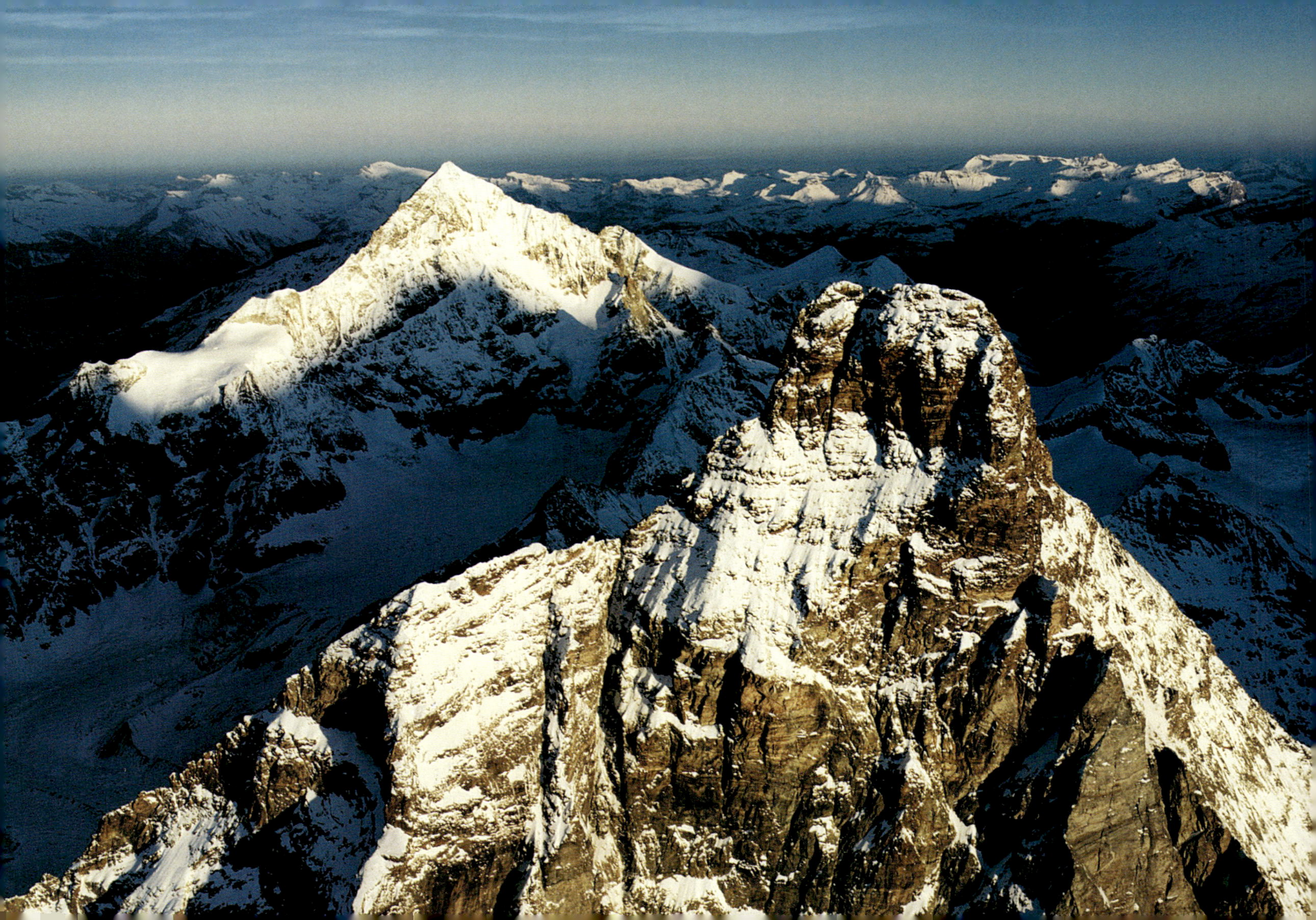

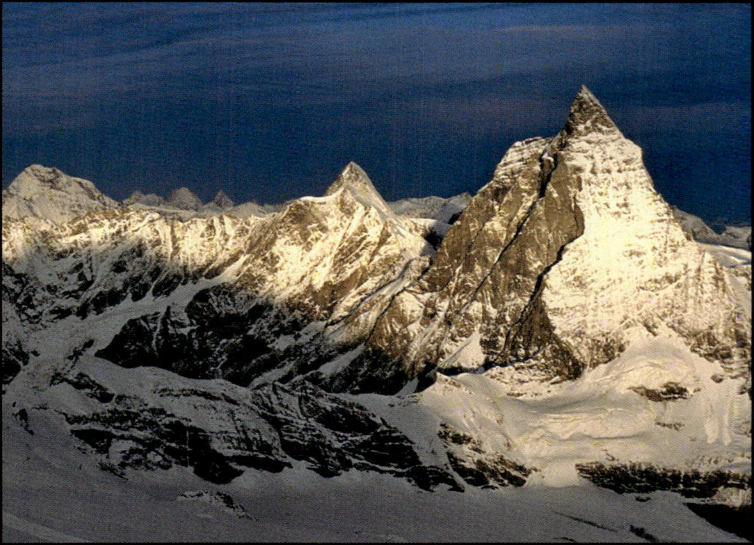

216

One of the most climbed peaks in the world, every face of the Cervino has been explored, and today ropes, ladders, and pitons can be found on all its walls.

217

The inaccessible pyramid-shaped peak of the Matterhorn is easy to observe in this photo: the mountain was climbed for the first time in 1865 by Edward Whymper.

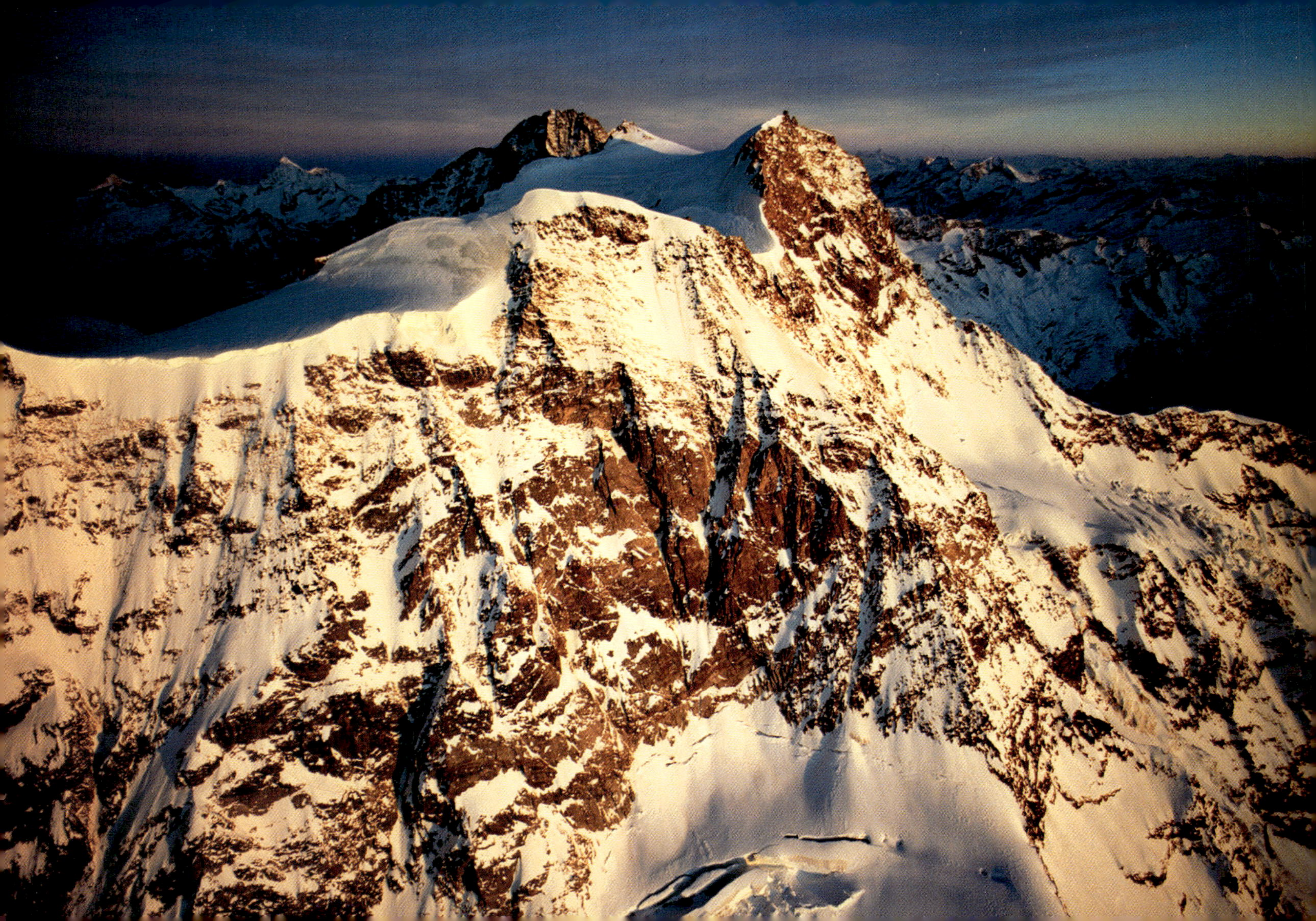

218
Mount Rosa, in the Italian Alps, reaches up to 15,204 feet with its highest peak, Point Dufour. Legend has it that the mountain's name comes from the fascinating pink color it takes on at sunrise and sunset.

219
The Regina Margherita Hut, the highest shelter in Europe, stands at 14,942 on Point Gnifetti, the fourth highest peak on the Mount Rosa massif.

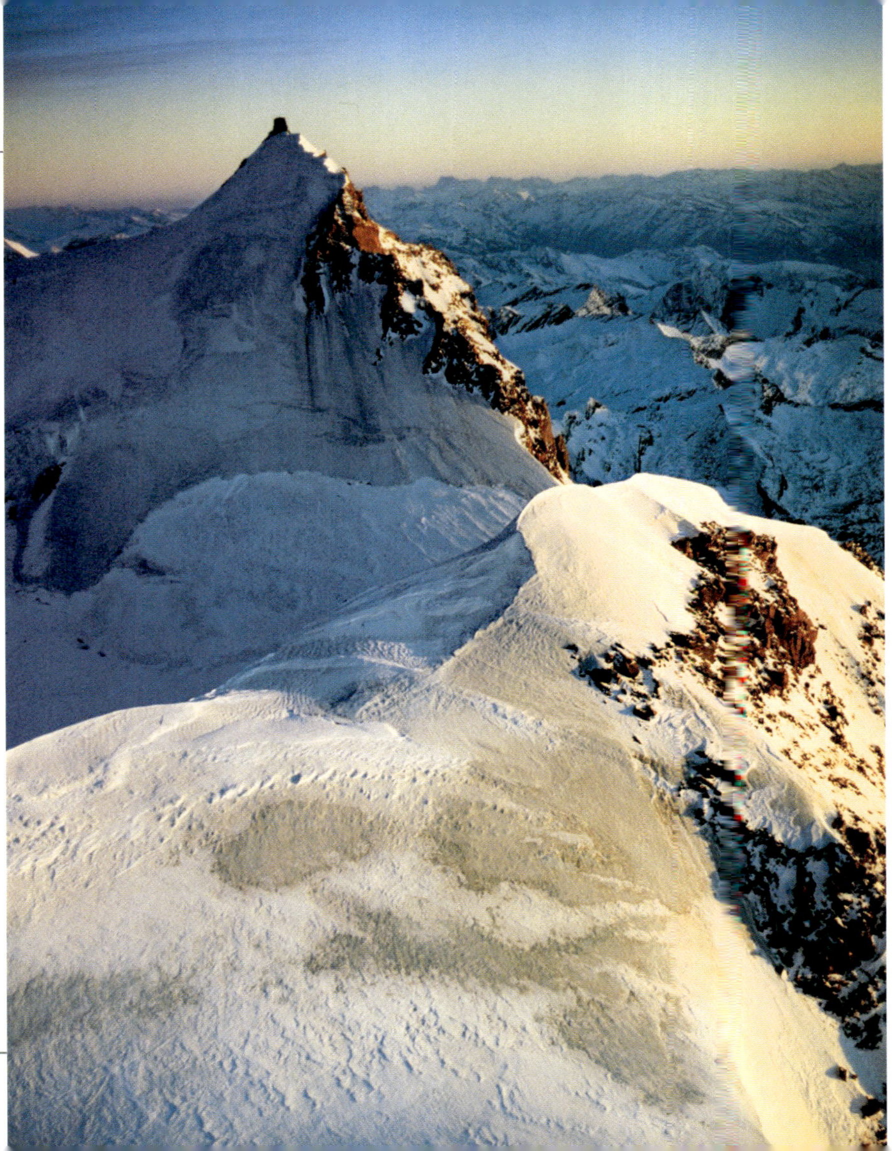

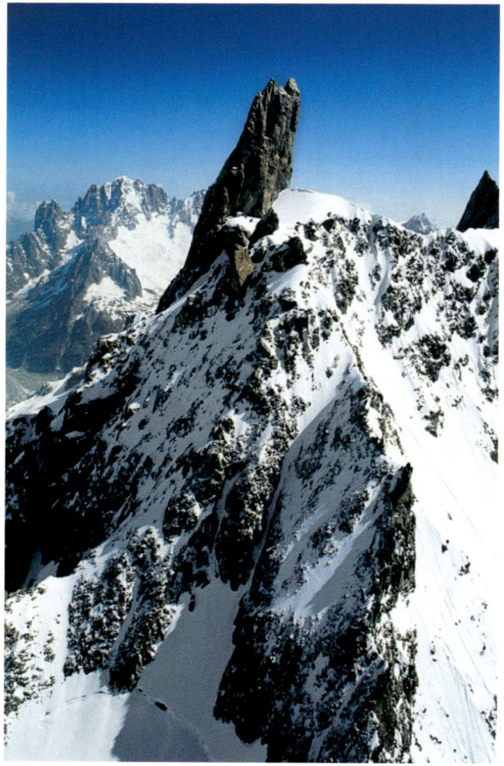

220
The Dent du Géant is one of the most amazing peaks on the Mont Blanc massif.

221
Mont Blanc is the highest peak in the Alps. Though it marks the natural border between Italy and France, the 15,772-foot peak is located entirely within French territory.

222-223
Mont Blanc has been a main character in the history of mountaineering since its conquest in August, 1786, and a destination chosen by thousands of climbers from around the world every year.

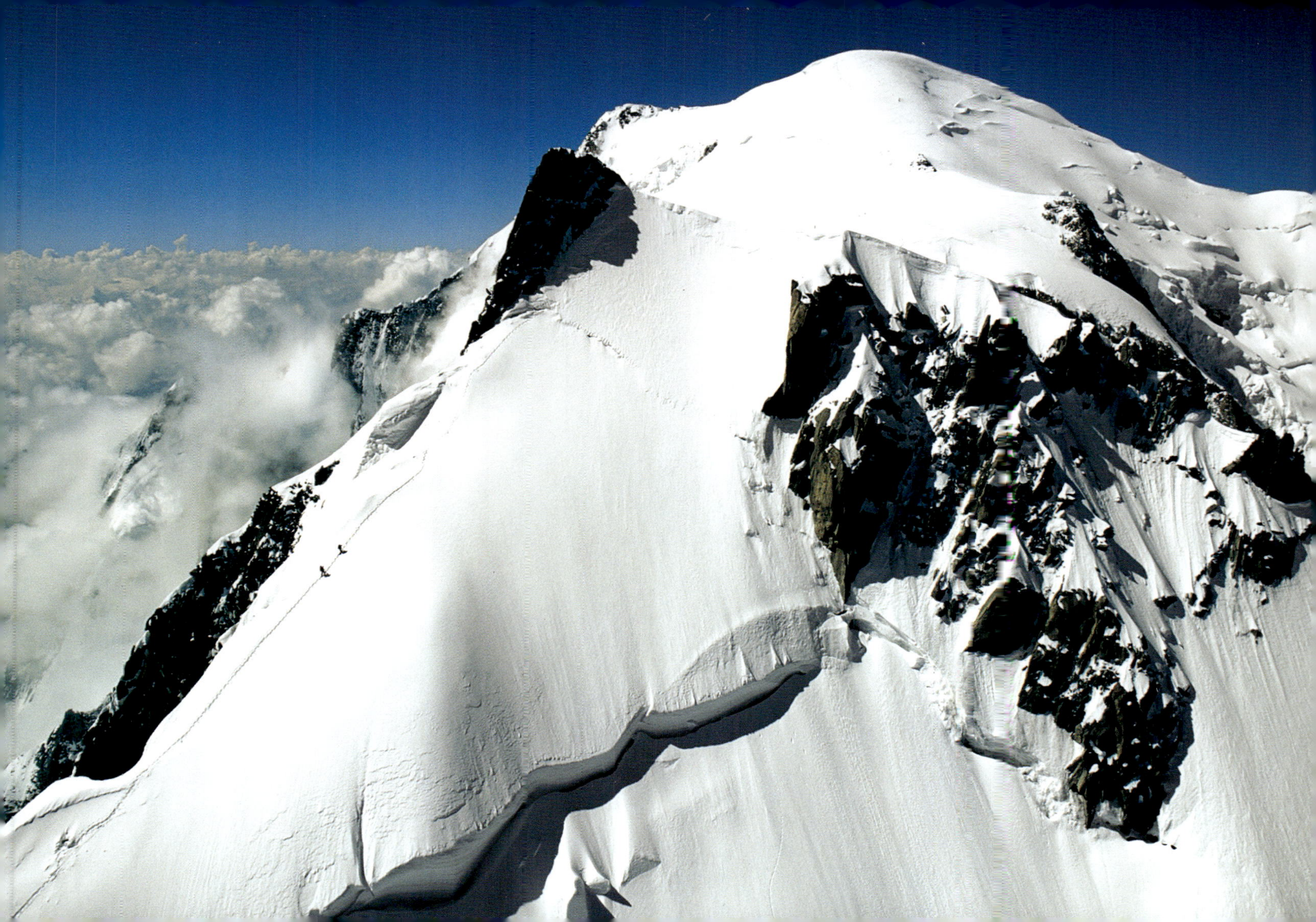

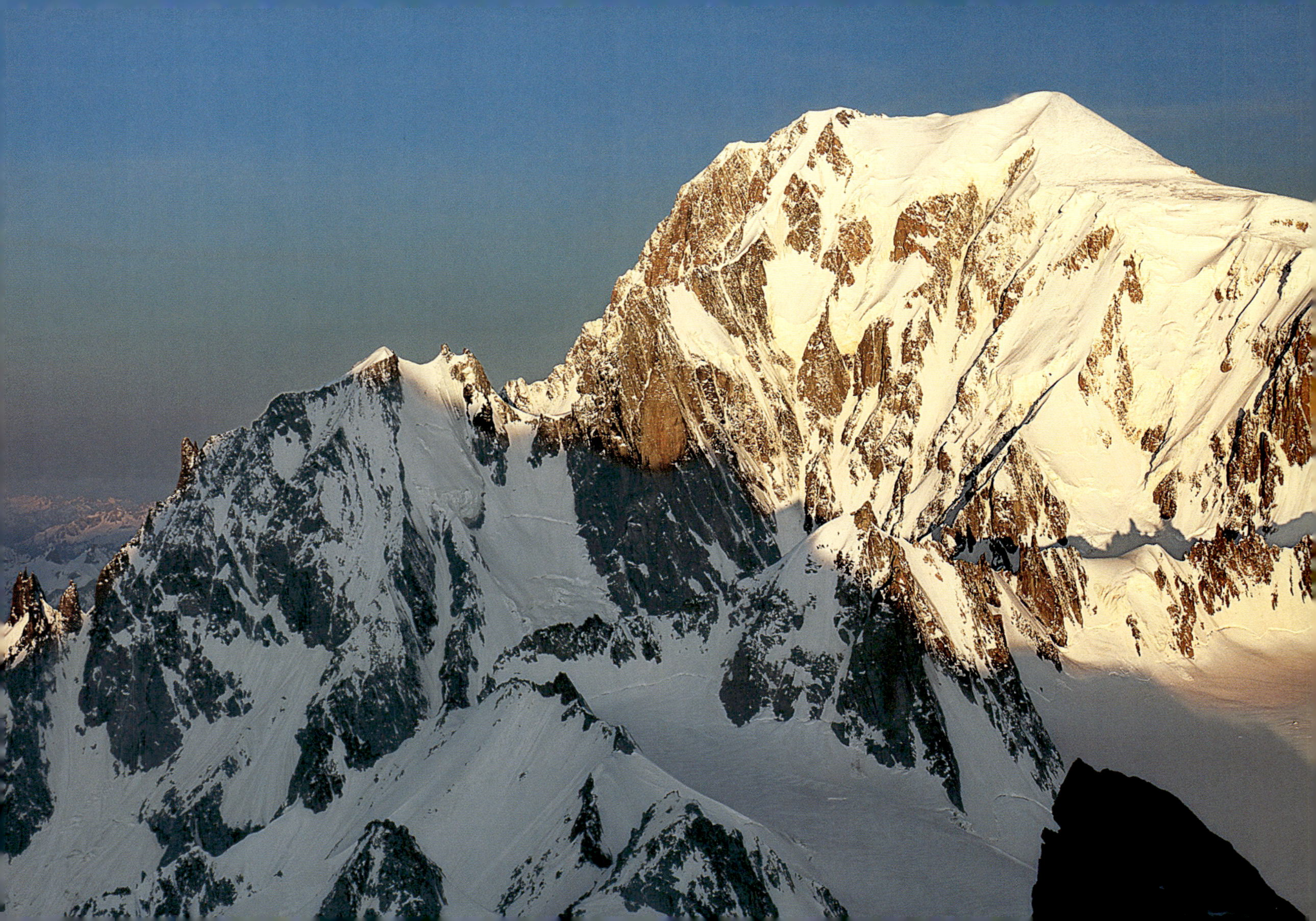

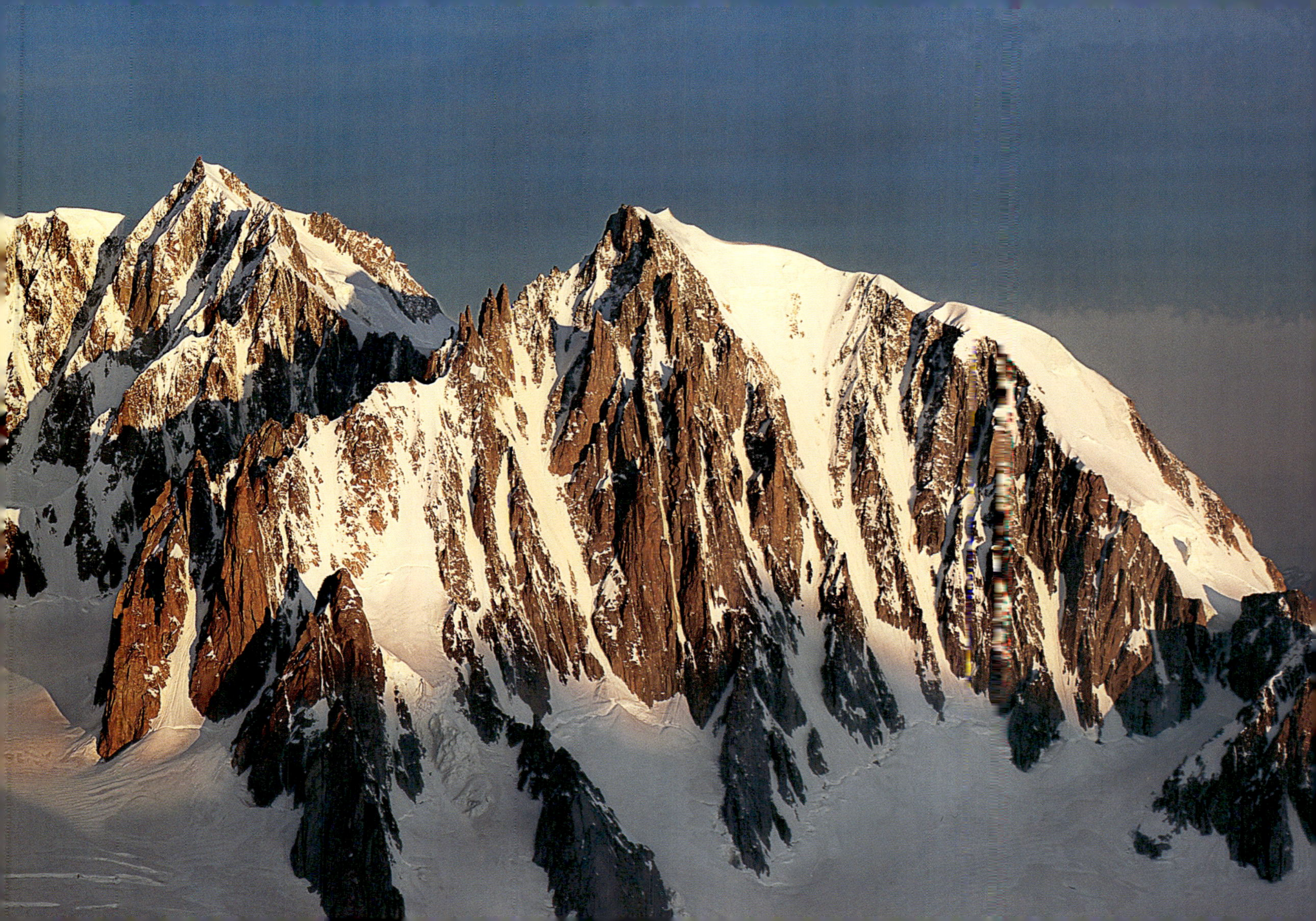

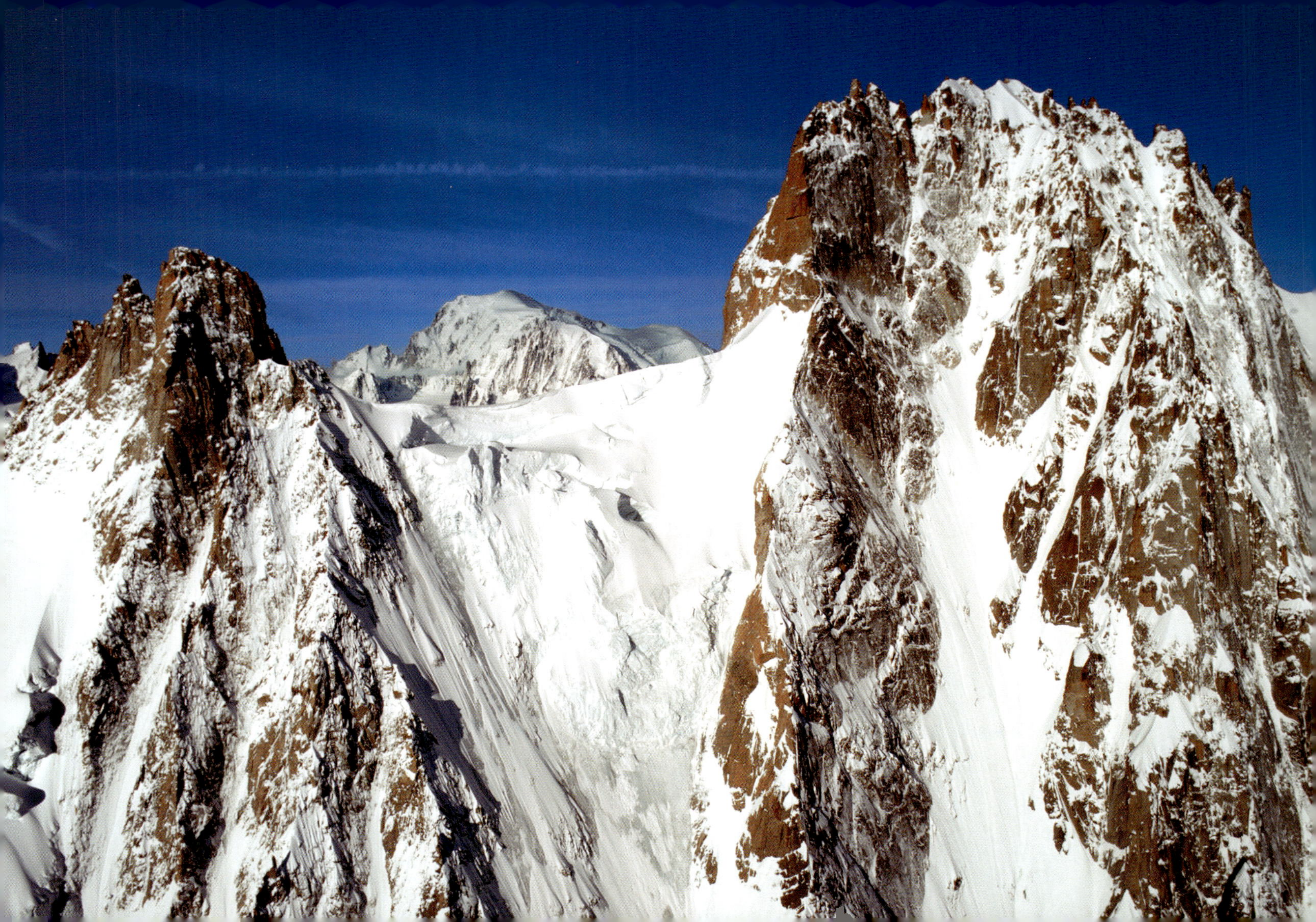

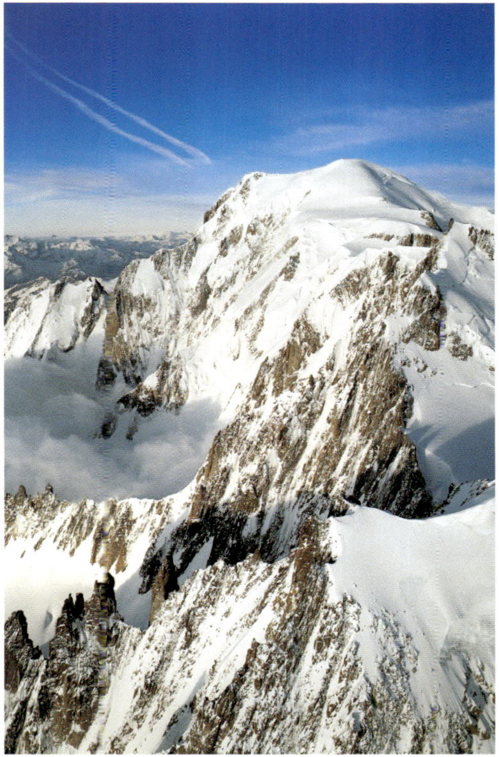

22[illegible]
The top of the Droites is a peak in the Mont Blanc massif that reaches up to 13,000 feet. Its north face is considered one of the most difficult to climb in the Alps.

22[illegible]
This view of Mont Blanc emphasizes the impressive crests that only a few expert mountaineers are able to climb.

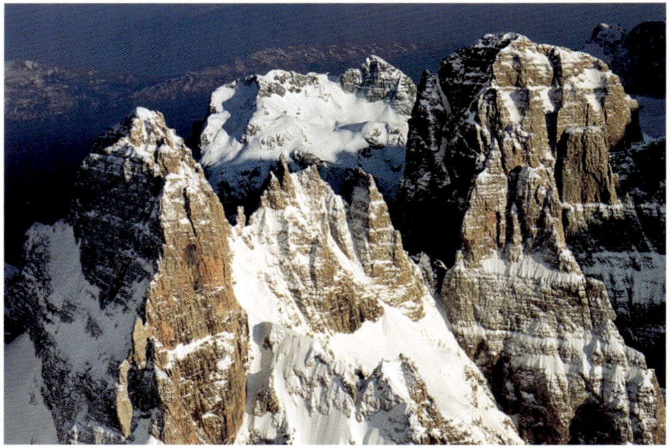

226 and 227
The Brenta Dolomites in Italy preserve intact the formidable rocky formations and slender shapes that were softened over time by erosion in other areas of the Dolomites.

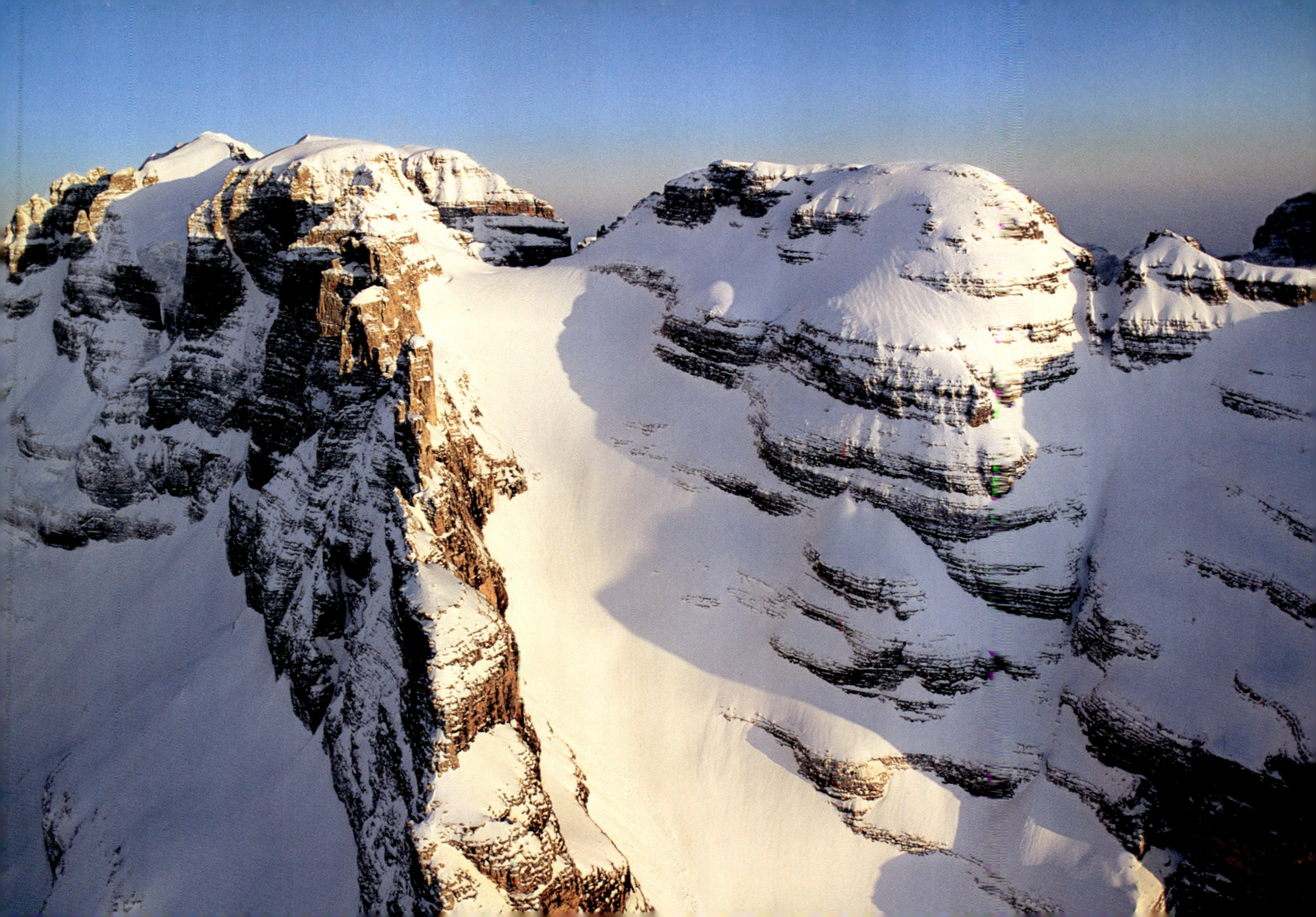

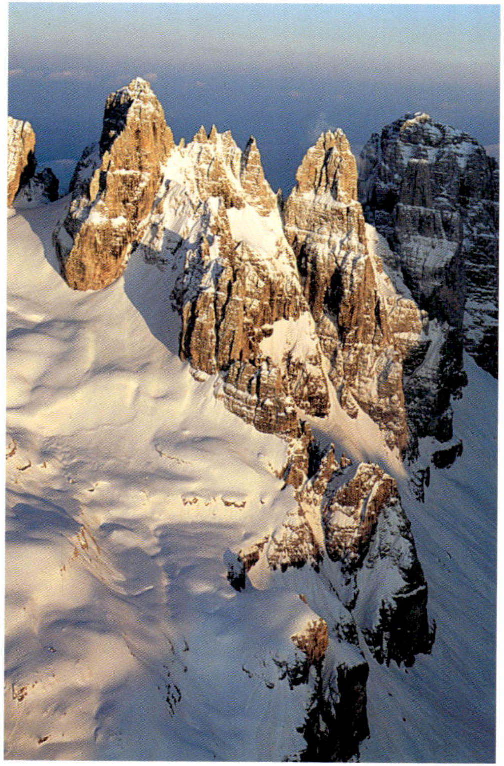

228
The group of the Brenta Dolomites extends from north to south for over 25 miles. The entire territory of the Brenta group is encompassed by the Brenta Adamello National Park.

229
The Catinaccio group, also known by the name of Rosengarten (rose garden), is a fascinating succession of striking mountain faces and rock towers.

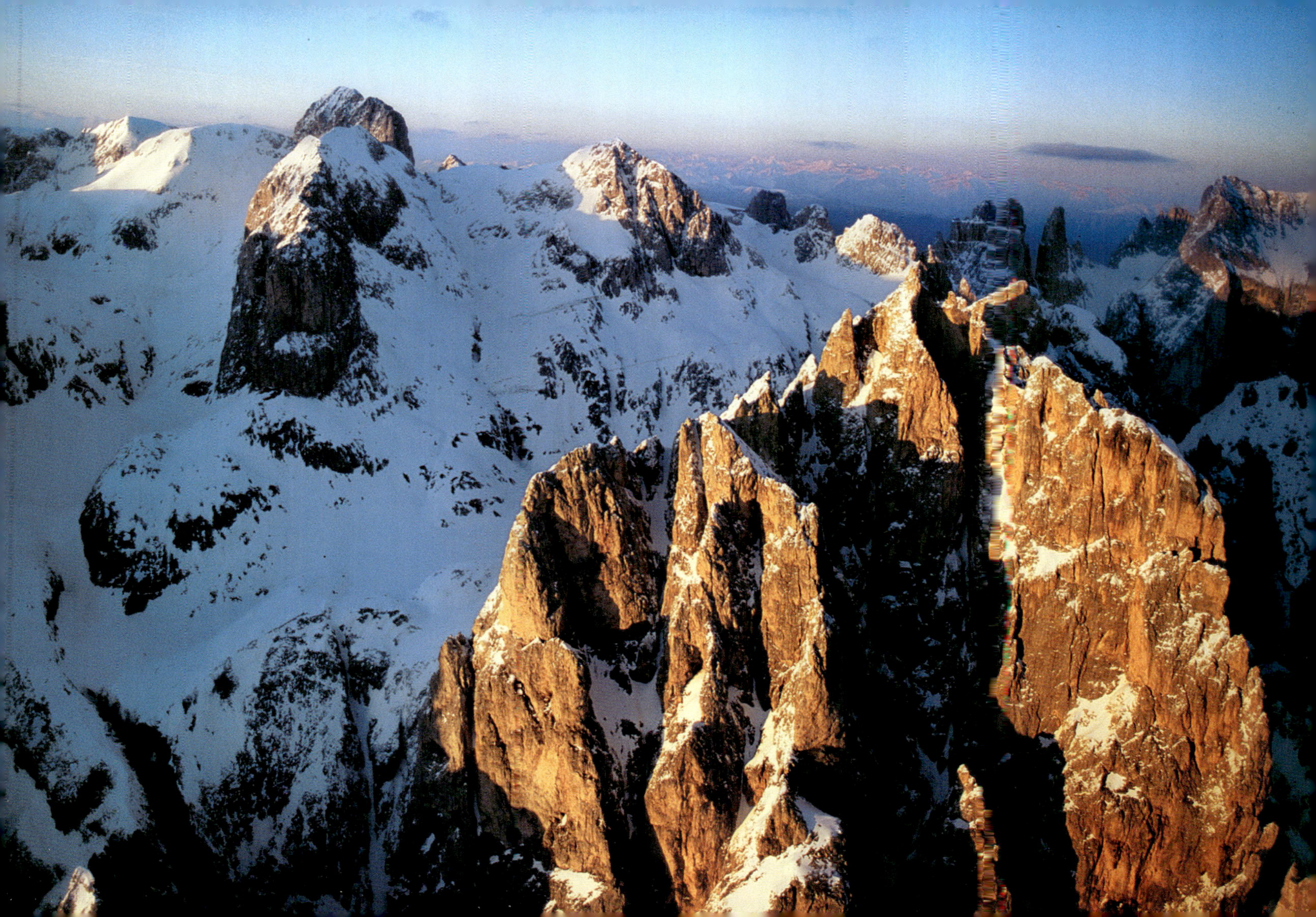

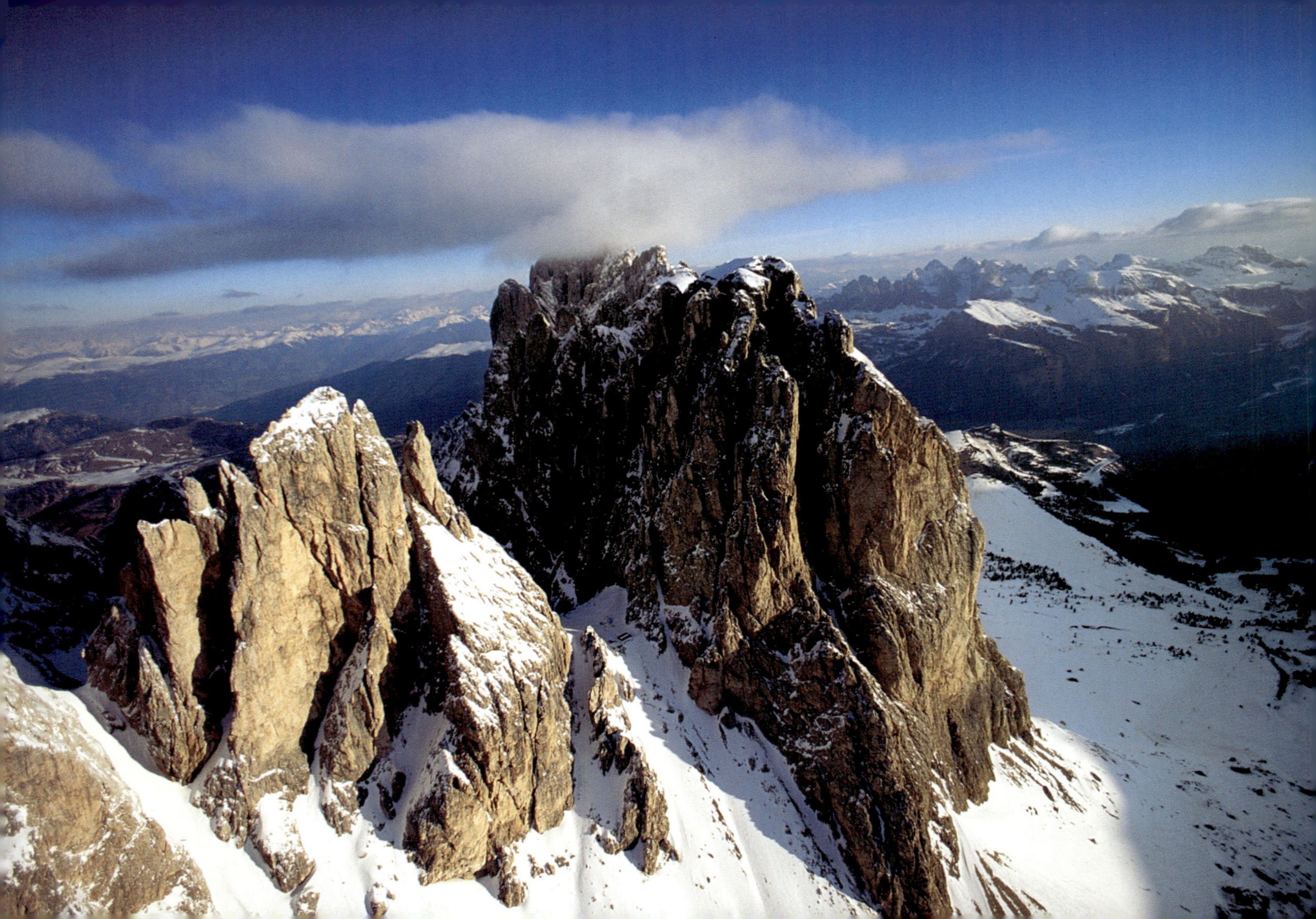

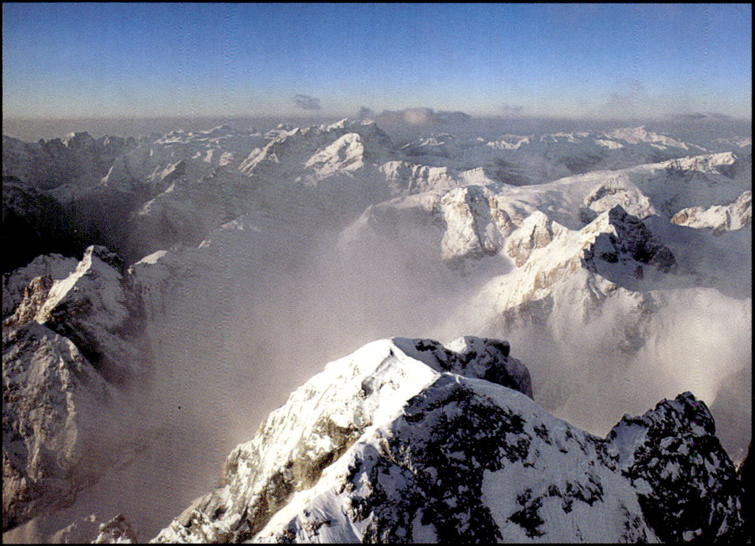

230

The name of Sassolungo (10,437 feet), in Val Gardena in Italy, is closely tied to those of Paul Grohmann, F. Innerhofer, and P. Salcher, who were the first to climb it in 1869.

231

The Marmolada, the "queen" of the Dolomites, is a massif reaching up to 10,965 feet tall with the Penta Point. This peak, together with Rocca Point, constitutes the main chain, which goes from east to west.

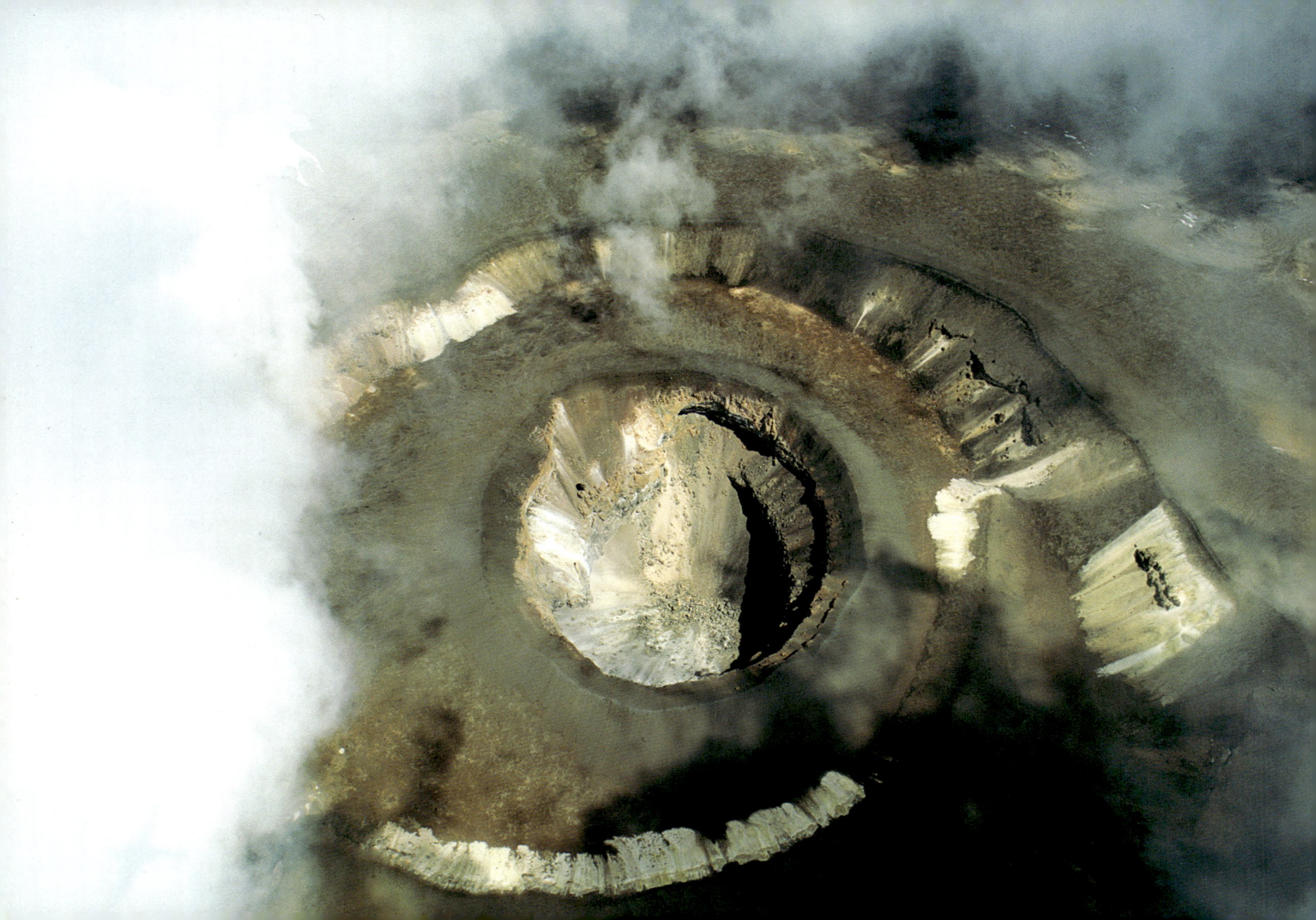

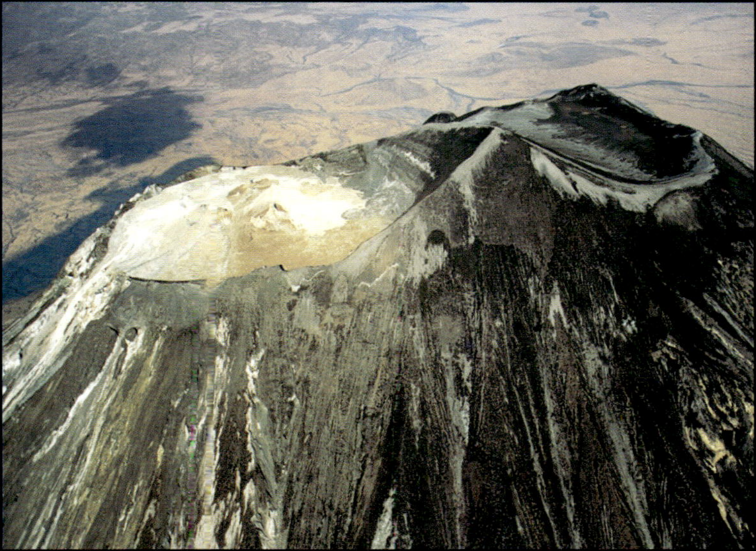

232

A spectacular view of the crater on the top of Kibo, the extinct volcano located on Mount Kilimanjaro that, with its 19,342 feet, represents that tallest mountain in Tanzania and Africa.

233

The Doinyo Lengai, in Tanzania, is an extremely fascinating volcano located on the African tectonic trench, whose name, in the Masai language, means "mountain of God."

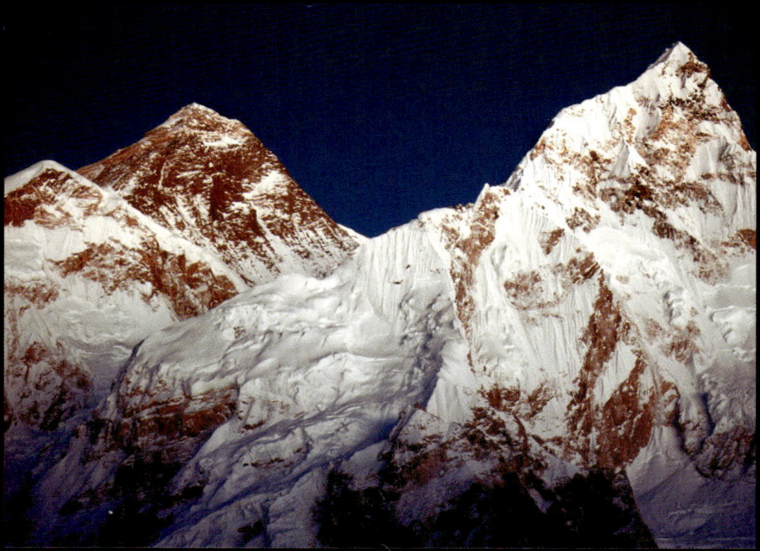

234 and 235
In these two photos, Mount Everest, on the left, and Nuptse, on the right, can be admired – two of the most impressive Himalayan mountains.

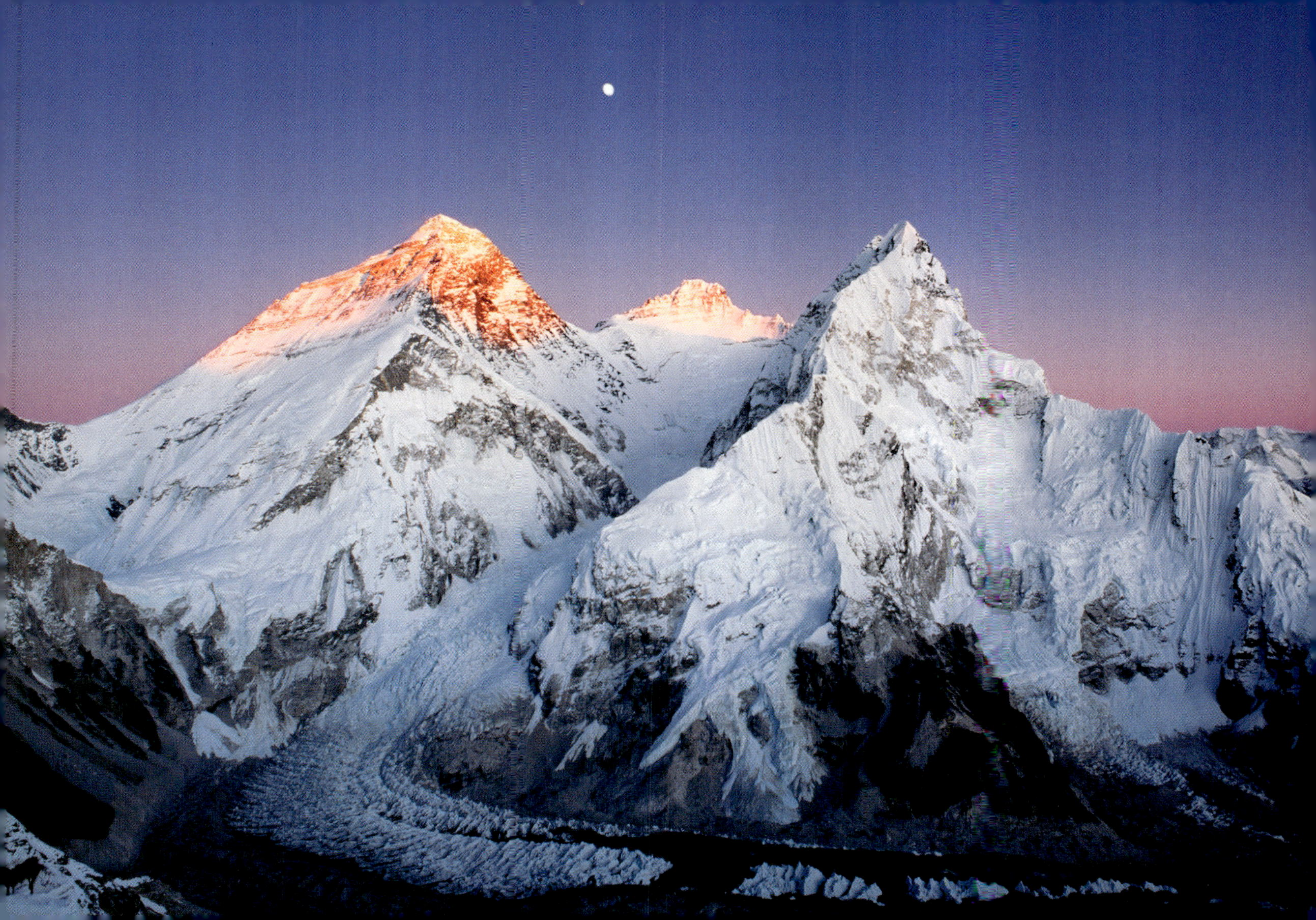

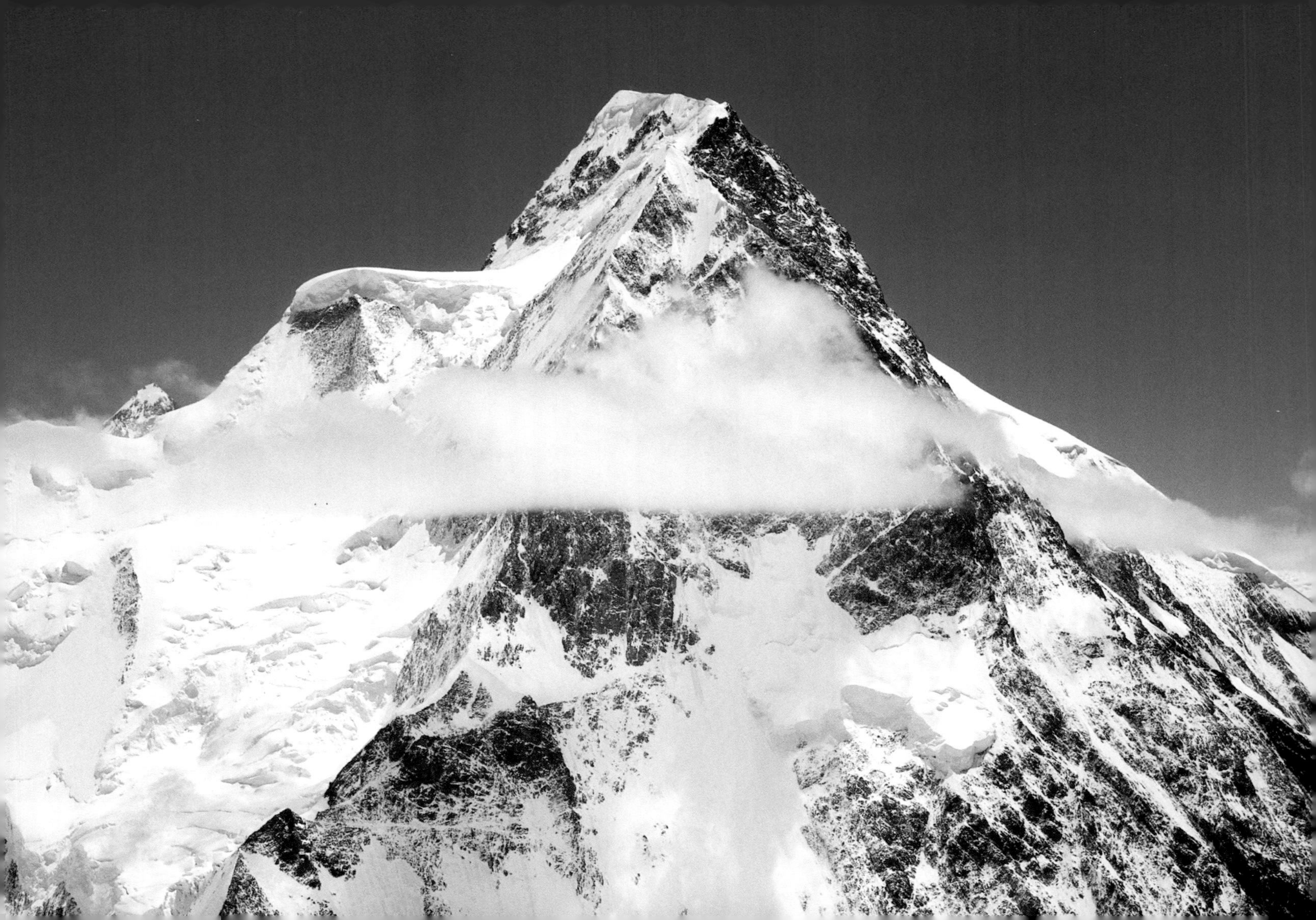

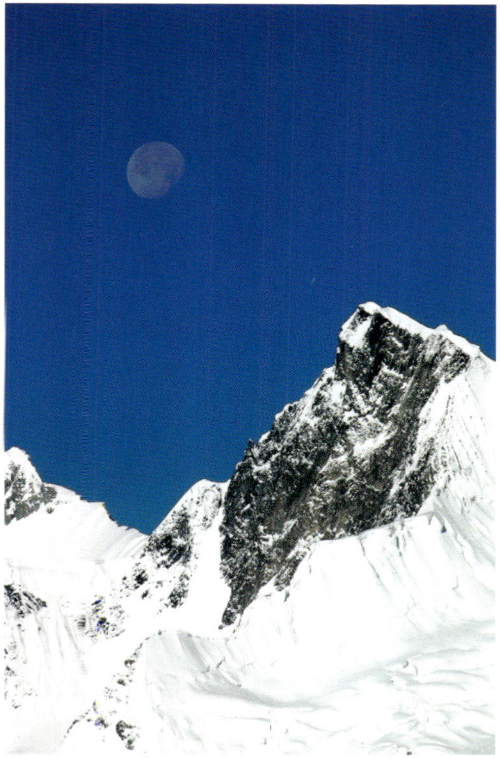

236 and 237
K2, between Pakistan and China, with its 28,253 feet, is the second tallest peak in the world. Its peak was finally conquered for the first time in 1954 by an Italian expedition.

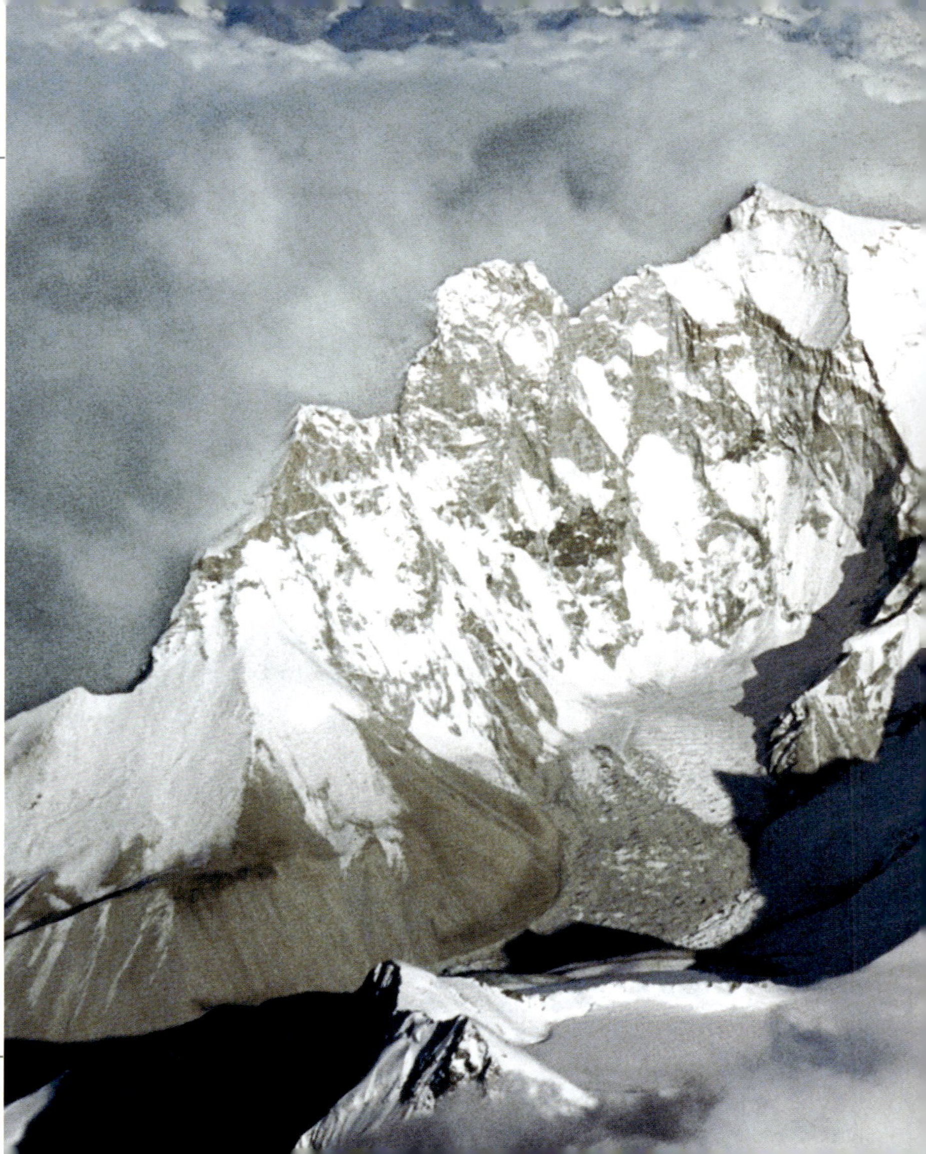

238-239
Mount Makalu in Nepal is the fifth tallest in the world with its 27,767 feet.

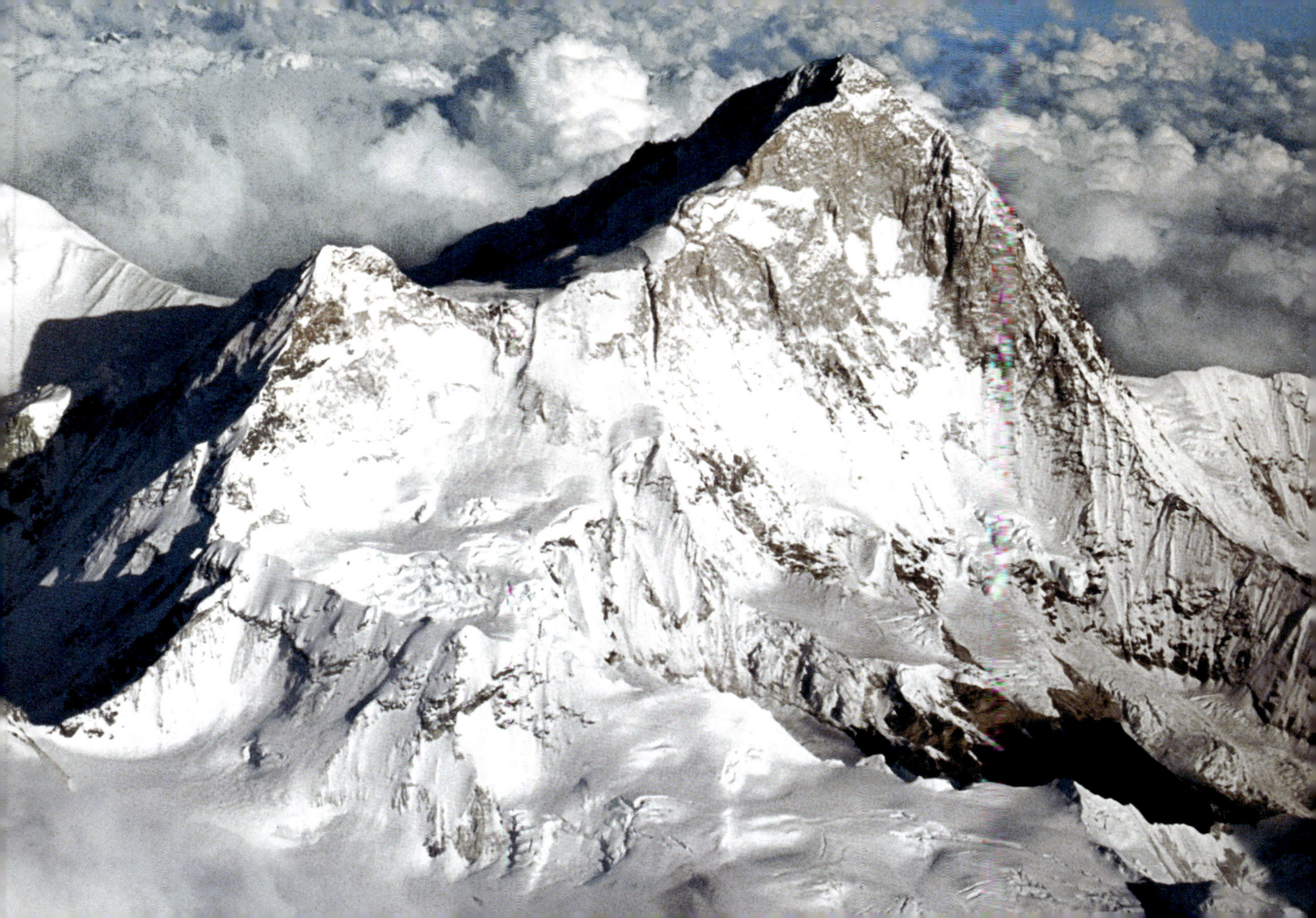

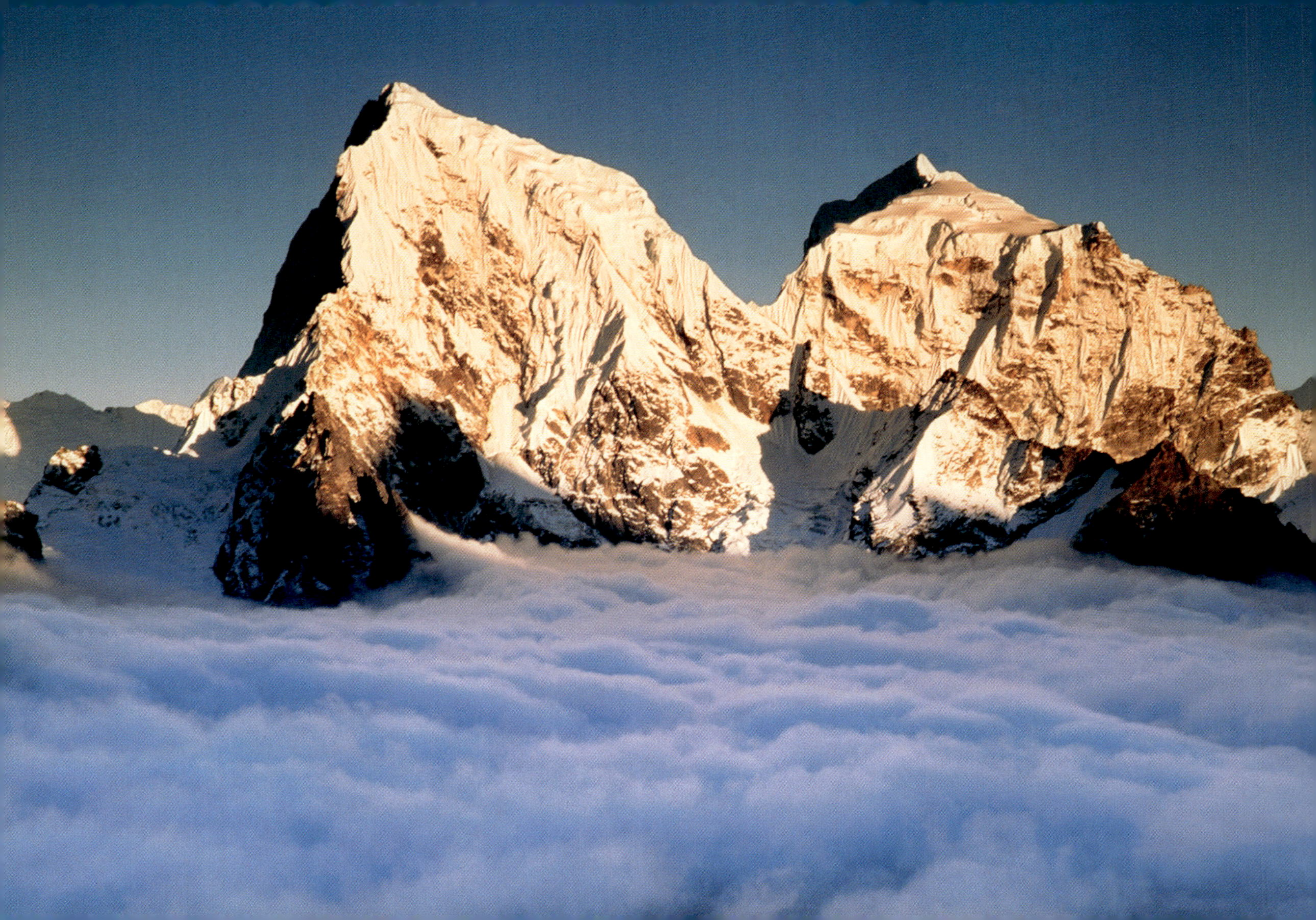

240
The last rays of the sun illuminate the Cholatse (21,130 feet) and Taweche Mountains (21,464 feet) in Nepal.

241 left
Ama Dablam, whose name means "mother of all jewels," is a splendid sacred mountain located south of Everest, in the Khumbu region of Nepal.

241 right
Tramserku rises over 21,000 feet above the predominantly mountainous territory of the Khumbu region in Nepal.

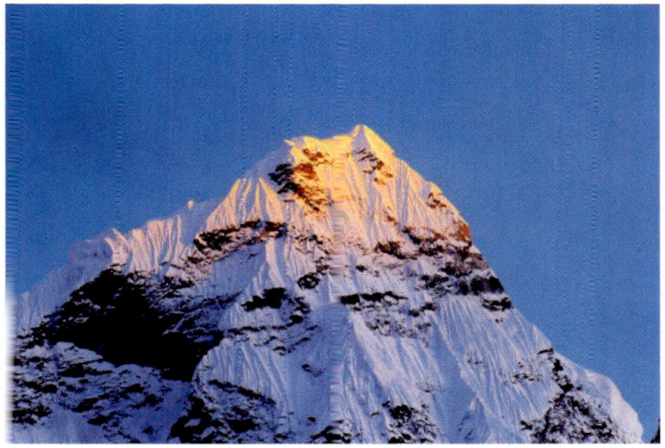

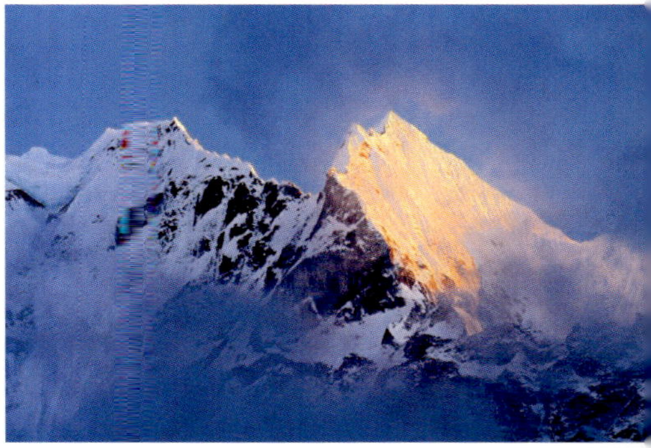

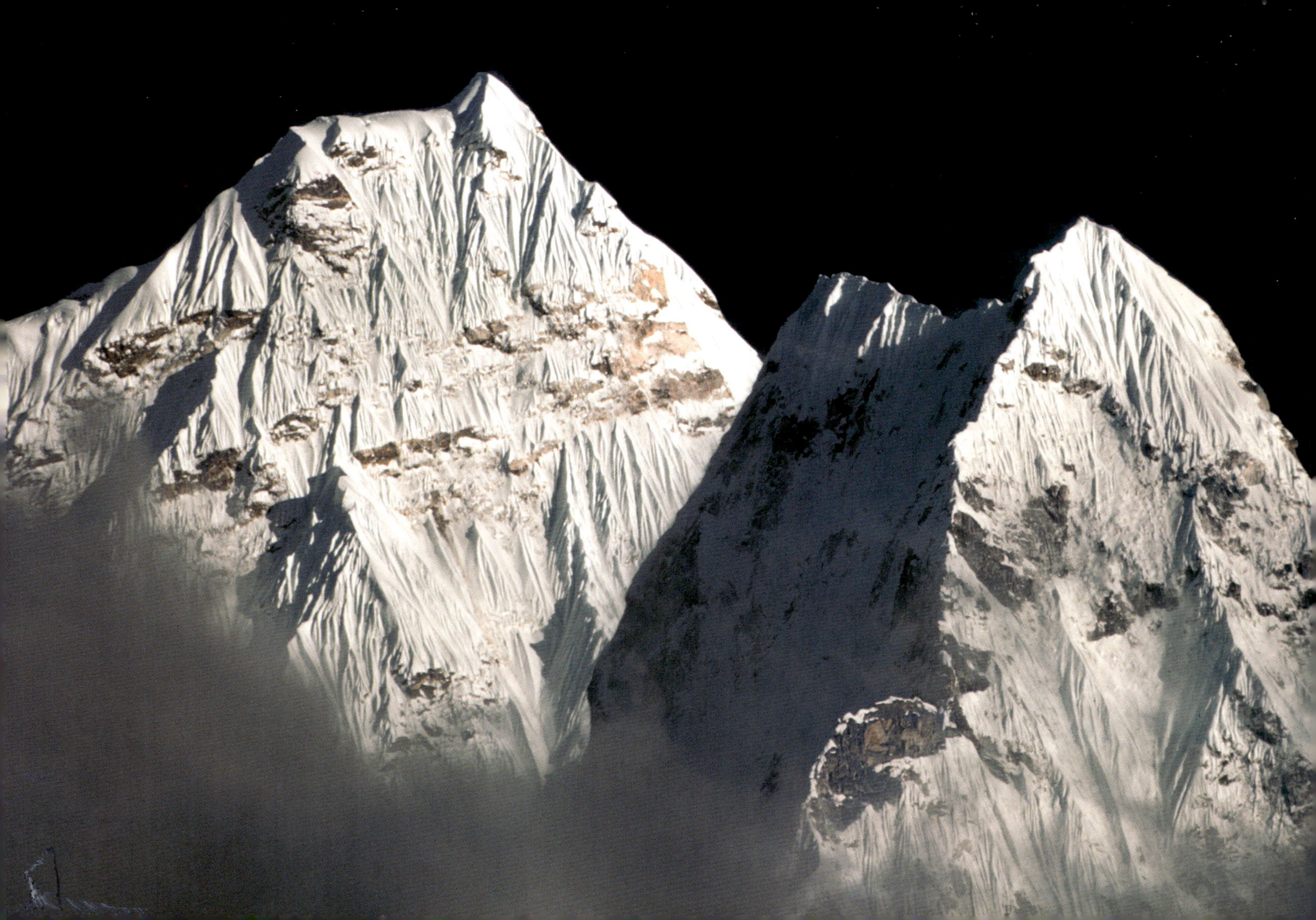

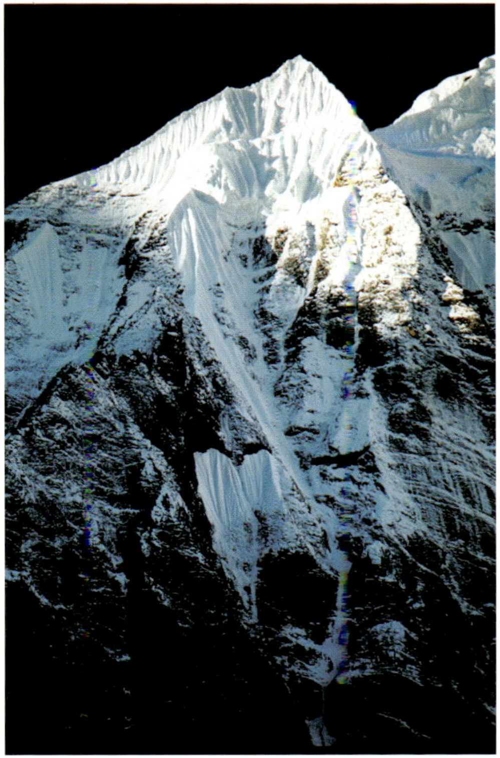

24

Climbed for the first time in 1961, the extremely sharp crest of Ama Dablam, in Nepal, is probably the best known peak after the 26,000-foot colossi.

243

As the sun sets, Annapurna, which comes from Sanskrit and means "goddess of the harvest" seems even more enchanting.

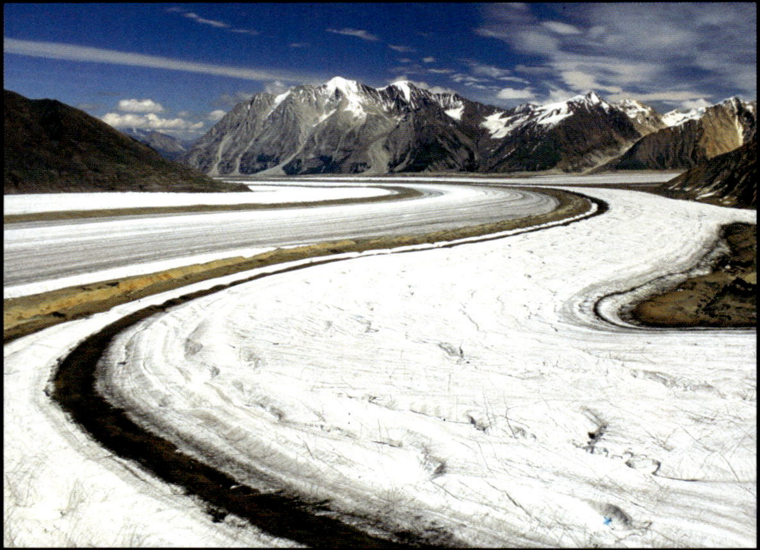

244 and 245
A true gem in the family of Canadian National Parks, Kluane National Park covers an area that includes Mount Logan that, with its 19,552 feet, is the tallest in Canada.

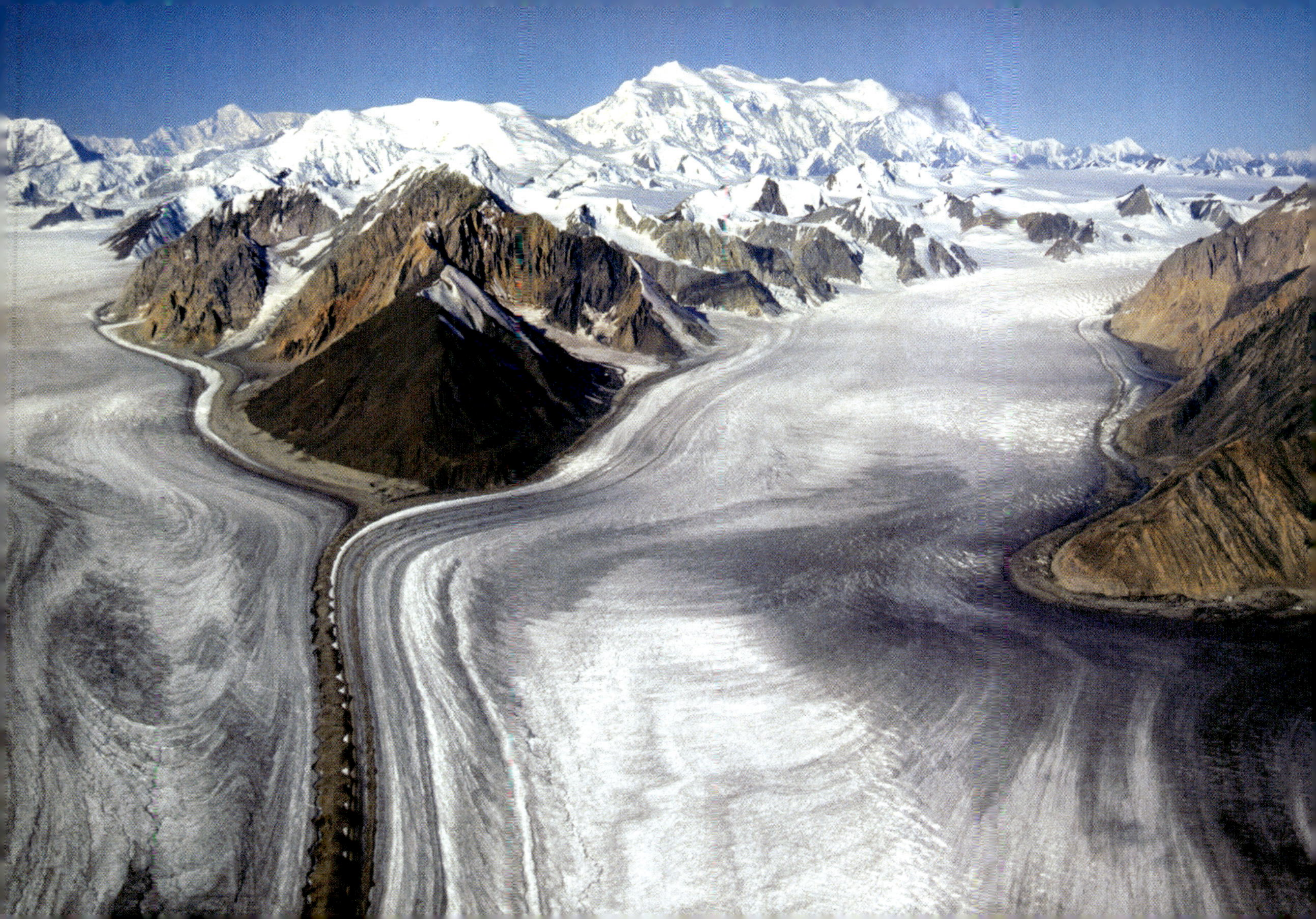

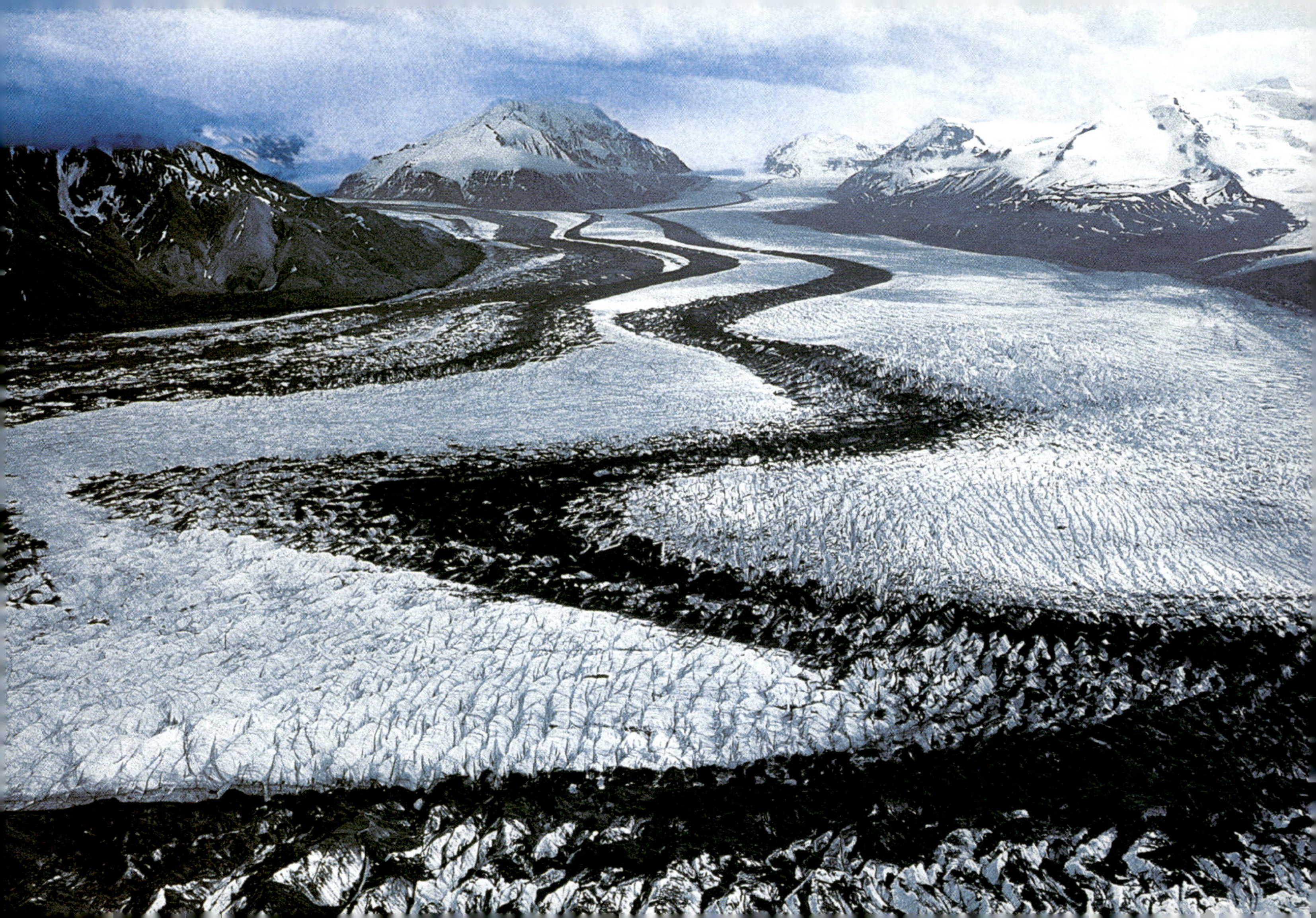

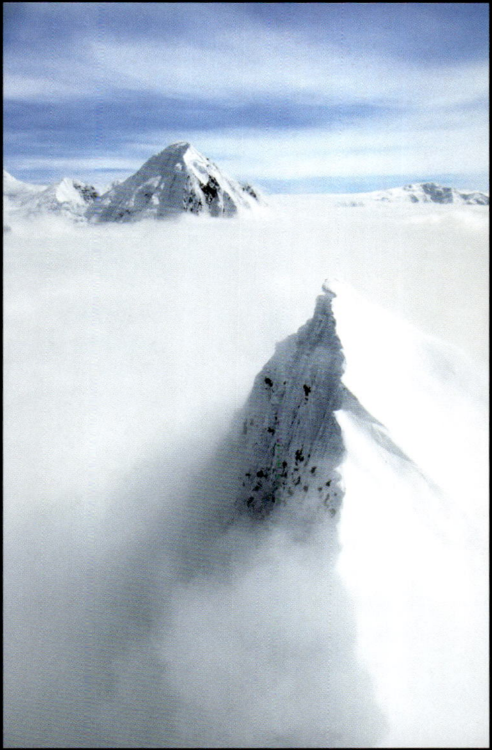

245

Big Russell Glacier is located on the St. Elias Mountains, the tallest coastal mountain chain in the world, found in Alaska.

247

The Wrangell Mountains, in southeastern Alaska, are an extension of the St. Elias Mountains and are composed of peaks exceeding 11[illegible]00 feet on average.

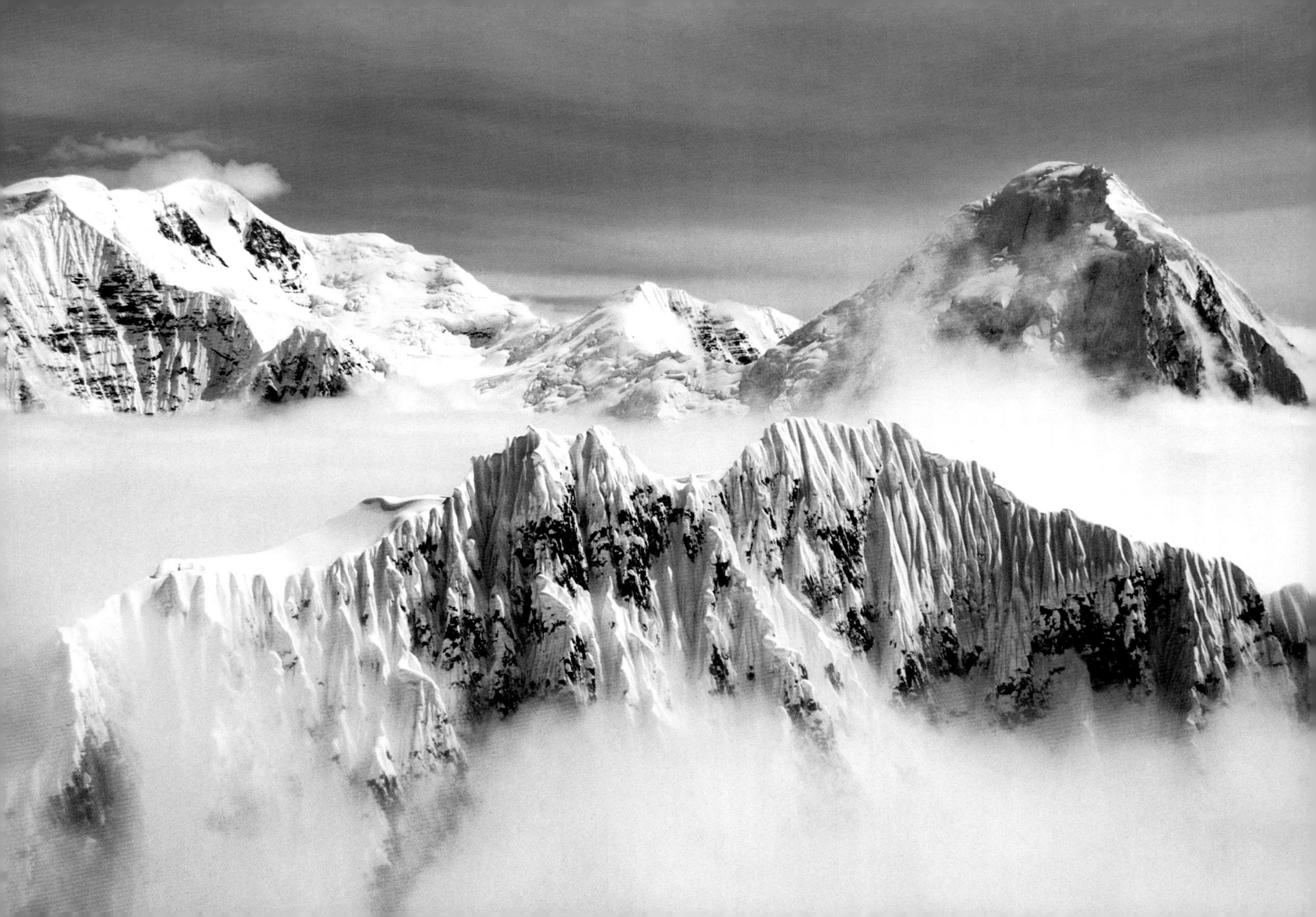

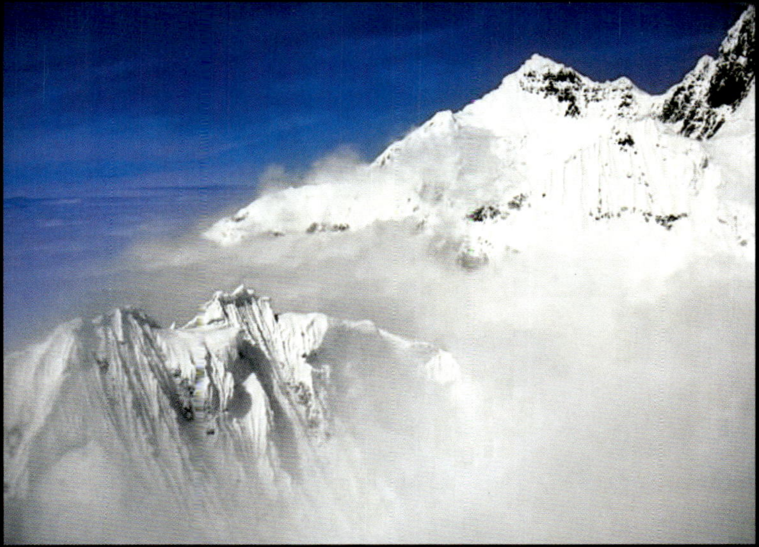

248 and 249
Mount Wrangell, in Alaska, is an ice-covered volcano that erupted for the last time in 1907 and whose peak is today used by the American military for study and research.

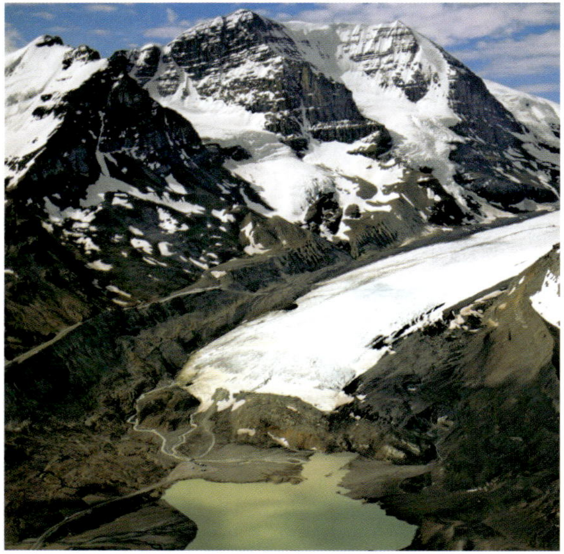

250 and 251

The Columbia Icefield is located on the border between Banff and Jasper national parks in Canada and, with a surface area of 3,500 square feet, is the biggest expanse of ice and snow south of the Arctic Circle.

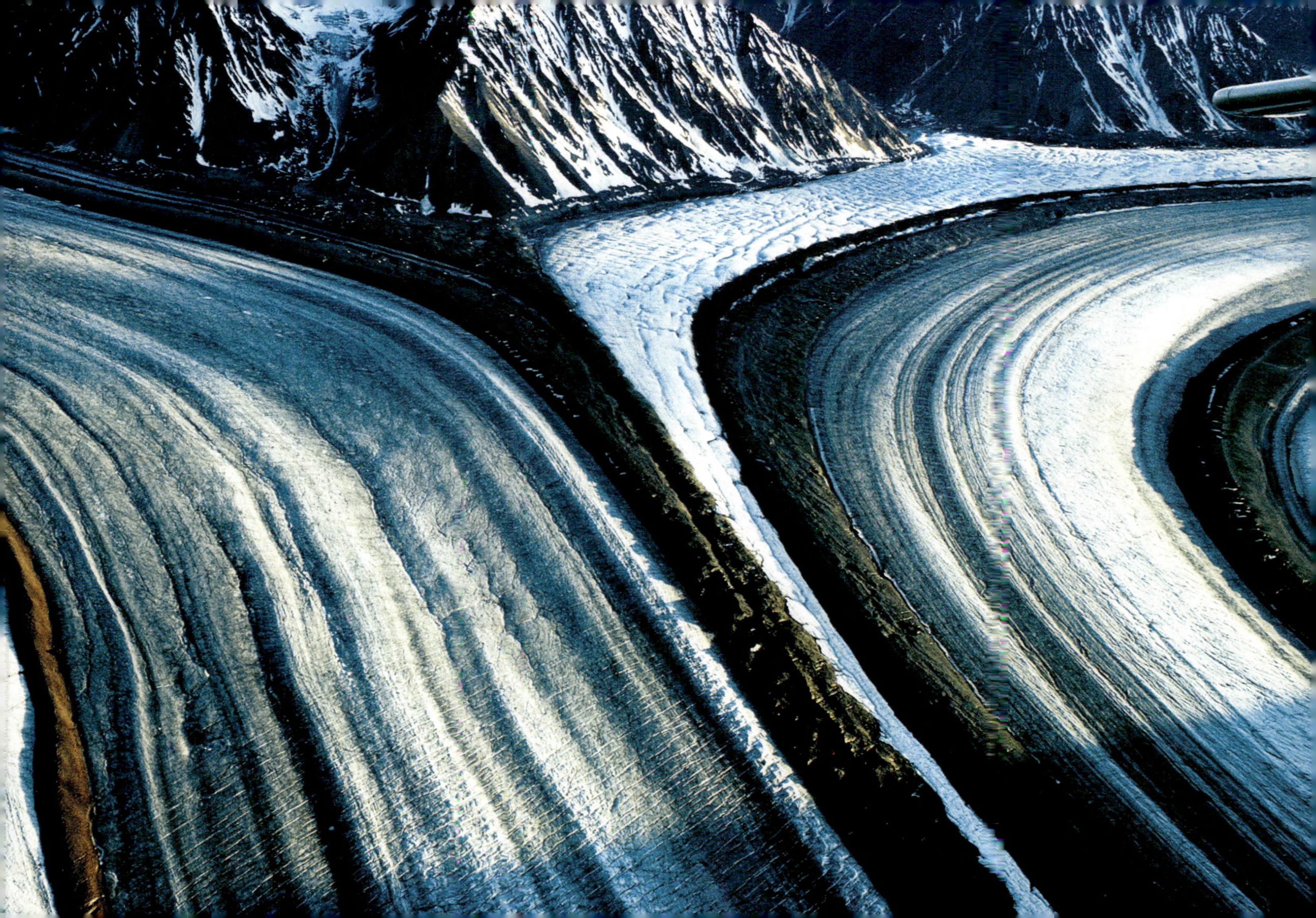

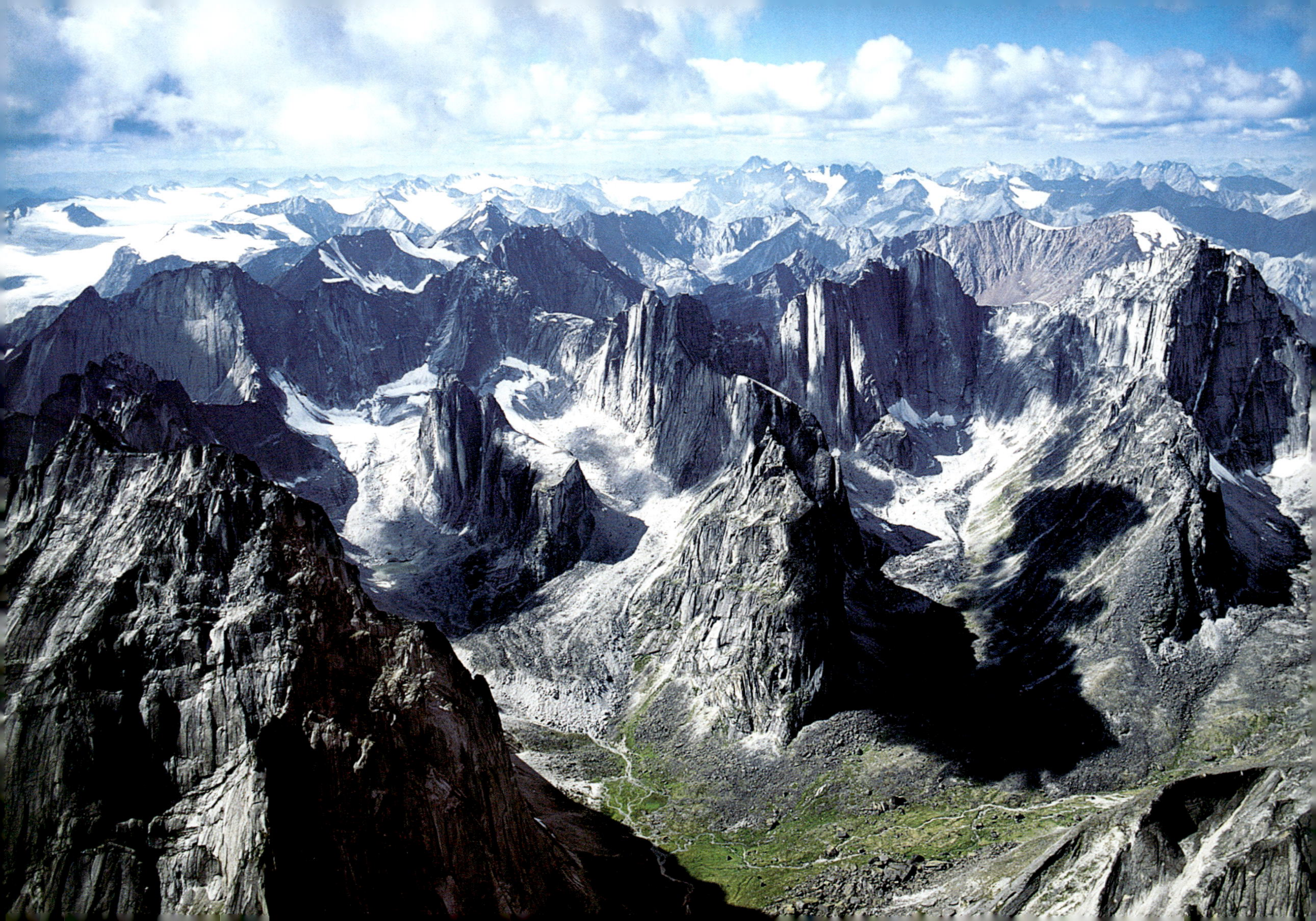

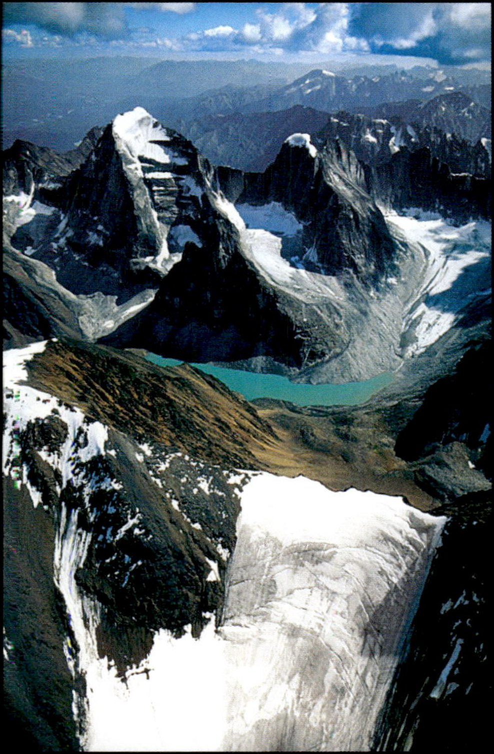

252 and 253

Two spectacular views of the Selway Mountains, a small group of peaks and vertical walls found in the extreme north of Canada, in the Northwest Territories.

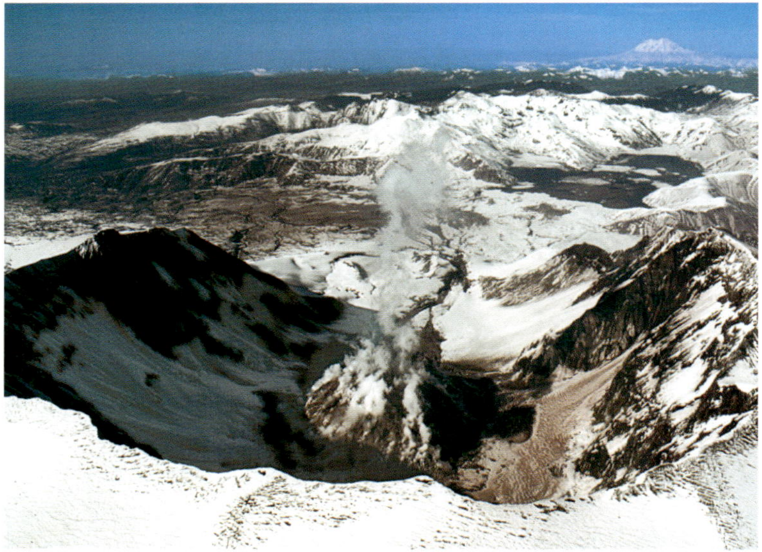

254 and 255

Two views of Mount St. Helens and the Lava Dome, in the state of Washington, from which continuous vapor puffs, demonstrating that the volcano is still active.

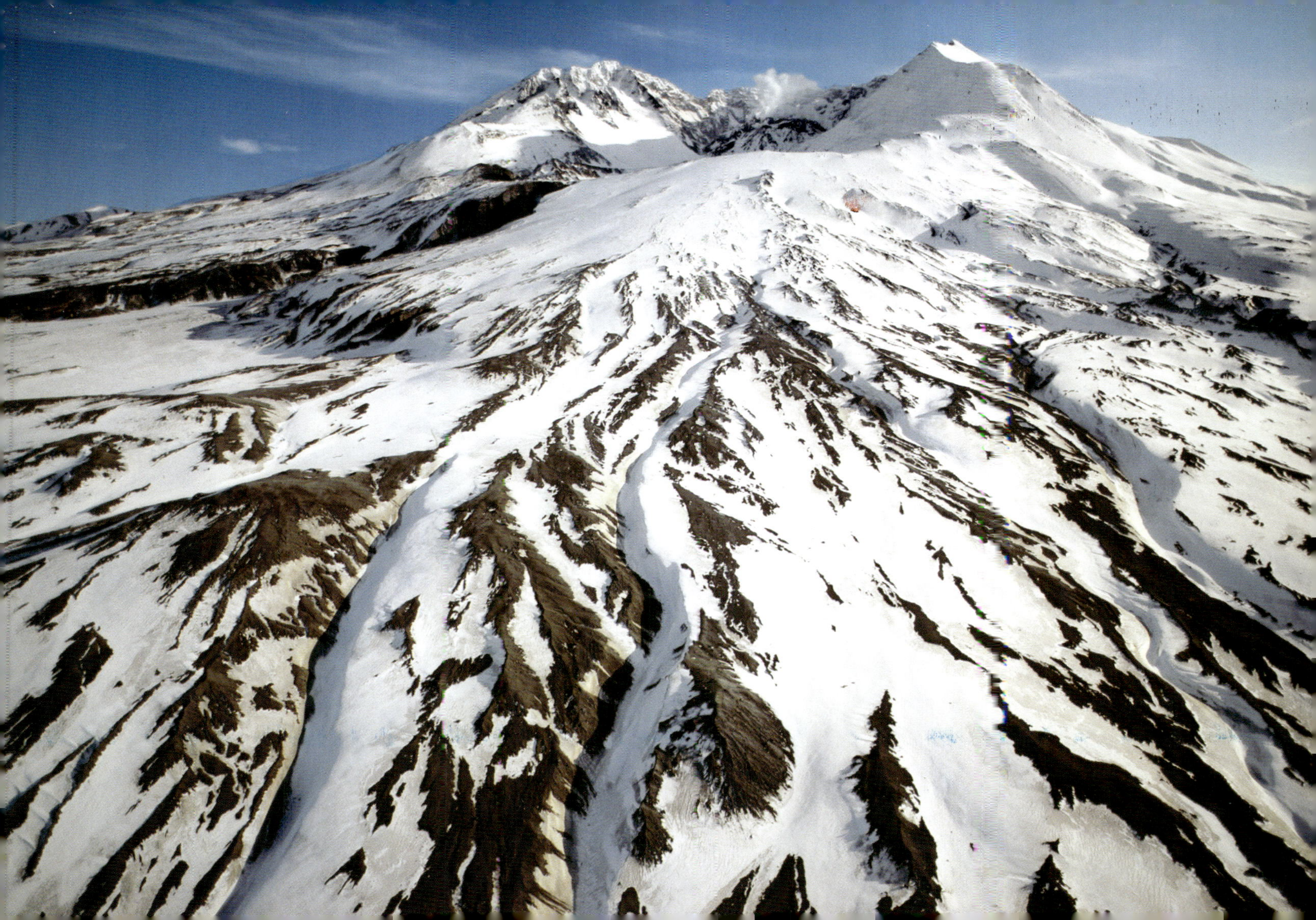

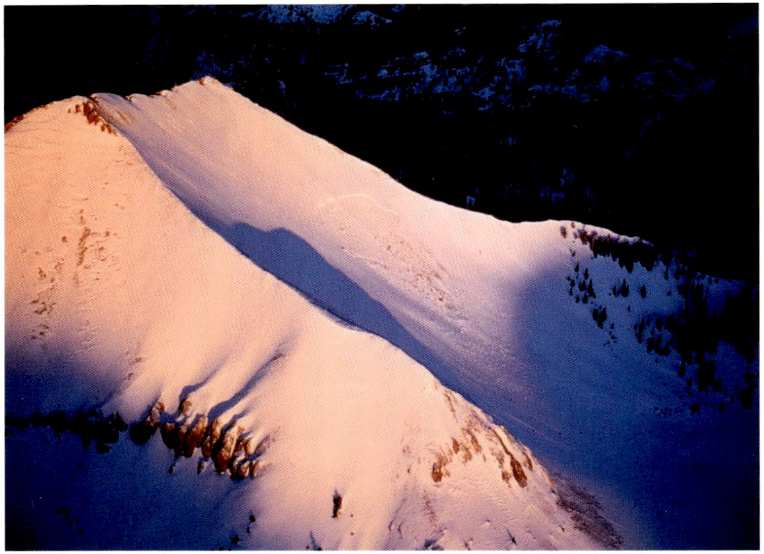

256

The early light of dawn evocatively illuminates a snowy peak in the San Juan Mountains, in southwestern Colorado.

257

Mount Rainier, in Washington State, is an inactive volcano that reaches up to 14,410 feet tall and is climbed successfully by thousands of people every year.

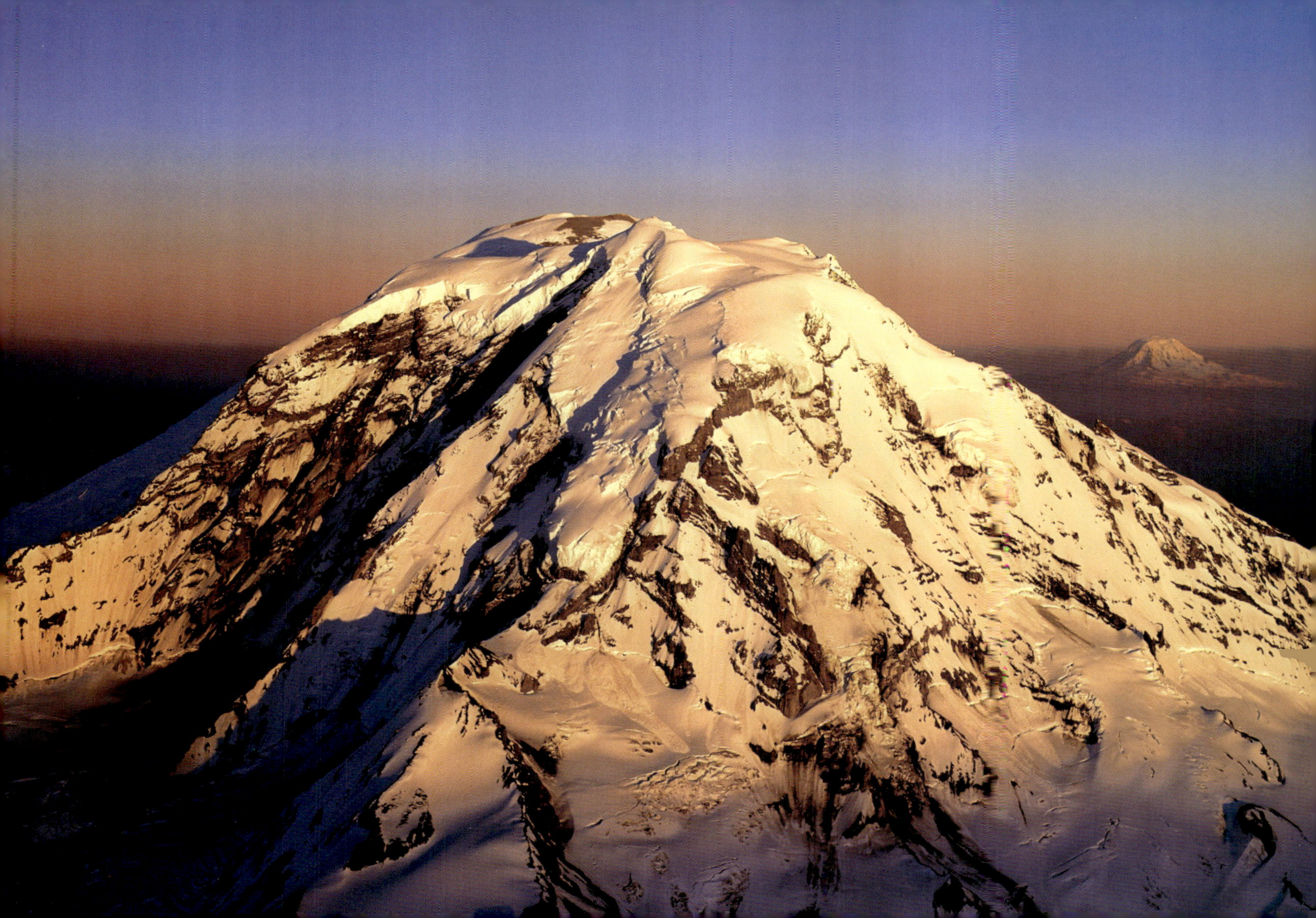

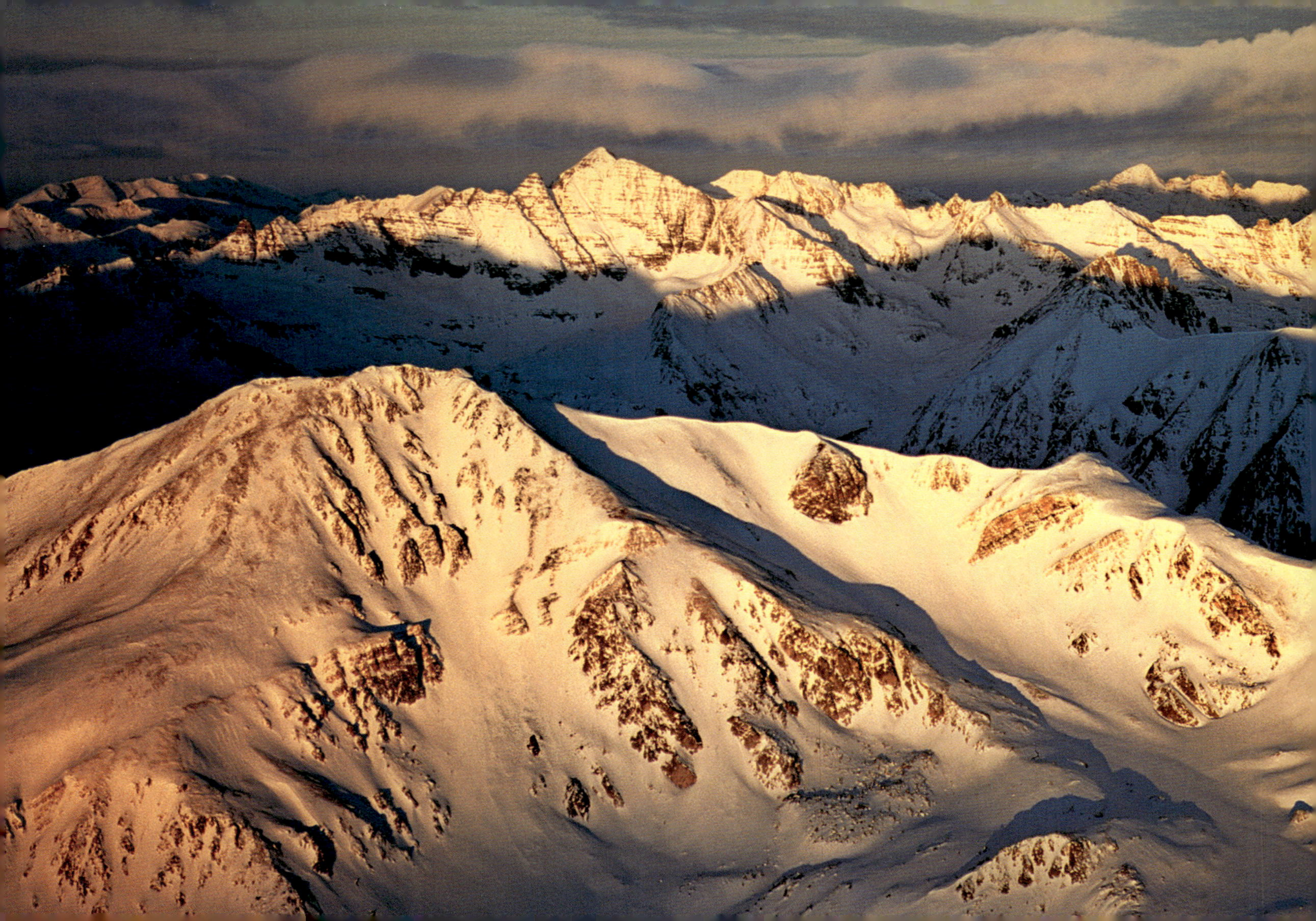

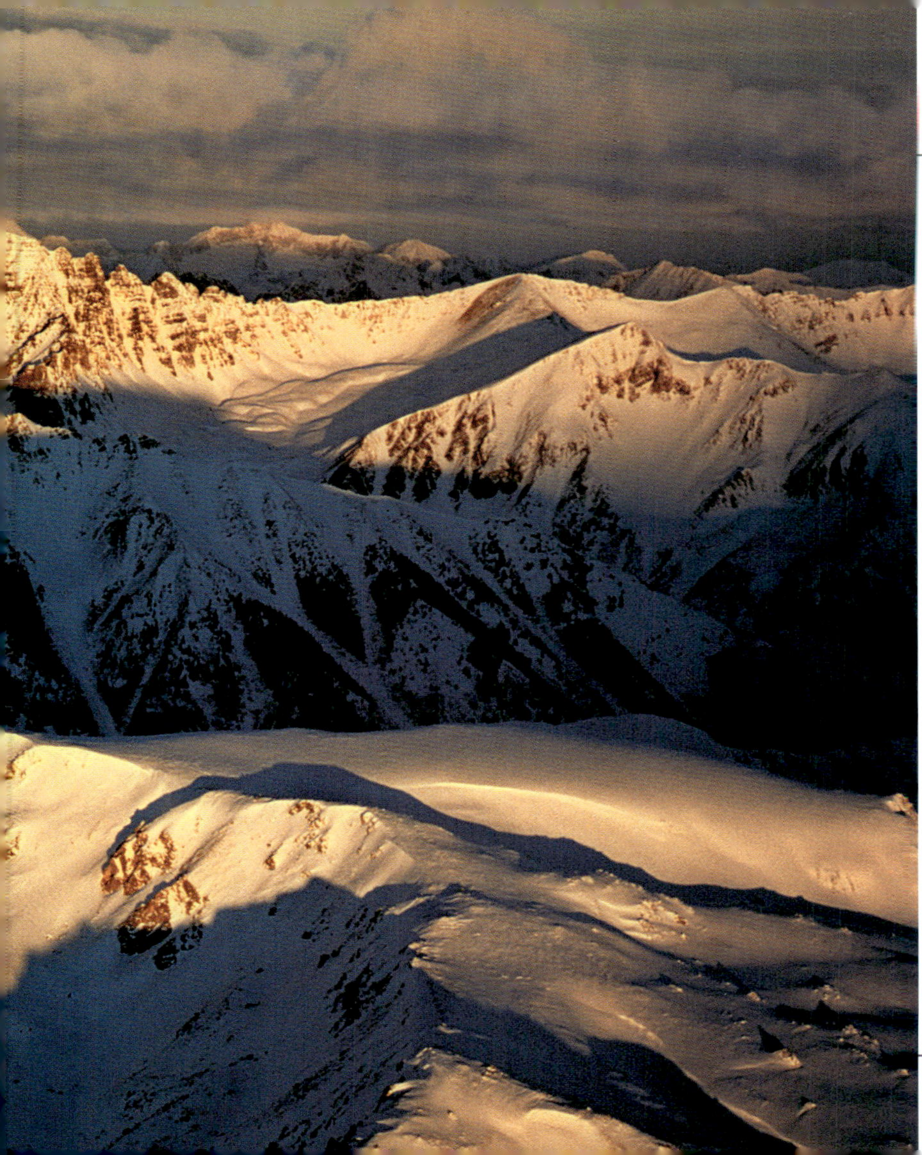

58-259

A magnificent dawn paints the Elk Mountains of Colorado red, making the panorama almost surreal.

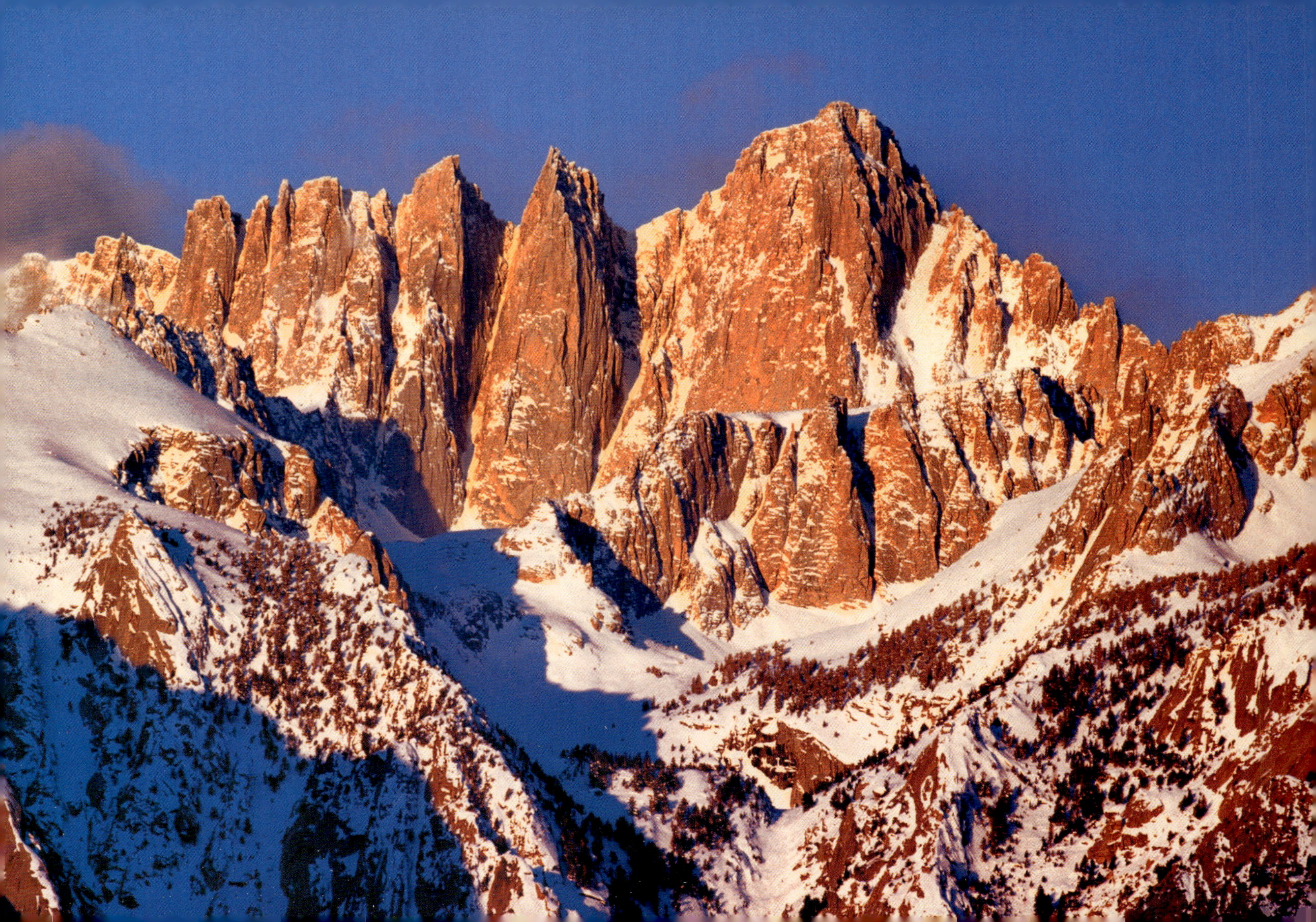

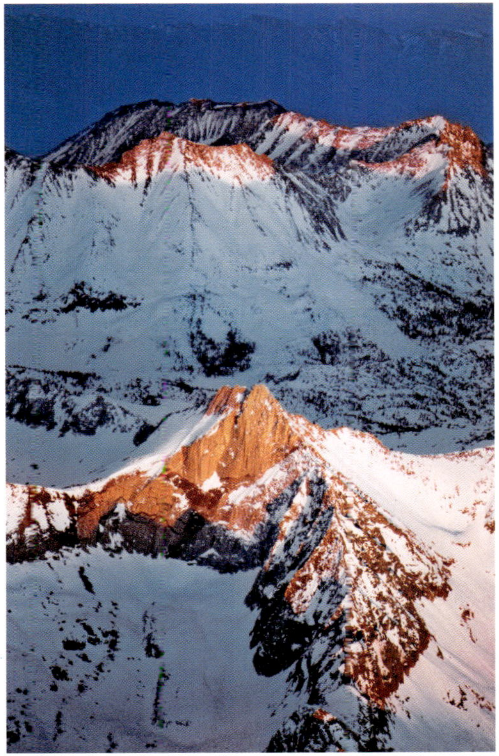

26[illegible]

Mount Whitney, in the Californian Sequoia National Park, is a highly visited tourist spot and also the most frequently climbed peak in the Sierra Nevada.

26[illegible]

The Sierra Nevada extend for about 400 miles down the state of California. The continuous erosion of the mountain chain has created and sculpted spectacular valleys known throughout the world.

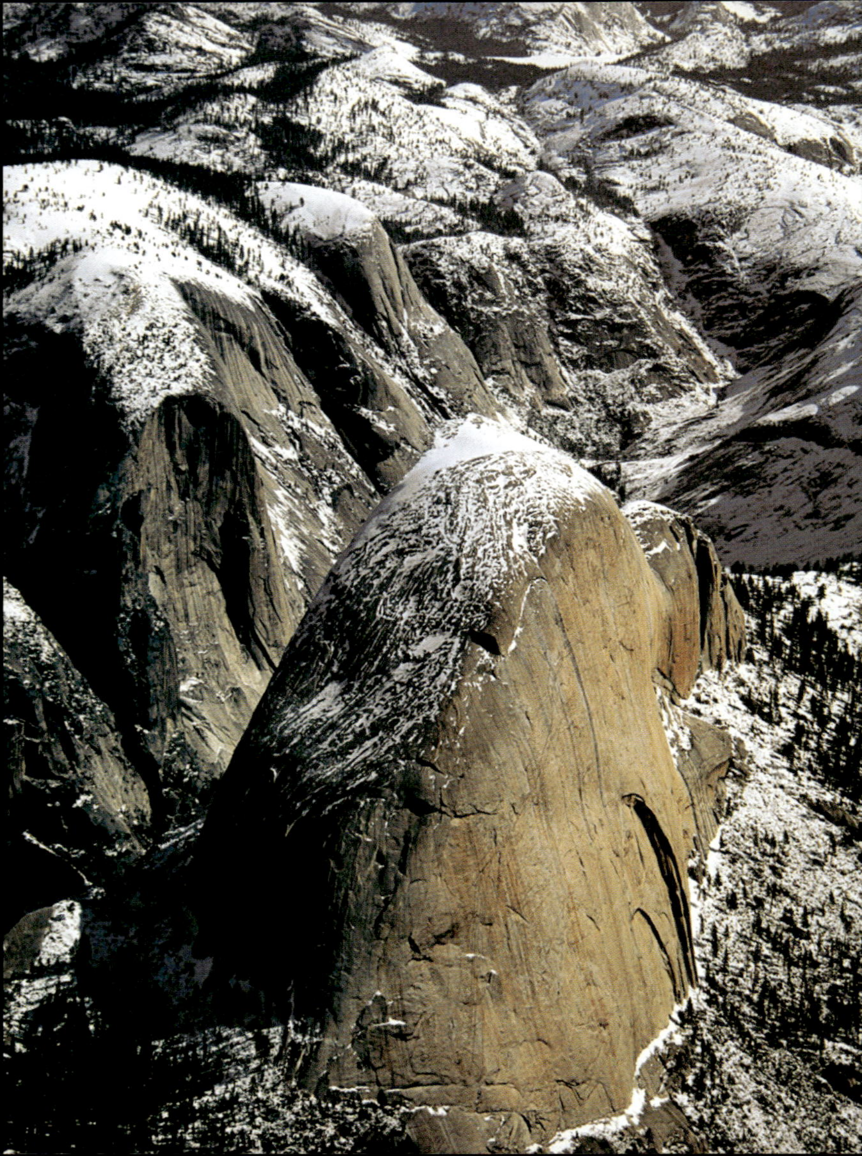

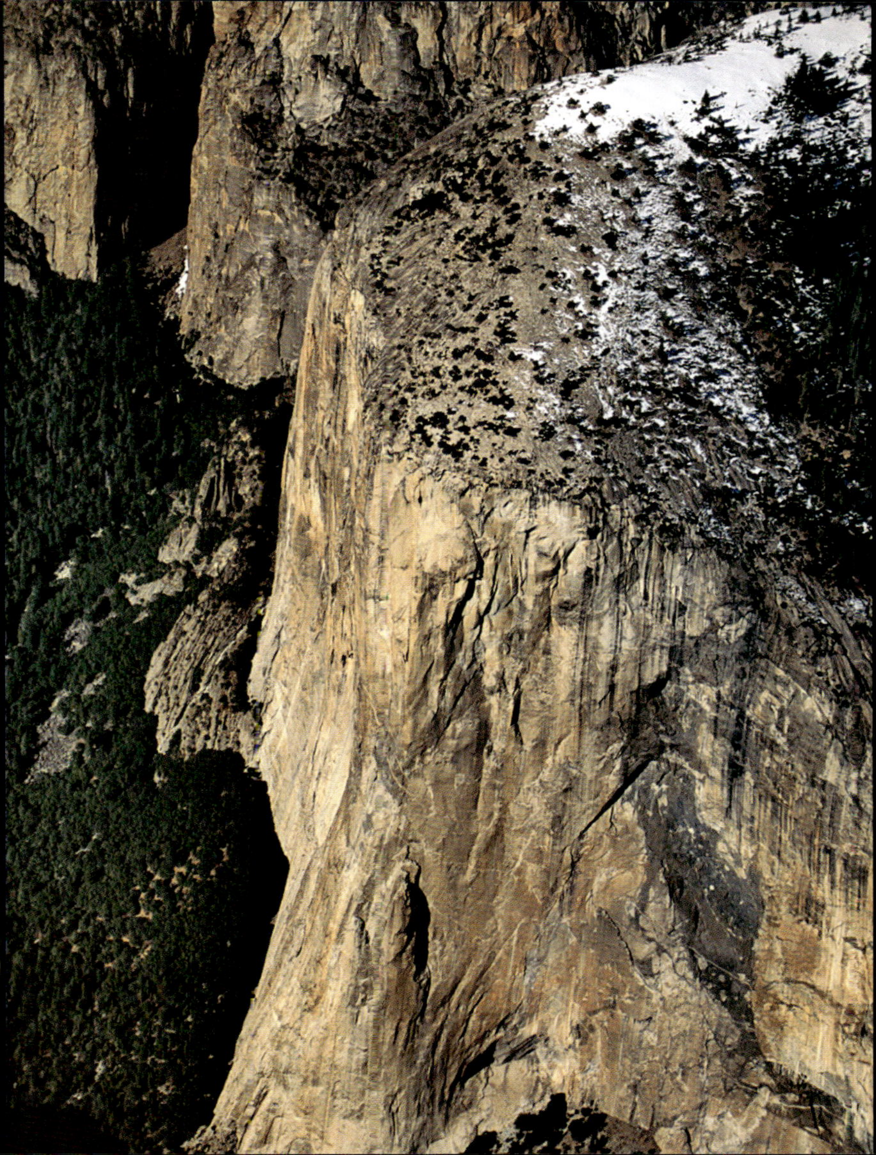

262
Half Dome, in Yosemite National Park in California, reaches up to 8,842 feet. The other half of the Dome is believed to have sunk after the great ice ages.

263
El Capitan, located within Yosemite National Park, is the biggest monolith in the United States and is one of the favorite spots for expert and amateur climbers.

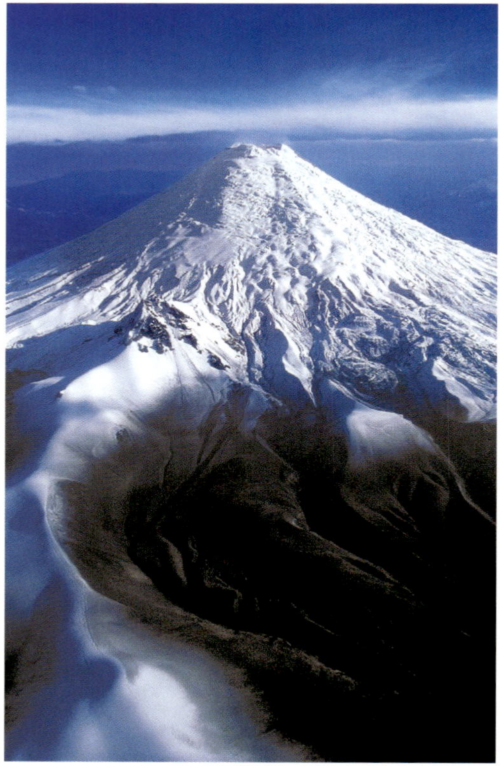

264 and 265
Snow and mist shroud Cotopaxi in Ecuador, a stratovolcano reaching up to 19,394 feet that, from 1738 to today, has erupted 50 times.

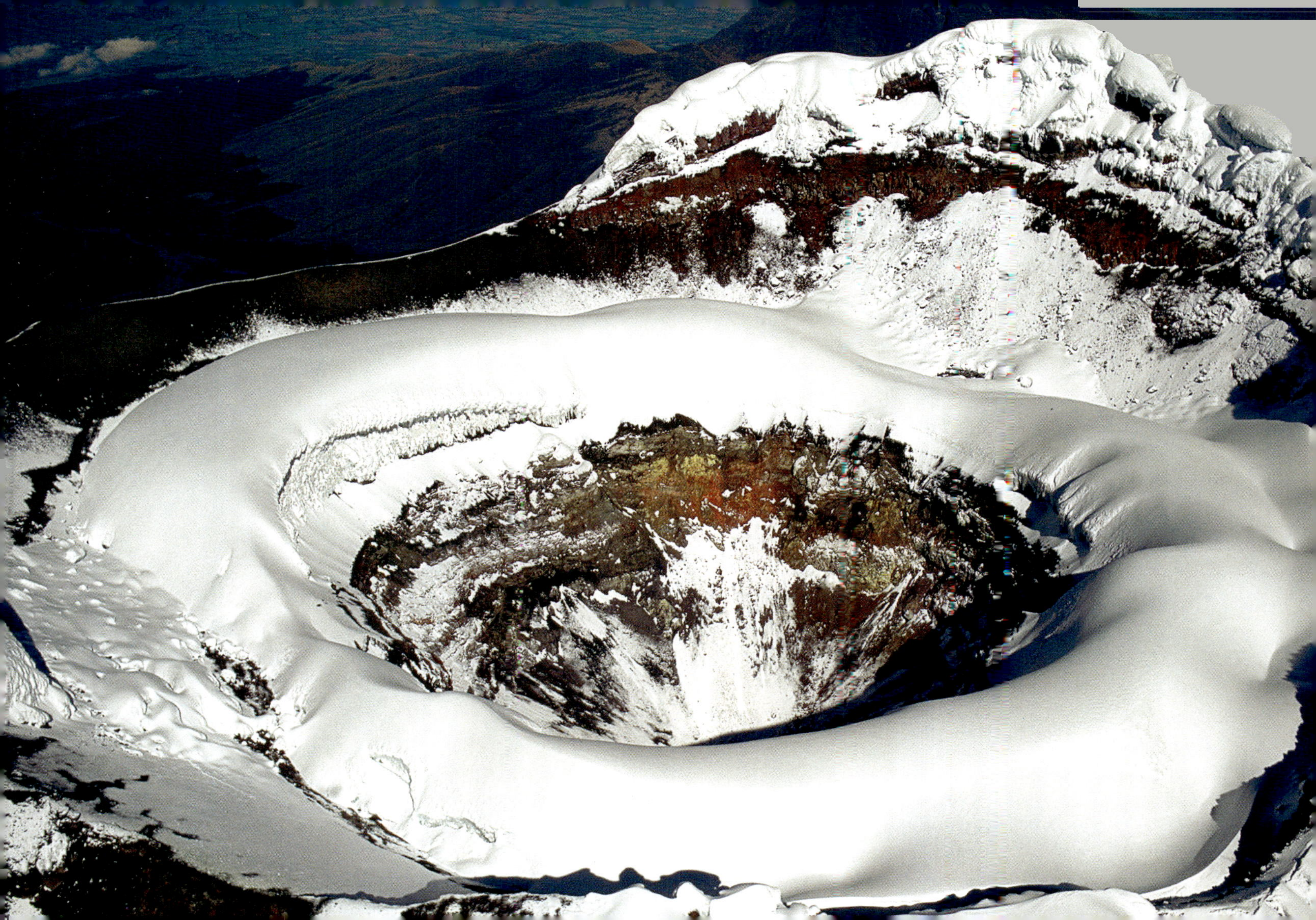

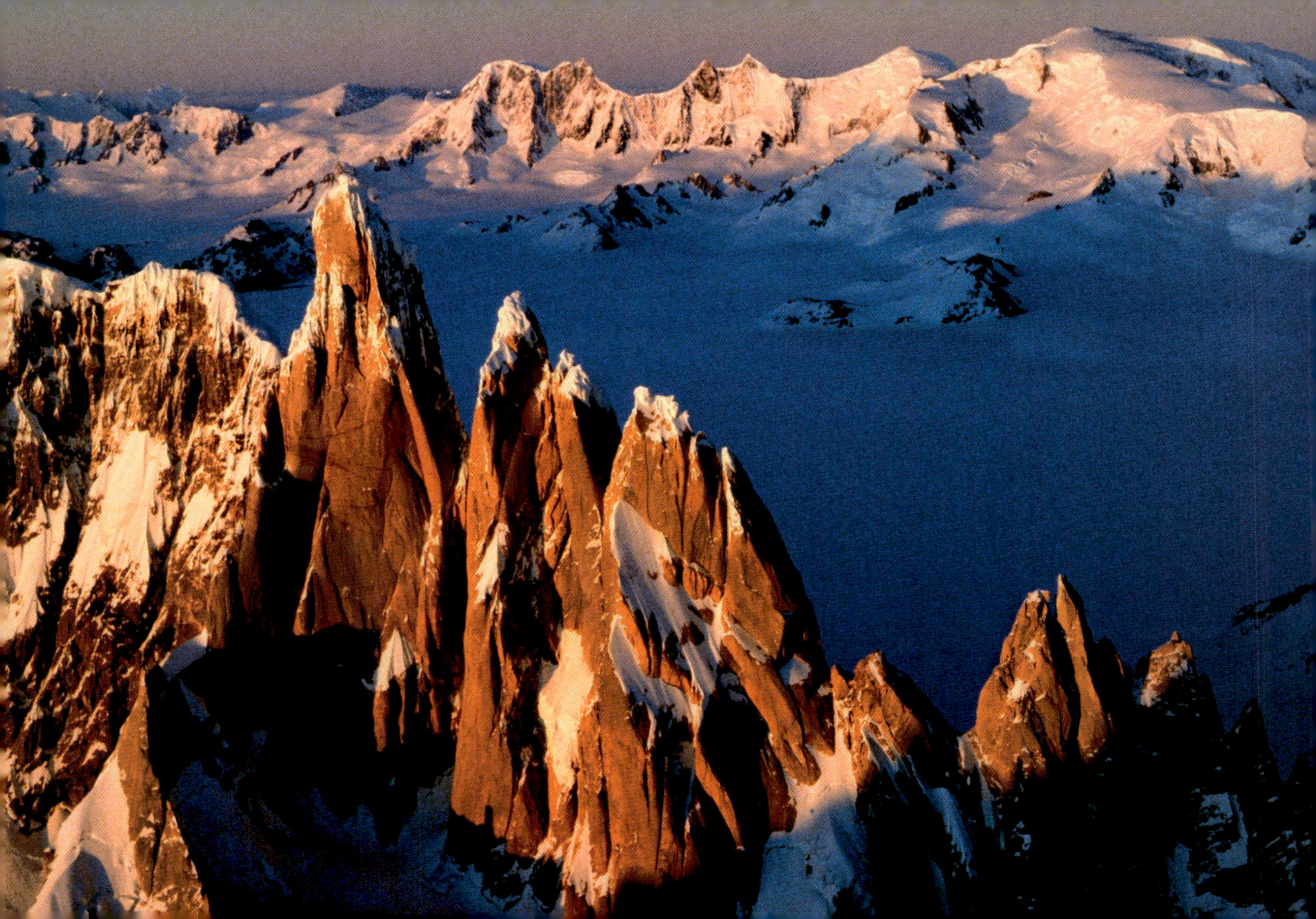

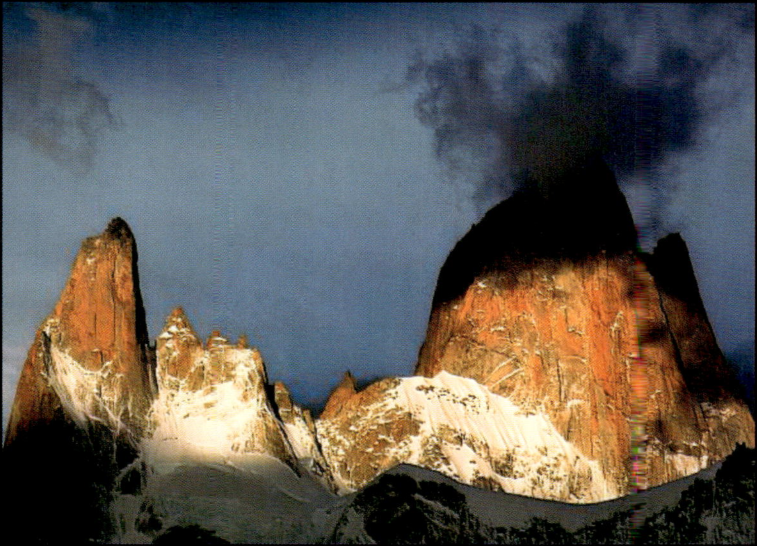

266
The peak of Cerro Torre stands out from the others in Patagonia, at the border between Chile and Argentina.

267
A cloud shadows the peak of Mount Fitz Roy in Patagonia, which the indigenous peoples call *El Chalten*.

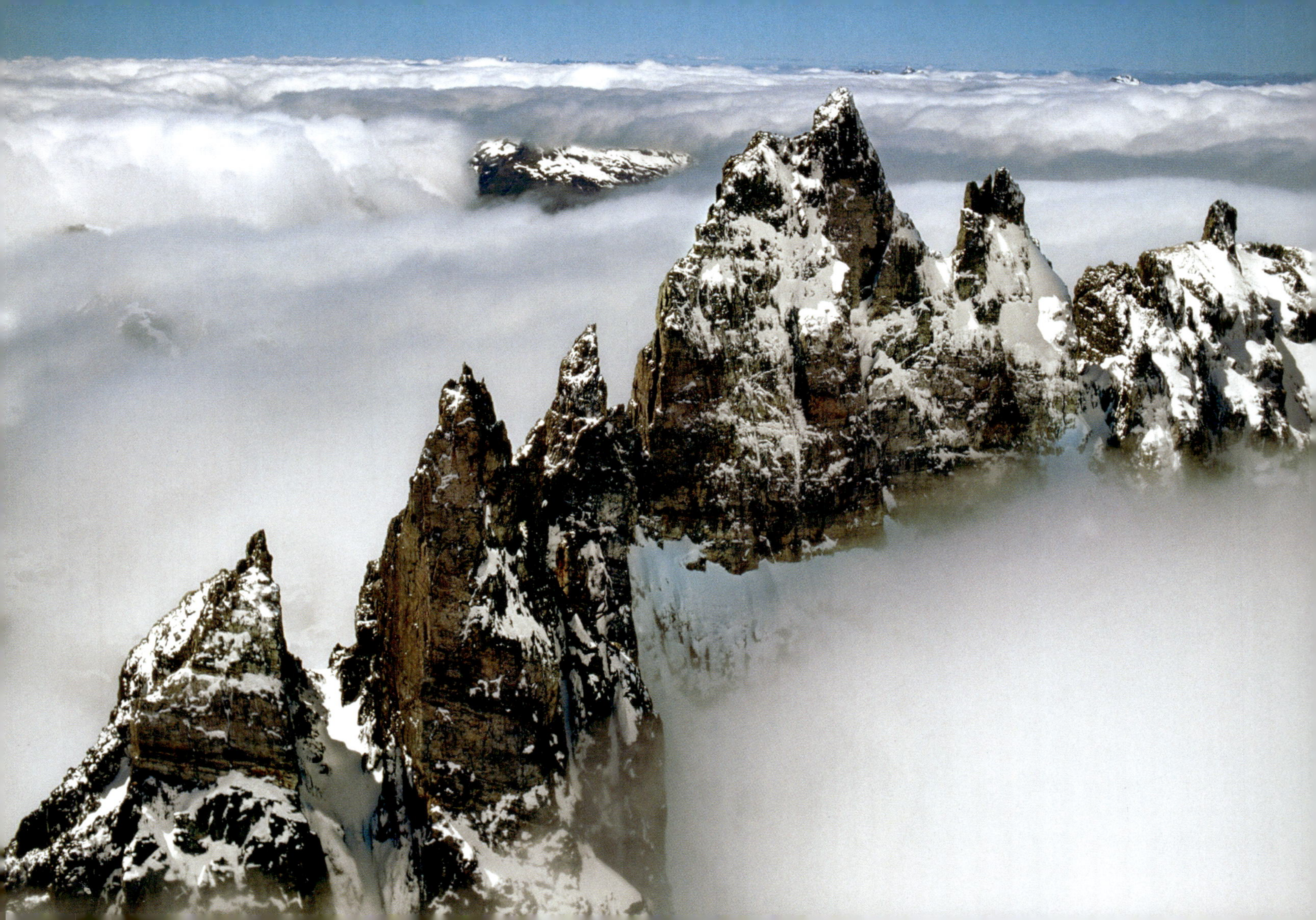

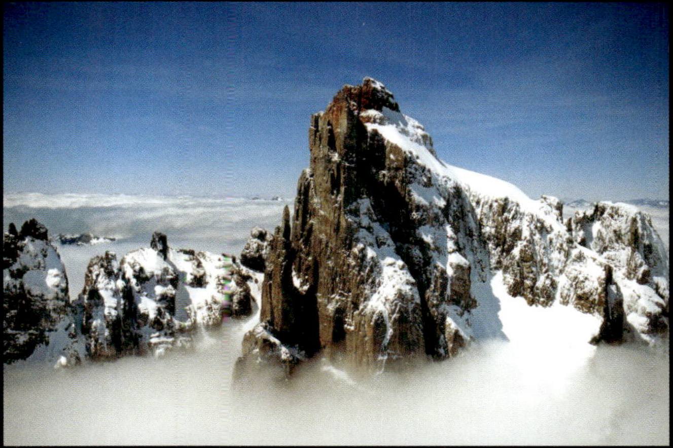

268

The indented peaks of the Andes, in Patagonia, seem to perforate the dense blanket of clouds stretching as far as the horizon.

269

An ice-covered Andean peak rises towards the blue sky of Patagonia, in Chile.

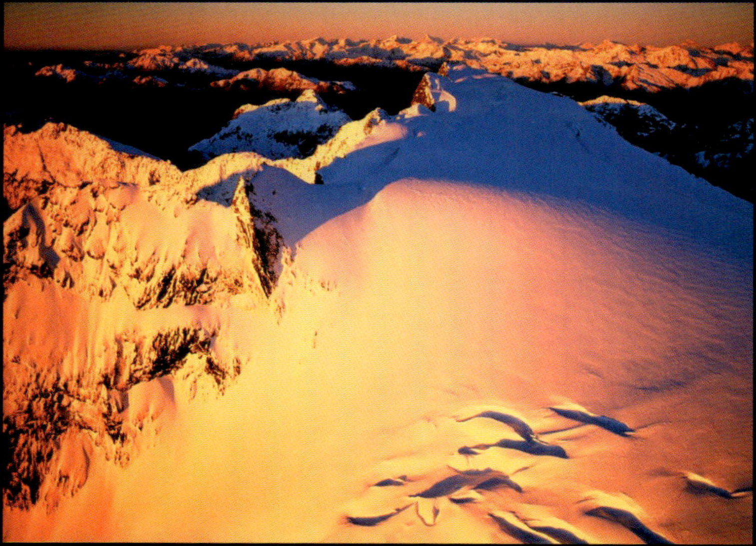

270
The Southern Alps are the biggest and highest mountain chain in New Zealand. A very recent alpine formation, they still continue to grow higher.

271
Sunset creates a magic play of light and shadow on Mount Cook, the tallest peak in New Zealand (12,317 feet), where sudden and violent snowstorms are very frequent.

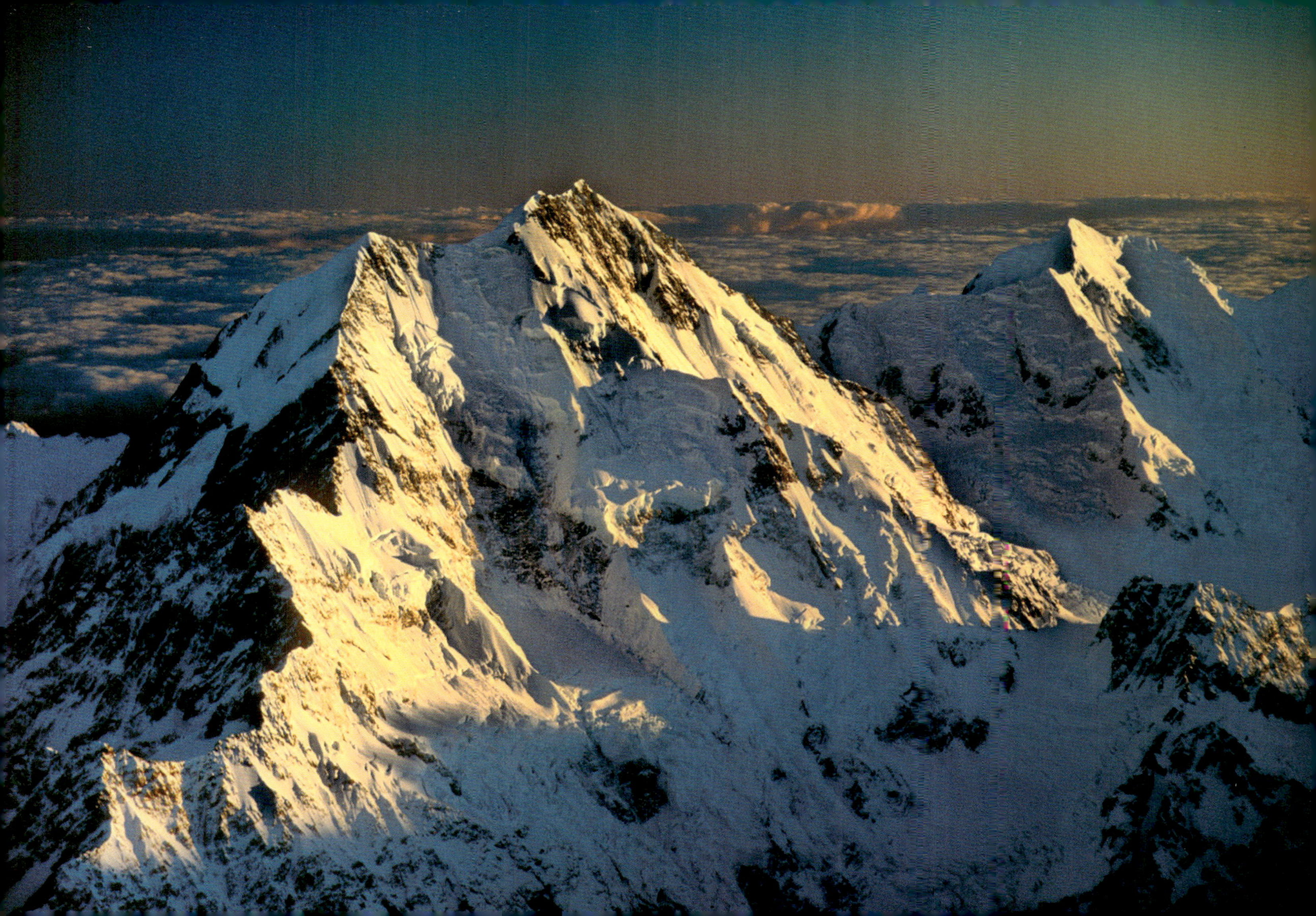

WHERE THE WORLD BREATHES

FLYING HIGH

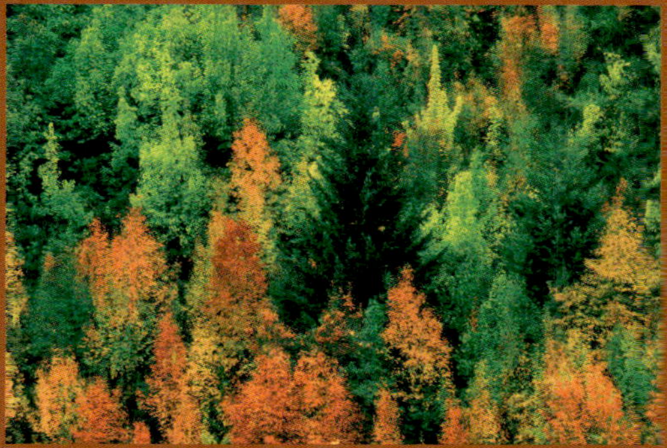
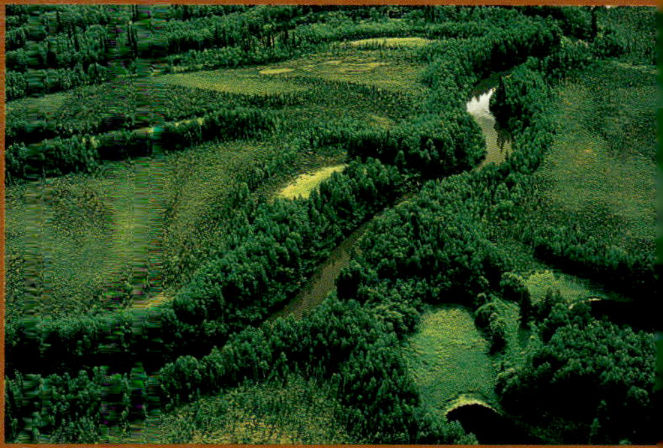

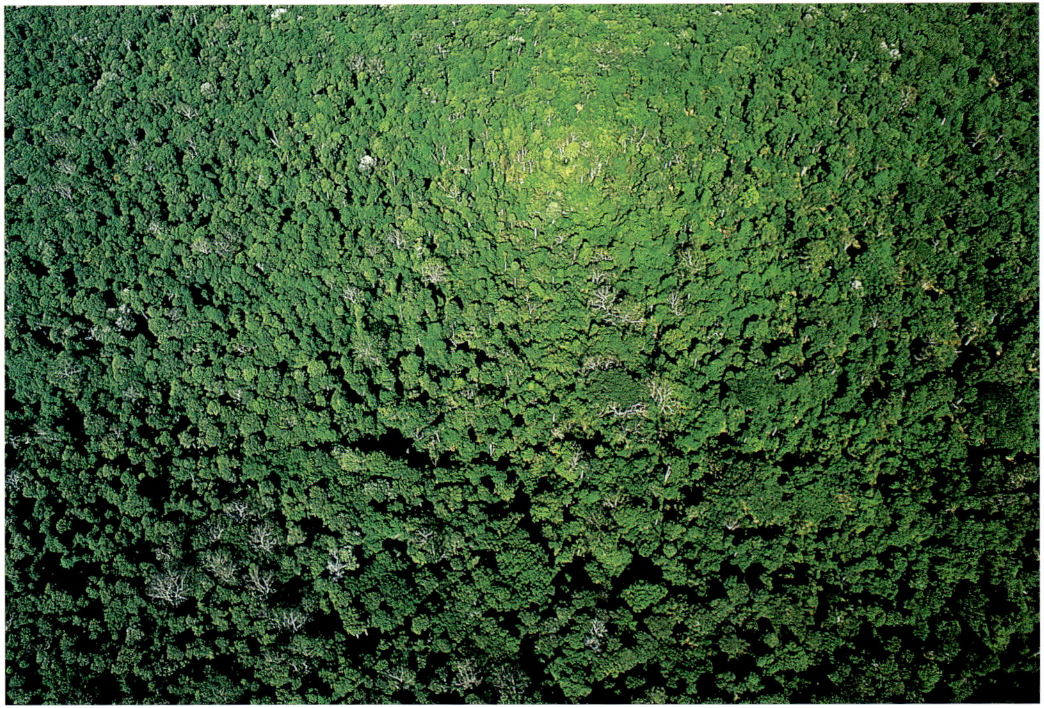

273
Woods near Arrowtown, in New Zealand (left); the Canadian taiga in the area of Fairbanks (right).

The forest, like the sea, is divided into more than one visible level. There is a "bottom" and a "top" in the world's great forests, like the surface of the ocean, which separates two environments as different as air and water can be, or the upper atmosphere and the ever denser void of space. A comparison proposed by some for the Amazon, for example, is actually extreme: it mentions hell, a green inferno, the underworld, Hades. A certain basis in truth, at least to the eyes of anyone who was not born in the forest, cannot be denied: "spider-eating birds and bird-eating monkeys" are the best one can hope for, according to Nick Nichols, a nature photographer for National Geographic, in the event of an emergency landing in the middle of that inconceivable extension of land covered by enormous trees. Thus, the lower level is hostile. Seen from the sky, on the other hand, and observed from "the top," the taiga, the forests of Congo and Queensland, and the huge expanses of conifers in Canada are distant oceans, dotted by islands that may be plateaus like that of Venezuela from where Angel Falls – discovered just in theme with the subject-matter of this book, by an American explorer-aviator in 1930 –, the tallest waterfall on the planet, hurdles 3,000 feet into the void, or the green domes drawn by the foliage of the tallest of the giant trees.

The Amazon offers some of the most impressive views from the sky in the world. It is truly difficult to not think of an ocean when one flies over the biggest forest on the globe, in addition to being the

274
The island of Rubondo, a floating nature park on Lake Victoria in Tanzania, is a reserve reachable only by air, from which it can be admired in all its beauty, or by boat.

Where the World Breathes

most threatened simply in terms of size. Instinctively, something seems to be missing. Anxiety over having mysterious depths below you is inevitable. Then, consciously, you notice another strident note echoing among the centuries-old trees. Ever larger clearings start to appear in the mantle of primary forest, essentially intact for the last 80,000,000 years, covering the basin of the Amazon River, but also that of the Congo River and the thousands of short rivers in Sumatra, Borneo, and New Guinea. The famous Trans-Amazon Highway cuts a perfectly straight line across thousands of miles of forest: the visual impact is a marvel, whereas the environmental impact is disastrous.

There are two main types of forest: tropical and temperate. They have the domineering natural tendency to expand their territory wherever they encounter no obstacles and to fill any void where the conditions of the soil, climate, and human settlement patterns allow it.

This tendency is clearly visible: just think of the incredibly precise border marking the passage between the Oregon forests and the deserts to the east, winding along mountain crests like the back of an antediluvian monster. Here, the woods rule; a few feet in and even grasses no longer grow.

Temperate forests like the Siberian taiga are among the most impressive in this sense. It is an enormous river of tall thin conifers – often separated by just enough space to throw long shadows onto the fields of snow or the prairies – running across northern Asia, between a wide tundra shore and another of continental desert. No less remarkable are the enormous temperate broad-leafed woods of the eastern regions of the United States, often made up of primary forest never touched by man, full of maple, beech, birch, chestnut, and oak trees. They are all trees that make the ancient mountains east of the Great Plains burn in autumn in a flameless and heatless fire, boiling on the slopes of the shallow valleys.

The Black Forest, in Germany, bears this color even

Where the World Breathes

from the top level, quilted with conifers in schwarz grün, a *black-green* so intense it swallows the sunlight. One can understand why the trolls and witches of the Grimm fairy tales sought a life there, far from man, in that ambiguous era when the forest was much, much bigger. Straight roads cut through all that darkness, stretching on across a territory that must not be disturbed by invasive curves. Clearings open a passage like islands in negative relief within this sea smelling of resin.

A more "domestic" aspect characterizes the woods sprinkled around the long-colonized countryside, like those of Devon and Wiltshire in England, or the vast forest areas of France and Germany, in a certain sense under siege by civilization but still big enough to be considered the prized "lungs" of Europe. The state of New Hampshire, in the northeast United States, features an open fan of hills with ample slopes, which divide equally airy valleys, 200,000,000 million years old. The whole area is empty, expect for along the perfect bends of the Saco River, rounded and continuous for miles. Every foot of its shores and the countryside of the valley is lined by wild but controlled woods. Order, the *mundus*, exudes everywhere, in the settled areas and in the primary areas, integrated in a perfectly natural fashion, almost as if they were arranged to create one of the most tranquil panoramas imaginable.

The familiar aspect of the copses, with which we have integrated, is apparent even among the bizarre shapes of the giant rhododendrons growing on the southern slopes of the Himalayas, together with the up to 200-foot-tall decdar cedars (at 6,500-10,000 feet high), other conifers, and further down, a leafy population of banyan fig trees, oaks, and beeches. All of this is found at the base of or in the folds of those high-altitude deserts in which the sun, wind, ice, and rock are the only natural elements to resist.

They are places that, because of the elevated altitude, normally only feature barren lands. However,

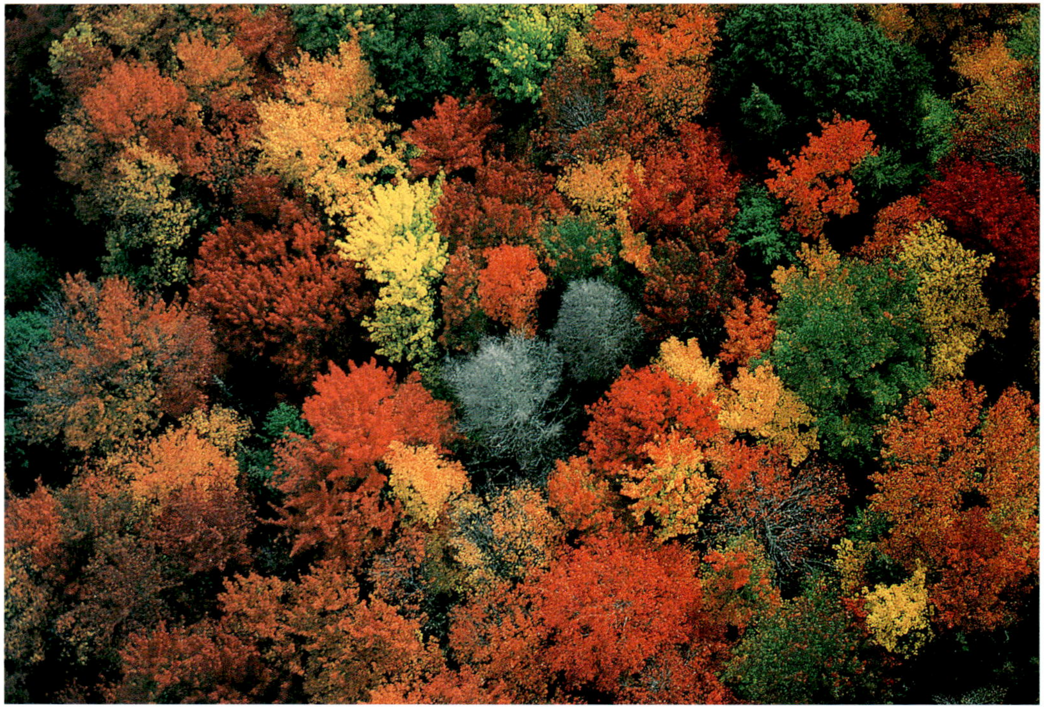

Where the World Breathes

thanks to the rather mild climate, favored by humidity from the plains of northern India, a sort of Asian Switzerland or Austria presents itself to the sky. The woods, duly delimited, give way to large pasture lands dotted with flocks, rolling slopes, and stone villages flying flags unraveled to offer prayers to the Abode of the Snows.

The degree of imperviousness of the forests, much more conveniently evaluated from above than from land, has ensured their own survival and that of the populations living there, human and non, for thousands of years. The woods, places of mystery, Druid altars, and witches' Sabbaths, have been able to conceal their secrets for a very long time. We have only known for less than two centuries that we all depend on the forest mantle in order to breathe. The strange thing is this: until science had clarified the vital relationship between us and plants, the only thing that made us respect them and in part keep us at a distance were ancestral fears, taboos, or even the childish chills inspired by myths and fables.

Today, it is the opposite: we know, but we do not want to see, that the forests are disappearing. Let us observe them, then, these forests; let us study them and convince ourselves that flying over the Amazon in a few years – some maintain not more than 10 to 15 – will be like flying over the desert if nothing changes. Over our desert, created by our own demands.

278
A highly varied spectrum of colors enflames the foliage of New England woods in the northern United States.

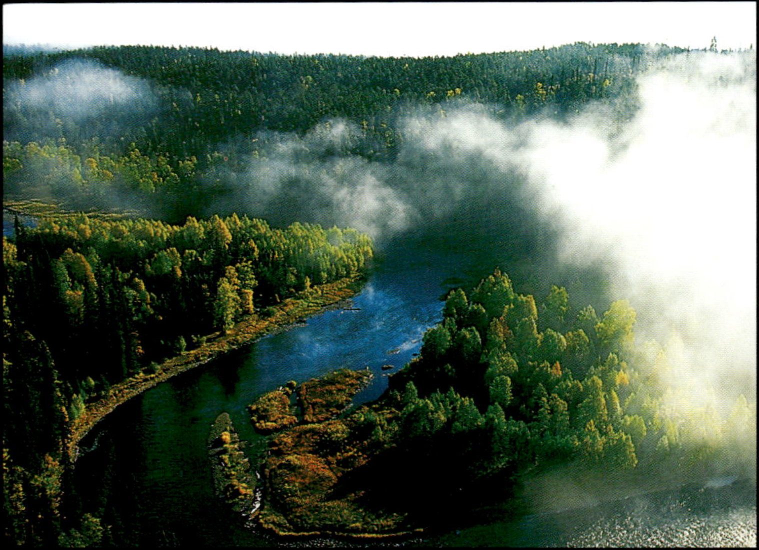

280 and 281
The forests in the Oulanka National Park, in Finland, are crossed by the Kitka River, which runs very swiftly in tracts, with rapids and spectacular waterfalls.

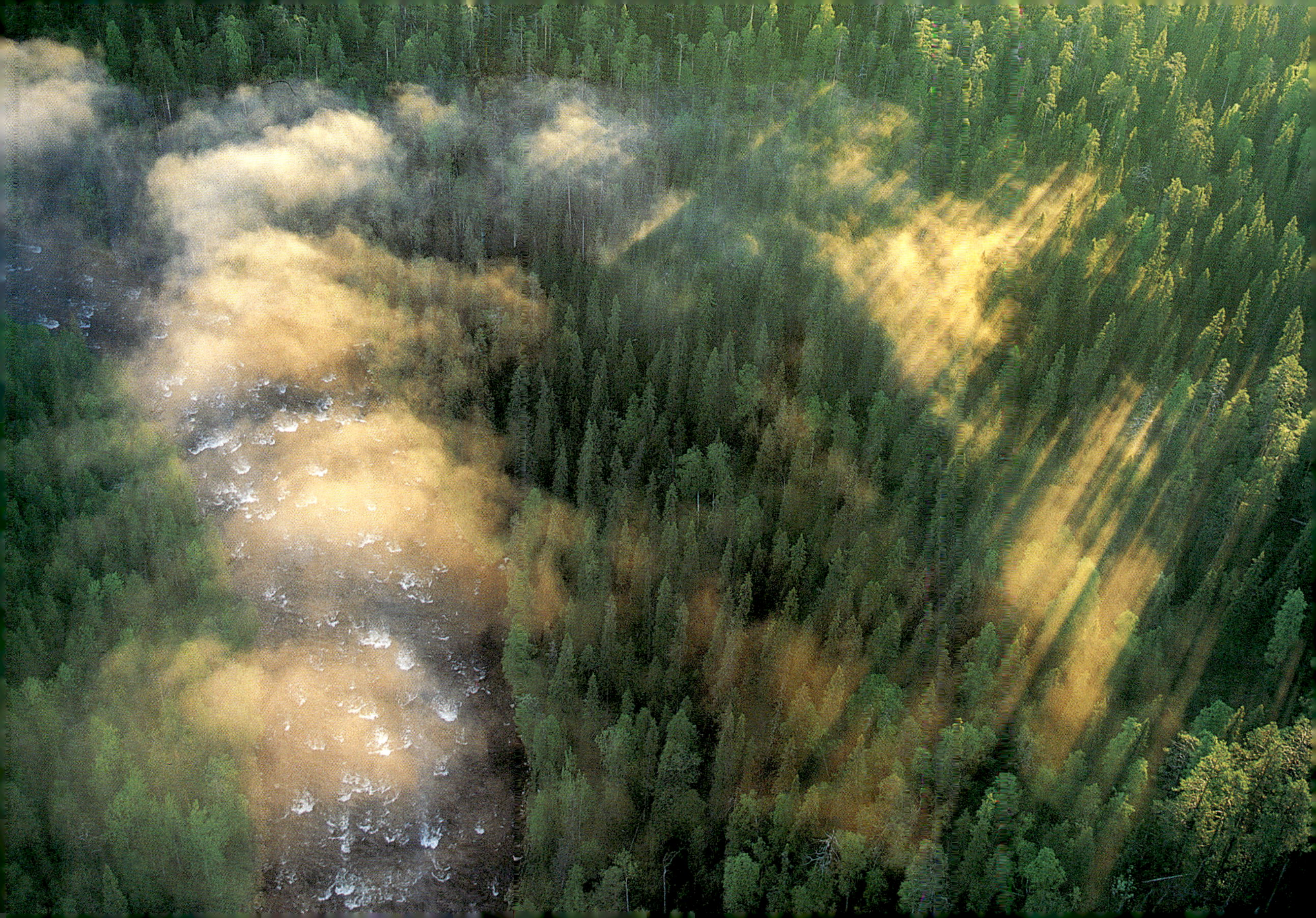

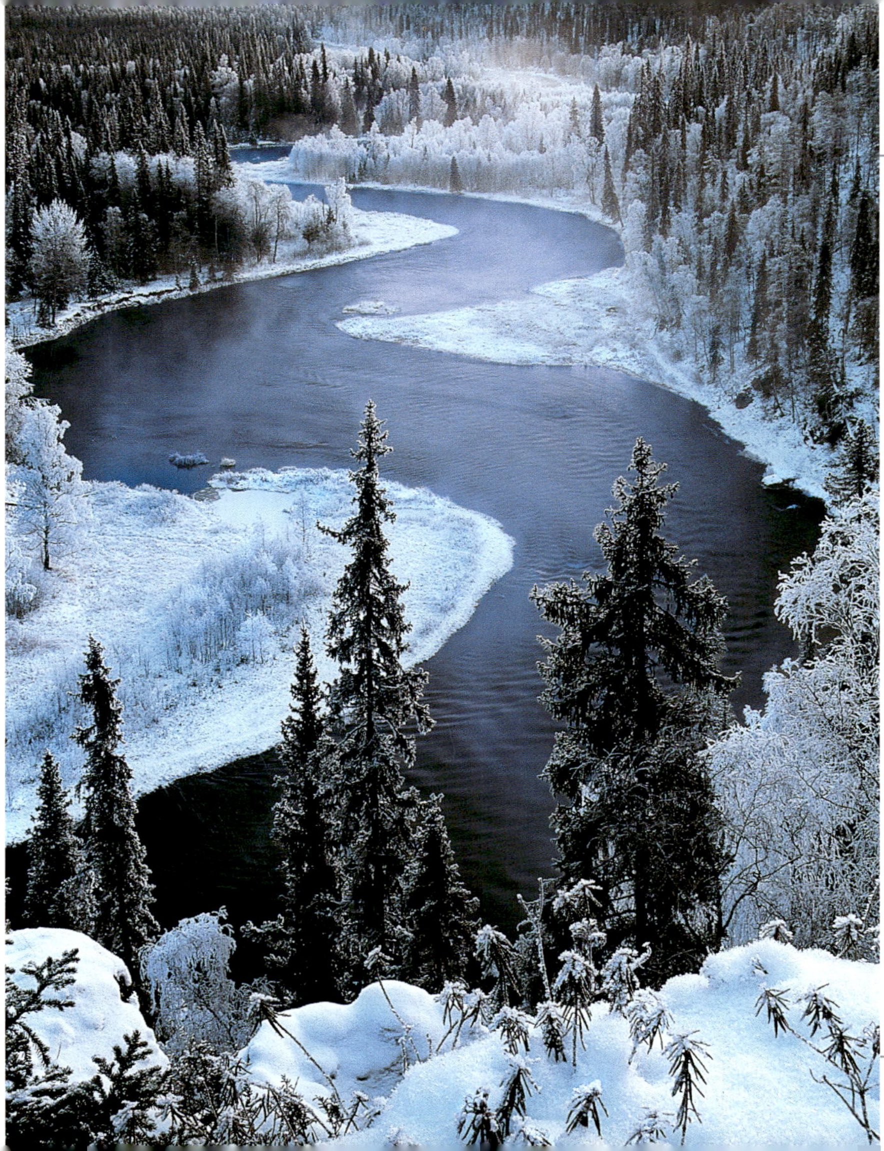

282
During winter, the Finnish Kitkajoki River, which originates near the Kitkkajarvi Lake and flows into the White Sea, is surrounded by frozen woods.

283
The play of shadows on the snow seems to multiply the number of trees in woods in the Oulanka area, in Finland.

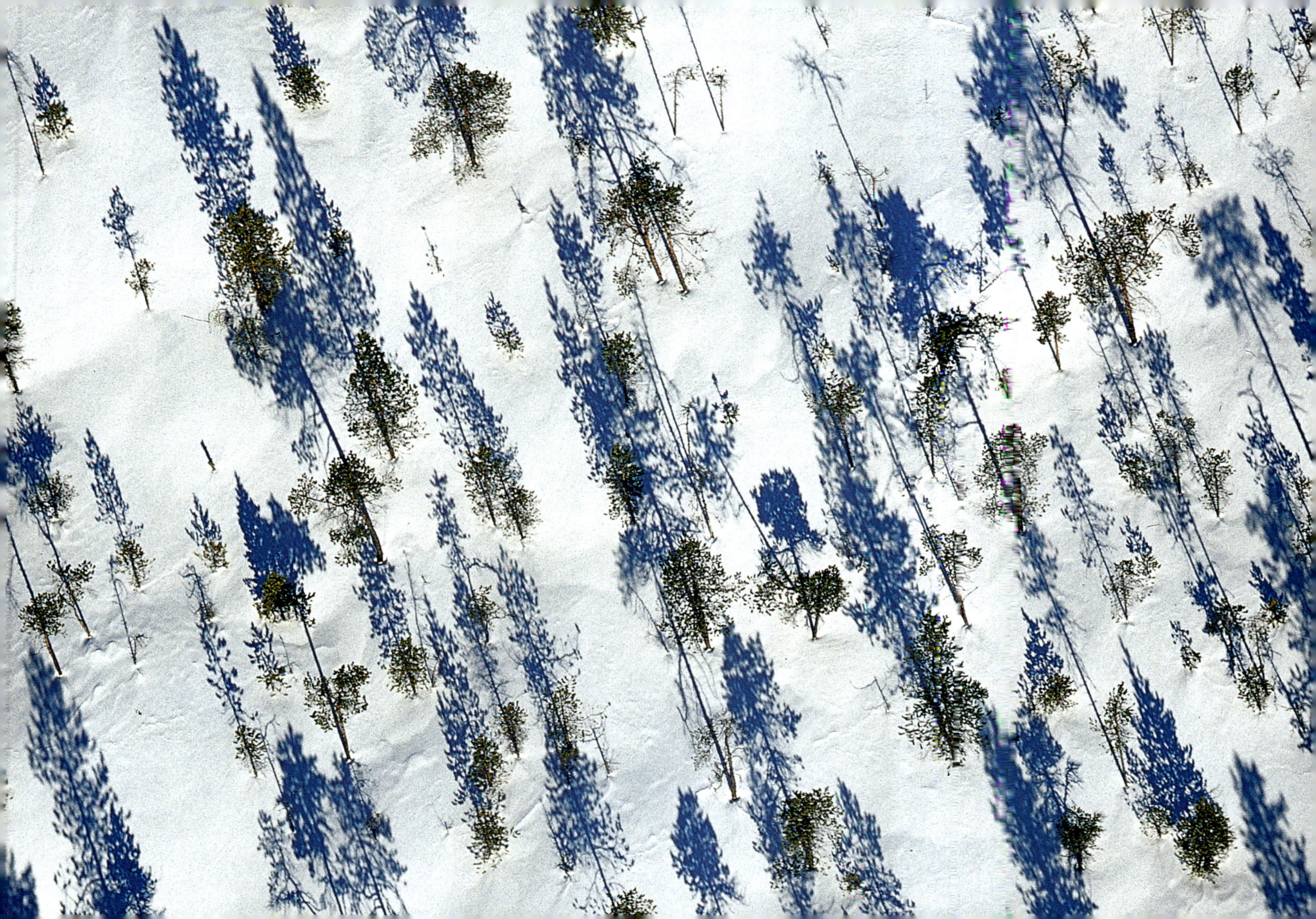

284-285
The forests of the Buskerud highlands, in Norway, are crossed by rivers and dotted by lakes, often created by the river inlets themselves.

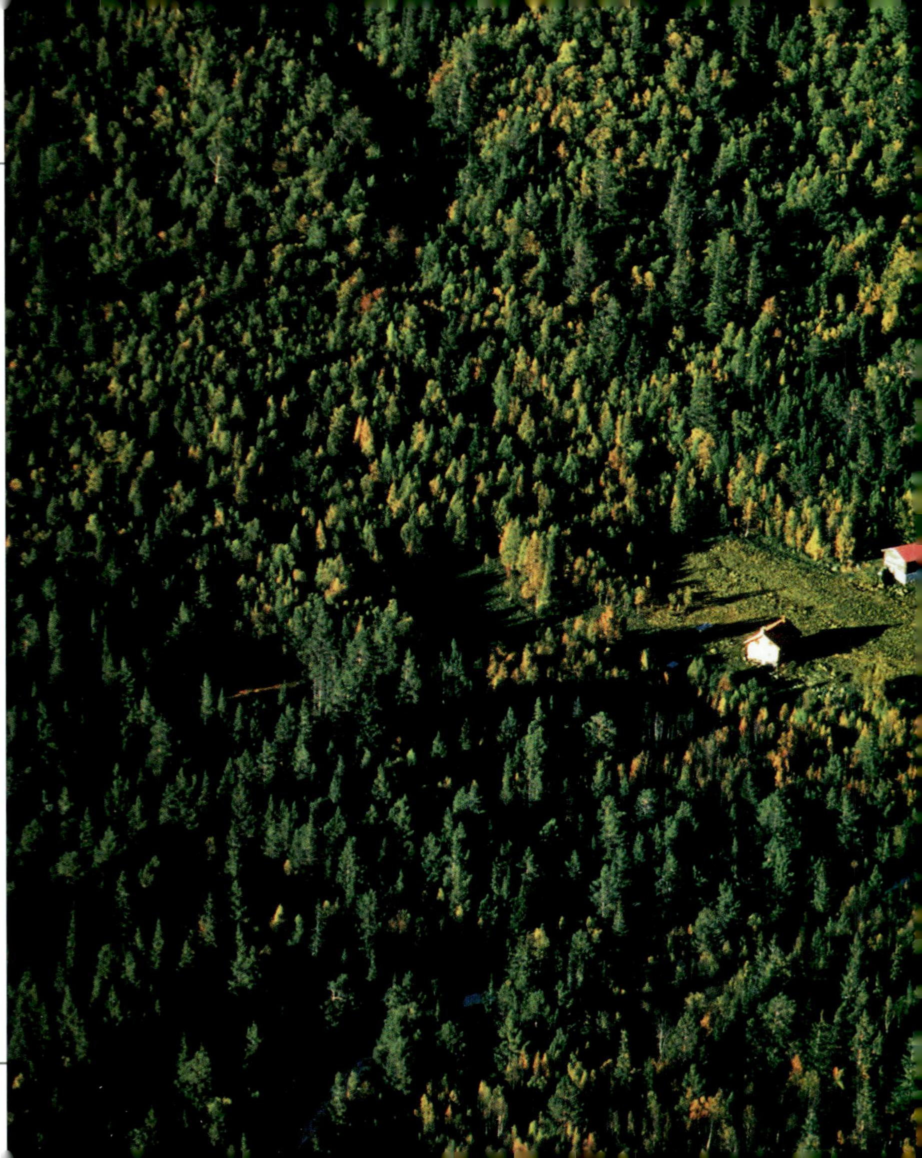

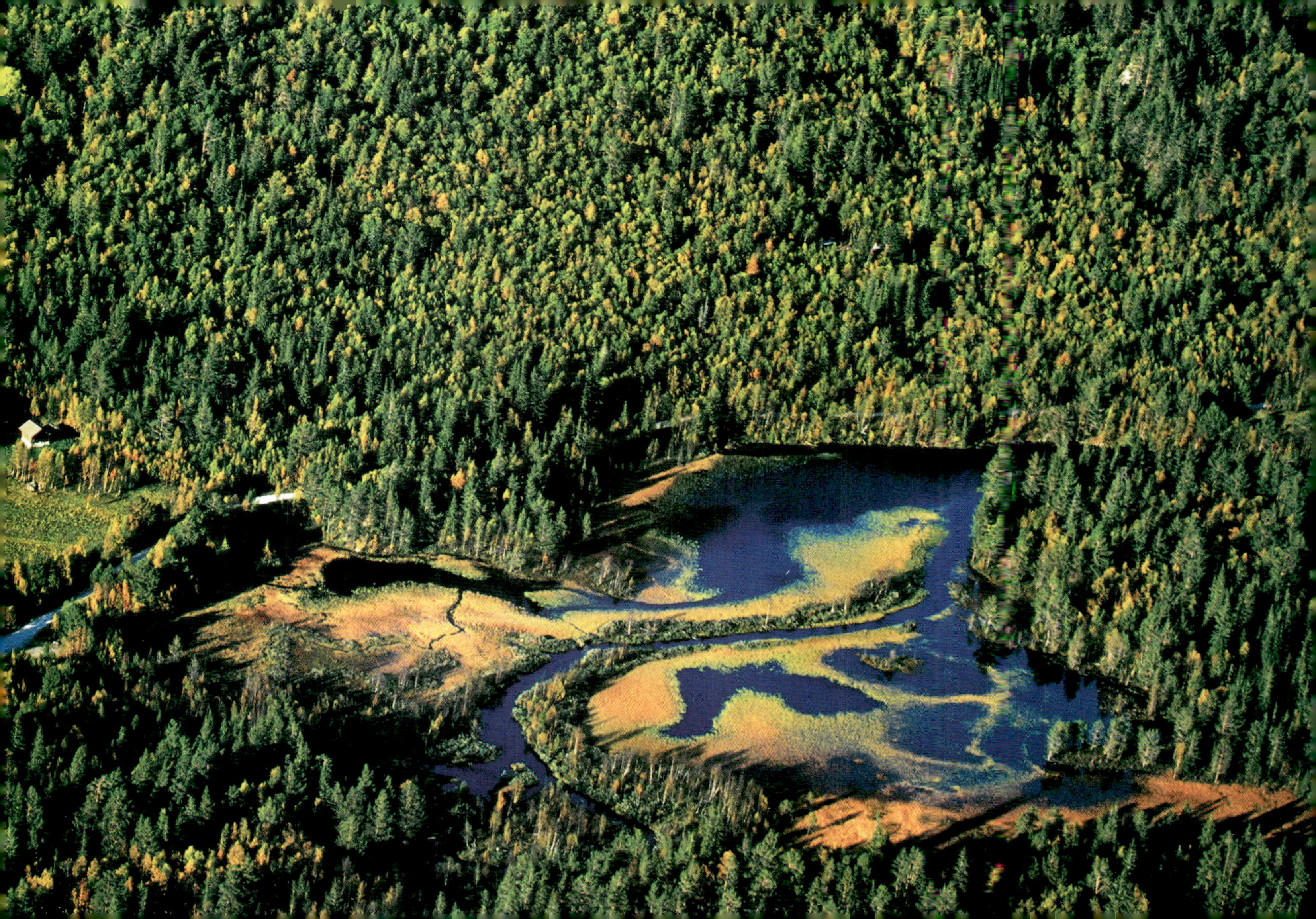

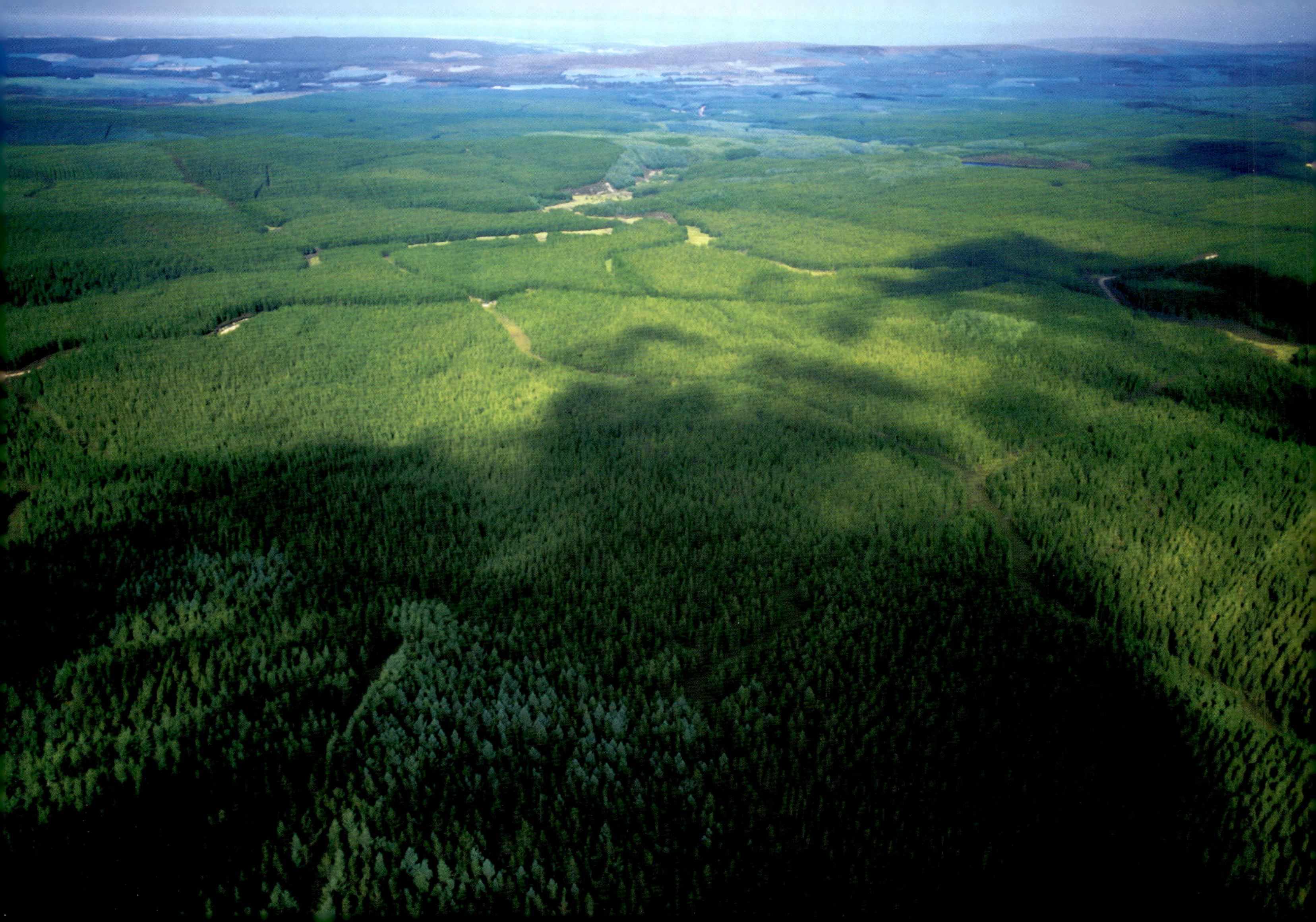

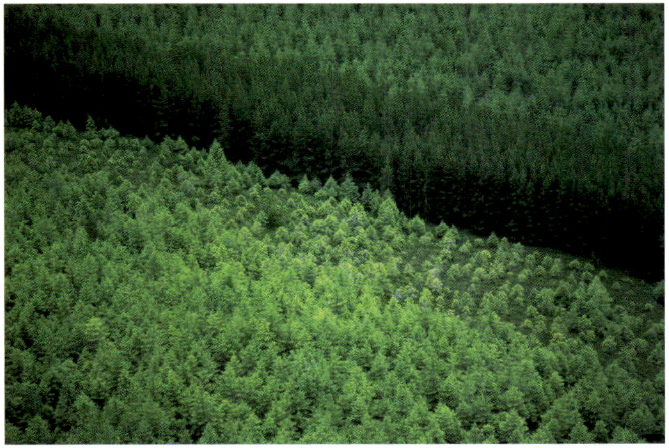

286

The pine forests, an icon of the Scottish Highlands, are considered a fundamental element in the territory's equilibrium, from an ecological but also economic and touristic point of view.

287

The forests lining the course of the Lossie River, in Scotland, are inhabited by countless species of birds and for this reason are excellent for bird watching.

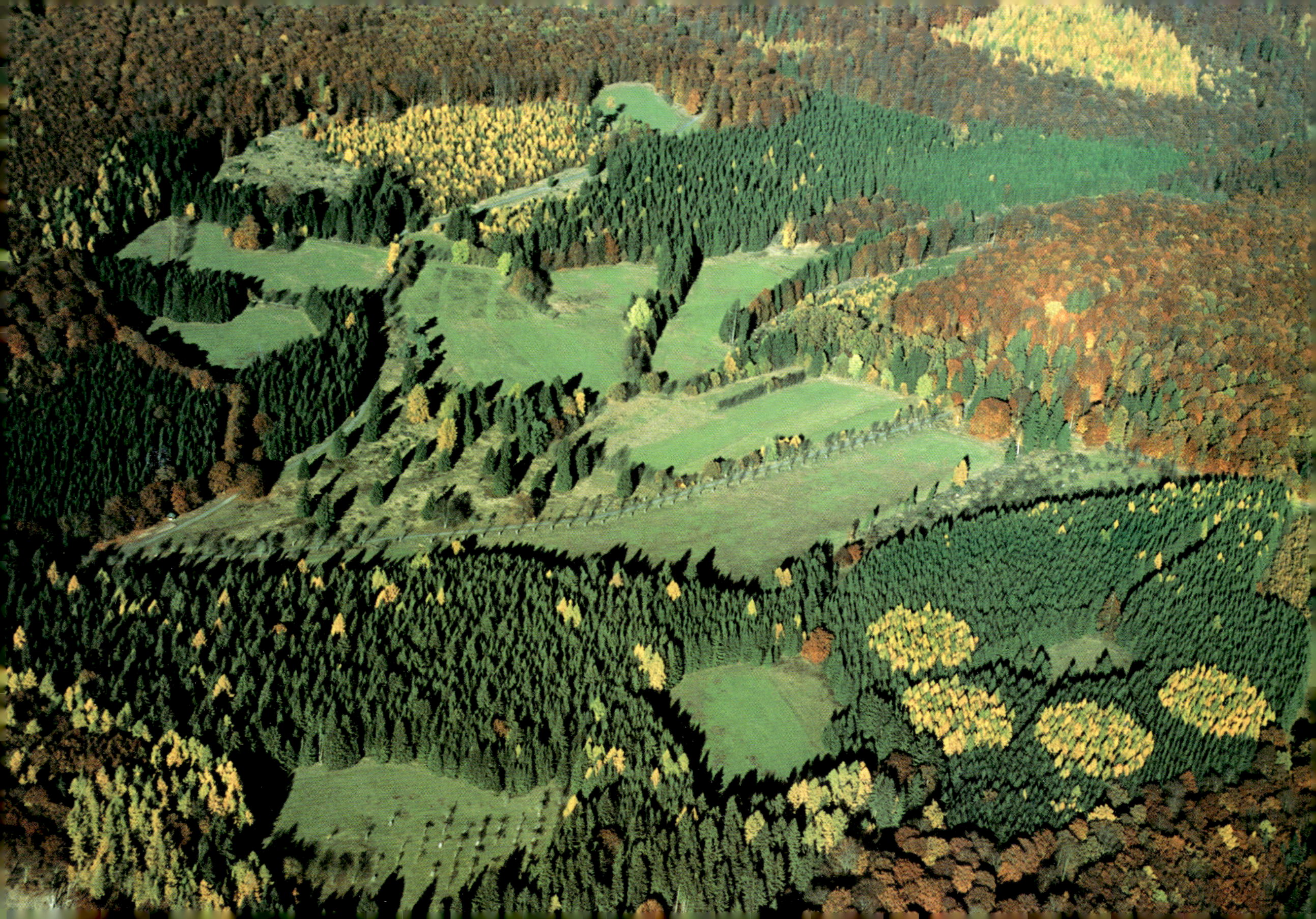

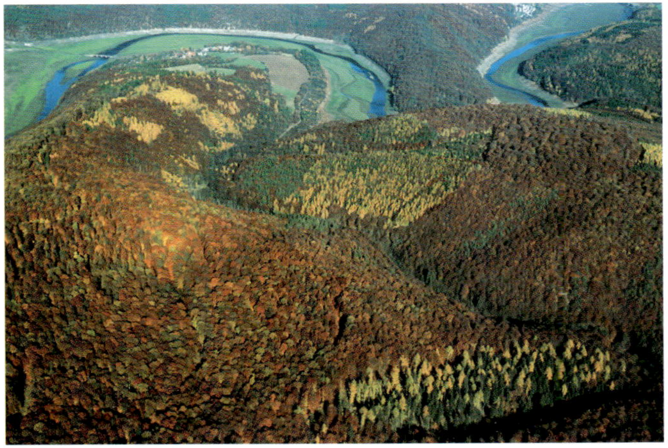

288 and 289
The play of color and the contrasting volumes of the woods, fields and rivers give movement to the natural scenery in the Kellerwald National Park in Land Nordhessen in Germany.

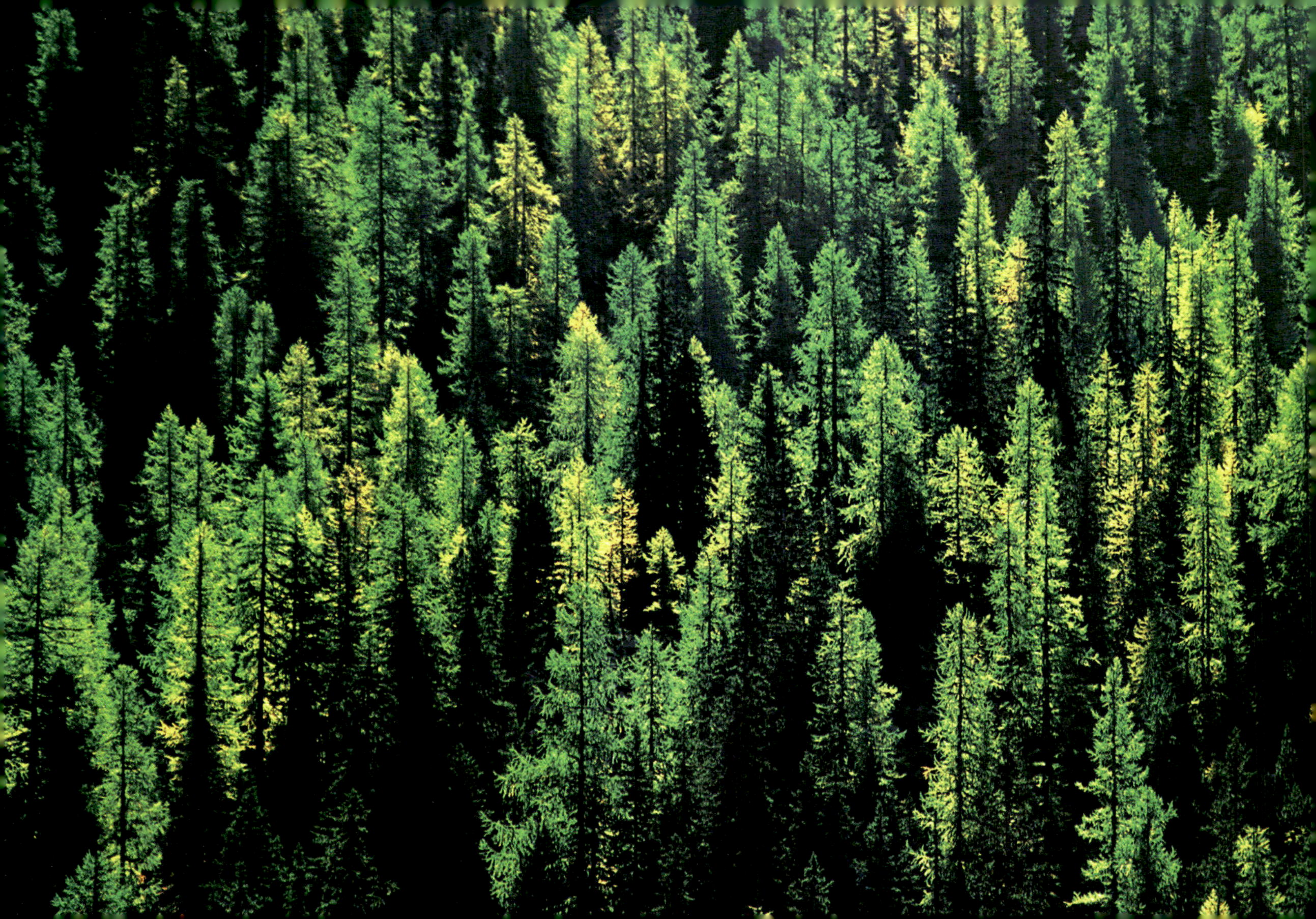

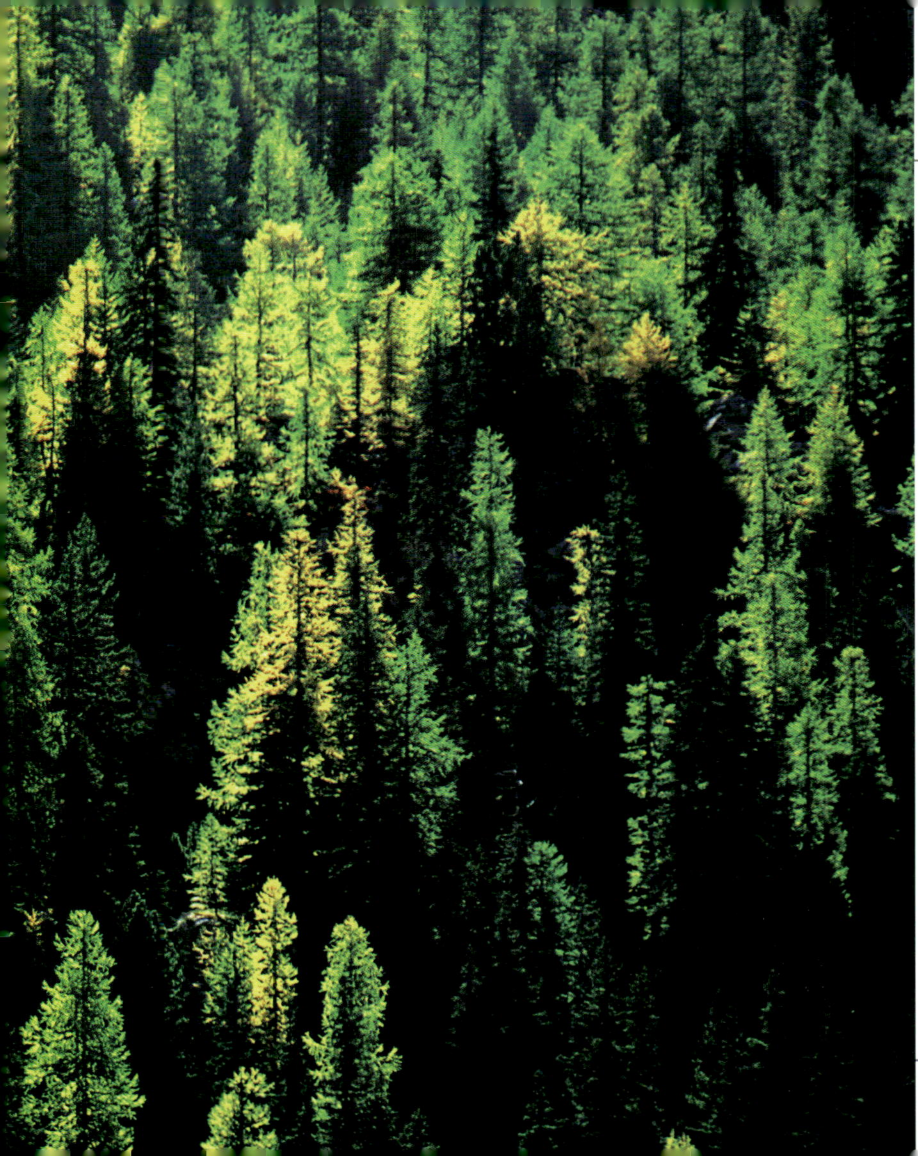

290–291
Beyond the line of broad-leaved trees and larches, in the Lombard valley of Valmalenco in Italy, coniferous forests dominate up to an altitude of 6,500 feet.

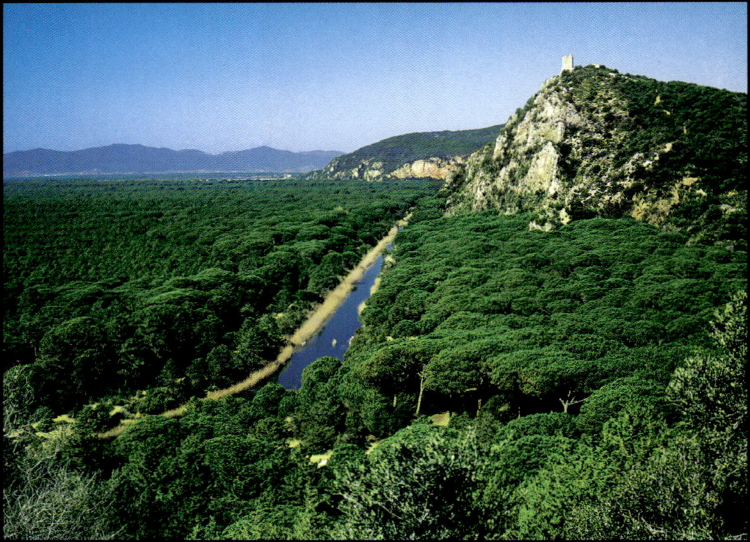

292
The Tuscan nature reserve of the Uccellina, in Italy, constitutes a precious mosaic of ecosystems, whose main form of vegetation is represented by Mediterranean scrub.

293
In southern Italy, coniferous woods, like this one between Salerno and Paestum, consist mainly of Mediterranean stone pines, unmistakeable with their characterisitc umbrella-shaped foliage.

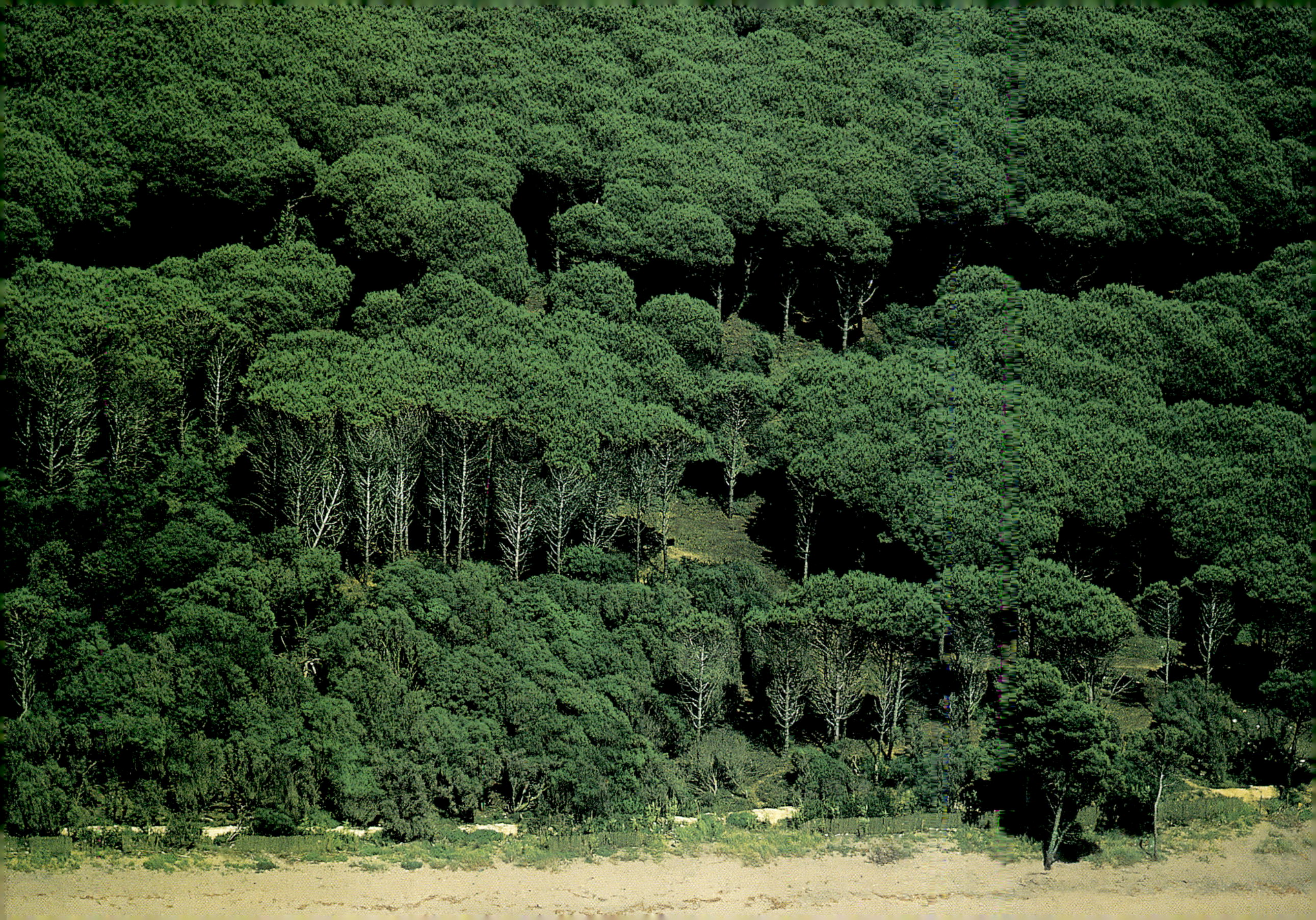

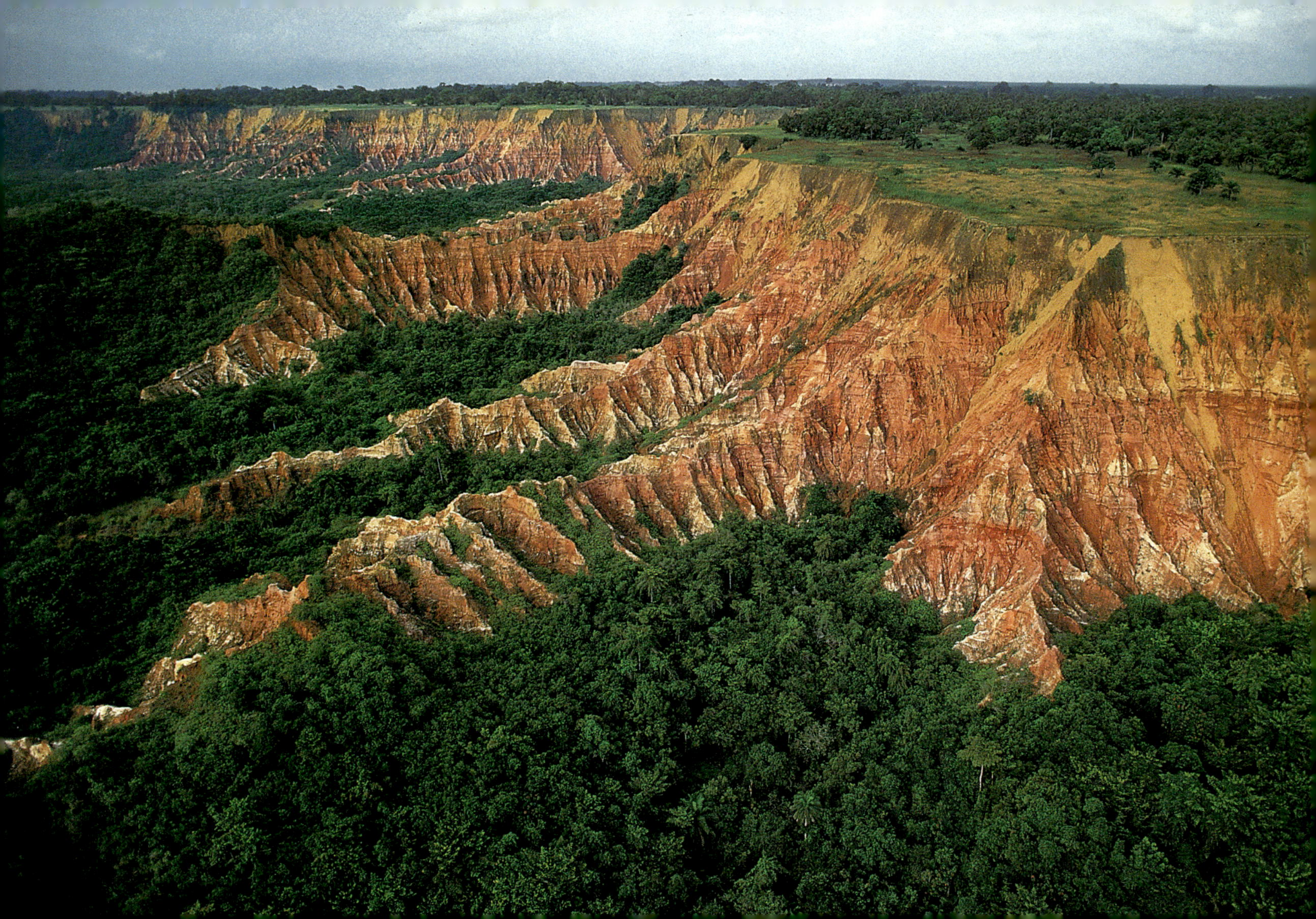

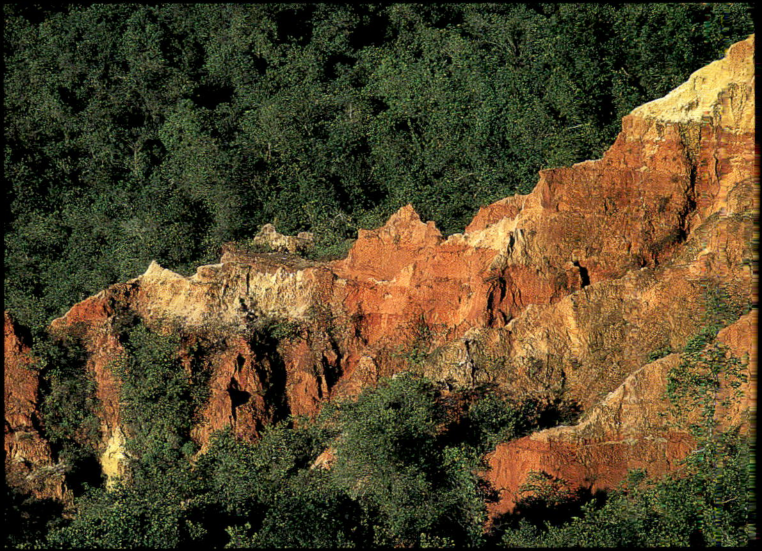

294 and 295
The Diosso Gorges are a sort of reef in the middle of the forest: their modern-day appearance is in fact due to the erosive action first of the sea and then the wind.

296
The savage spectacle of the forests surrounding Lake Victoria in Tanzania has fascinated generations of explorers, such as Burton, Speke, Grant, Baker, and Livingstone.

297
On the shores bordering Lake Victoria, in Tanzania, vast woodland areas alternate with swamps and evergreen forests.

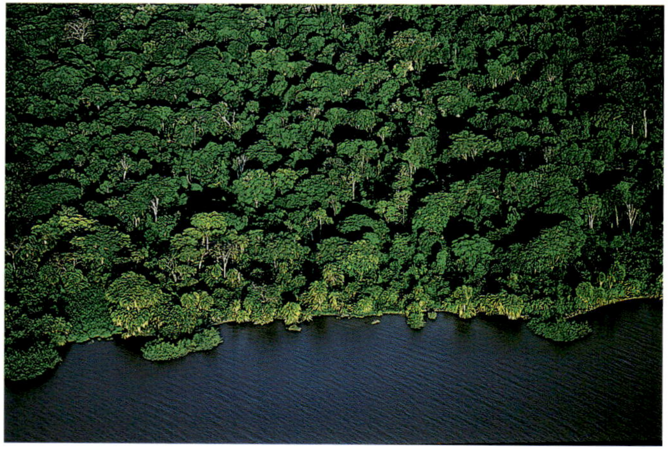

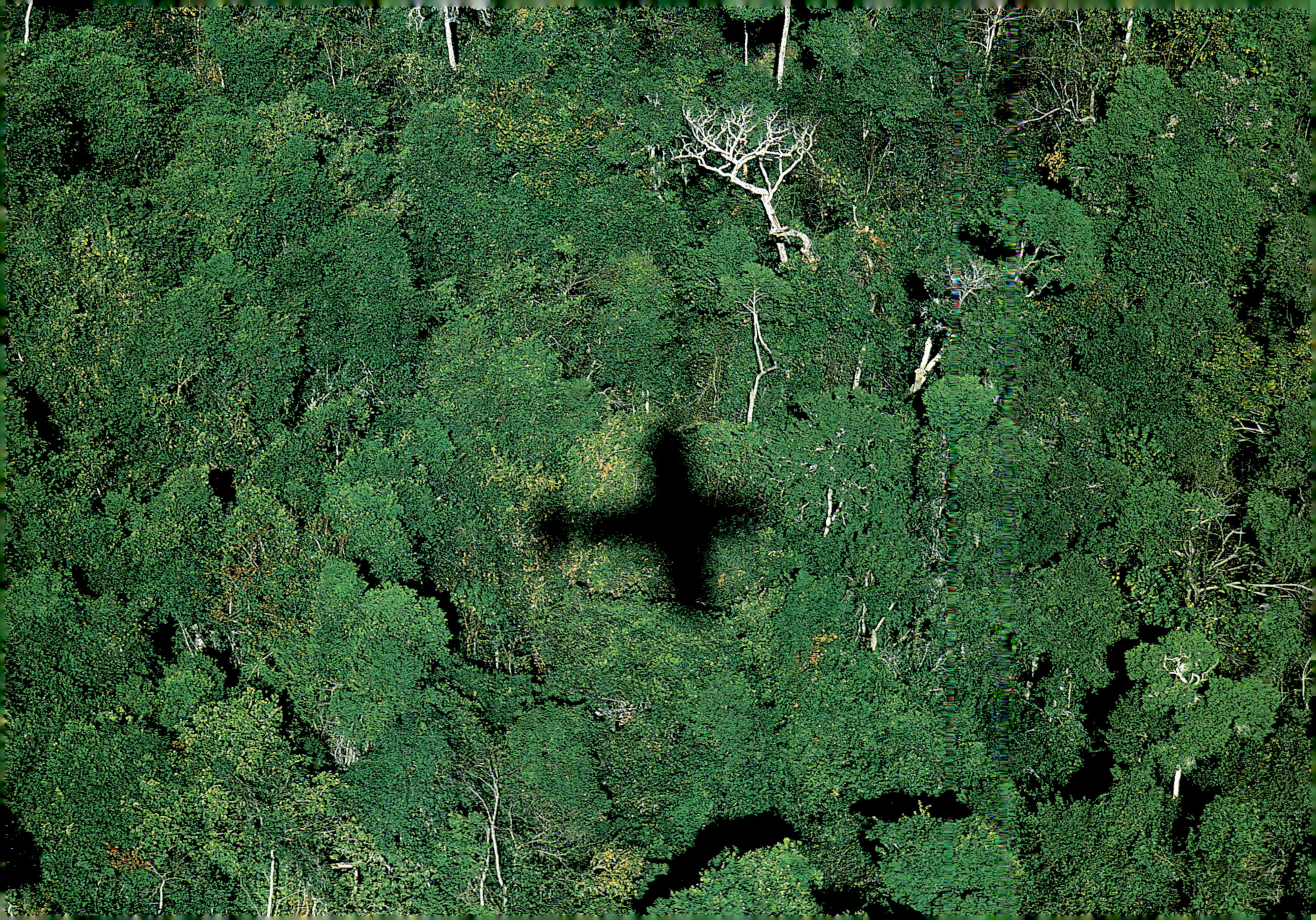

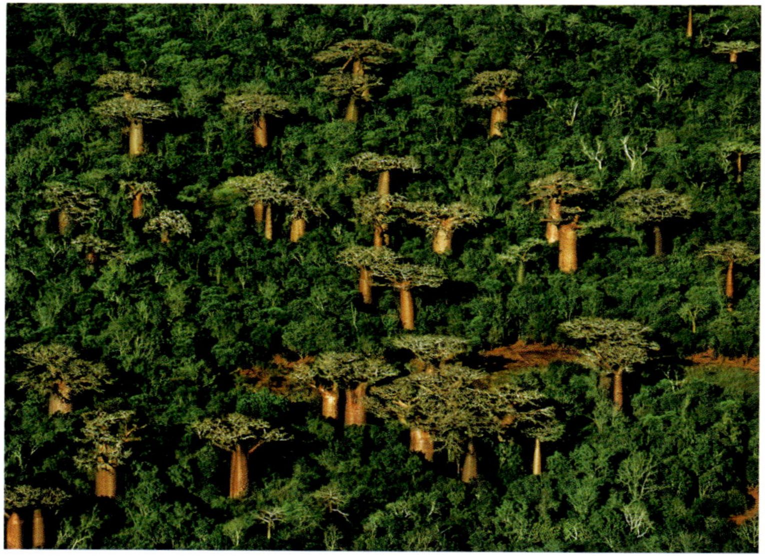

298
In the forests of Madagascar, a special species of Baobab tree grows with an enormous trunk and a tuft-like kind of foliage.

299
In the forests of the Seychelles, unique plant species grow that have totally peculiar characteristics. The islands' symbol is the coconut palm known as "Maldivian," whose fruit can weigh up to 55 pounds.

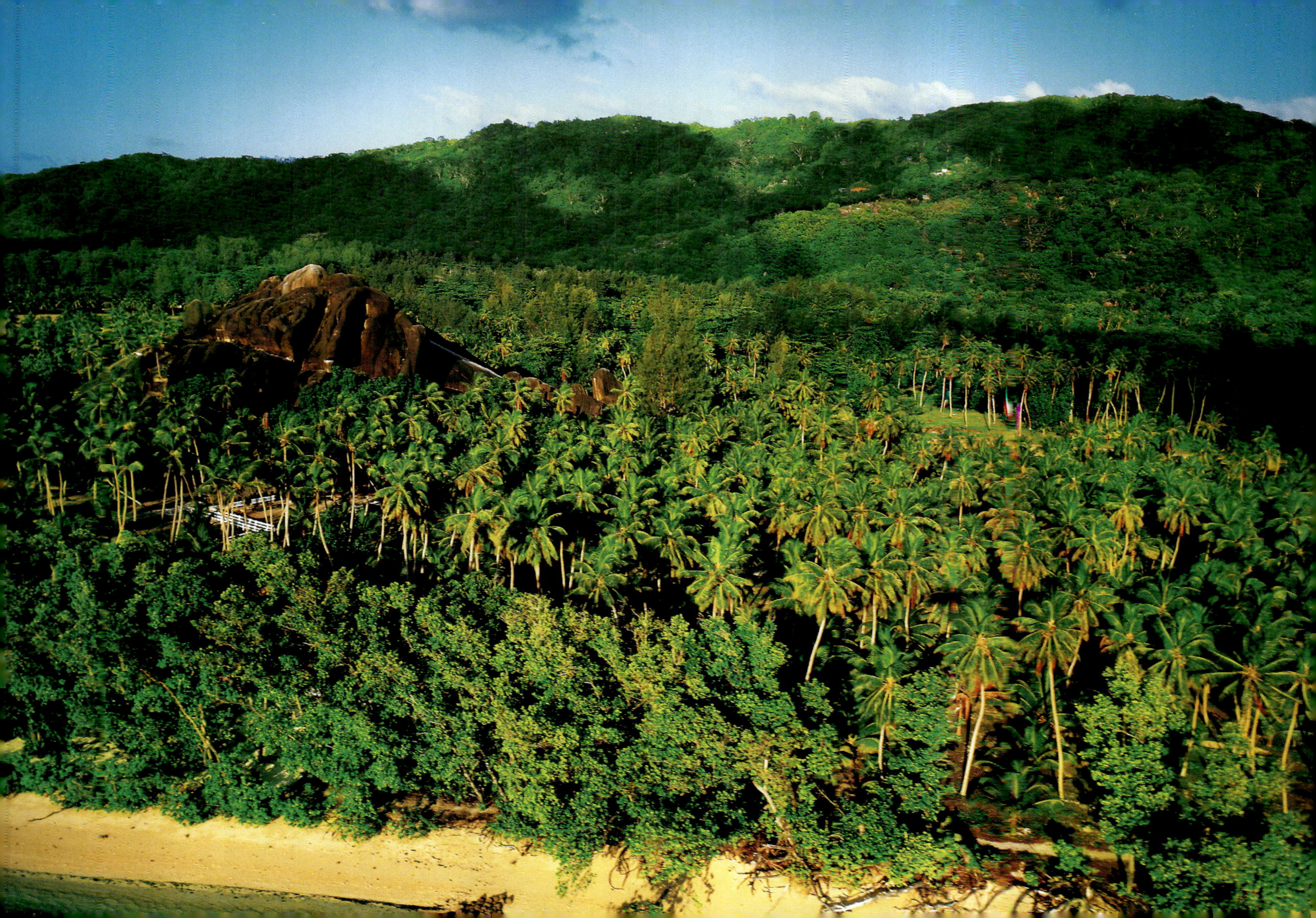

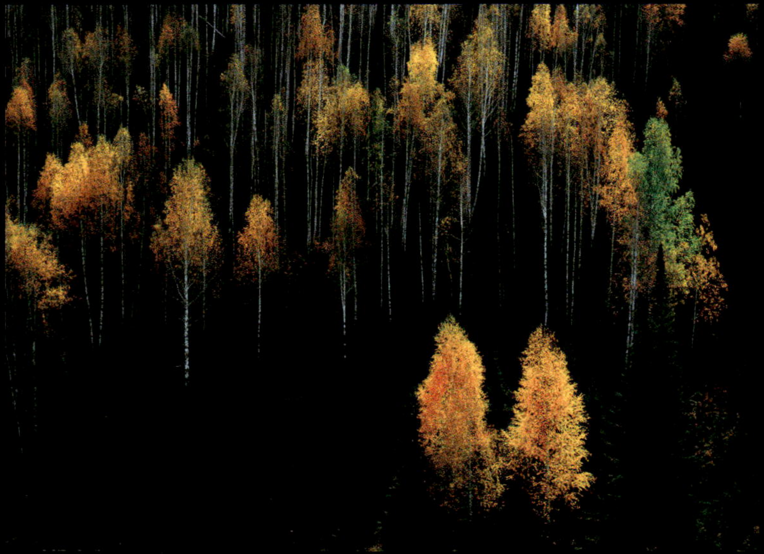

300
In autumn, the copses in the Xi Jiang Valley, in China, take on warm tones.

301
Each year, in the month of October, numerous tourists visit the parks in the Chinese region of Miyaluo, attracted by the spectacle of the maple woods tinted red.

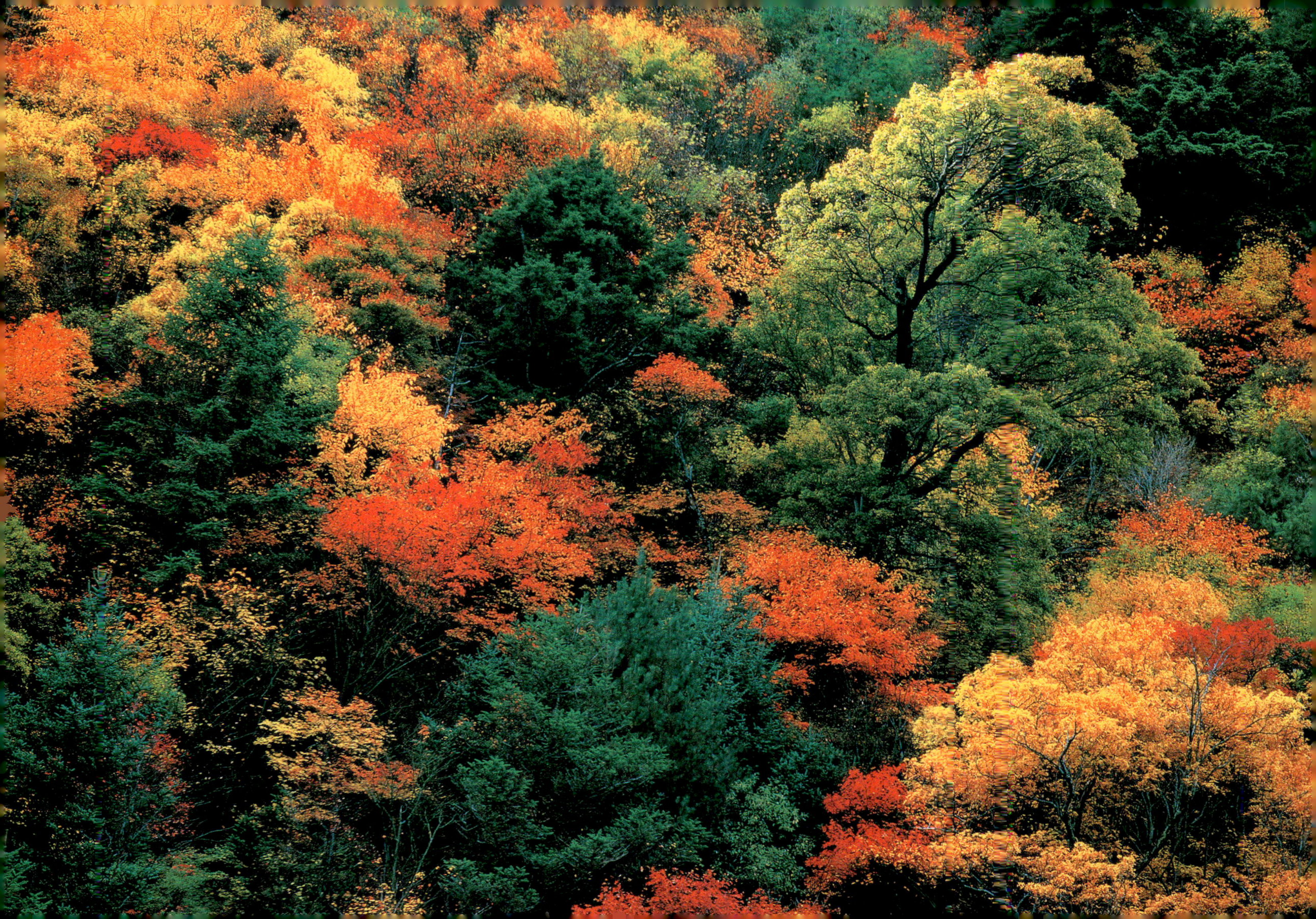

302
The rain forest is one of the many woodland varieties forming the plentiful ecosystem of the Western Ghats mountain chain, in the Indian region of Tamil Nadu.

303
Irian Bariat, the western part of New Guinea under the Indonesia government, is covered by forest reaching altitudes of up to almost 984 feet.

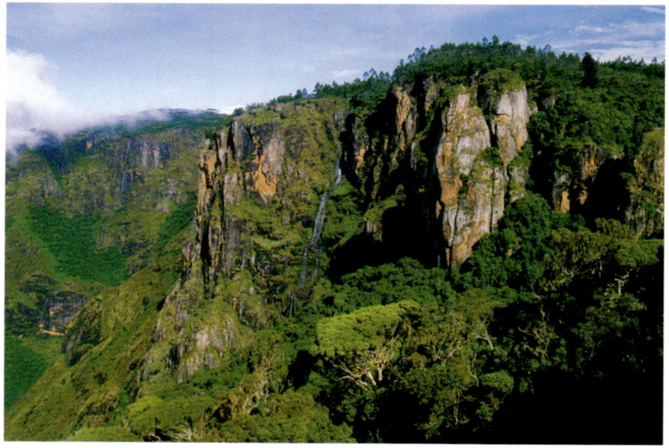

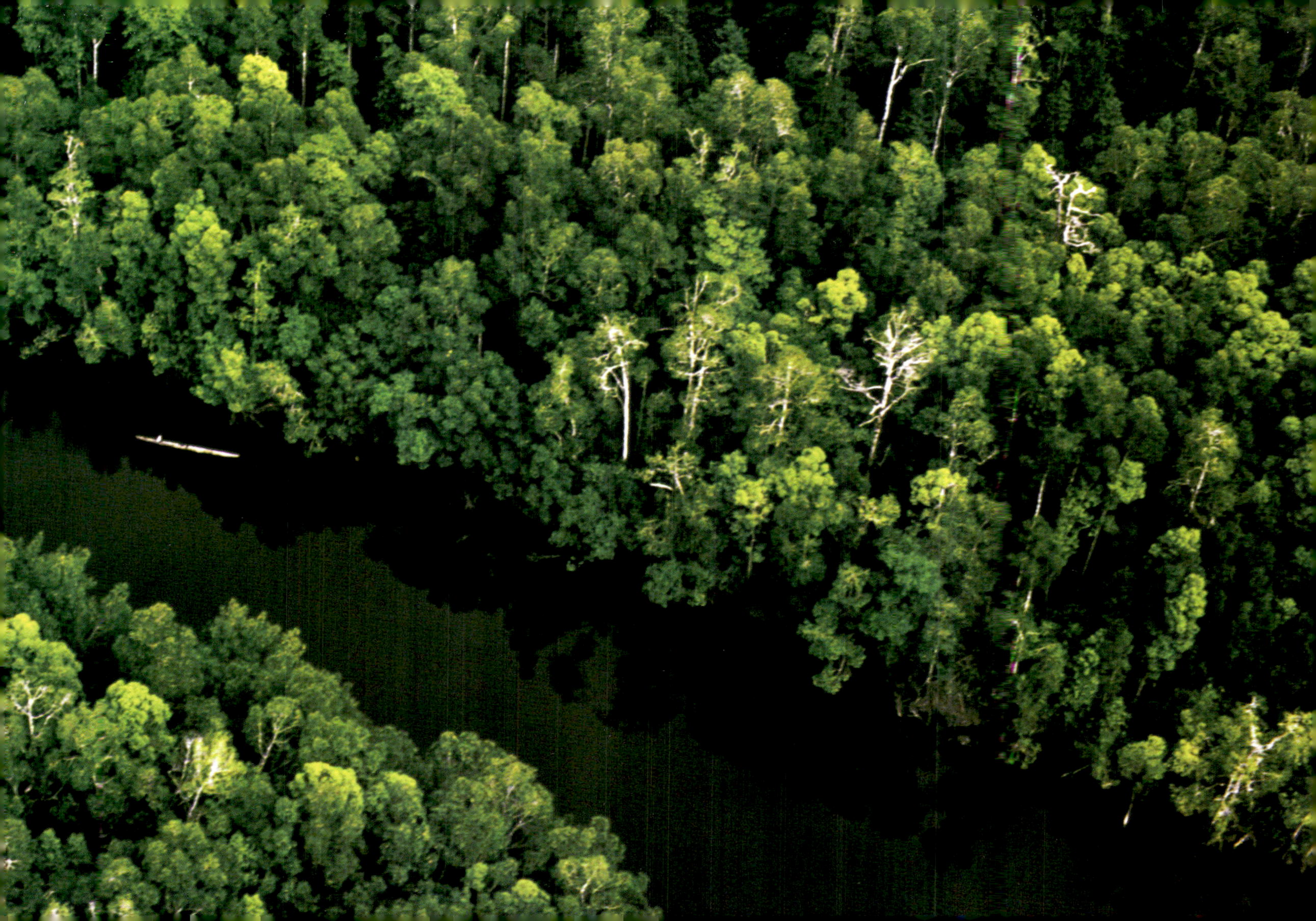

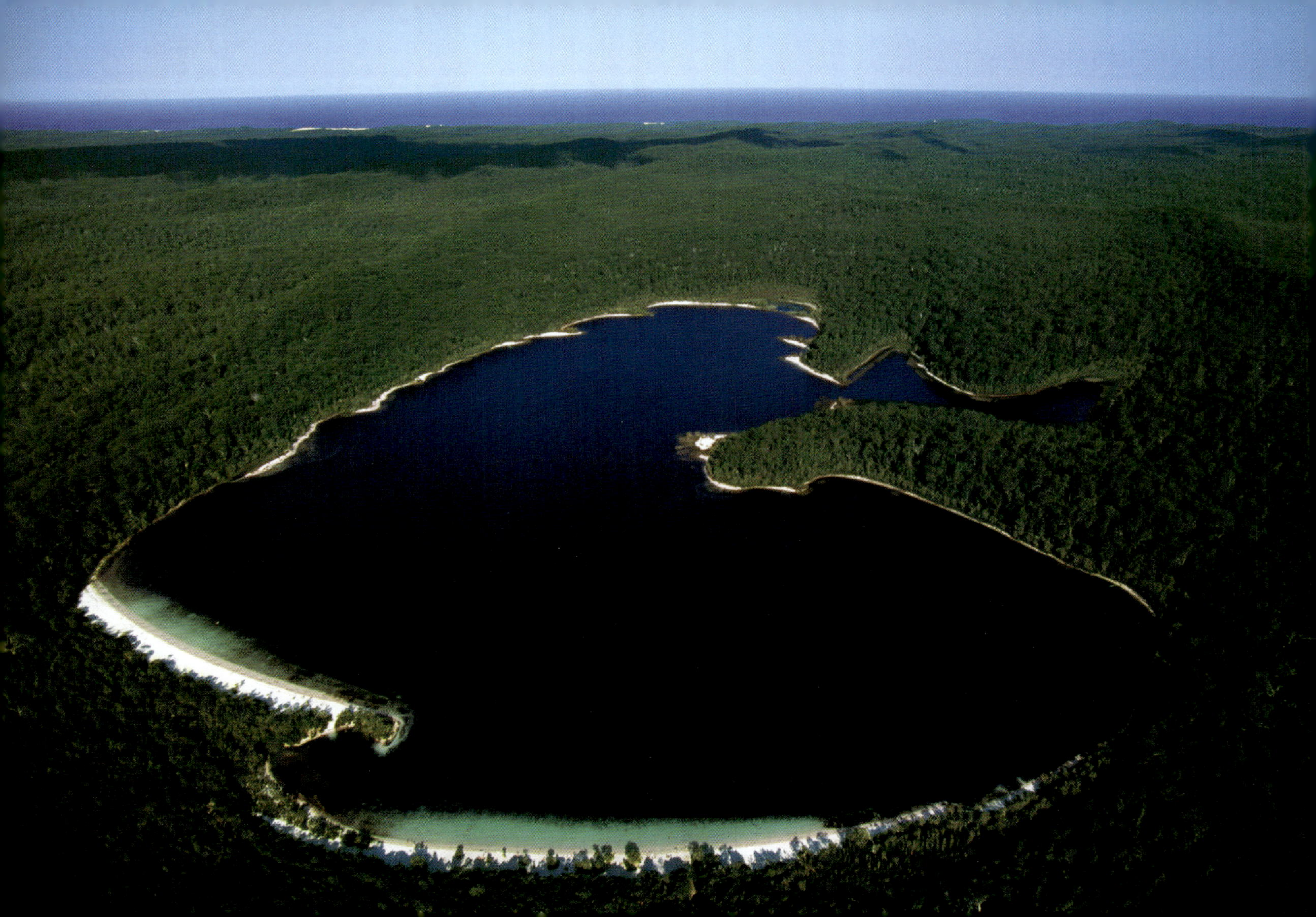

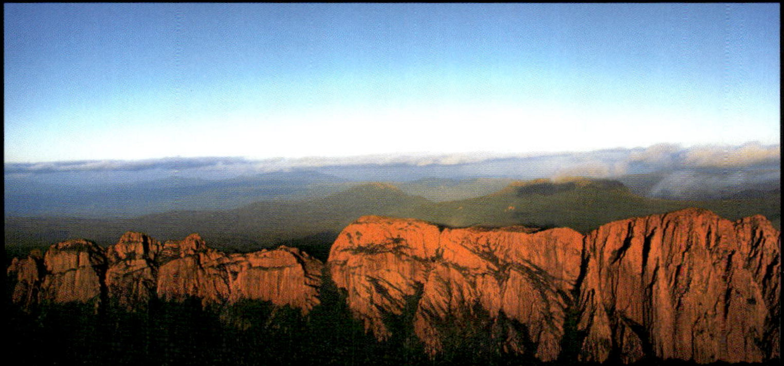

304

On Frazer Island, in Queensland, diversified plant life exists: big rain-forest areas alternate with lakes or sandy expanses.

305

At the end of the 1970s, the calcareous stone formation of Precipitous Bluff, in Tasmania, was incorporated into Southwest National Park.

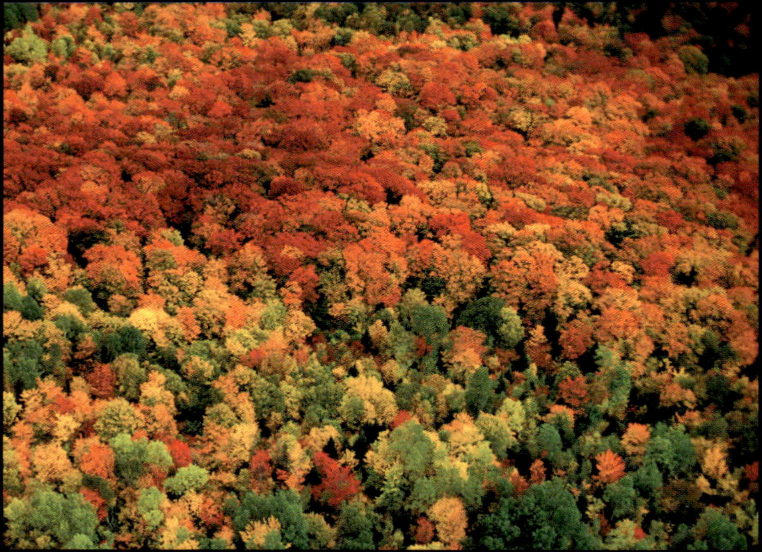

306
During the so-called Canadian "Indian Summer," in the months of September and October, the leaves of the trees in the region of Charlevoix take on warm autumn tones.

307
The Canadian mountains of the Laurentides, with their 4,500 lakes and uninterrupted expanses of woods, rise parallel to the San Lorenzo River, from which they get their name.

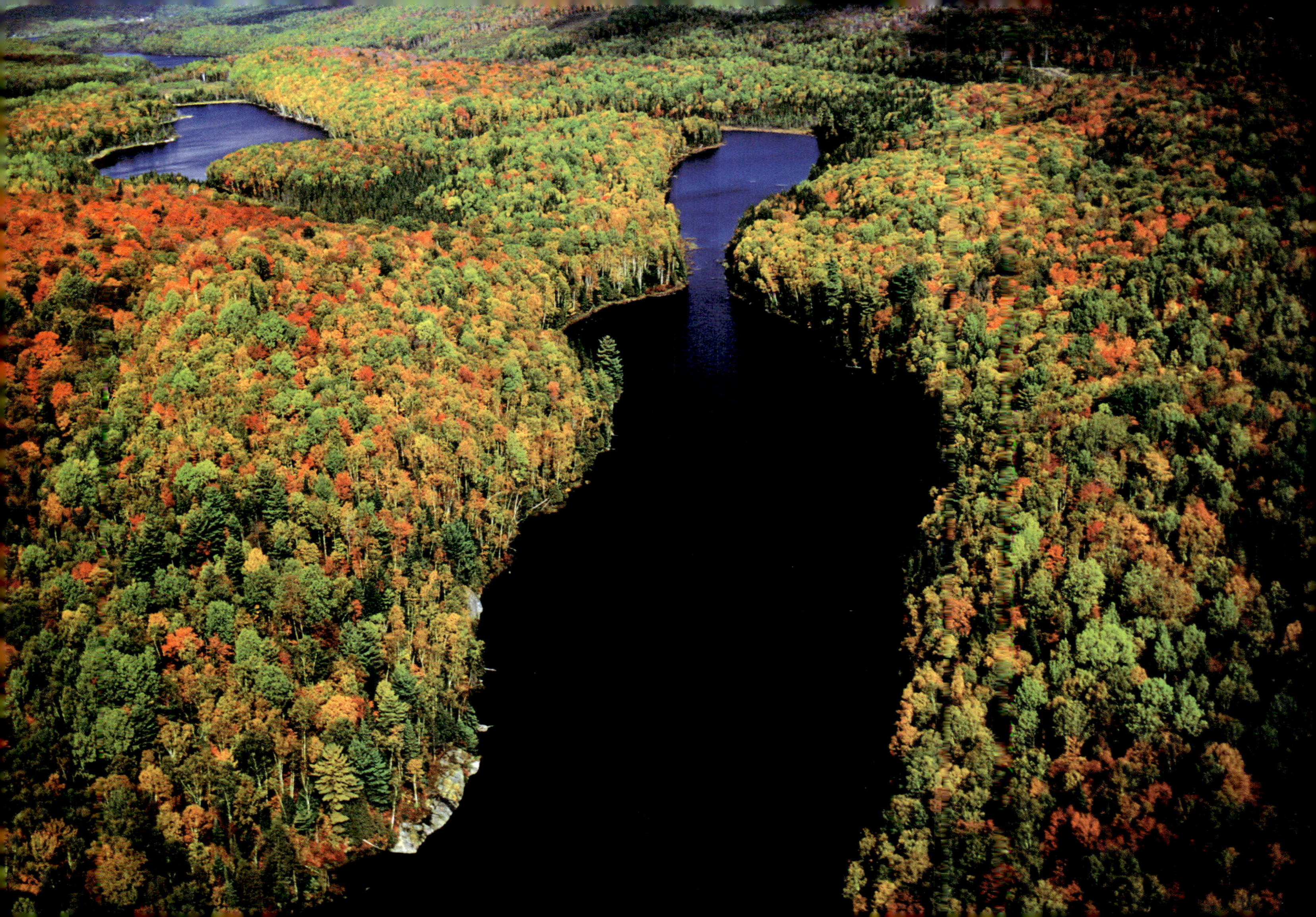

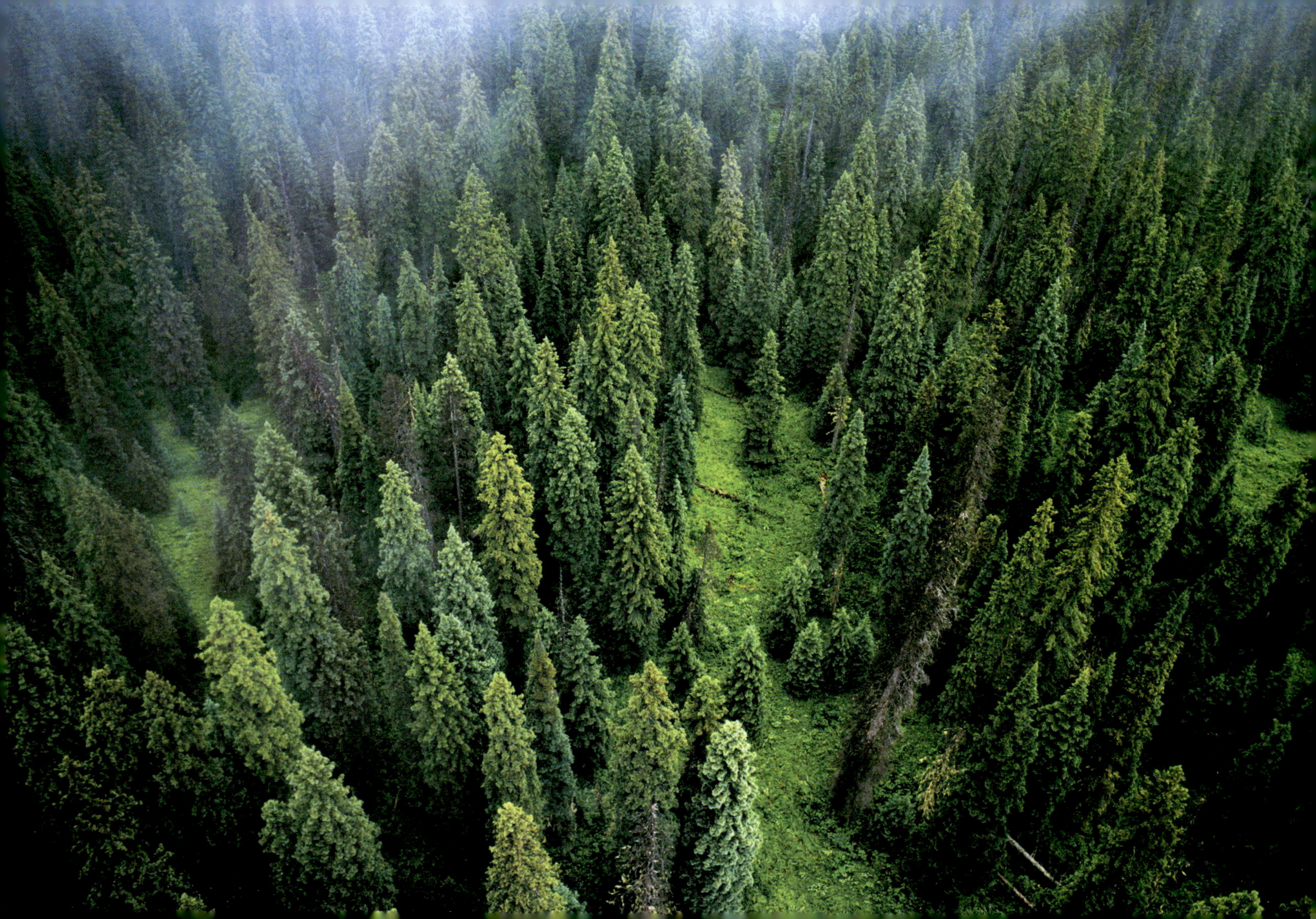

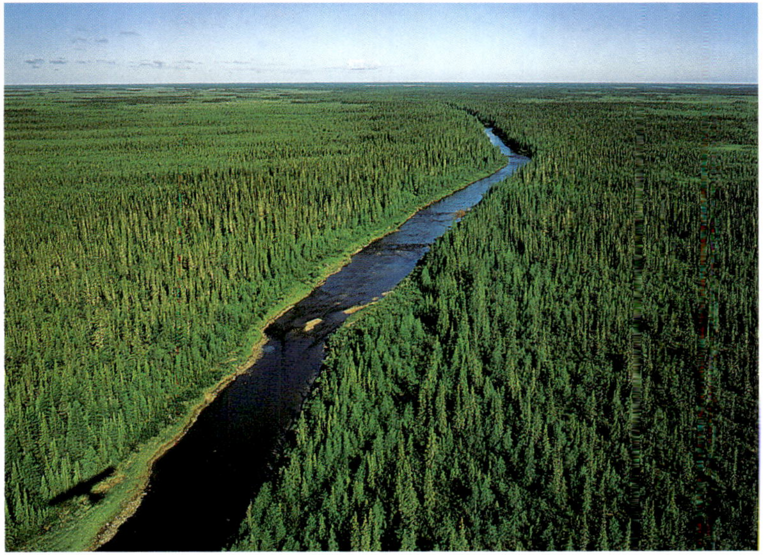

308
The terrain of internal British Columbia, in Canada, is covered by 37,000,000 acres of forest, composed predominantly of pines.

309
In the Manitoba region in Canada, 65,000,000 acres of the territory are covered by forests, the majority of which are of the boreal type, wi h a predominance of fir trees.

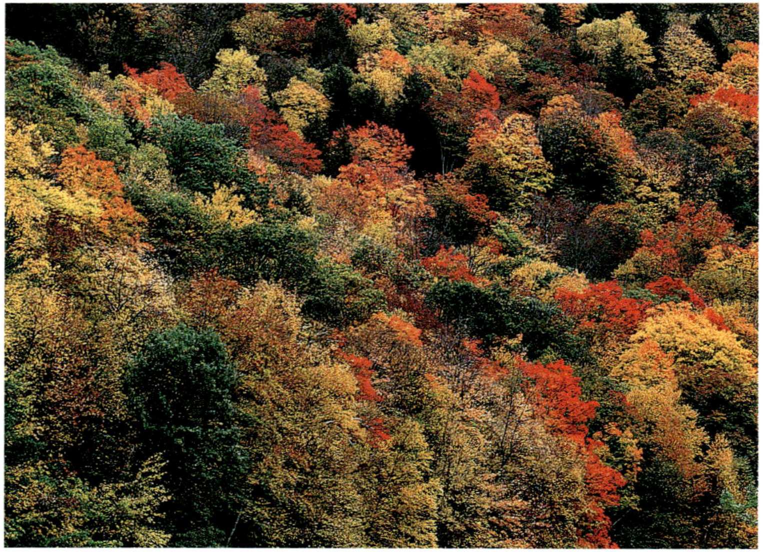

310 and 311

These two photos of New England woods emphasize the process by which the leaves of periodical vegetation die in autumn, when their carotenoids are visible, giving the foliage the typical yellow and red tones.

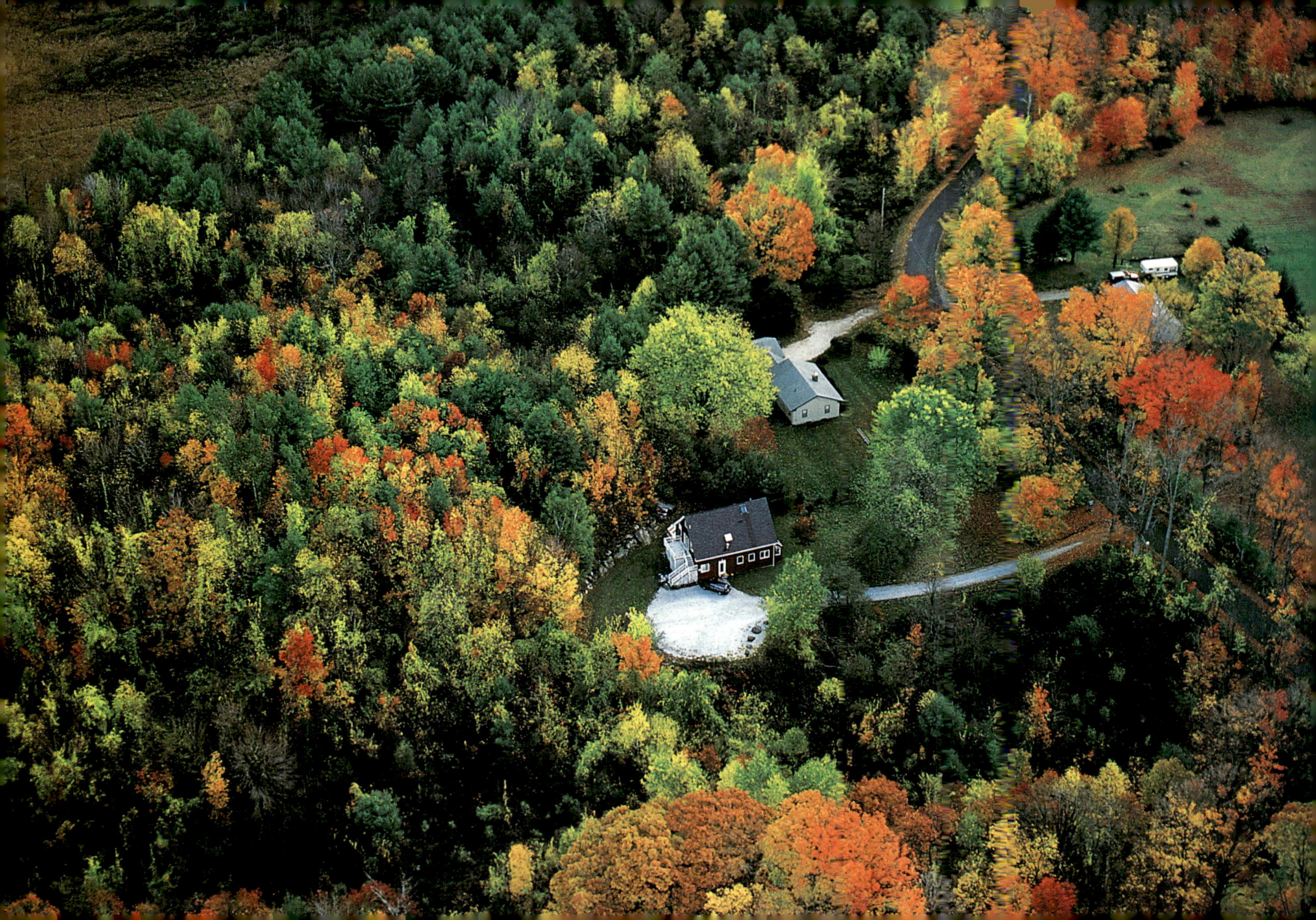

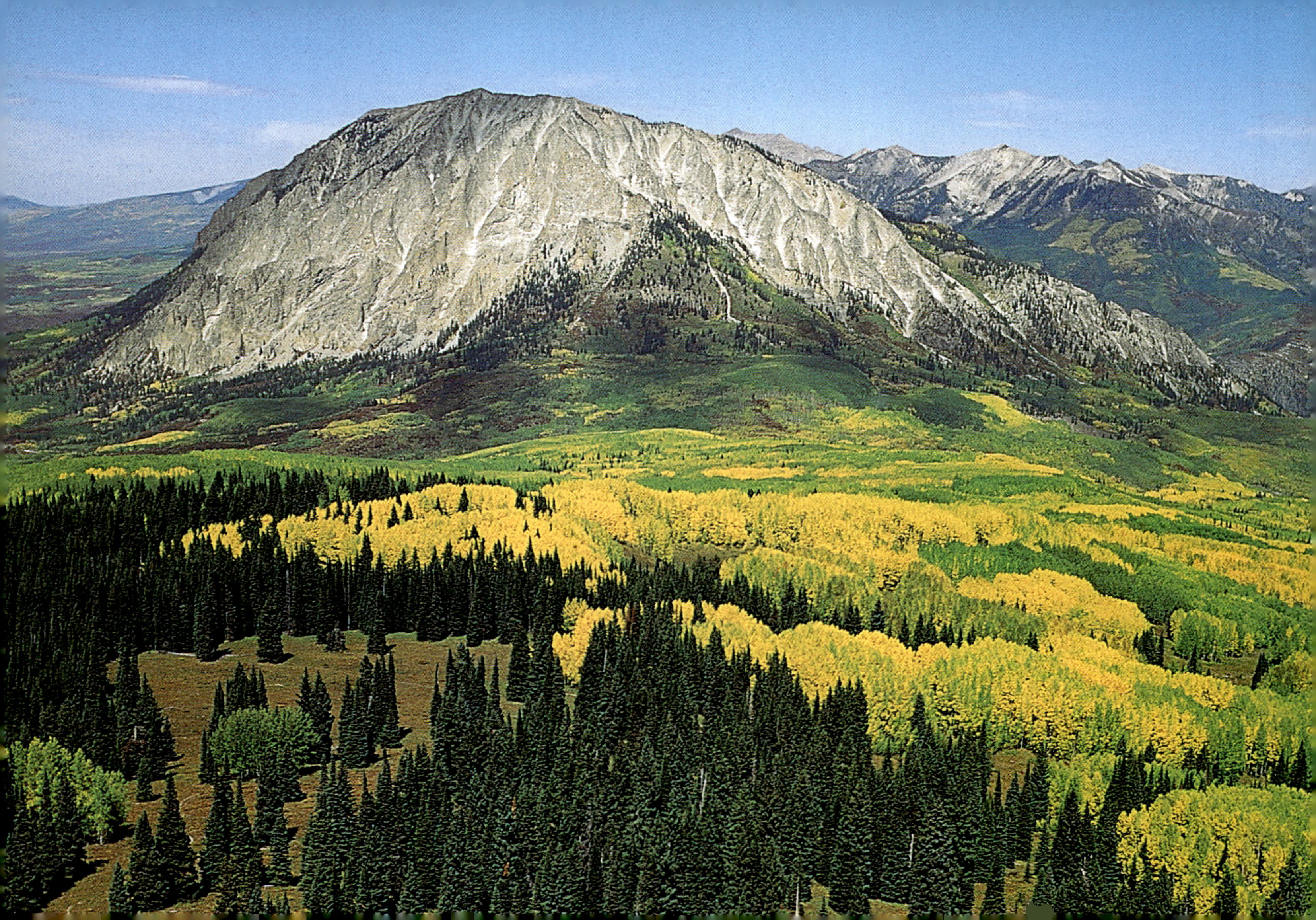

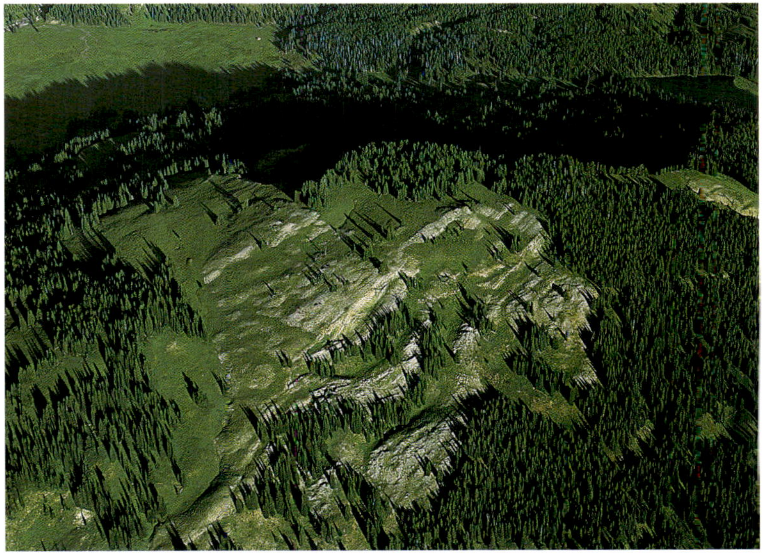

312

Marcellina Mountain rises from seasonal woods, tinted yellow, and coniferous forests in Gunnison County in Colorado.

313

Grand Teton National Park in Wyoming is located in the central portion of the Rocky Mountains and is covered by big green expanses and coniferous forests.

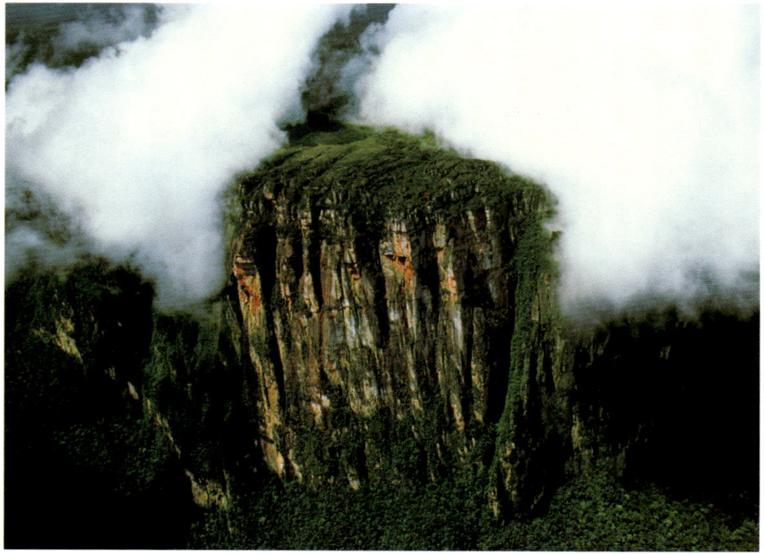

314 and 315
The highlands of Auyantepui (the Devil's Mountain) in Venezuela are covered by an impenetrable forest.

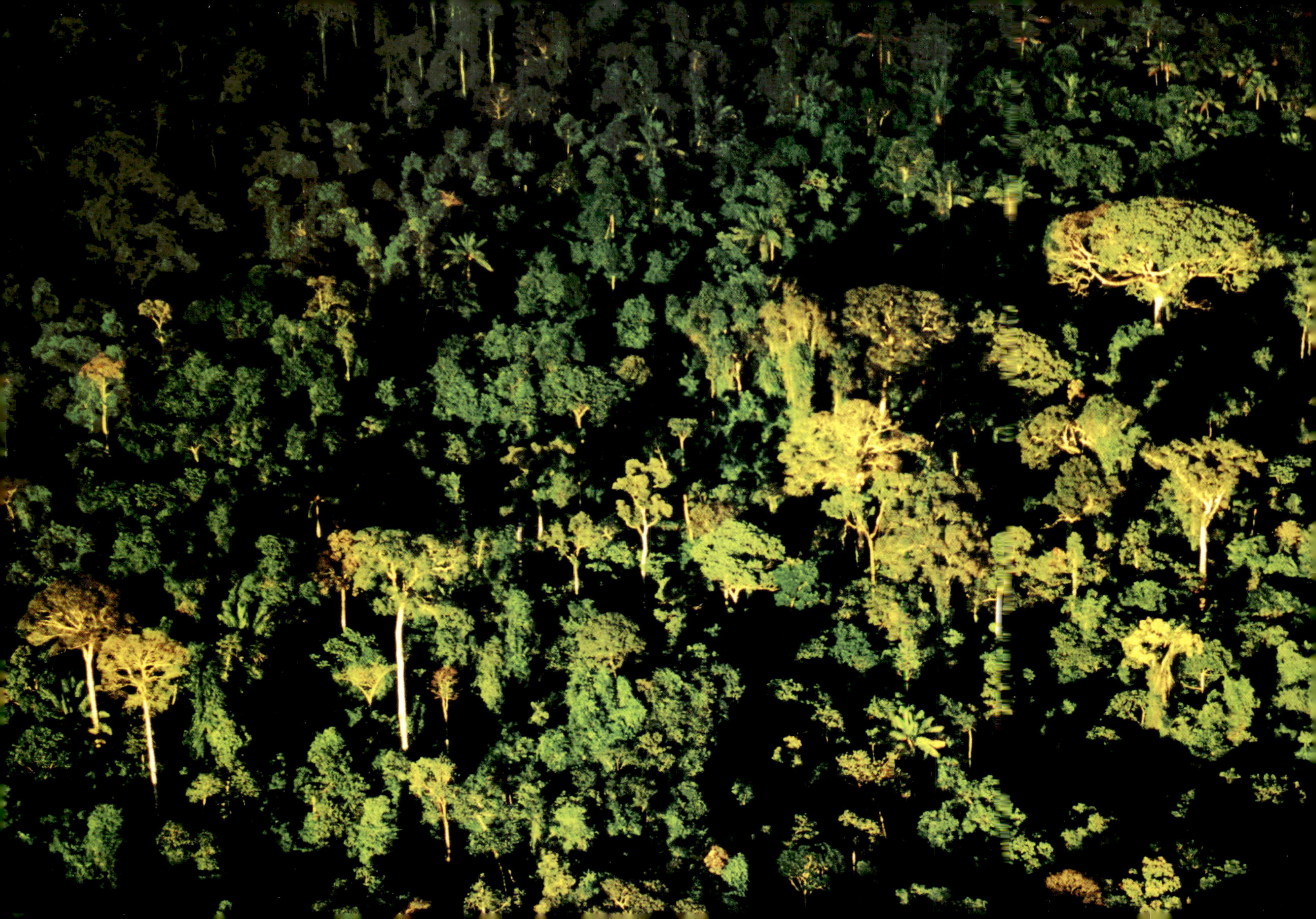

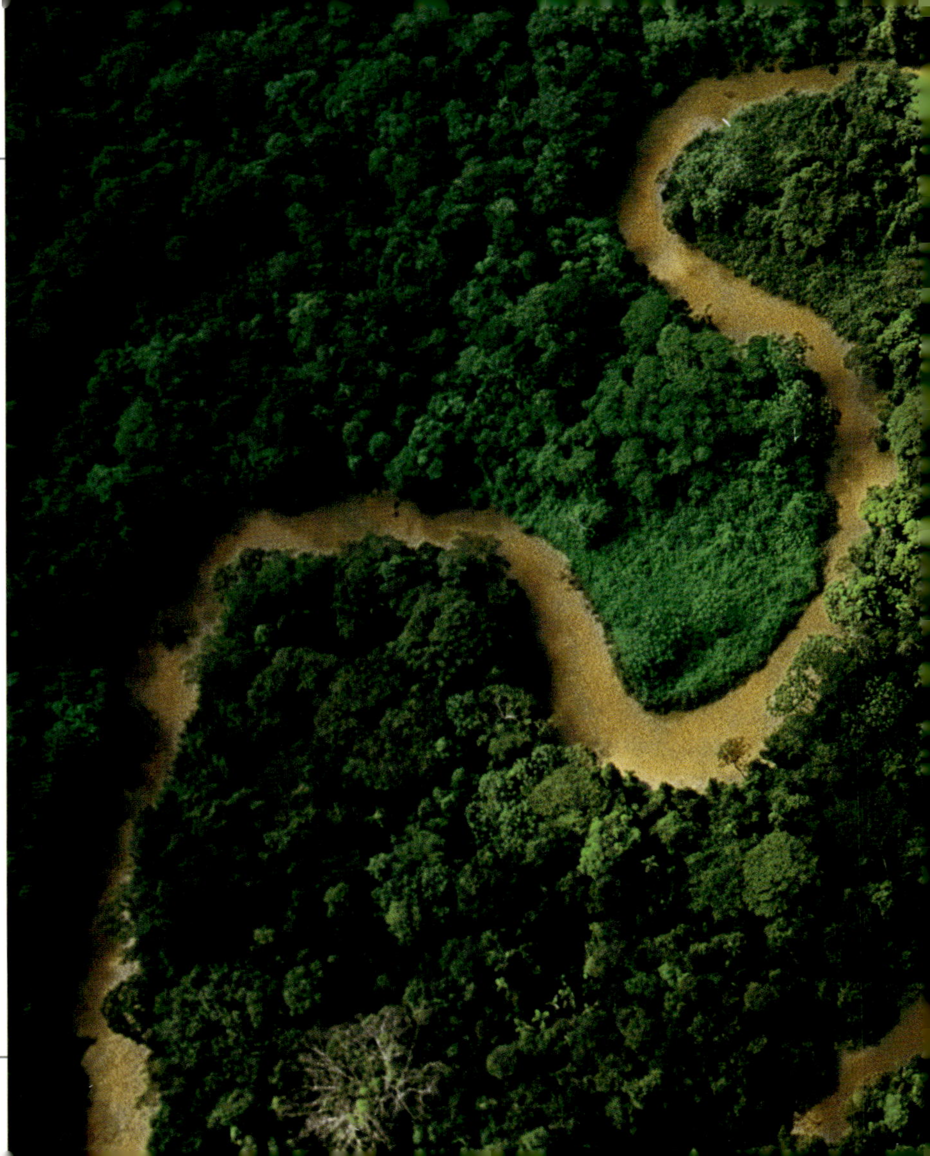

316-317
Rain forests are found in many countries on the South American continent. In this photo, the Rio Conaco, overflowing with water, crosses the Ox-Bows River in Ecuador.

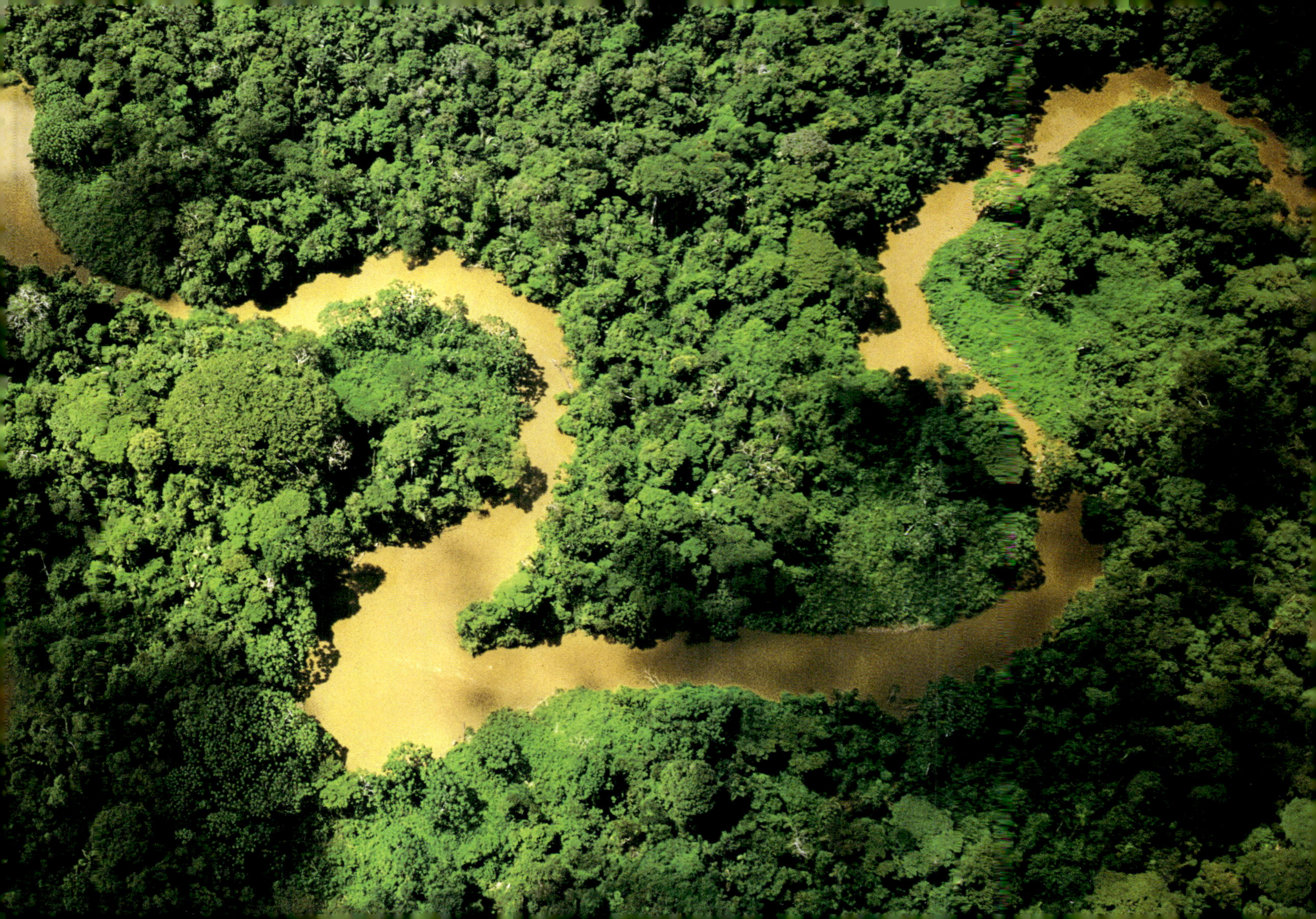

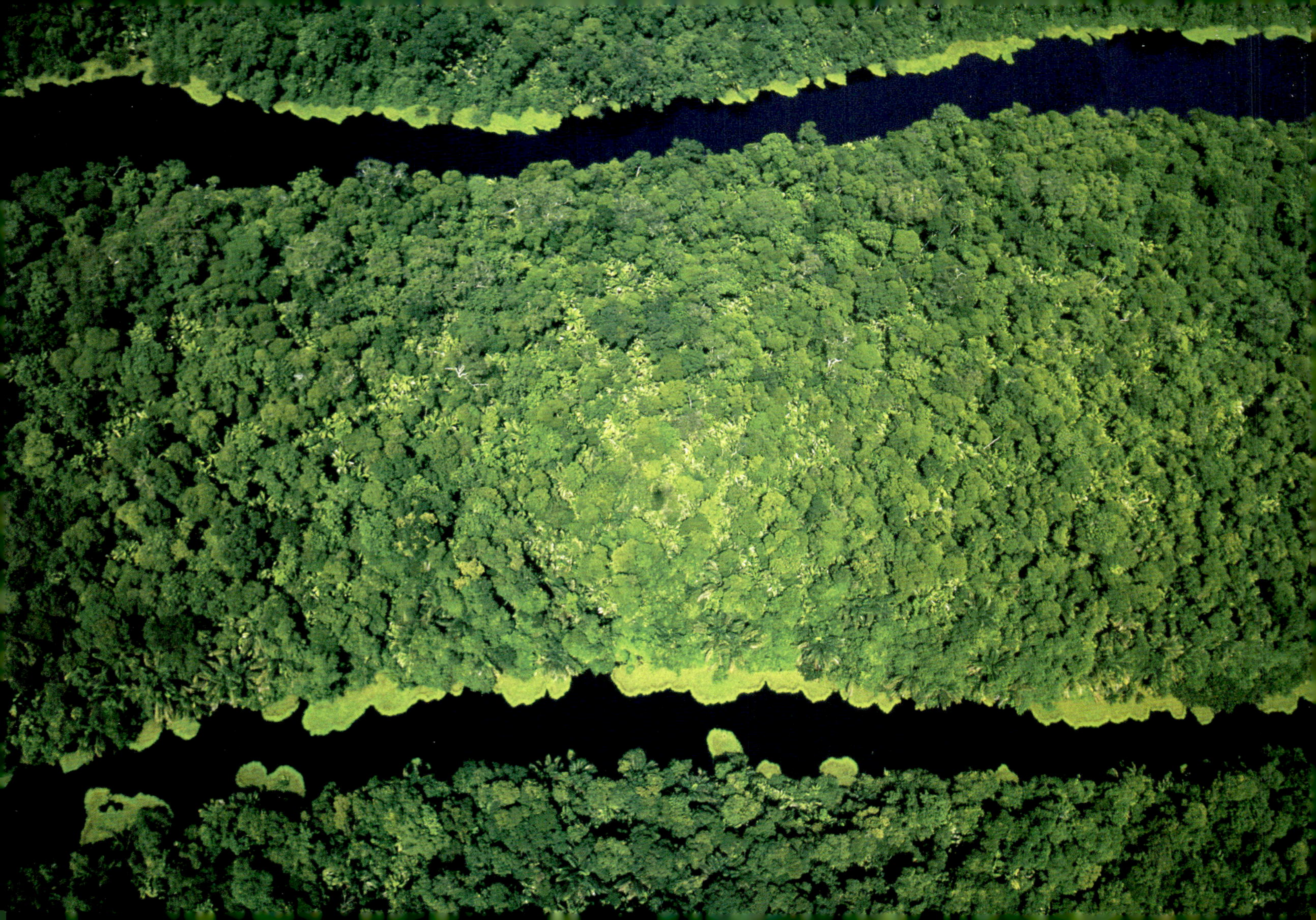

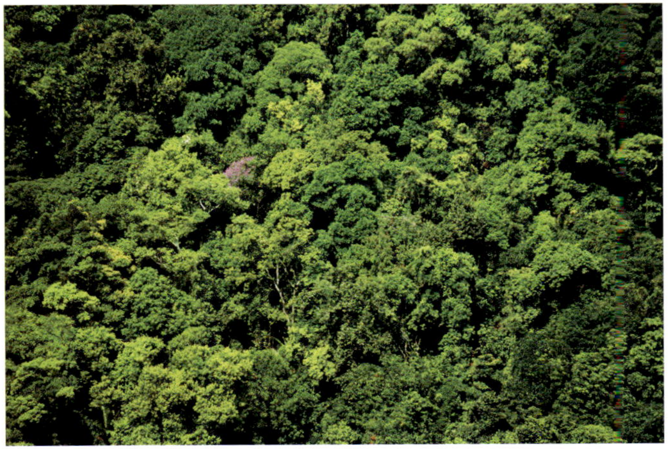

318
Tortuguero Nature Reserve in Costa Rica is an important ecosystem, thanks to its dense rain forest and beaches where green turtles nest.

319
The green lung of the world is the Amazon Forest in Brazil, full of plant and animal species of which only a small percentage has been identified.

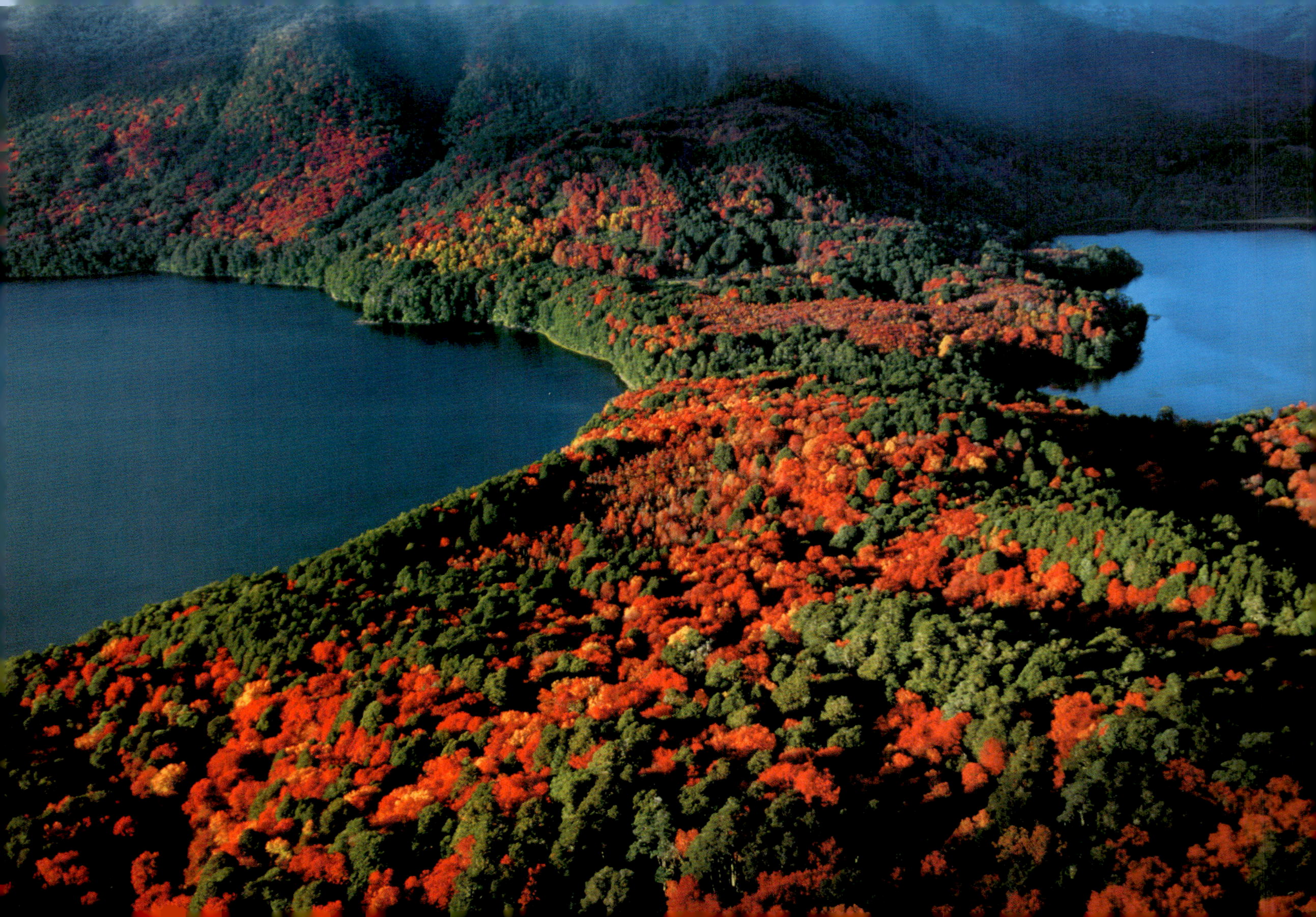

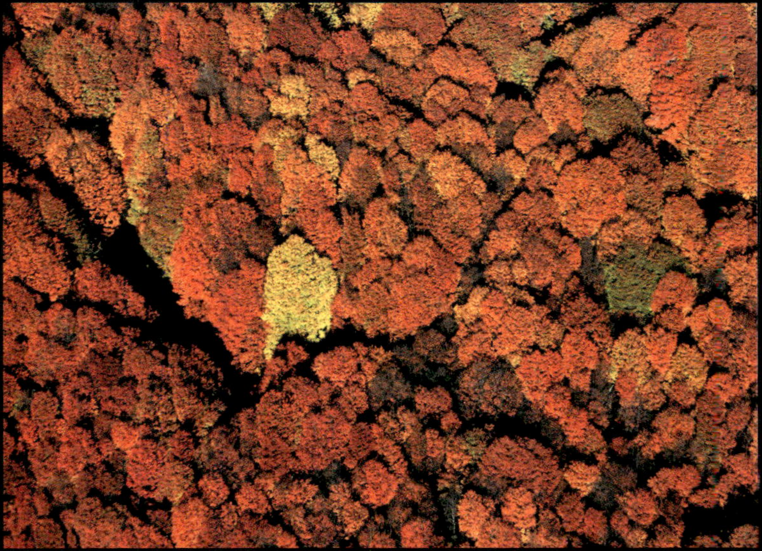

320 and 321
Lanin National Park in Argentina has the purpose of preserving autochthonous plant species like the roble pellin, a variety of oak, and the rauli, an evergreen beech that becomes red in autumn.

THE CYCLE OF WATER

FLYING HIGH

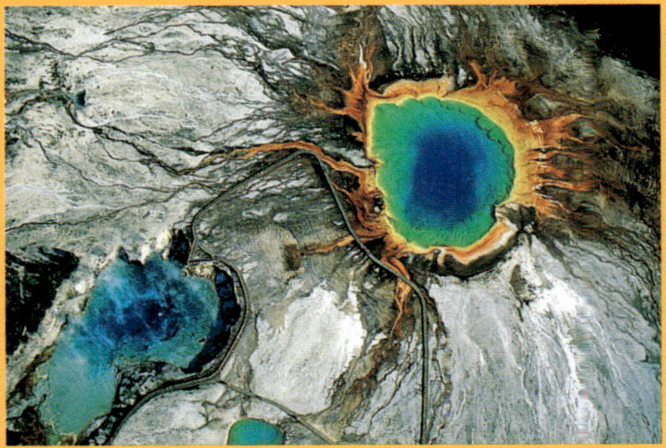
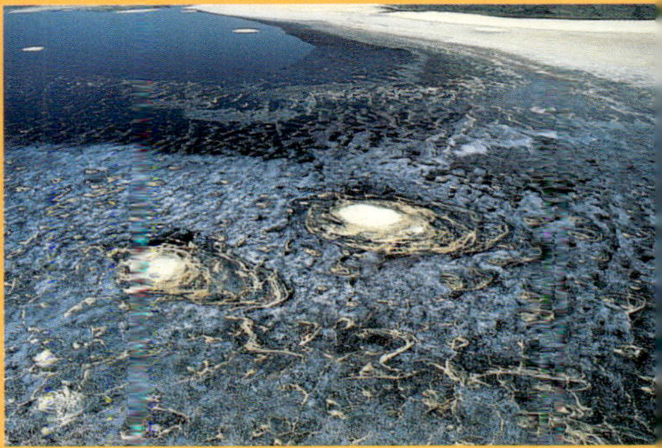

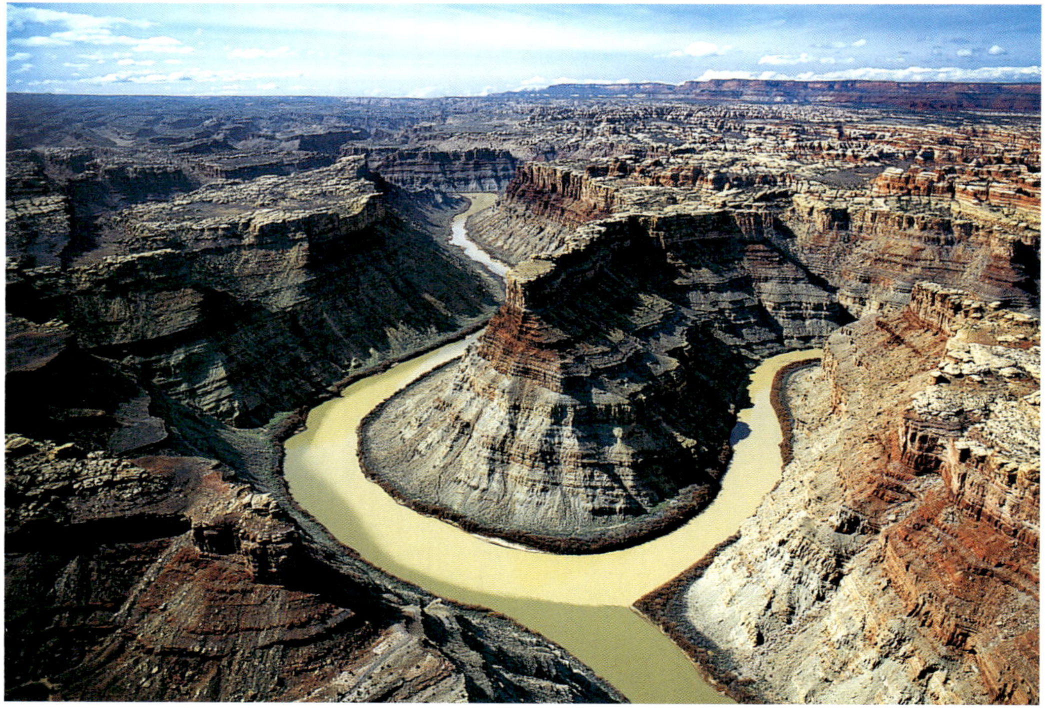

323
Pools of sulfurous waters in Yellowstone National Park (left), and Lake Natron in Tanzania (right), rich in sodium bicarbonate.

The roof of the world, Tibet, deserves this name for the evenness of its terrain and its height, like any good roof. Between 10,000 and 16,000 feet high, some of the vastest highlands on the planet extend like a sort of enormous hillside, slightly inclined to the east-northeast, towards East and South Asia, collecting enormous quantities of fresh water from big glaciers and perennial snowfields. In a less spectacular way, all above-water lands hold the same function. Whether little islets, big islands, or continents, they all act as watersheds, receiving billions of tons of fresh water from the condensation of ocean waters in the form of clouds and rain. From the heart, or rather from the spine, of the mountains of the continents depart blue, winding veins of rivers that have been the father or mother – depending on the culture – of entire civilizations, largely still active on the planet. The eternal cycle of water, from the sea to the earth and from the earth to the sea, acts like a wheel to the continents during this phase, first forming into rain and then high-altitude lakes, narrowing into waterfalls proceeding with the primordial force found in Yellowstone or the majesty of the Mississippi, Nile, or Amazons rivers, crossing gorges and plains that do nothing but collect more water and, from our point of view, other visible forms of beauty from the sky.
Lake Manasarowar in Tibet, the Bamian Lakes in Afghanistan, and Lake Titicaca in Peru and Bolivia are relatively close to the barely visible sources of those great waters: the surrounding territories are among the most arid, yellow soil and rock under

324
A confluence along the Colorado River, in Utah.

328
In the area of the Venezuelan city of Bolivar, two waterways with very different colors flow into one river.

The Cycle of Water

the sun, where the lakes can capture all the blue of the sky and transfer it to the earth. They are mirrors reflecting the keystones of the highest layers of the atmosphere, as all tiny mountain lakes do, left behind by glaciers at the highest places in the world, and certain questionable artificial wonders like Lake Powell, in the United States, and Lake Nasser, in Egypt. In these last two cases, seen from the sky, the chromatic impact is the same: strong blue contrasts fill the bottom of ancient flooded valleys almost totally dry beyond the surface of the water. The difference is found in the boats crossing them from one crest to another, always white: dozens of feluccas, sails, and motorboats.

Descending to the valley, where the earth's crust forms ample steps created according to fault lines or the edges of great plates, open waters reach the height of the expression of their force. Magnificent natural amphitheaters, hidden under the hundreds of thousands of cubic feet of water that falls per second, receive the great waterfalls of the planet. It is more often not height that creates impressive views: frequently, as in the case of "short" Niagara Falls, a drop of just a hundred or so feet is enough to create a liquid inferno of frightening force. Victoria Falls, along the Zambezi River, features a curtain of water that is the widest in the world, a 5,600-foot fan whose presence, basically impossible to observe just from the ground unless situated at the point of the drop, can be heard thundering from miles away. It is difficult to say whether these "squat" waterfalls or the slender columns boasting the world record for height are the most impressive, but certainly the latter are the most dizzying. It is not uncommon to sense a hollowness in the stomach, transient, sudden, and intense, when one flies over the above-mentioned Angel Falls in Venezuela (3,110 feet), Tugela Falls in South Africa (3,110 feet), or the dozens of "extreme" Hawaiian waterfalls like Olo'Upenal, the third tallest in the world at 2,953 feet. The record-holders in this field are contended for by the two Americas and Norway, where the cascades are

The Cycle of Water

veils 2,300 to 2,600 feet long, white threads stretching between the crests of the valleys and the blue of the fiords.

Where the plains make the rivers run lazily, tiring them out over increasingly more ample twists and turns like those in Missouri and Mississippi or the Jenisei in Siberia and the Chiang Yang (Blue River), the tiniest depression is enough to create great freshwater lakes. Following a perfect diagonal on the globe, from the Canadian Northwest Territories to Michigan, a strip forms where water and the mainland compete to dominate the surface and be in the sun. The tundra and birch trees give way to the Great Lake of the Bear, the coniferous forest embraces Athabasca and Winnipeg, and Chicago's skyline is reflected in Lake Michigan.

But the Great Lake of the Slaves exhibits a special appearance, where the slopes of the above-water land stretch deeper down along the general route of the water. The nature of the land and the minimal altitude, as if at the bottom of basin, trap the water, forming labyrinthine bogs, a sort of temporary and chaotic fusion of the land and the river. The swamp environment is among the most disturbing for symmetry-loving creatures like ourselves, used to – but also forced into – maintaining control over our surroundings as much as possible. Vast swamps often form at the mouths of big rivers or at the bottom of vast hydrogeological basins, creating somewhat alien-looking aerial views, absolutely opposite to our anxious need for cosmos, for "order." Such magnificent complexity is evident in different parts of the world. The case of "sea of grass" that defines Florida's boundless Everglades is quite eloquent: in effect, the mixture of plants and water is absolute in that flat and impenetrable expanse of tenacious, several foot tall grasses, the perfect refuge for dozens of animal species long disappeared from other places. On the other hand, this description does not do justice to the canopy of mangrove trees hiding canals, bogs, and shadowy pools. The Nile Delta has al-

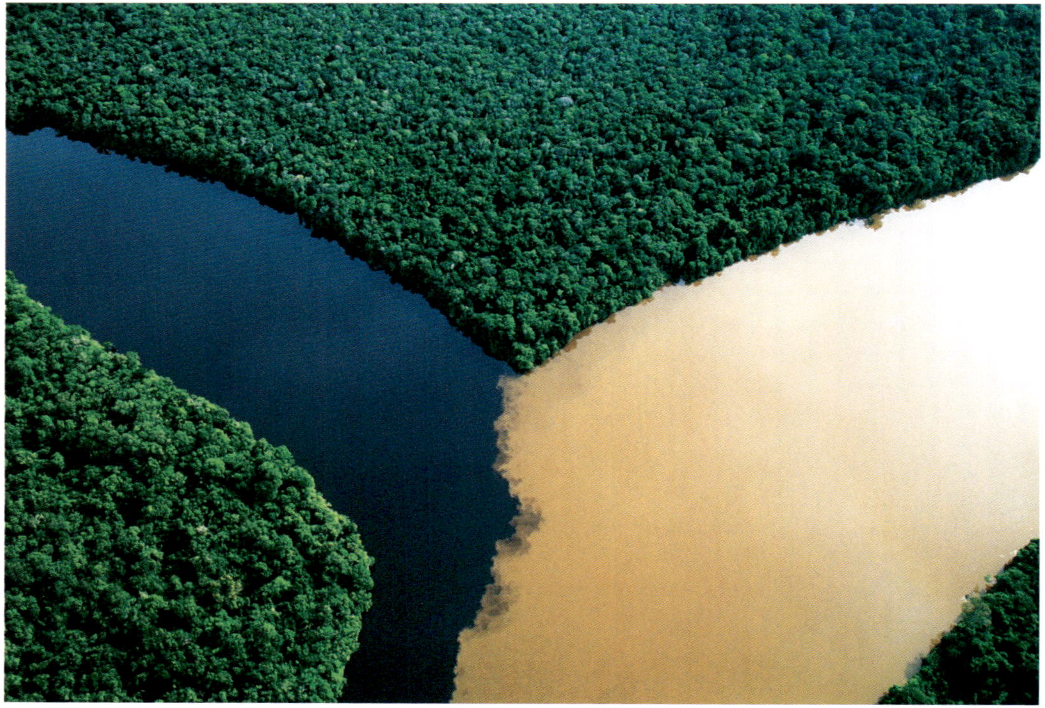

The Cycle of Water

ways been famous for its relative impenetrability. Threatening gods like Seth, the murderer of Osiris, kept their dwellings there, among the dense foliage of the resistant papyrus, like fortresses against the advance of humans. The Hawaiian Islands, always amazing despite threatened environmental conditions – much reduced and contained in recent years, since it was discovered that the wealth of endemism in that still-evolving archipelago risked inexorable extinction – contain high-altitude marshes and bogs. The intense humidity creates vast swamp areas in the mountain depressions supporting highly fragile natural "greenhouses" for a number of plant and animal species unique in the world. From the sky, even the delicate catwalks up to several hundreds of feet long that give access to botanists and scholars hired to monitor and take care of the fortunate plant and flower varieties that are still able to prosper there can be seen.

As for river mouths and swamps, Africa contains a very special form of delta, associated with vast flood zones. The Okavango River ends in a decidedly *sui generis* mouth: no lake, no less a sea, collects its lazy waters, which before being absorbed are lost in the plains, flooding them for vast tracts, forming one of the greatest marsh systems in the world. At times, from the sky, "roads" of dark water can be seen, opened by the hippopotami passing through the layer of vegetation covering the labyrinthine canals, squeezed between one island of grass and another.

The cycle of fresh water, at this point, temporarily abandons above-water lands to return to the sea and re-acquire salt lost during evaporation. Then, under the effect of the sun, vapors will continue to rise from the surface of the ocean, gliding like giant white galleons over to the continents and condensing into rain. The Roof of the World, at this point, becomes the world itself, and the wheel that nourishes life on the planet's surface will complete another turn.

Europe

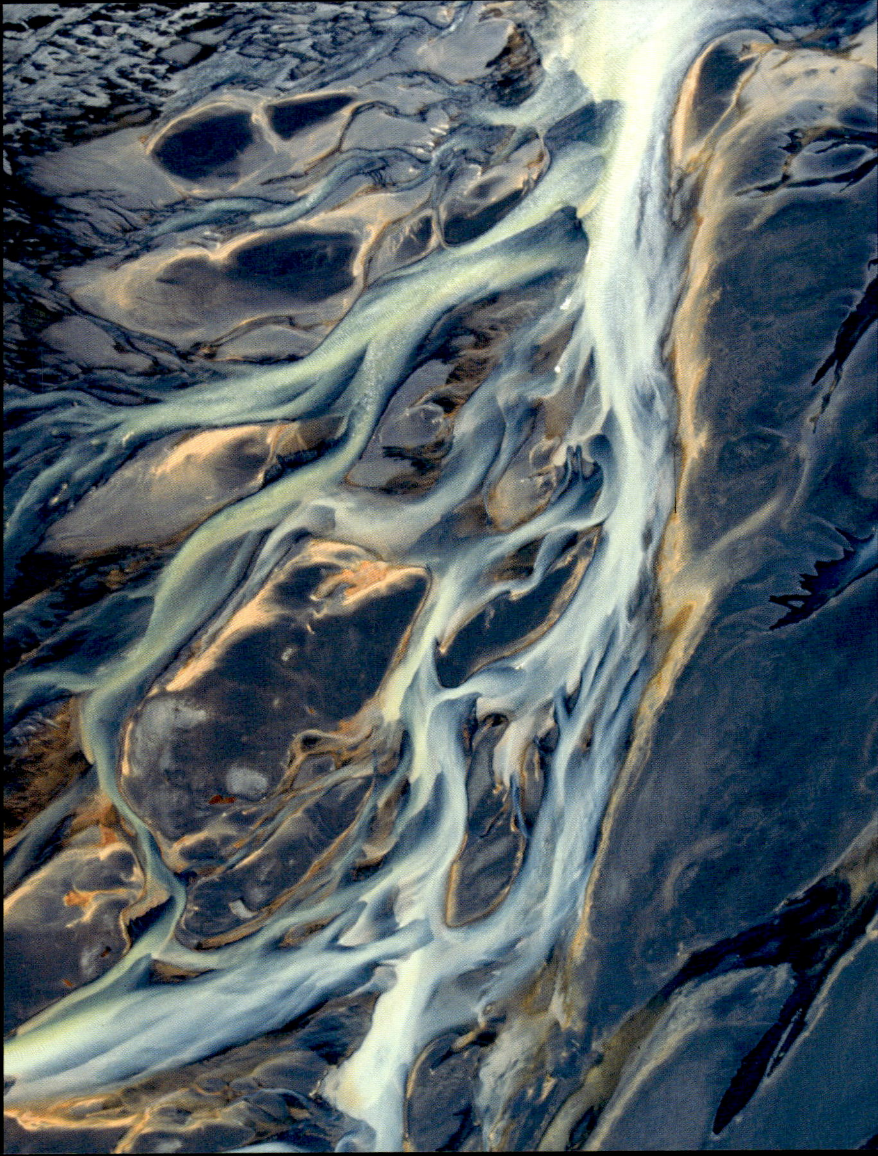

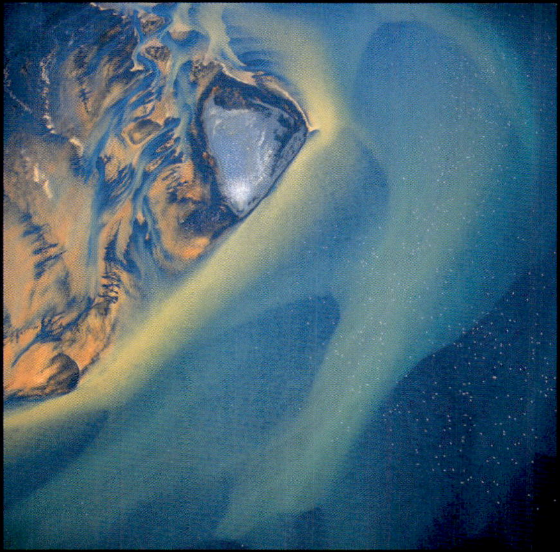

330 and 331

The Pjorsa River is the longest one in Iceland. Its bed rests on lavitic terrain, from which it lifts mineral deposits giving the waters their specially colored shading.

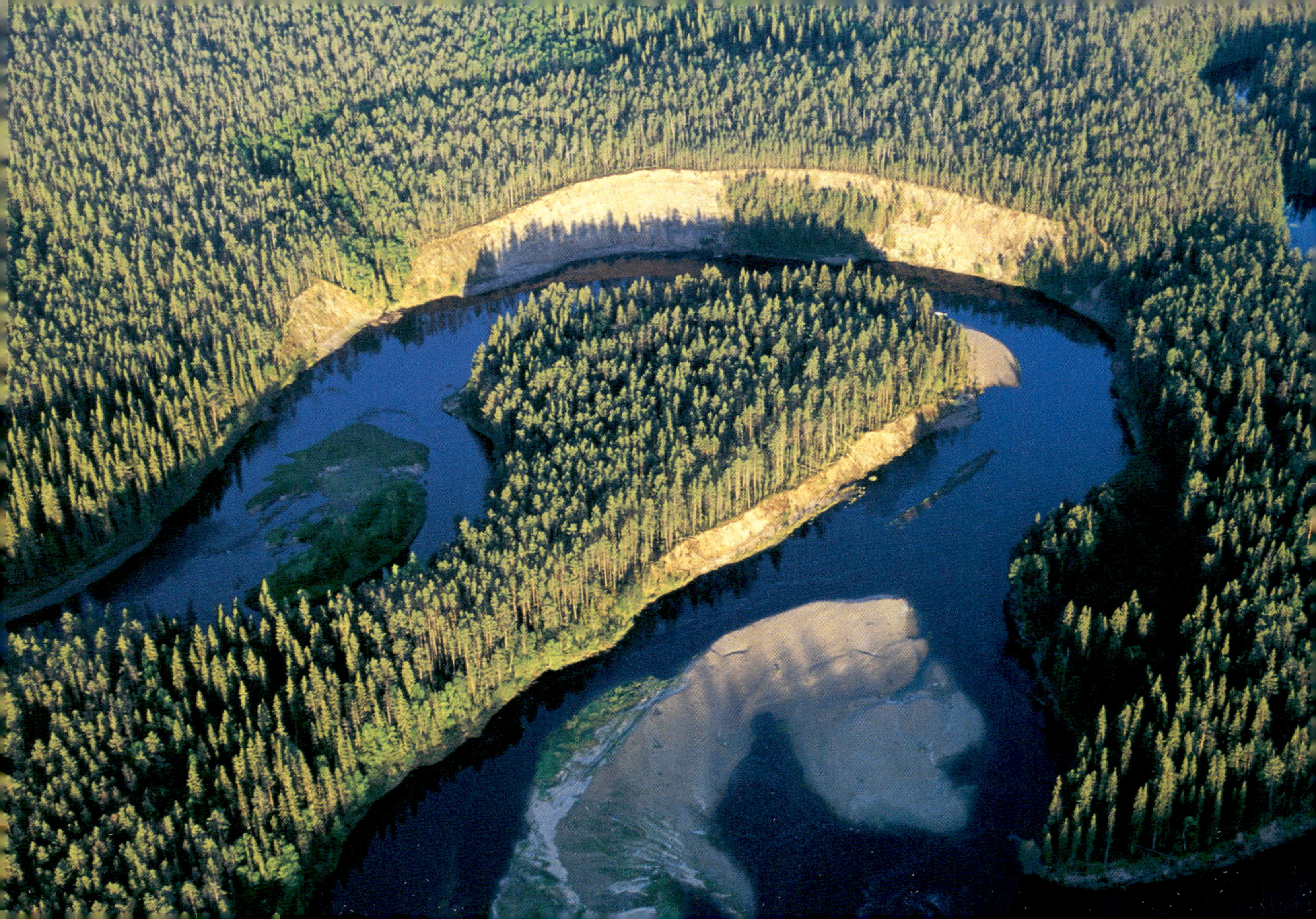

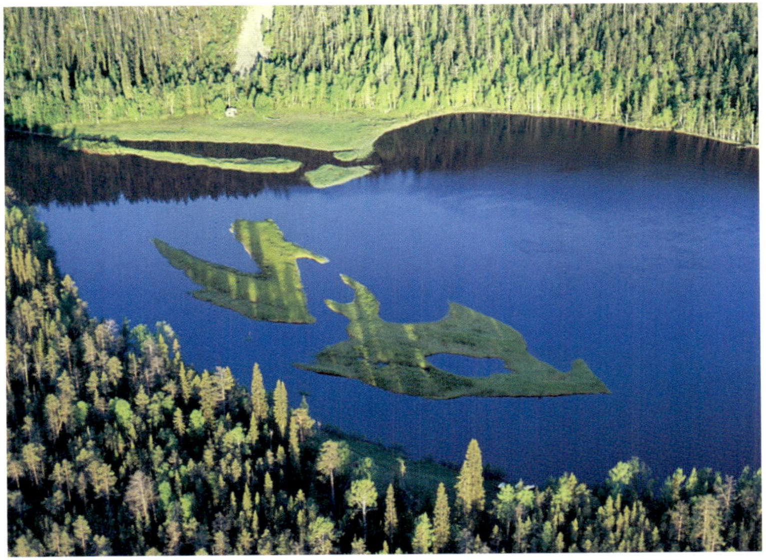

332

Despite the fact that it flows near the Arctic Circle, the Culanka River favors the growth of green vegetation along its course.

333

Under the June sun, the foliage of the conifers throws the shadow of their long silhouettes across a lake in the Finnish region of Kuusamo, near the Arctic Circle.

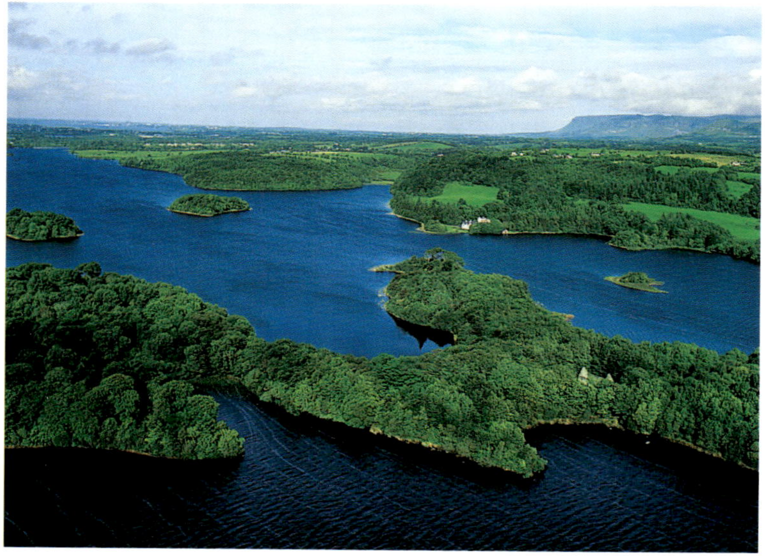

334
Lough Gill, in the Irish county of Sligo, hosts numerous varieties of fish, among them trout and salmon.

335
Lough Ree, located in the heart of Ireland, is a dilatation of the basin of the Shannon River, surrounded by fertile terrain under cultivation.

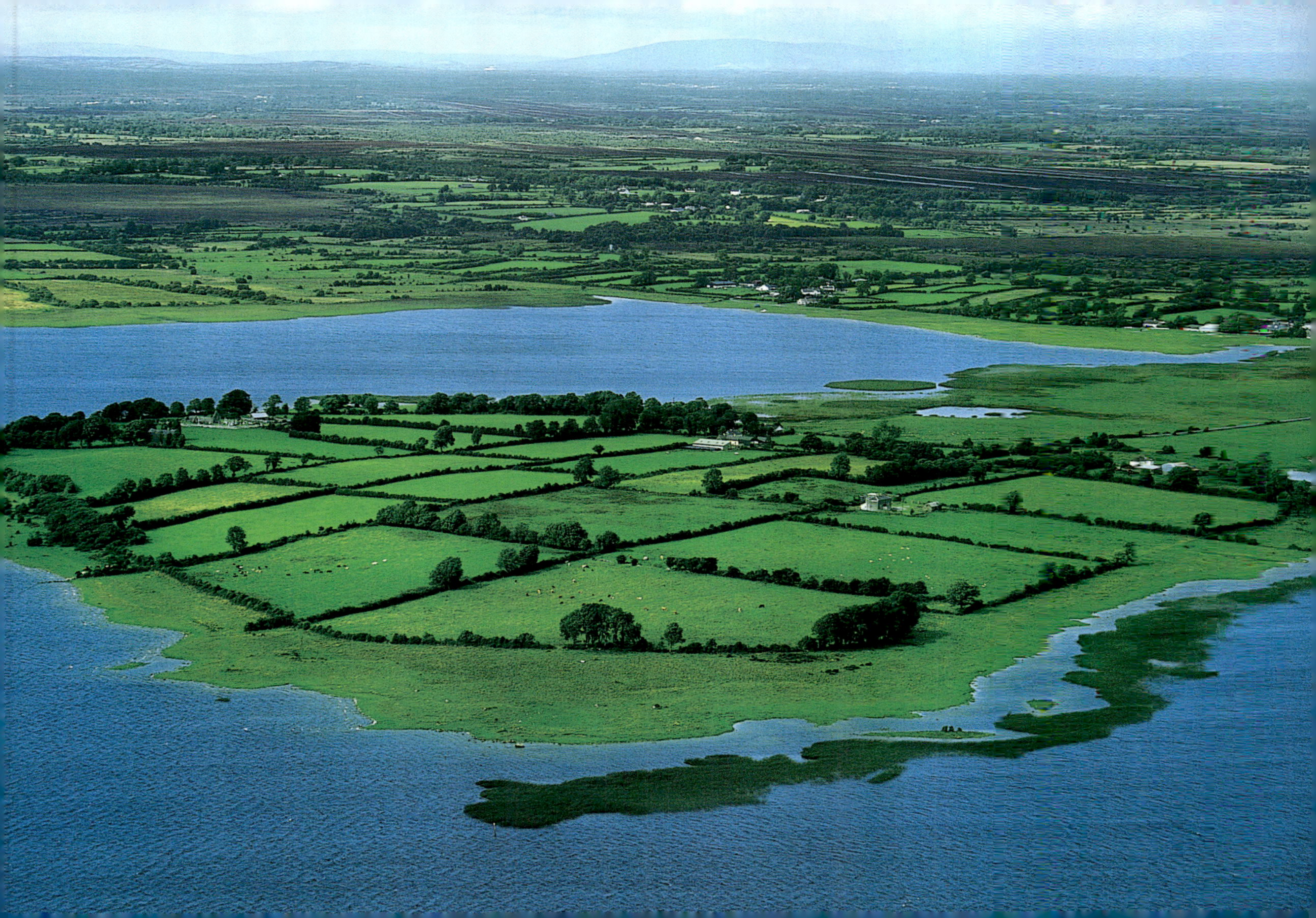

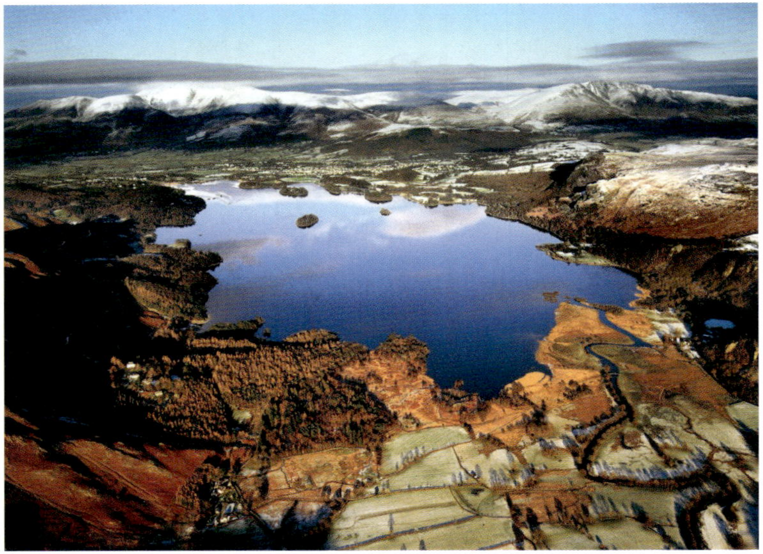

336

In British Cumbria, north of Lancaster, the Lake District is found, a region famous for its lakes, of which one of the biggest is the Derentwater.

337

One of the symbols of England, the Thames, seen here in the Swinford Bridge area, has a short but almost entirely navigable course.

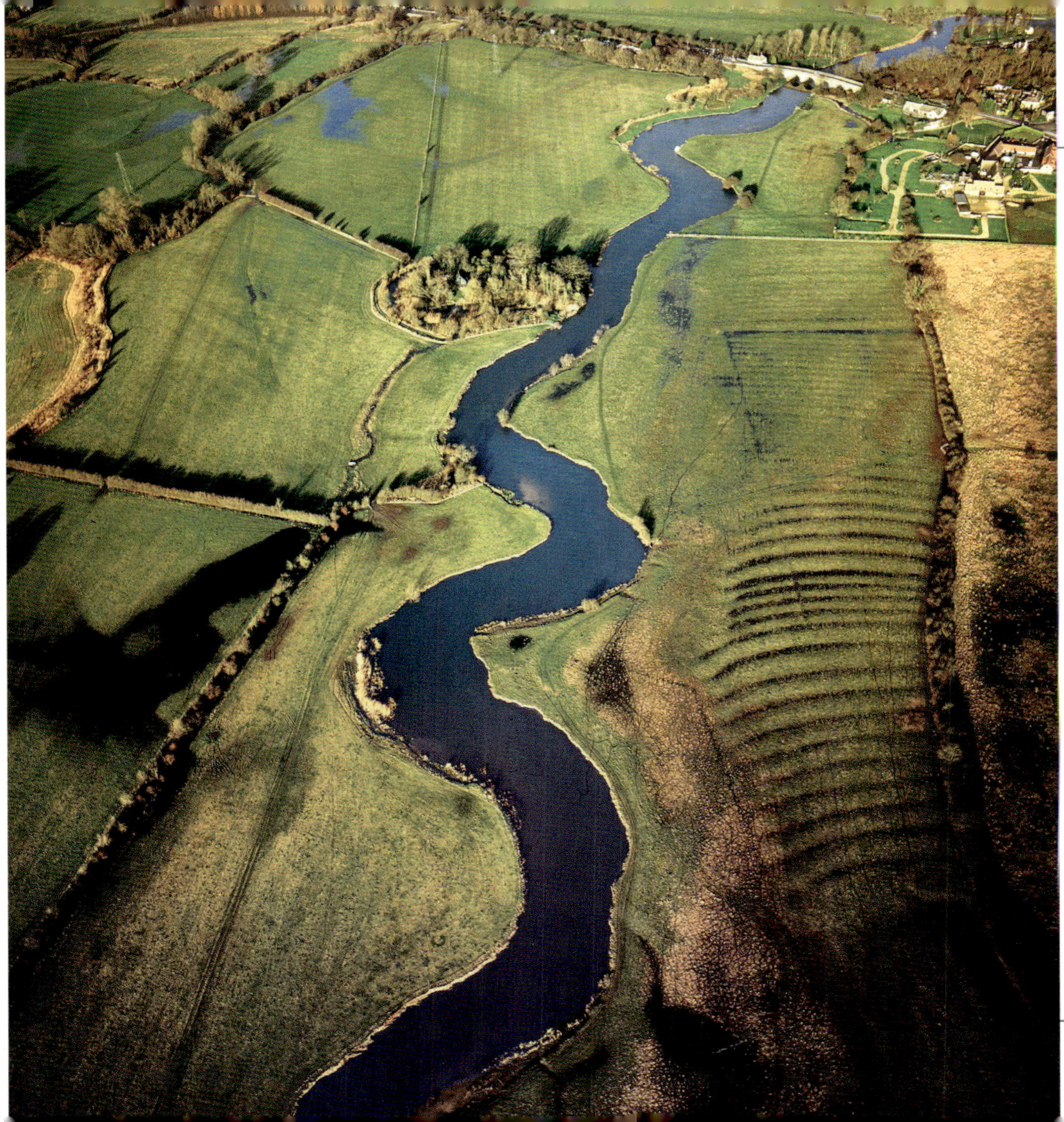

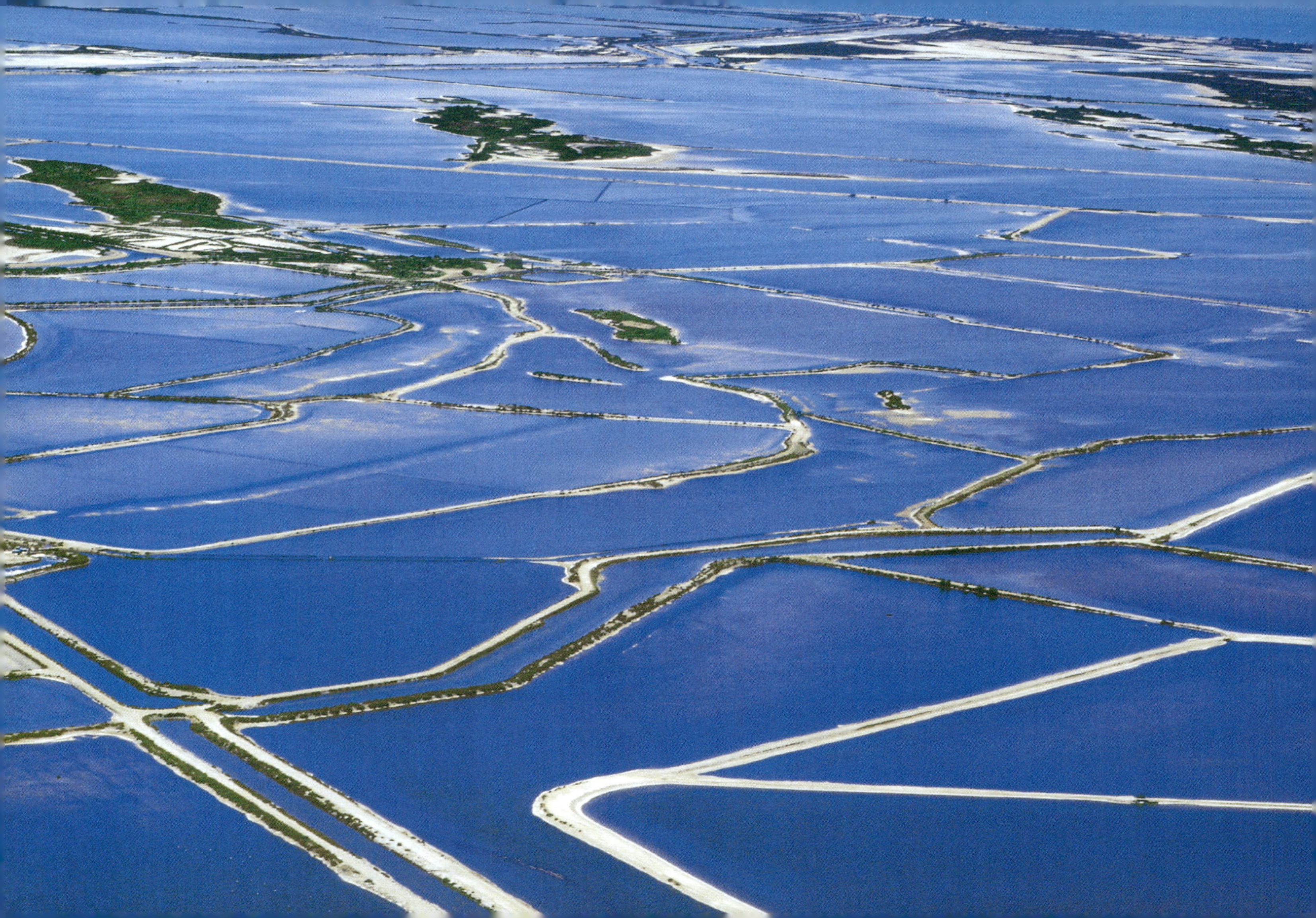

338

A chain of saltwater evaporation pools stretches for thousands of acres in Camargue, in France.

339

The Canal du Midi, in France, links Toulouse, on the Atlantic, to the Mediterranean Sète, traveling 149 miles.

340-341

Fishing pools in the Venetian lagoon, known as "barrier-style," are formed by a pond surrounded by earth dykes furnished with drains, mechanisms making it possible to change the water.

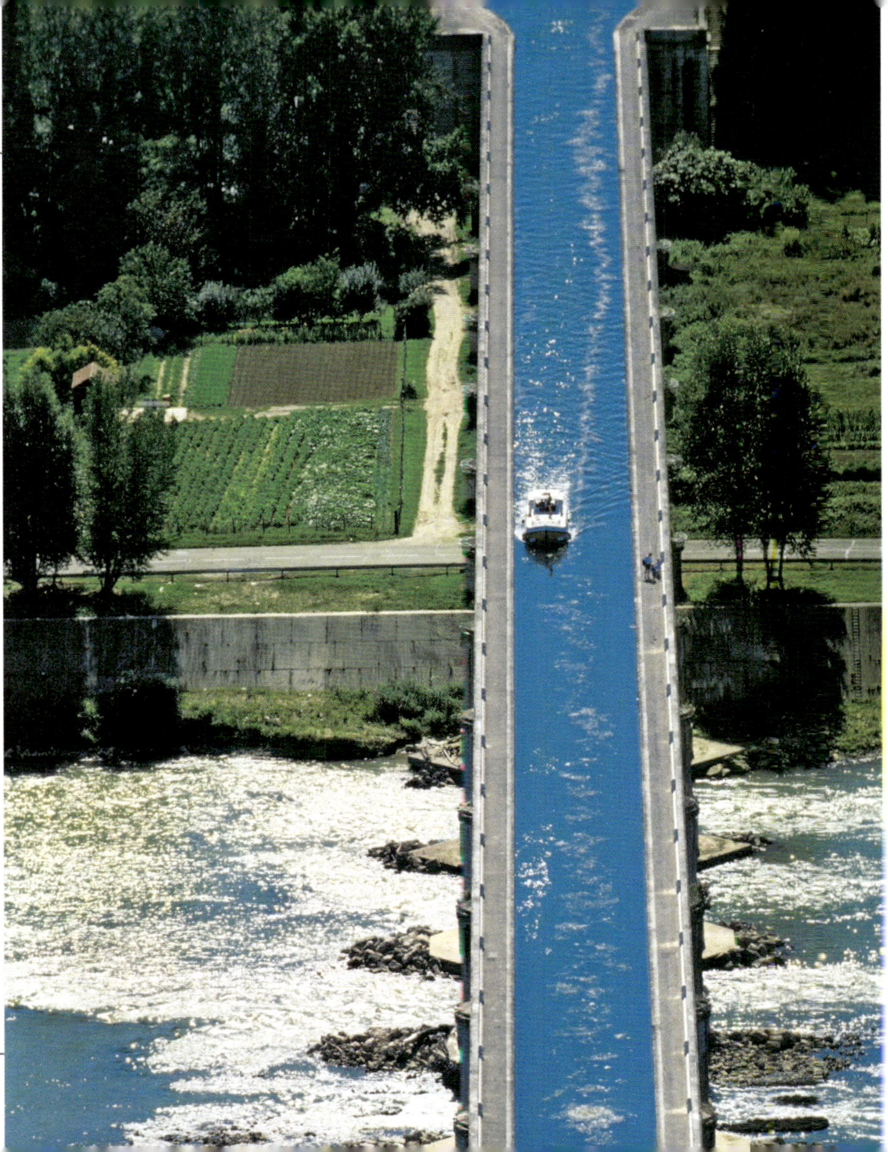

339

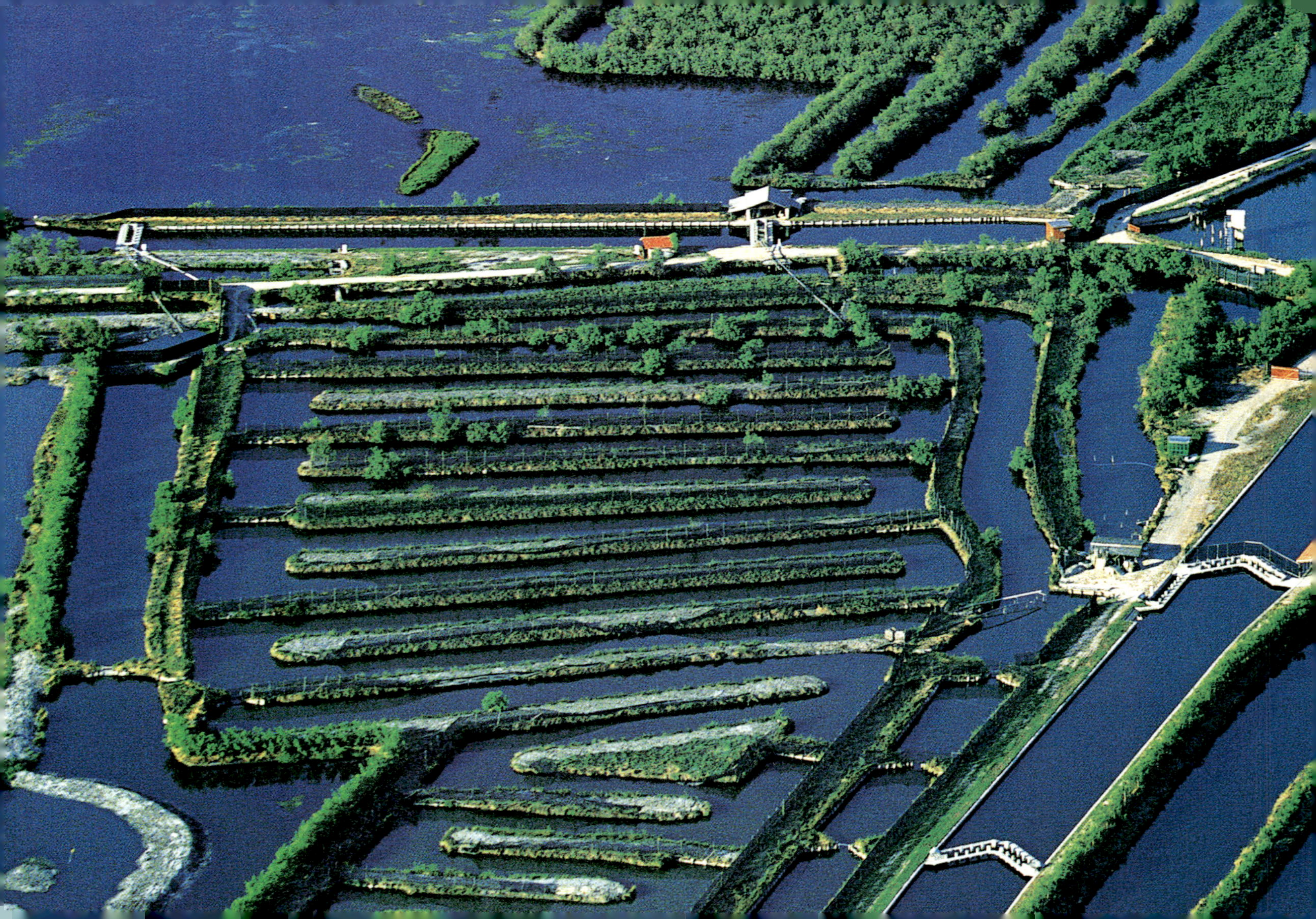

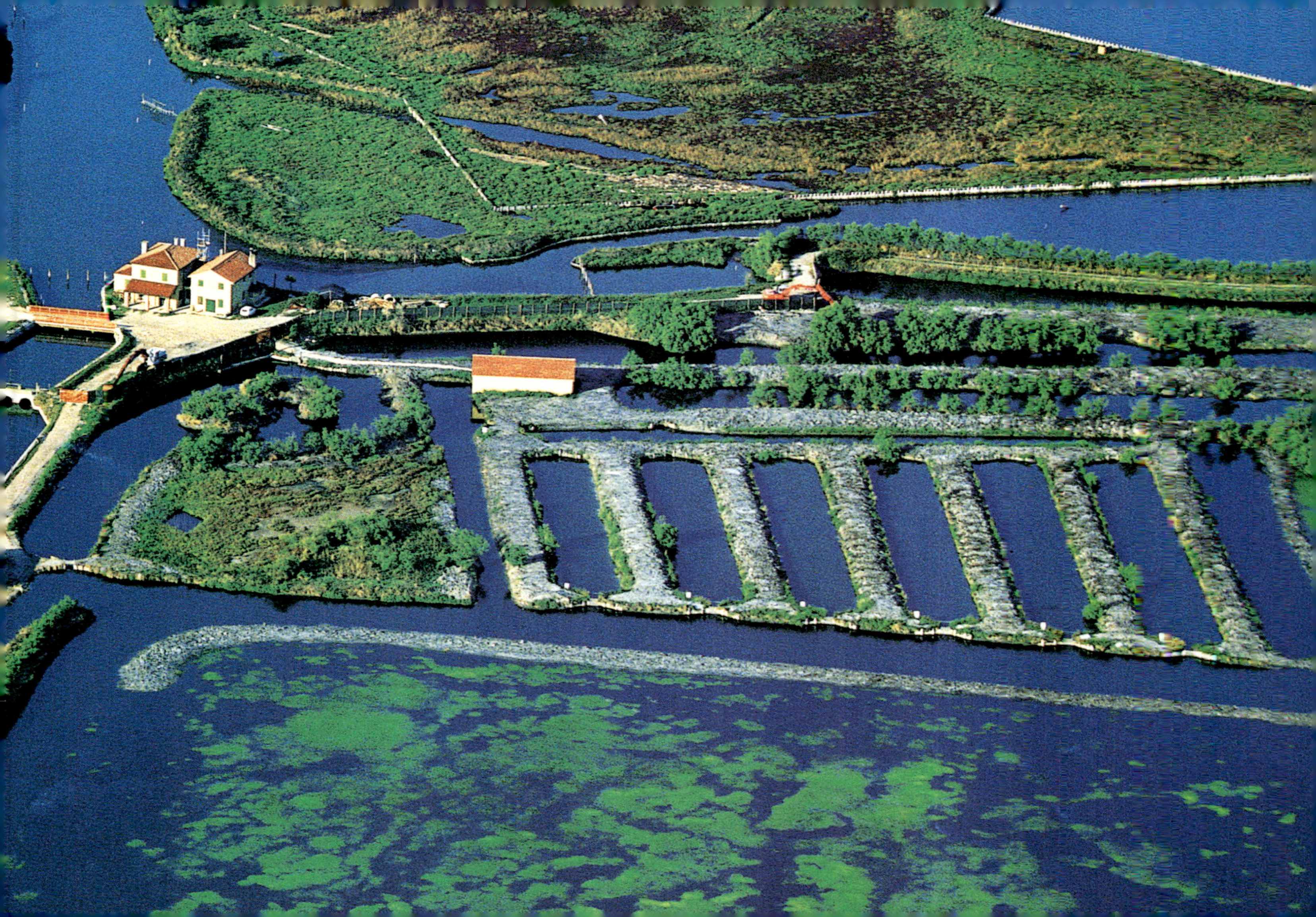

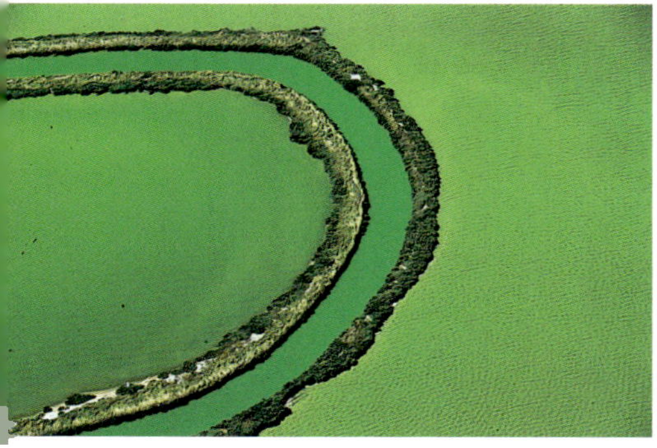

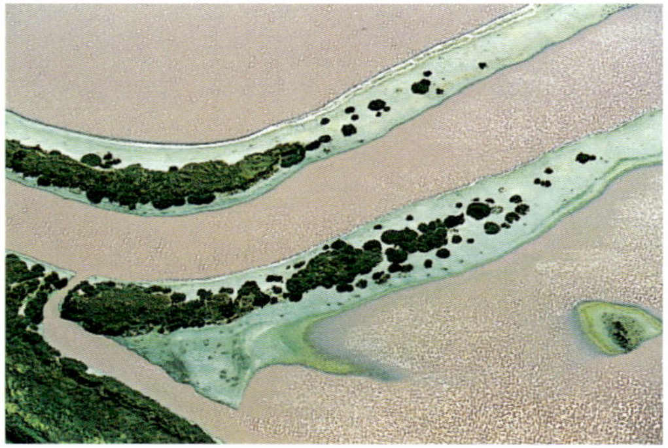

342
In the Po Delta area, in Italy, natural aquatic habitats of different types coexist: depending on the zone, brackish ponds or freshwater humid zones can be found.

343
In the sixteenth century, the shallow course of the Po River started to be regulated through hydraulic engineering works permitting the collection of saltwater in artificial reservoirs.

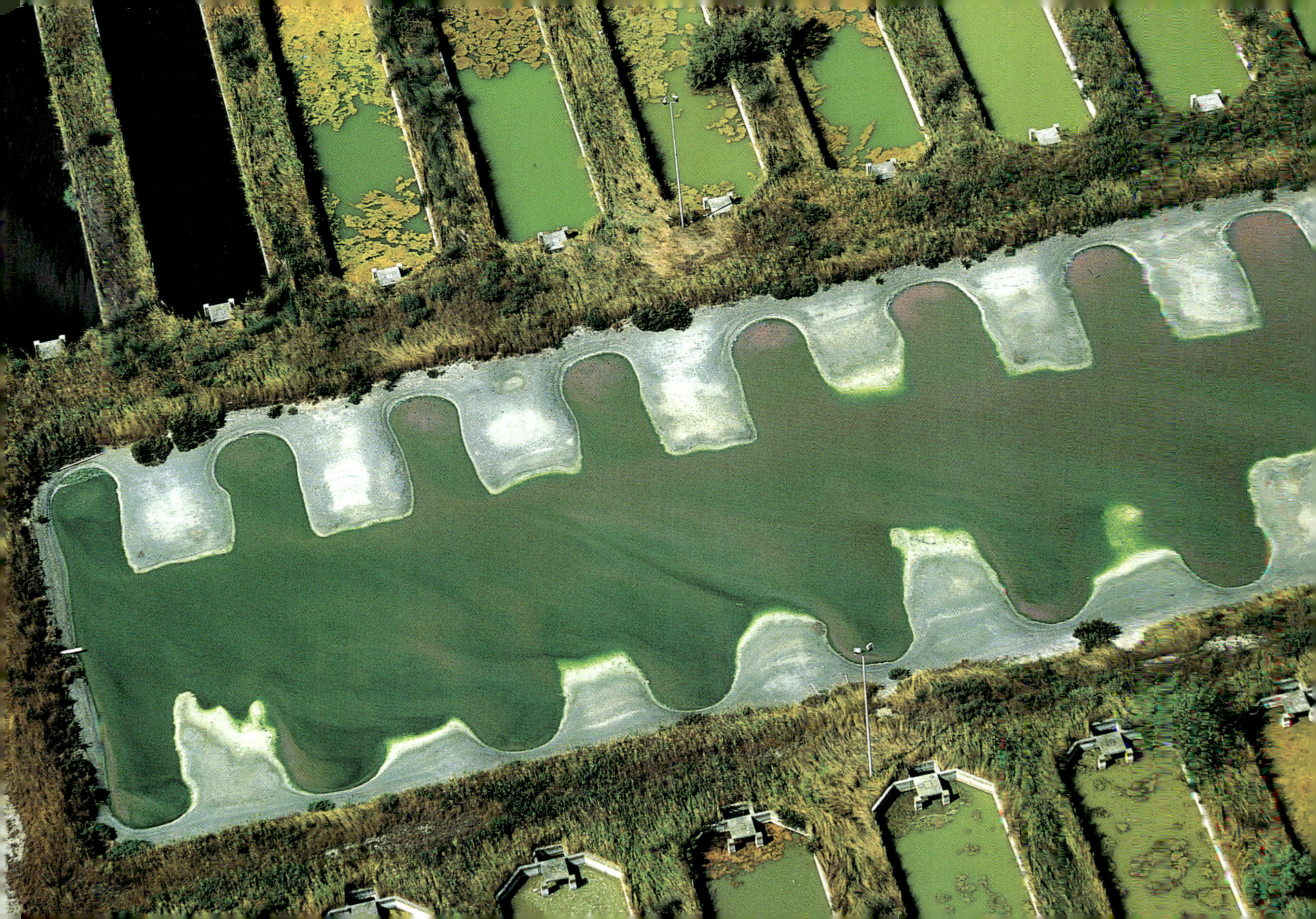

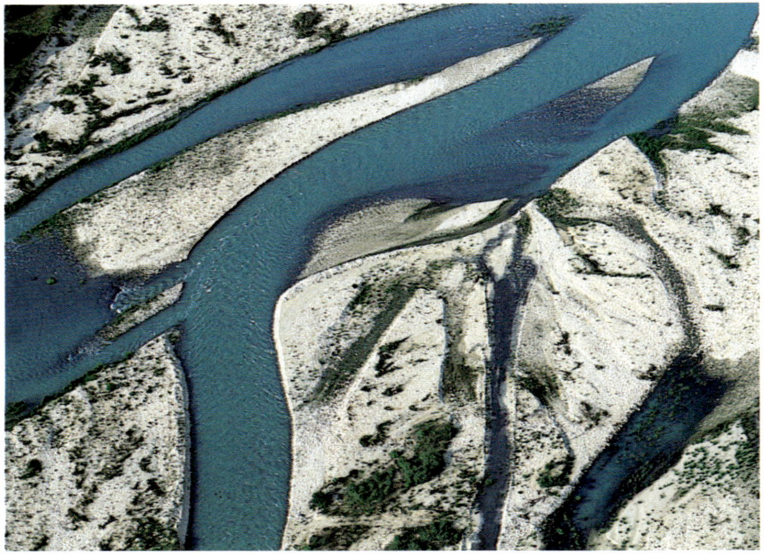

344 and 345

The Italian rivers of the Po Valley (photo on the left), along its course through Piedmont and Tagliamento (photo on the right), in Friuli-Venezia Giulia, are affected by the phenomenon of resurgences: rain and river waters, finding permeable ground composed of porous material, are absorbed only to then return to the surface once they encounter the impermeable layers of the low plains.

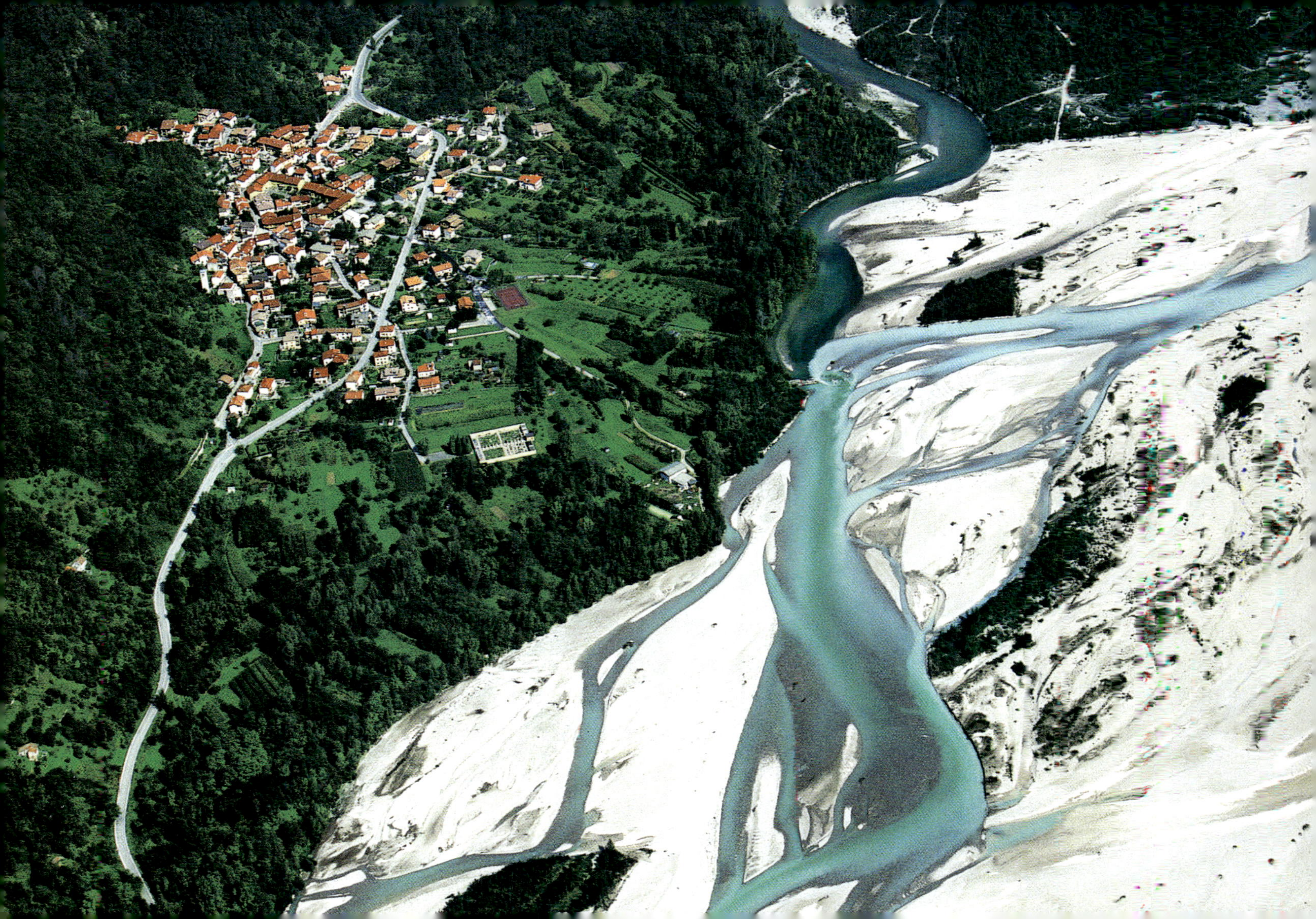

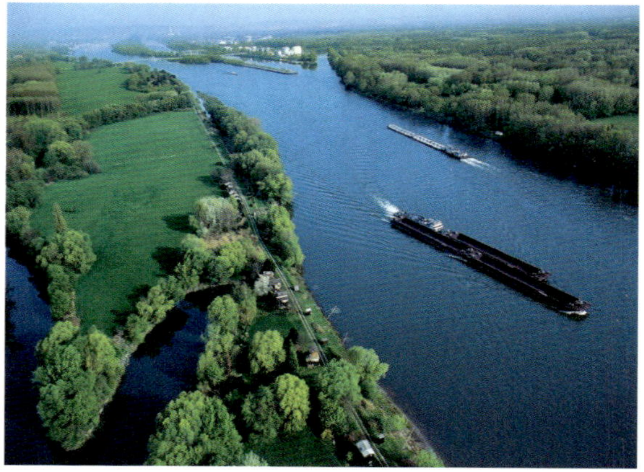

346
Once it reaches Austria, the course of the Danube becomes flat for about 600 miles, travelable on long flatboats.

347
The Velika is the second longest river in Serbia, whose fertile plains it crosses, and is an important tributary of the Danube.

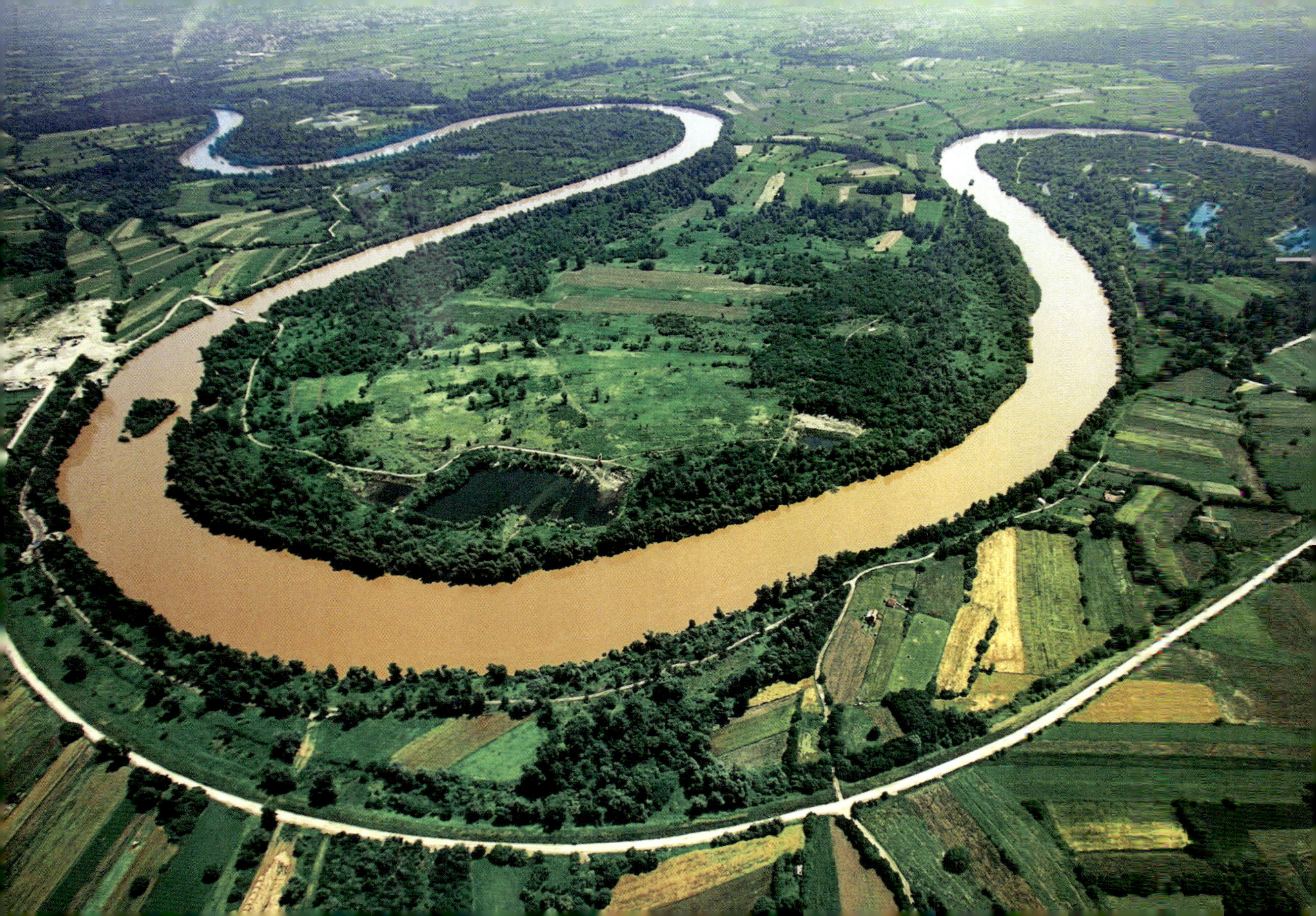

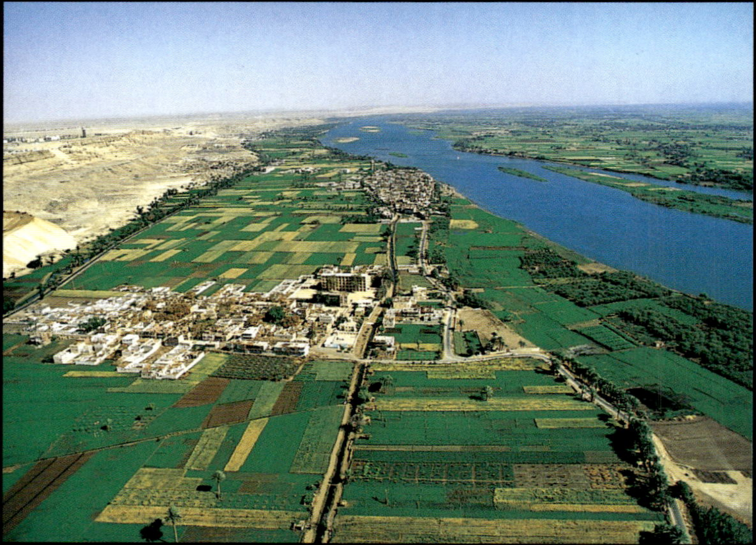

348 and 349
The countryside lining the Nile in the Luxor area is green and densely cultivated.

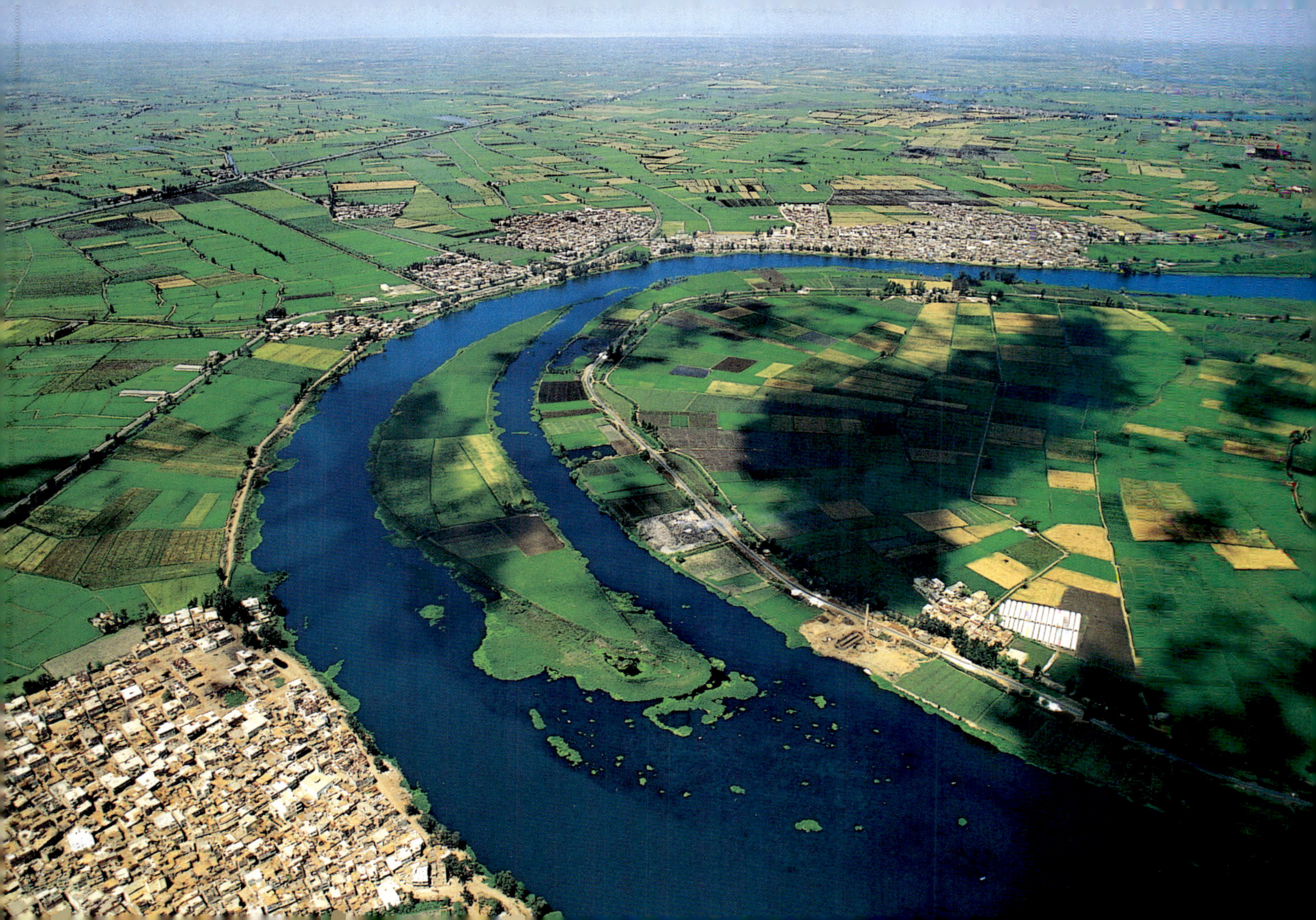

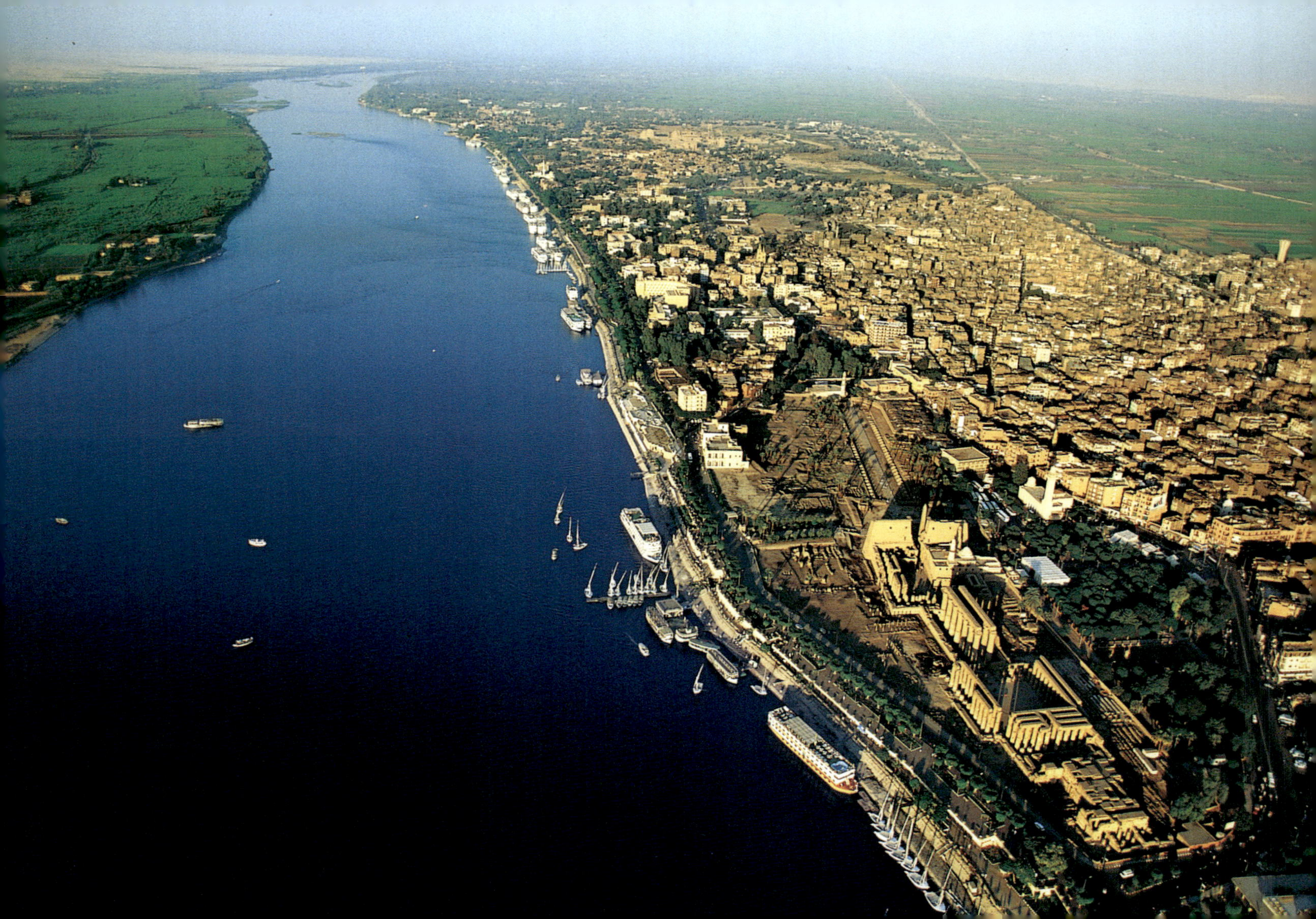

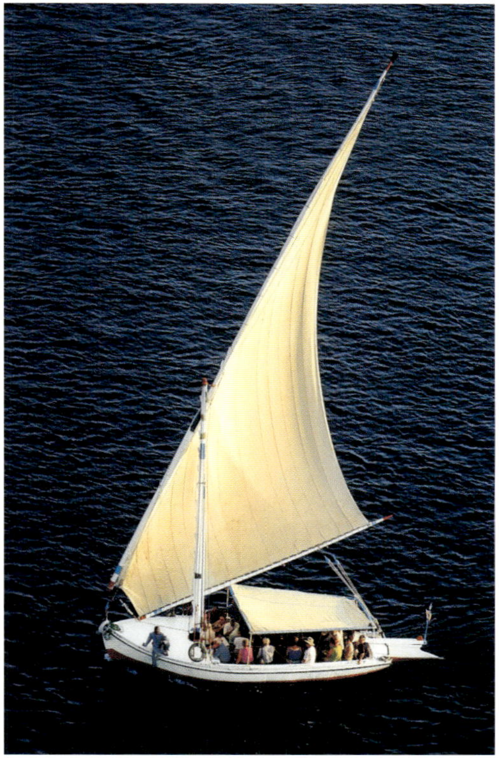

350 and 351
Luxor looks onto the right bank of the Nile, which is crowded with numerous crafts used by the local population or, along this tract, by foreign tourists.

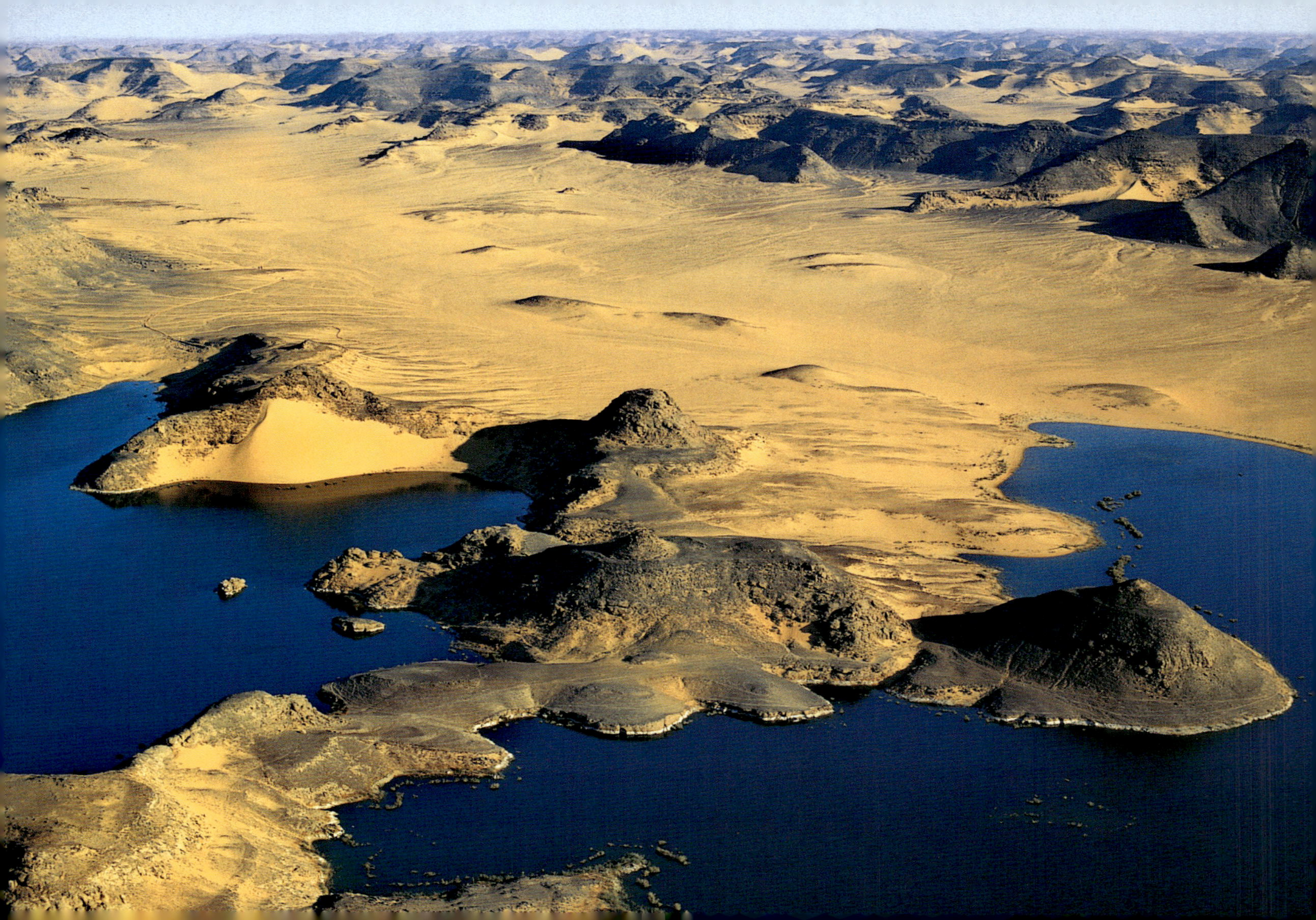

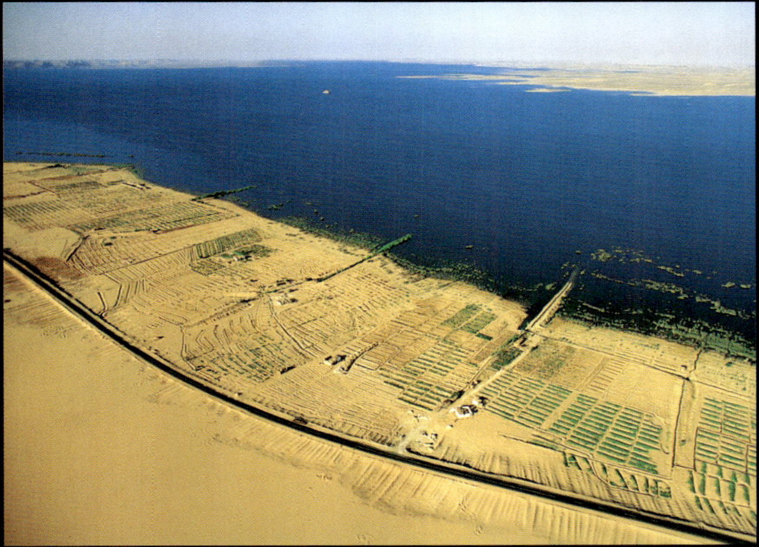

352 and 353
Lake Nasser in Egypt, created thanks to the construction of the Aswan Dam in 1971, which blocked the course of the Nile, flooded 191 square miles of desert; aridity is the dominant feature of the basin's shores.

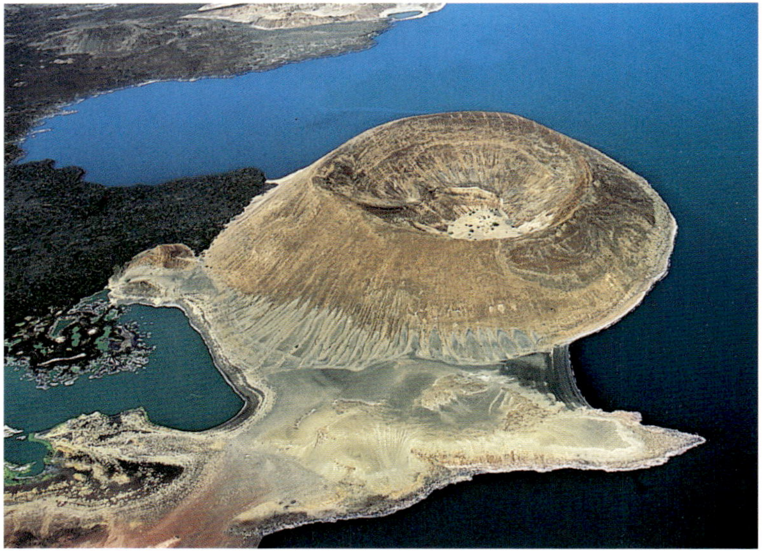

354

At the northern border of Kenya with Ethiopia, Lake Turkana is found in a desolate-looking continental depression, with fields of lavitic rock interrupted by volcanoes like the Nyabuyatom.

355

Lake Natron in Tanzania is a saltwater basin located at 1,970 feet, surrounded by arid savannah broken in tracts by stony desert.

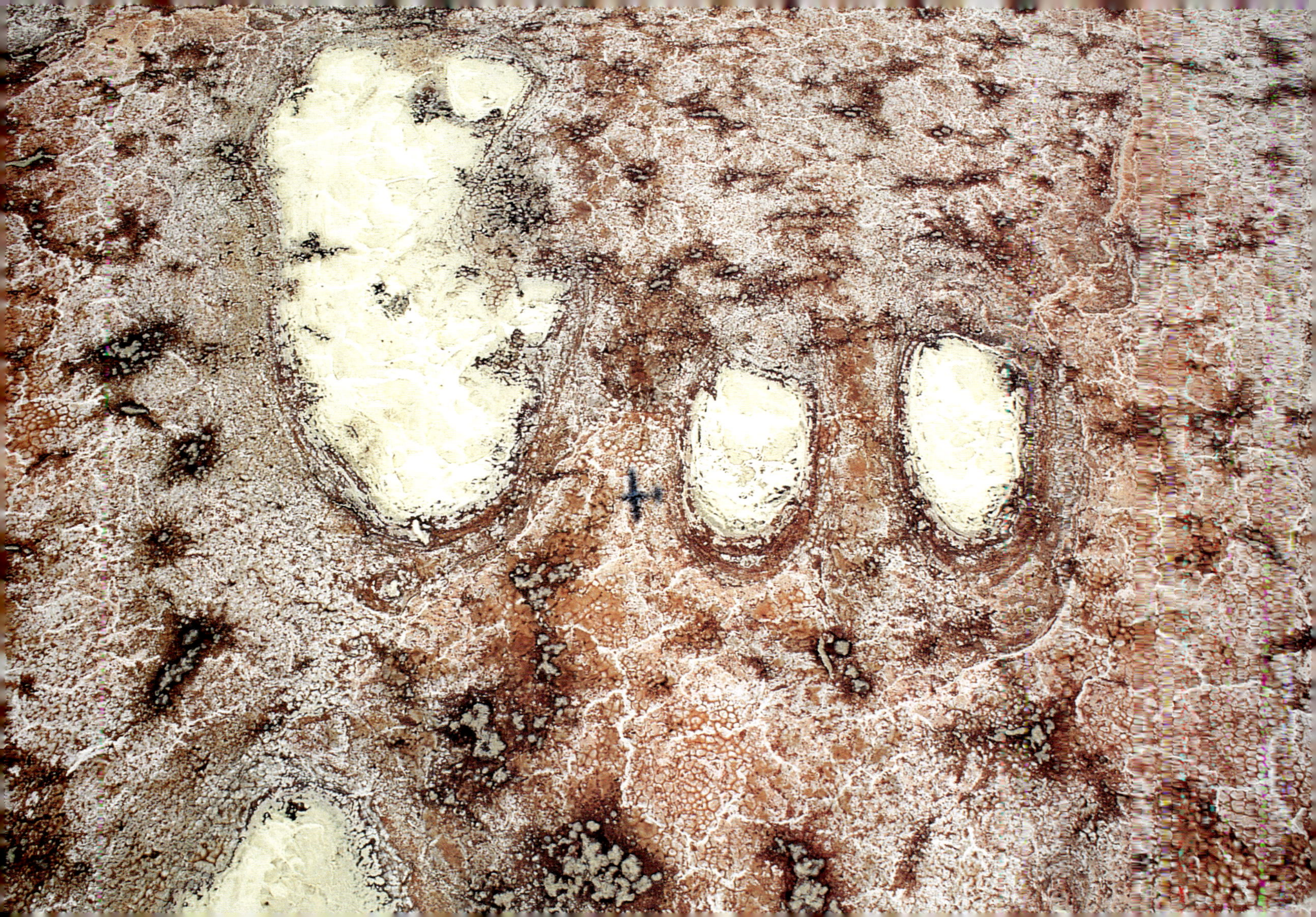

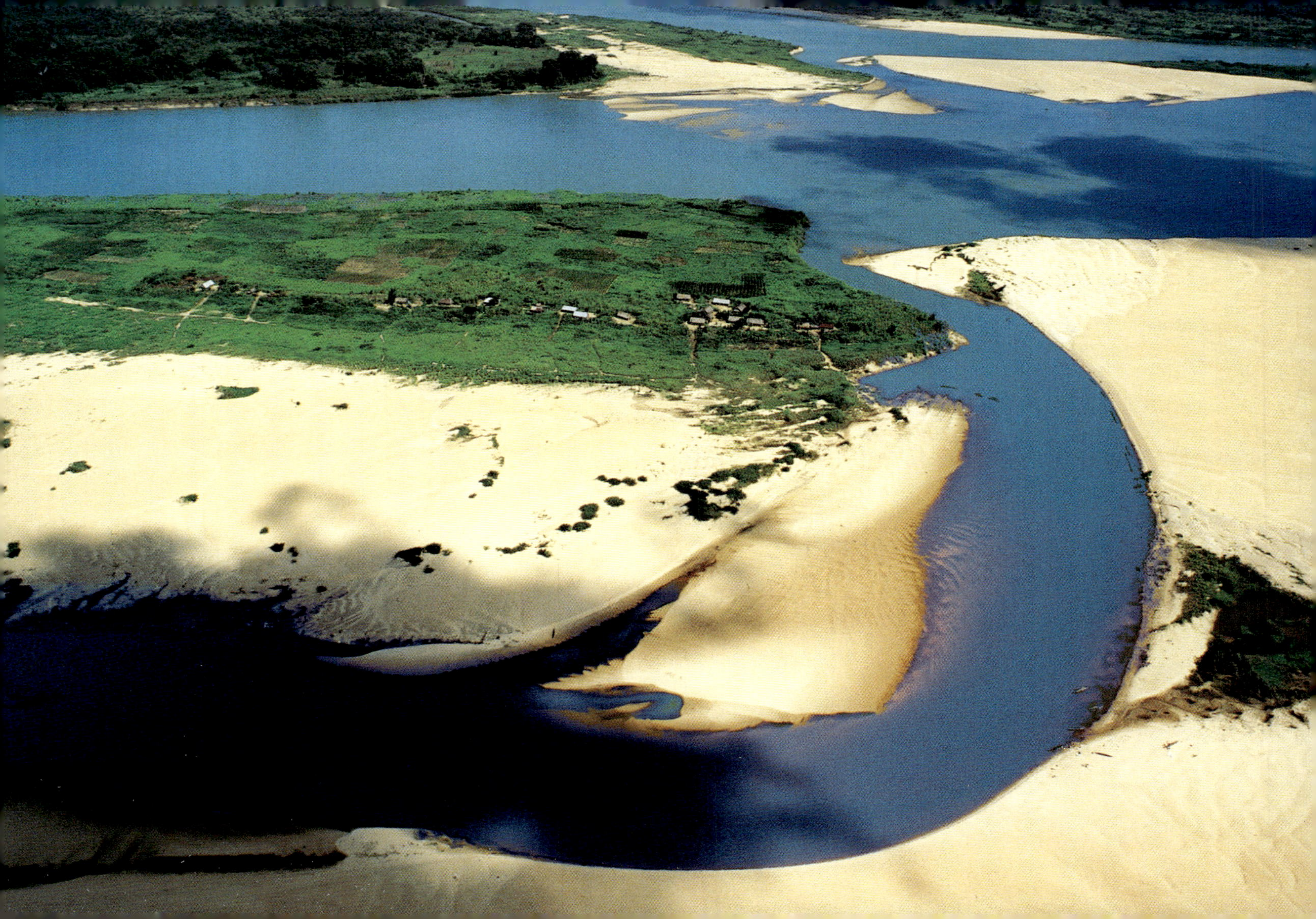

356

A small village at the mouth of the Niger River in Nigeria can take advantage of both the fresh river water and the saltwater of the Gulf of Guinea.

357 left

The Kuilou Basin covers about 60 percent of the surface in the northern and central coastal areas in Congo before flowing into the Atlantic Ocean.

357 right

The area of the Nigerian delta is at 2,500 miles distance from its sources.

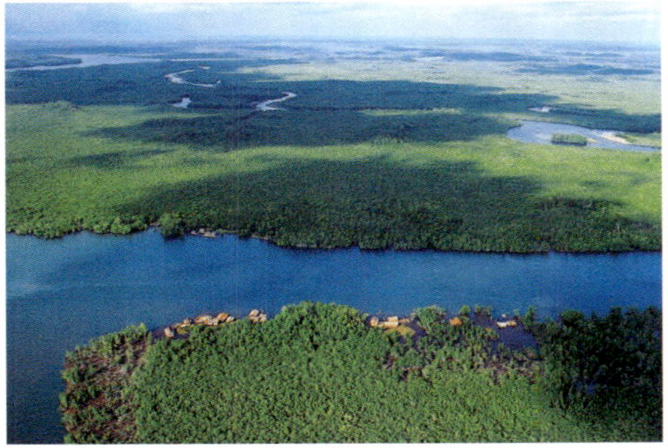

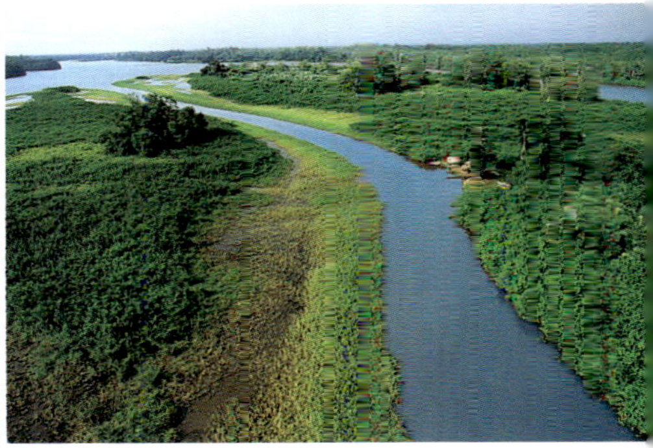

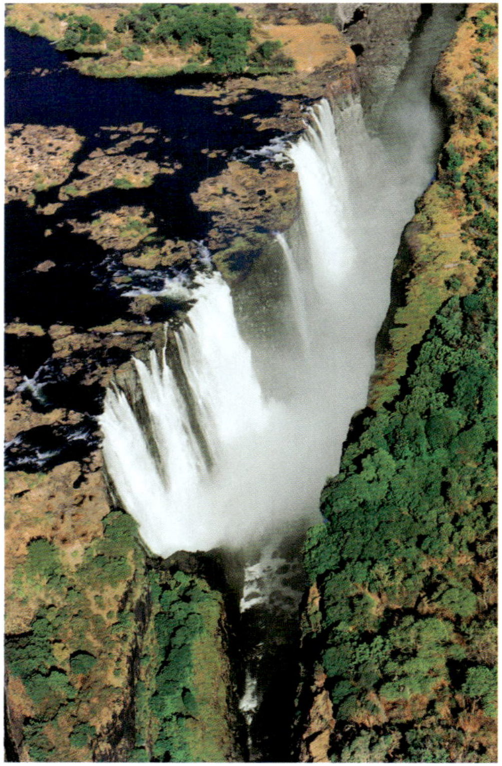

358 and 359

At the Zambia-Zimbabwe border, Victoria Falls form, when the Zambesi River is at its fullest between February and March, the longest curtain of water in the world, with a capacity of 132,000,000 gallons of water per minute.

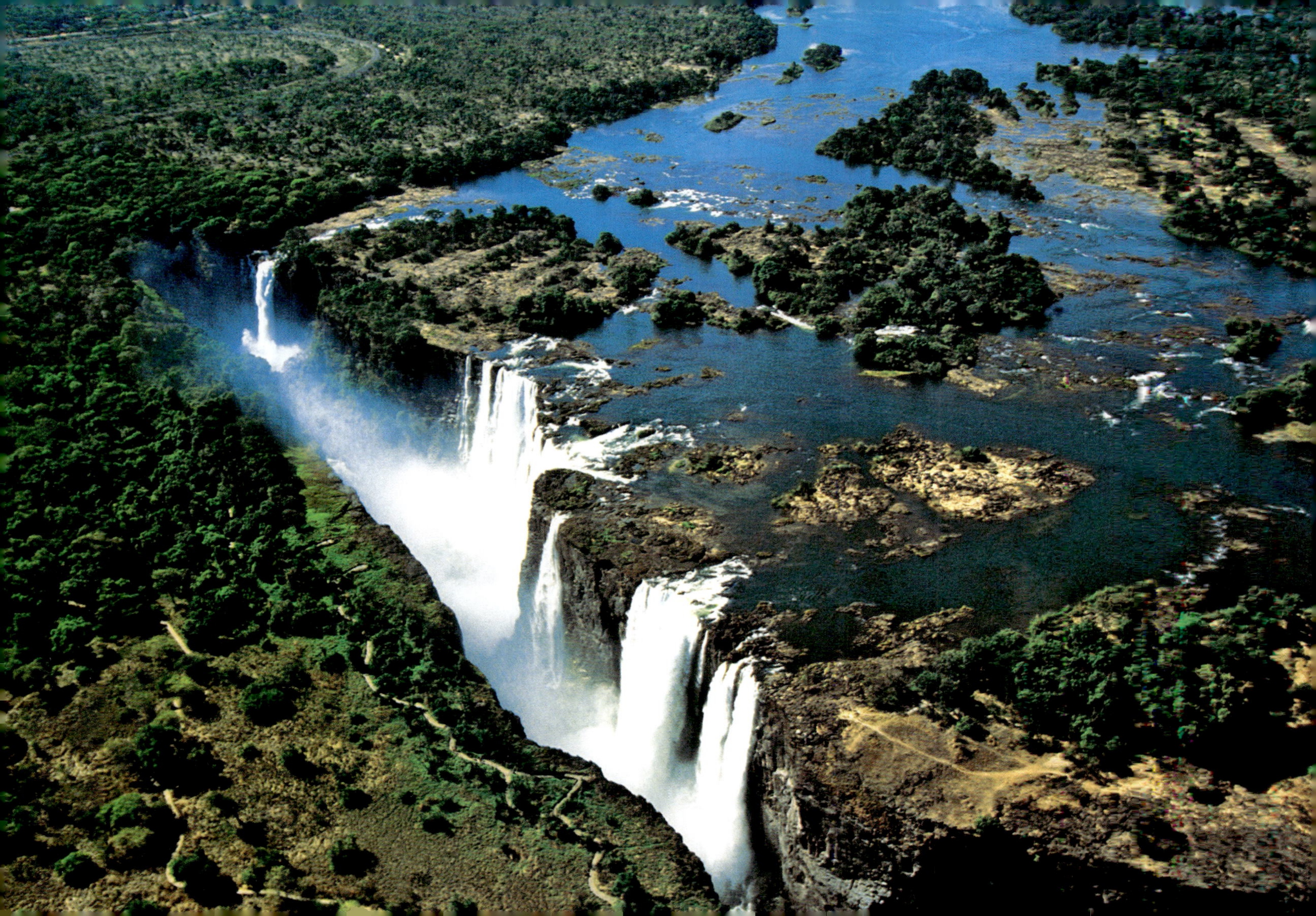

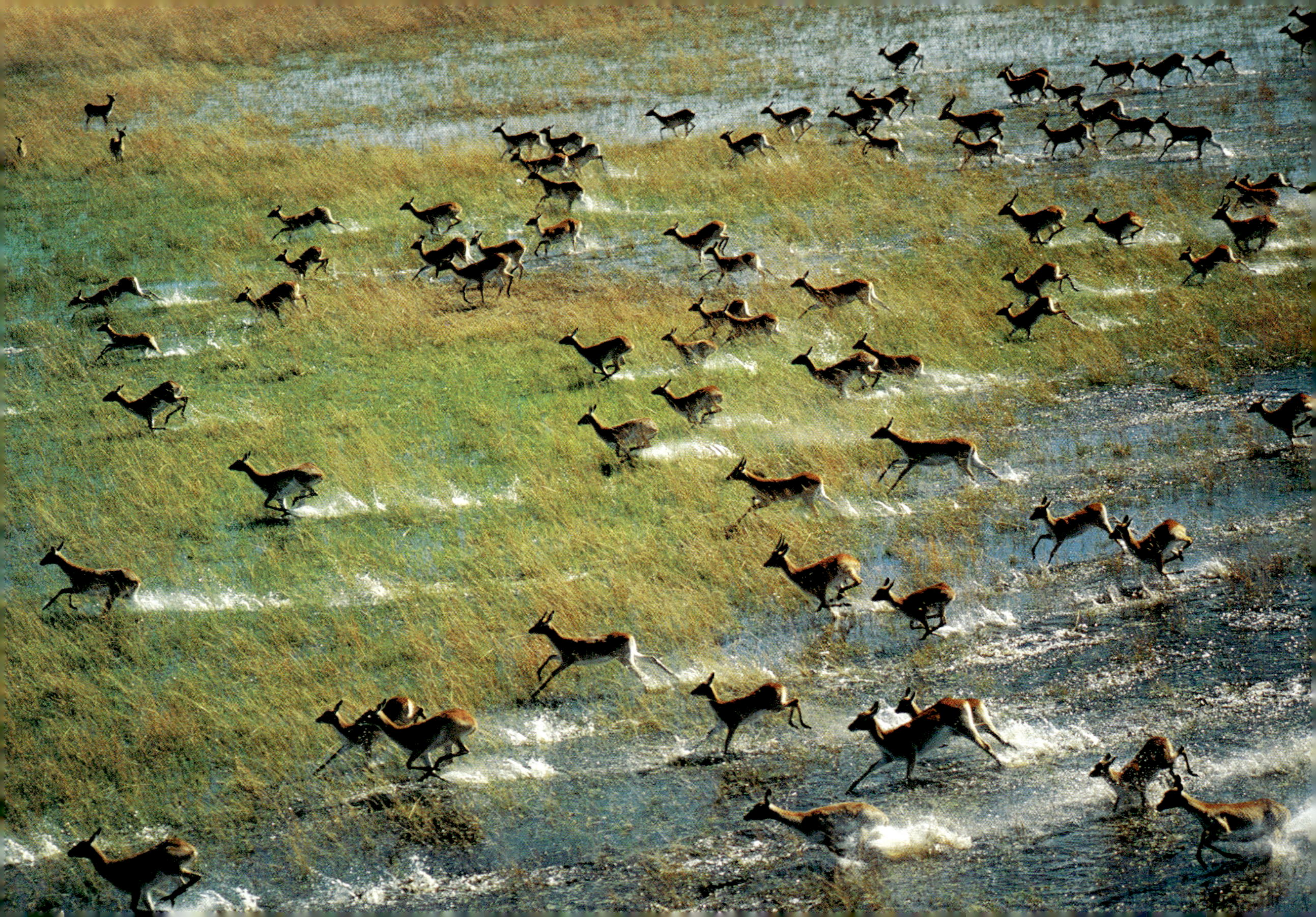

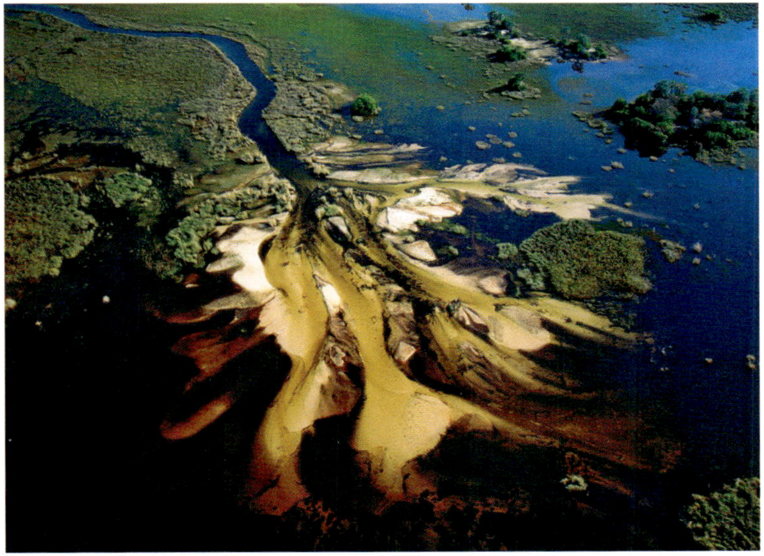

360
A herd of kobus run through a marsh created by the delta of the Okavango River in Botswana.

361
The system of the Okavango River deposits more than 2,000,000 tons of sand on the bottom of the river's delta every year, which spreads out into thousands of streams and ponds.

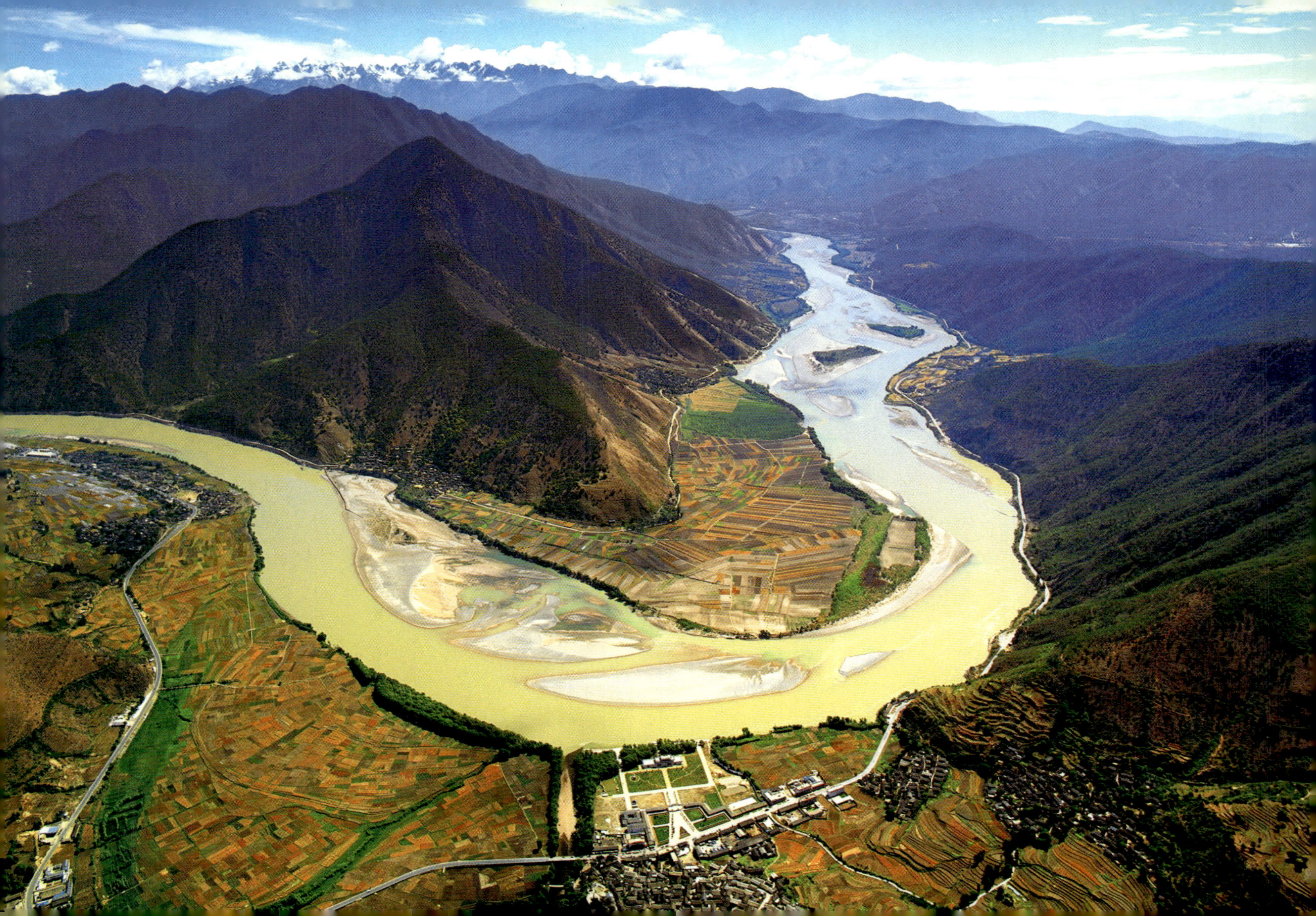

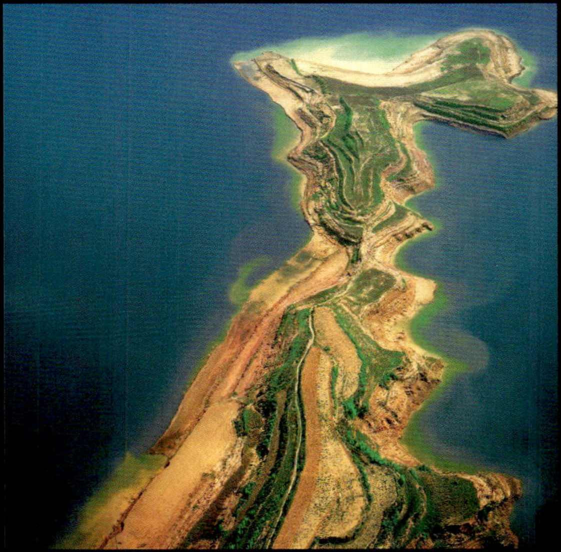

362 and 363

The Blue River, Chiang Jang (left) with its length of about 4,500 miles, is the longest river in China. The second river is the Yellow River (right), which crosses Chinese territory towards the east for about 3,100 miles.

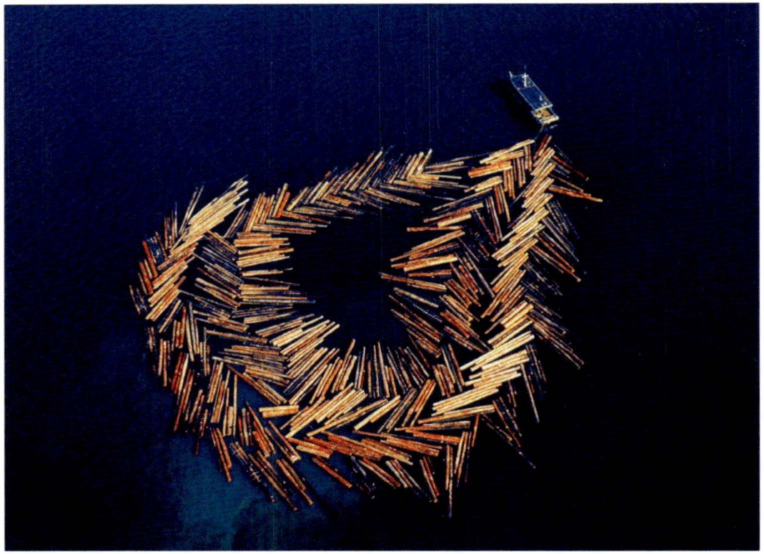

364 and 365
In the Indonesian regions of Sabah and Sarawak, transport occurs above all by way of a river network because of the presence of rough hills in the interior that impede the development of a road network.

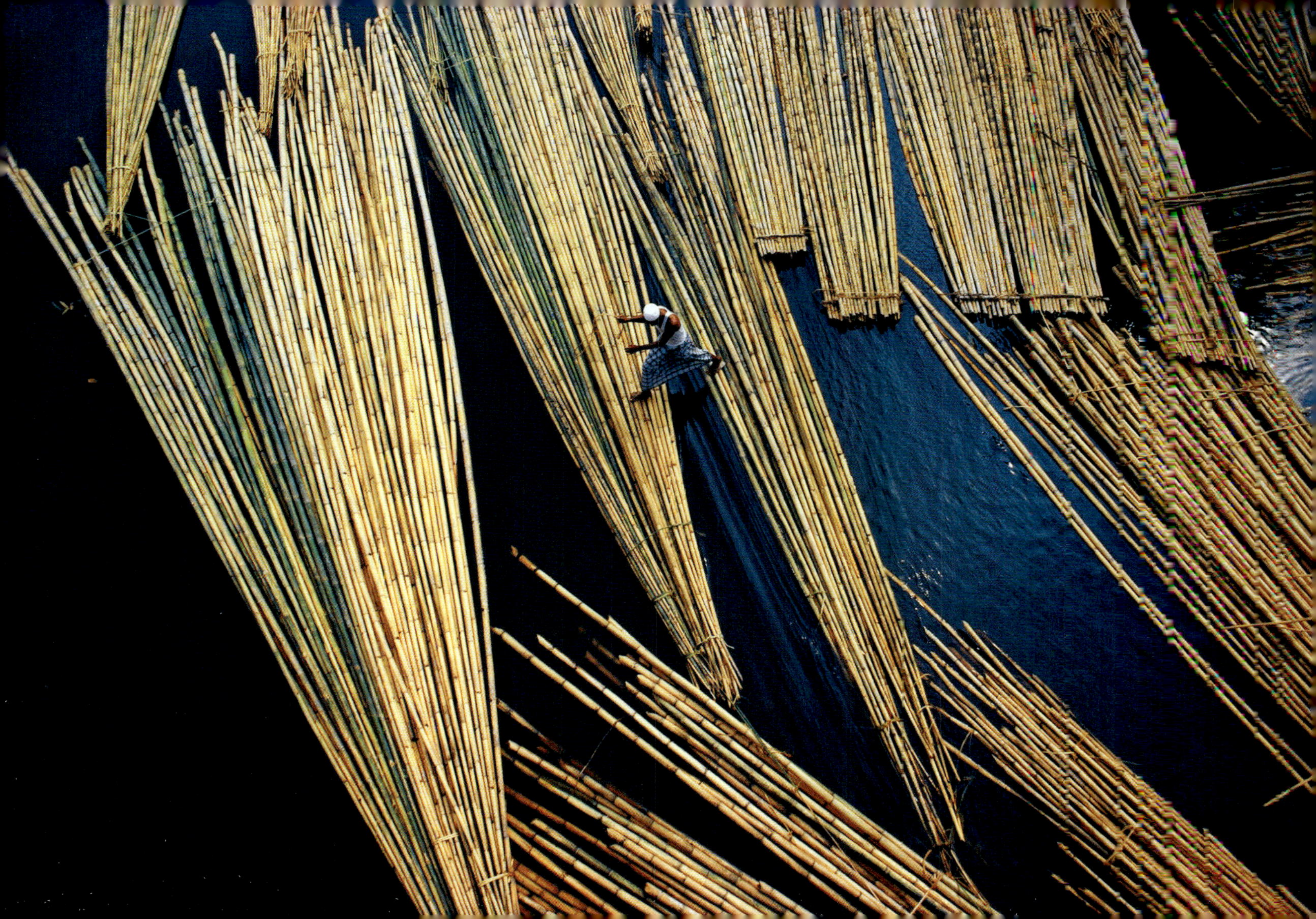

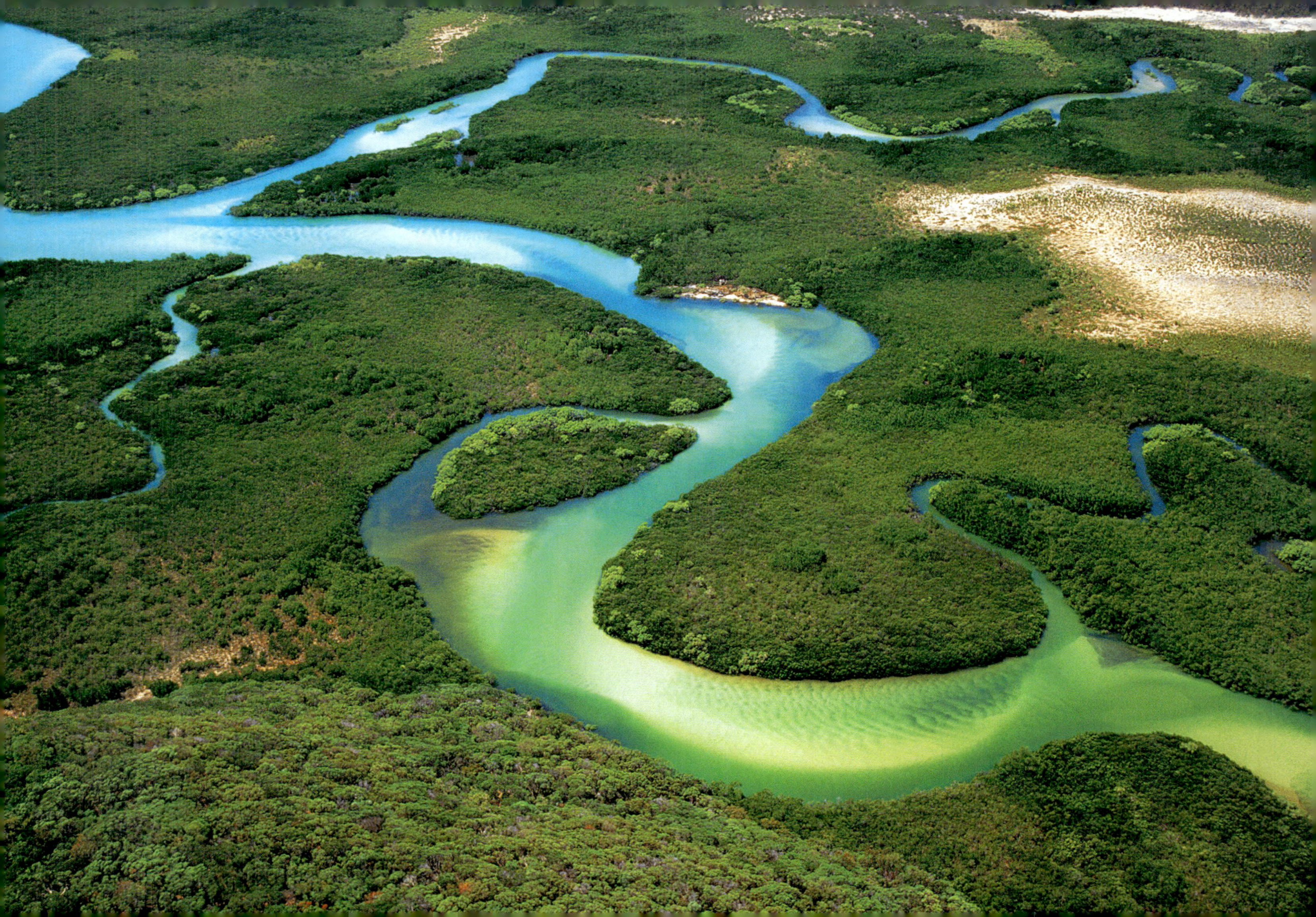

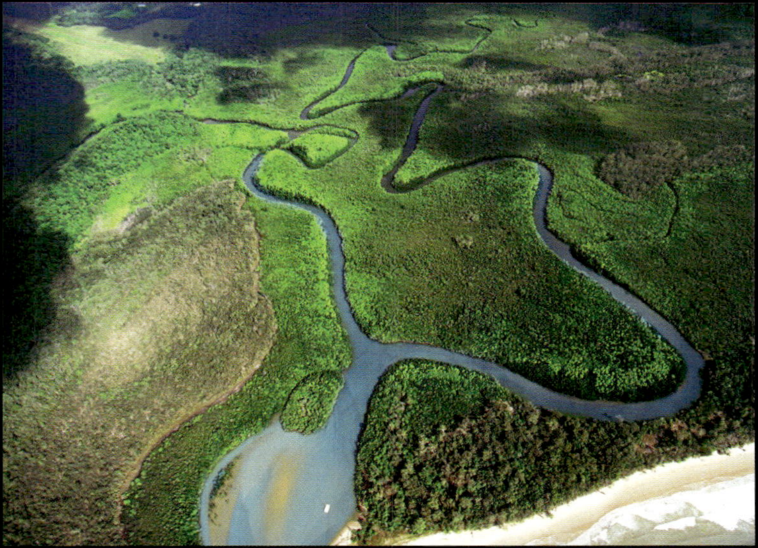

366
A turquoise-colored waterway snakes through the woodsy areas in the immediate interior bordering Whiteheaven Beach, in the Australian Whitsunday Islands.

367
The final tract of the course of the Daintree River, near the Coral Sea, is lined by the rain forest of Australian Queensland.

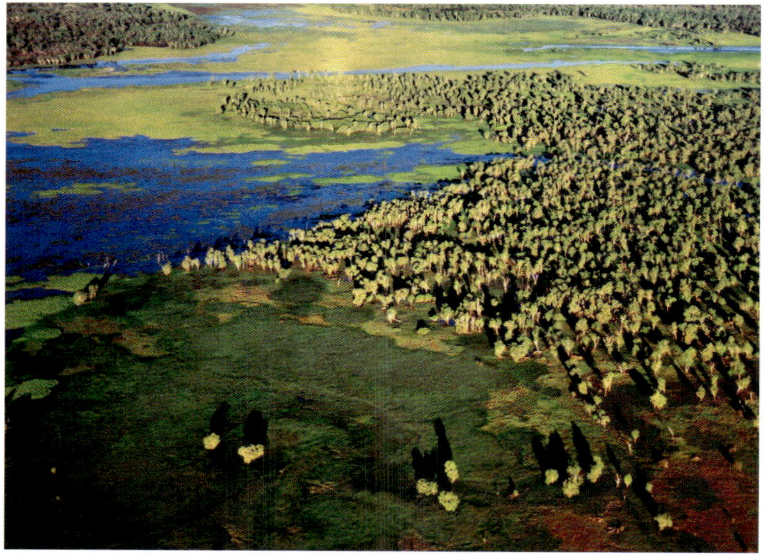

368 and 369
During the dry season, the humid zones of the so-called "Yellow Waters," in the Australian Kakadu National Park, attract numerous animals that come to drink.

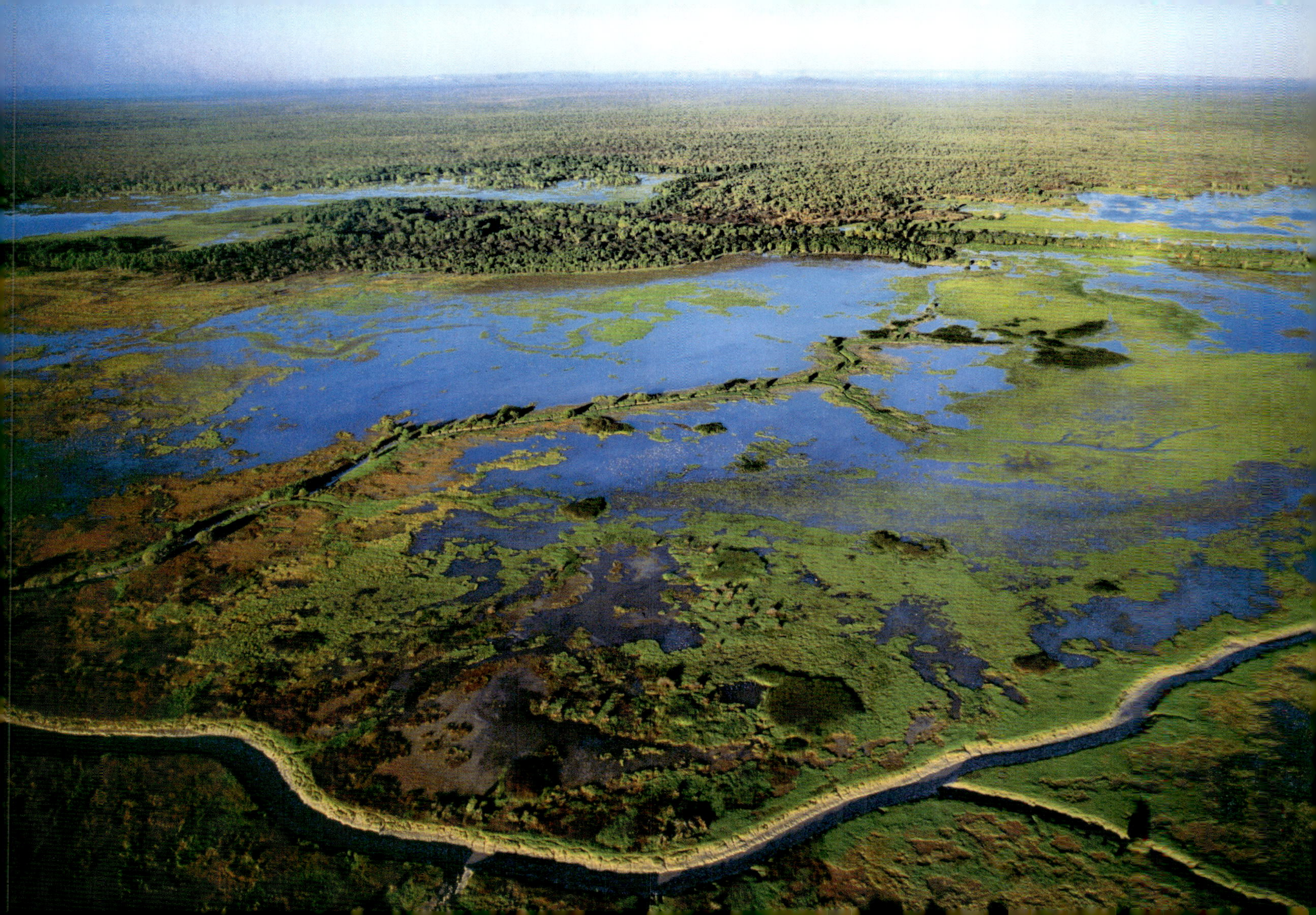

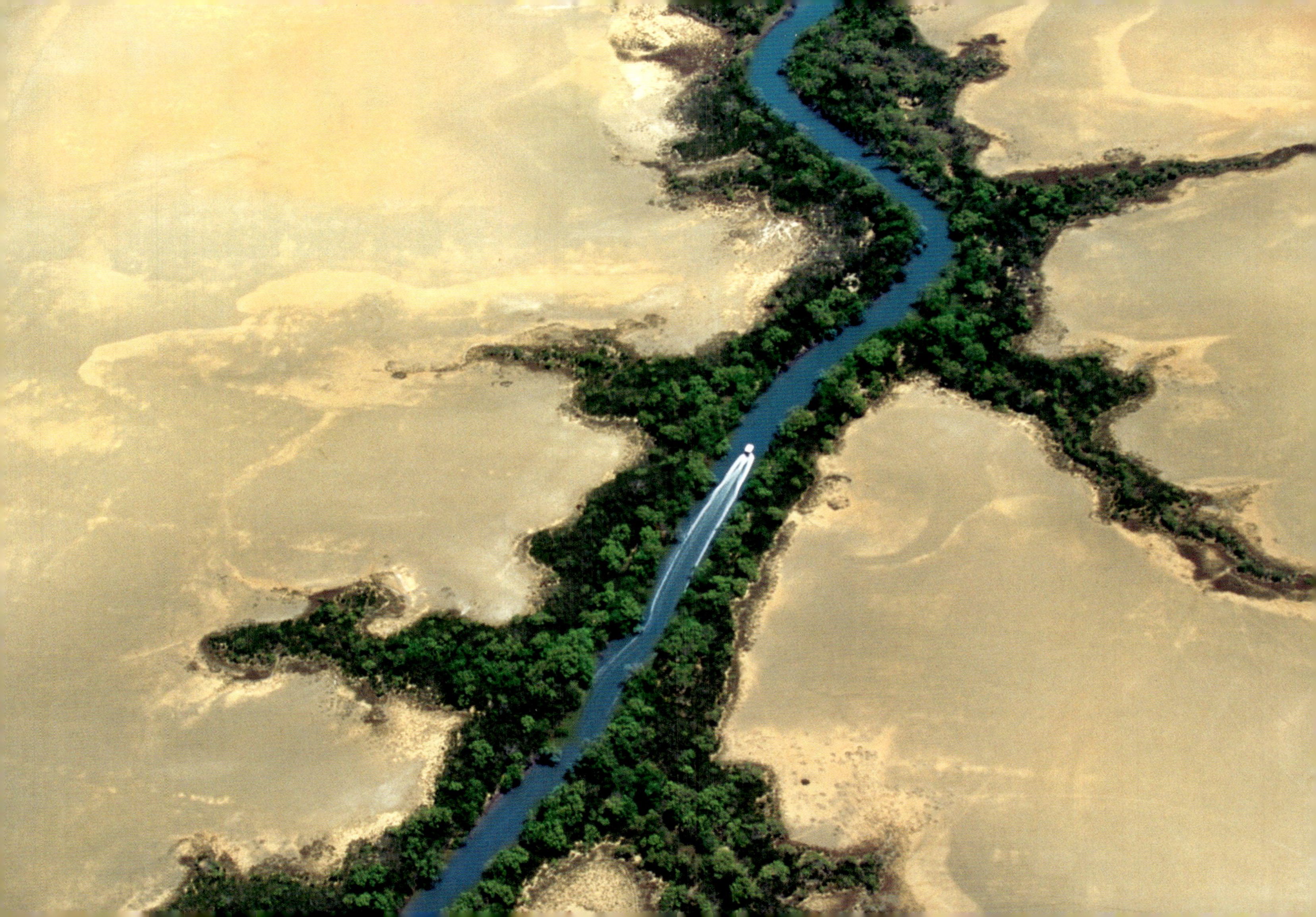

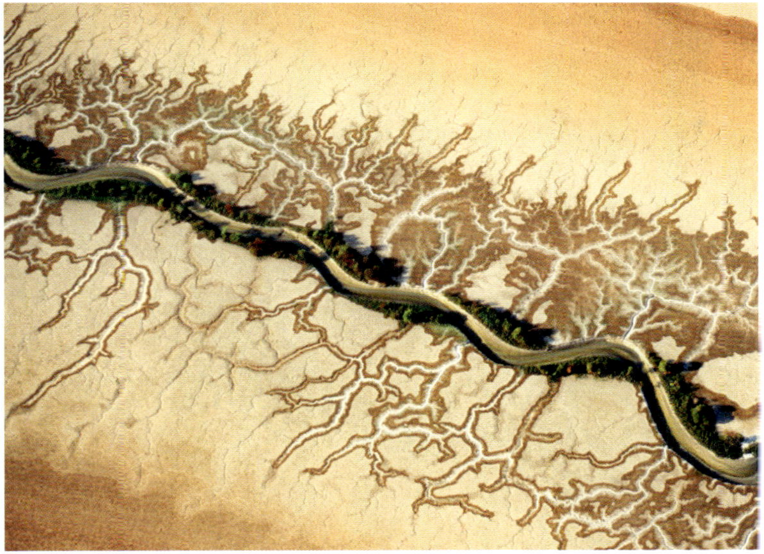

370

A boat shoots down a waterway lined by lush vegetation within a sandy expanse in the national park of Bowling Green Bay, in Australia.

371

A river slides with winding bends across the sandy flatlands of Arnhem, in the Kakadu National Park in Australia.

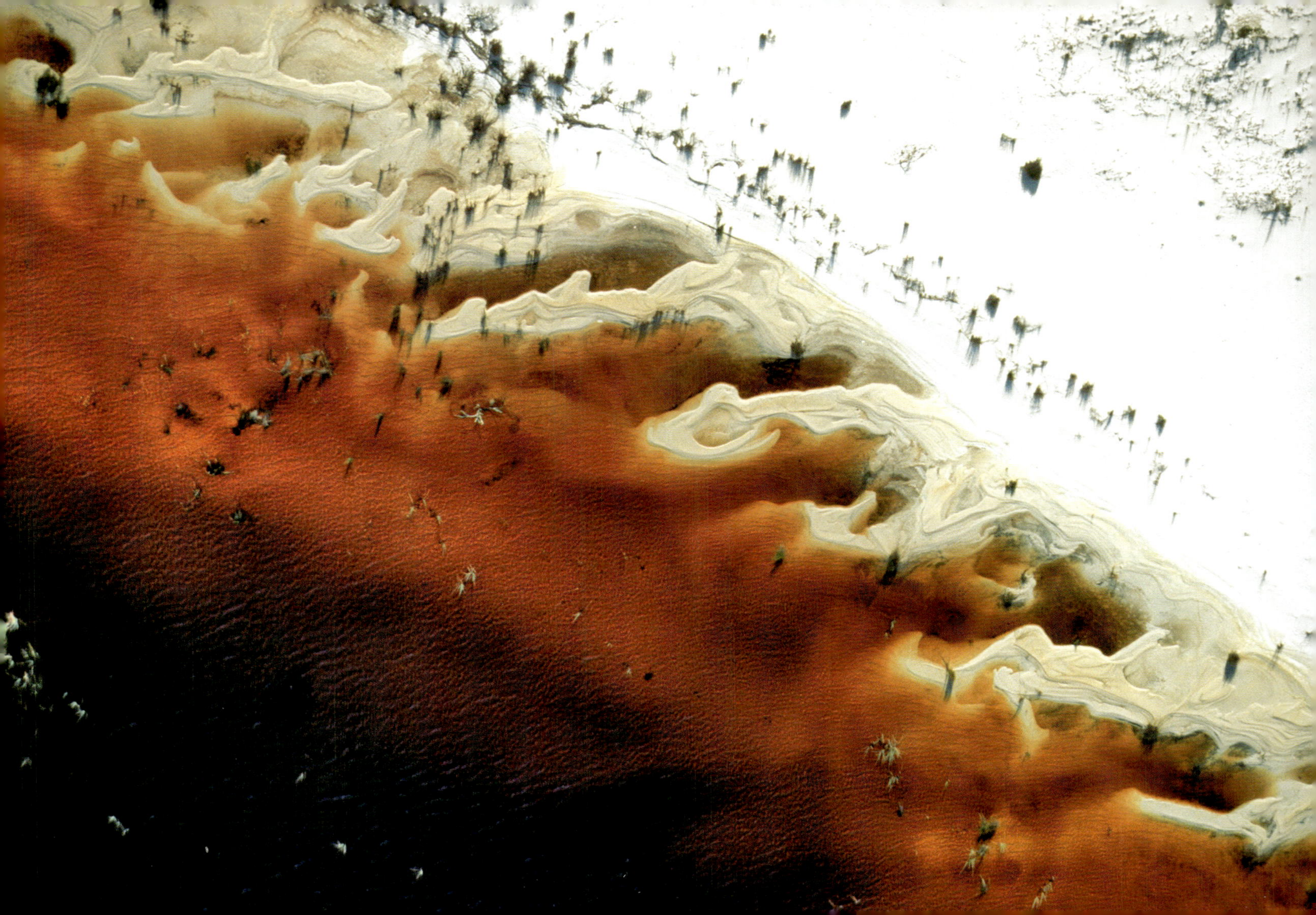

372

Australian Frazer Island is dotted by generally crystalline-colored lakes. Ponds like this one are exceptions called "lakes like peat," whose waters are tea colored.

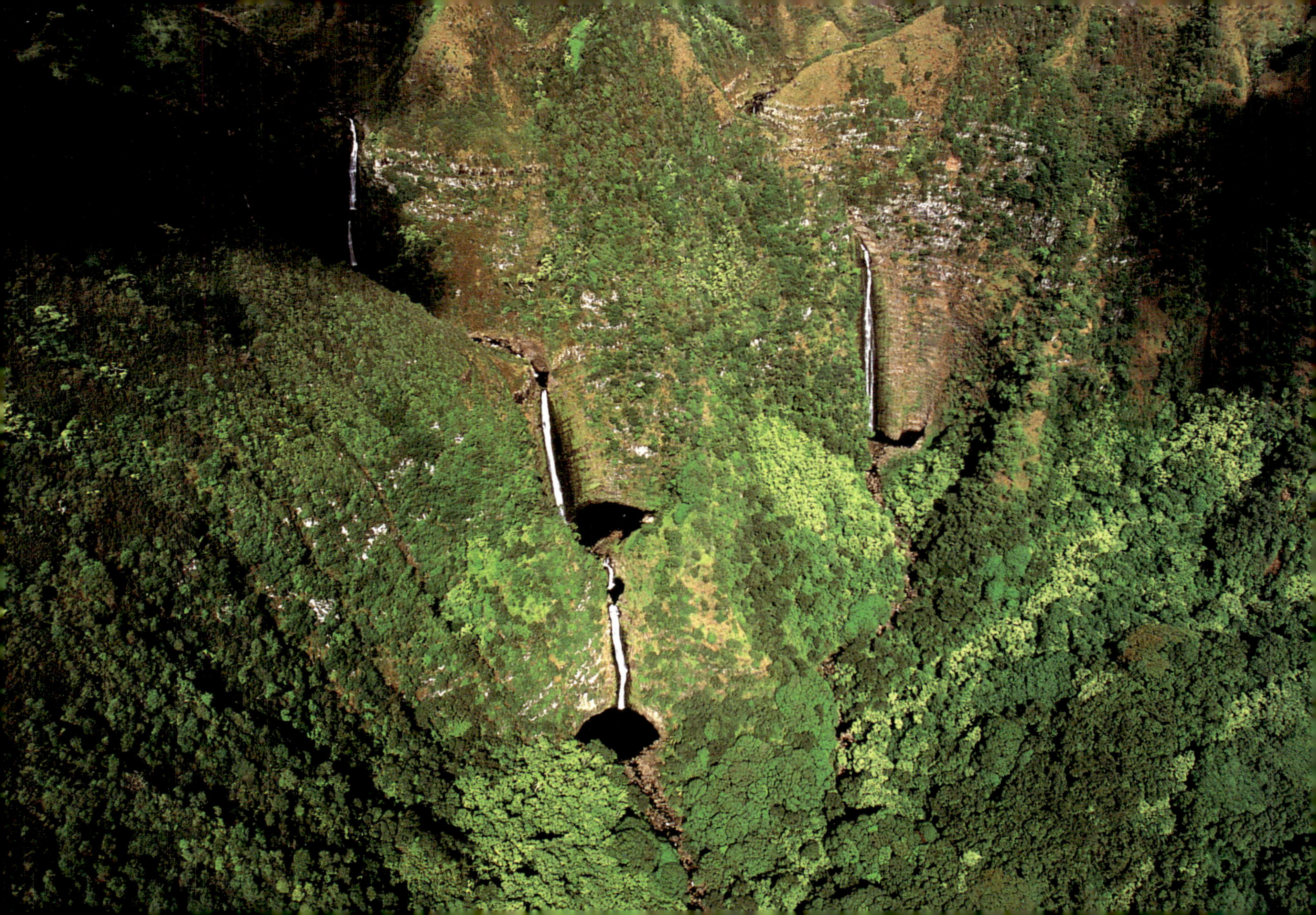

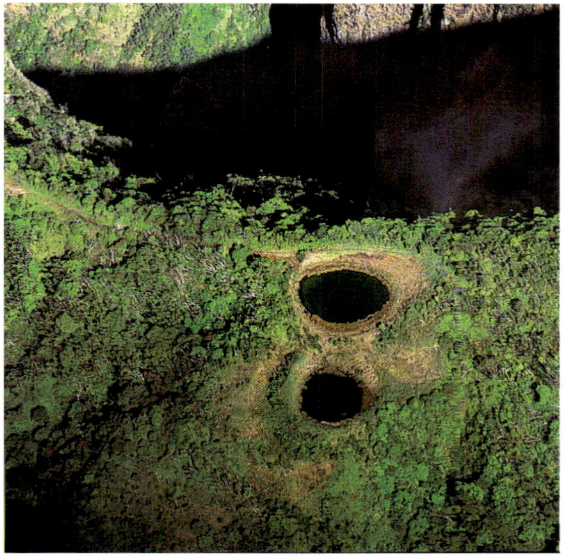

374

The valleys of the Kalaupapa National Park, on the Hawaiian island of Molokai, are scored by a series of waterfalls linking a constellation of small ponds.

375

Two ponds sit at the top of a crest in the Iao Valley, in the Maui Archipelago, which is in turn part of the Hawaiian Archipelago.

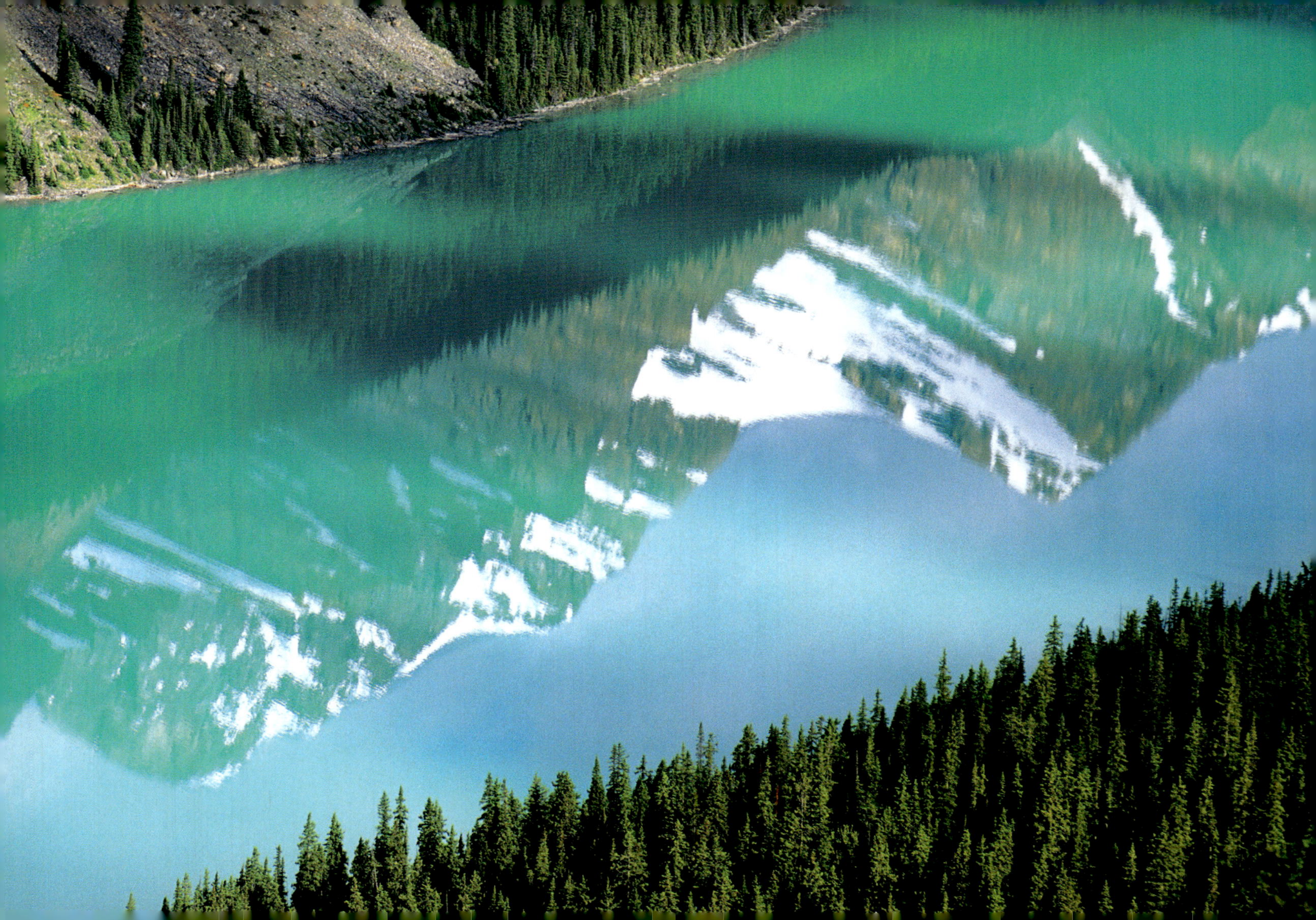

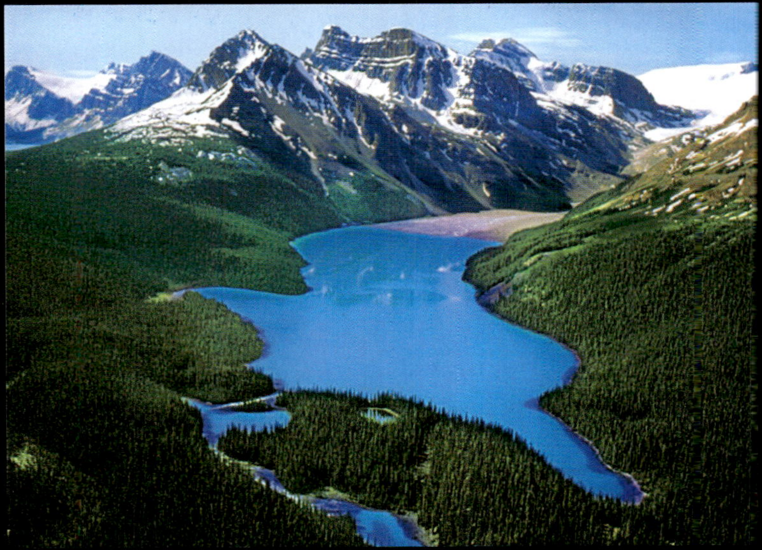

376 and 377
The Canadian Rocky Mountains are reflected in the numerous lakes in Banff National Park, famous for its hot springs.

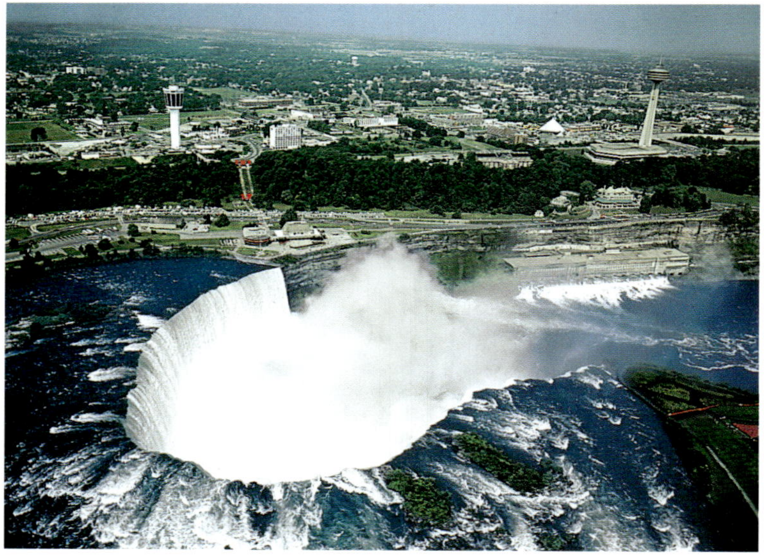

378 and 379

Niagara Falls are formed by two cataracts: the Canadian Falls (seen in these photos), 161 feet tall and 2,592 long, with the characteristic horse-shoe shape, and the American Falls, 167 feet tall and 1,001 long.

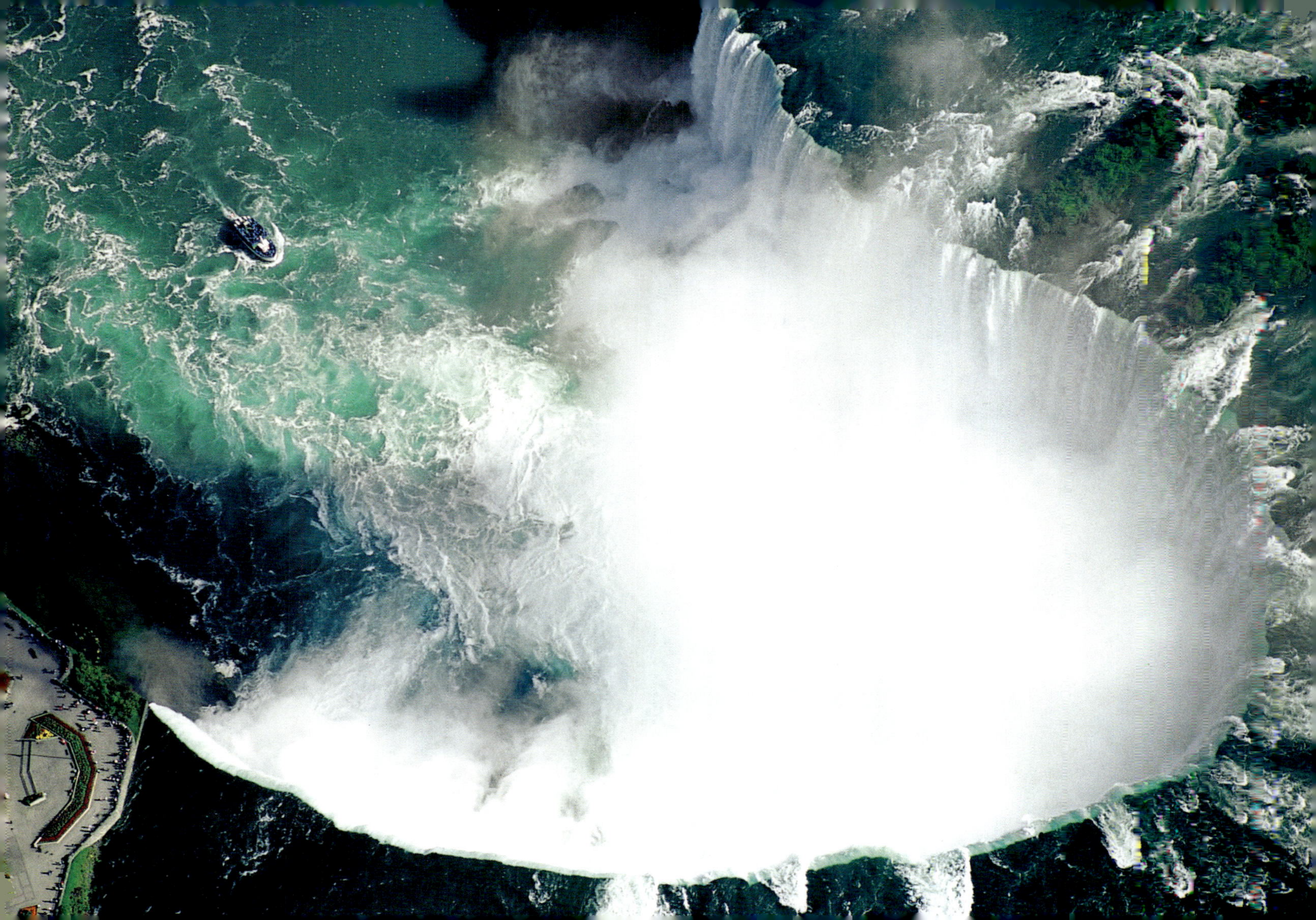

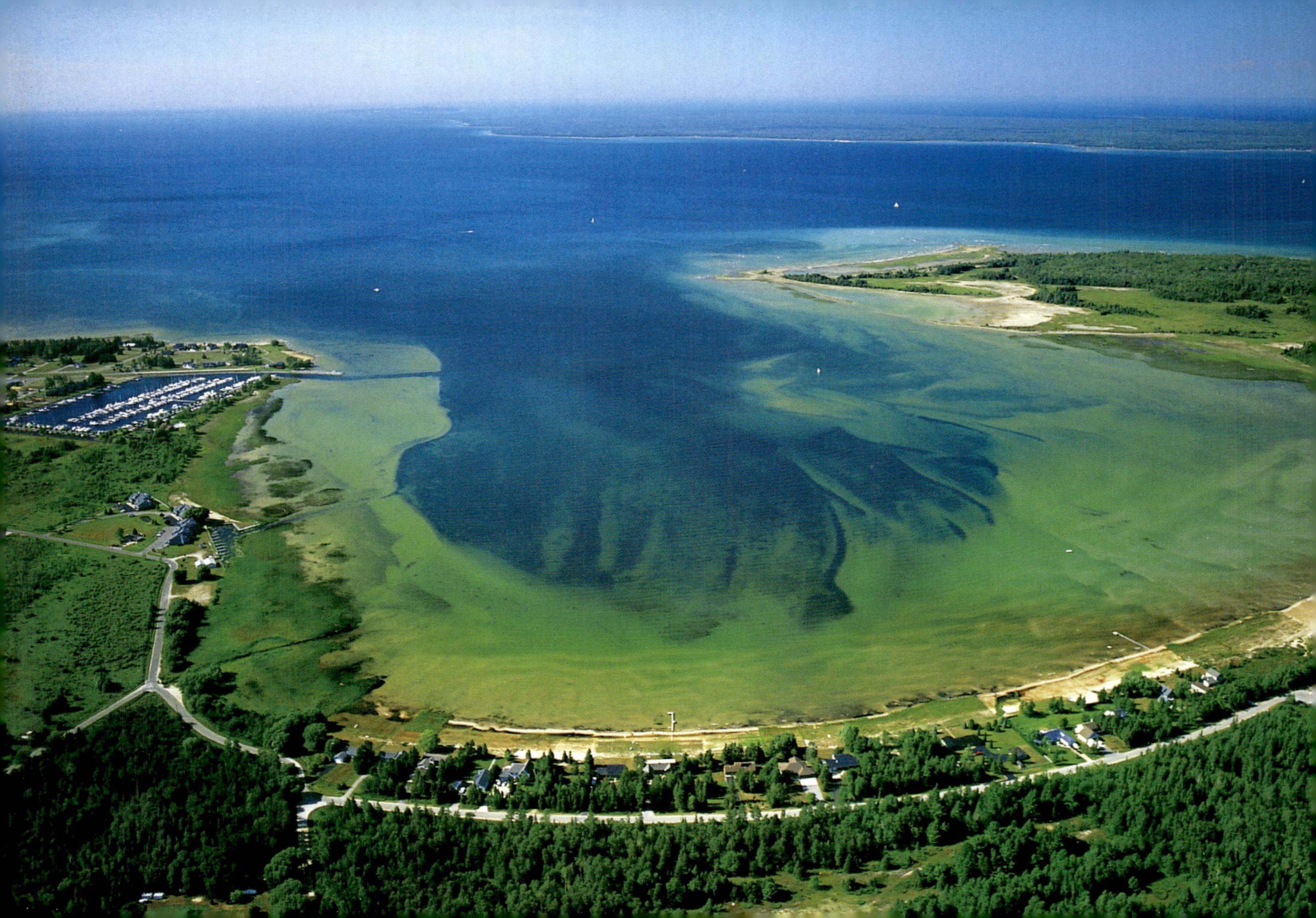

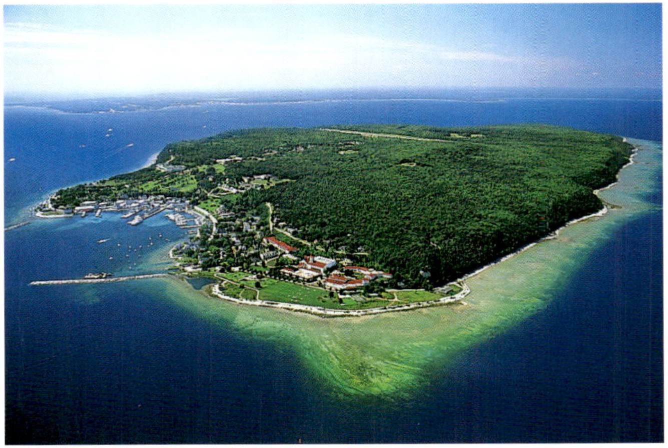

380
Green and blue hues give texture to the surface of a bay on Lake Huron in Michigan.

381
Mackinac Island, whose diameter measures only eight miles, emerges slightly from the waters of Lake Huron.

The Cycle of Water

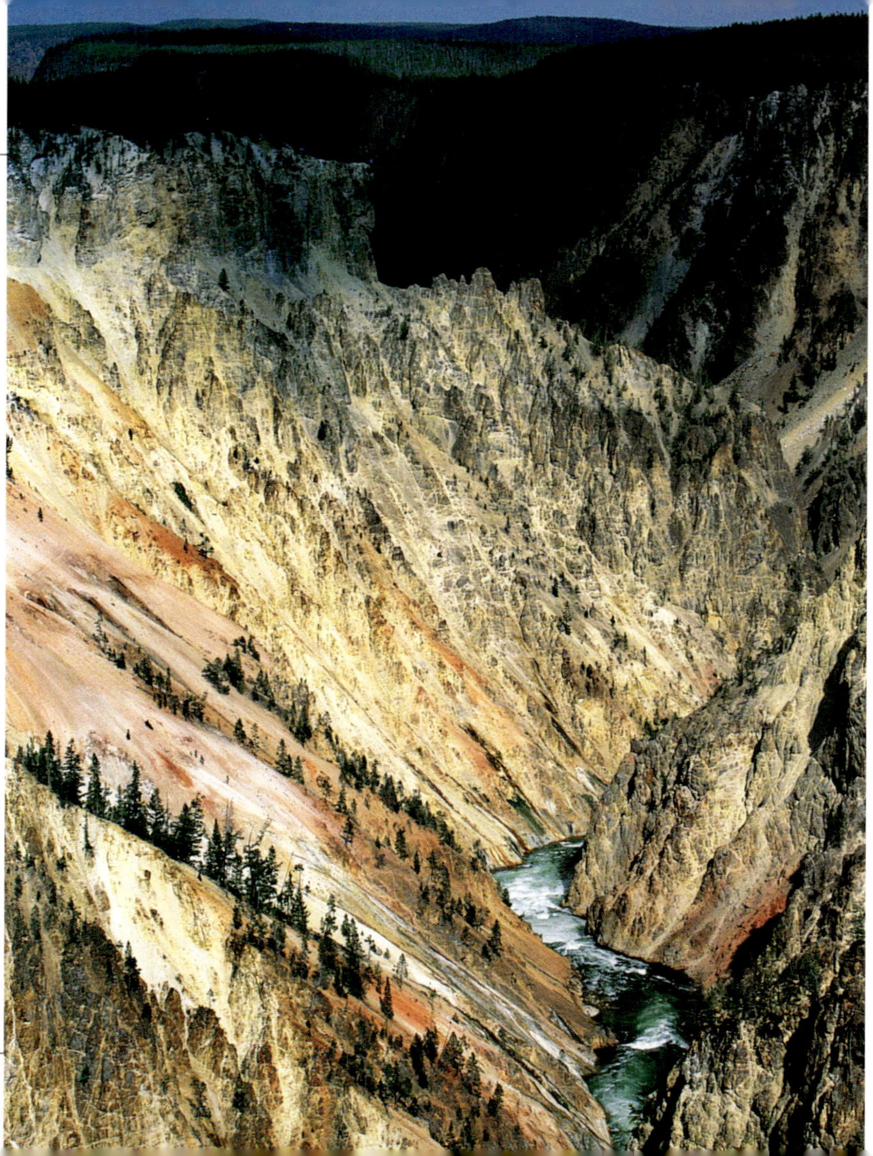

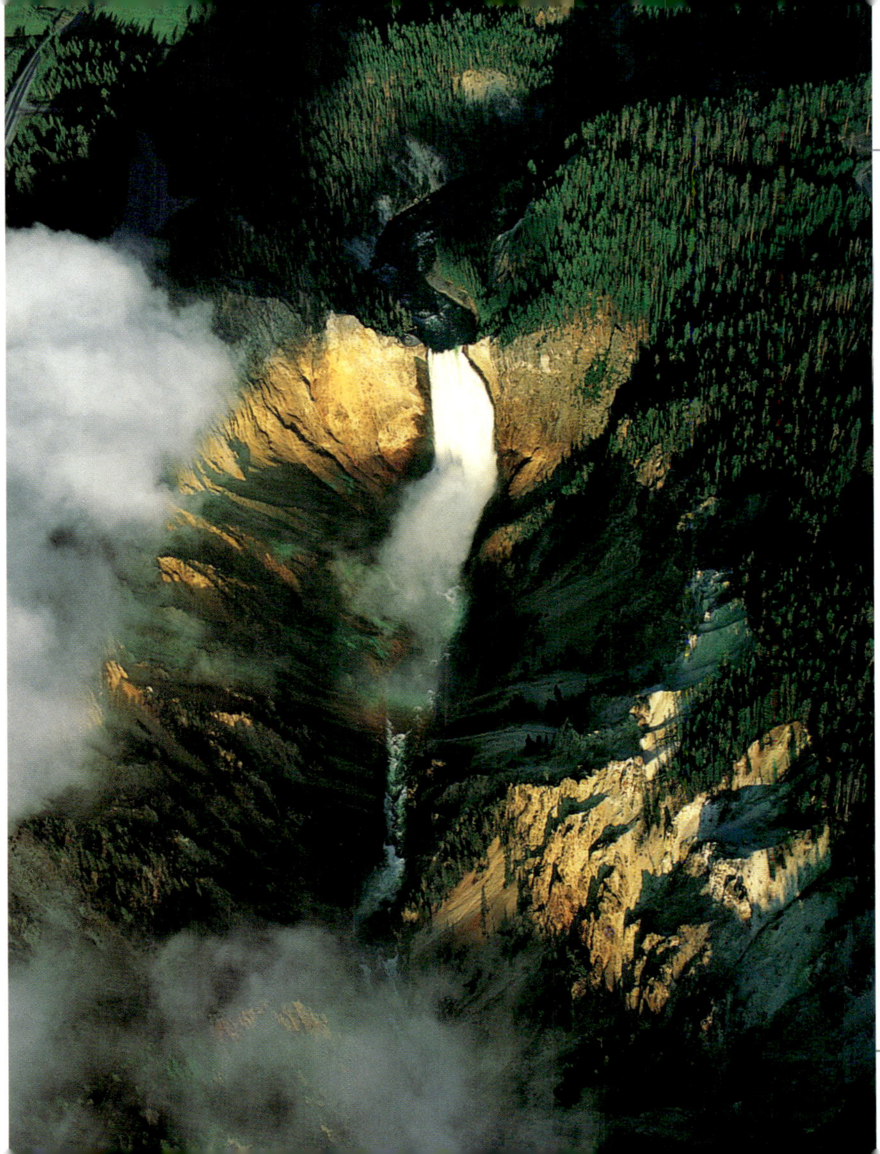

382 and 383
Lower Yellowstone Falls drop their waters into Yellowstone Grand Canyon, exceeding a jump of 308 feet.

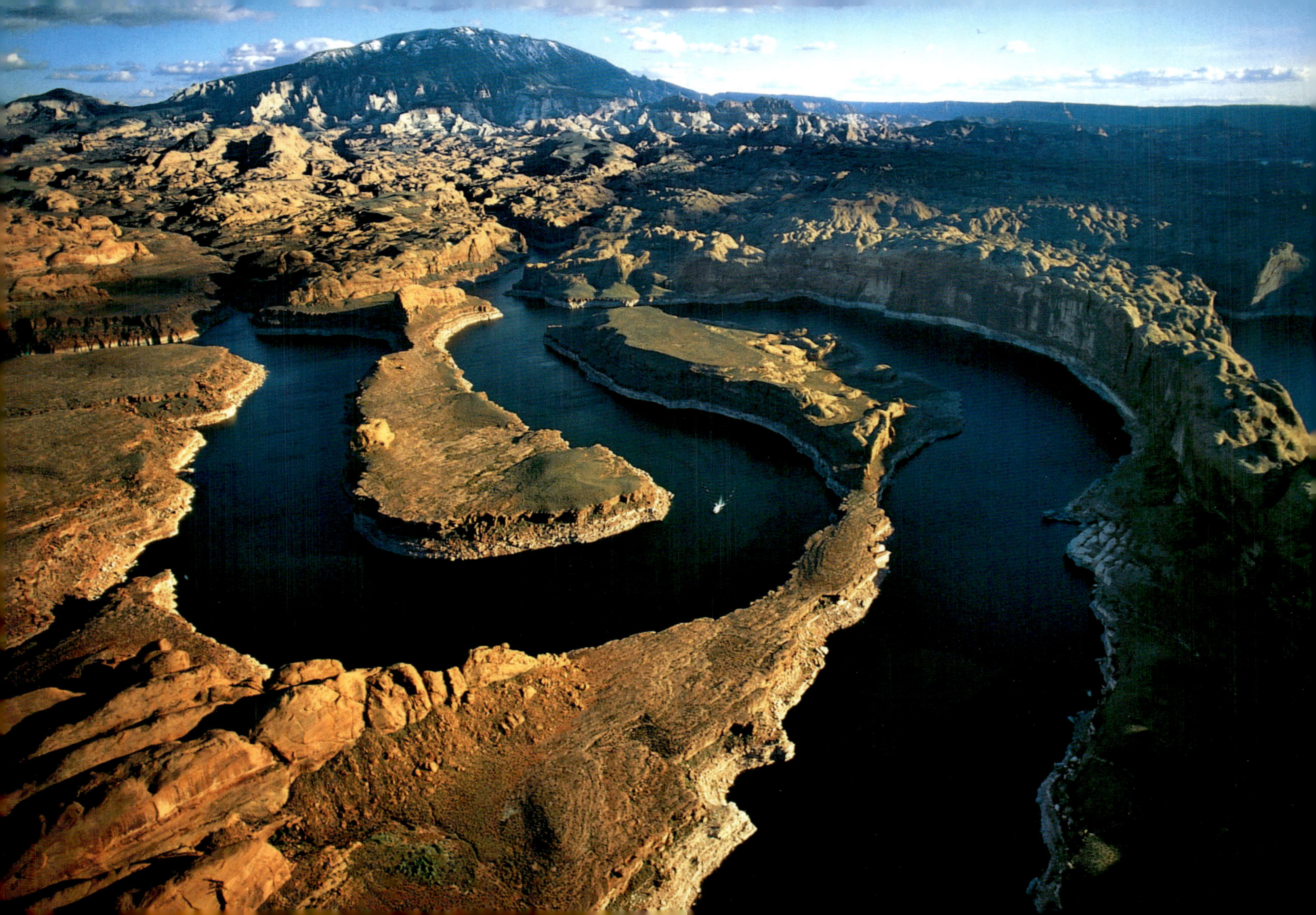

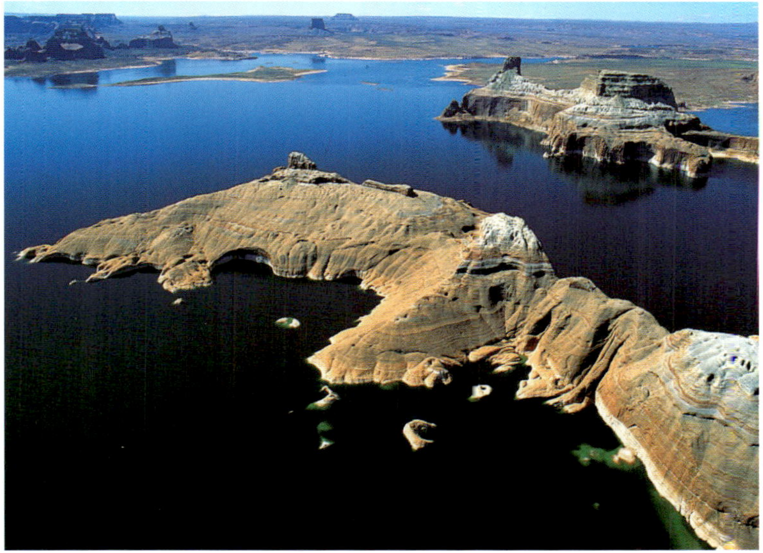

384 and 385

The blue waters of Lake Powell encounter protrusions of sandstone rock in the desert surrounding the basin.

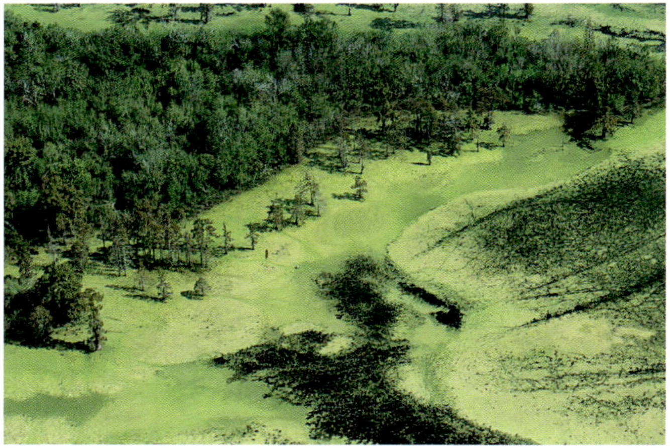

386 and 387
The tall-trunk vegetation is not clearly distinguishable from the greenish sheen covering the surface of this lake in Devil's Swamp in Louisiana.

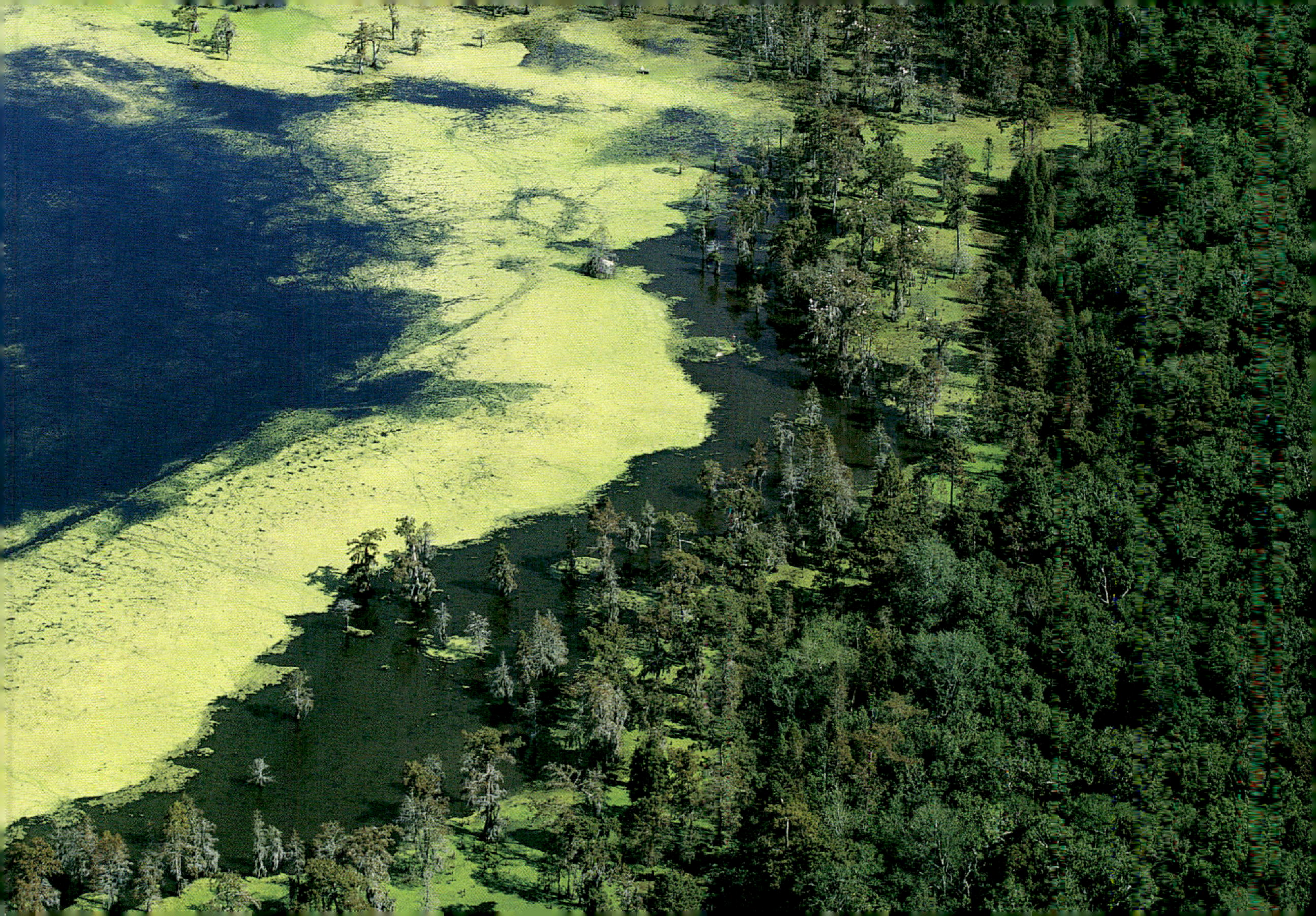

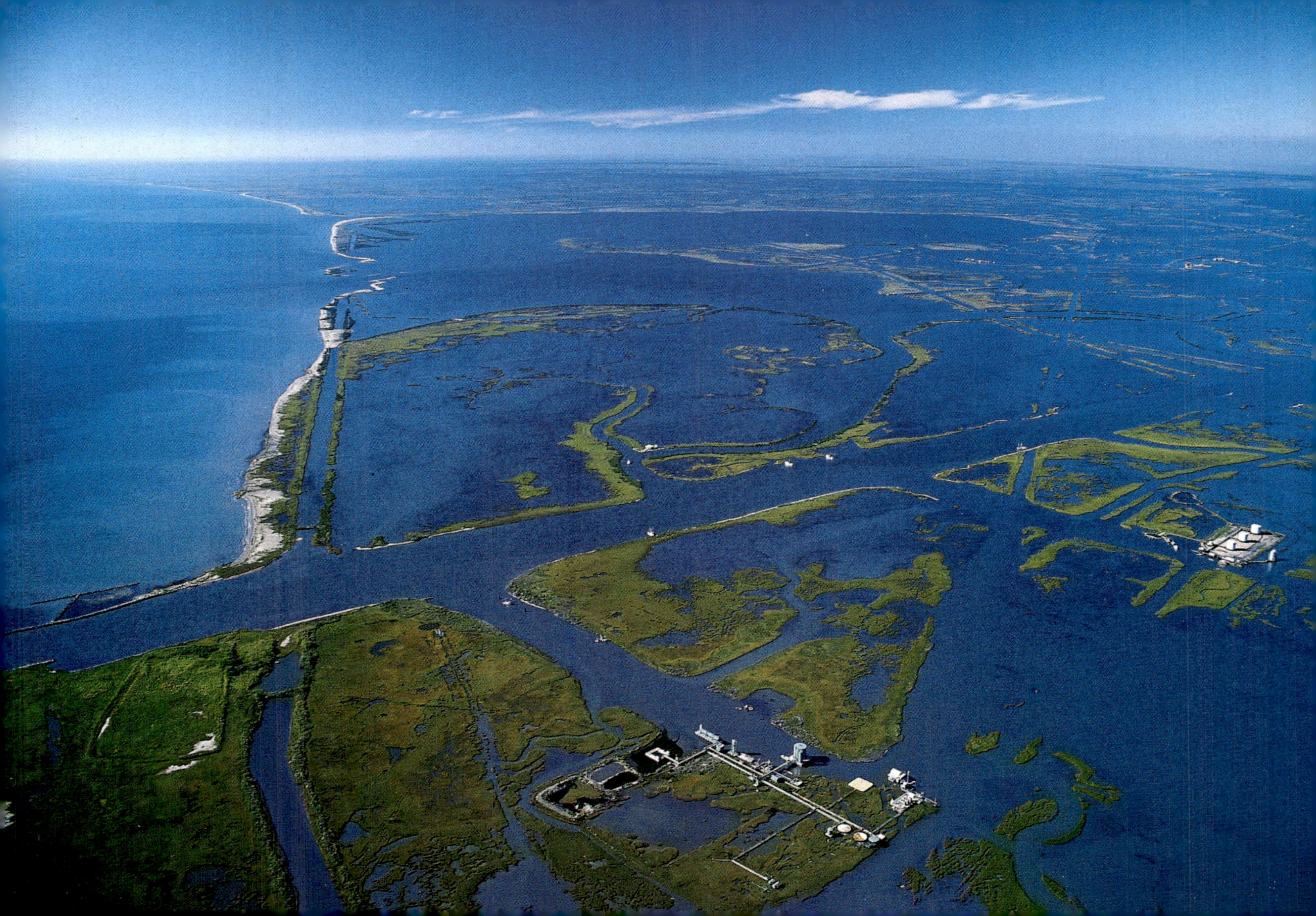

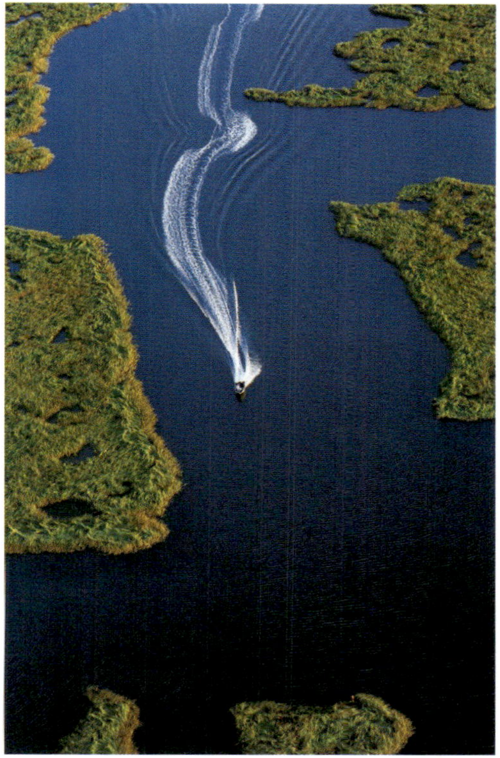

388

The delta of the Mississippi River in Louisiana, photographed here at the point where it encounters the Gulf of Mexico, has a surface area of 14,942 square miles, composed of flood debris.

389

The famous bayous of Mississippi are branching, shallow canals whose waters, often stagnant, flow lethargically.

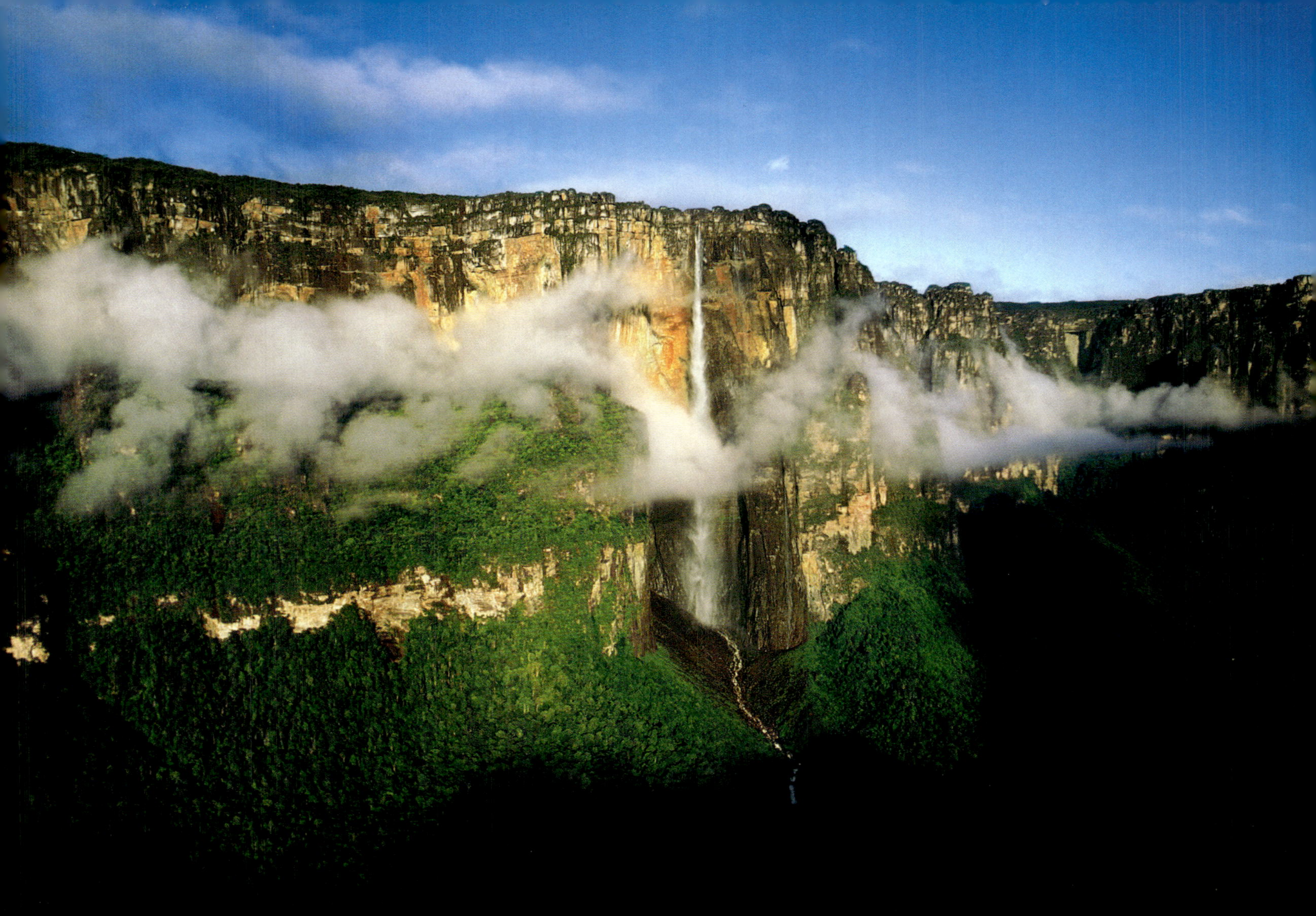

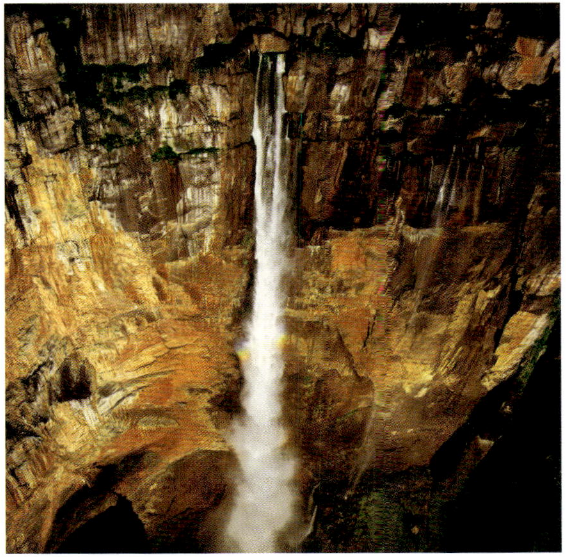

390 and 391

Angel Falls in Venezuela, at a height of 3,215 feet, are the tallest in the world.

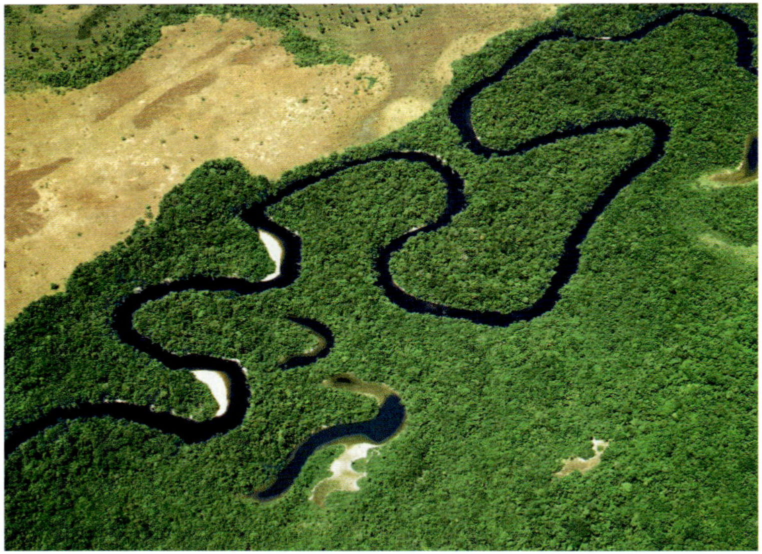

392

The enormous cushion formed by the foliage of the trees in a Venezuelan rain forest is sliced by the course of a river crossing the area.

393

The Pantanal is the biggest humid fresh-water region in the world.

394-395

The Brazilian river archipelago of the Anavilhanas contains 400 islands.

396-397

The Iguazu waterfalls, at the border of Argentina and Brazil, consist of hundreds of falls dropping from a height of 262 feet.

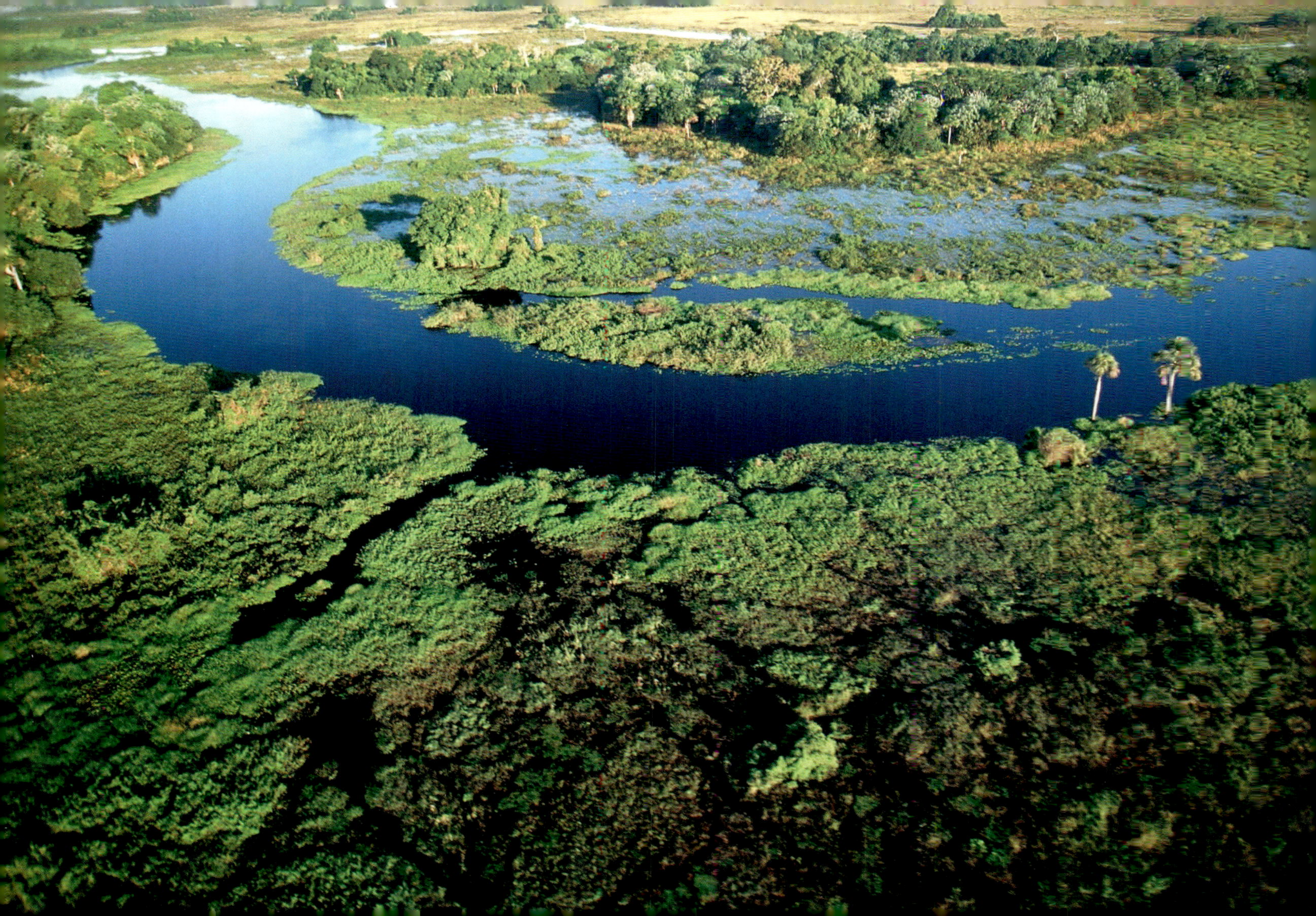

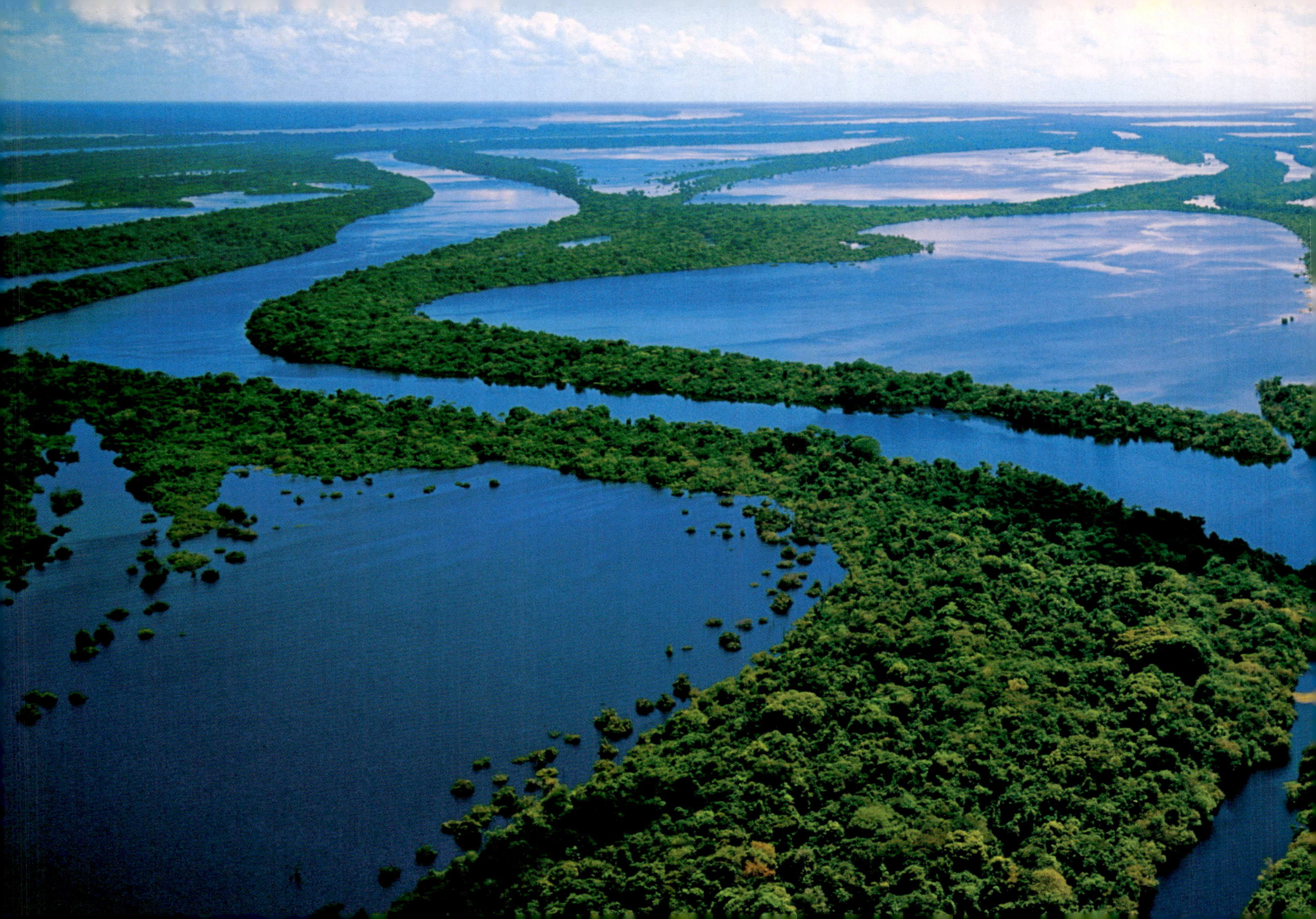

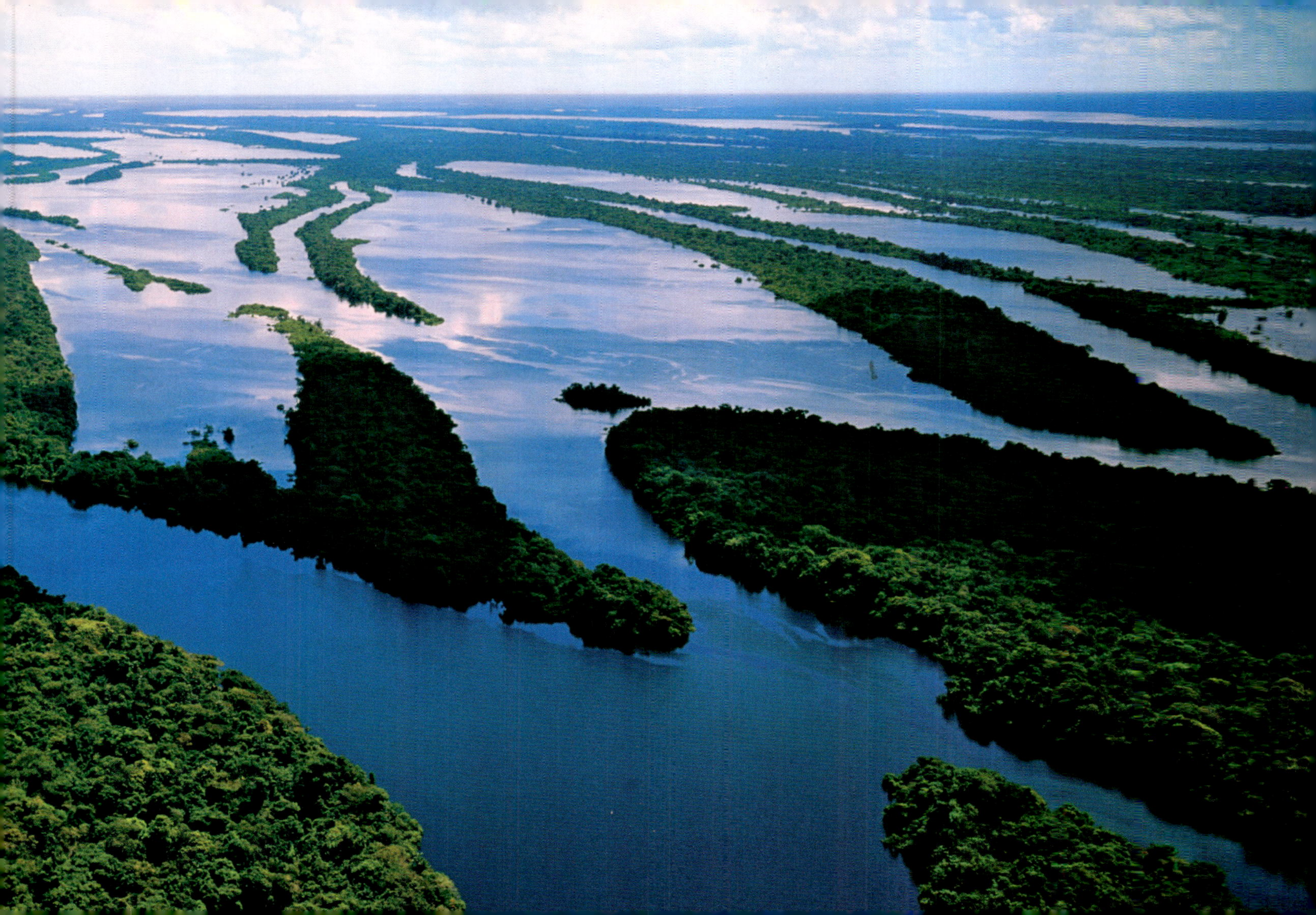

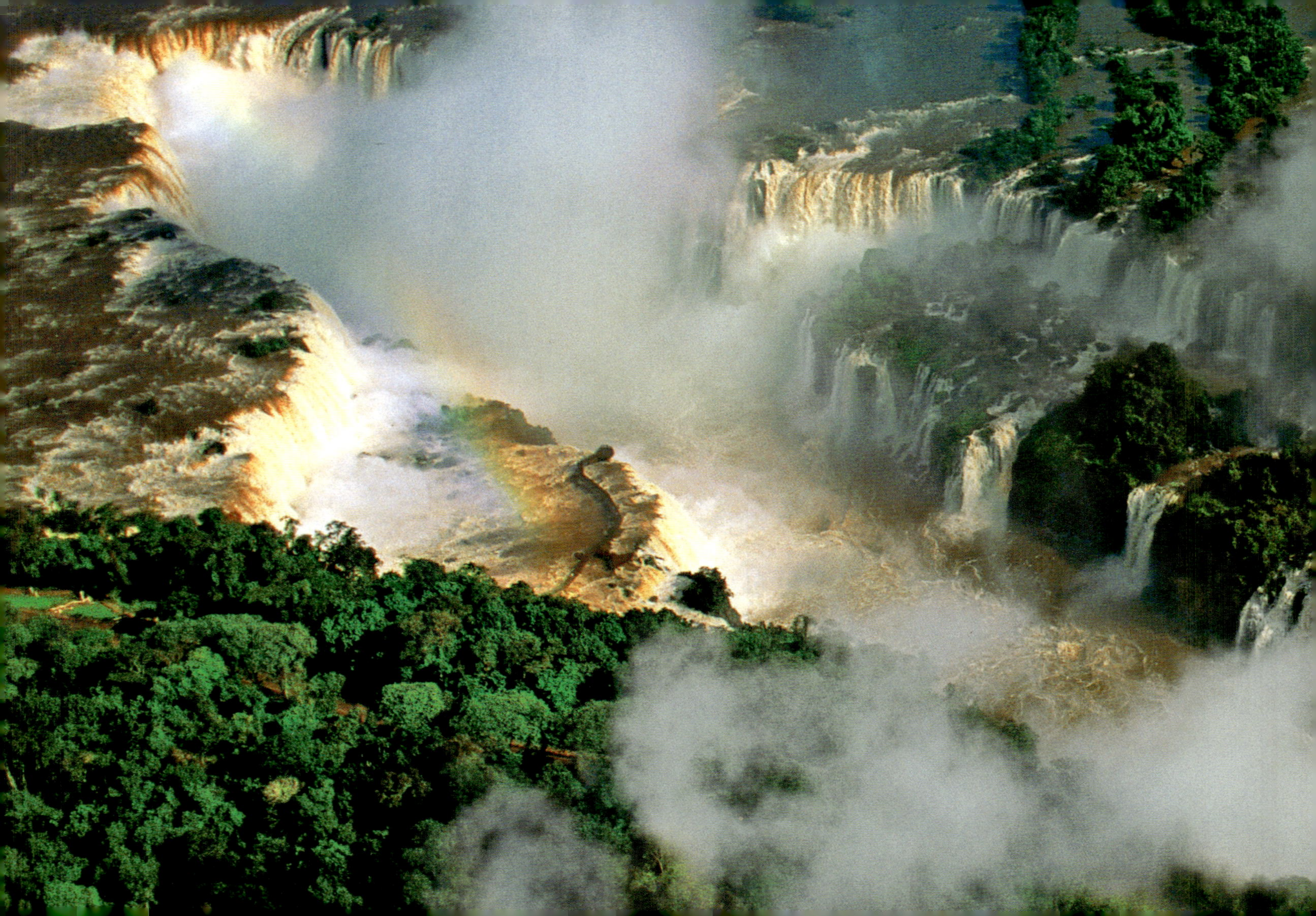

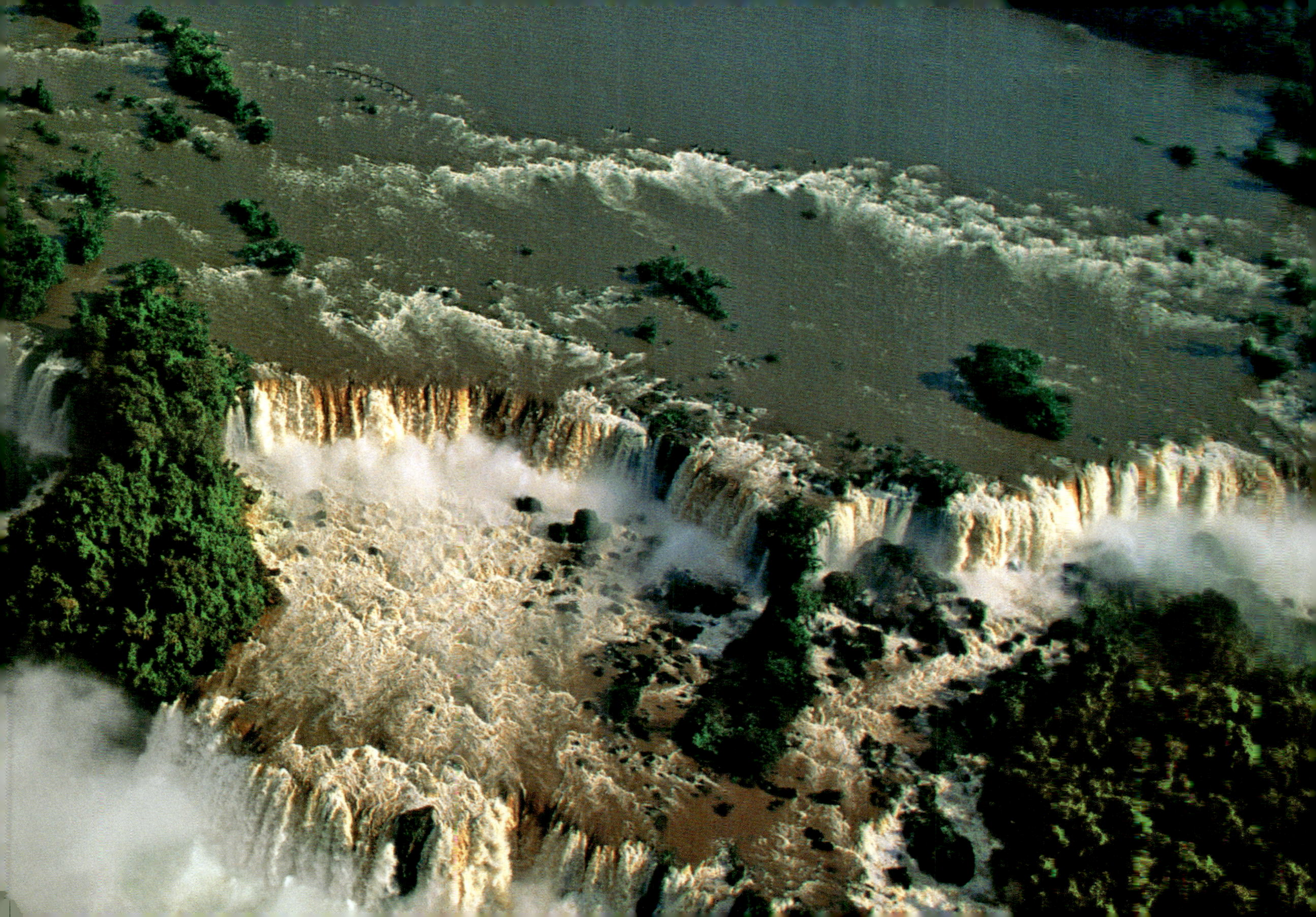

LANDS OF SILENCE

FLYING HIGH

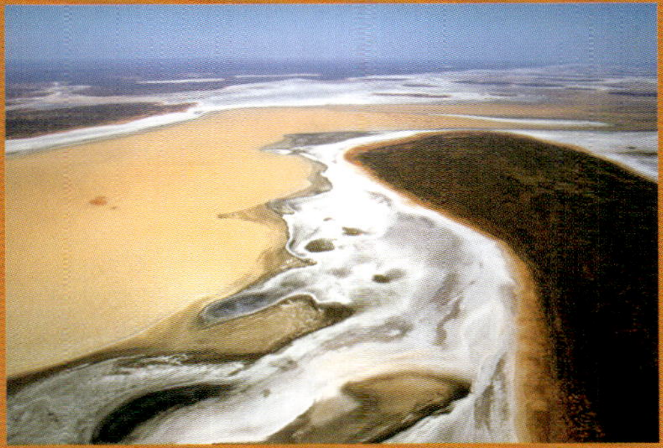
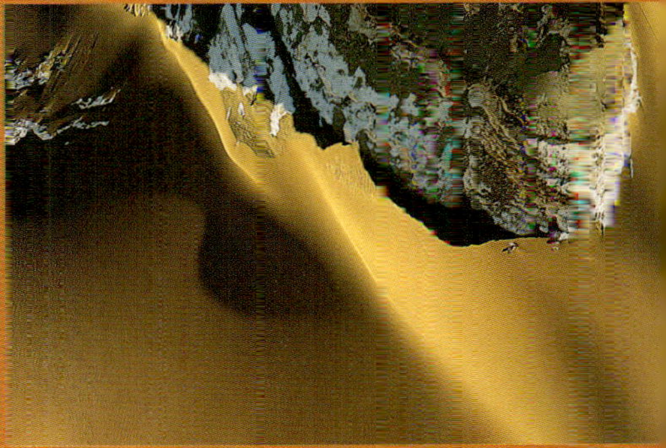

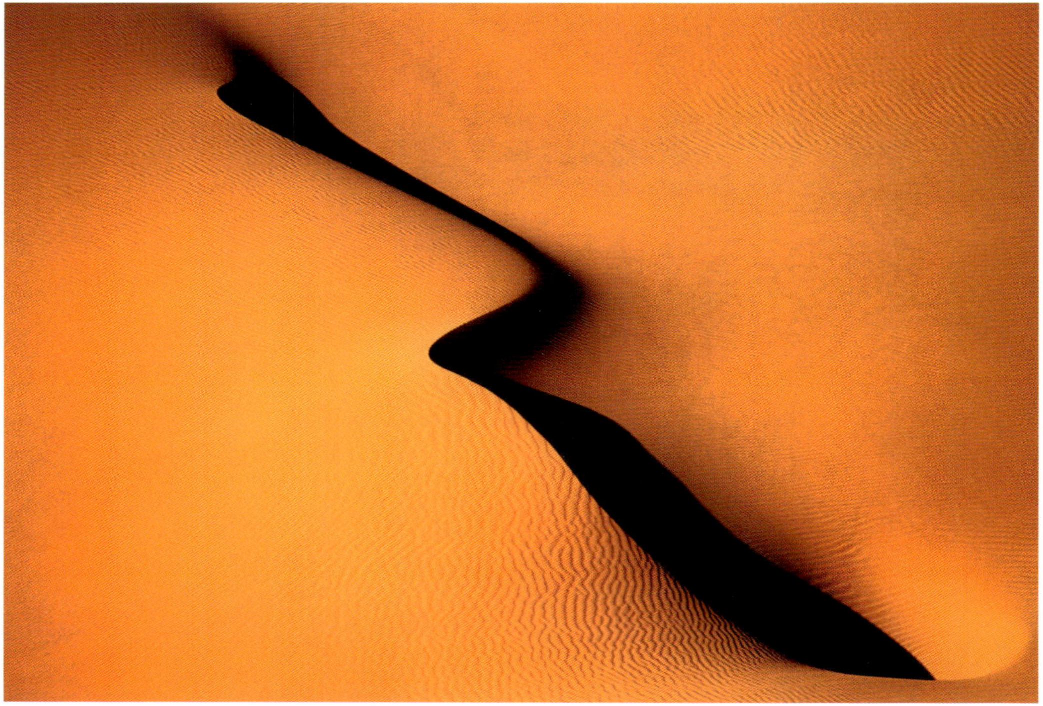

399
The basin of a salt lake in Uluru National Park in Australia (left); the White Desert in Egypt (right).

"How many desert plateaus, like the convex surface of a shield, have I crossed, which were never beaten by the eager legs of travelers, and which I dominated from beginning to end."

These words were written by a man who had found his refuge in the desert, the immense abode in which his enemies, frightened by his freedom, would never have dared nor known how to flush him out: Shanfara, the poet-bandit that lived in the deserts of Yemen and the Hijaz a few years before Mohammed's revelations would echo across those sands.

The desert, therefore, offers freedom. The peoples that still resist the adulation of the cities and "civilization" know that well. The few Tuareg who continue to cross the Sahara with their caravans of salt would never dream of doing otherwise. The desert is the realm of silence. Only the wind breaks the torrid air of day and the icy air of night. It is a mystical experience the land of that which it seems and which it is not, the place in which mirages and hallucinations are difficult to distinguish from reality. For thousands of years, the initiates of many cultures, various Ancient-Egyptian gods, obscure hermits, and prophets have been in the habit of crossing the threshold of the deserts, where the scarceness of sustenance honed their spirit to the extreme. The desert, for many, was the abode of demons like the *jinn* of Arab tales, or even the "backyard" of Satan himself, the place-elect of temptation, as implied by the gospels of Luke, Mark, and Matthew.

400
A shadowy mantle drapes over the top of the sandy dune of Sossusvlei in the Namib-Naukluft Park in Namibia

Lands of Silence

An image that comes often to mind when speaking of the desert is the spectacular sea of dunes of Lawrence of Arabia, but it is only a romantic and partial perspective. A large part of the deserts is bare rock, as demonstrated by the great *reg* and *hamada* of Algeria and Libya, scattered with pebbles and graced by mountain chains of magnificent beauty like the Tadrart Akakus, a dark bastion rising above the surrounding flatlands, reinforced by towers that are pinnacles of contorted rock, or like the Algerian Hoggar, whose granite cones reflect the blood-red glow of the horizon.

The Namib Desert, extending along the southwestern coast of the African continent, is a strip of territory over 700 miles long but not terribly wide at its most arid section (60 to 140 miles). Considered among the most inhospitable on the planet, it is also one of the most ancient, remaining tenaciously dry since the beginning of the earth's crust's history. Dark sand, of a unique earth-brown color or blood-red in the evening shadows, accumulates on dunes that are at times as big as medieval fortresses, seemingly hostile to any type of life. However, overcoming the crests of those scimitar-shaped hills, never still and yet always there, one might happen to see a caravan of wild elephants traveling unknown roads across the Namib, certain to arrive where only they know. Even a green-leafed acacia tree manages to pop up in remote places, miles away from their closest neighbors. The strange thing is that, to create such a scorched basin, not only heat was responsible but also cold: the Antarctic current of Begula that laps the coast does not actually produce true rainstorms but only a salty mist that, depositing itself, manages to spark the miracle of life, sustaining insects, sporadic plants, and even large animals like elephants, as we have seen.

Many deserts contend for first place in terms of aridness. Some parts of the Jordanian and Sinai deserts, for example, have not had a single drop of water in 400 years, and yet even there, life survives,

Lands of Silence

even though practically invisible, and more so from the sky. However, the landscape can reveal hidden wonders like Petra, a city excavated from the rock, where an entire people lived and prospered for centuries, ingeniously exploiting the scarce rainfall through a network of canals.

The western coast of South America is covered in large part by Peru and Chile, by a strip of desert including the Atacama Desert, overlooking the Pacific Ocean in the north part of the Chilean coast. This thick ribbon of white sand, stretching for thousands of miles between the north and south, is at times interrupted by the right-angled path of the rivers and streams descending from the ever-present Andes, sustaining farming settlements that stick out like oases from the sterile sand.

The deserts of North America do not belong to this ranking of totally inhospitable places, being generally evaluated as "extremely arid," which is also true for the immense, blazing basin covering the large part of central Australia and for the Gobi Desert, forsaken in the most remote and shadowy part of Asia. However, its attraction is not less for this reason. The Desert States – Utah, Colorado, and Arizona – boast fragile sandstone structures, perforated over millions of years of incessant wind. The well-known Delicate Arch is only the most famous example, but the entire region seems an enchanted realm of improbable castles hewn by erosion. On the other hand, Death Valley boasts many first place prizes. The Backwater Basin depression, the lowest point on the western hemisphere at 925 feet below sea level, is an oven heated by a desperate sun that calcines everything, creating a landscape in which life becomes as delicate as the spirit.

The merciless sun lays bare colors that cannot be seen in any other part of the planet. In fact, thinking about the desert as a land lacking in colors other than golden yellow or the red of sand and rock does not do justice to the places in which erosion and the consequent direct irradiation of the lower layers of the soil brings to light minerals that oxidi-

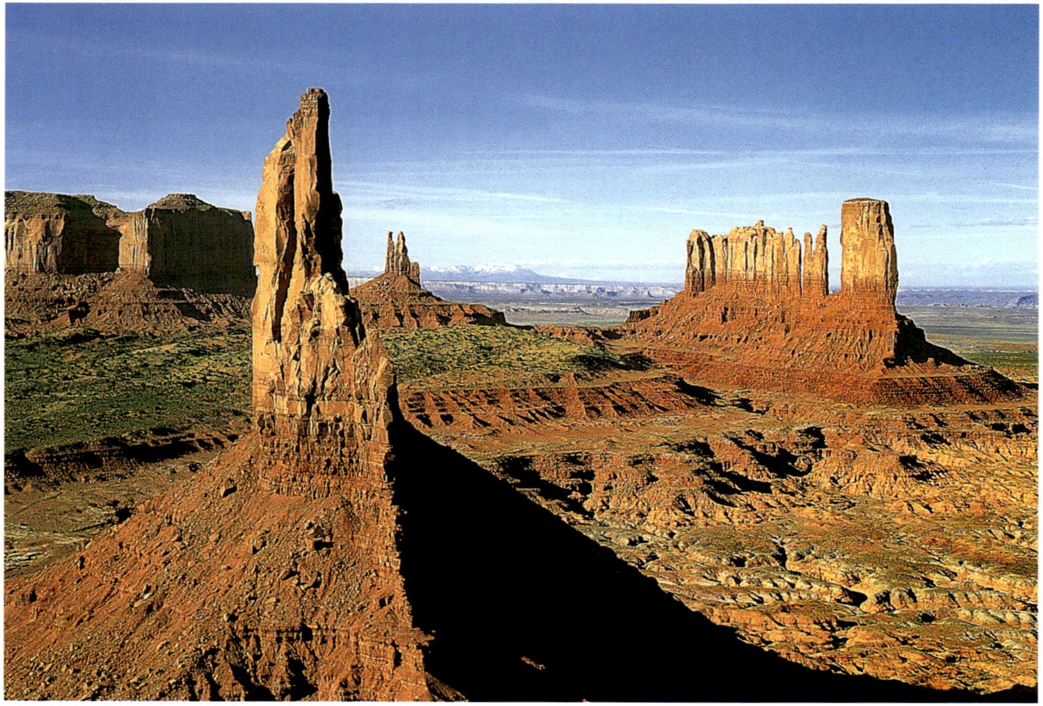

Lands of Silence

ze, bond to other elements, and create new combinations of greens, browns, purples, and deep reds. Otherwise, there are whites as immaculate as fresh snow, like in the White Desert near the oases of Farafra, in Egypt, where the calcareous substratum is laid bare by the wind, forming patches that can truly make one think of a mirage of some strange sort, so out of place do they seem in the scorching air. From the sky, then, even the deep tracks left by water can be seen well, despite the aridity that, except for the extreme cases we have seen, is never total. The dried-up wadi and creeks of the world channel torrents of rainwater that seasonally transform the hard ground into a shambles of gurgling mud, carrying off everything in their paths and digging clear-cut river beds heavy with dark shadows in the light of dawn and sunset. Here, this sweeping away, unlike what happens in well-irrigated areas whose soil laden with water can barely absorb the rain, the flood brings everything back to life. The desert, after the rain, fills with yellow, red, periwinkle, and green flowers. Some batrachians, adapted to drought, emerge from the broken-up mud, reawakening in the sun even when years have passed since they last saw it. Then, as the desert commands, everything goes back to sleep, following the rhythms of nature, which is never in a hurry and never forgets.

404
Reddish monoliths, isolated or in groups, dominate the plain in Monument Valley, between Arizona and Utah in the United States.

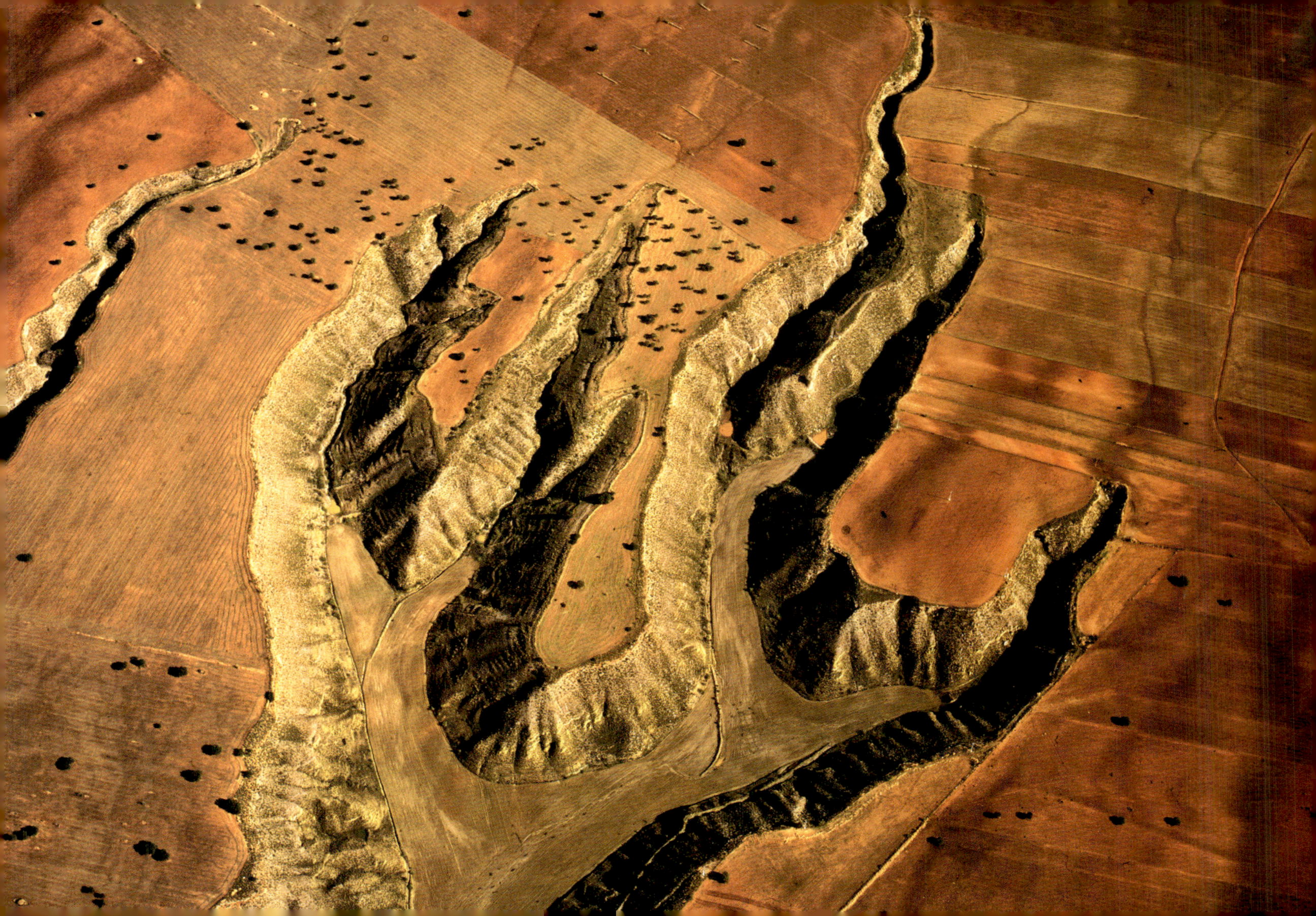

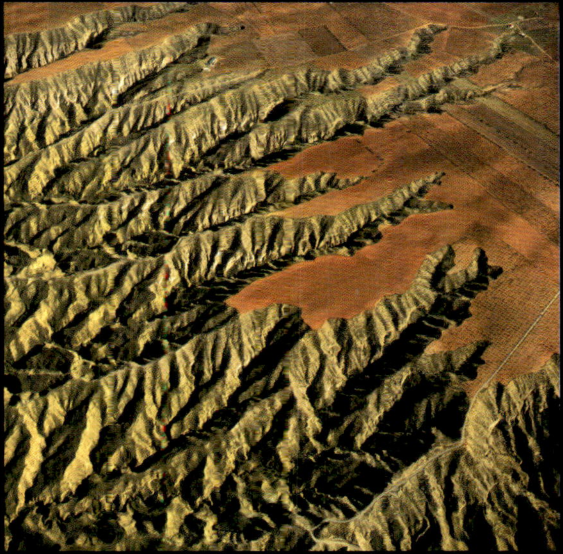

406 and 407
The erosive action of rivers has left deep tracks dug from the clayey soil in the northern Sierra Nevada in Spain.

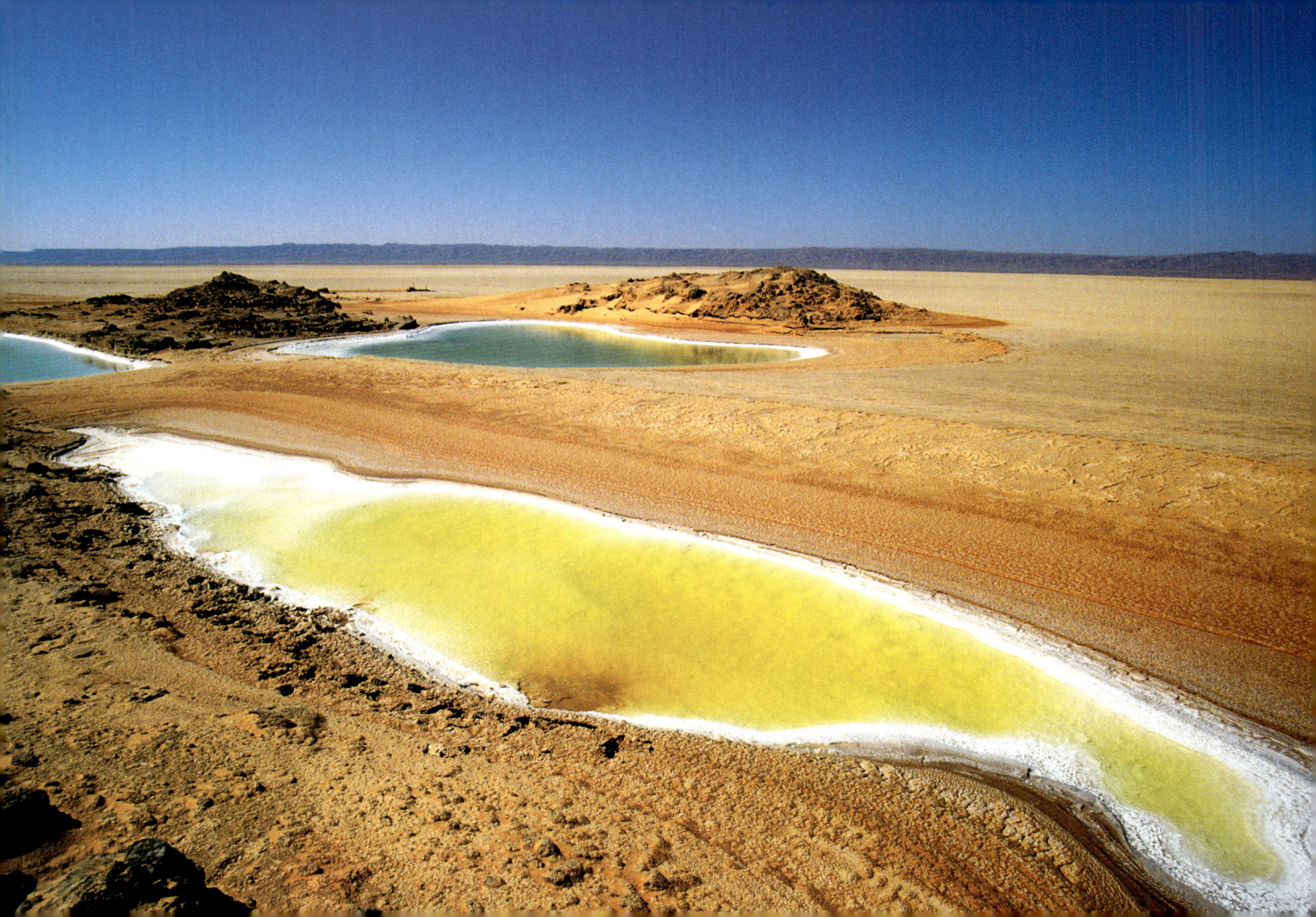

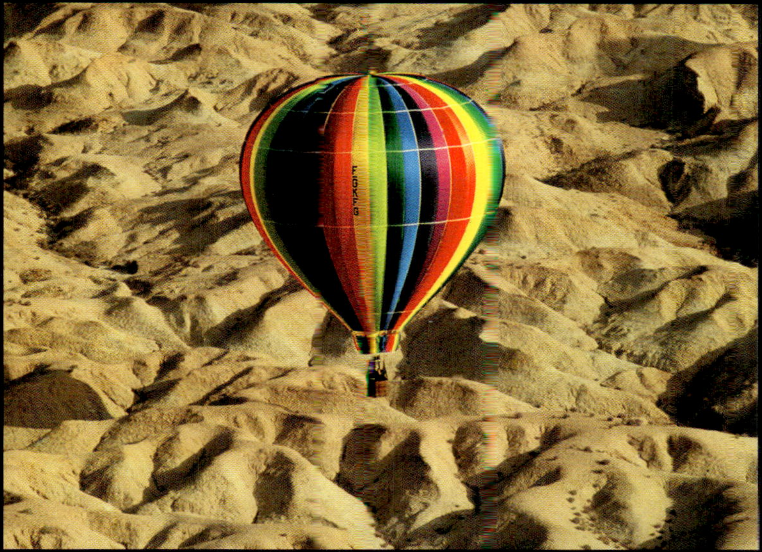

408
The Erg of Chott el-Jerid, in Tunisia, presents unusual sights, like these saltwater puddles recalling the deformed clocks of Salvador Dali.

409
A hot-air balloon crosses a rocky desert in the area of Tozeur, in Tunisia, exploiting the rising air currents fueled by heat radiating off the rocks.

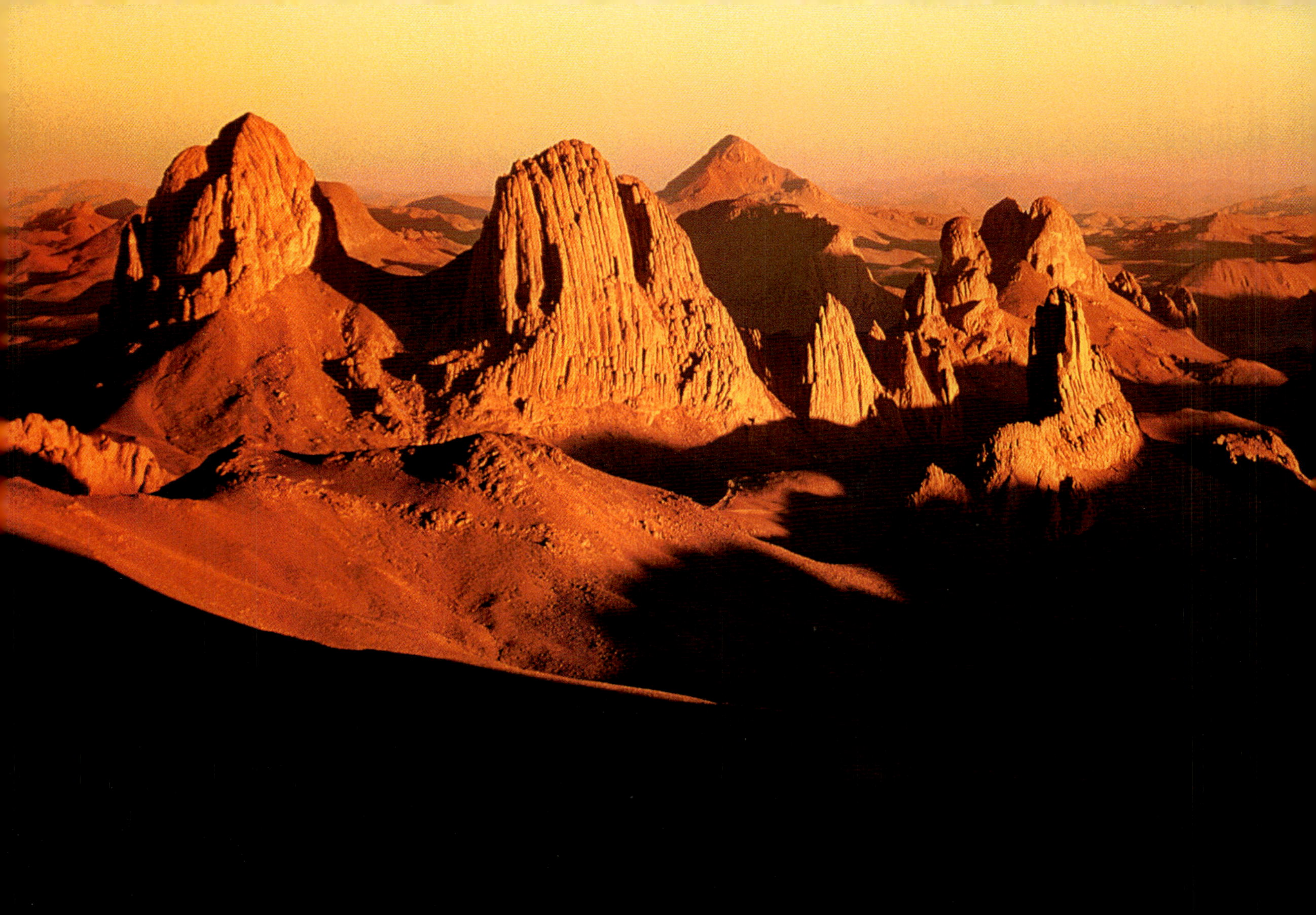

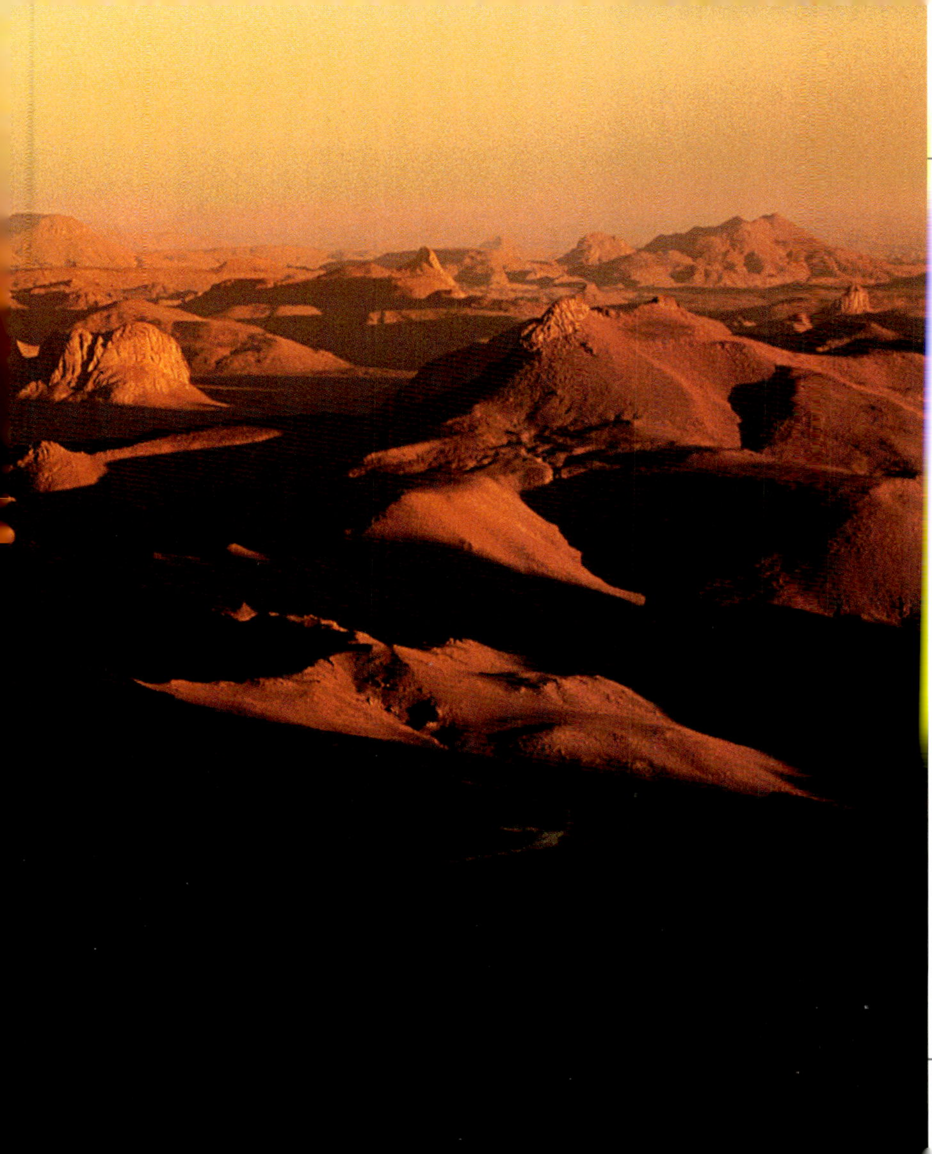

410-411
The peaks of the Atakor region, in Algeria, were places chosen for seclusion by the hermit Foucault, enchanted by the charm of this territory and the Tuareg culture.

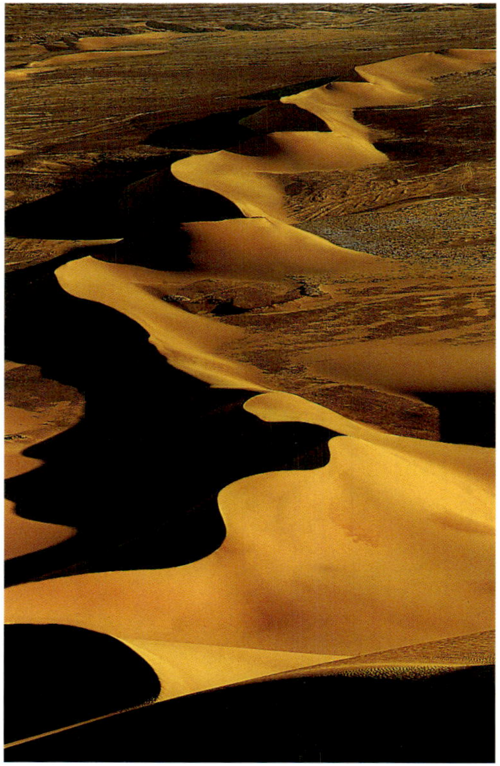

412 and 413
Interacting with the sands of the Sahara, here photographed in Libyan territory, atmospheric agents create undulating designs recalling the sea floor.

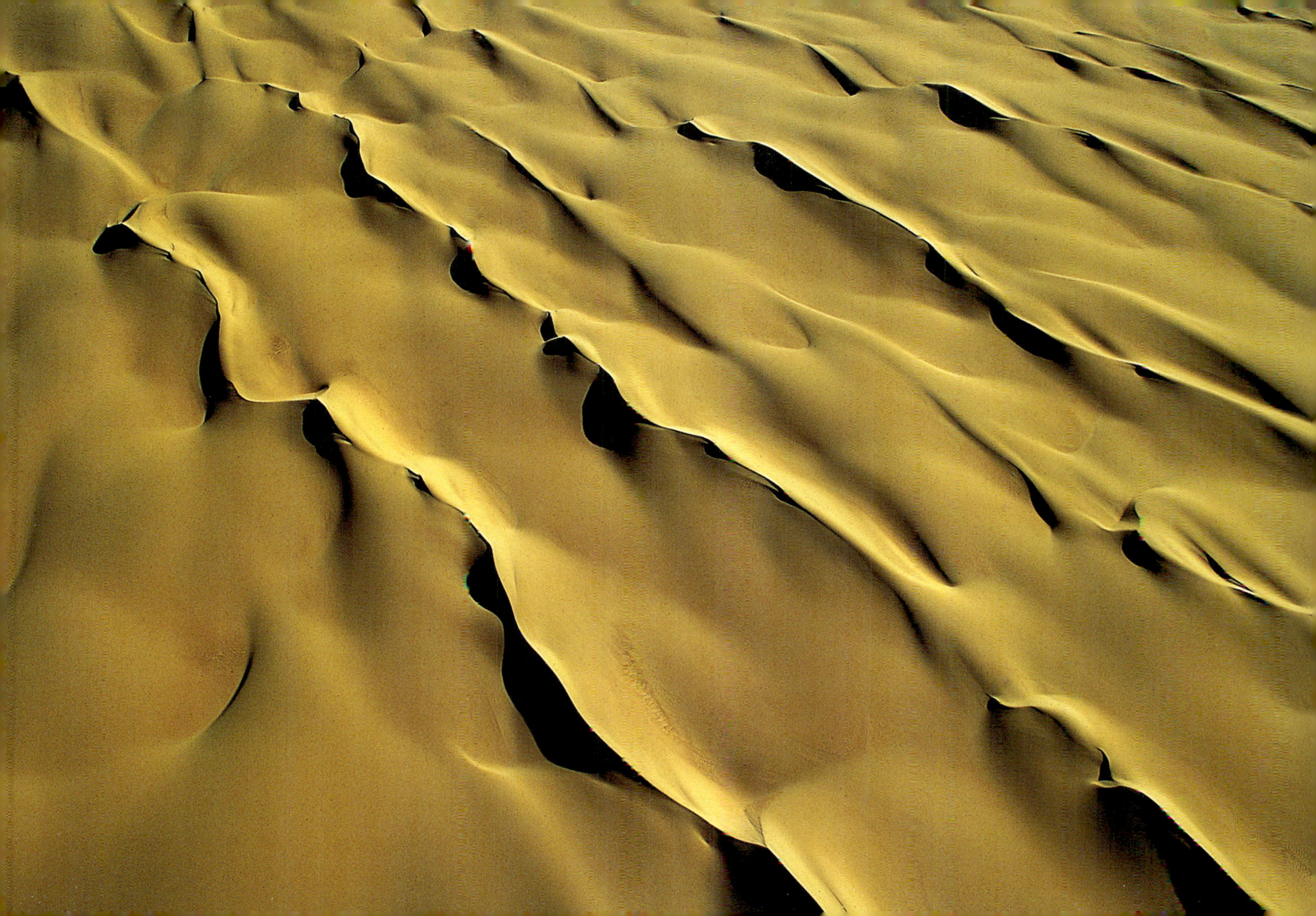

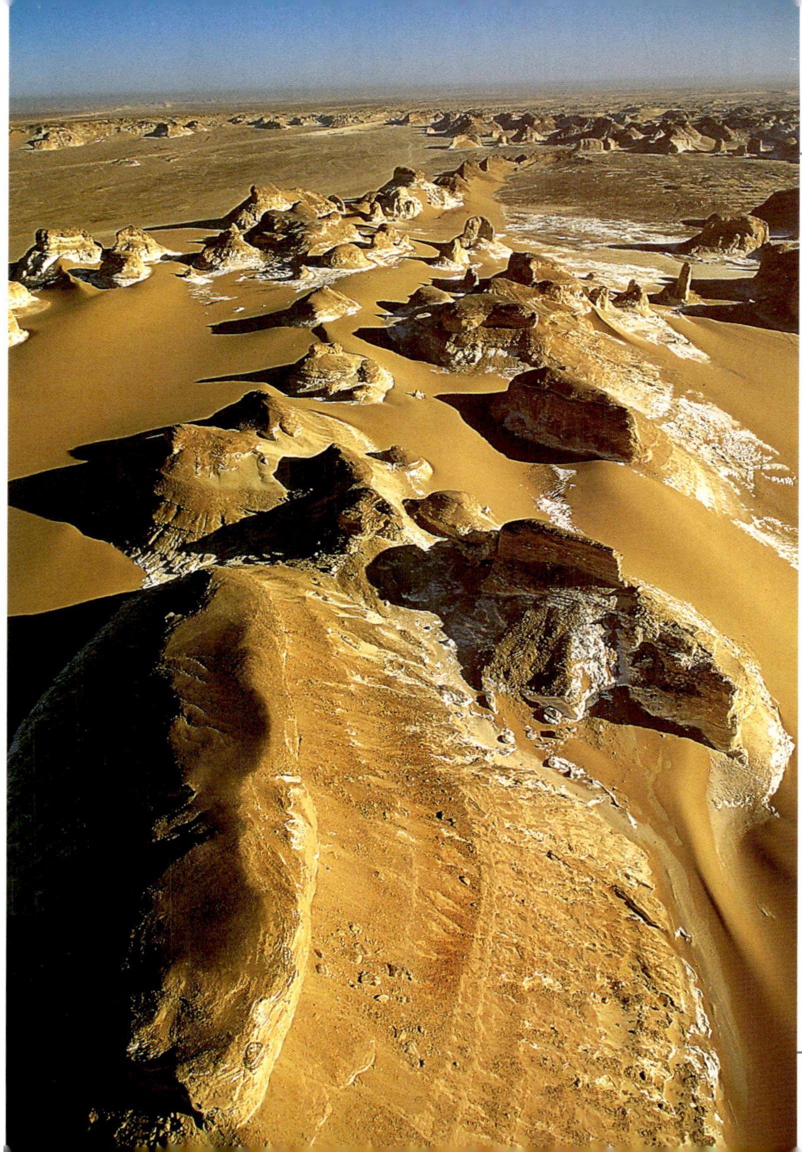

414 and 415

In the Egyptian White Desert, once covered by expanses of water that later receded, chalky formations subjected to constant erosion, giving them an almost lunar appearance, dominate the landscape

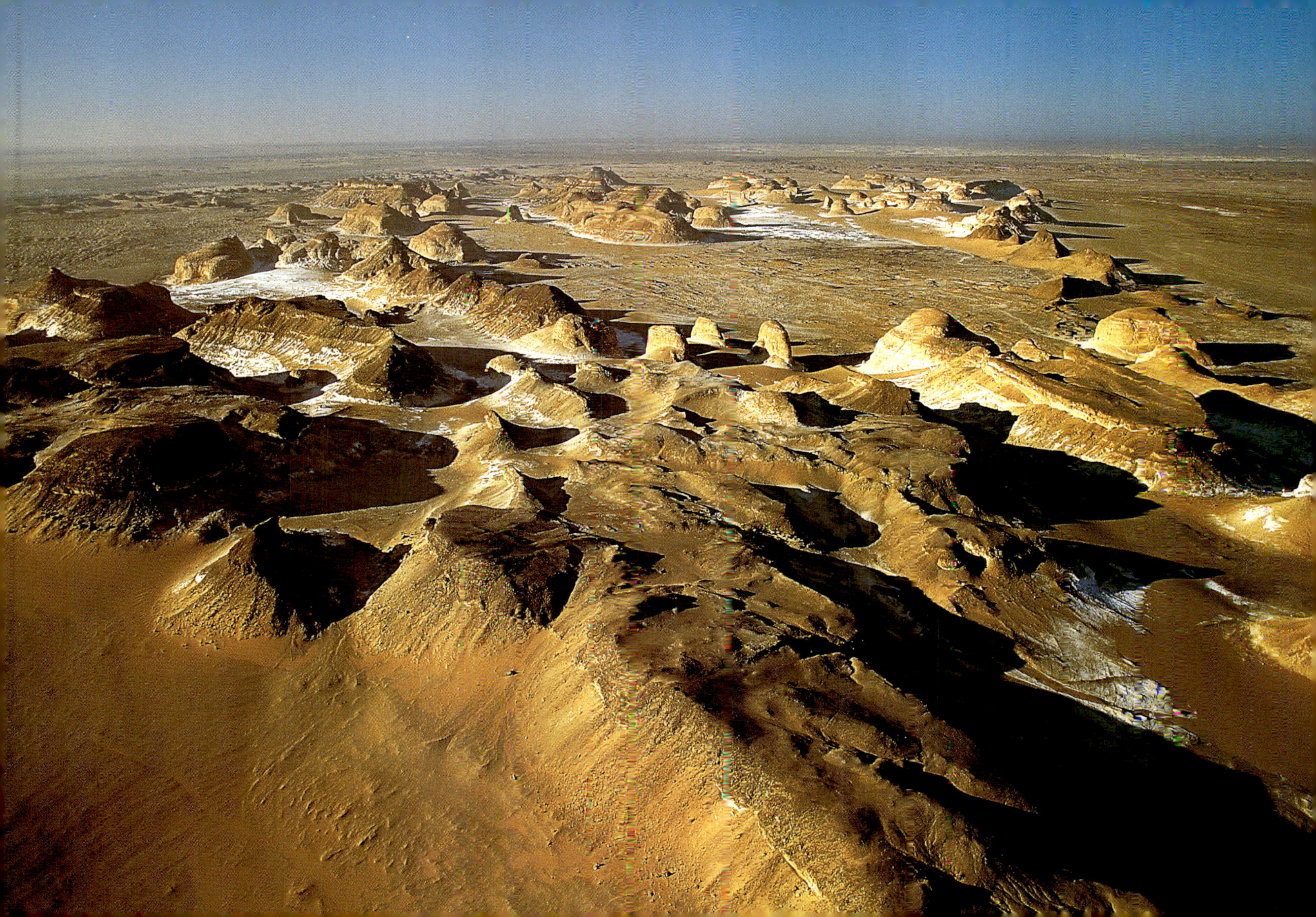

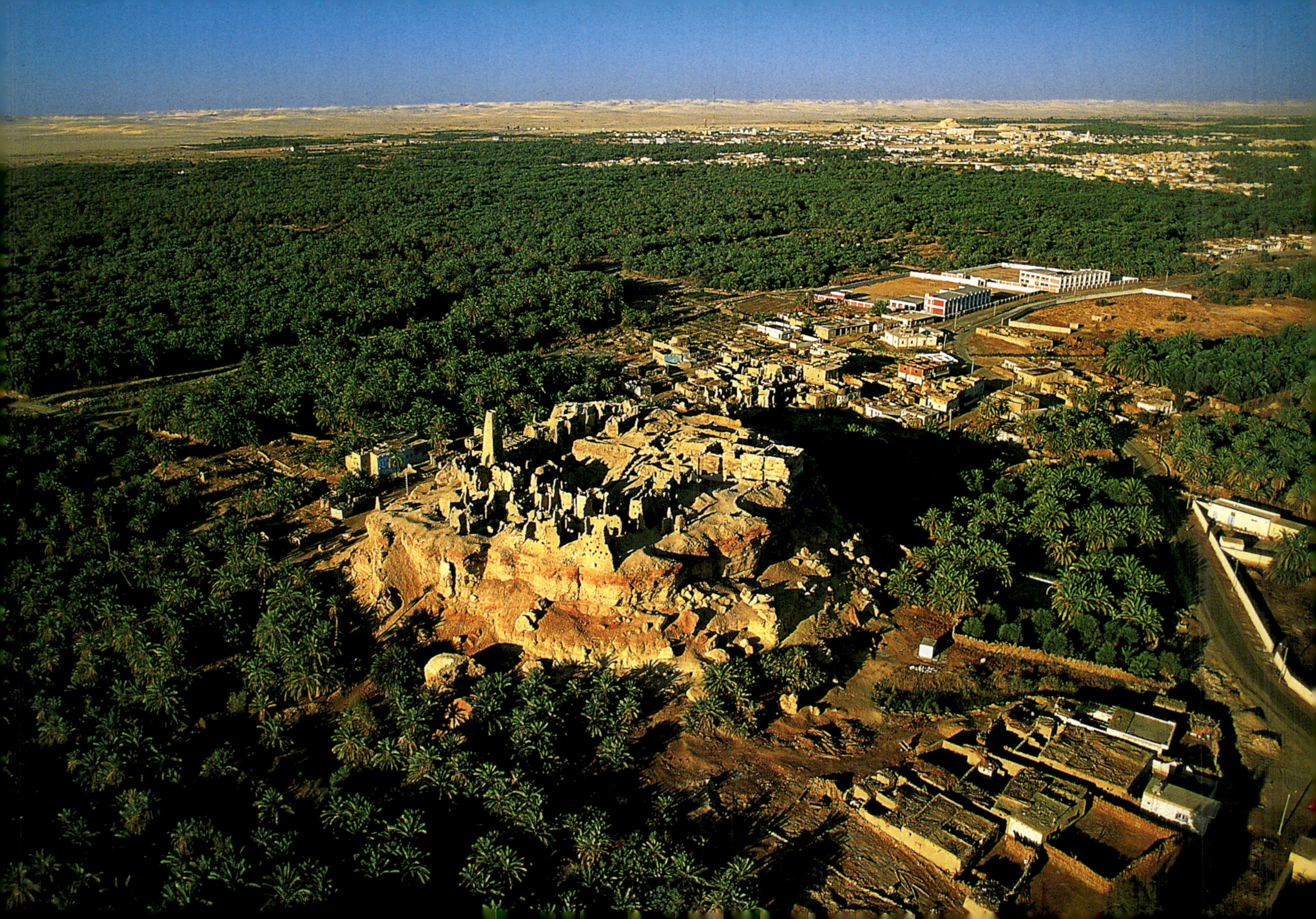

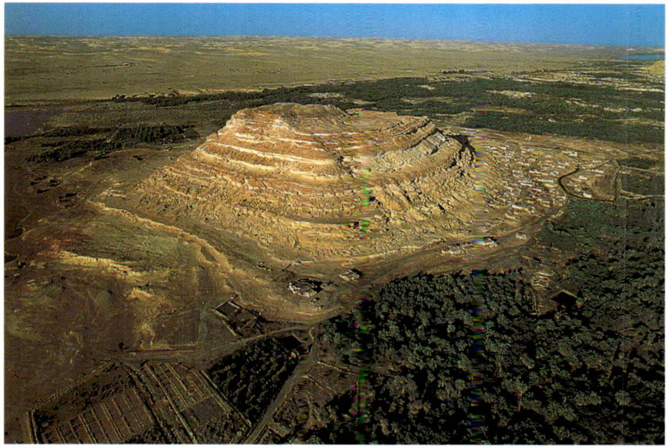

416
Aghurmi stands out from the green palm-tree groves in the Siwa Oasis, in Egypt, where the ruins of the ancient fortress of Shali and the temple of the oracle of Amon are found.

417
Besides those built by man, magnificent natural temples, like this calcareous formation, can be found at the Siwa Oasis.

419
A caravan crosses the dunes of the Sahara in Mauritania, in the area of Nouakchott, creating a chiaroscuro design in the sand similar to those of Chinese etchings.

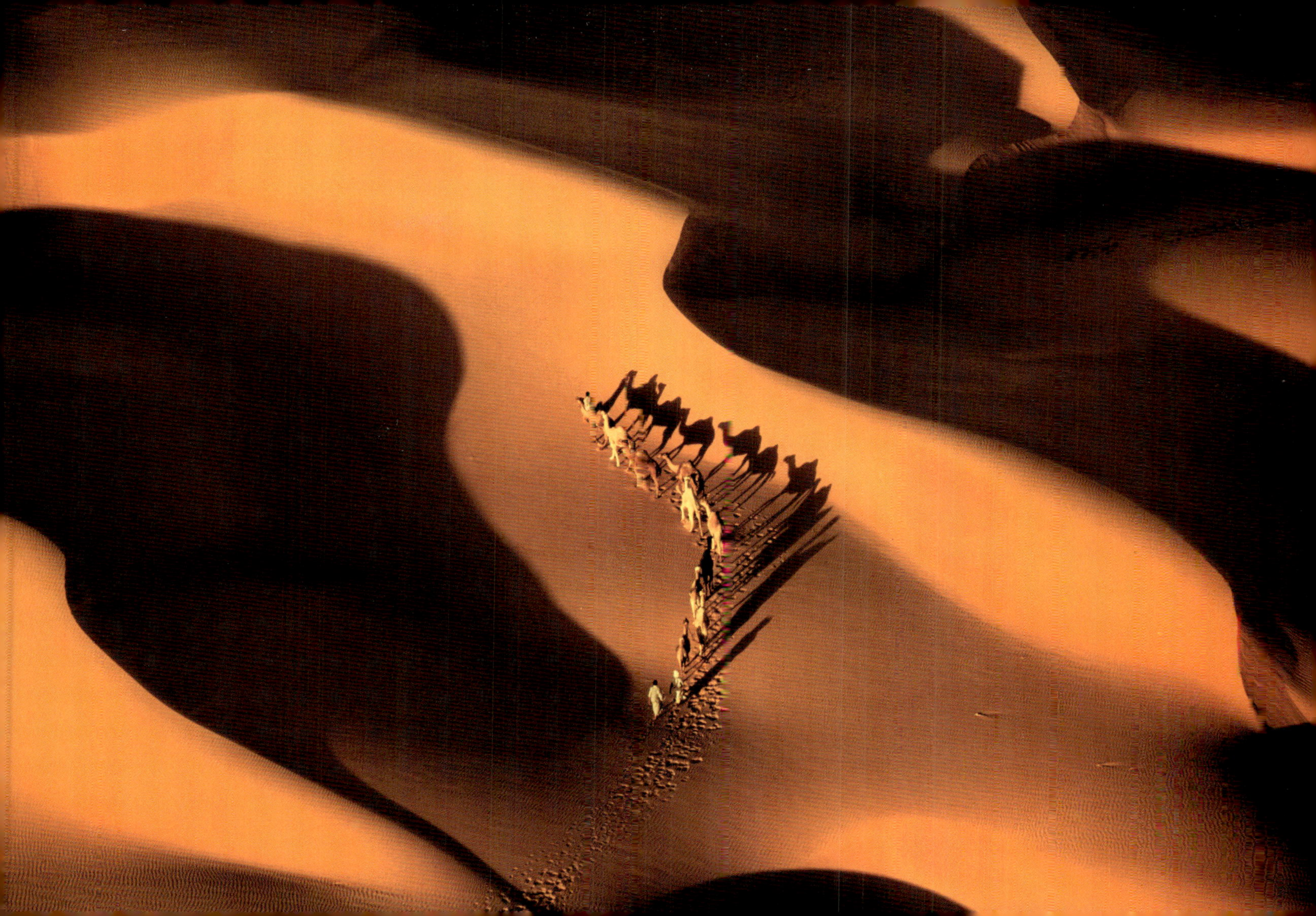

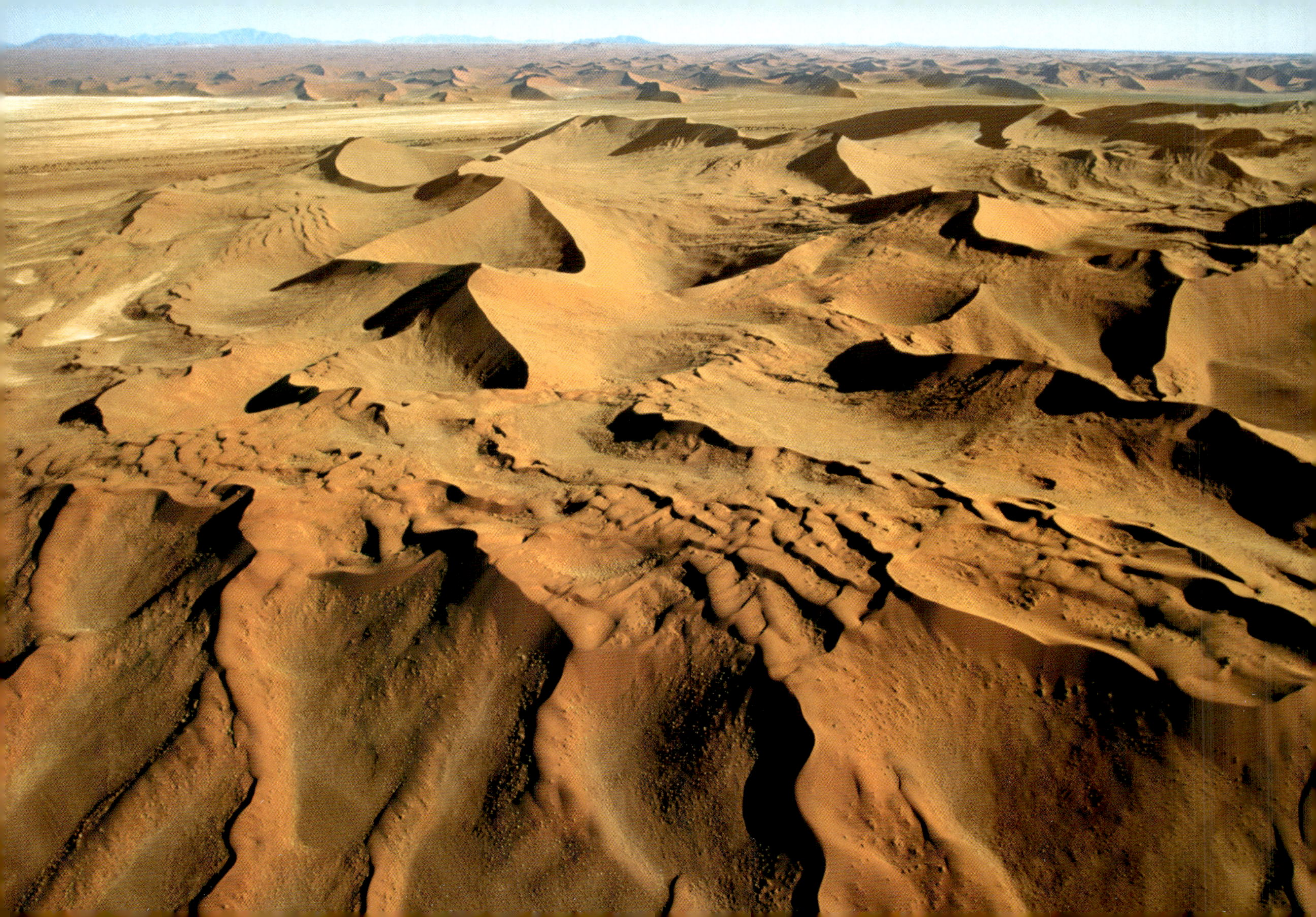

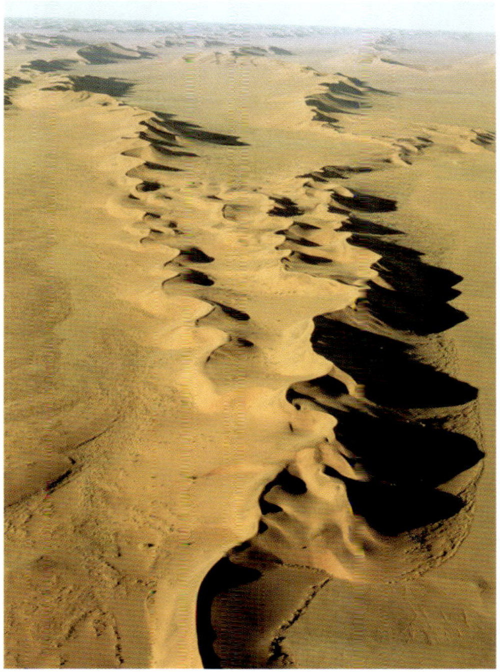

420 and 421

In the Namib Desert, from which Namibia gets its name, mountainous red dunes alternate with plains and *inselbergs*, isolated mountains with steep sides and flat tops.

422-423

A herd of gemsbok run across a clearing in Namibia.

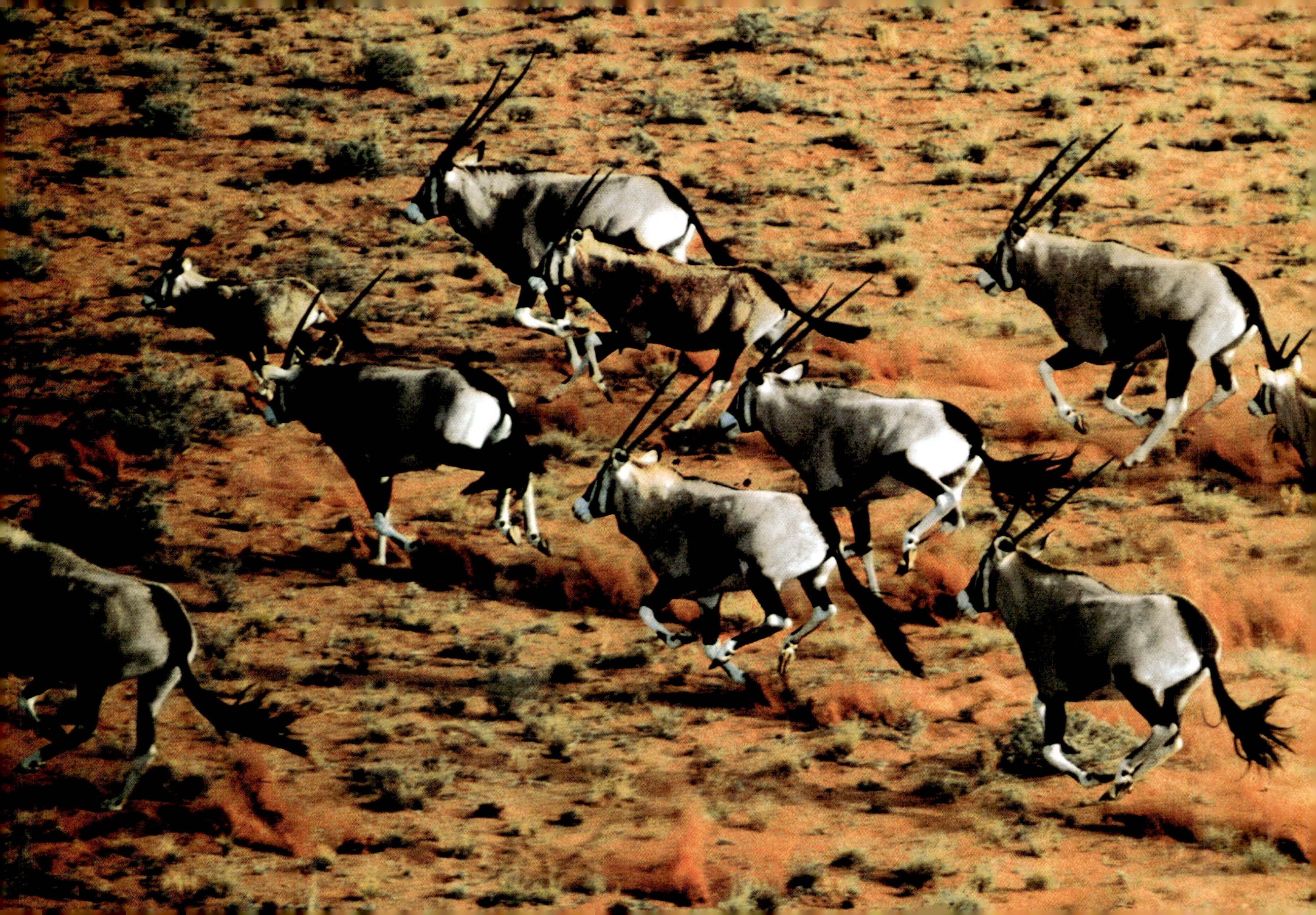

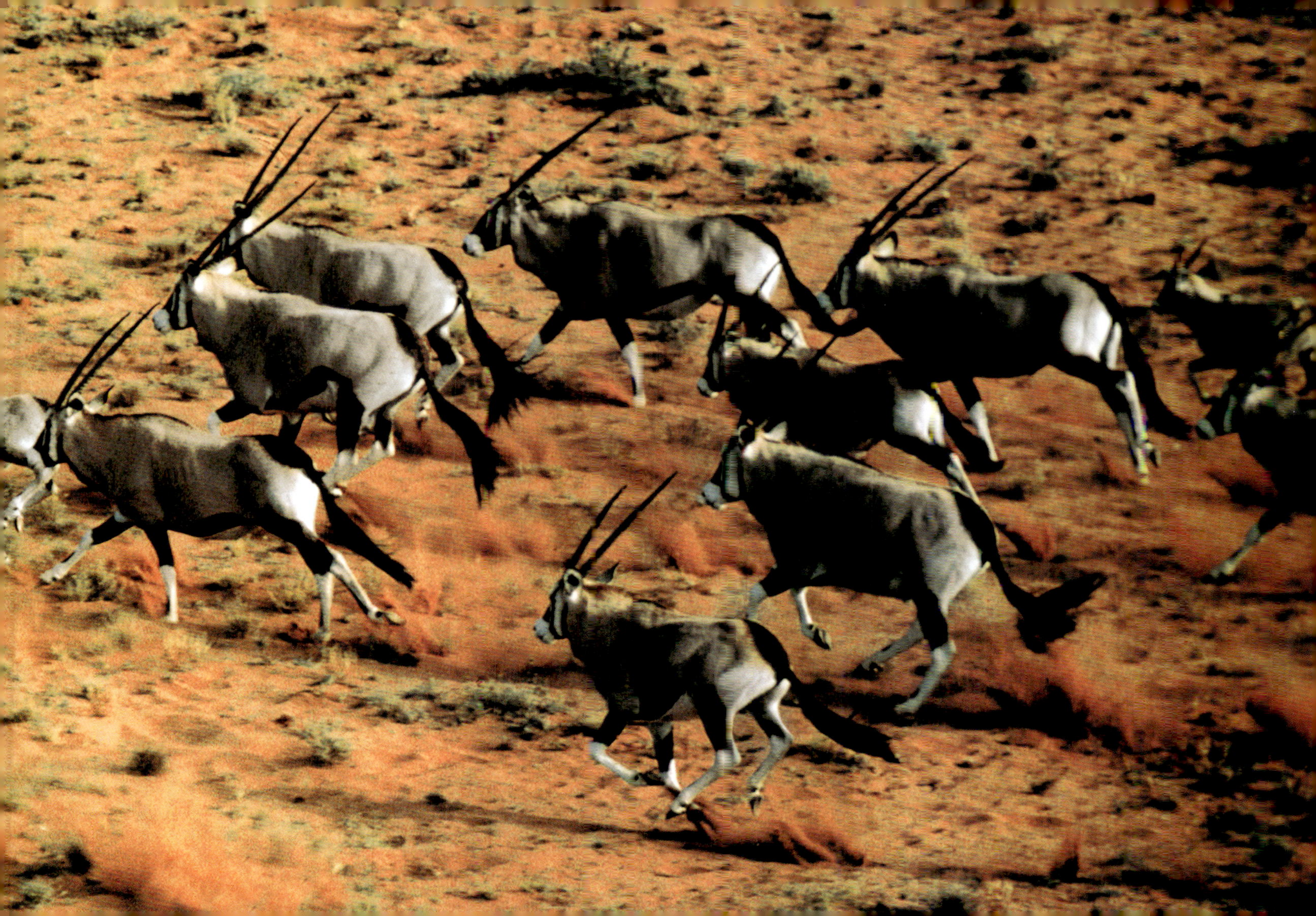

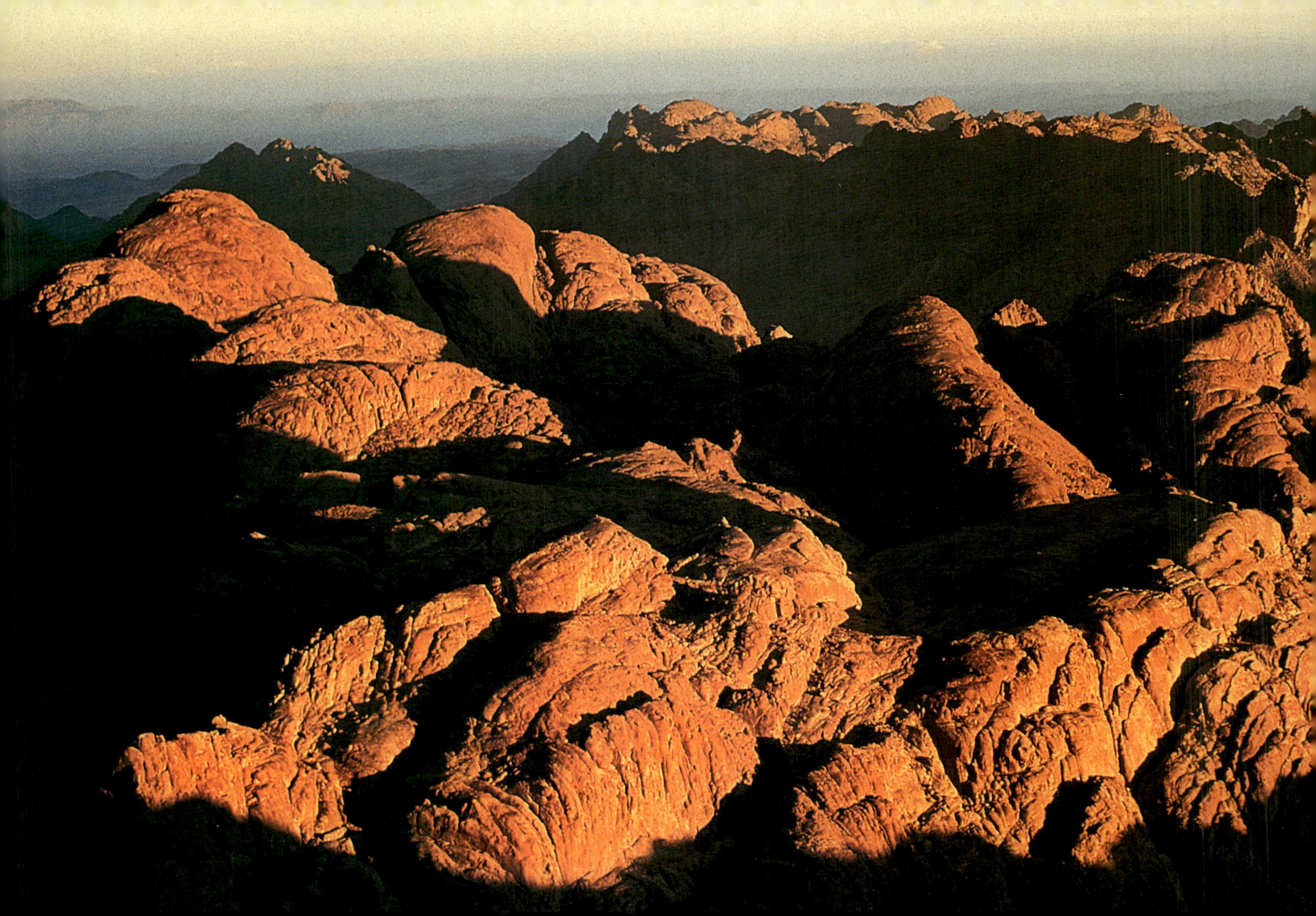

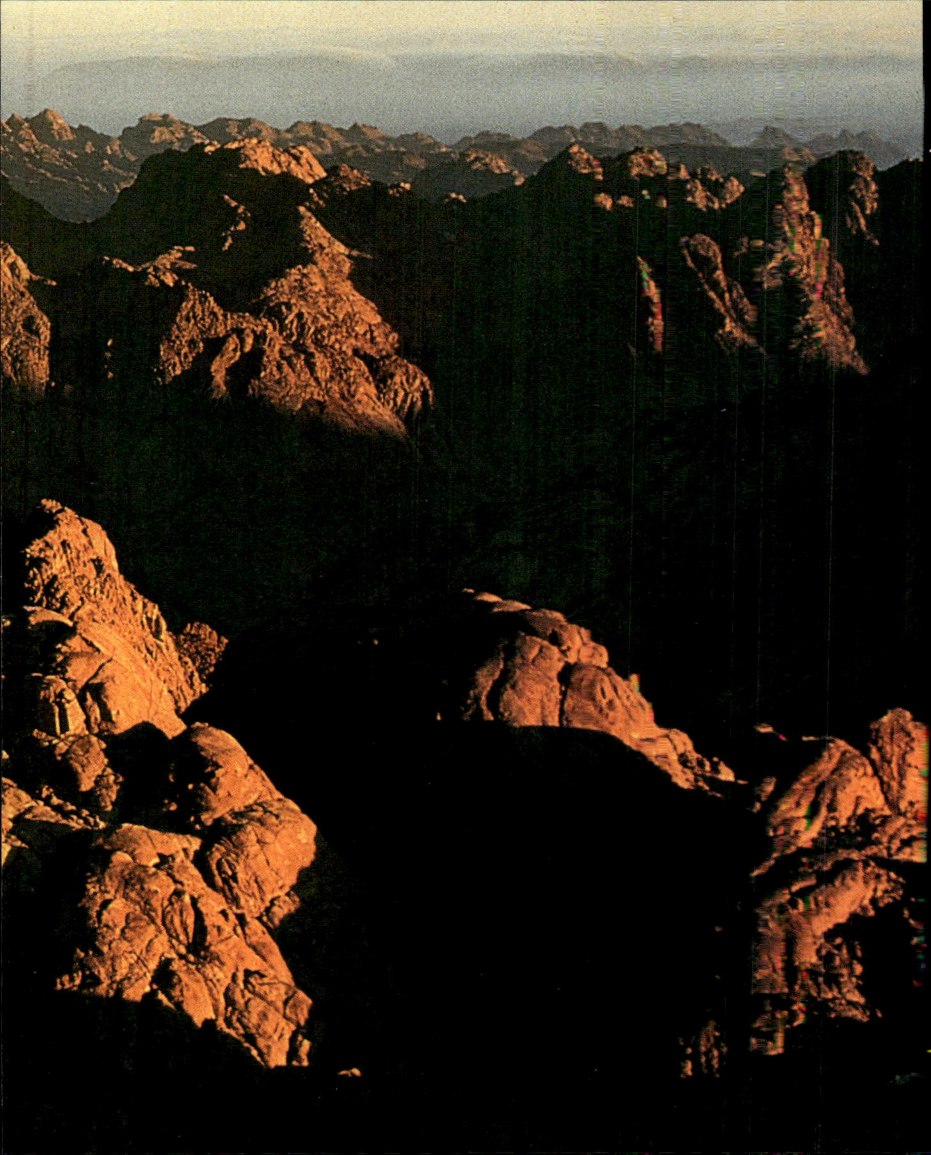

Asia

424-425
Mount Sinai, or Gebel Musa, Moses' mountain, holds great charm thanks to its natural beauty, emphasized by its colors especially at dawn, and to its religious significance for the Christian religion: Moses received the tablets of the ten commandments here.

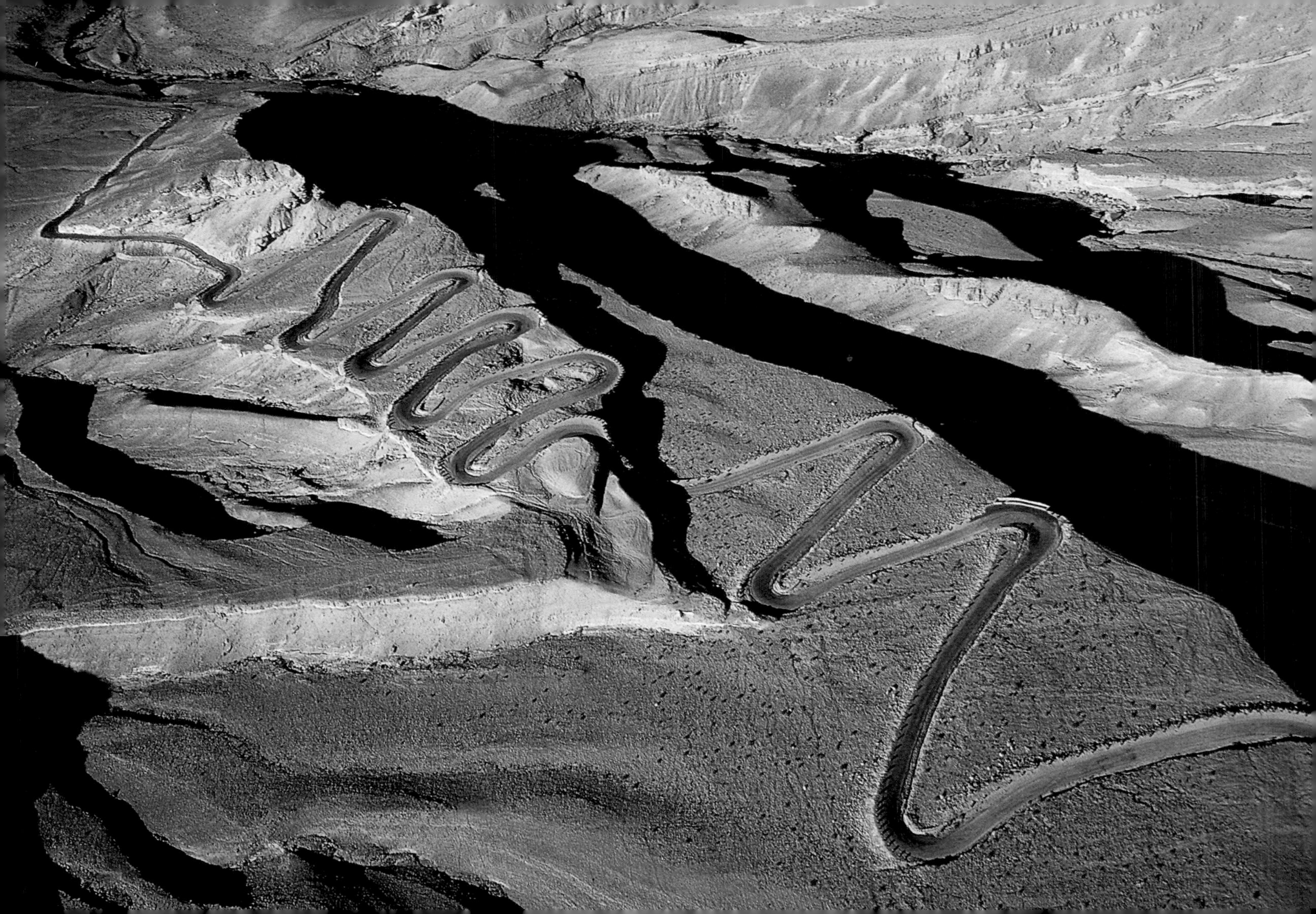

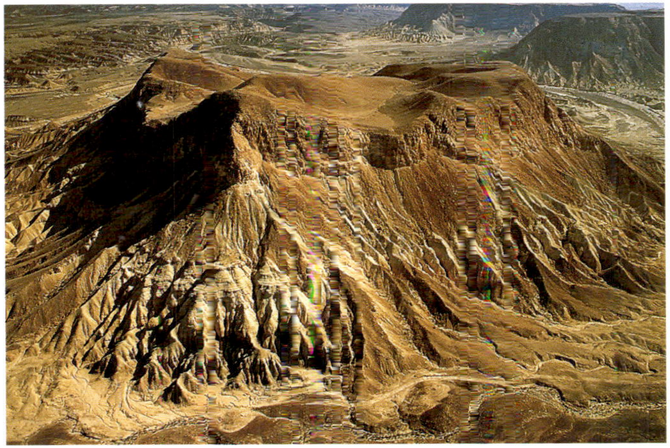

426

Ma'ale Akrabim, in Israel, is a tract of an ancient road between Beersheba and Eilat that winds like a serpent up the arid mountainous territory it crosses.

427

The top of Mount Nishpeh, in Israel, is formed by rock resistant to atmospheric agents, whereas the underlying stone is more easily weathered.

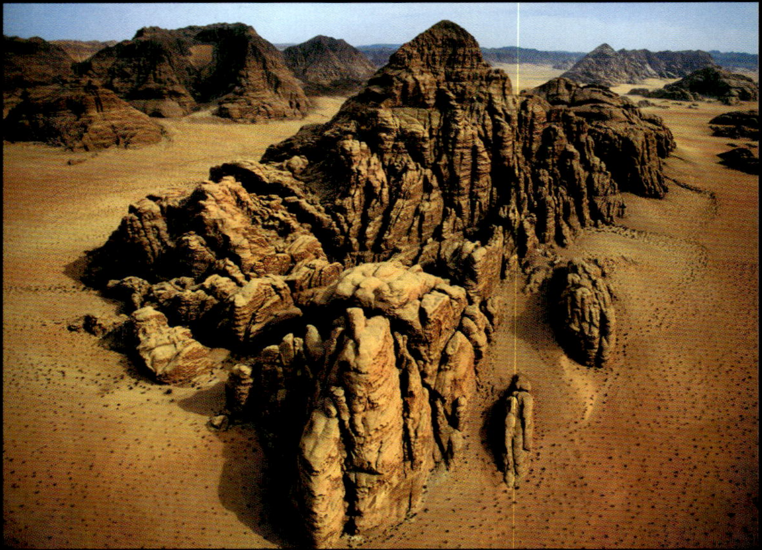

428 and 429
Iwadi Rum is the biggest desert in Jordan. Labeled "immense, echoing, divine" by T.H. Lawrence, who was enchanted by its charm, it is formed by expanses of sand from which rise the *jabal,* sandstone hills.

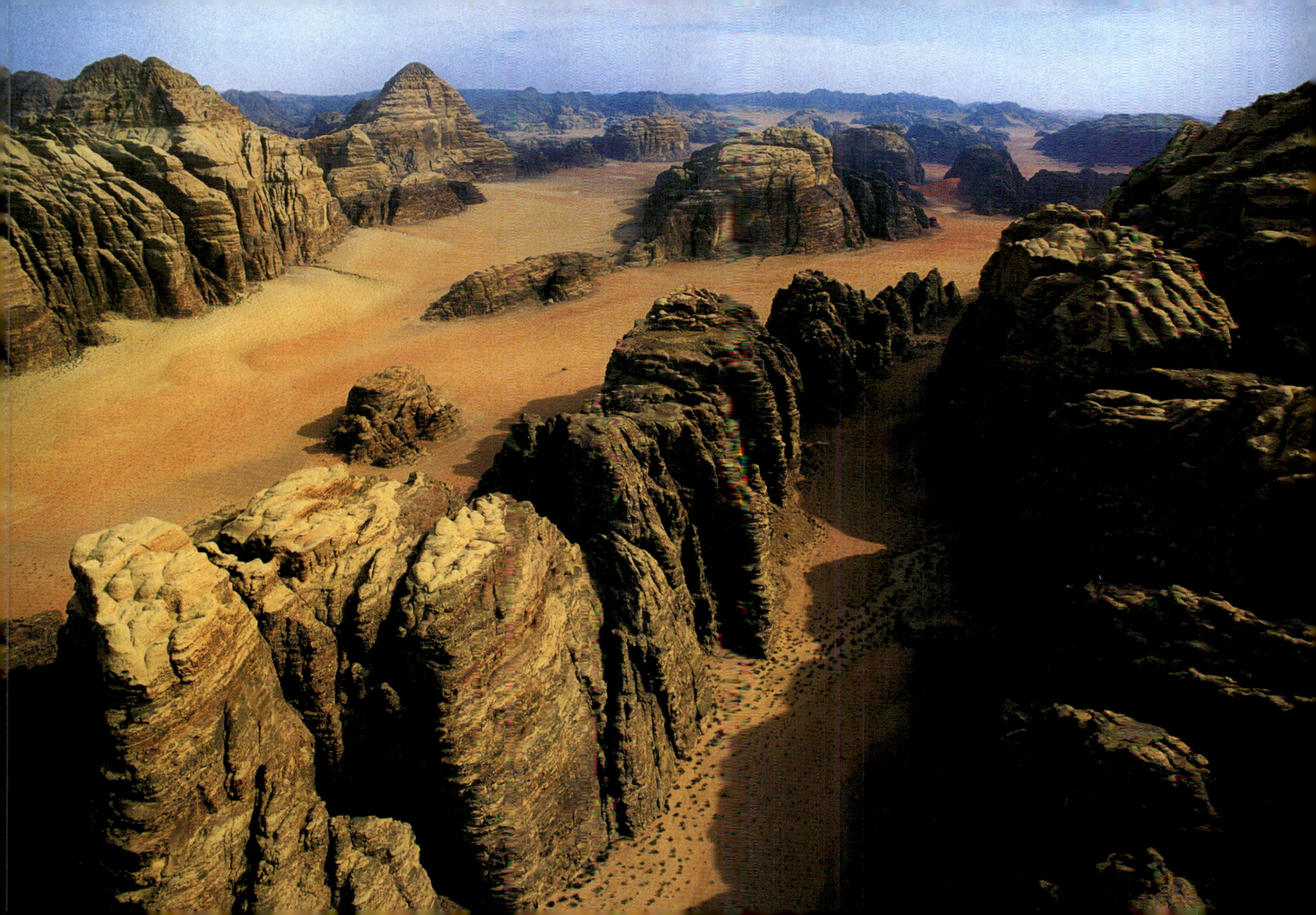

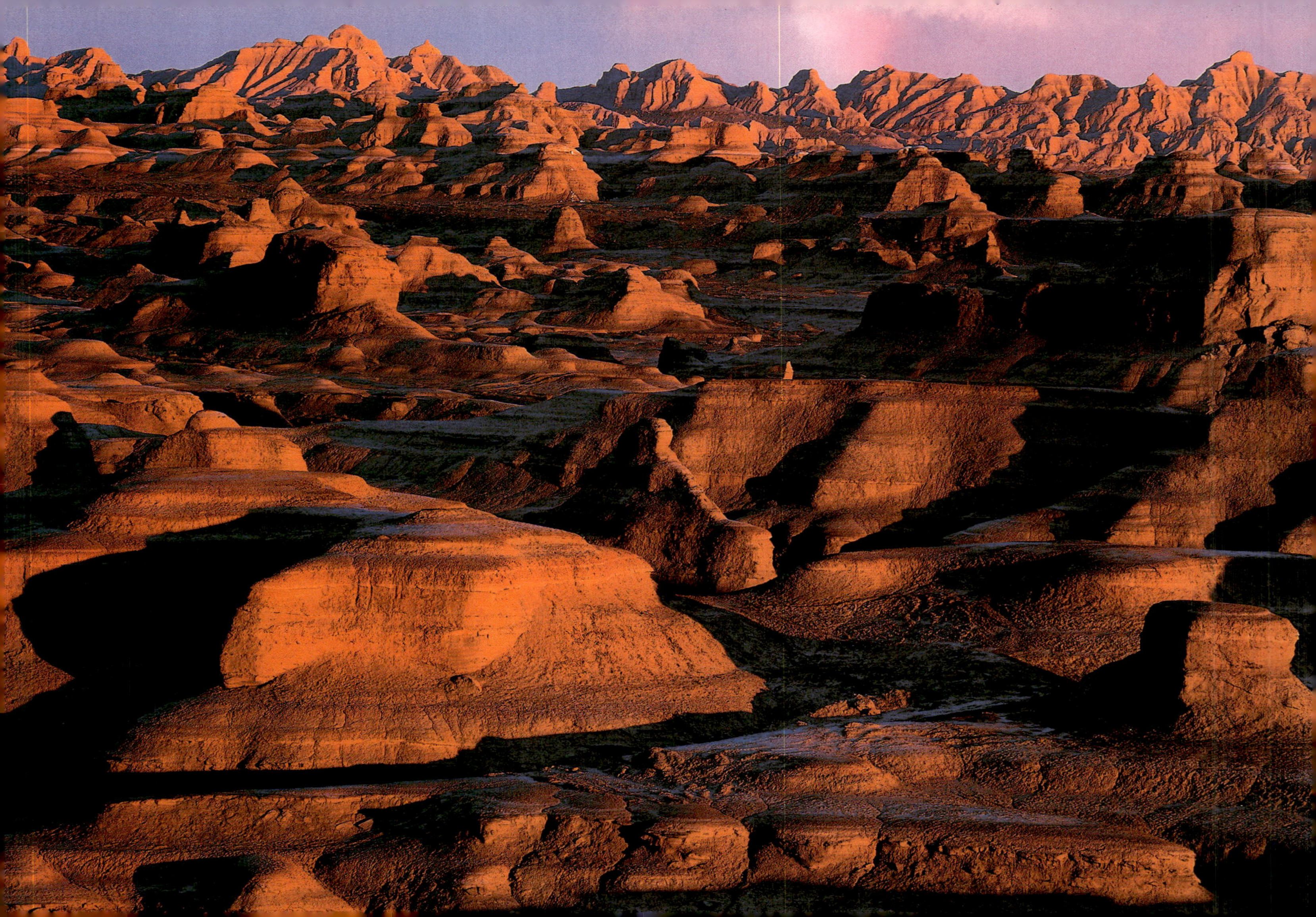

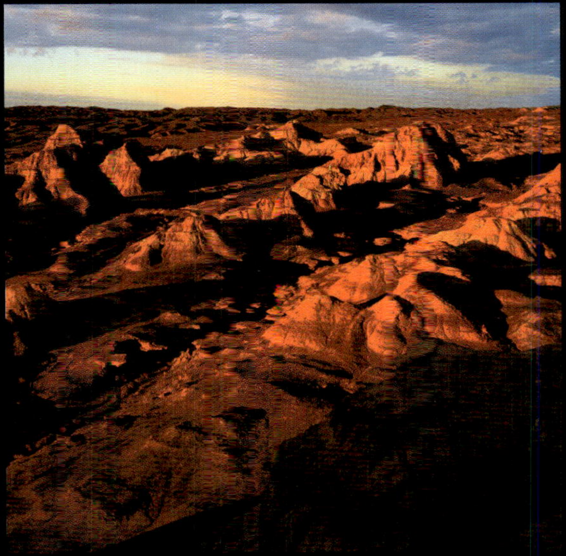

430 and 431

One of the forms that the Gobi Desert, in China, can take is the *yadan*, a term meaning cliff in Uygur, indicating landscapes composed of protruding solitary rocks.

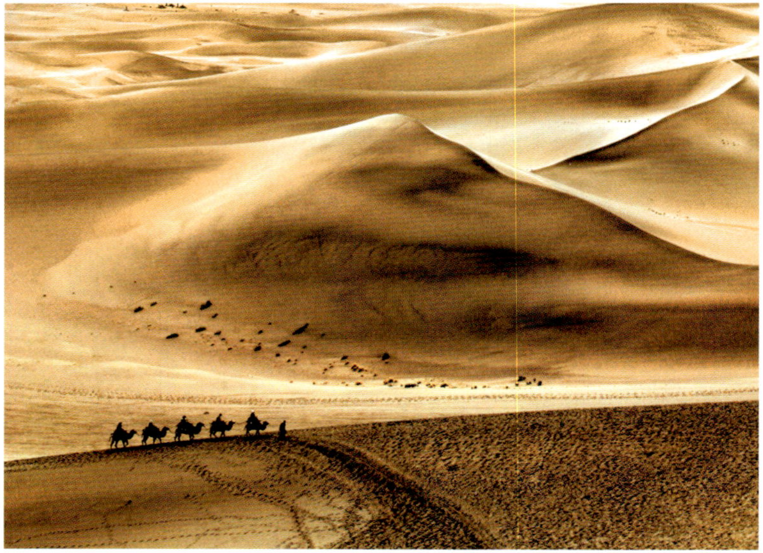

432 and 433

The contrast in size between man and the vastness of the desert stands out in these photos portraying camel-drivers in the Taklimakan Desert in northwestern China.

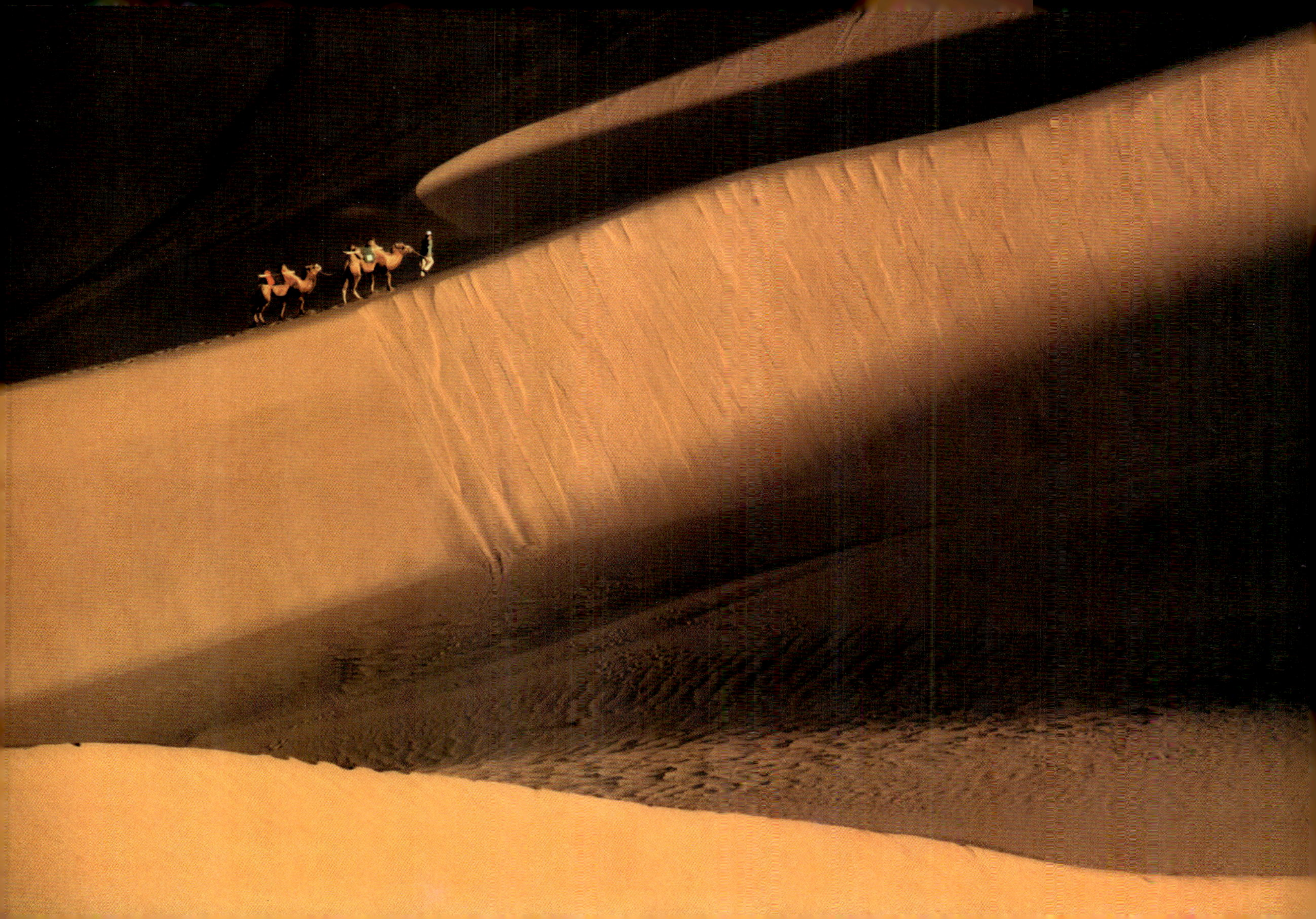

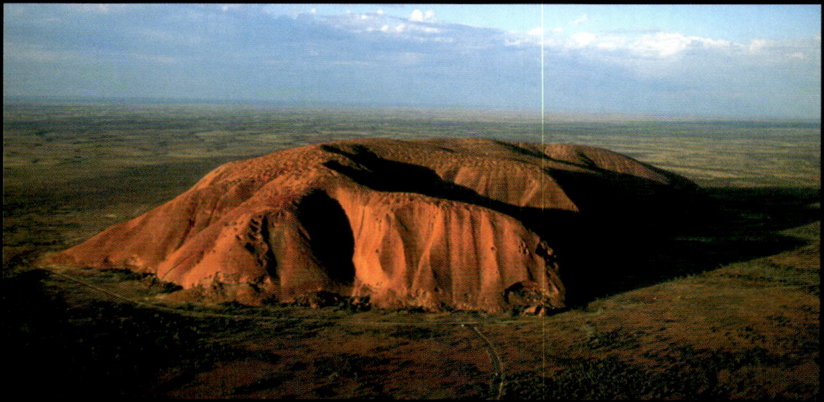

434
The rocky monolith of Ayers Rock is an icon of the Australian continent: it rises 1,142 feet and has a circumference of about six miles.

435
Kata Tjuta, in Australia, is composed of more than 30 rounded, red-colored massifs considered sacred by aborigines because of their finger-like shape.

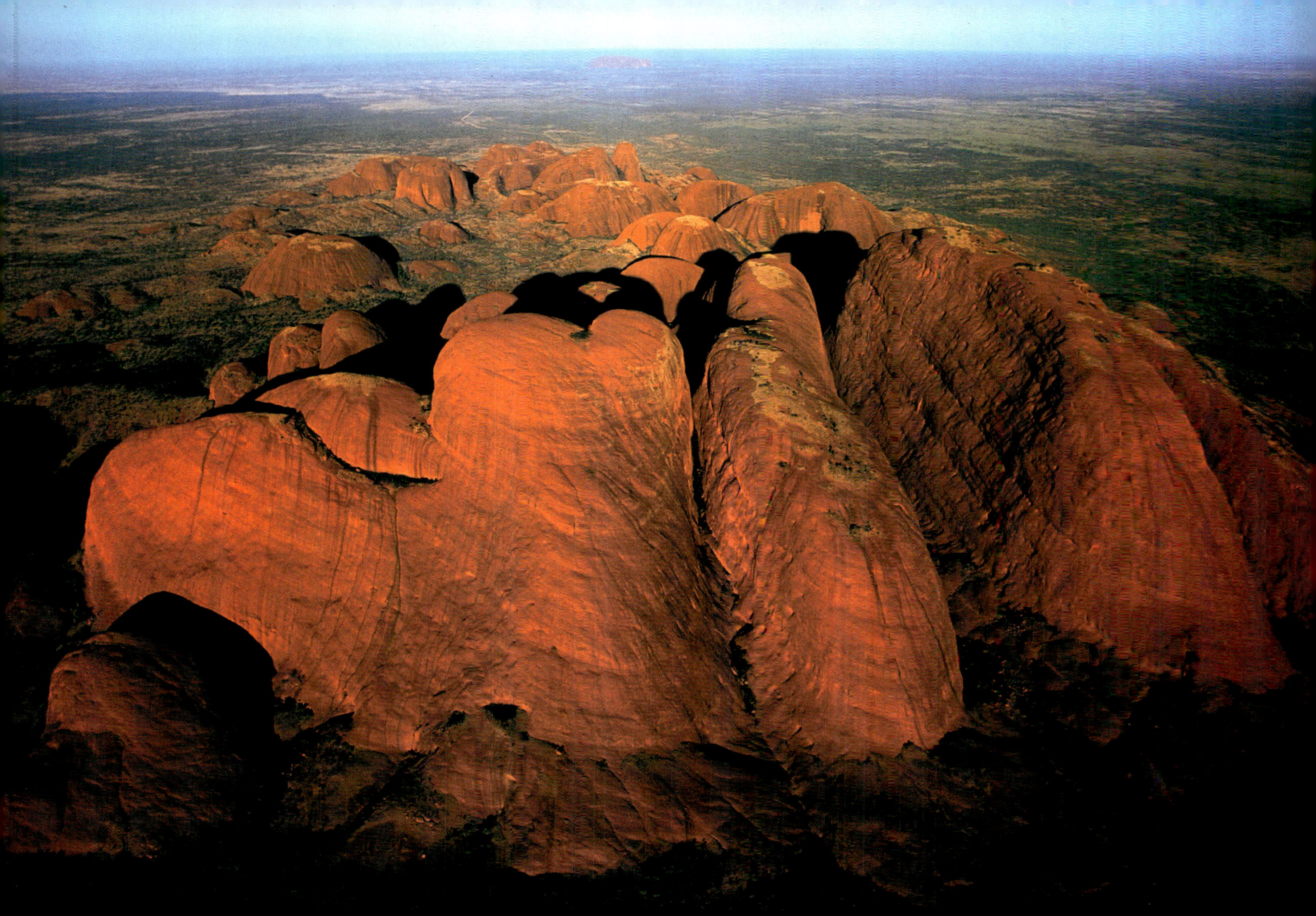

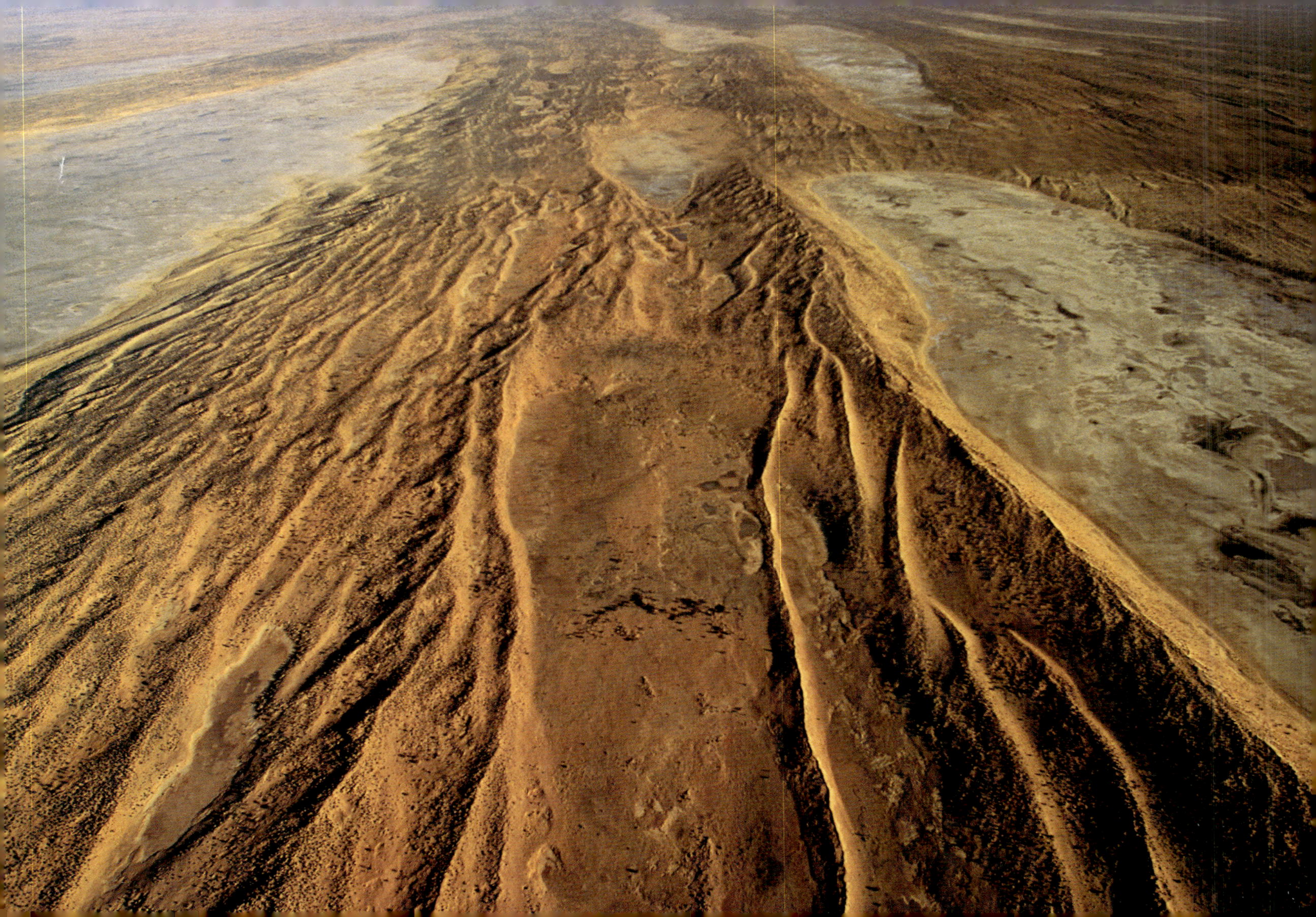

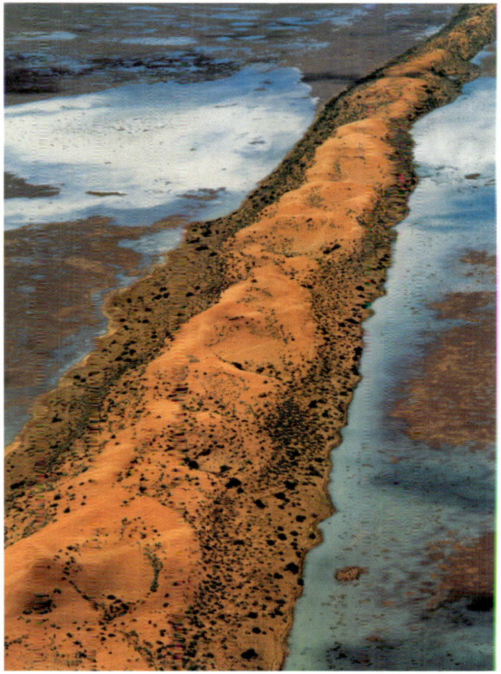

436 and 437

According to many, the landscape of the Australian Simpson Desert, in which sandy dunes alternate with salt lakes, is similar to the terrain on planet Mars.

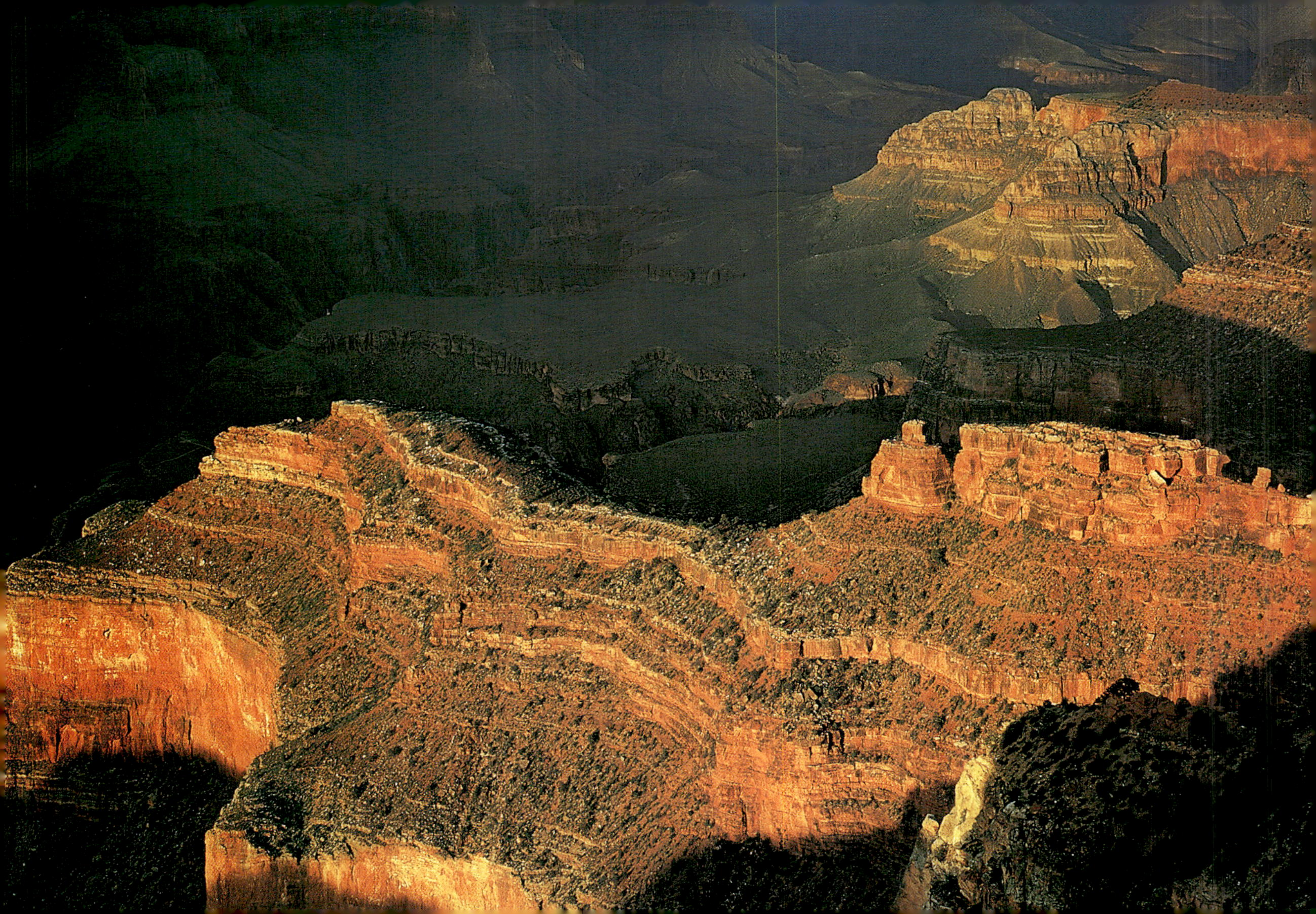

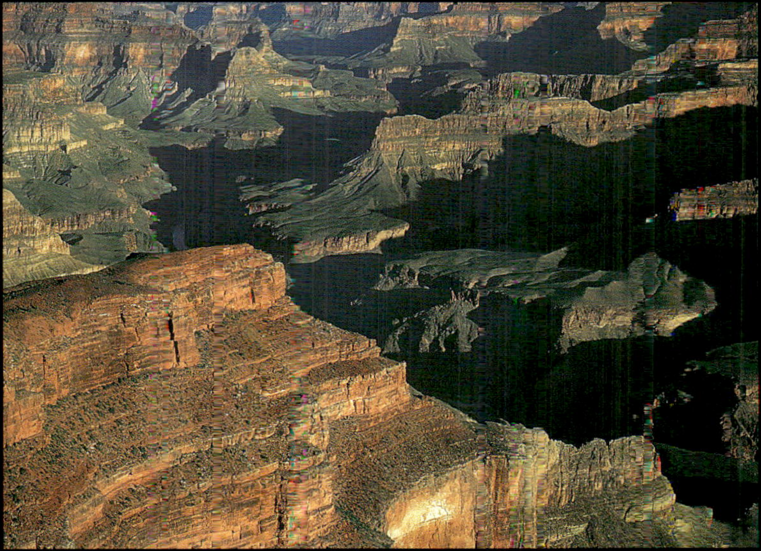

438 and 439

Two hundred and seventeen miles long and from four to 19 wide, the Grand Canyon in Colorado was created over thousands of years of erosion and flooding and represents one of the most spectacular settings in the United States and the world.

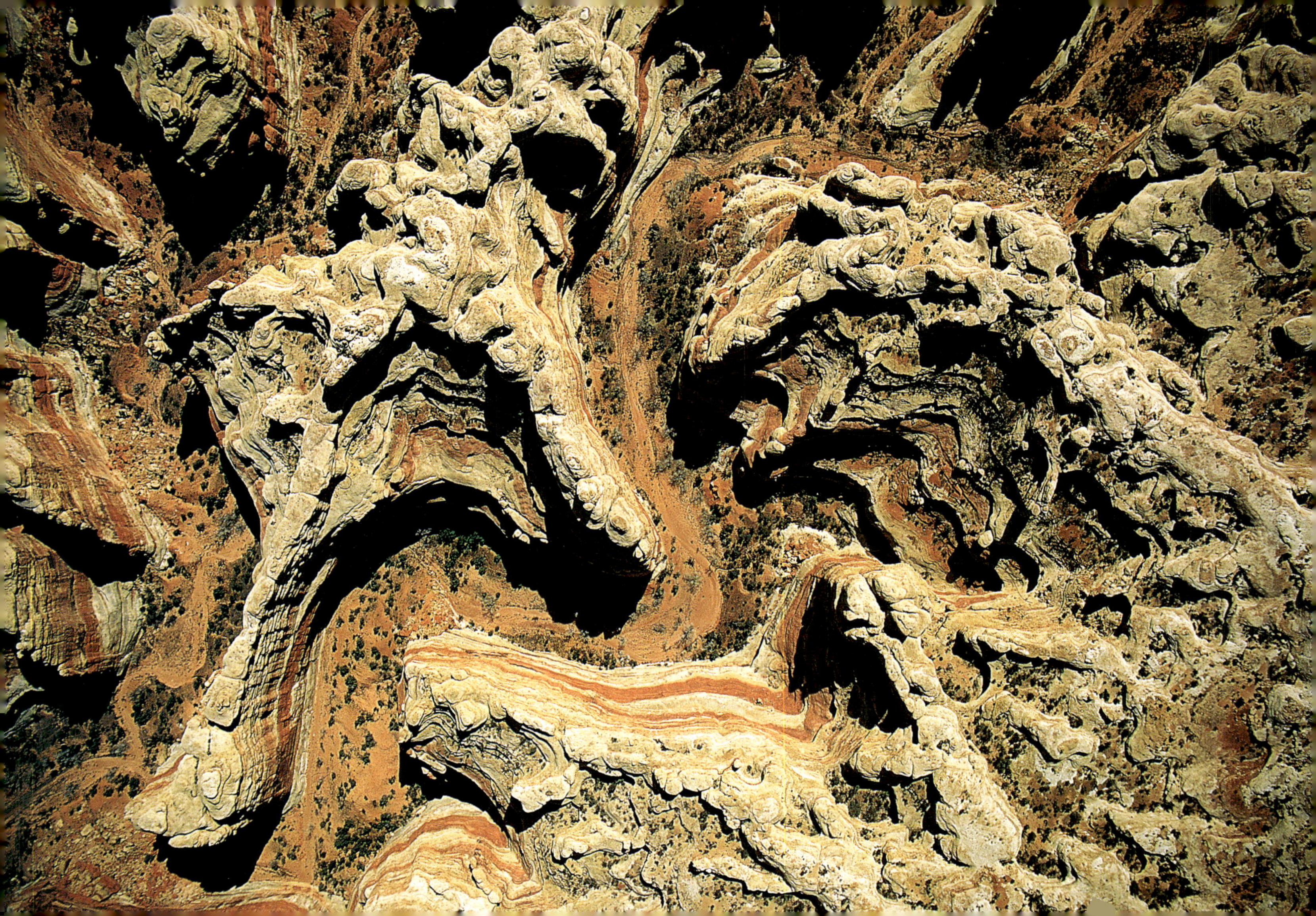

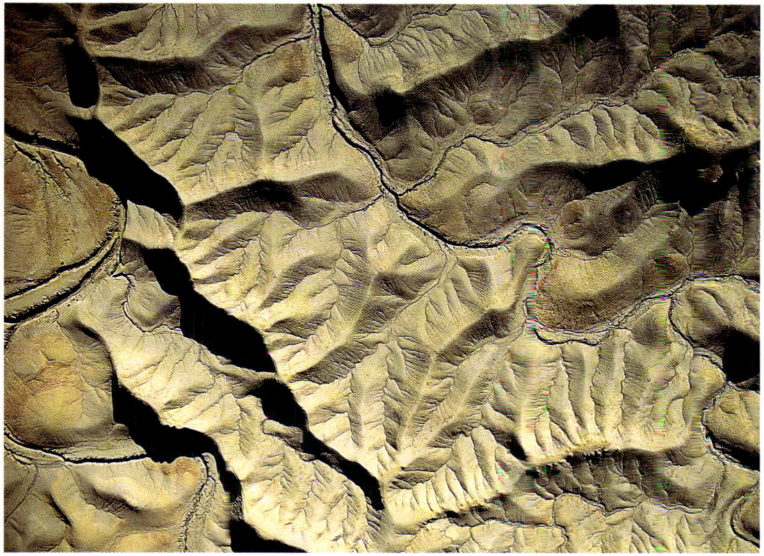

440

The Maze, the most remote area in the Canyonlands National Park, in Utah, is characterized by canyons shaped like labyrinths, with tall rocks and sandy fins.

441

The San Rafael Desert in Utah is a completely arid territory where the light reflecting off the rocks has an almost blinding effect.

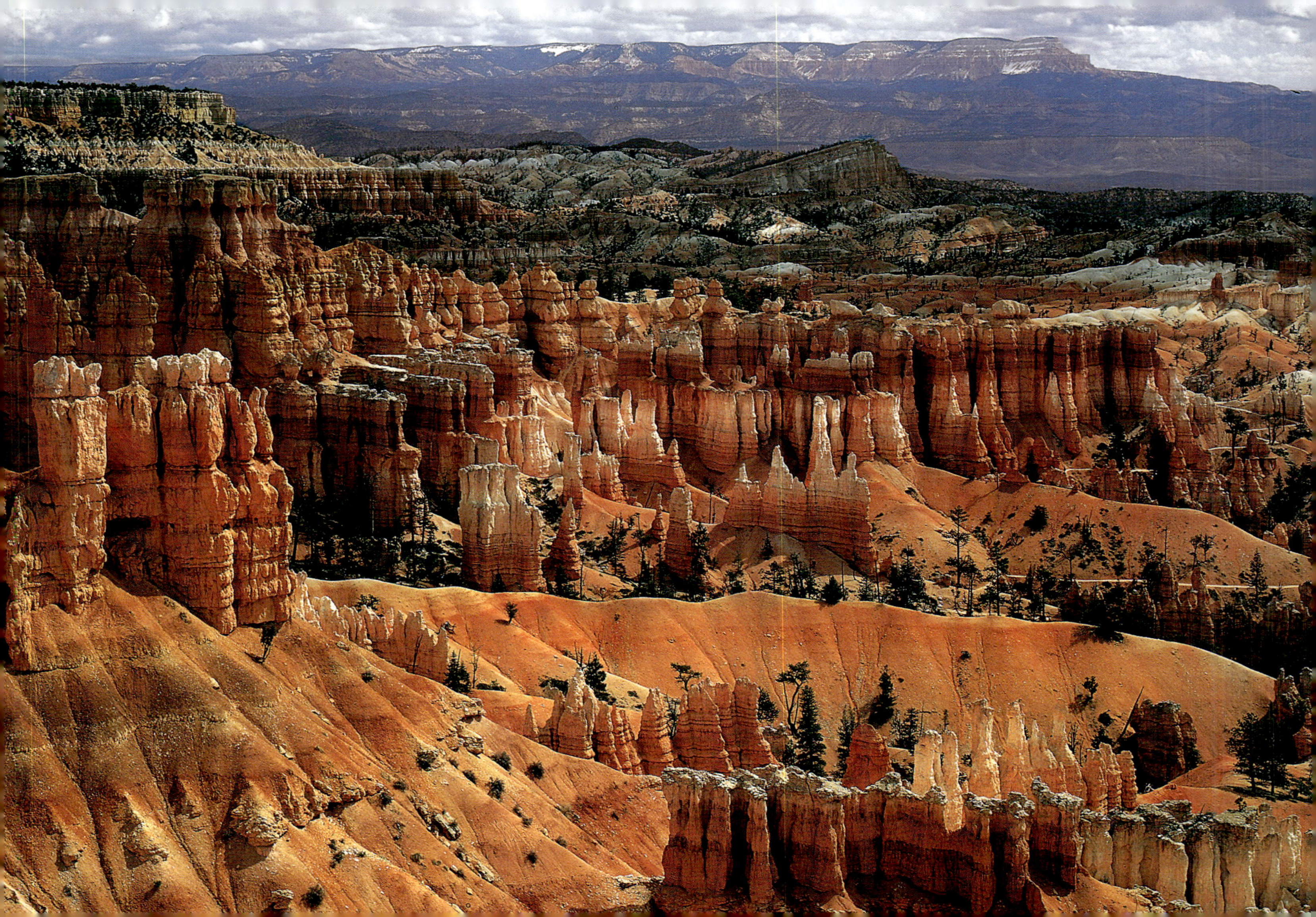

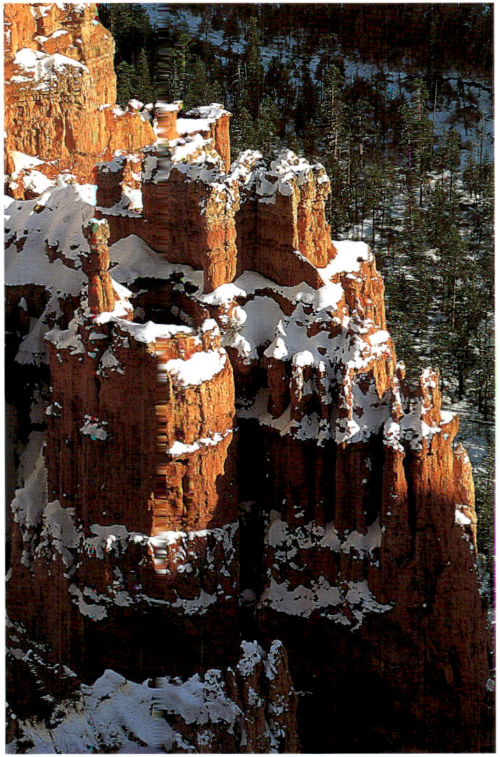

Lands of Silence

442 and 443
Bryce Canyon, in Utah, is an ensemble of natural amphitheaters formed by spires sculpted out of the rock, which reveal their full splendor at dawn and dusk. In winter, the red rocks are partially covered by snow.

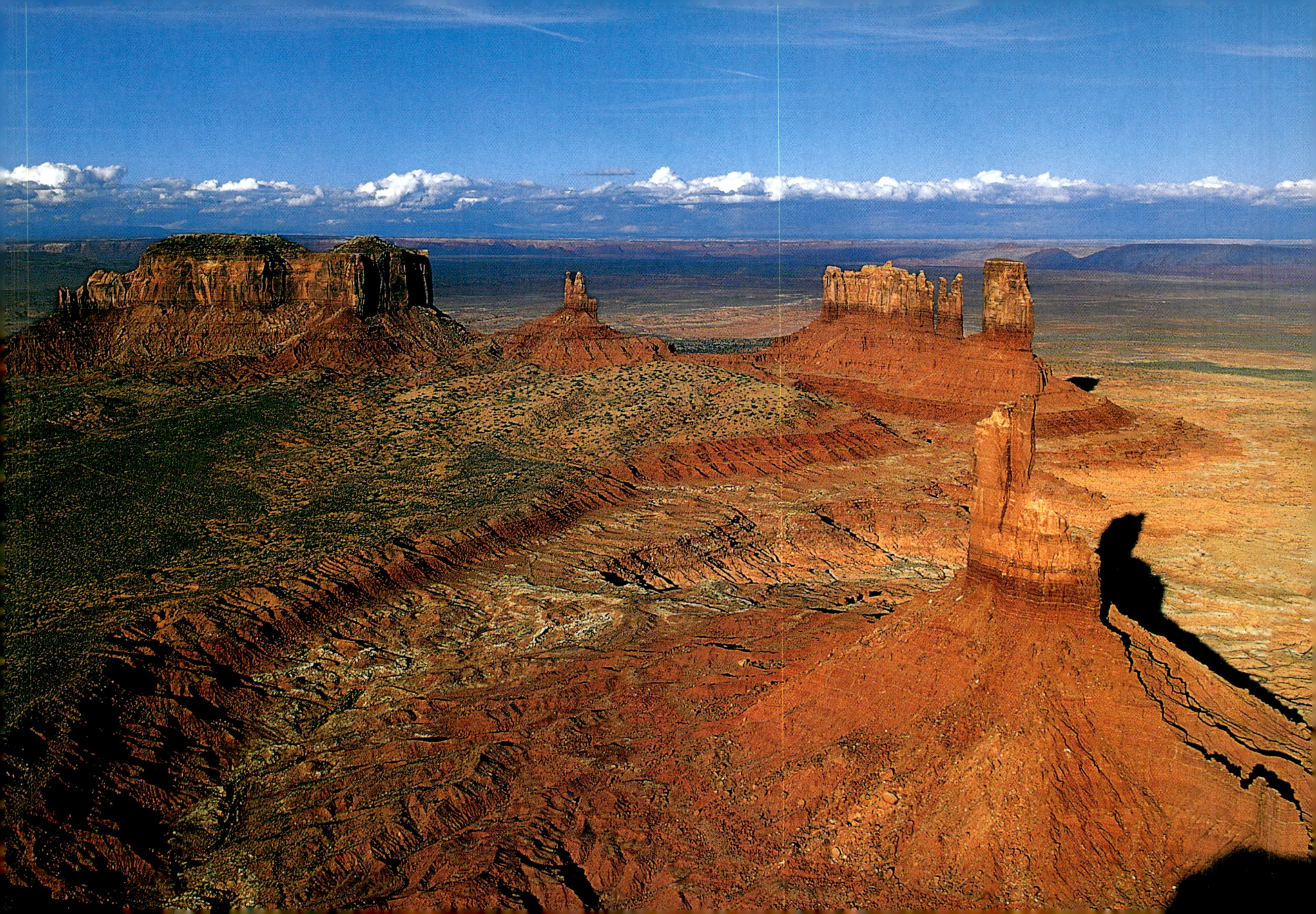

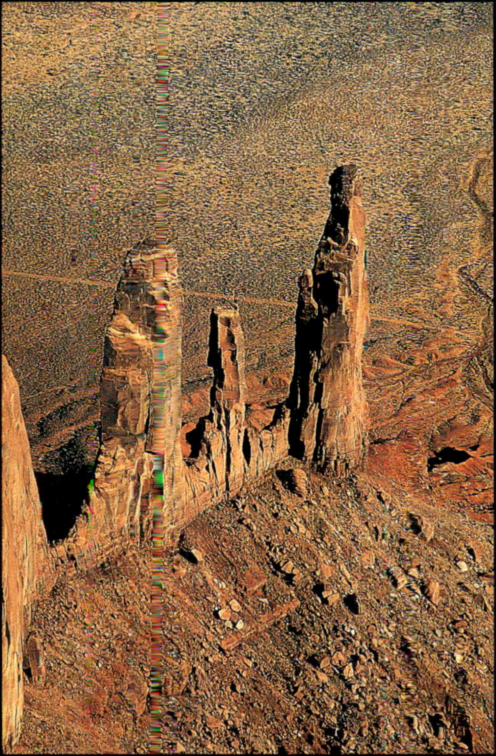

444 and 445

The scarce pinnacles of red sandstone in Monument Valley in Arizona are silhouetted against an infinite sky, emphasizing their great height, often reaching up to 1,000 feet.

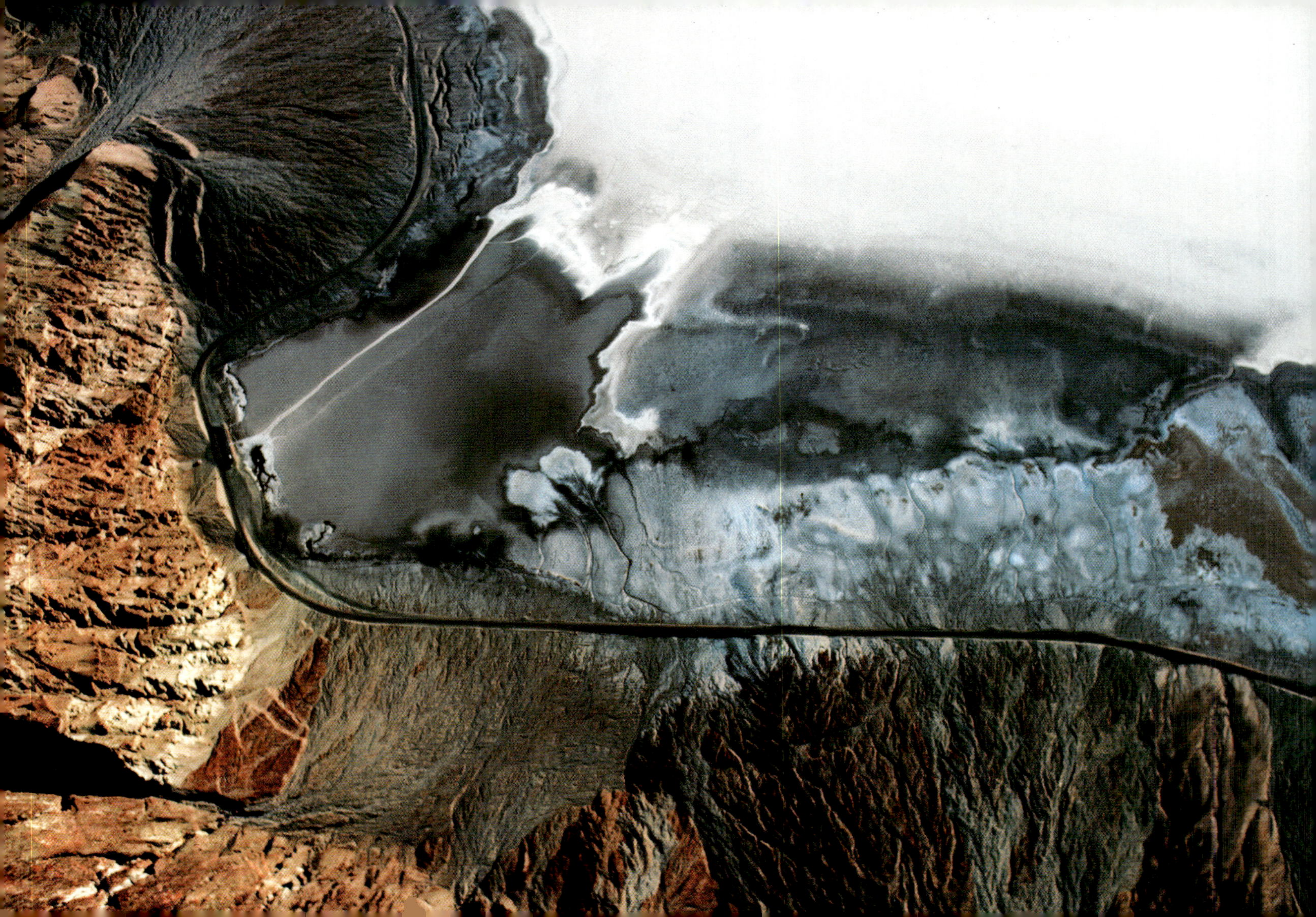

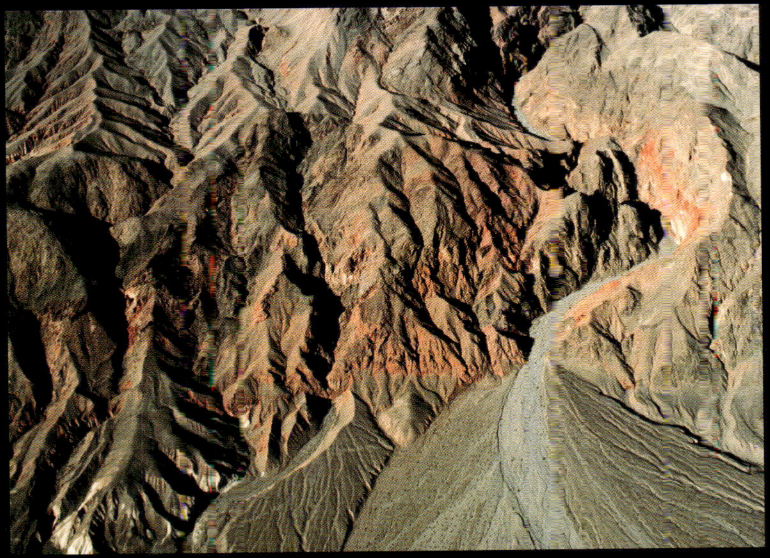

446

Particular chromatic effects occur on the waters of the salt lake located 282 feet below sea level, in Death Valley in California

447

Titus Canyon in Death Valley is a typical slot canyon, a valley dug out from the rocks, lined by tall walls and a narrow floor.

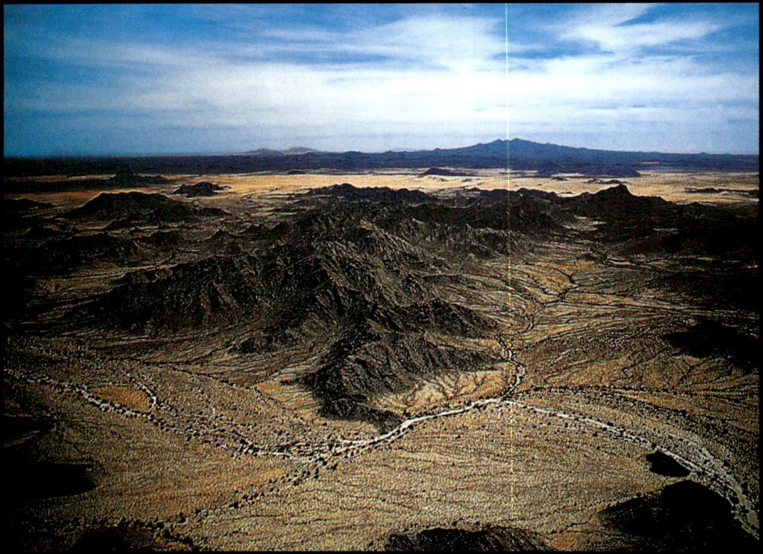

448
The Mexican Altar Desert, on the border with the United States, is a stark, sandy region, which in summer reveals its immobile harshness in the extreme temperatures that can be reached there.

449
A sandy dune gives movement to the flat setting of Laguna de San Ignacio, in Mexico's Baja California.

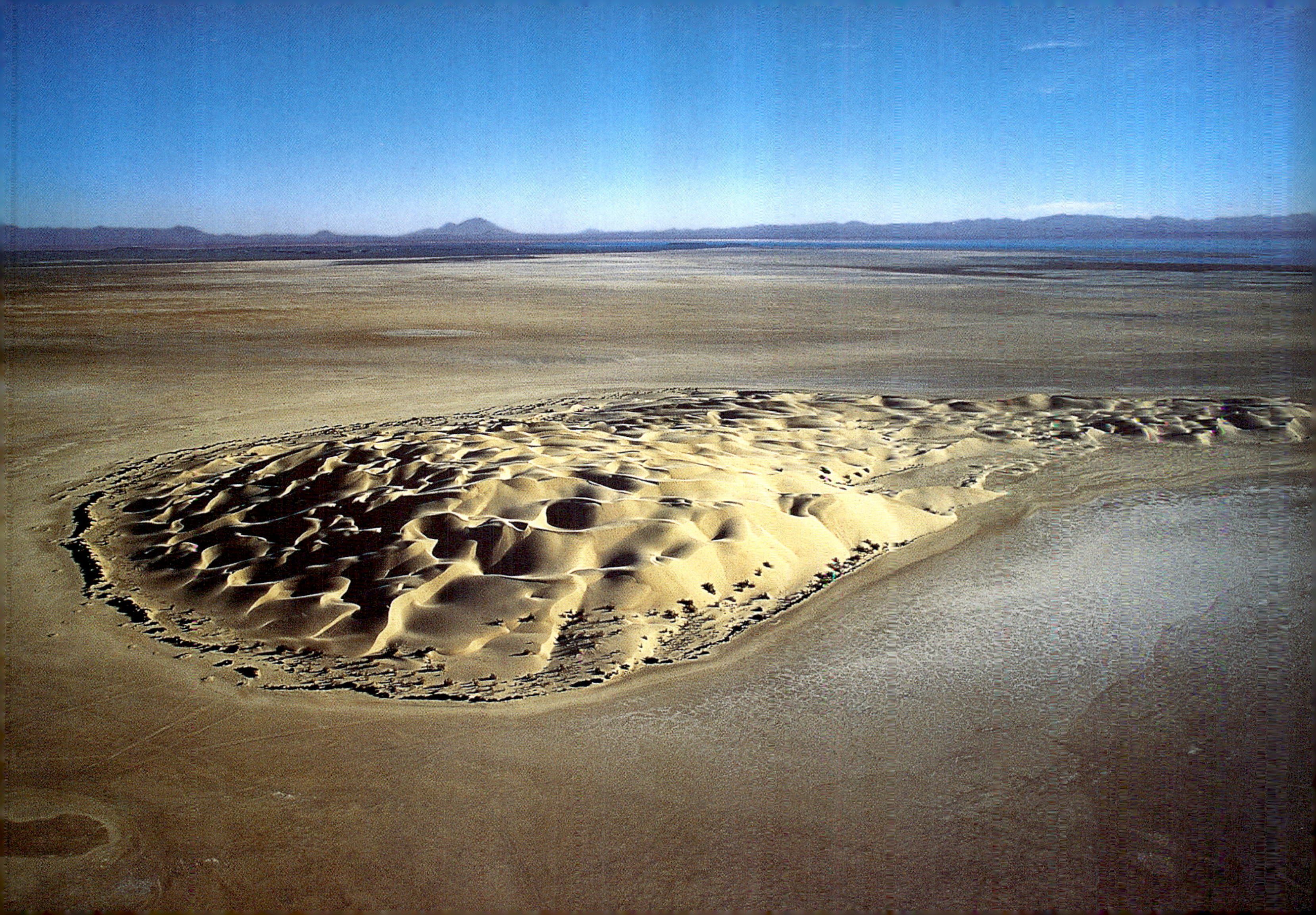

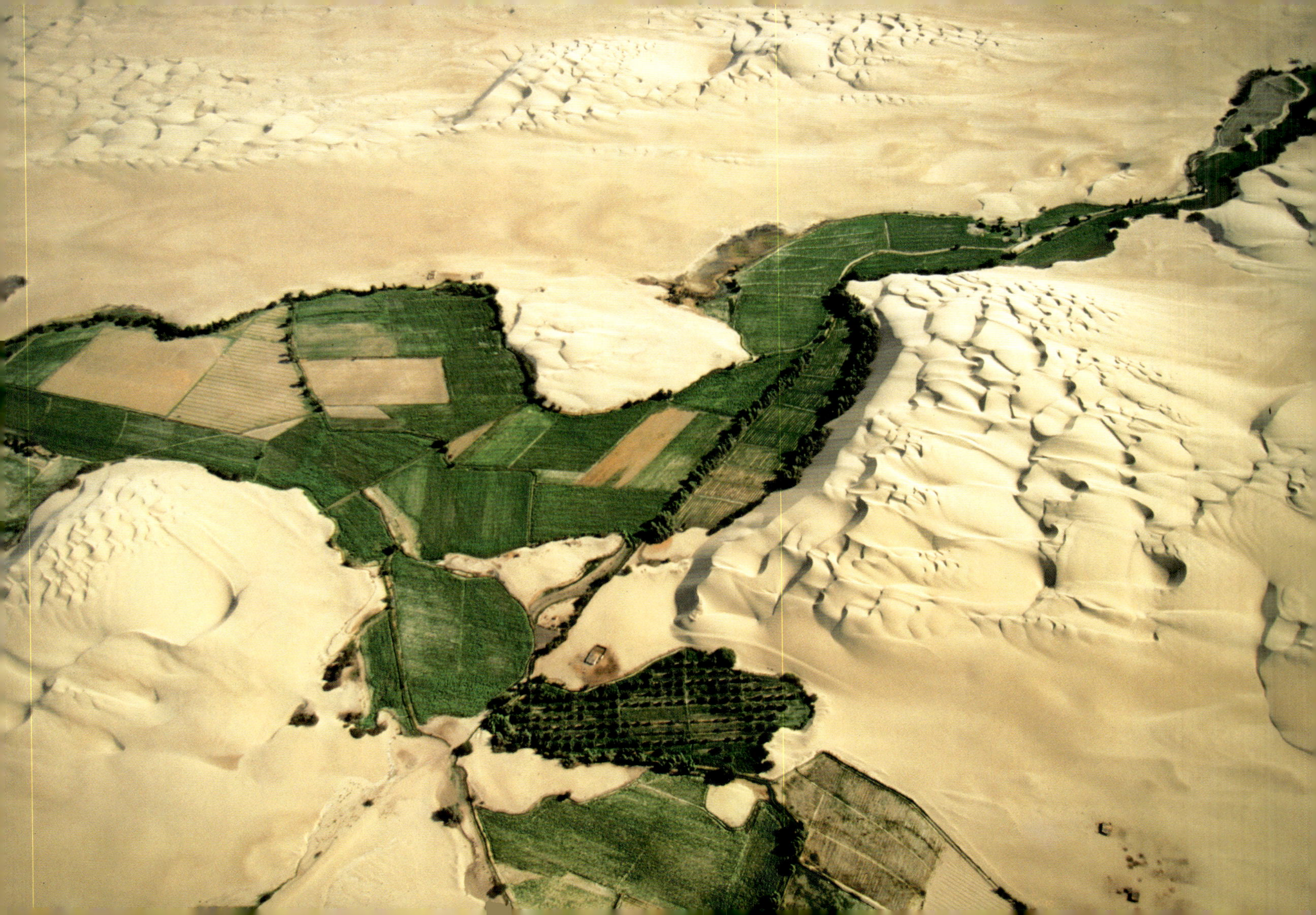

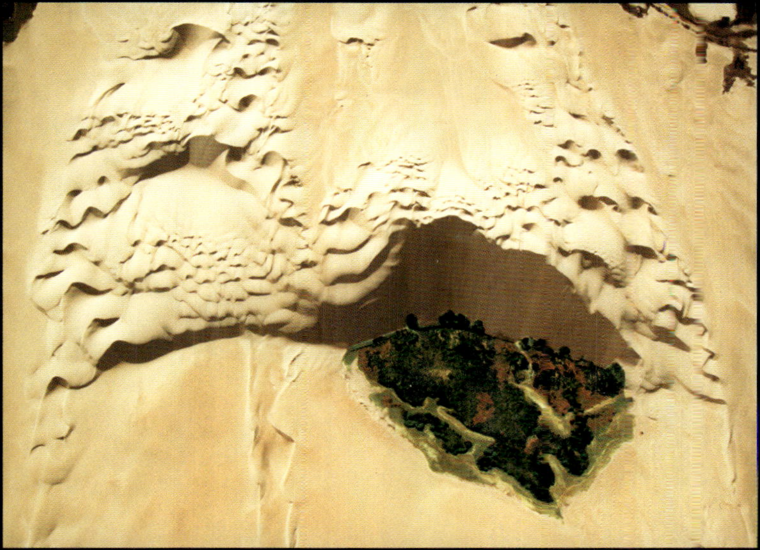

450 and 451

Patches of vegetation or cultivated fields alternate with desert expanses in the territory surrounding the city of Ica in Peru.

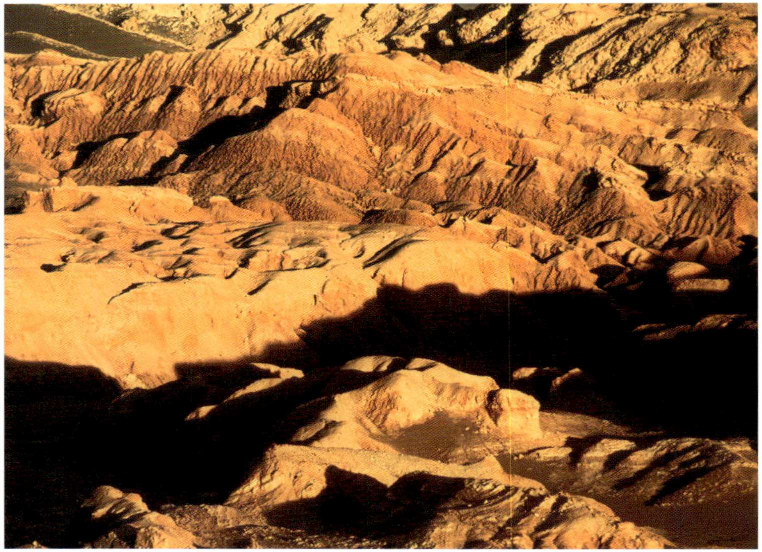

452 and 453

The Valley of the Moon, in the Chilean Atacama Desert, is an immense depression featuring differentiating geological formations, such as salt lakes, active volcanoes, and salt outcroppings.

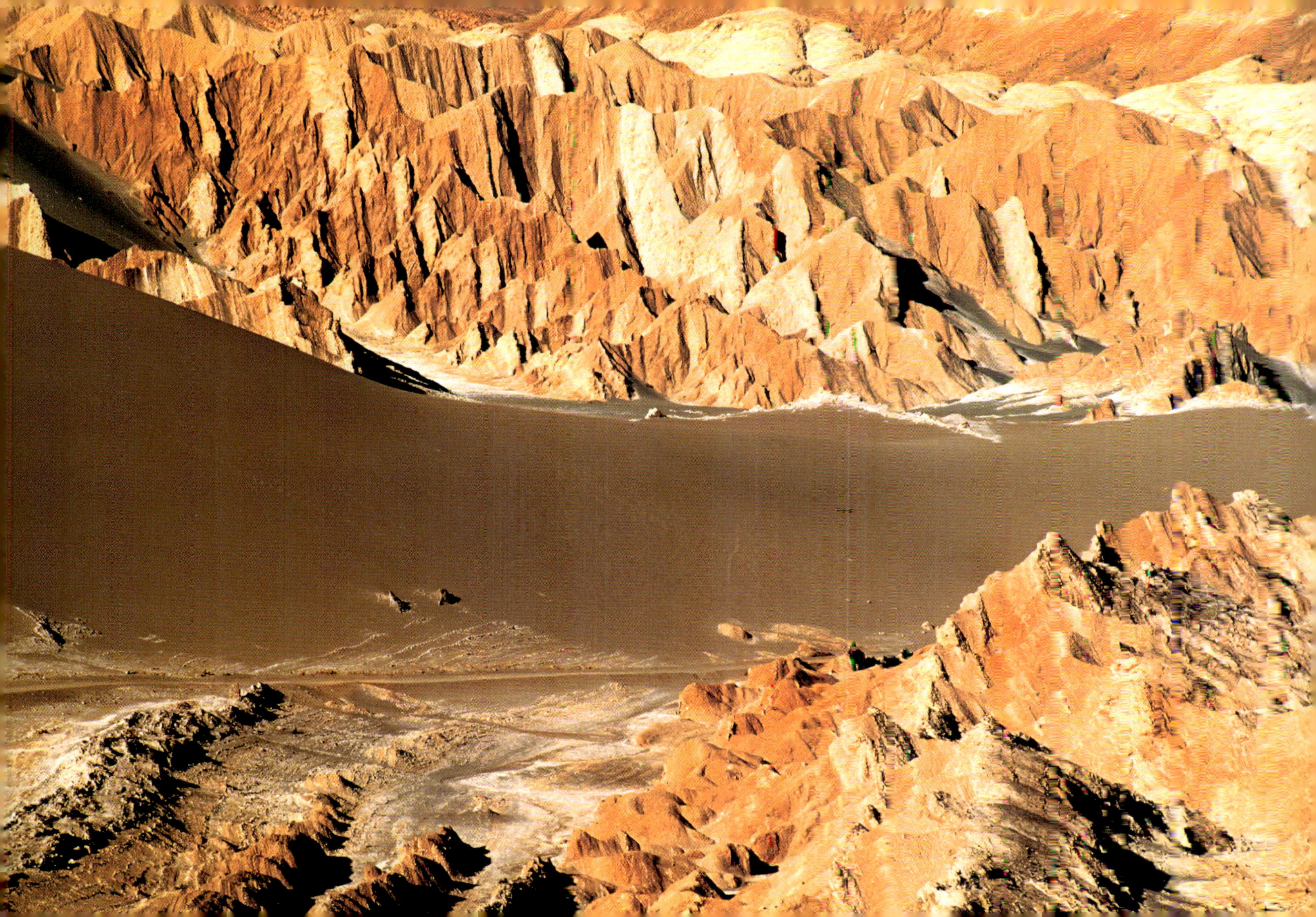

THE REALMS OF MAN

FLYING HIGH

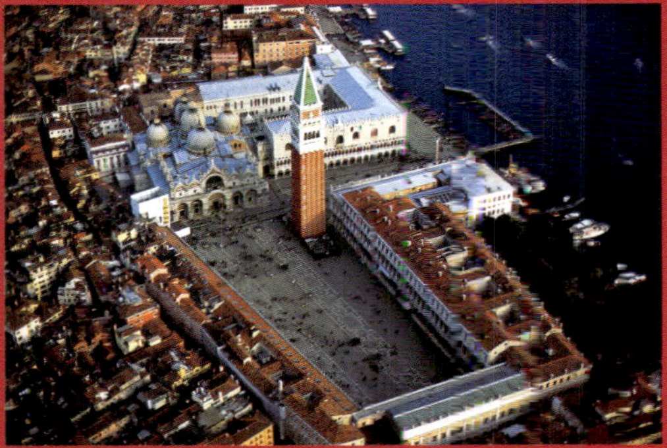

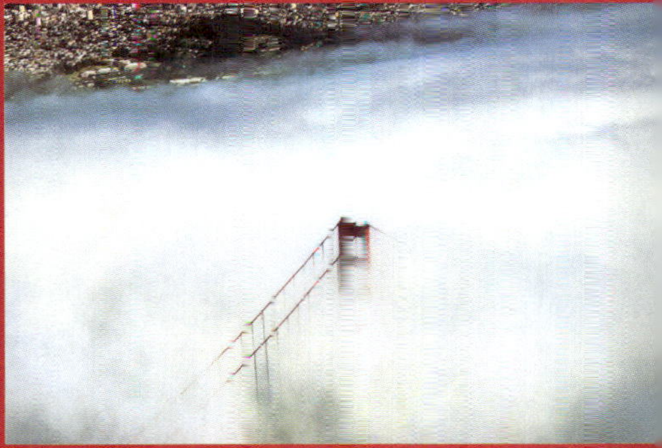

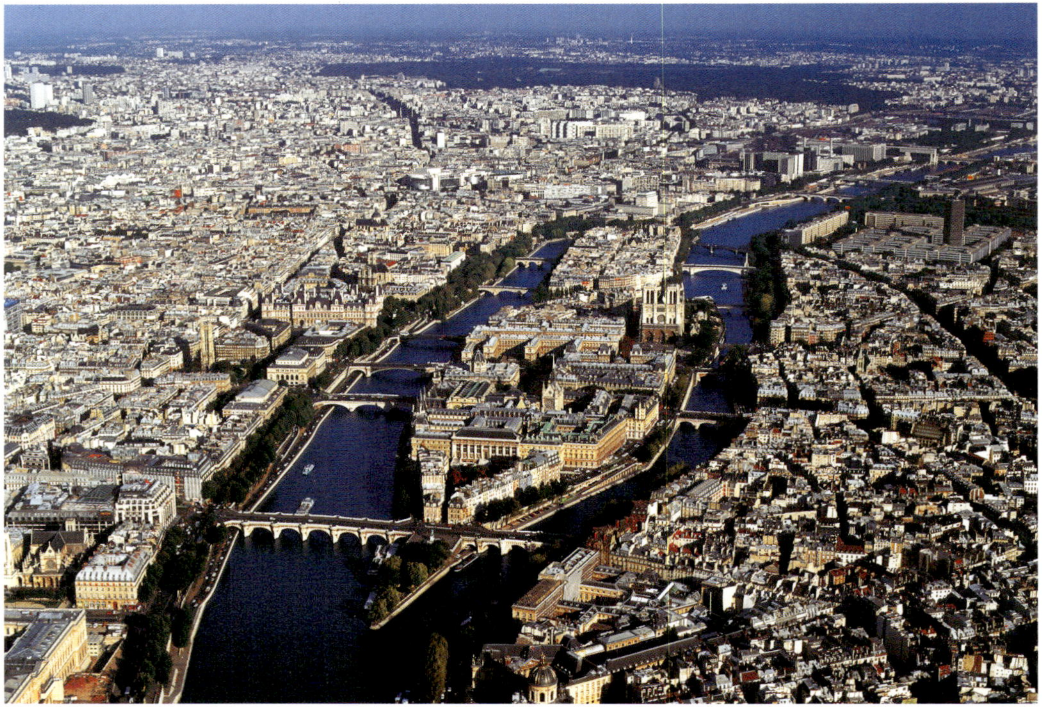

455
San Marco Square in Venice (left), Golden Gate Bridge, San Francisco (right).

More than just an agricultural environment, human space is the realm of man par excellence. The cities are entirely of man, built from the foundation up to their towers, stone by stone. The labor of centuries or millennia – but not always, as we will see – has raised cities that by their nature, and thanks to particularly favorable conditions, have seen their natural tendency to expand, both horizontally and then vertically, met with compliance. Thus, venerable architectural wonders have sprouted from Lisbon to London, from Berlin to Paris (perhaps the richest of all of them in "symbolic" construction was left to us by Gustave Eiffel), and from Cairo to Bangkok.

Then grew, in a truly pioneer spirit, the unexplainably thrilling pincushions of downtown New York and Chicago, which between the end of the nineteenth and the beginning of the twentieth centuries became disproportionate lots for experimental new technologies. When the number of floors achievable using basic construction techniques had been exceeded, despite being reinforced by increasingly better techniques and steel, no small leap in creativity became necessary.

No one actually knew if the high-rise buildings would endure and support the stress to which they would be subjected – gravity, wind resistance, the sudden brutality of earthquakes, and even simple everyday use – nor does anyone really know today how long reinforced cement in a structure built 100 years ago can hold up. The point is that a certain number of the historic colossi have well surpassed the threshold of antiquity. It is not without reason, cautiously speaking, that some buildings holding

456
Île de la Cité seen from the west: on the right, on the south side of the island, rises the cathedral of Notre Dame.

457

less historical or symbolic value are slowly being dismantled, to be replaced by others more advanced and trustworthy.

Thus, the downtown of the twenty-first century almost always appear as sophisticated art galleries on a disproportionate scale, true museums intended to show off ever greater power, but also, more prosaically, dedicated to that art so useful to man's survival that is architecture.

In fact, masters like Niemeyer, Piano, Tange, and Pei, some of the prophets of an enlightened and profoundly symbolic urbanism, "exhibit" in big cities, and not always the most prosperous.

Most likely, not even the proudest opponent of modern, gigantic buildings can deny the beauty of the cone-shaped Petronas Towers, slender twin towers embracing across a mid-air bridge of glass that links them. At 1,483 feet tall, the Petronas seem to almost squash downtown Kuala Lumpur under their circular bases, though they have lost the world record for height despite being perched on the threshold of the impossible: today the record is held by Taipei 101, in Taiwan, at 1,670 feet tall. In third place stands the top of the Sears Tower in Chicago, just 187 feet shorter and much more severe looking with its mass of black overlapping parallelepipeds on the main body and avant-corps, composing a modern Tower of Babel against the incredibly crystalline background of Lake Michigan. Limiting the discussion to the top three places, given that by now almost every capital of the world and all the great cities without exception can boast their own splendid towers, in third place is the Jin Mao Tower in Shanghai, which is also one of the most symbolic.

A 1,381-foot-tall bamboo shaft, a disproportionate pagoda reflecting the cultural and traditional universe of the Far East. In its own way sacred, and not just as a temple of the most aggressive business approach that the twenty-first century has produced, this fascinating creation may be the one most removed from the image of the hyper-tech-

The Realms of Man

nological high-rise building in its "natural" existence, with its segments ever-so lightly accented by slightly upward-curving horizontal lines. It truly seems to be a plant shaft burrowing its roots into the Asian earth, extracting from it the lifeblood that makes it so tall, unique, and beautiful.

The skill of the masters of advanced architecture has apparently hit the mark. Their creations have passed the exam for the moment unable to be critiqued by those who see them from above. In fact, despite their proliferation, the present-day skylines – as were those "under construction" a half century ago – are never haunting; rather, they are inviting.

A very interesting, and impressive, aspect of modern cities is their elusiveness. The bigger they are, the more difficult they are to get to know. Censuses have always been problematic, so much so that today it is not known which urban center is the largest in the world. Despite having perfected statistical instruments, it has never been very clear whether Cairo or Mexico City or even the combination of Tokyo-Yokohama has the largest population. Cities such as Istanbul, which until 30 years ago contained a million souls today far exceeds more than 10,000,000 inhabitants without showing signs of stopping. It is not terribly important to know which is the largest, however it seems incredible the number of Chinese, Indian, and Russian cities that exceed 1,000,000 inhabitants.

Isaac Asimov, scientist and writer, in creating the setting for one of his most famous series, took it upon himself to hypothetically count the number of souls that could inhabit a planet like earth if it were entirely developed. The amount hovered around 40,000,000,000 and was probably far underestimated. The actual most believable information speaks of 50 percent of the total population being concentrated in cities, meaning more than 3,000,000,000 souls that, at the highest peaks, live in no less than 22 huge cities with over 8,000,000 inhabitants each.

The Realms of Man

Not all the big cities can boast venerable origins. Brasilia is the most famous example of an "artificial" capital and features an appearance exemplary of "from scratch" planning. The masterpieces of Niemeyer compose an urban panorama made up of vast empty spaces, ringed by functional but also attractive buildings, in a sort of real-life version of the oneiric squares of De Chirico. Open space is the most attractive characteristic of planned cities built in the second half of the twentieth century. Islamabad, in Pakistan, stands out remarkably from the other cities in that country; as does Canberra, in Australia, so spread out over vast parks it seems to elusive at first sight, from Capitol Hill to the City, with expanses harmoniously placed in concentric circles on the shores opposite Lake Burley Griffin.
History has accustomed us to great constructions, but unfortunately also to big collapses. At this point, it is necessary to remember something that no longer exists. From the empty socket of the World Trade Center, a warning to the world continues to be launched. Maybe, it is to overcome the idea of conflict itself and, even, architecture. In fact, an intangible "structure" of pure light stood for a short time where the rectangles with the gothic ribbing drafted by the genius of I.M. Pei once towered. The towers are no longer there, but in their non-existence has taken on a new and even greater role, at once symbolic and charismatic of that which they once played during their brief existence, as if to underline the fact that the removal of a visible trait from the face of the earth is automatically equivalent to the defeat of whomever sought its eradication.

461
The Empire State Building is currently the tallest building (1,050 feet) in Manhattan, in New York. In the background, Central Park can be seen.

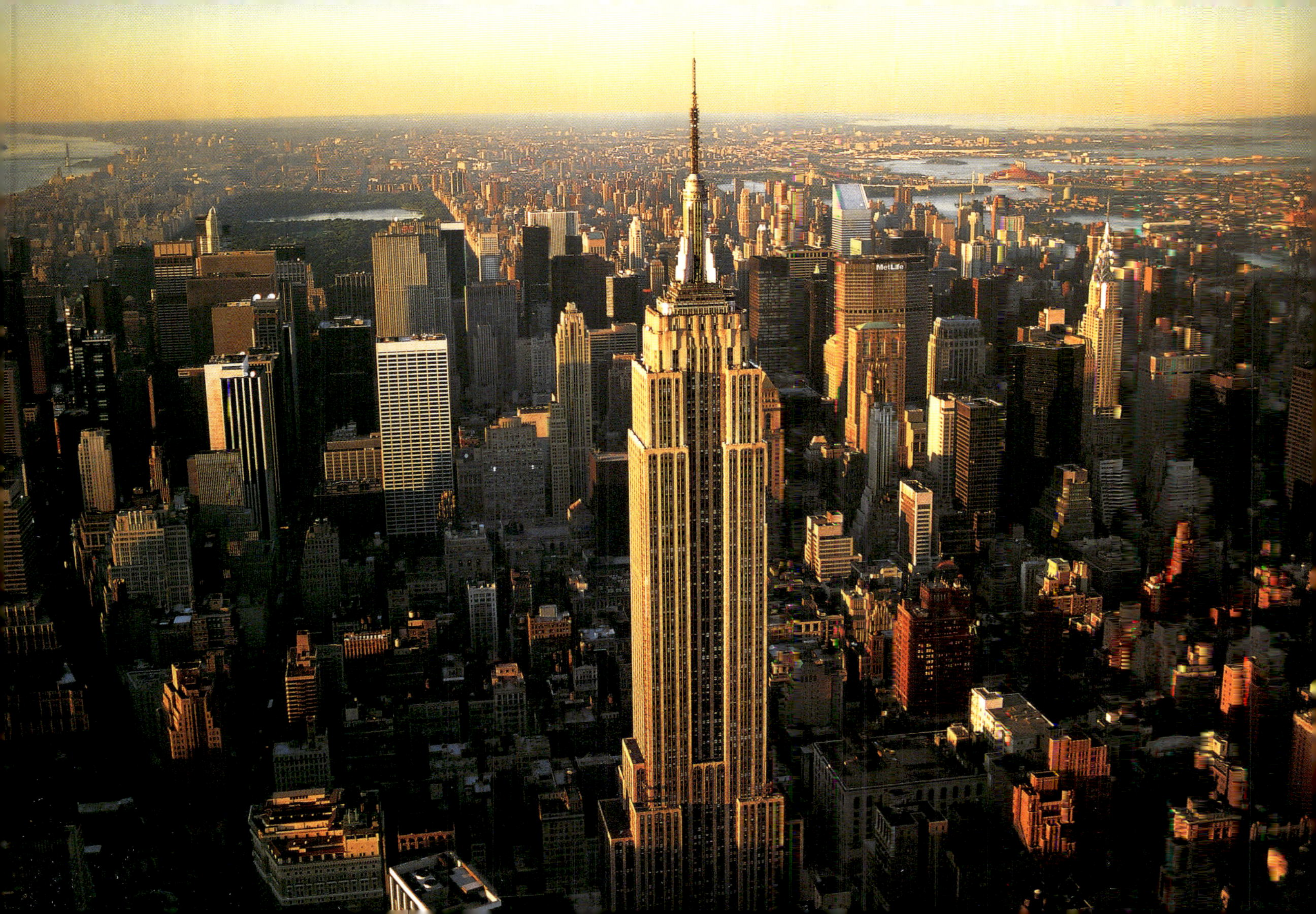
MetLife

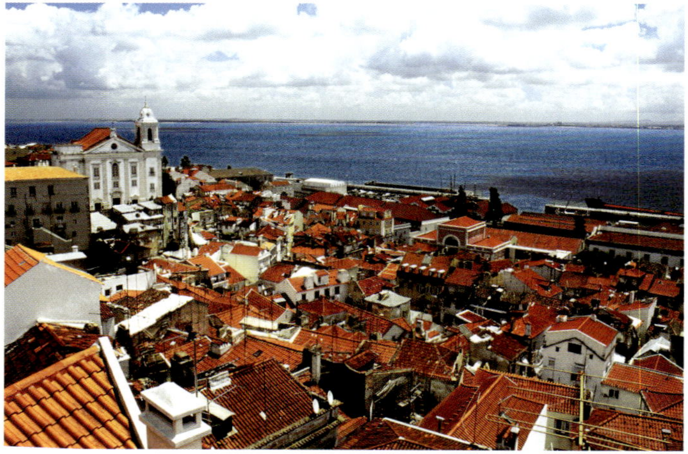

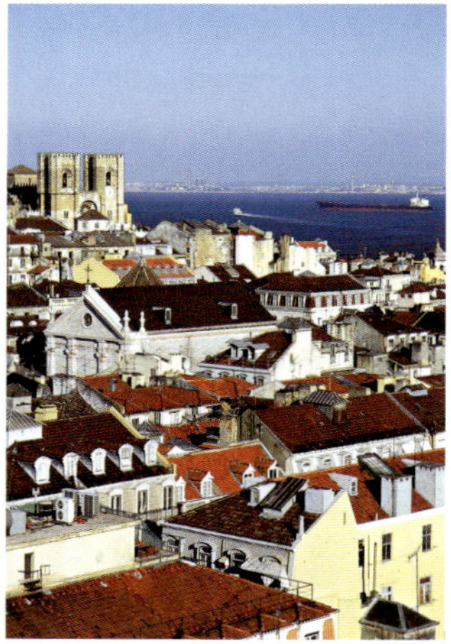

462 left

On the southern shore of the Tago River, a sea of red roofs announces the Alfama Quarter.

462 right

Since the twelfth century, the square towers of the Cathedral of Sé have towered over the city center.

463

The statue of Dom Pedro IV (1798-1834) dominates the façade of the Lisbon National Theater, in the square named after the king but better known as Praça Rossio.

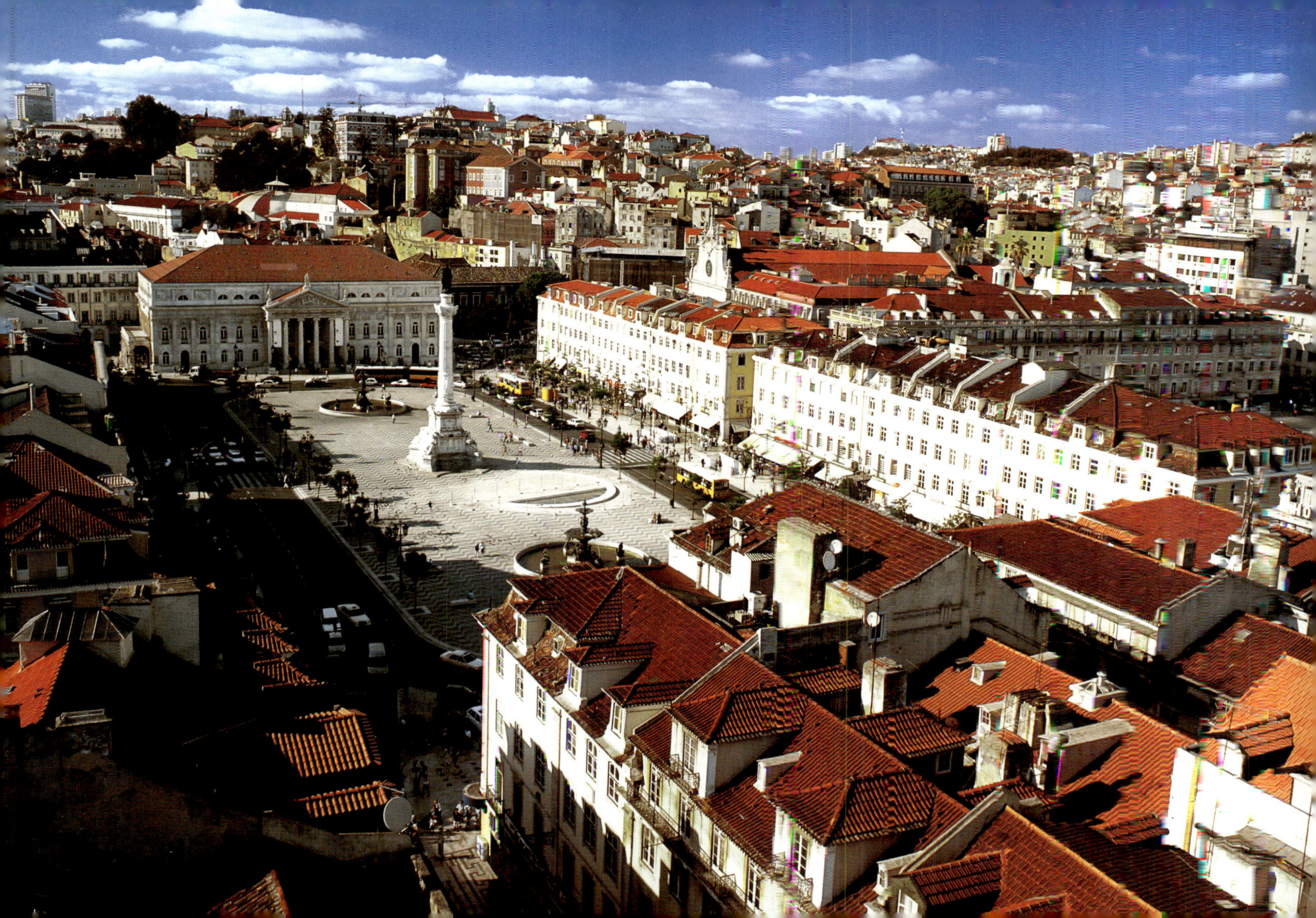

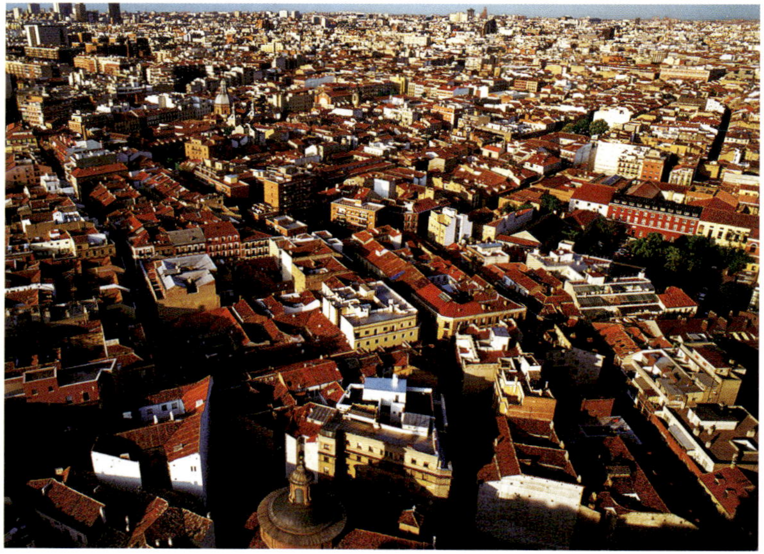

464
Located on the highlands of the Meseta at 2,625 feet high, the capital of Spain, Madrid, has a huge historical center that is more striking in its entirety than for its single monuments or age.

465
Madrid boasts one of the biggest arenas in the world: the Plaza de Toros de las Ventas, where the ancient tradition of bullfighting takes place.

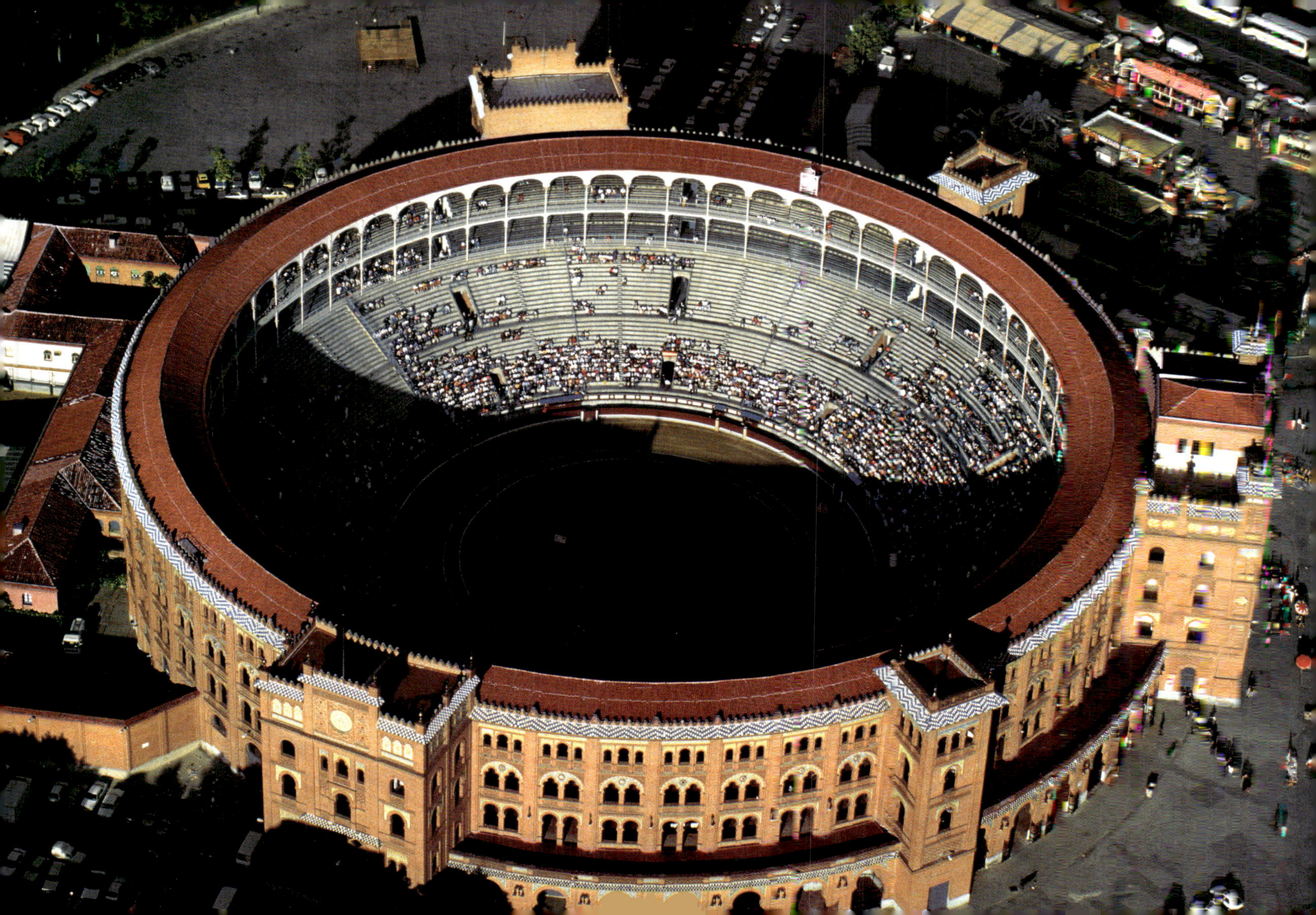

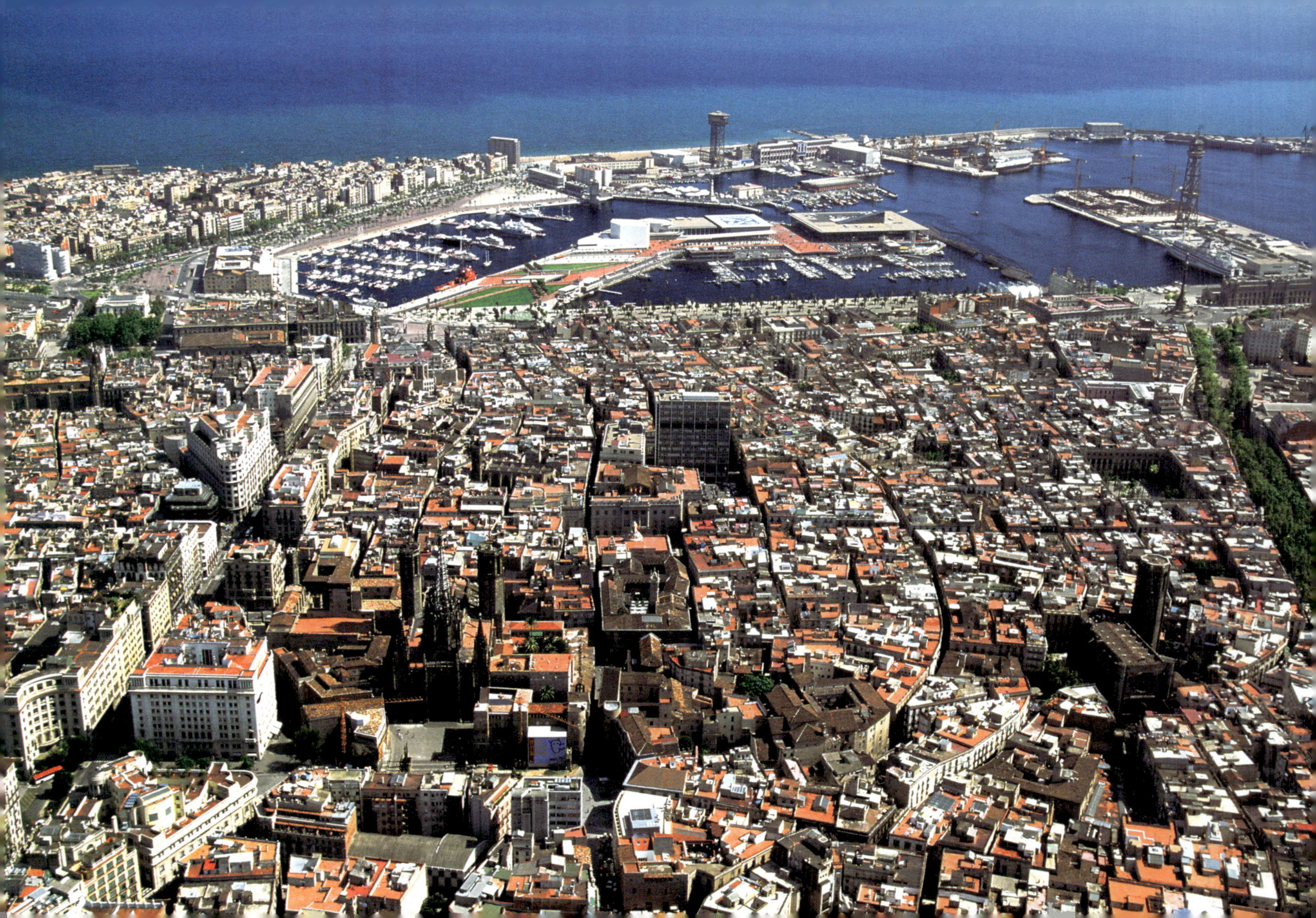

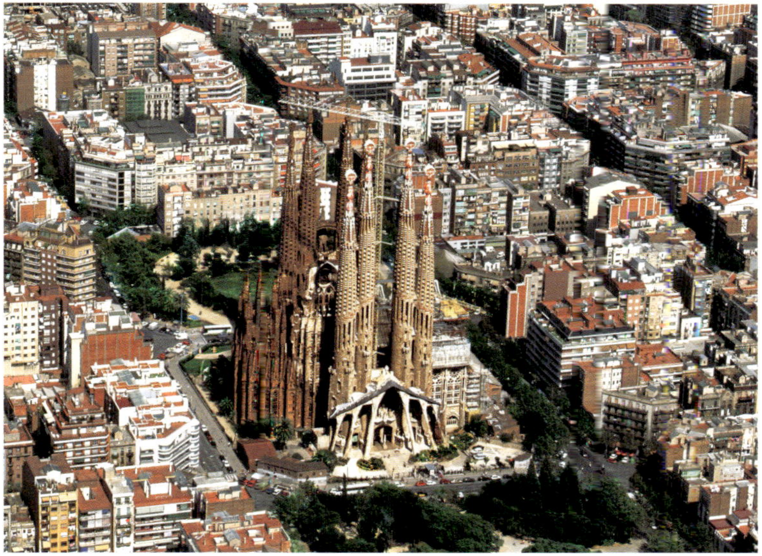

466

Cosmopolitan like all great port cities, Barcelona, in Spain, boasts the most important port in the Mediterranean and the second most important in Europe.

467

Begun in 1883 and still underway, construction of Antoni Gaudí's masterpiece of the Cathedral of the Sagrada Familia in Barcelona advances only thanks to offerings by worshipers.

Dublin

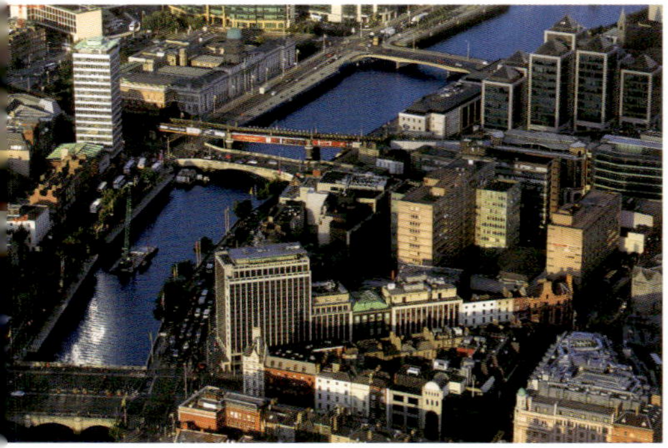

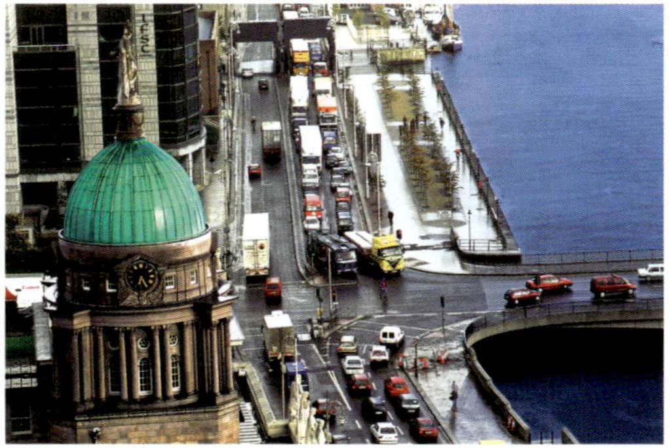

468 left
Dublin is located on a bay a the mouth of the Liffey River. Its port has a monopoly over the commercial naval traffic in the Irish Republic.

468 right
Grand Custom House, on the northern shore of the Liffey River, was built around 1780.

469
In the heart of the city, Trinity College of Dublin, founded by Queen Elizabeth I in 1592, is the oldest Irish university.

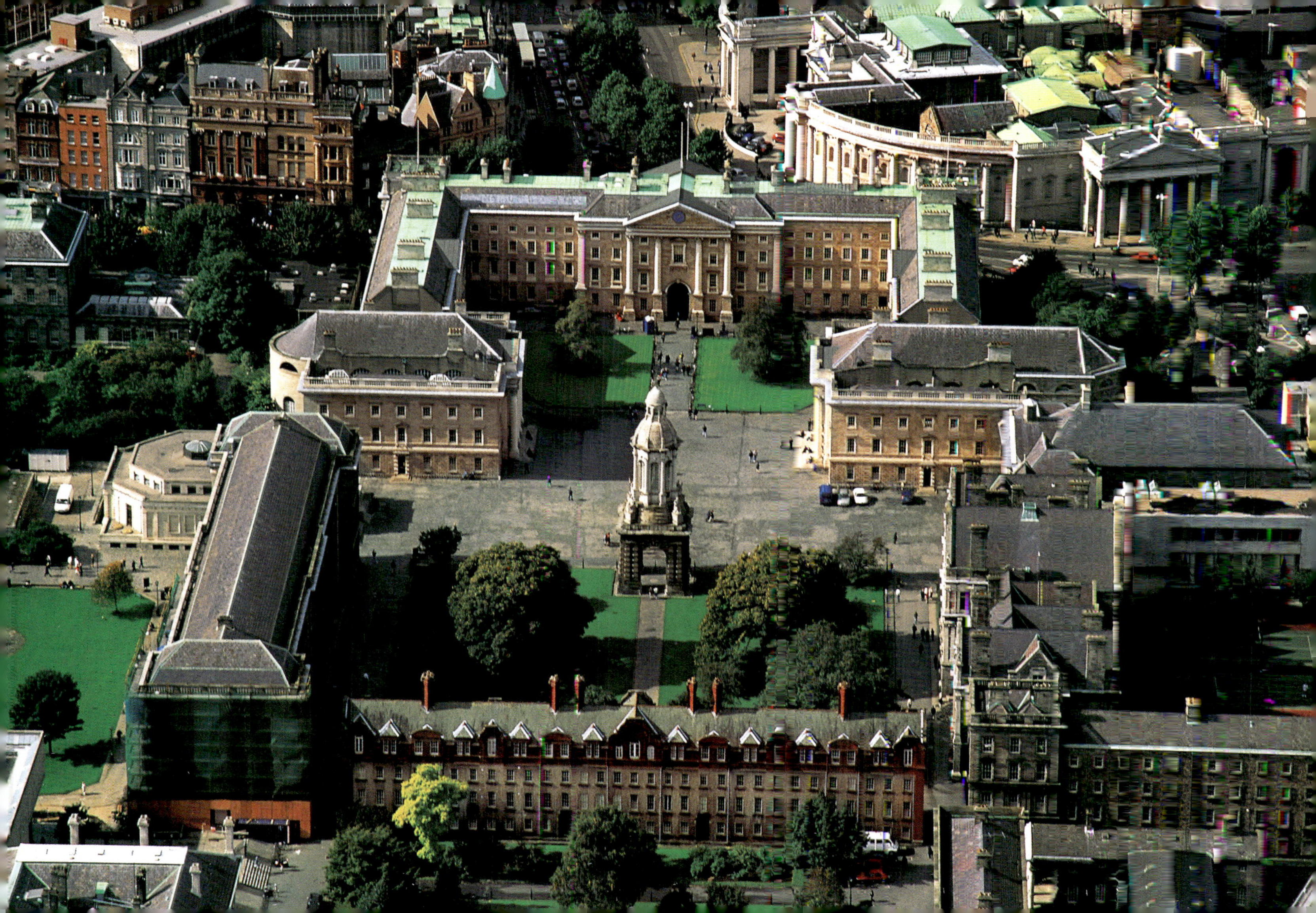

London

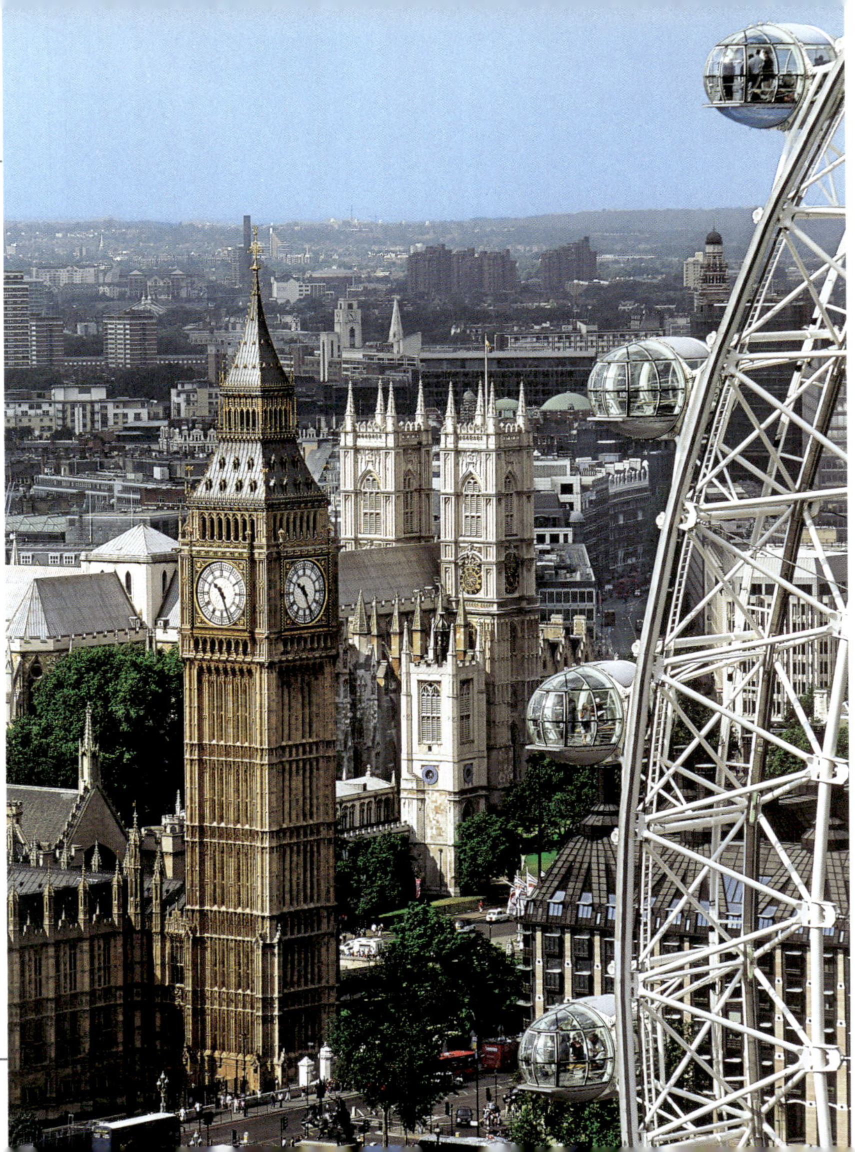

470
The tower of Parliament, containing the famous bell of Big Ben, flanks the spires of Westminster Abbey in London, which upon comparison seem almost ethereal in their purity.

471
An extraordinary glass roof towers over the Great Court of the British Museum, so big it occupies an entire block in central London.

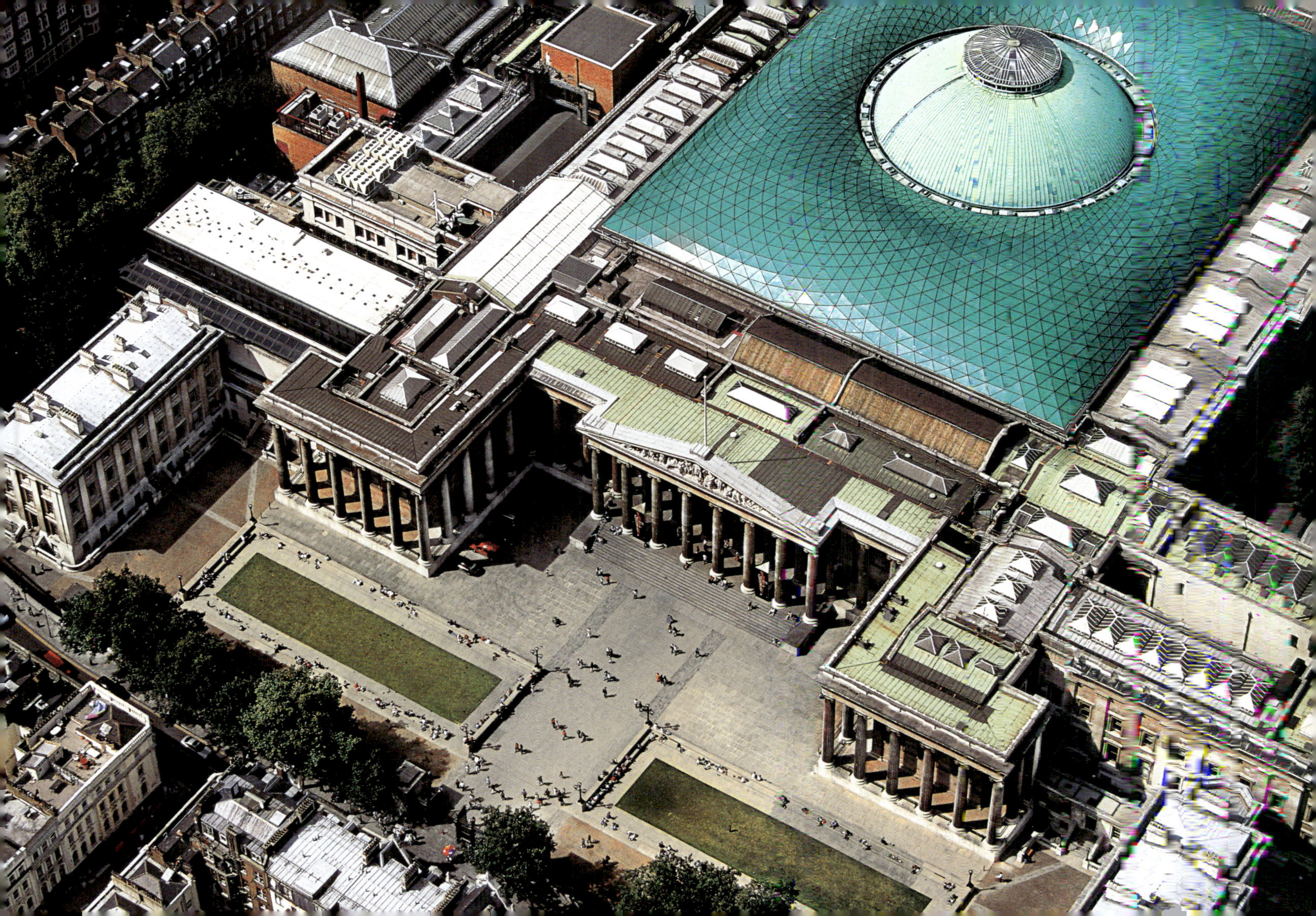

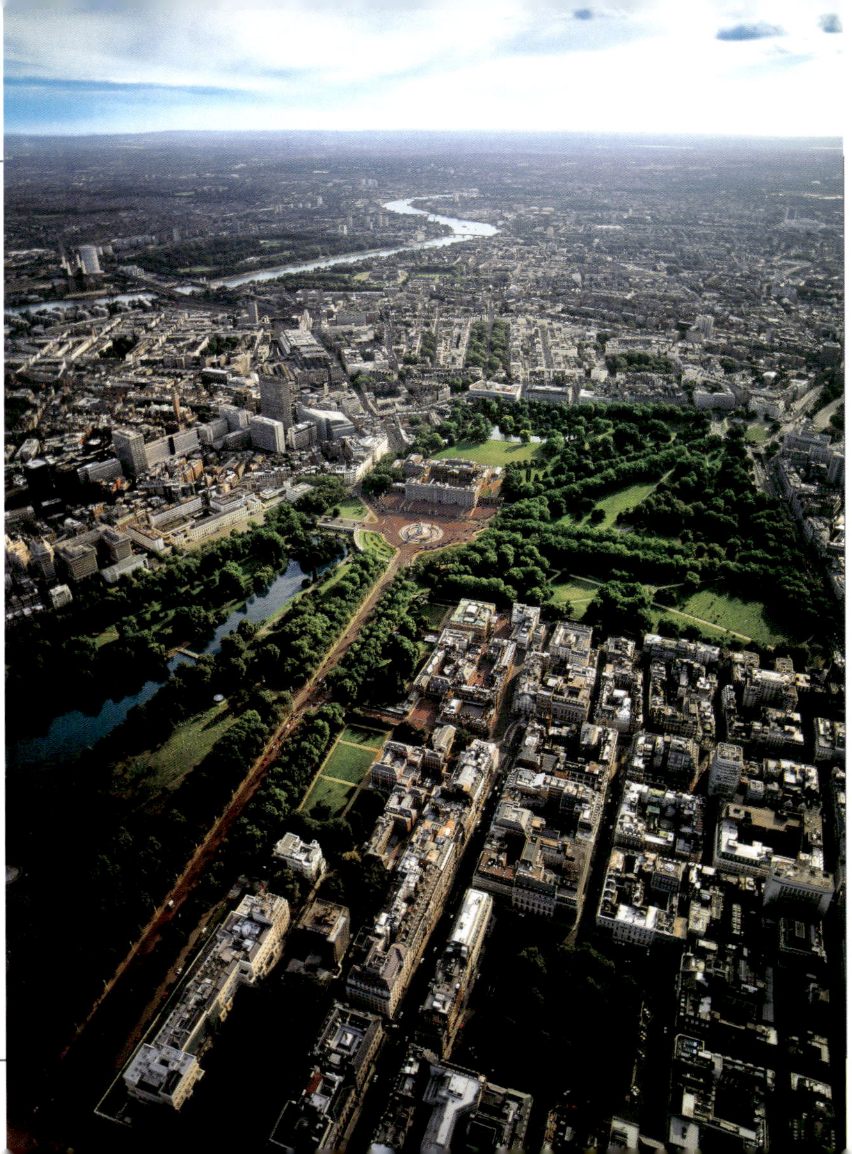

472

The green cloak of Saint James Park is cut in half by the long lawn of The Mall, a ceremonial avenue opened in 1910. In the back rises Buckingham Palace, one of many symbolic places in London.

473

Vast green areas separate the built-up zones in the airy north-eastern neighborhoods of London, facing onto the winding Thames River.

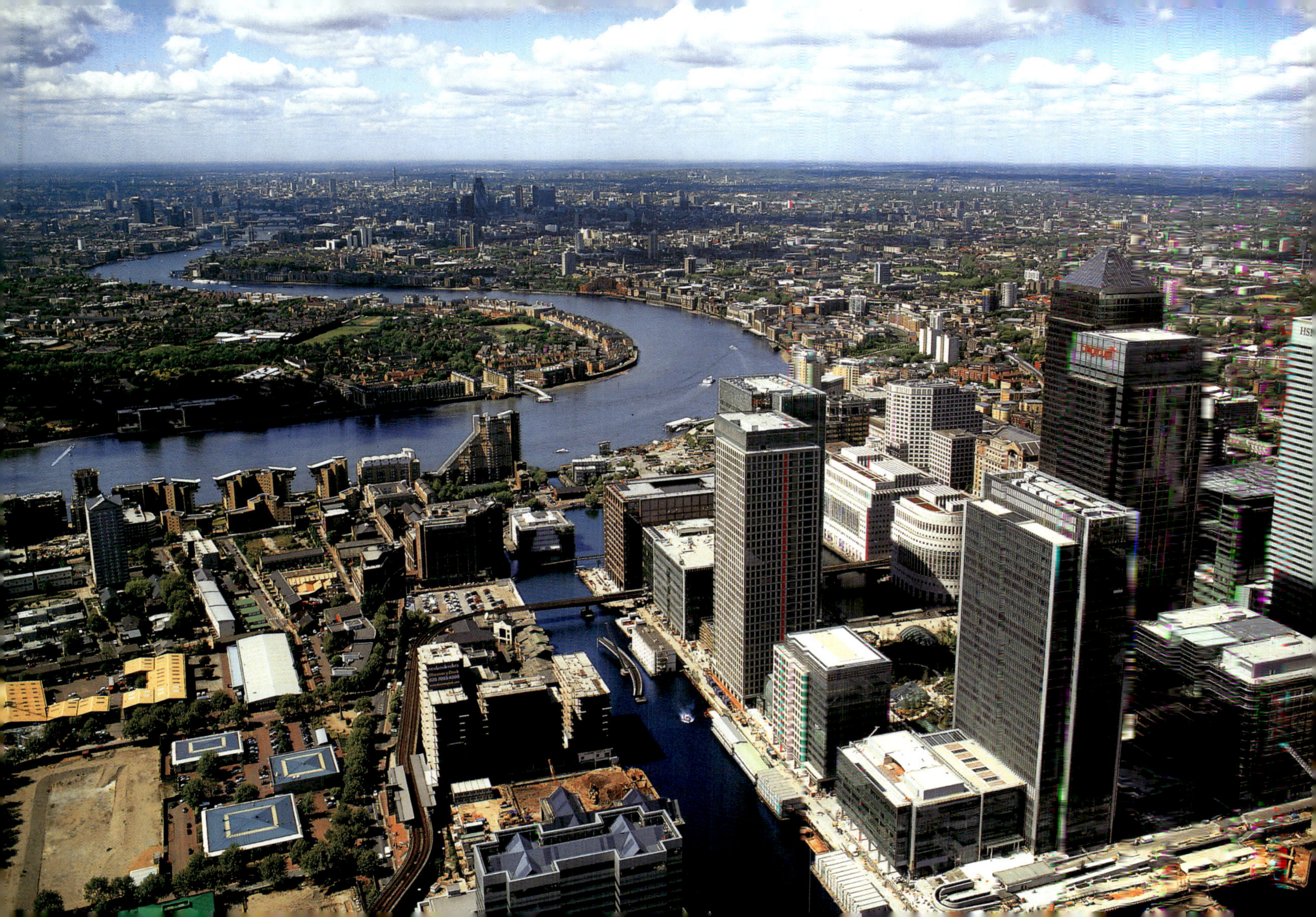

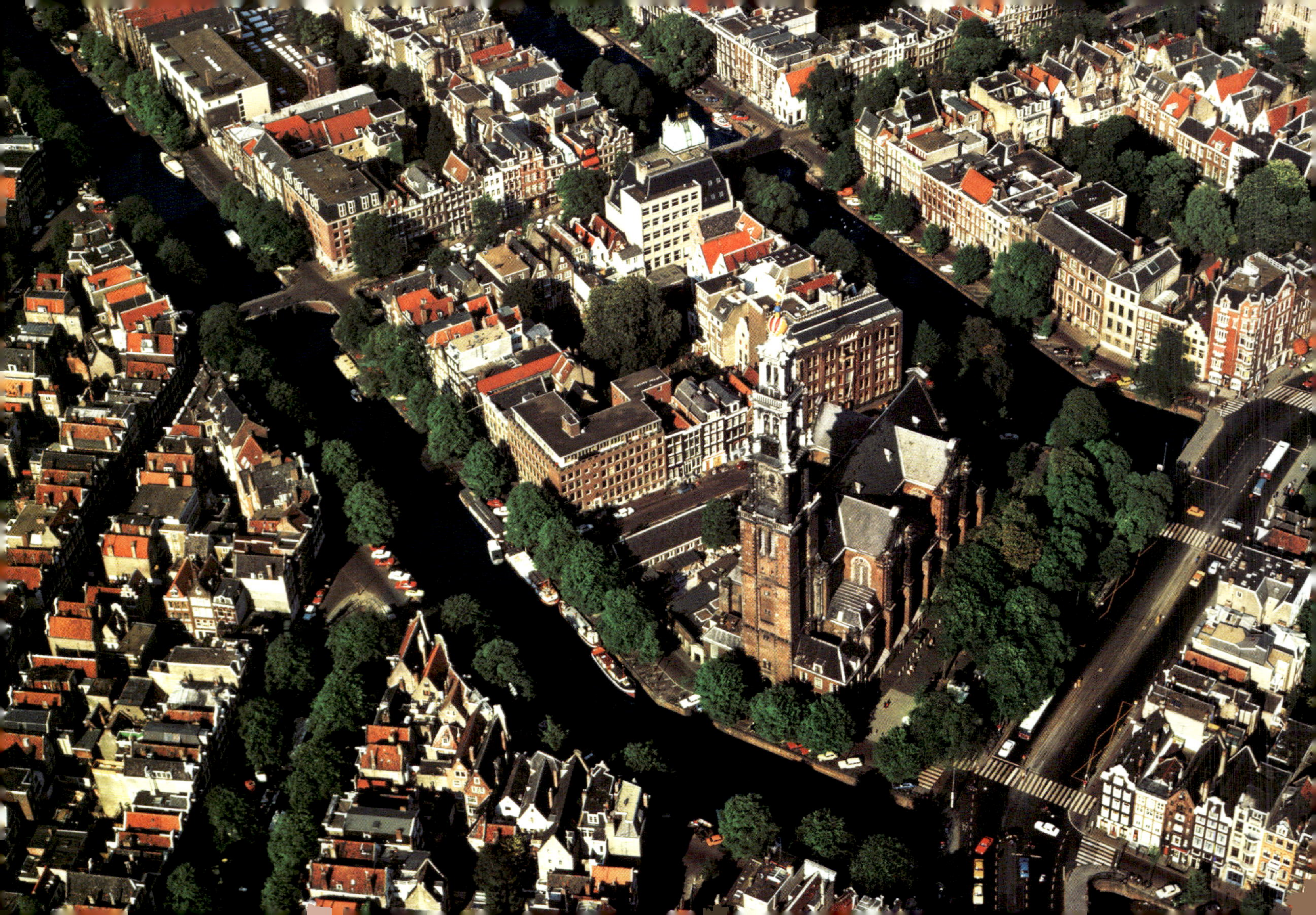

Amsterdam

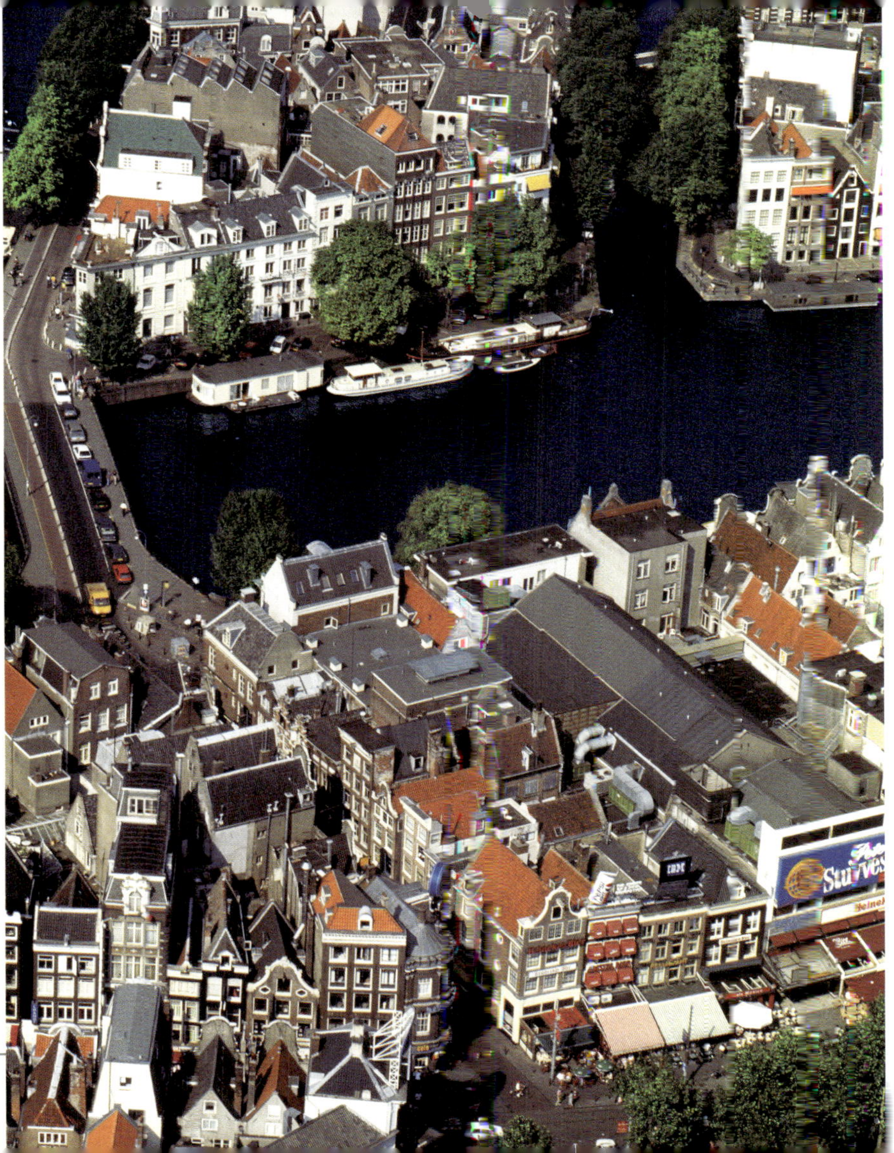

474 and 475
Waterways and "conventional" streets, often tree-lined, compose the urban plan of Amsterdam, the capital of Holland. The network of canals, in concentric circles, owes its layout to the fact that the city developed along the perimeter of the ancient walls.

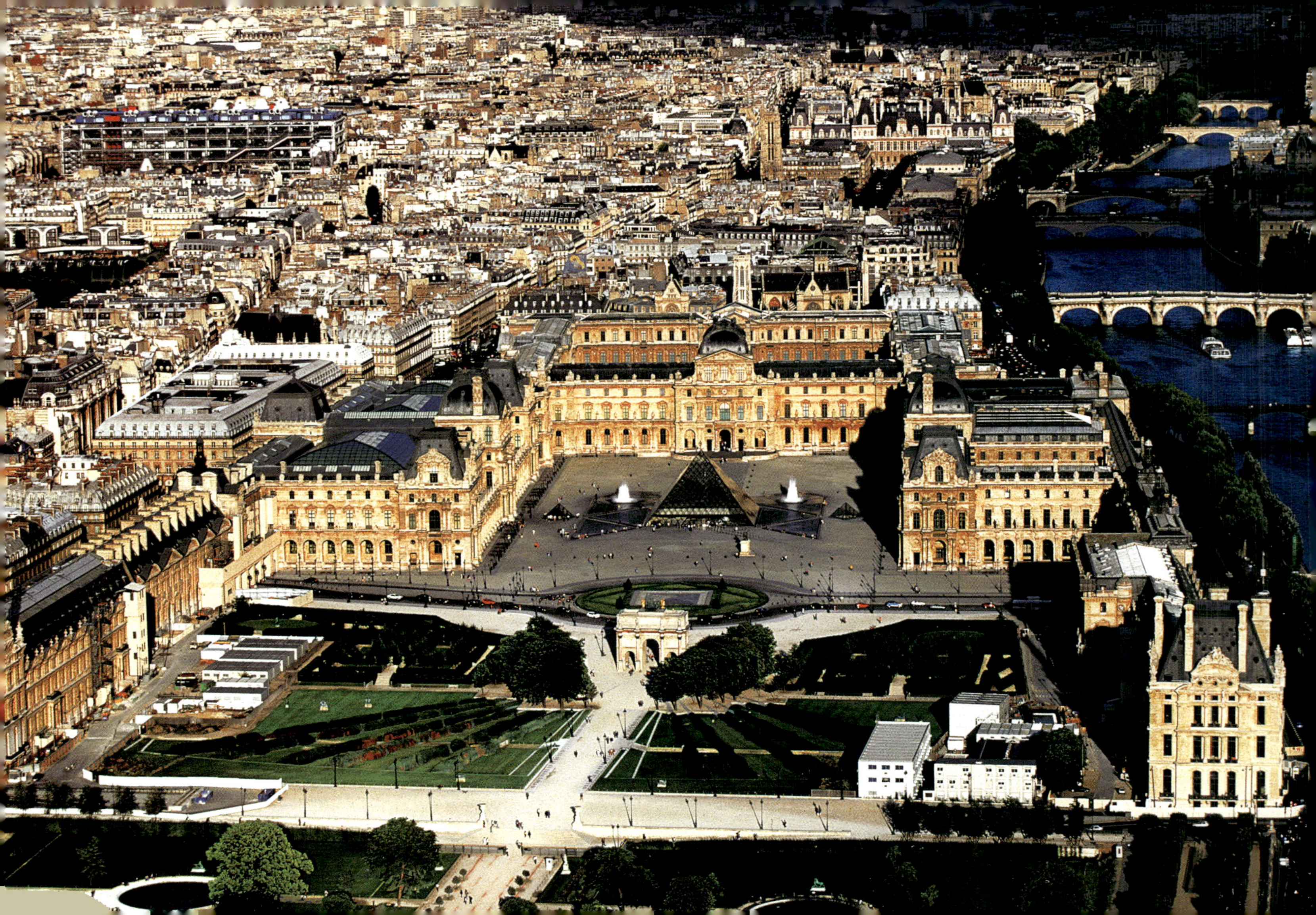

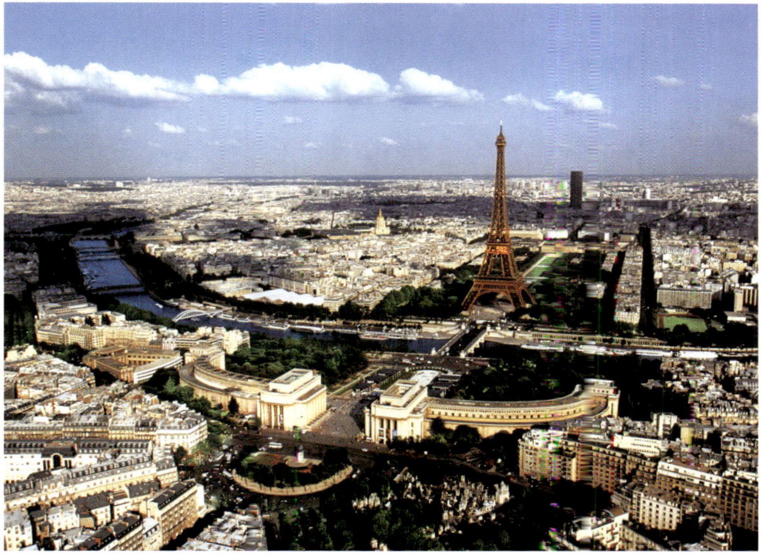

476

Place du Carrousel, with the Arc de Triomphe and the palace of the Louvre, offers a truly magnificent view of the dense fabric of central Paris.

477

An engineering wonder completed in 1889, the Eiffel Tower rises high above Paris.

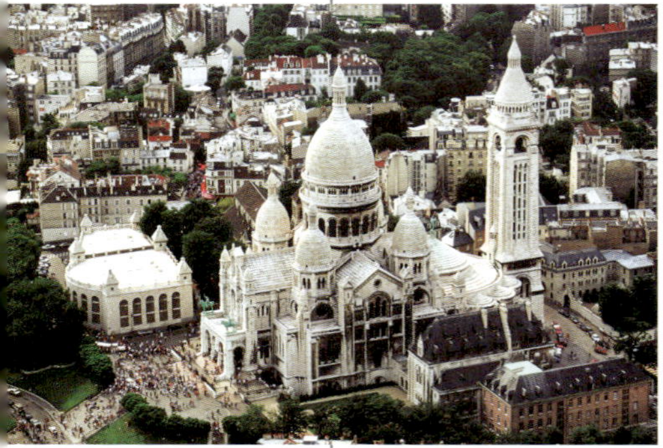

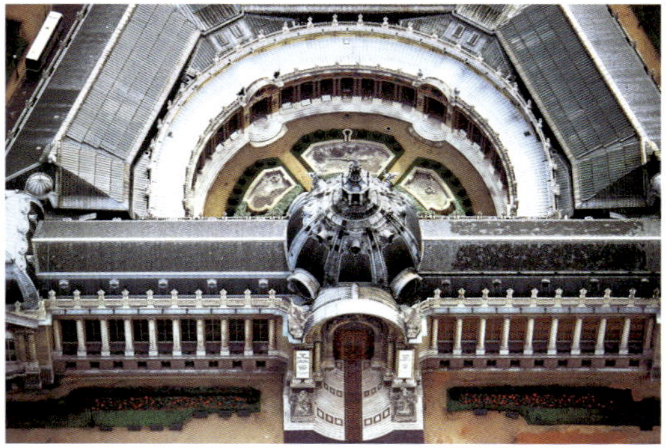

478 left

On Monmartre Hill, the white Basilica du Sacré Coeur is one of the most beautiful and symbolic constructions in Paris.

478 right

Parisian "elegance" is not just a question of fashion, as demonstrated by the Petit Palais' exquisite architectural grace.

479

An aerial view of Place d'Etoile immediately explains the reason behind the square's name: it is a "star" of boulevards converging at the nerve center of the French capital.

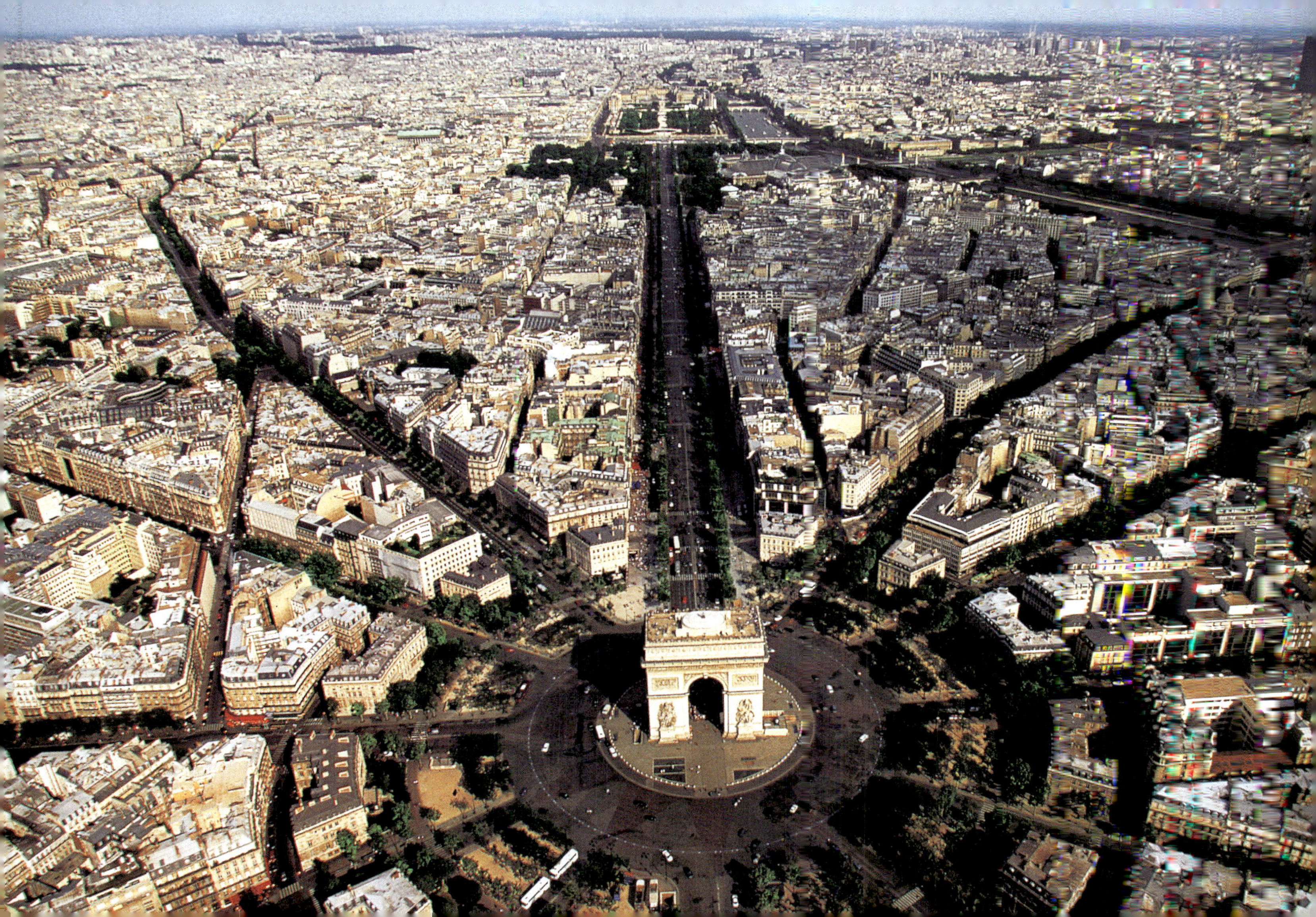

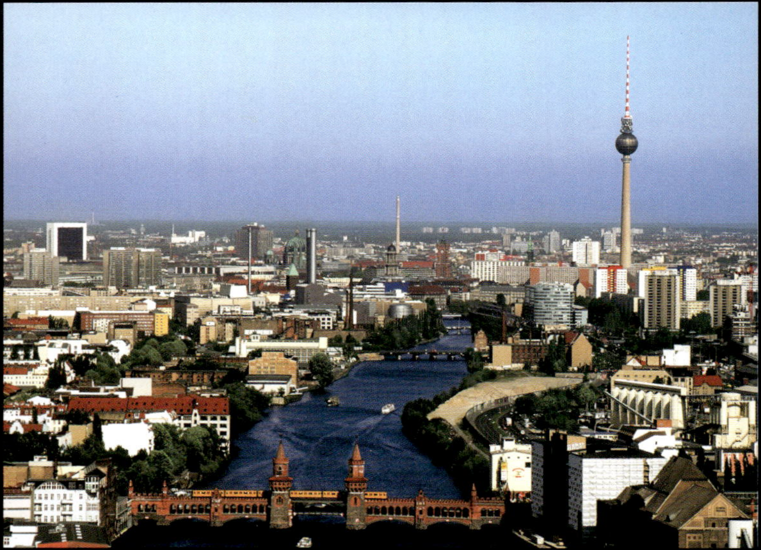

480
The Oberbaumbricke crosses the Sprea in downtown Berlin, dominated to the left by the Fernsehturm television tower, once part of the Soviet area of the German capital.

481
Dusk descends upon Kurfürstendamm, the main shopping street in Berlin. On the right rises the spire of the Kaiser-Wilhelm-Gedächtniskirche.

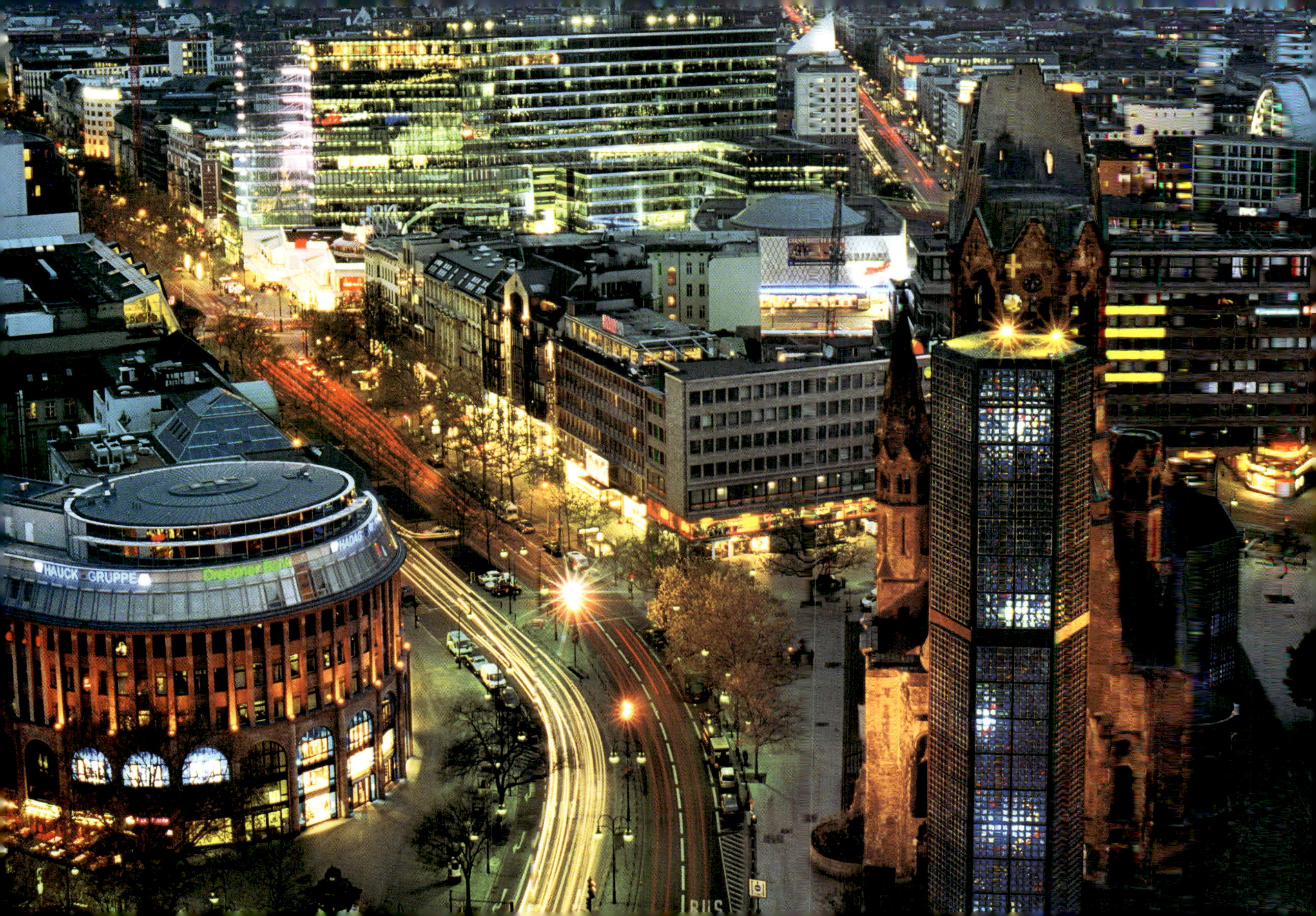
HAUCK GRUPPE
Dresdner Bank

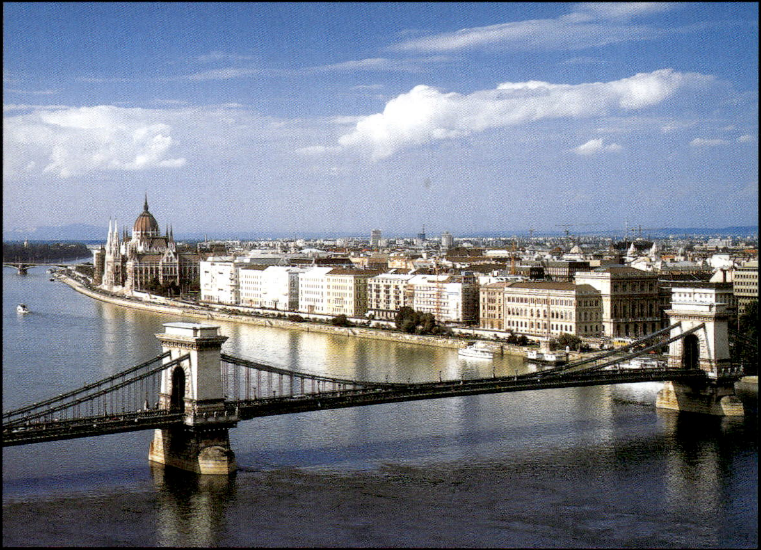

482
In the photo, the Chain Bridge can be admired in the foreground, whereas the majestic dome of Parliament can be seen in the background.

483
The church of Saint Stephen, which towers over the center of Budapest, is the biggest basilica in the city.

Budapest

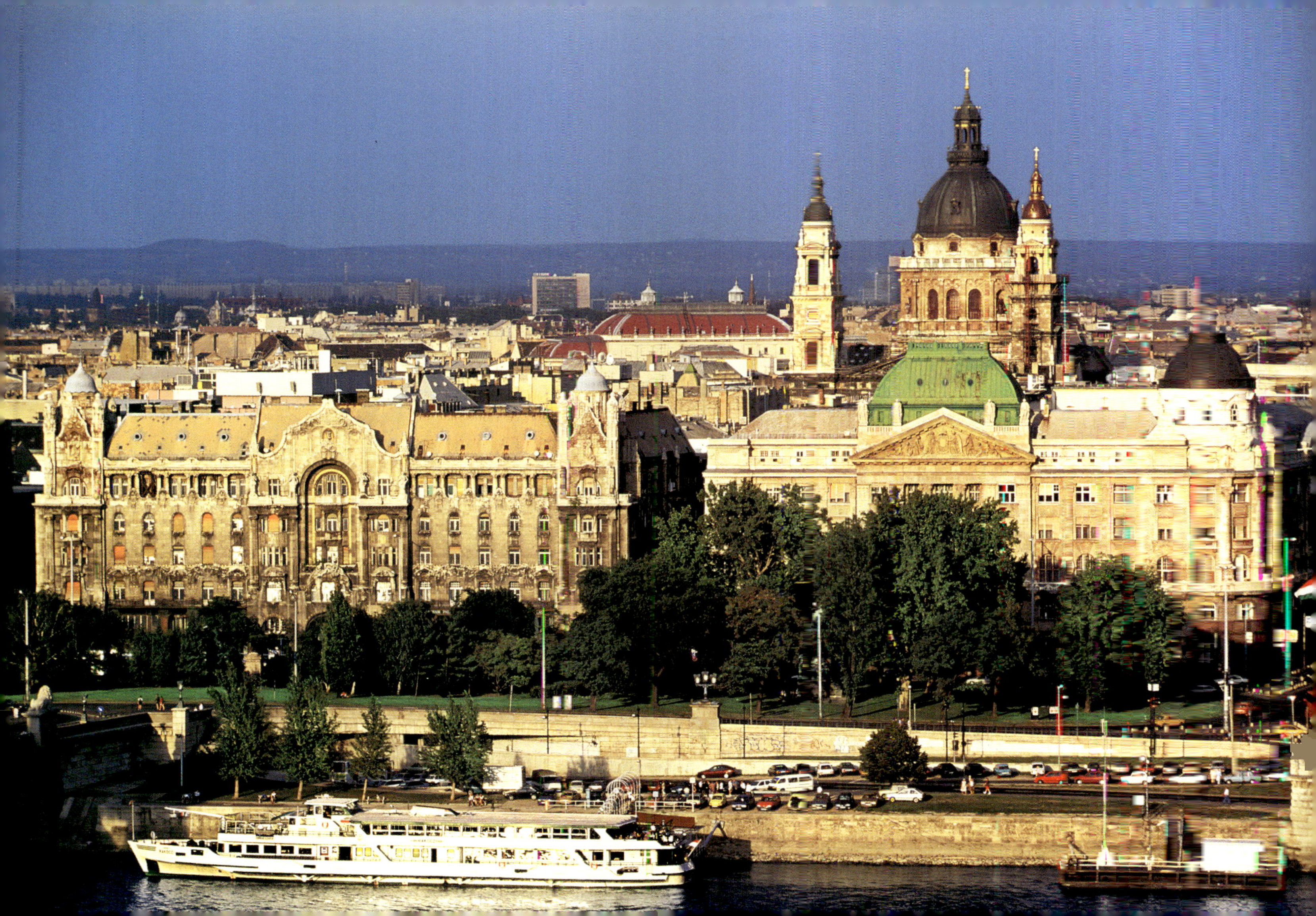

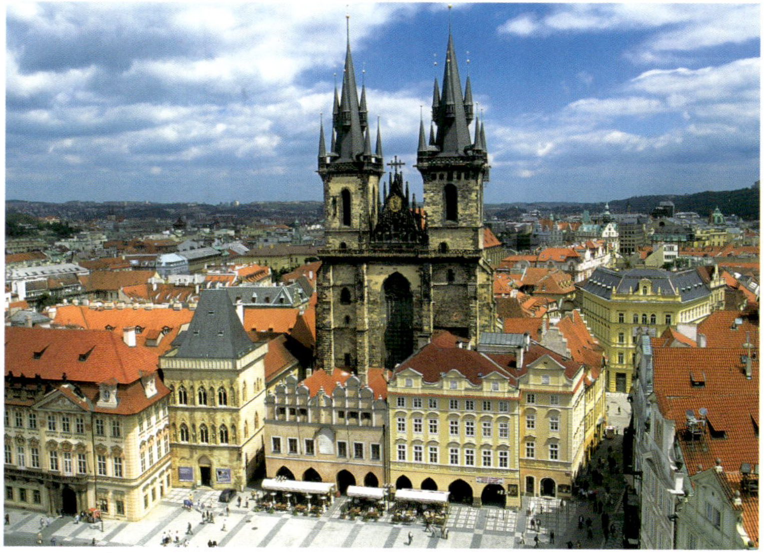

484
The shapes of the spires on the church of Tyn have no equal in terms of magnificence and uniqueness, standing tall on Staromestke Namesti, the main square not to mention the center of the Old City of Prague in the Czech Republic.

485
The Cathedral of Saint Vitus rises above Prague Castle and the Little City (Malá Strana).

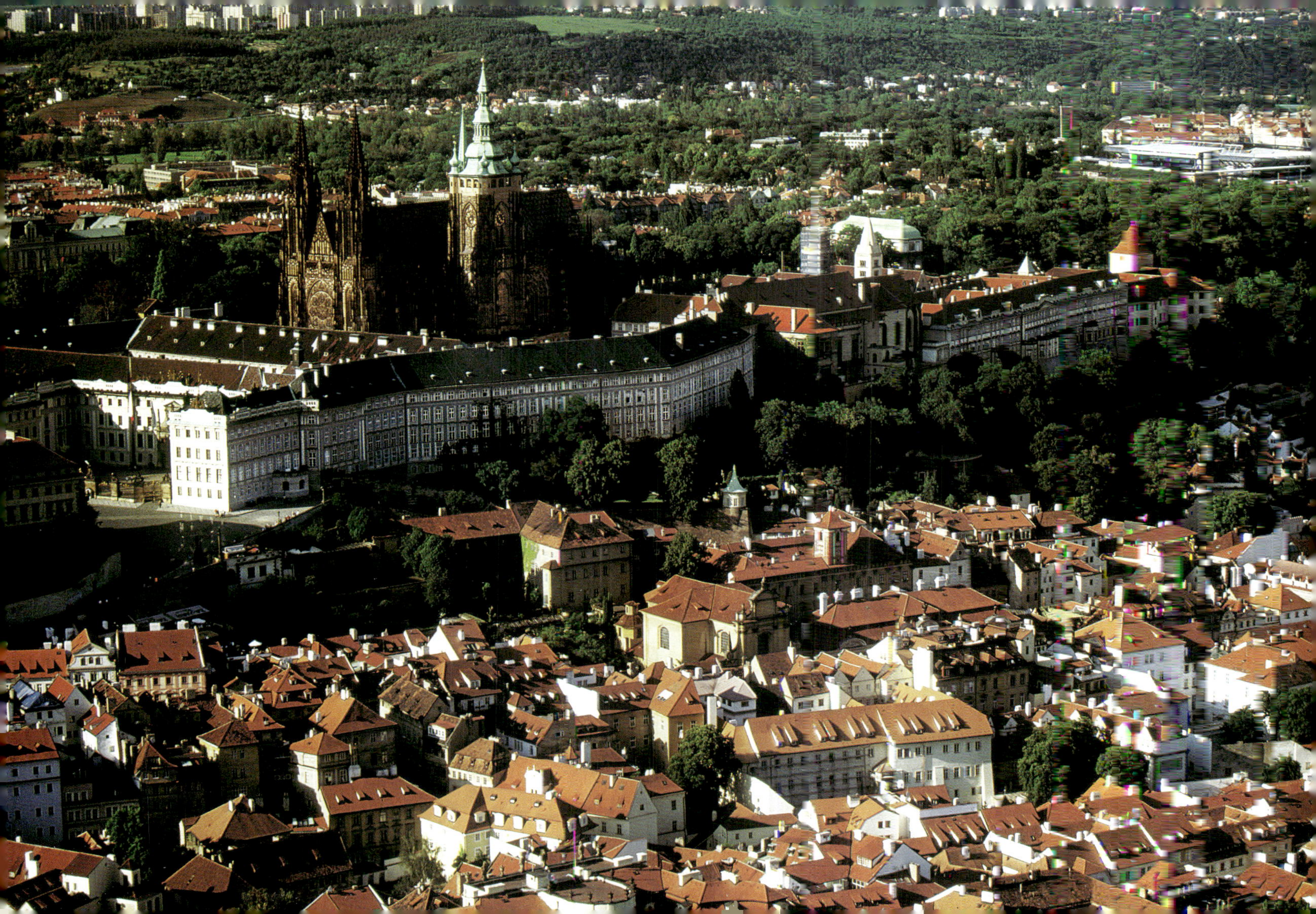

Vienna

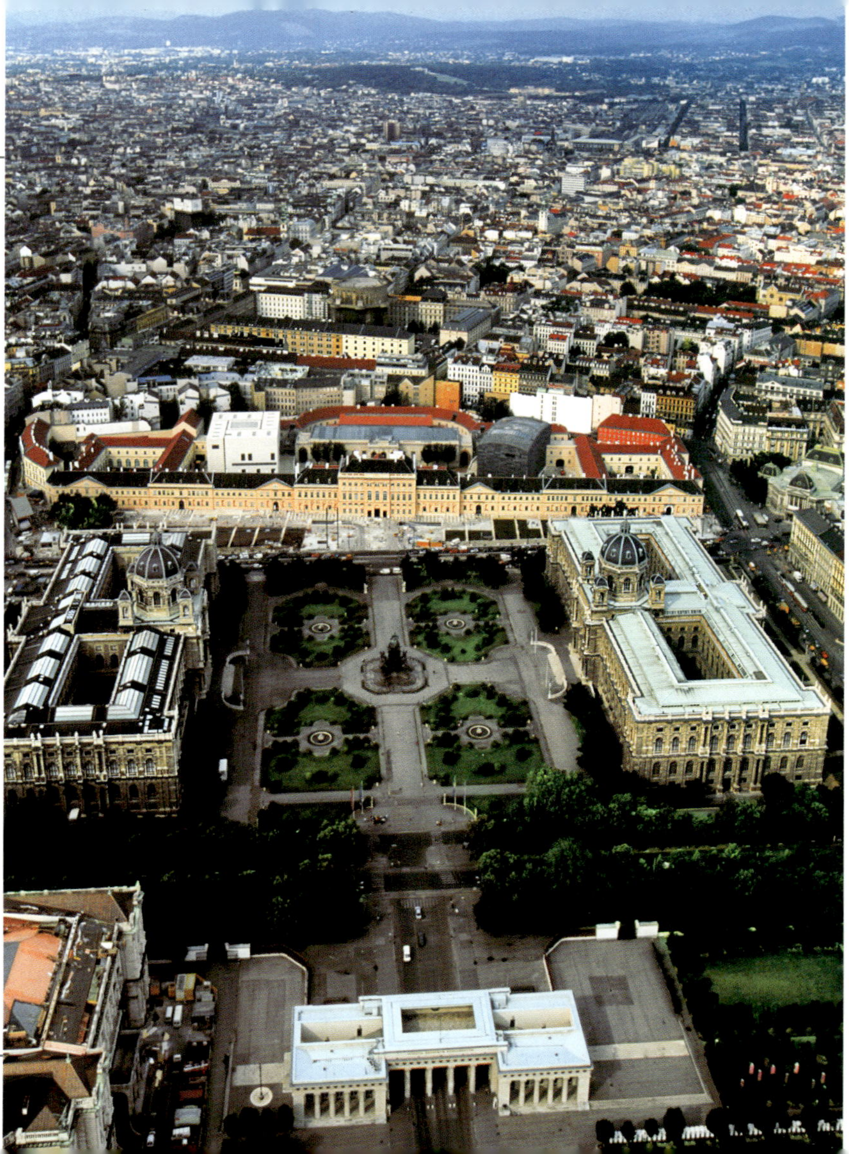

486
Several "temples" of the arts and sciences are found in Vienna's Museumsquartier, the capital of Austria. It is the largest group of buildings dedicated to cultural purposes in the world.

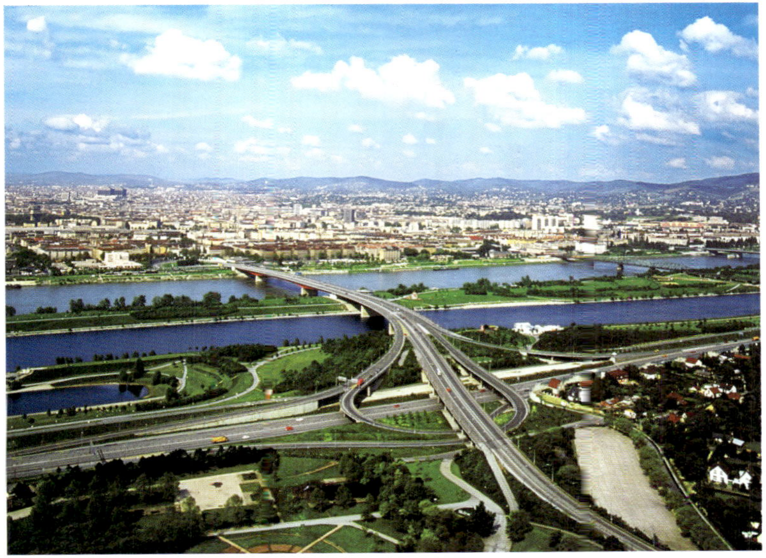

487

Vienna sits in a wonderful position on the northern side of the hydrographic basin of the Wiener Becken, on predominantly flat terrain. Some suburbs, however, are nestled into the hills west of the capital, visible in the background and on the right in the photo.

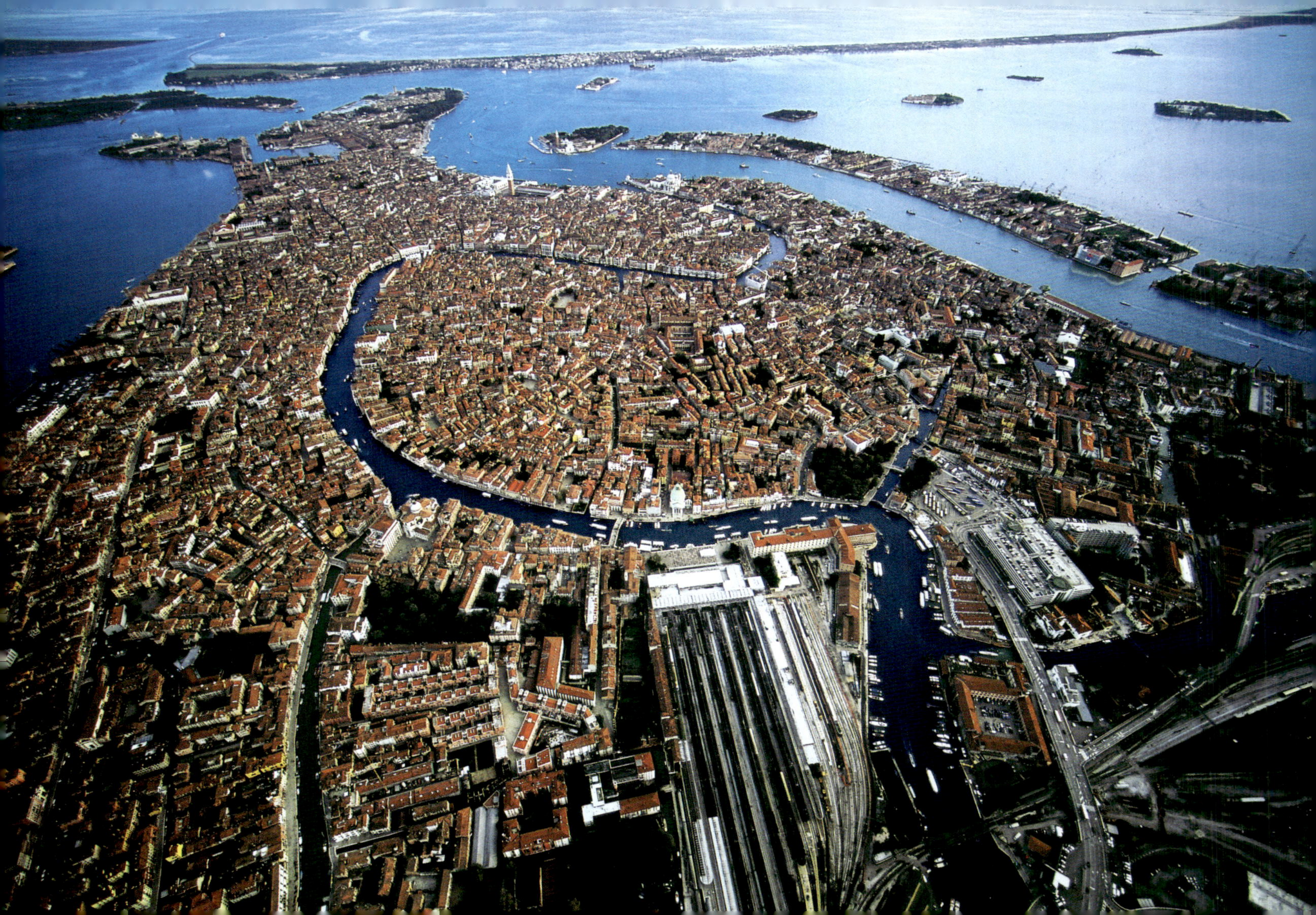

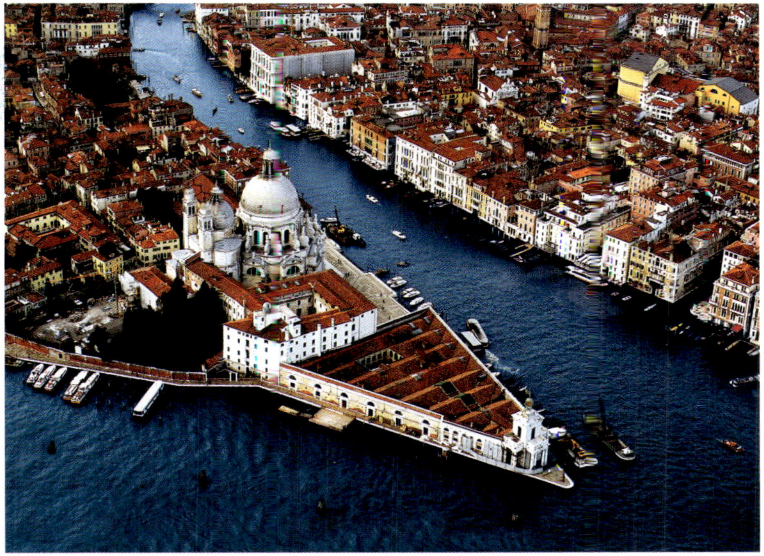

488

The platforms of the Santa Lucia train station create a unique geometric contrast within the intricate urban layout of Venice, built across 118 islets connected by 354 bridges.

489

The elegant domes of the church of Santa Maria della Salute, finished in 1674, stand on the eastern end of the Grand Canal.

490

Until 1854, the Rialto Bridge of Venice, built in 1588, was the only one crossing the Grand Canal.

491

Like a sign pointing to one of the most famous sights in the world, the bell-tower of San Marco Square in Venice draws the attention of observers. On the right, the domes of the basilica of the same name and the large building of the Ducal Palace can be seen.

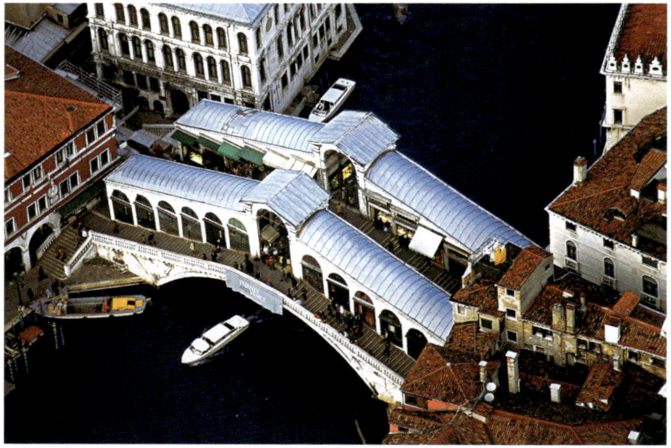

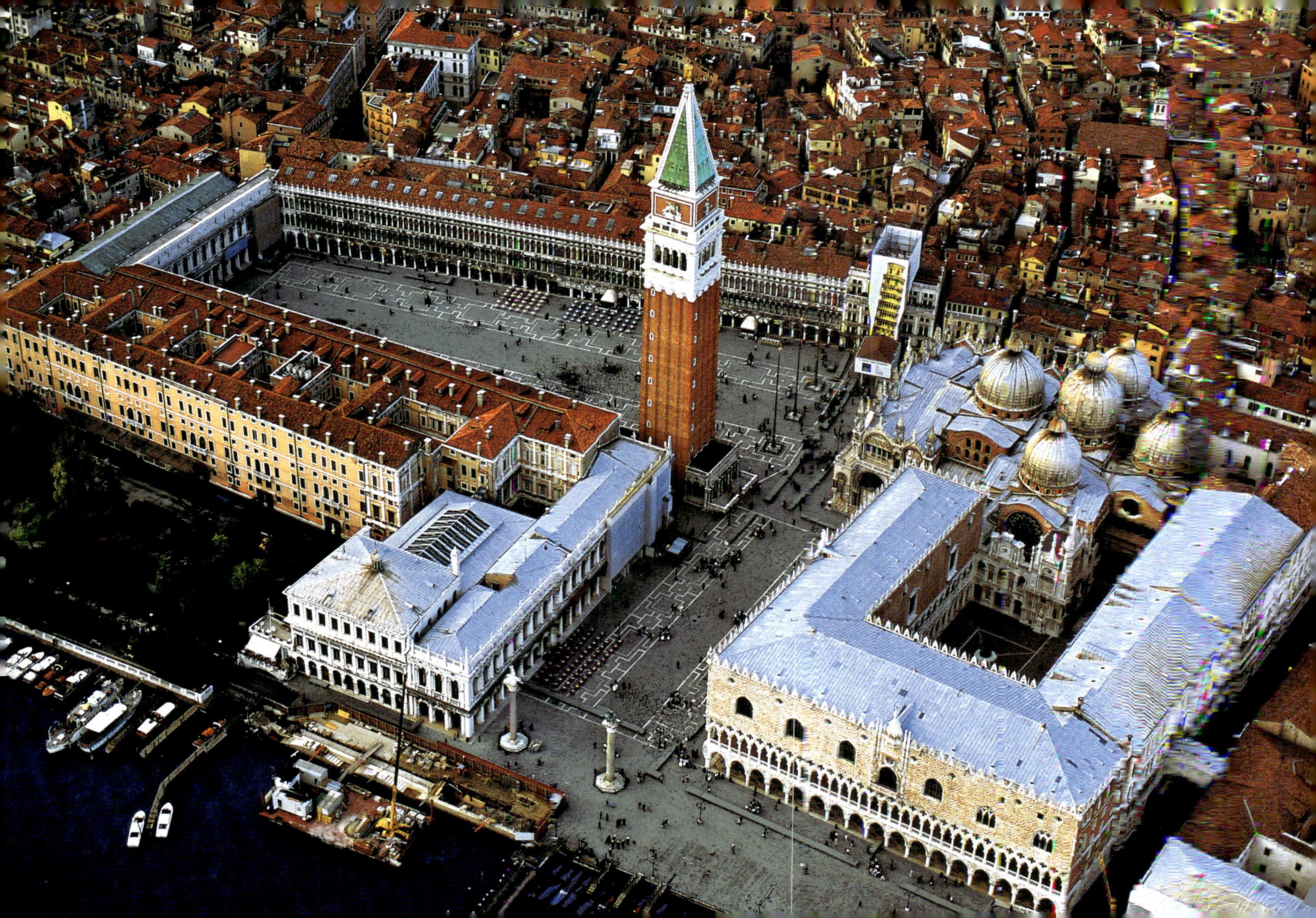

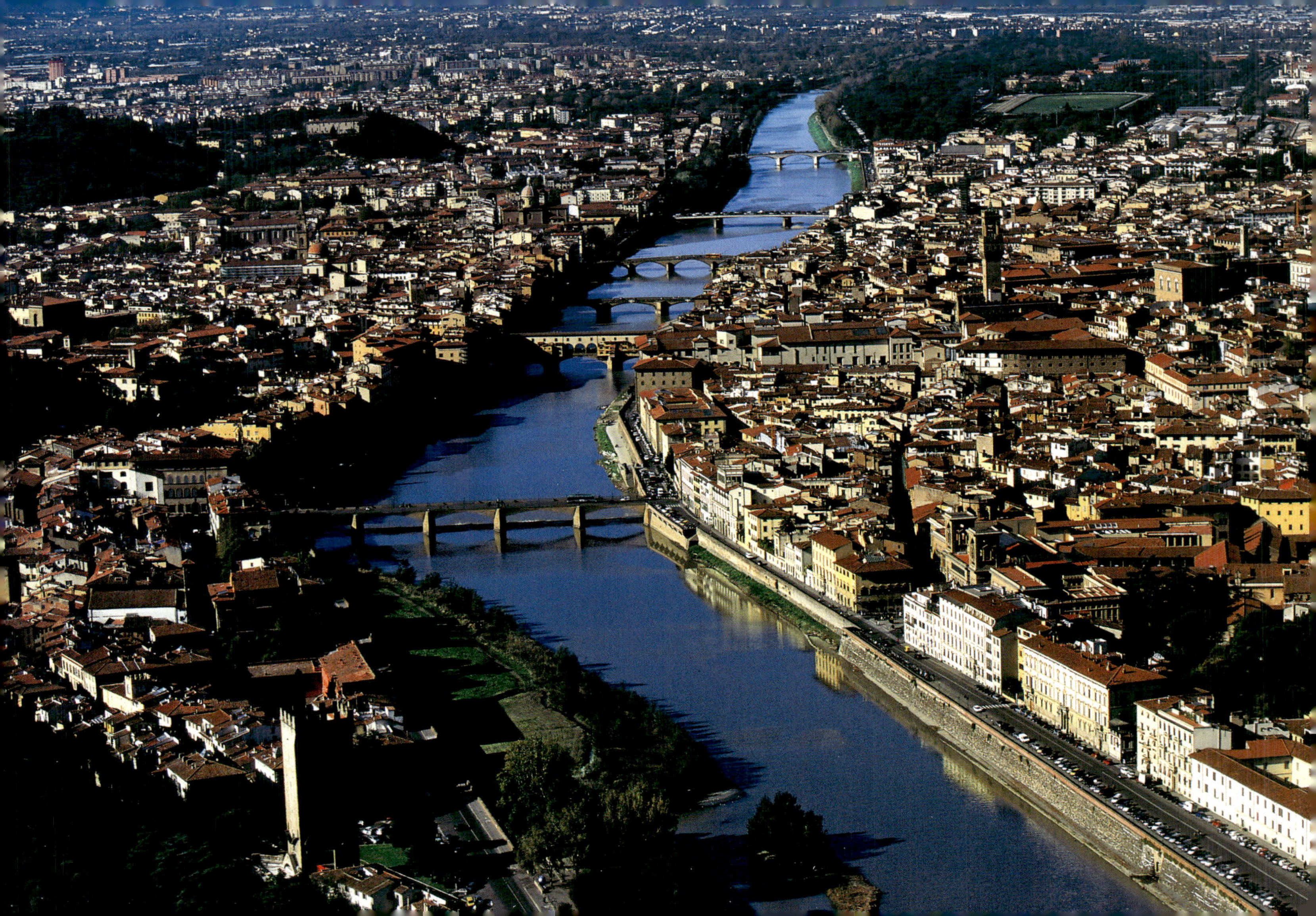

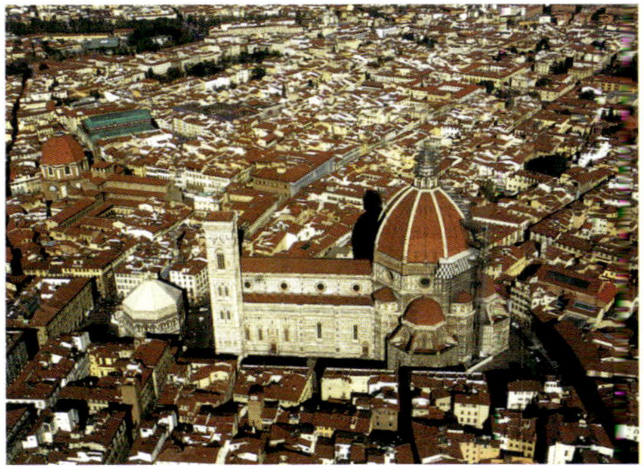

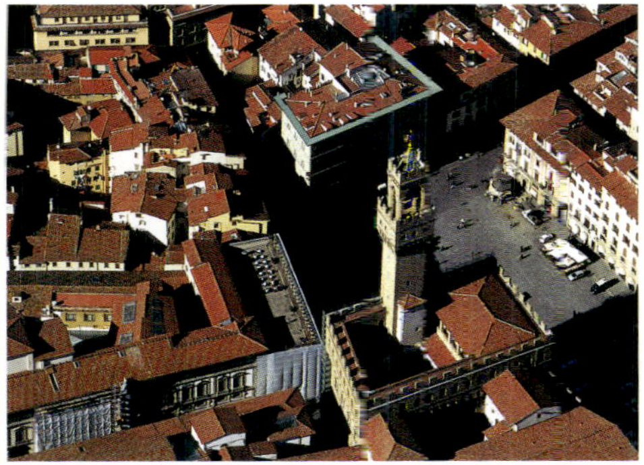

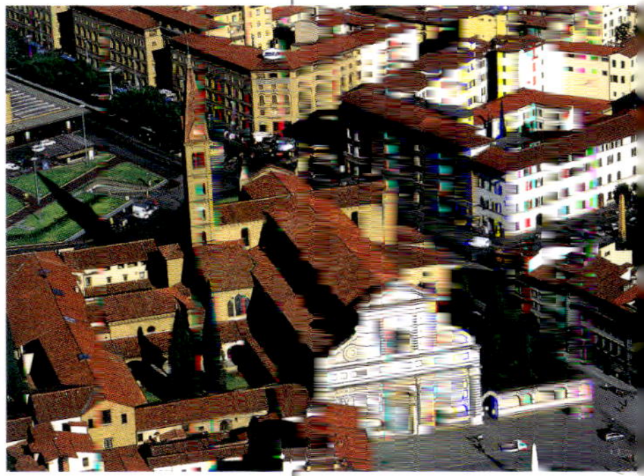

492

The Arno River, crossed by numerous bridges, cuts through the center of Florence diagonally from southeast to northwest. In this view, taken from the direction of the current, the fourteenth-century Ponte Vecchio (Old Bridge) is the second from the bottom.

493

Florentine masterpieces: the Duomo, or Cathedral, of Santa Maria del Fiore, Palazzo Vecchio (Old Palace) and Signoria Square, and the church of Santa Maria Novella. In Florence, it seems as if the Renaissance never ended.

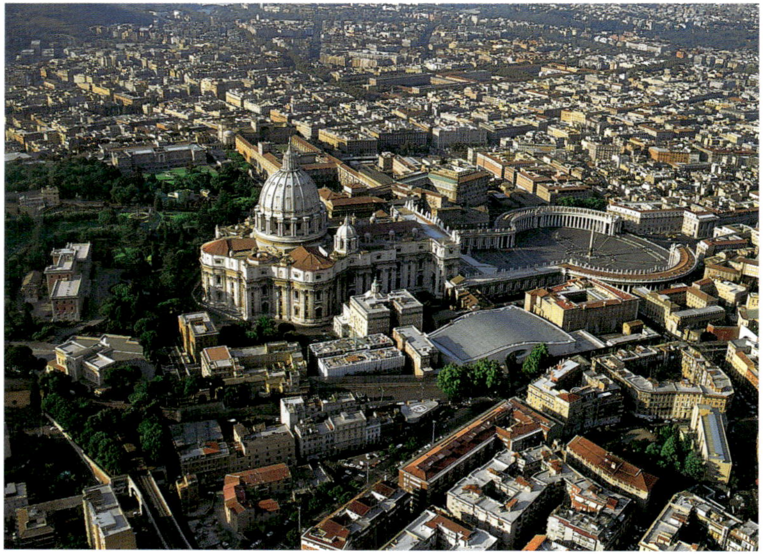

494
Rome surrounds on all sides the smallest sovereign state in the world, Vatican City, significantly featuring the biggest church on the planet: the Basilica of Saint Peter, seen here from the southwest.

495
The circular structure of Castel Sant'Angelo faces onto the Tiber River not far from the Vatican. Originally, the building was an imperial mausoleum.

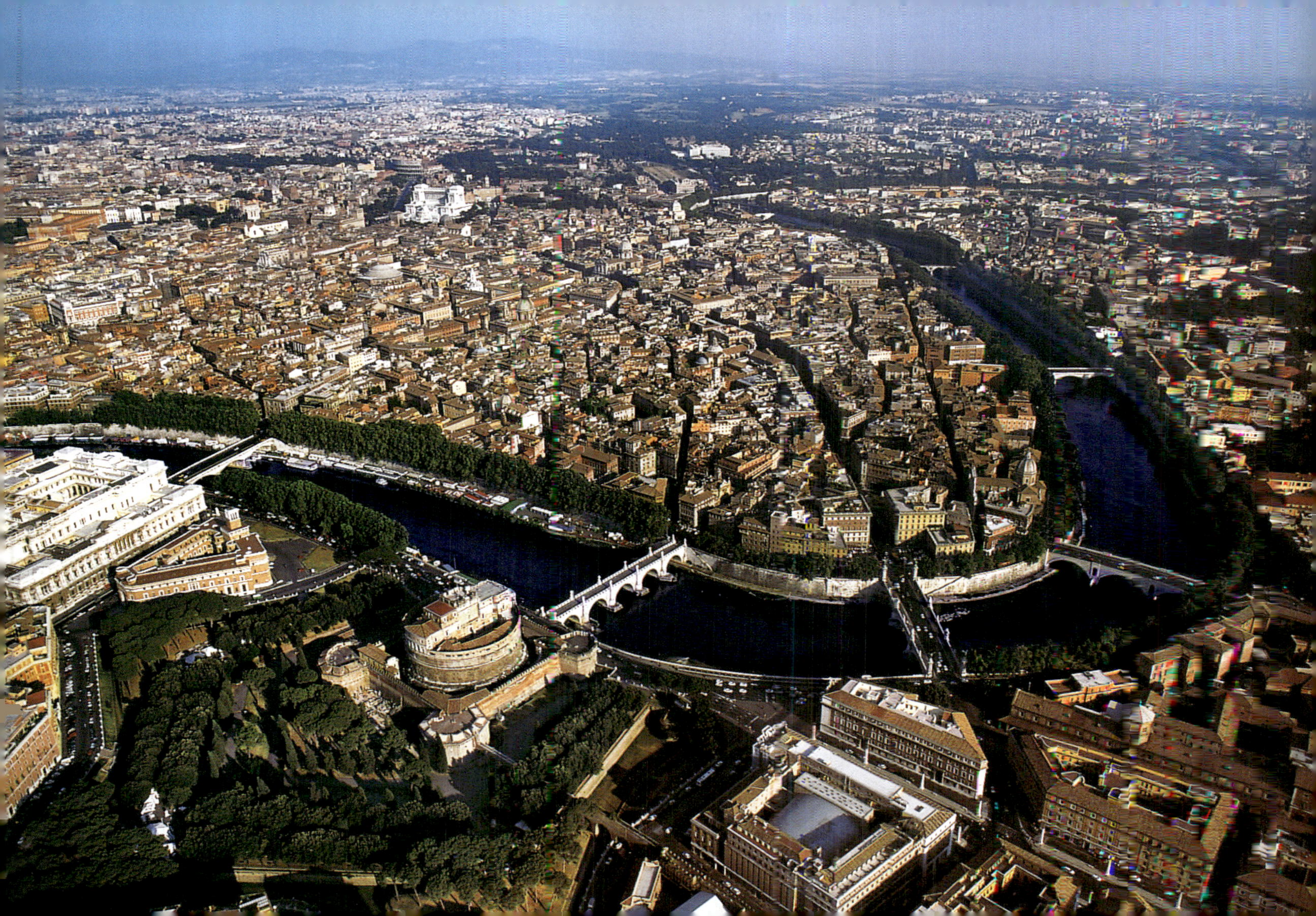

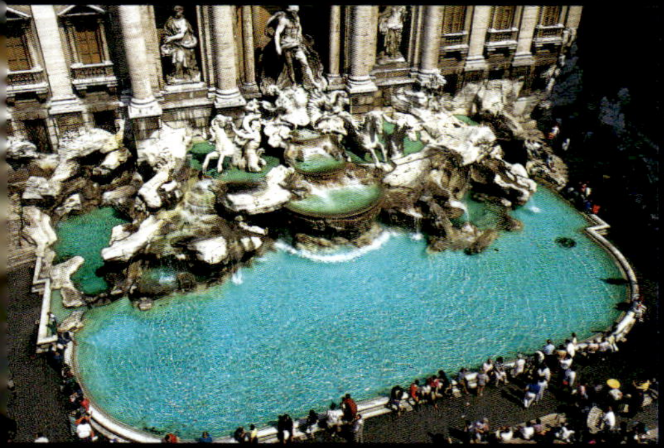

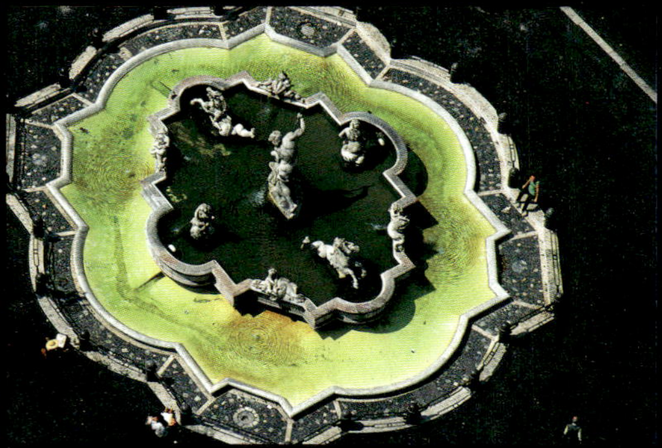

496
The eighteenth-century Trevi Fountain, on the left, blossoms at the base of Palazzo Poli. The Fiumi Fountain, sculpted by Bernini between 1648 and 1651, occupies the center of oblong Navona Square.

497
The famous staircase of Trinità dei Monti, a renaissance masterpiece, is one of the cult-places of the Rome of dreamers and non-realists from after the Second World War, in the days of the "Dolce Vita."

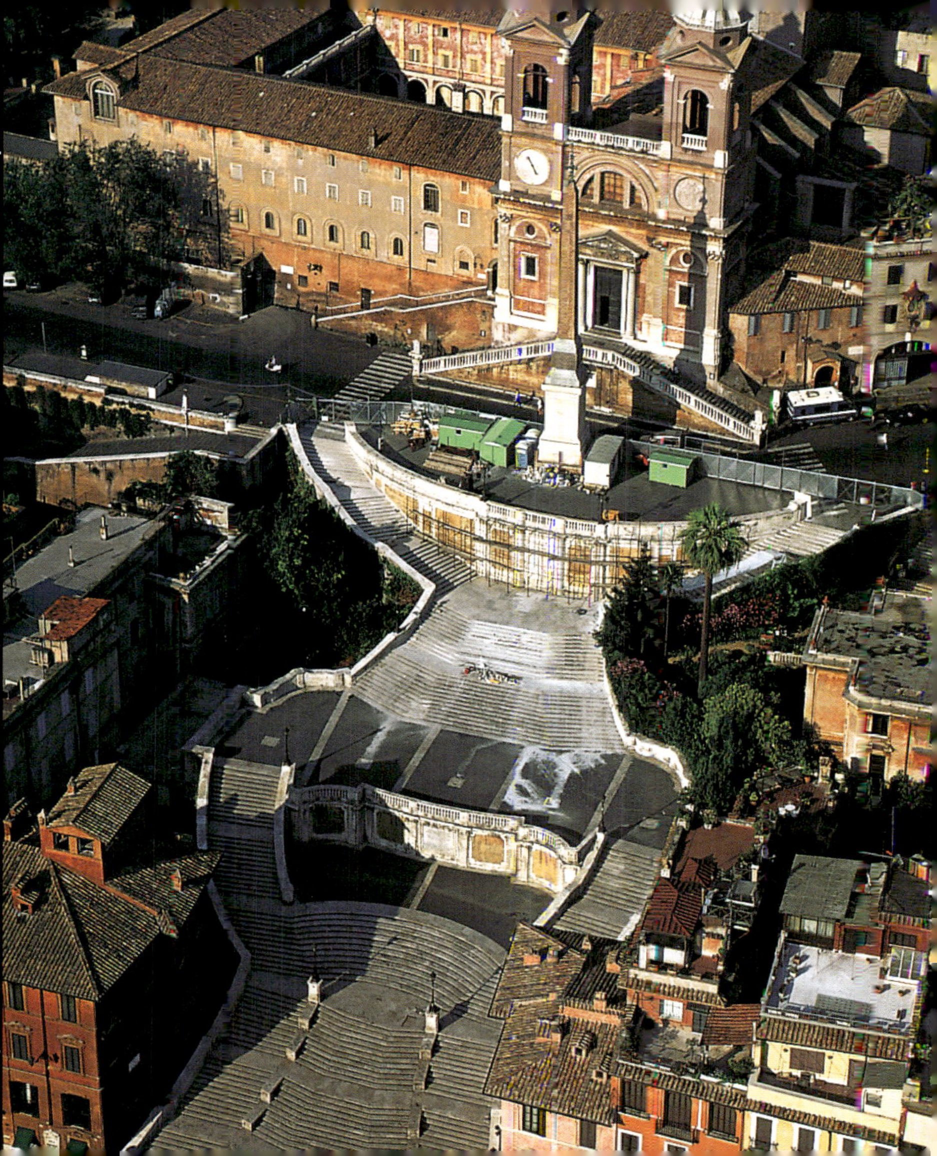

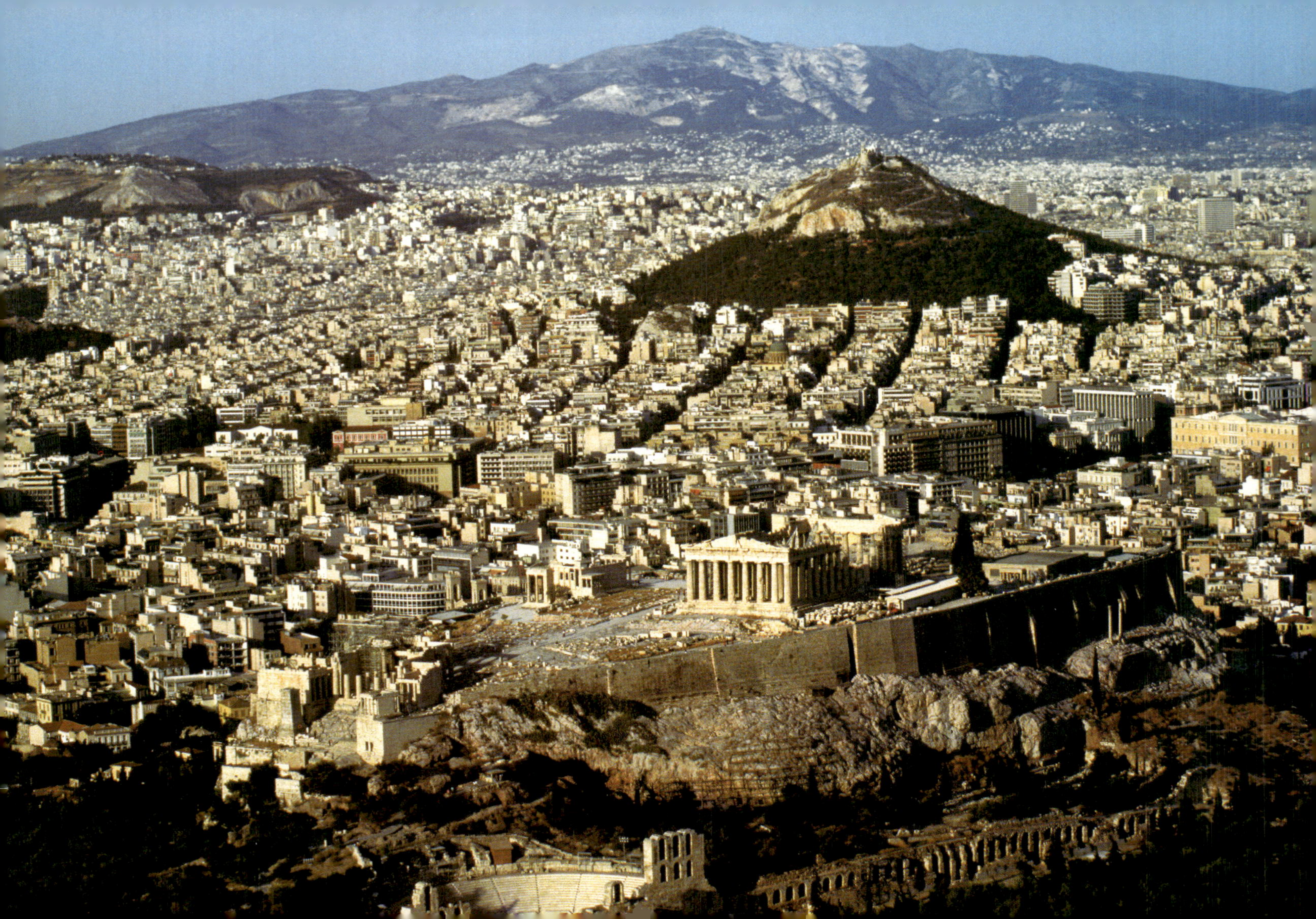

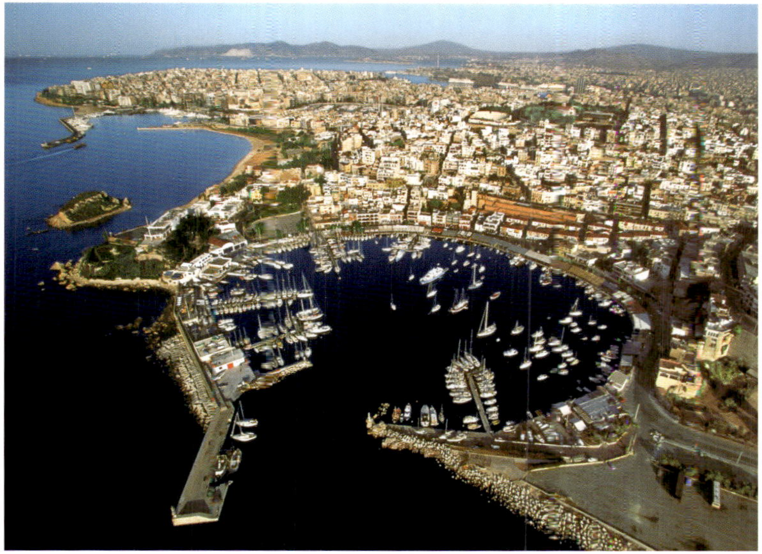

498

The ideal heart of classicism, the Acropolis of Athens rises upon a natural rock in the middle of Athens. At the center of the view stands another famous Athenian hill: the Lycabettus, the green lung of the Greek capital.

499

The Piraeus, also the port of ancient Athens, is formed by three inlets. The middle one, Zea, seen in the photo, was the military dock.

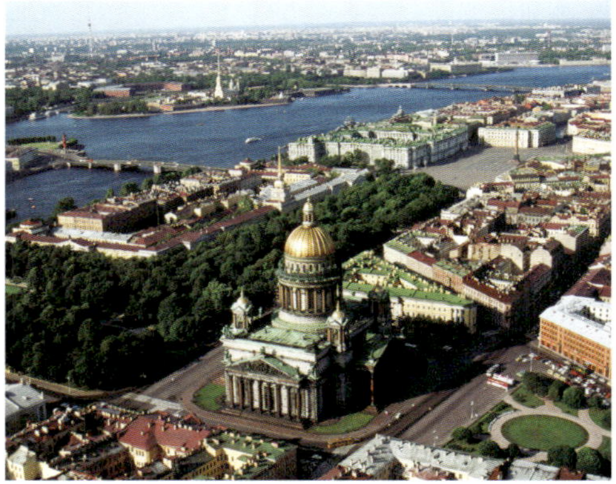

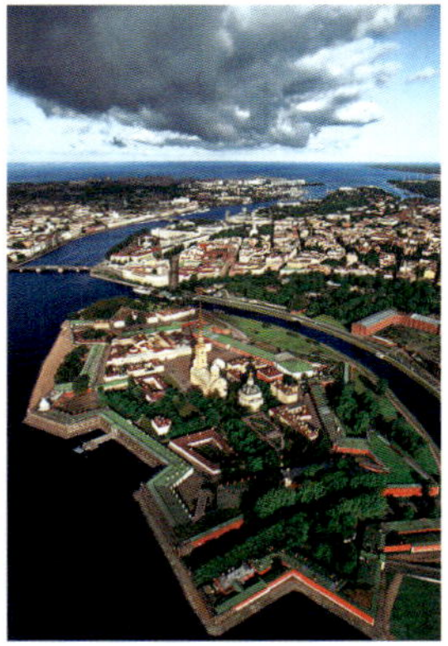

500 left

The gold-plating on the dome heightens the majesty of the cathedral of Saint Petersburg, in Russia, consecrated to Saint Isaac.

500 right

The fortress of Saints Peter and Paul occupies the entire Zayachy Island, in the estuary of the Neva River, where the Czar Peter the Great decided to build Saint Petersburg, his capital.

501

Alexander's Column, 154 feet tall, stands in the middle of the square of the Winter Palace (the Hermitage) in Saint Petersburg.

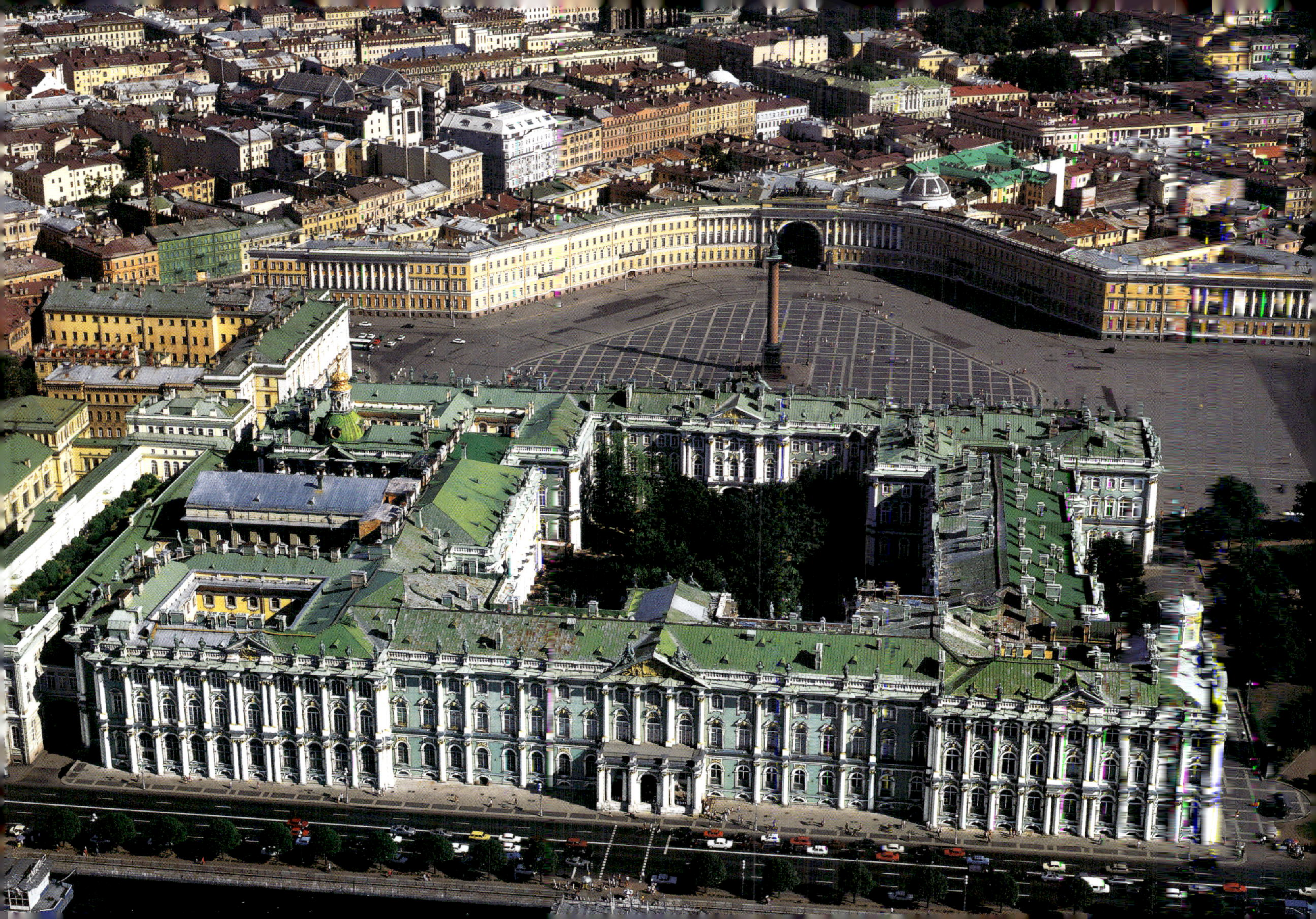

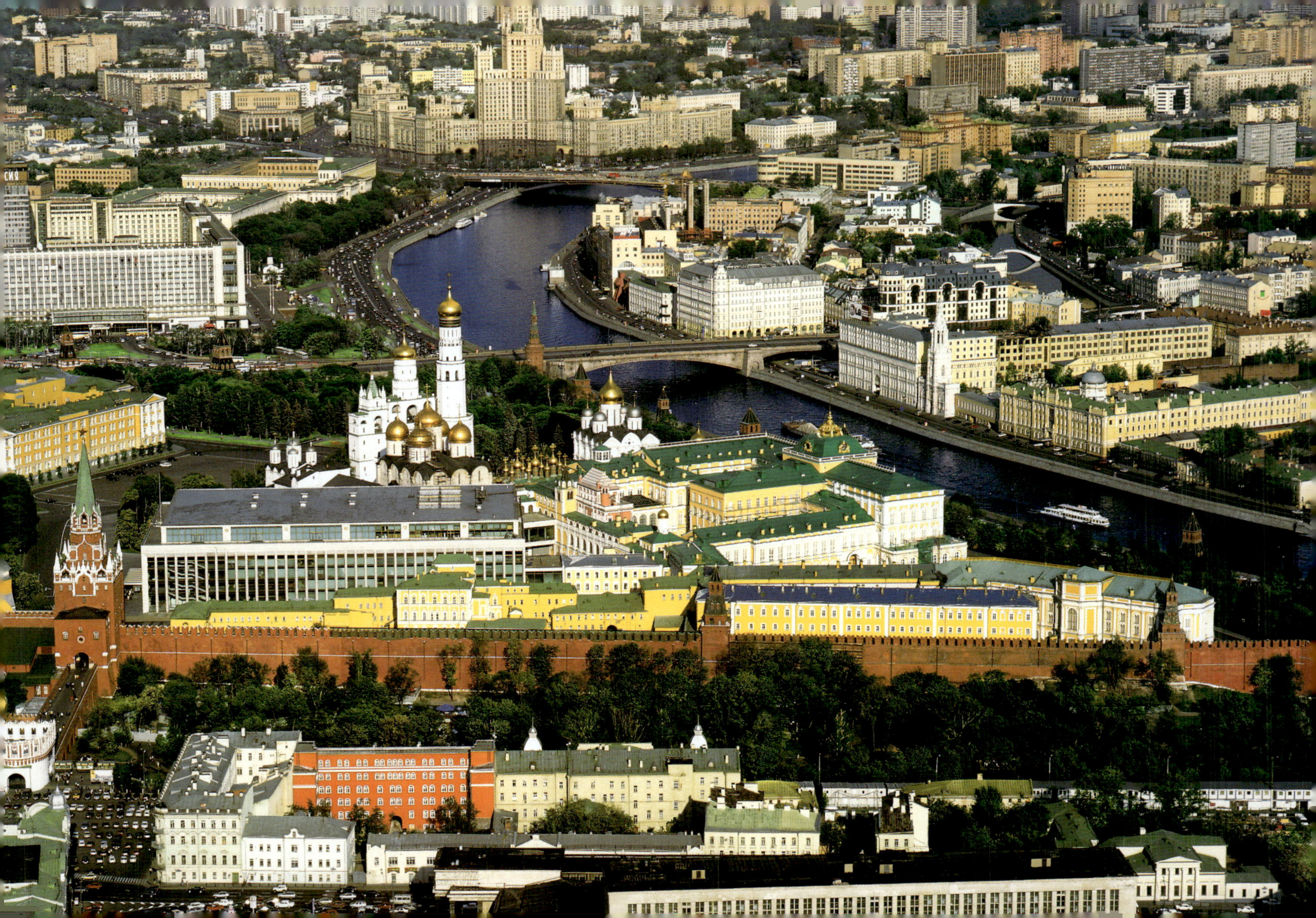

Moscow

502

Besides the red walls of Moscow's Kremlin, built starting in the fifteenth century, the enormous complex of the Great Palace is dominated by the golden domes of the Cathedral of the Assumption.

503 left

In the heart of Moscow, stands the nineteenth-century Cathedral of Christ the Redeemer. The unmistakable "Russian" style of the sacred buildings dates back to medieval models.

503 right

One of the symbols of Moscow is M.V. Lomonosov University. The central building, 787 feet tall, is currently the tallest in the capital.

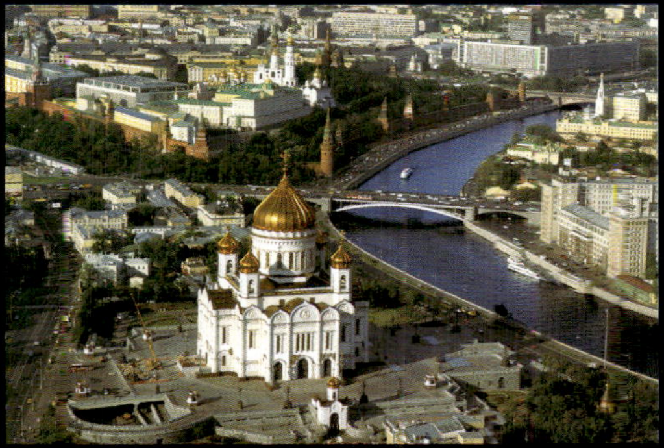

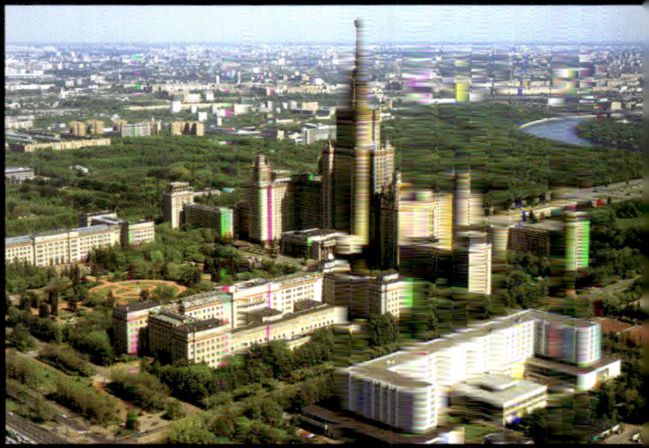

Cairo

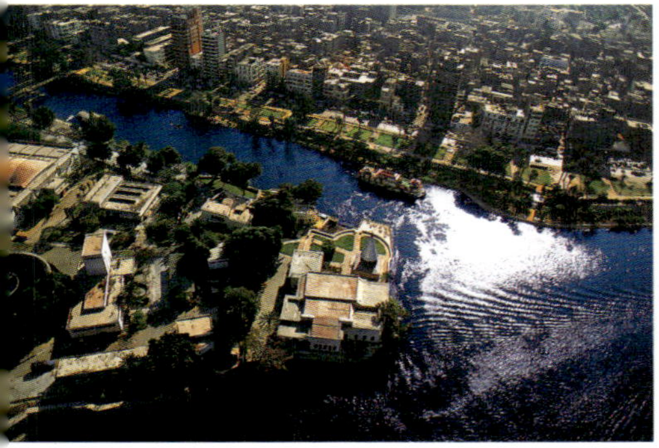

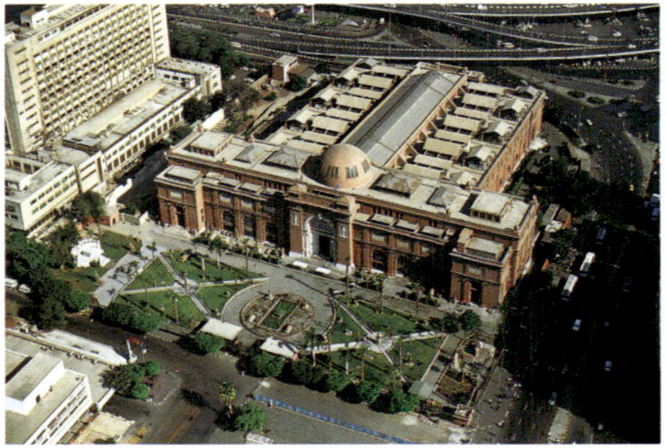

504 left
"Under siege" by modern Cairo on the two banks of the Nile, the island of Rawda features airier spaces within the center of the Egyptian megalopolis.

504 right
Completed in 1902, the building containing the Egyptian Museum of Cairo is topped by a characteristic dome with sunlights.

505
The spectacular domes of the Mosque of Mohammed Ali shine from the top of the citadel of Cairo, fortified by Saladin in the twelfth century.

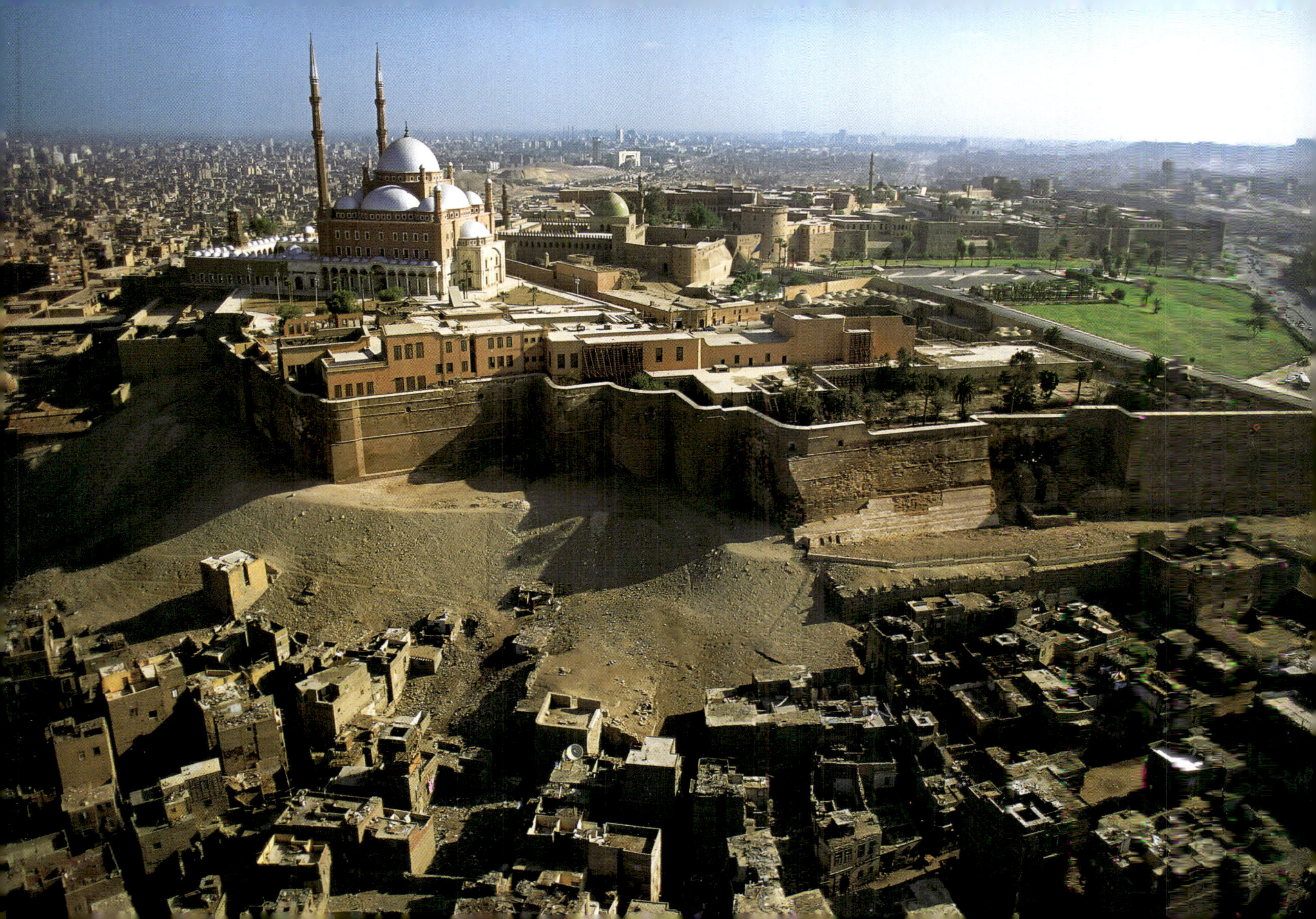

Cape Town

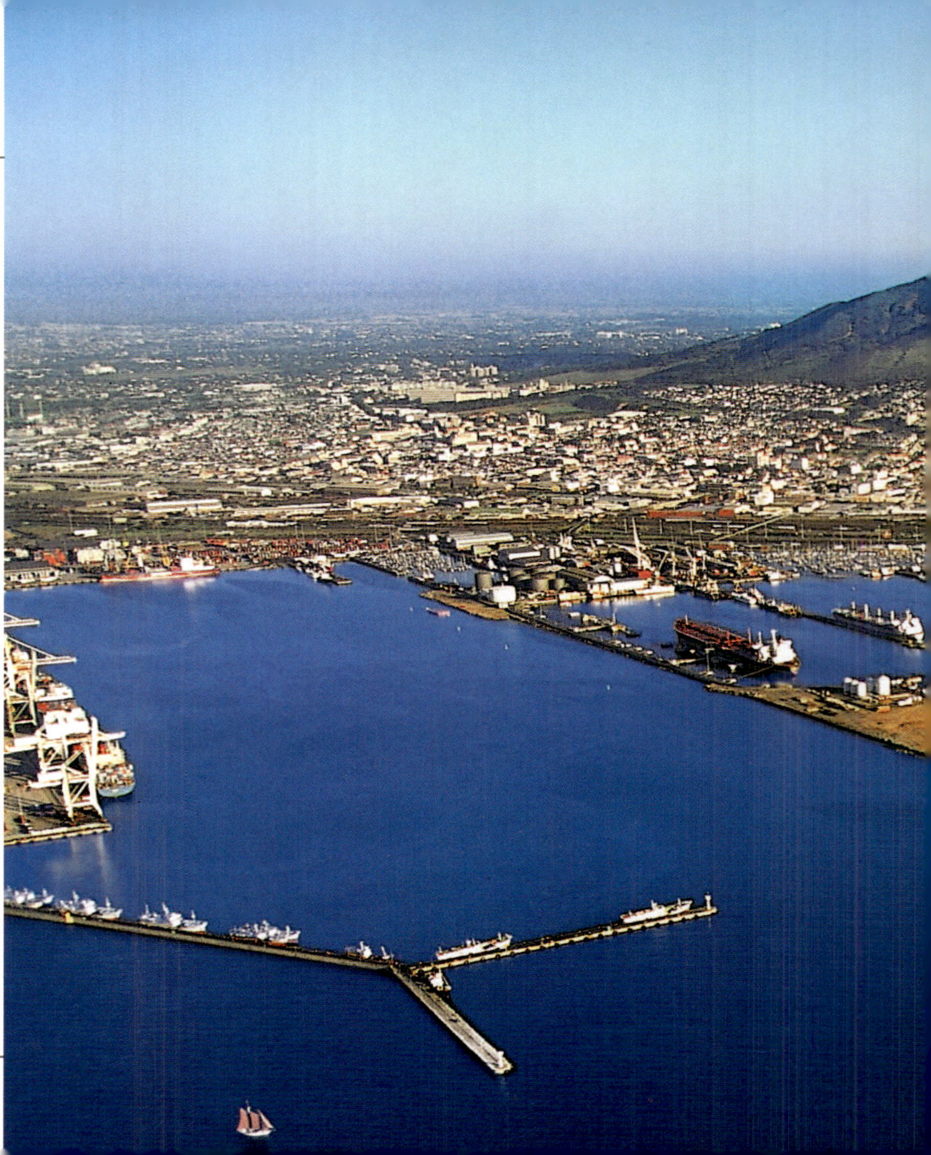

506-507
A view of Cape Town, the oldest urban settlement in South Africa, ends in the unmistakable profile of Table Mountain to the north. The city's harbor dates back to 1600.

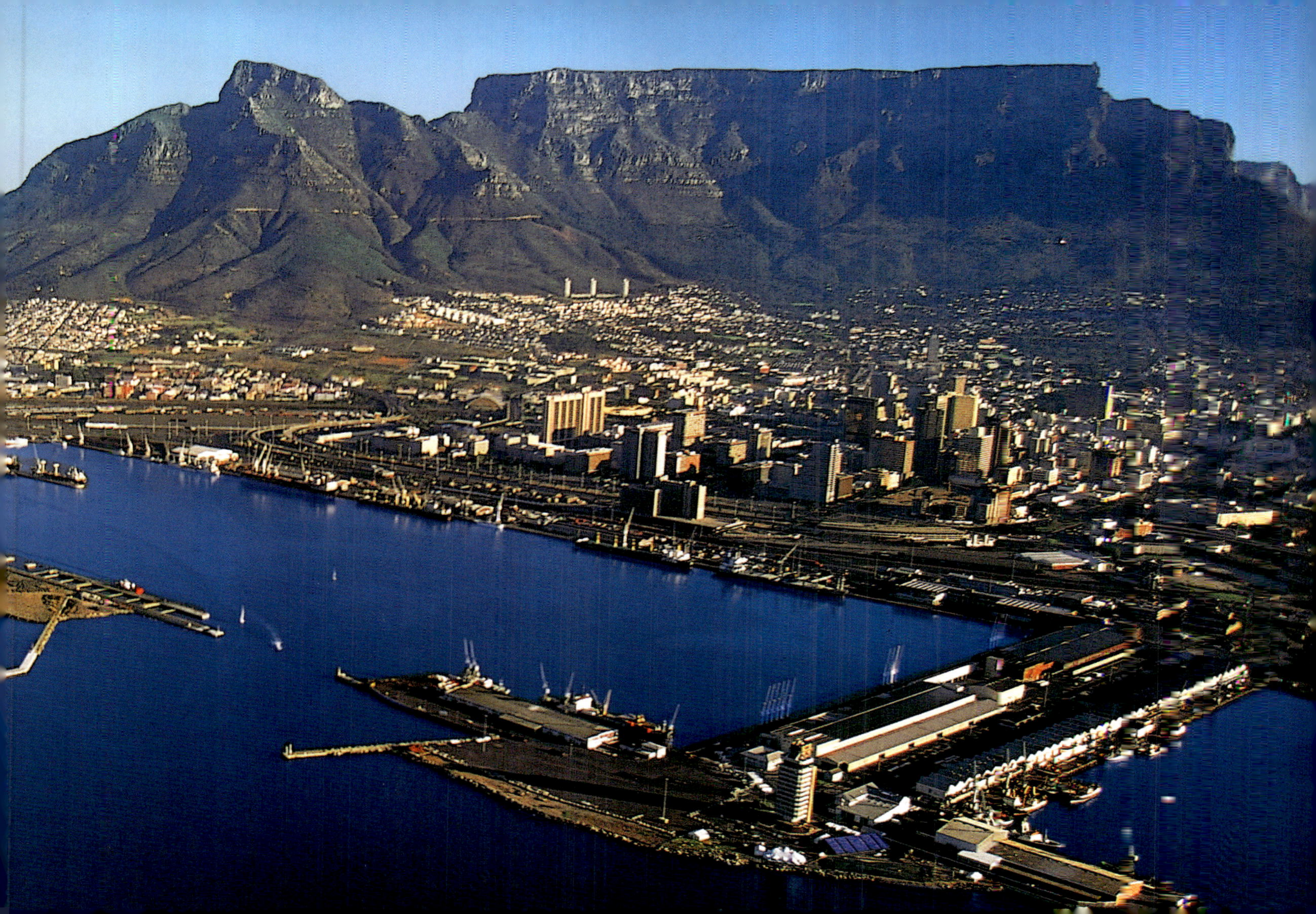

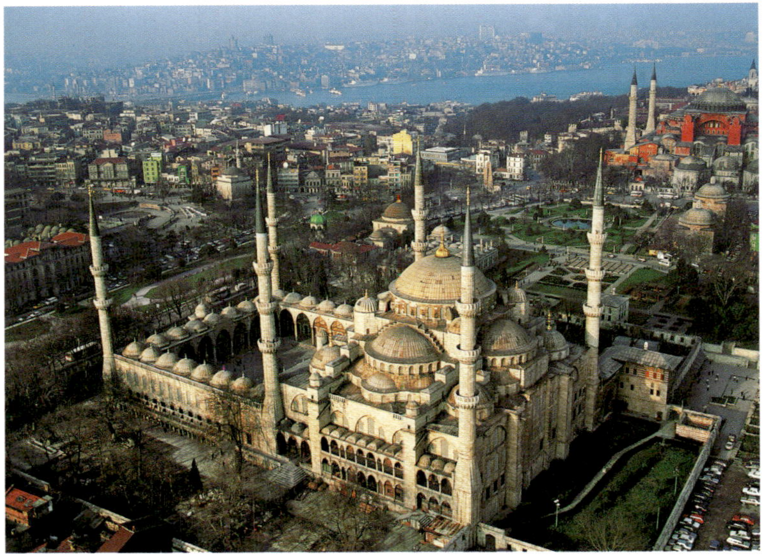

508
Sultanhamet Cami, or the Blue Mosque of Istanbul in Turkey, responds to the equally imposing mass of the red basilica of Santa Questo with its majestic volumes. The sight is one of the most exciting in the world.

509
The fairy-tale-like Topkapi Saray was the headquarters of the Ottoman sultans until 1853. The complex looms over the waters of the Golden Horn, on the left and all of the Bosphorus.

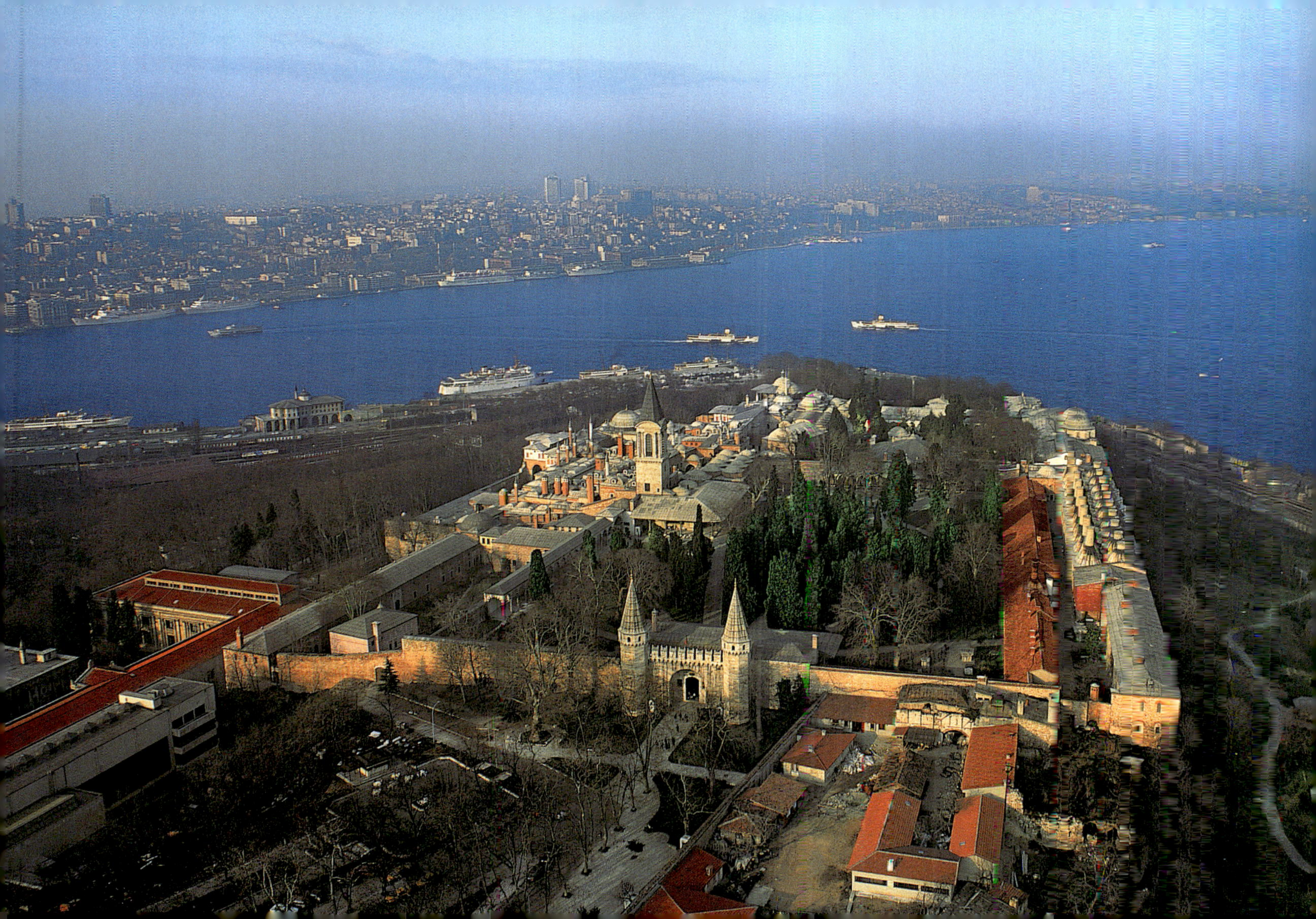

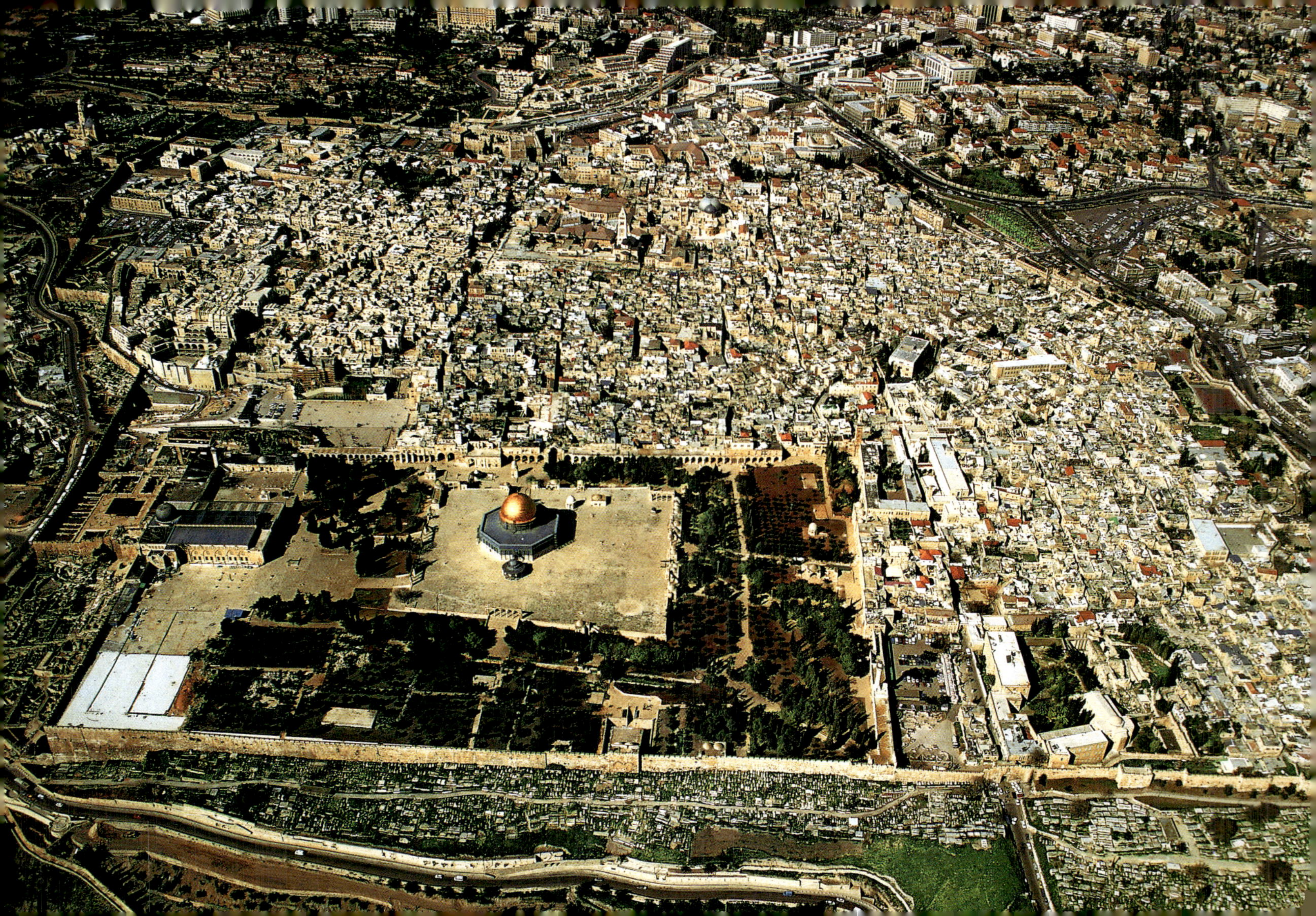

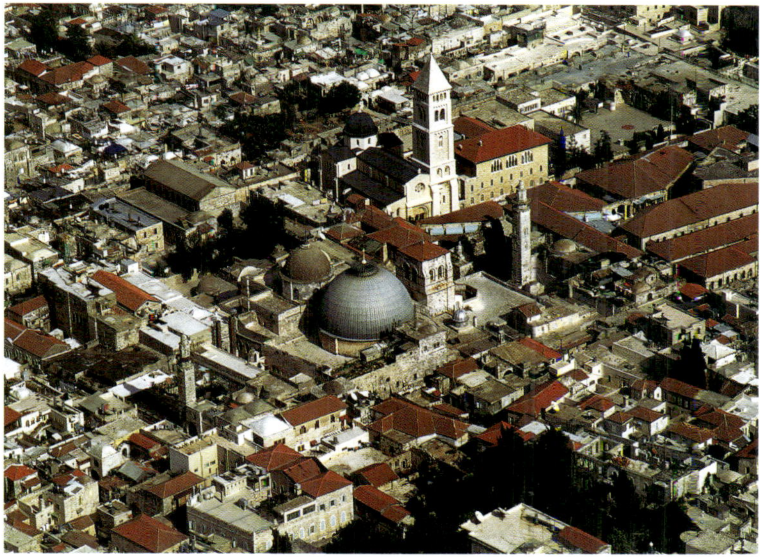

510

The Dome of the Rock, the mosque/memorial monument dating back the earliest days of Islam, sparkles with gold on the Al- Haram al-Sharif enclosure.

511

Less visible but equally venerable, the grey dome of the Church of the Holy Sepulcher in Jerusalem stands on one of the stations of the Cross, which extend from Golgotha Hill to the site of Jesus' burial.

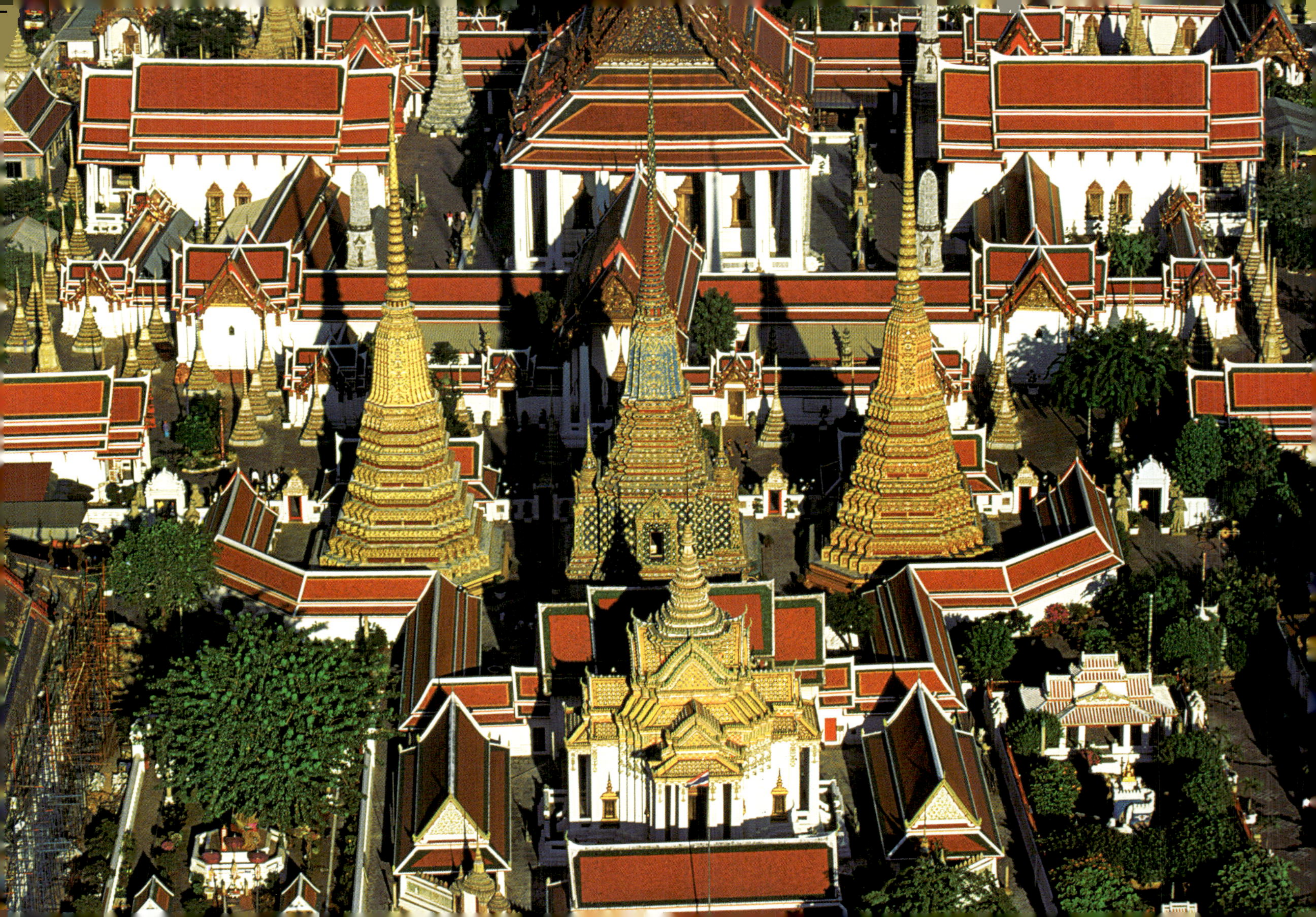

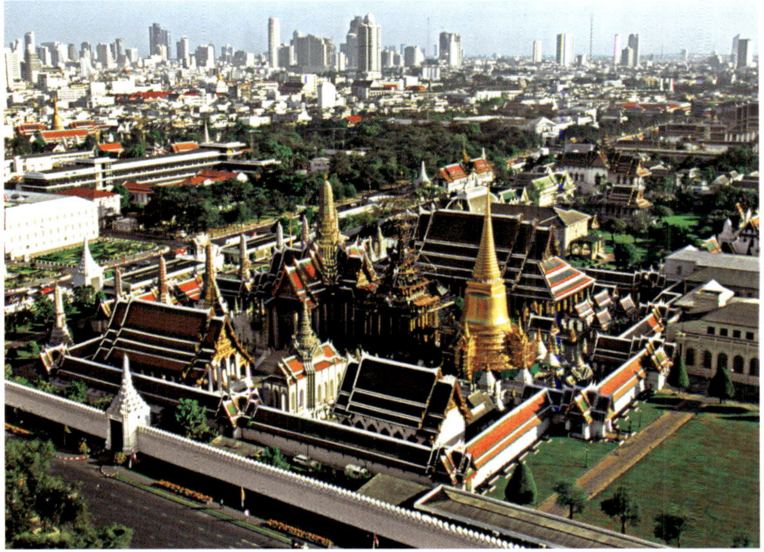

512

An seductive maze of roofs and spires rises above the temple complex of Wat Pho in Bangkok. It is one of the biggest and oldest Buddhist temples in the Thai capital.

513

No less striking is the temple of Wat Phra Kaeo in Bangkok, within the enclosure of the Grand Palace, the ancient seat of the rulers of fanciful Siam.

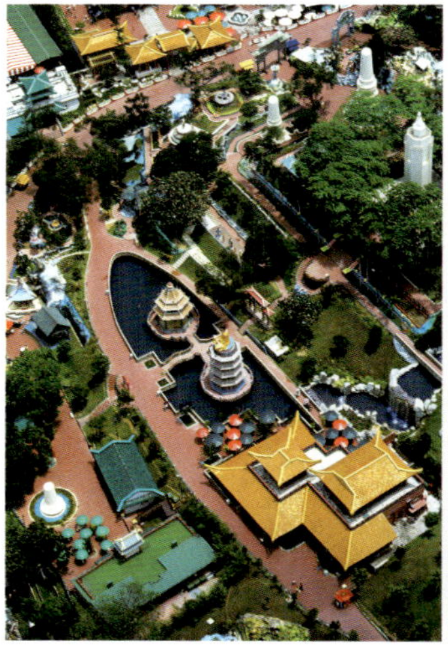

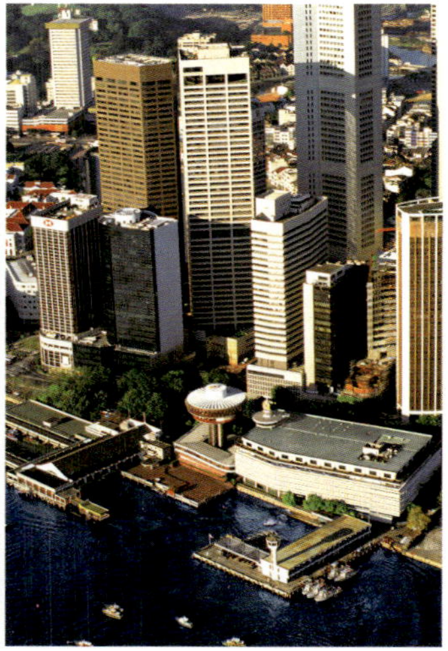

514

Singapore is a city-state in which strong religious traditions, represented by Buddhist, Hindu, Shinto, Confucian, Christian, and Muslim houses of worship, coexist with the symbols of a dynamic and developed economy, exemplified by the modern appearance of the Business District, seen in the view on the right.

515

The Business District dominates everything, but the glorious buildings in the Colonial District and the Padang cricket pitch remain to attest to Singapore's appearance until the 1960s.

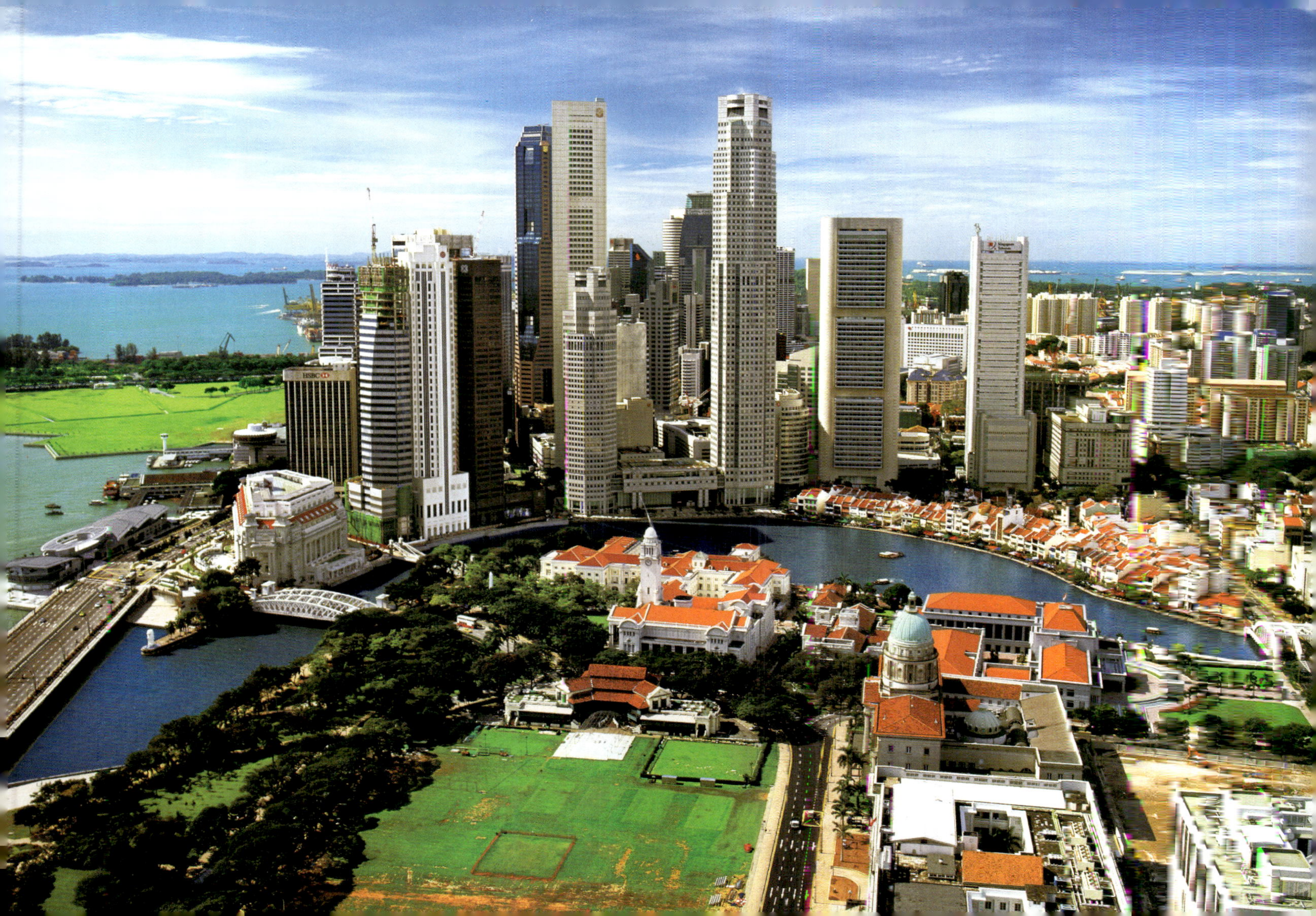
HSBC

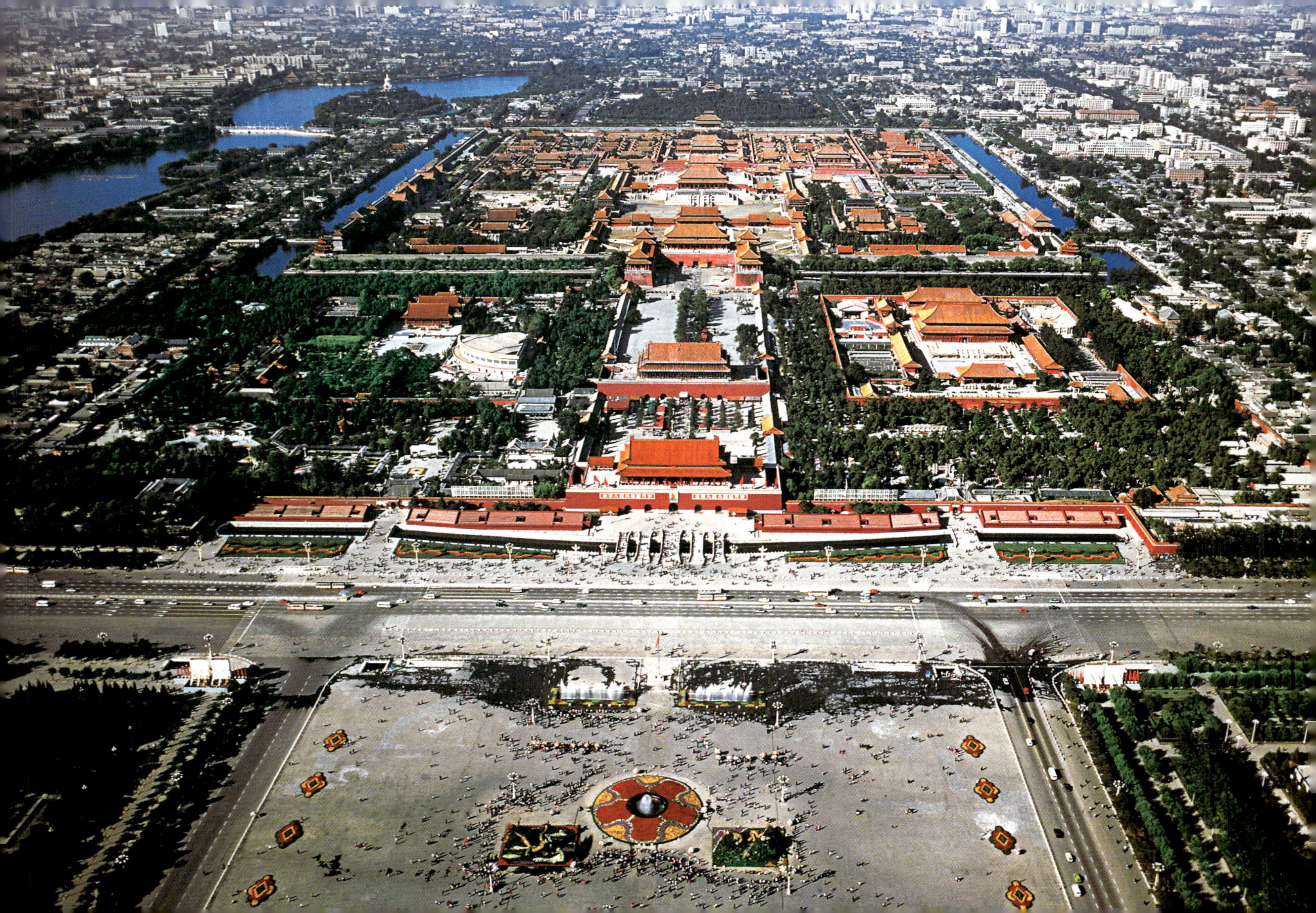

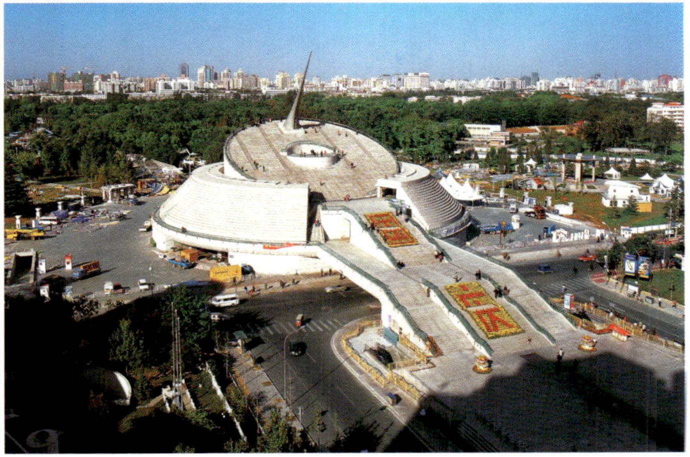

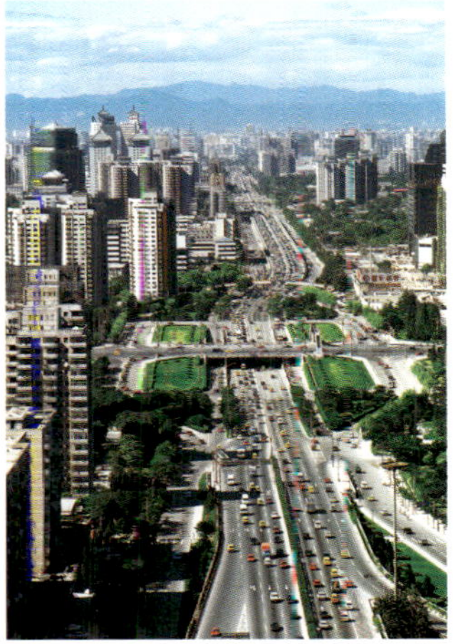

516

A perfect grid, with a symbolic as much as functional importance, characterizes the Forbidden City of Beijing, the seat of the Chinese emperors until 1912.

517

The futuristic Millennium Altar, on the left, is an example of the search for a more traditional monumentality. Contrarily, the main roads and skyscrapers represent the new "internationalist" China.

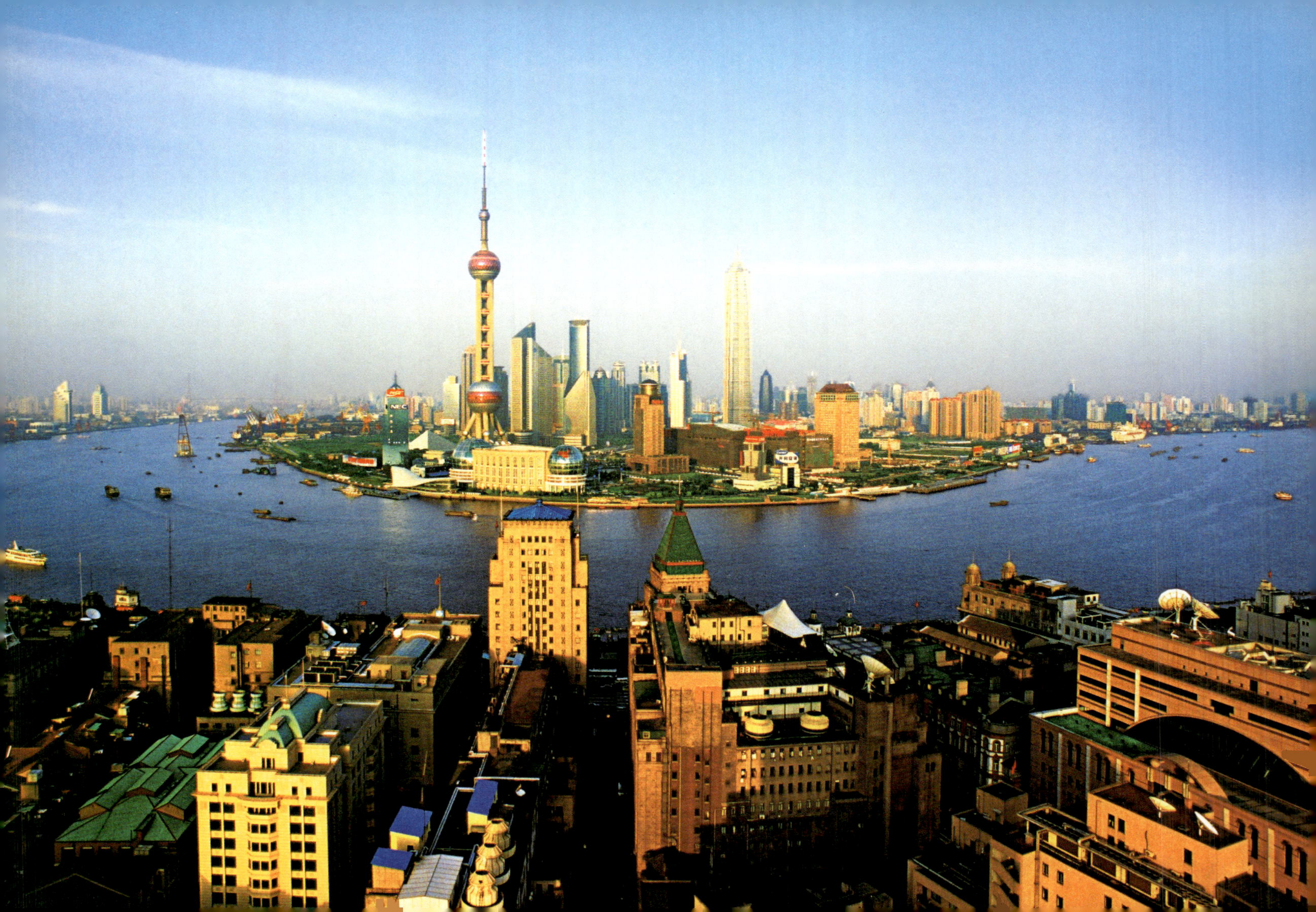

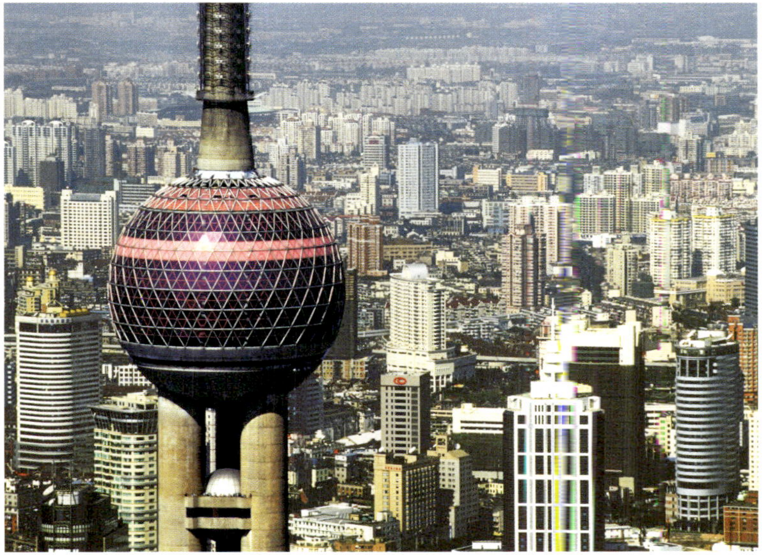

518

The skyline of Shanghai is one of the most spectacular on the planet the feather in the cap of the Chinese megalopolis is the magnificent Jin Mao Tower, seen in the center of the photo: at 1,381 feet, it is the fifth tallest in the world

519

Another feature boasted by Shanghai is the Oriental East Pearl TV & Radio Tower, a cement tower 1,536 feet tall in a futuristic style.

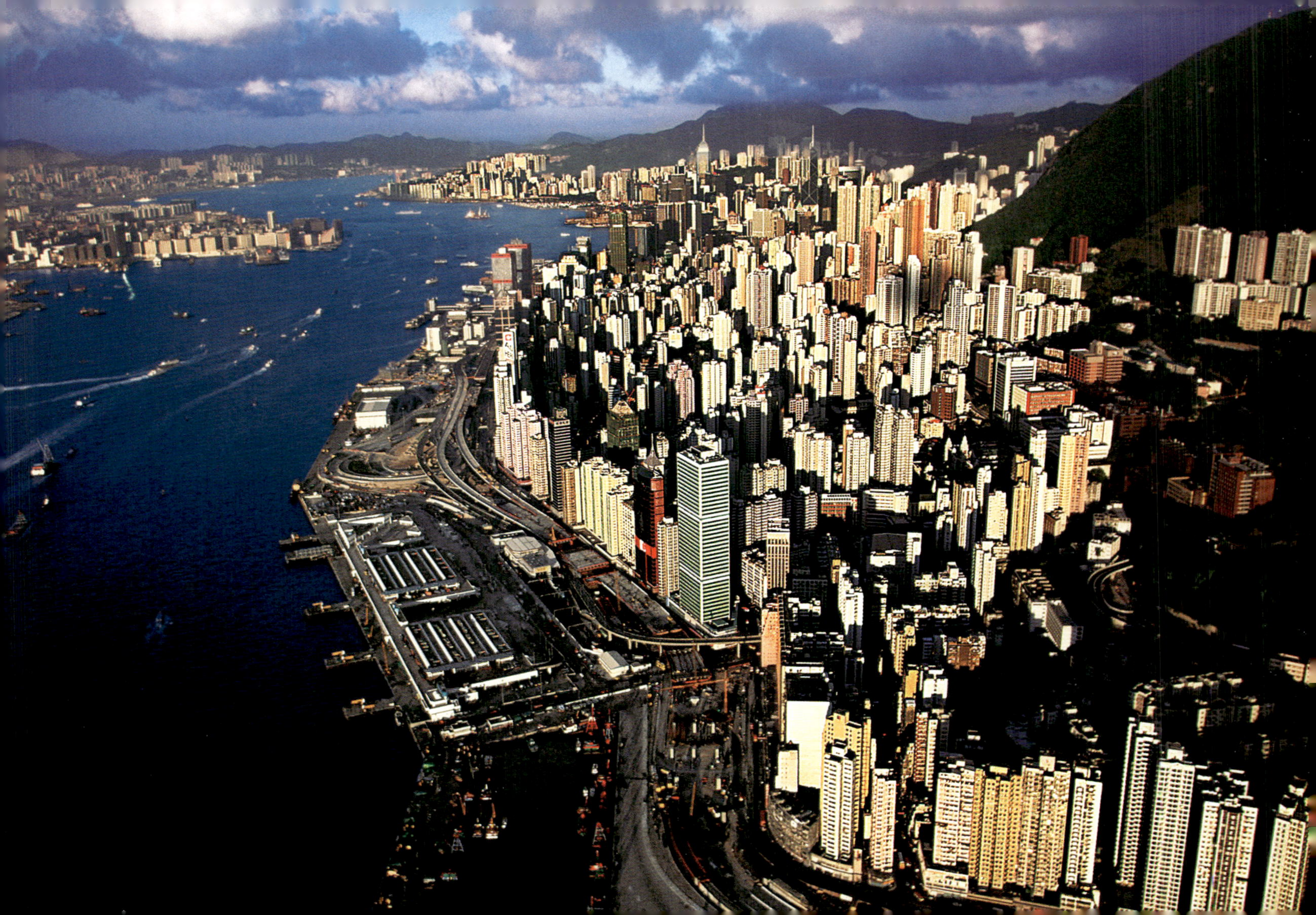

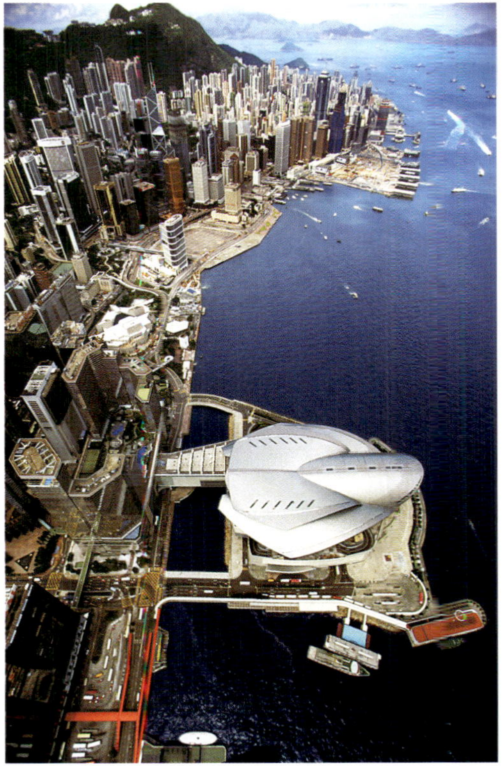

Hong Kong

520
A good part of Hong Kong is an impressive forest of skyscrapers, clustered along the narrow coastal strip facing onto the magnificent Bay of Pearls.

521
A strong conceptual push towards the exterior is noticeable in the structure of the Hong Kong Convention and Exhibition Center, whose aluminum roof was inspired by the shape of a seagull with its wings spread.

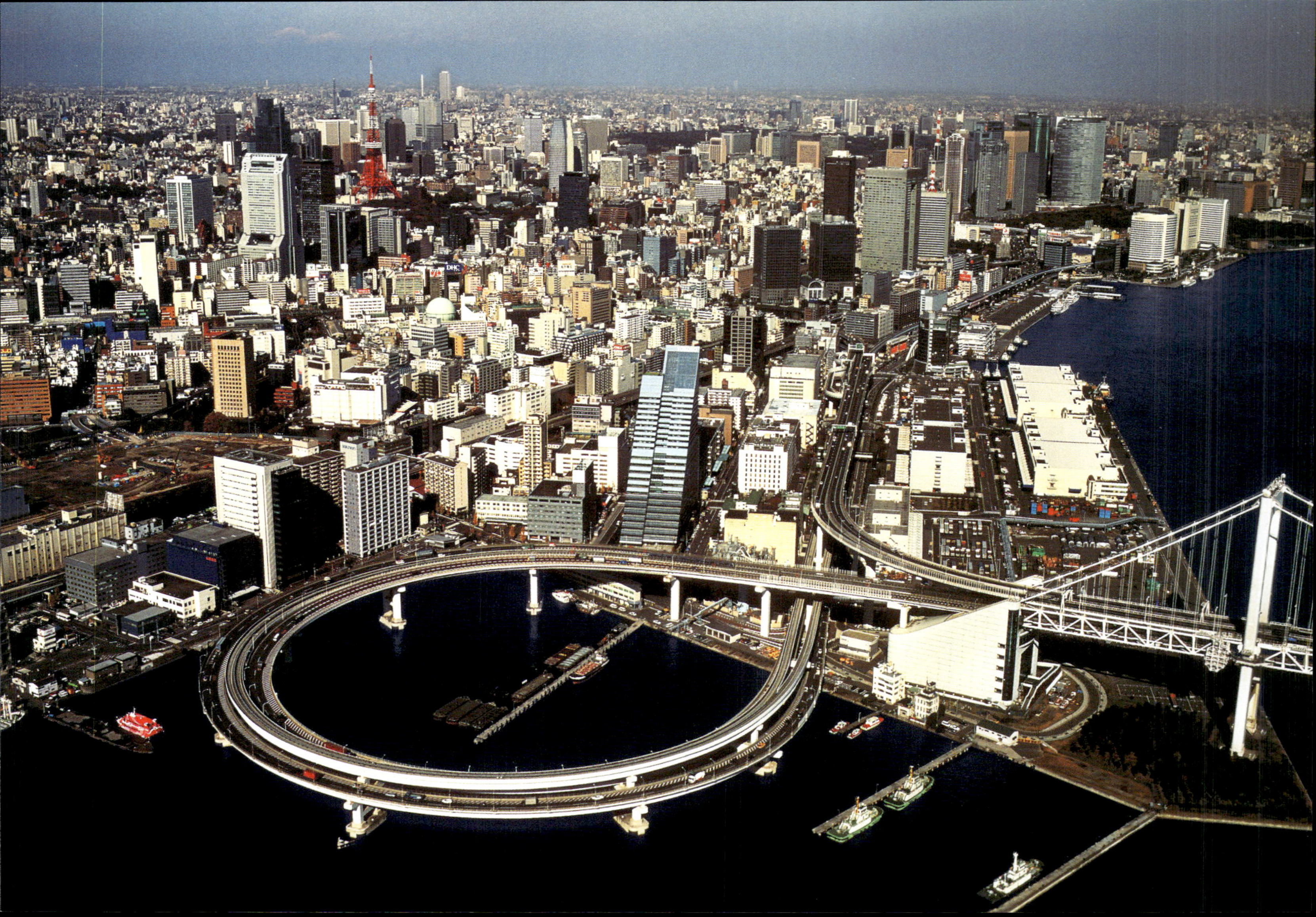

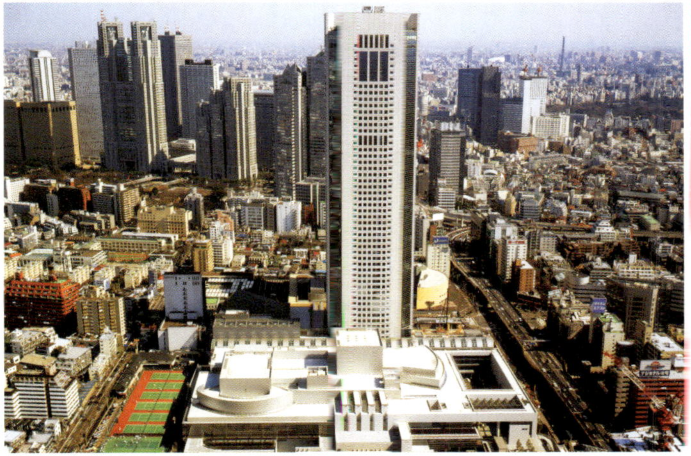

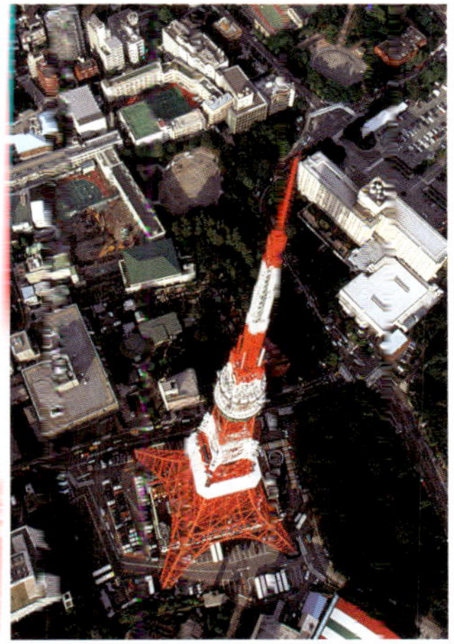

522

The two road levels on Rainbow Bridge, 299 feet long, flow into a circular ramp over Tokyo Bay.

523 left

The Shinjuku neighborhood is the most advanced of Tokyo's 23 districts.

523 right

Paris in Tokyo? Not exactly: Tokyo Tower is 1,093 feet tall, or three more than the famous original.

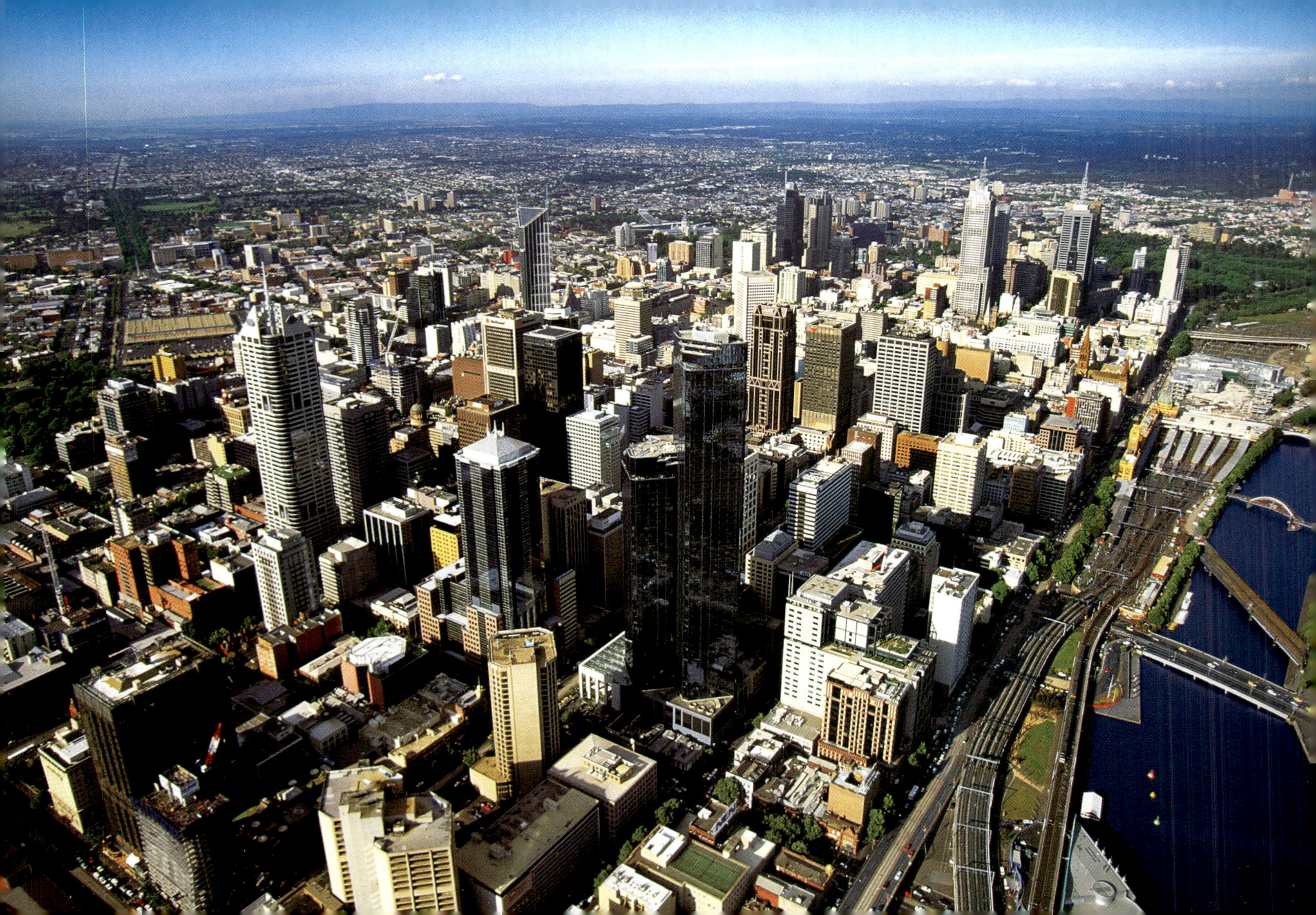

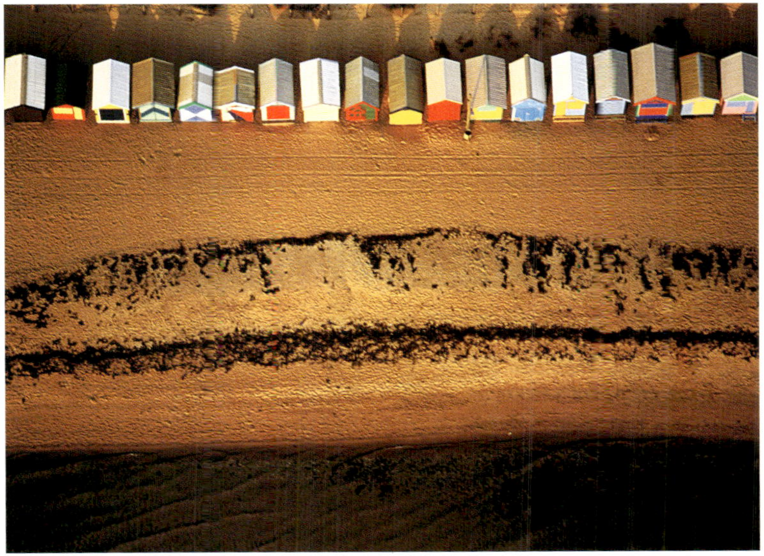

524

Downtown Melbourne, in Australia, boasts six skyscrapers over 500 feet tall, and this view includes them all. The nearest one, on the left, is Bourke Tower, 735 feet tall.

525

The opposite of the impressive giants of downtown, low beach cabins line the seashore on the outskirts of Melbourne.

Sydney

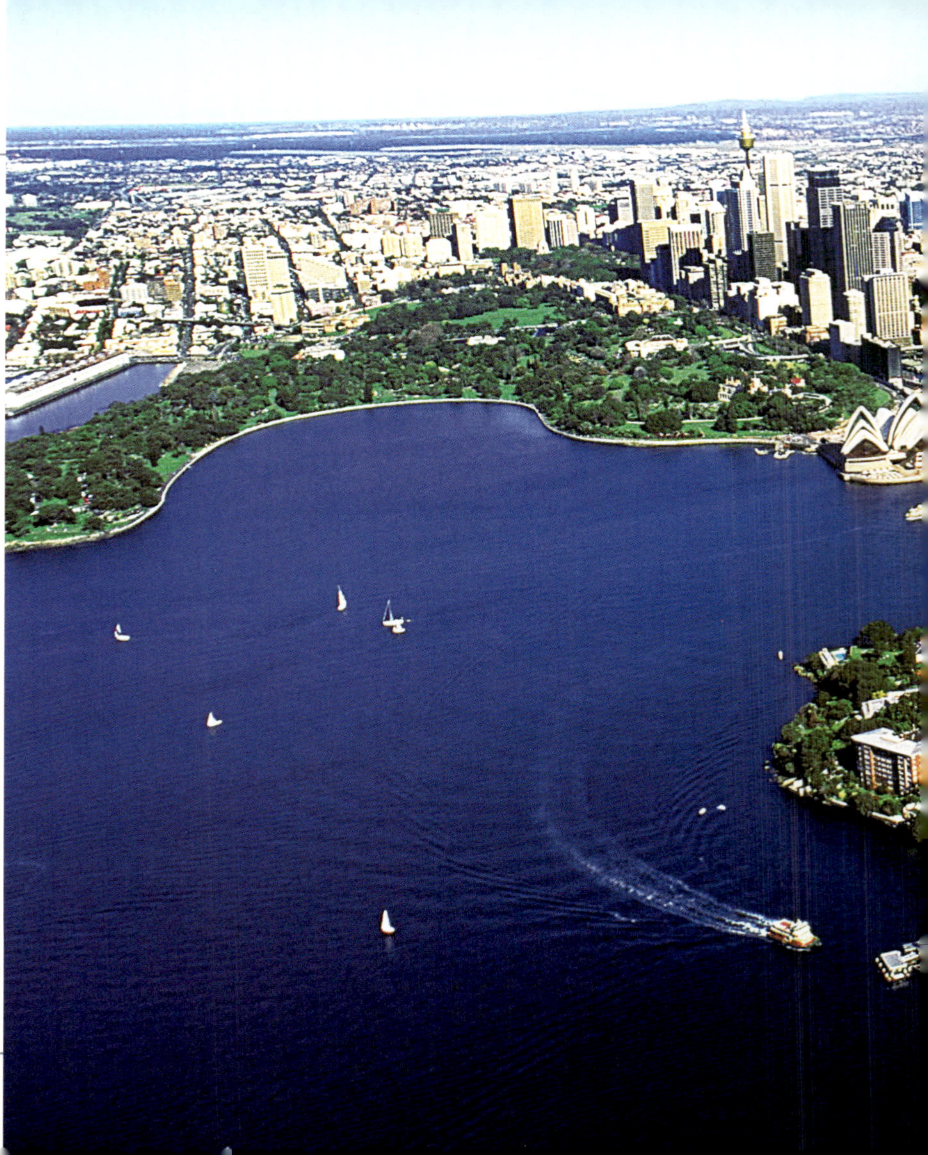

526-527

Sydney Harbour Bridge is a spectacular bridge crossing all of Sydney Bay. Sydney, the biggest city in Australia, along with Melbourne and Brisbane contain 50 percent of the continent's population.

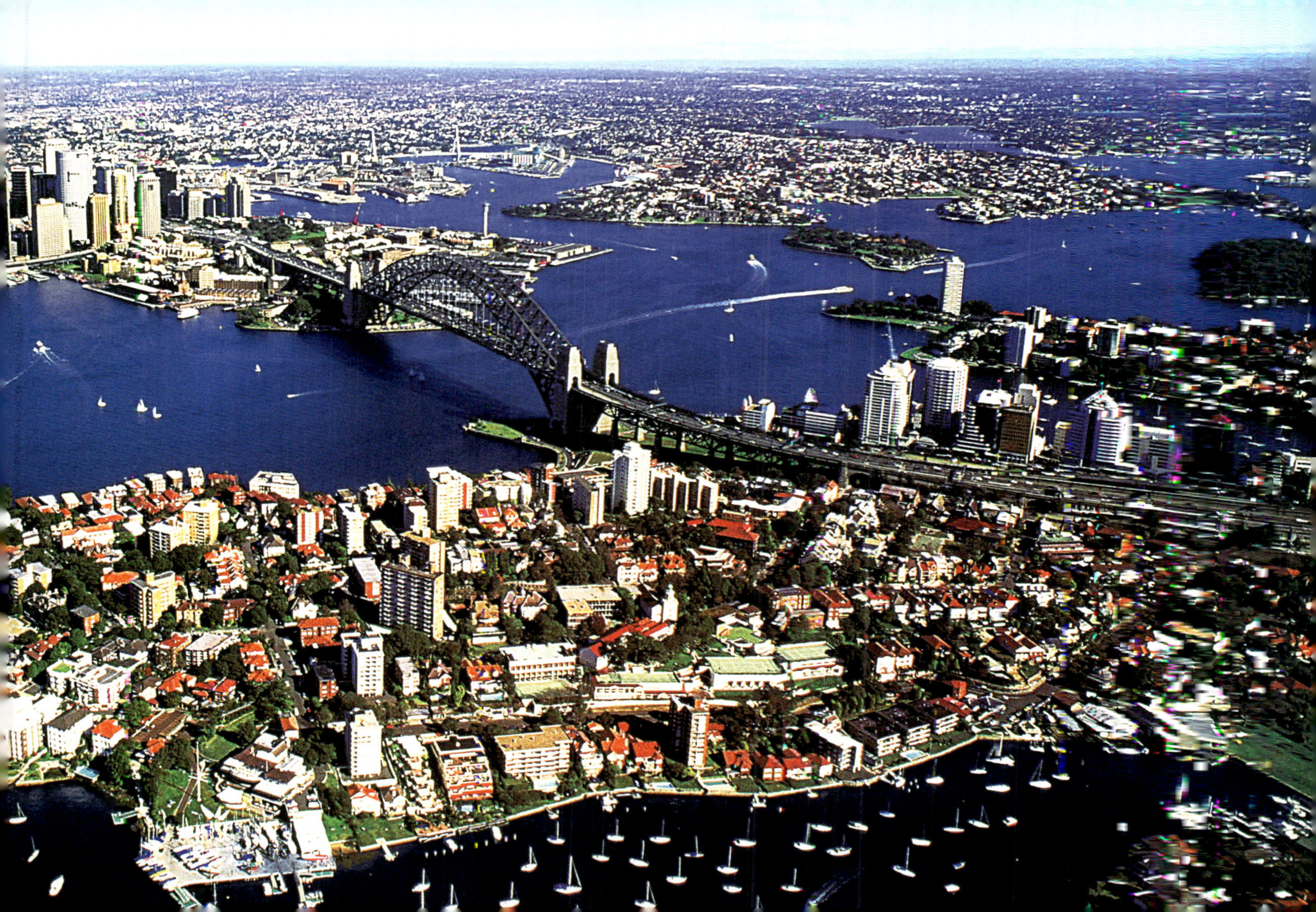

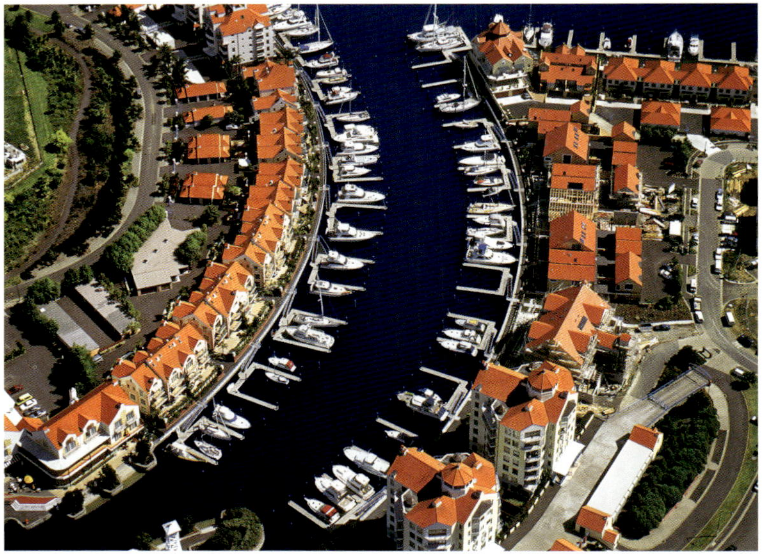

528
The red roofs of Gulf Harbour Marina, not far from the center of Auckland, the capital of New Zealand, trace a curve along the canal linking the port to the ocean.

529
Auckland may be more "contained" than other capitals, but nonetheless its Sky Tower, seen on the right, towers over it from a respectable 1,044-foot high.

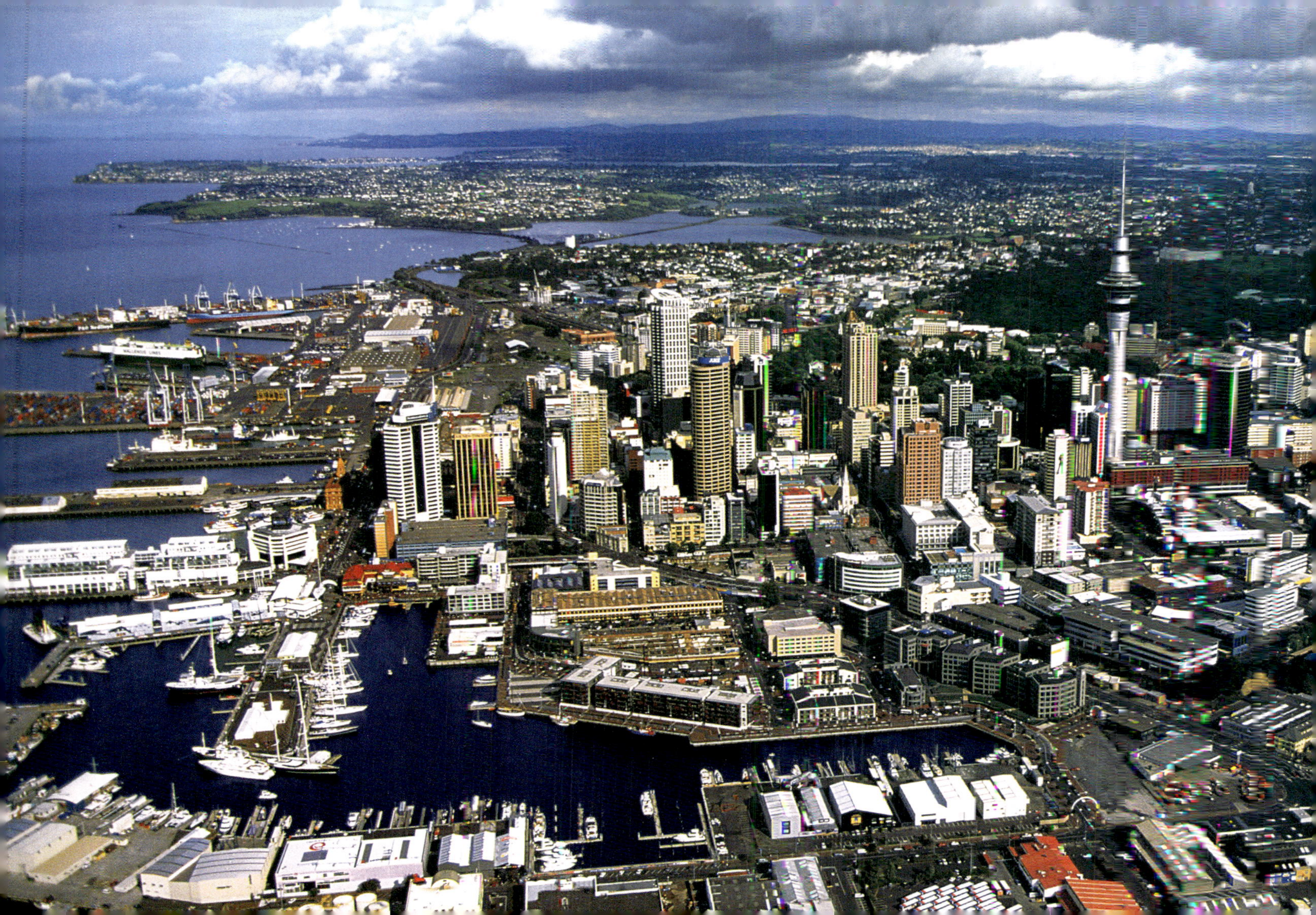

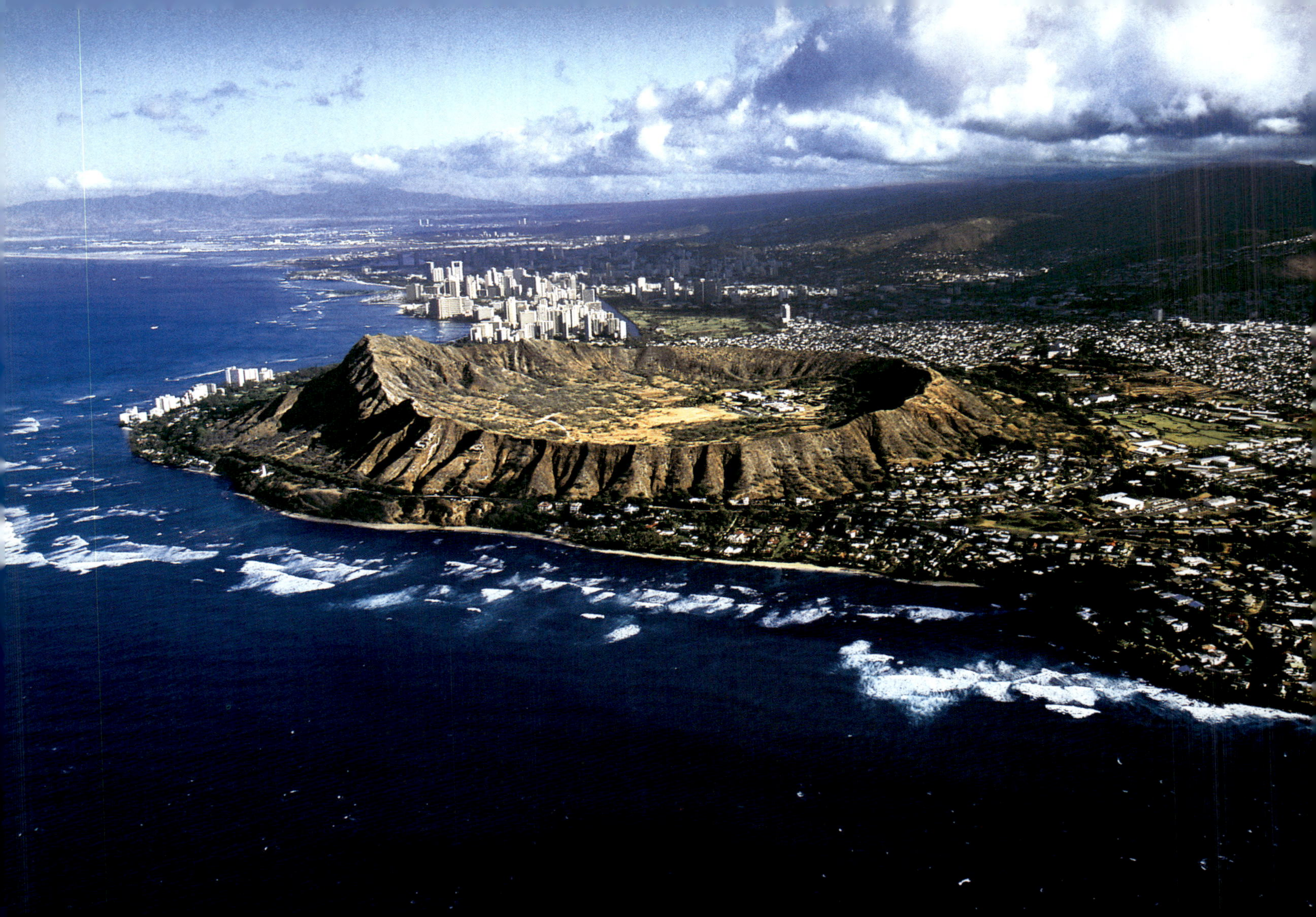

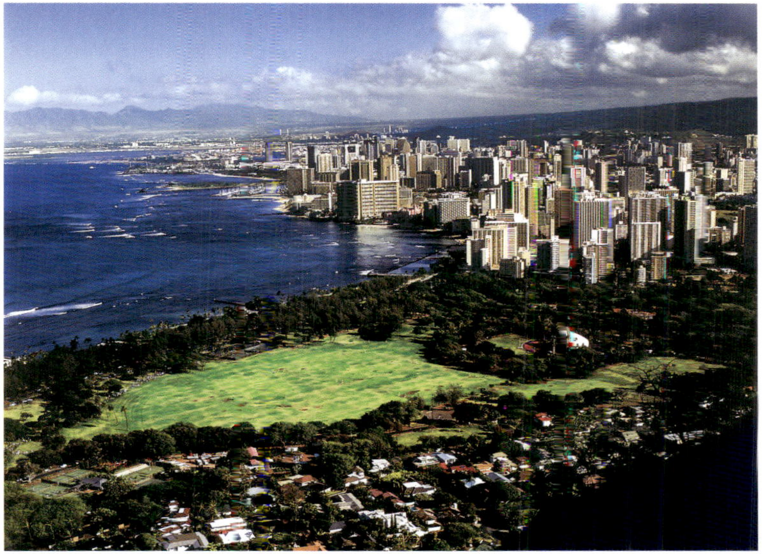

530

The panorama of Honolulu, the capital of the state of Hawaii, is immediately characterized by the magnificent "bowl" of Diamond Head Crater, a perfect circle 755 feet high.

531

Big golf courses mark the city limits of Honolulu, whose skyscrapers are located along the ocean, lining Waikiki Beach.

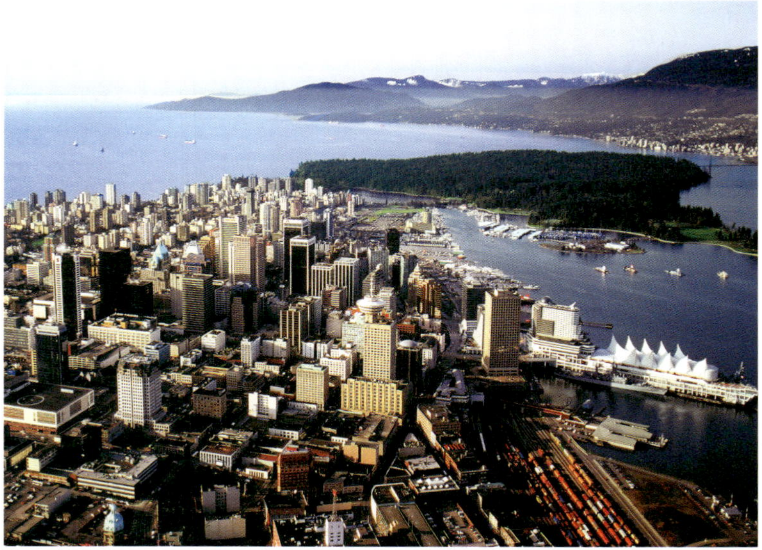

532 and 533

Vancouver, the capital of British Columbia in Canada, enjoys a magnificent position on a series of bays. In the photo on the left, the series of white "sails" contains a futuristic 3D cinema. Besides being a sophisticated residential city, it is a true garden-city, as demonstrated by the vast areas of trees seen within the view on the right, taken from the west.

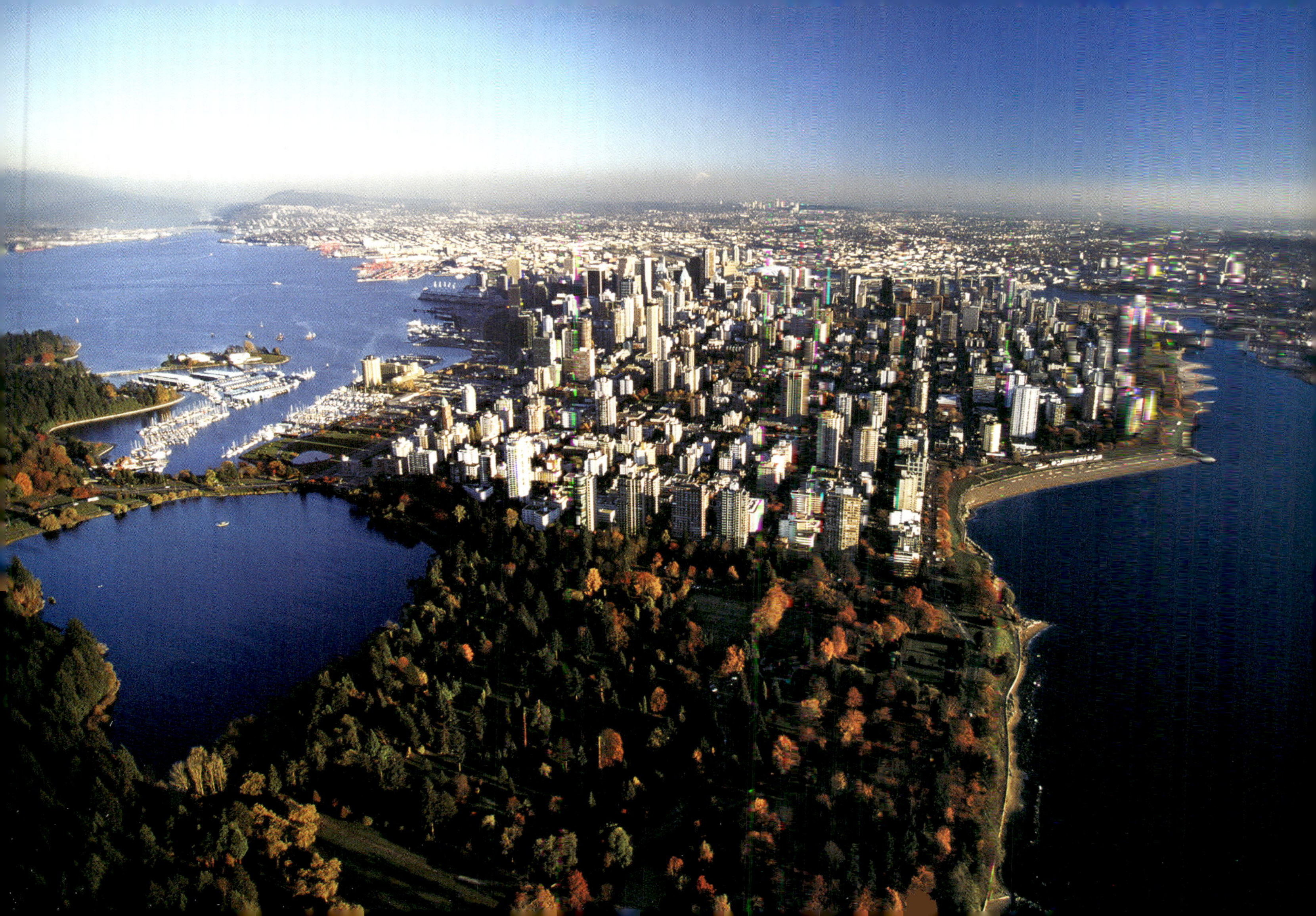

Montreal

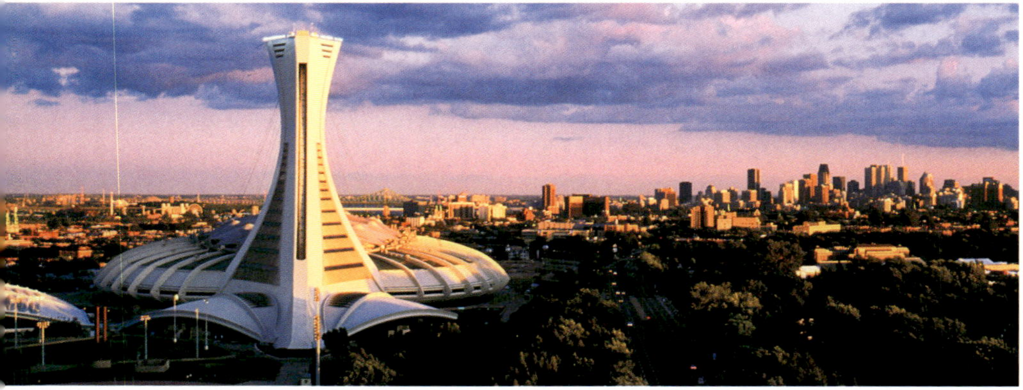

534
Truly oriented towards the future, the Biodome in Montreal, Canada, was originally built as an Olympic cycling area and later became an environmental museum: under the amazing roof, some of the most gorgeous ecosystems of the Americas have been recreated.

535
Much has changed in the attractive Vieux Port quarter of Montreal, since a gentrification program made it into an area dedicated to entertainment and a highly desirable residential neighborhood.

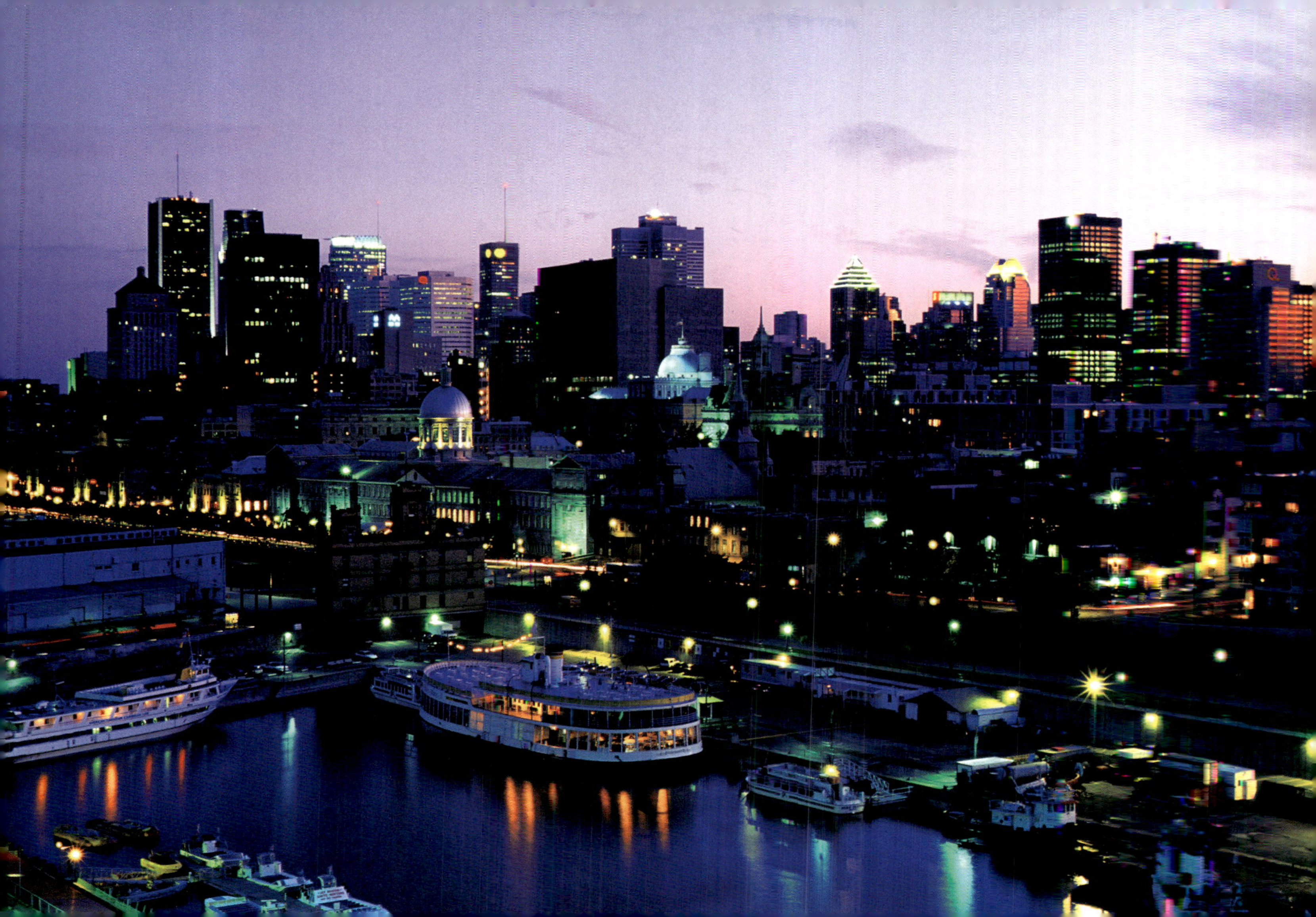

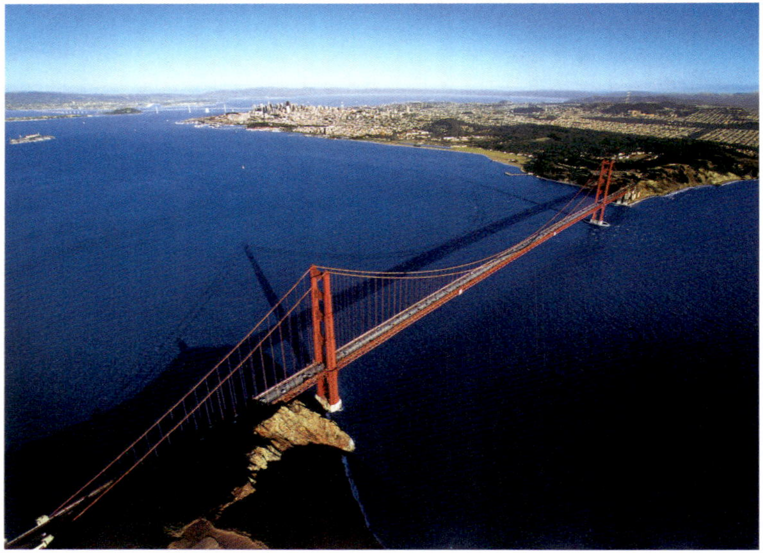

536
The San Francisco Bay can be a truly breathtaking sight, above all when the fog is not covering the daring 8,980-foot long Golden Gate Bridge, completed in 1937.

537
The Transamerica Pyramid, 853 feet tall, marks the true center of San Francisco. In the background, a pylon of the Bay Bridge can be seen.

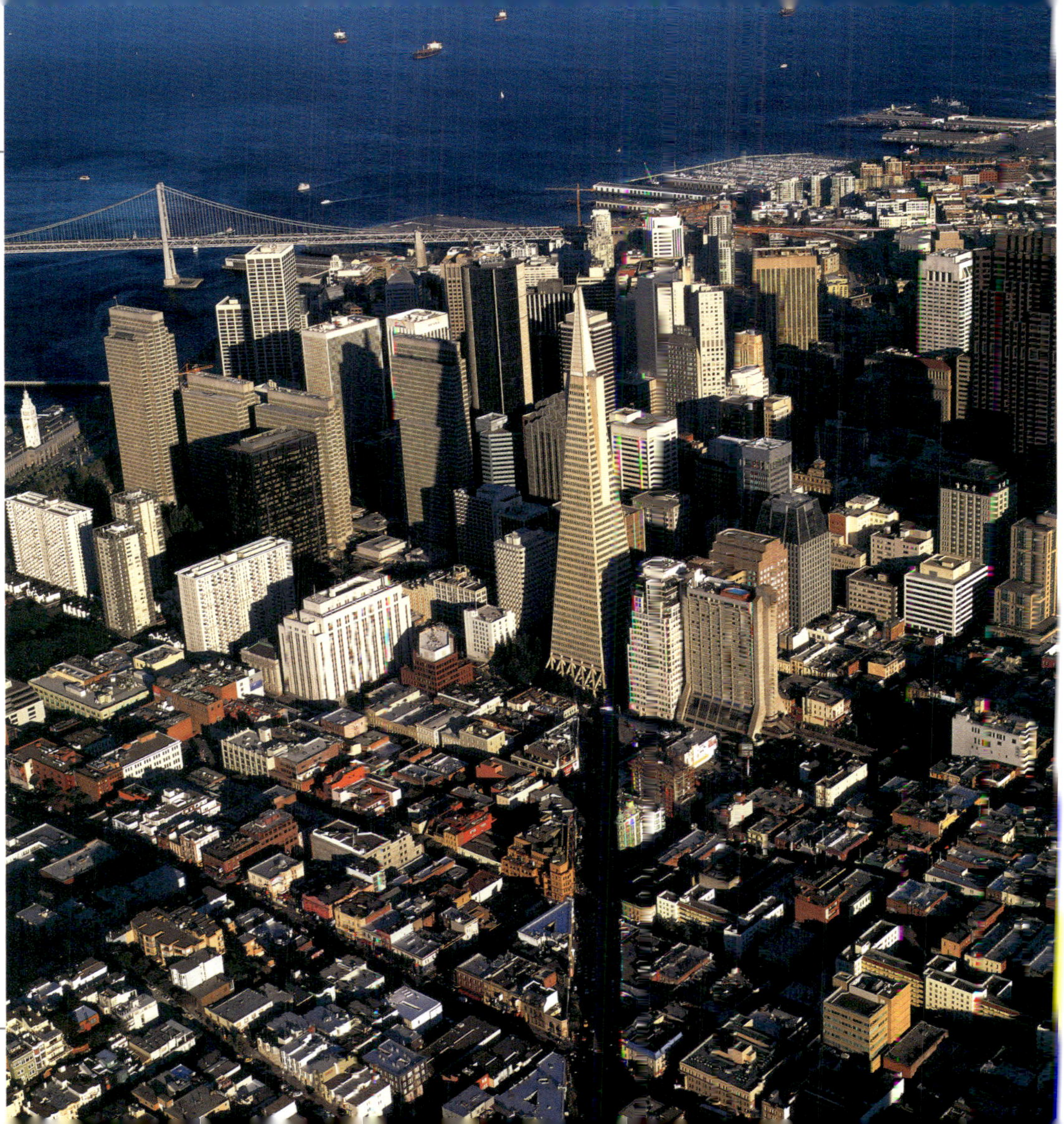

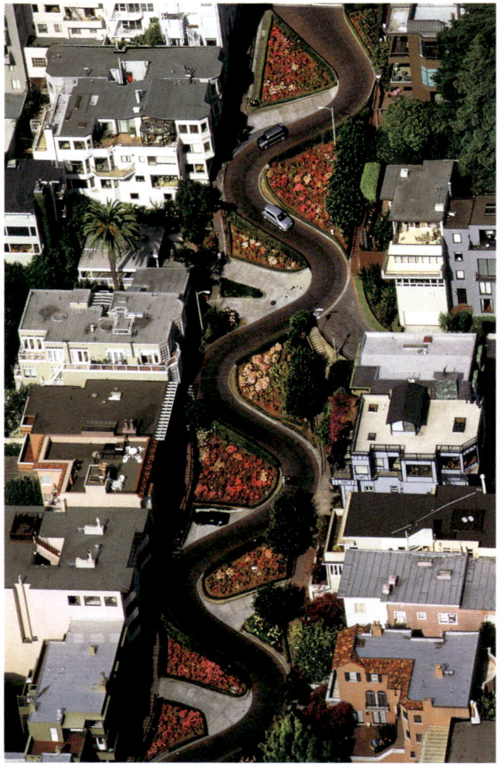

538
San Francisco is unique: in no other city in the world do the streets wind like Lombard Street does, in the Russian Hill neighborhood.

539
The elegant Pavilion of the Palace of Fine Arts in San Francisco holds the Exploratorium, dedicated to the spread of applied sciences and astronomy.

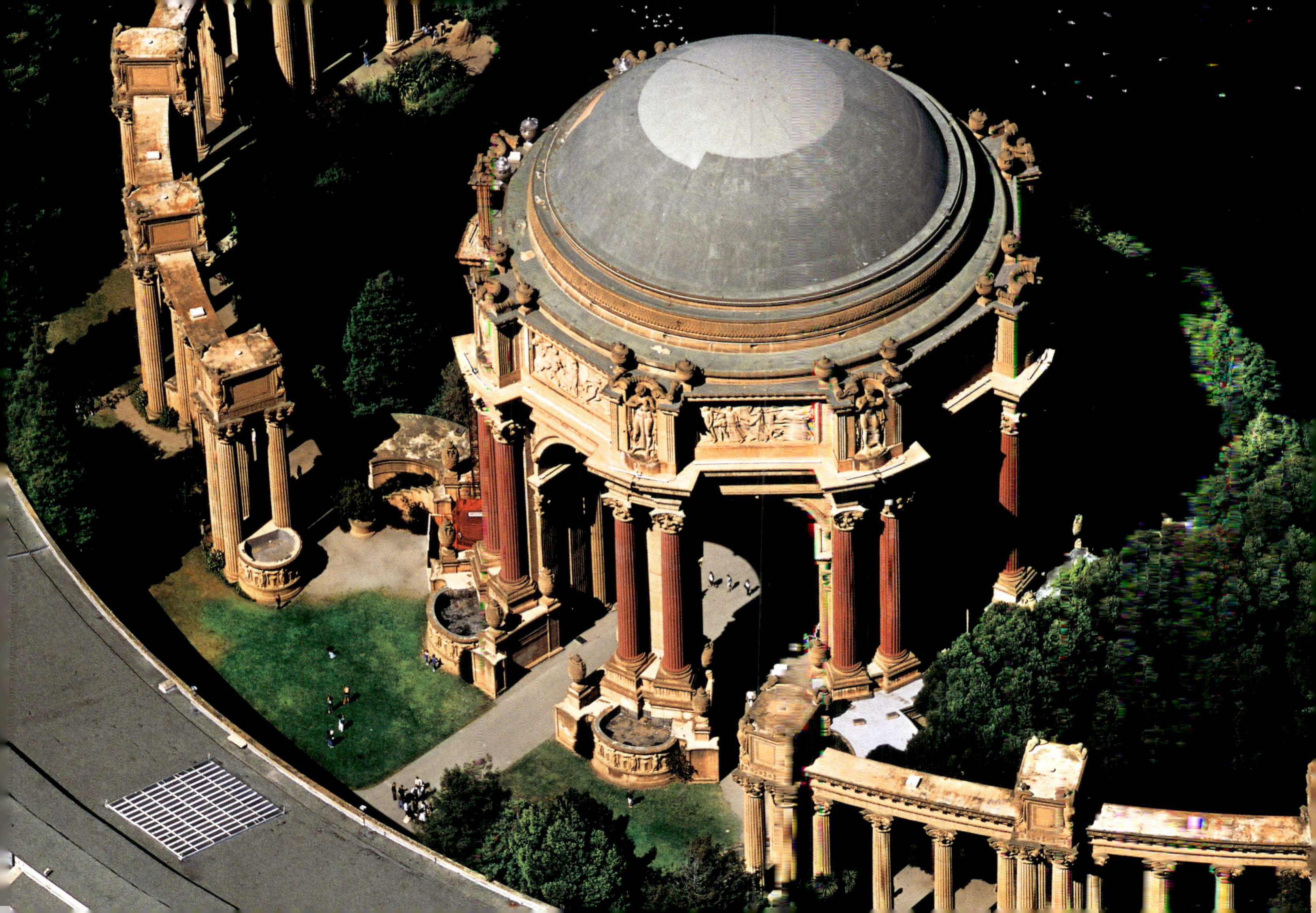

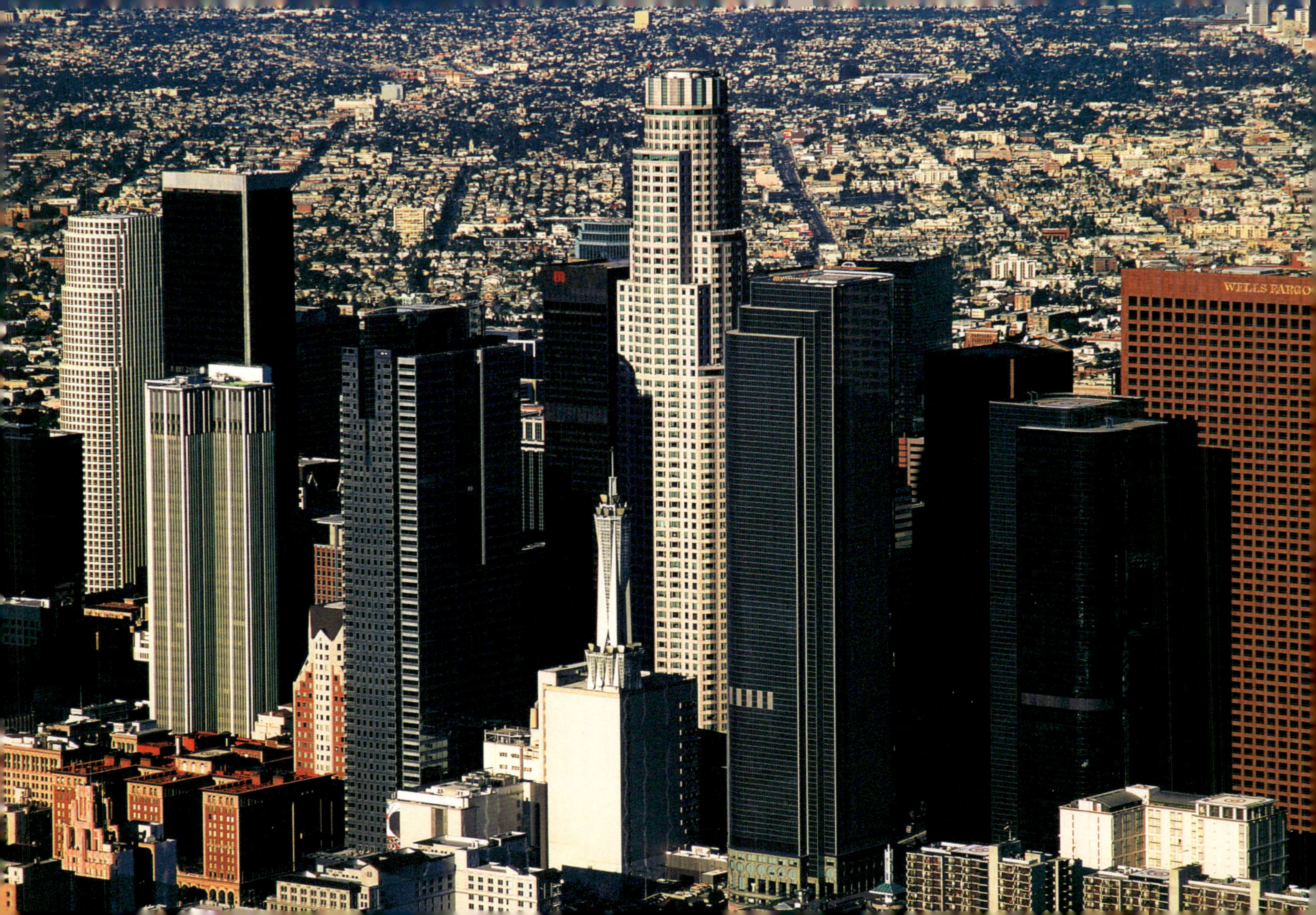
WELLS FARGO

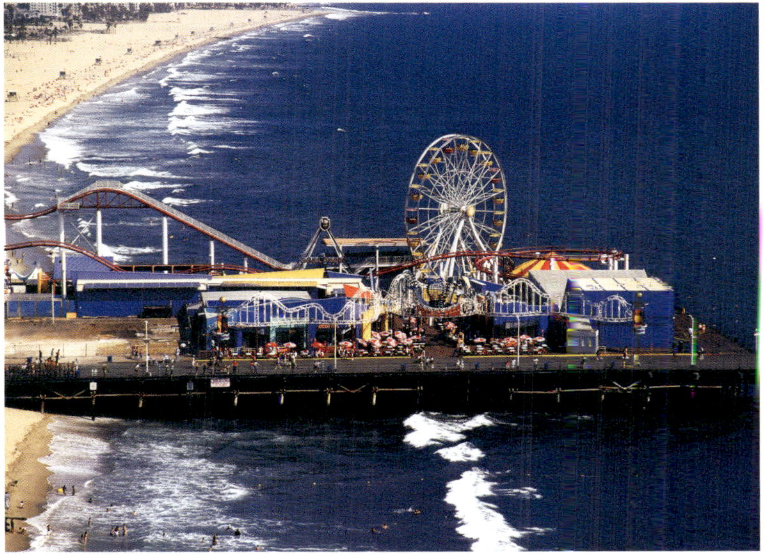

540

Downtown Los Angeles, California: an octopus-like city, this metropolis grown out of a Spanish mission culminates in the US Bank Tower, in the middle of the photo, 1,017 feet tall.

541

The atmosphere is completely different in Santa Monica Pacific Park with its Ferris Wheel from days of yore and a roller coaster that is not at all enormous.

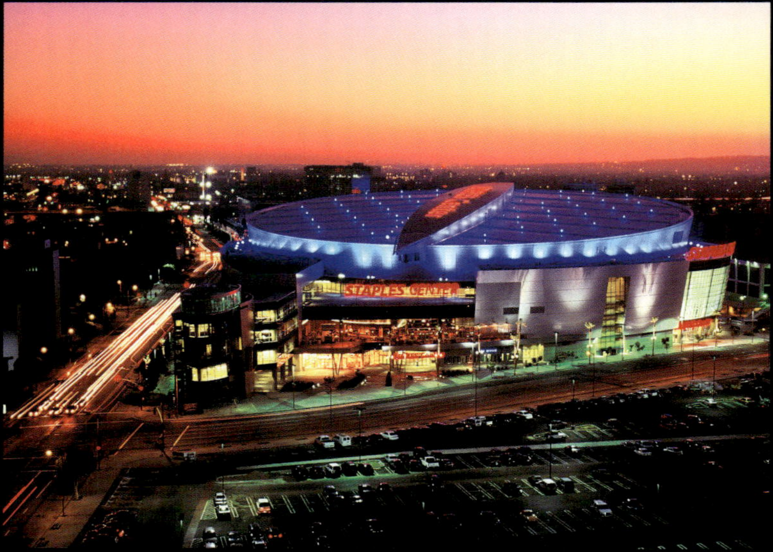

542
At dusk, the stadium of the Los Angeles Lakers and Kings, or the Staples Center, transforms into a sort of attractively-colored alien space ship. The modern structure can hold up to 19,000 spectators.

543
Los Angeles lights up as night falls. Over 17,000,000 inhabitants live in this boundless city, which extends over 60 miles down the California coast.

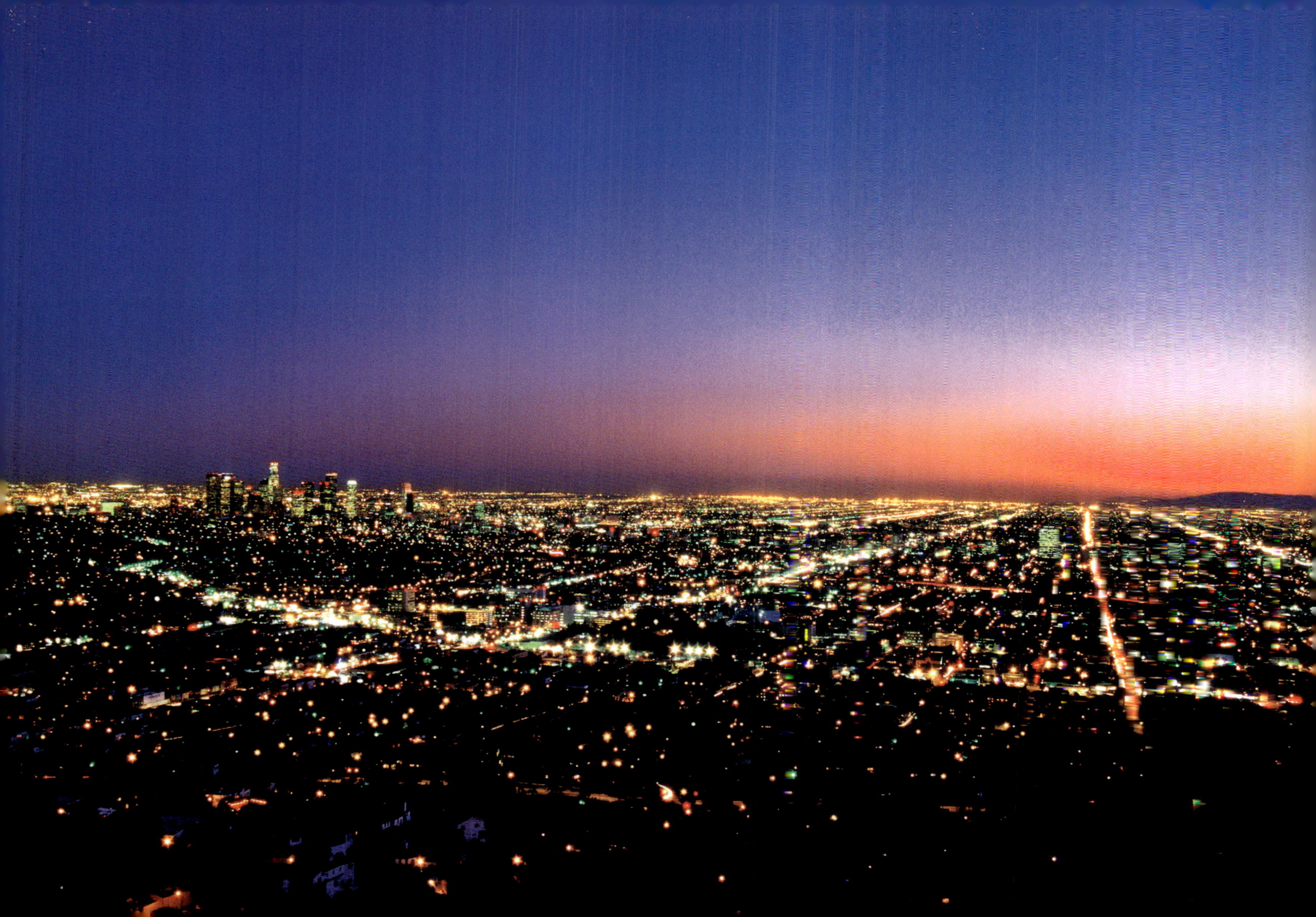

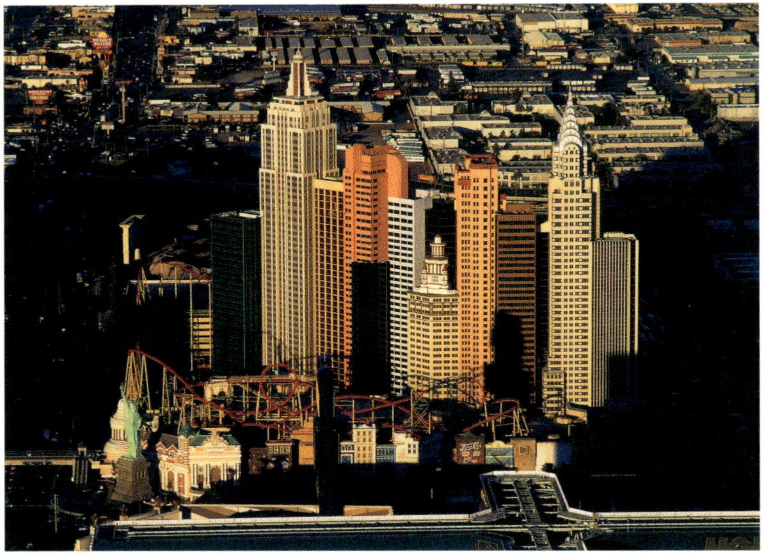

544

Las Vegas, Nevada, "plays" with everything: here there is even Manhattan, though on a reduced scale, with a big Empire State Building (obviously the tallest of the group) and even the Statue of Liberty.

545

This is the kingdom of light. The unique fact is that the darkness beyond the limits of Las Vegas conceals nothing, given that the city stands in the desert.

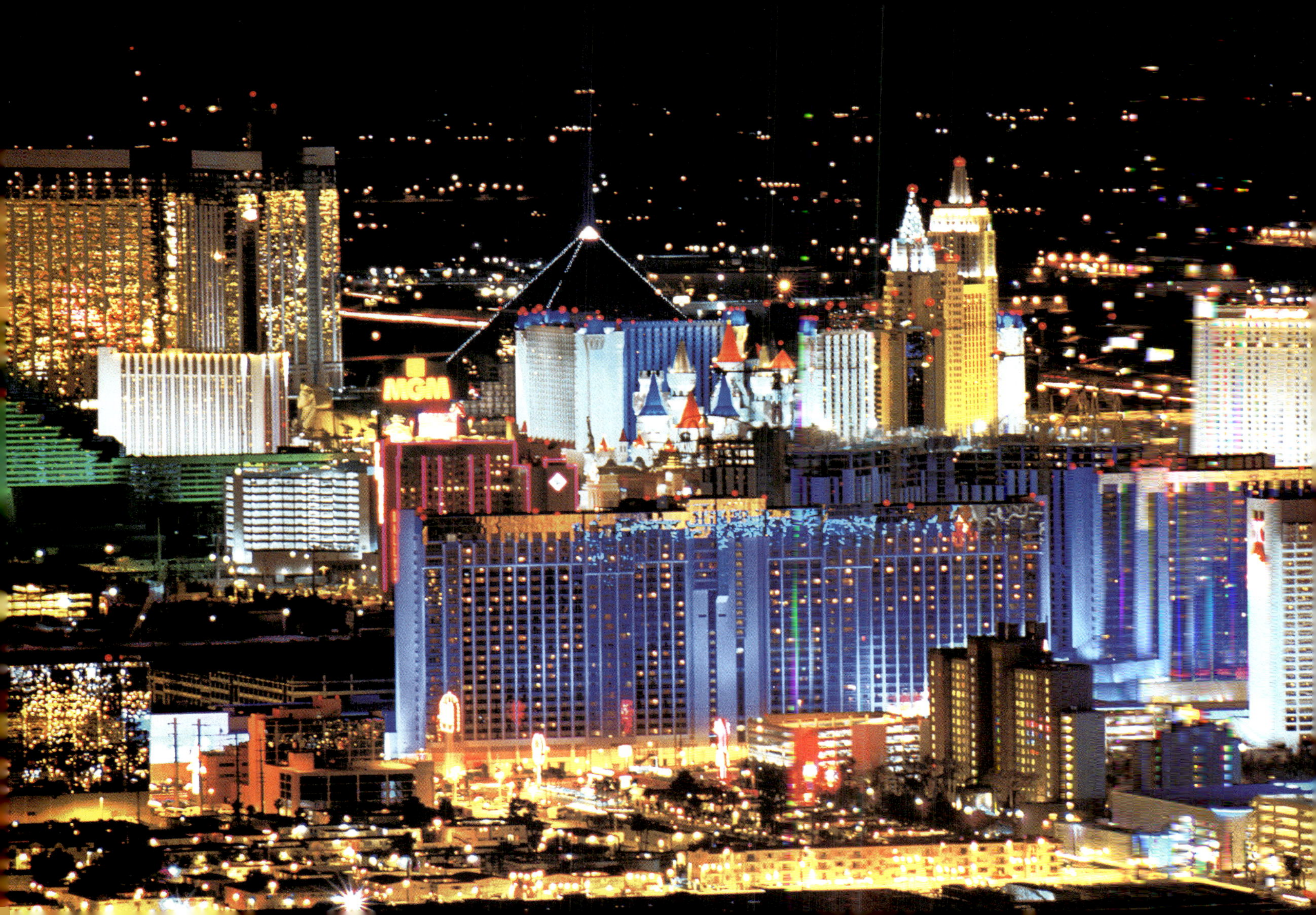
MGM

Chicago

546

The John Hancock Center (1,476 feet including its antennas) towers over the shores of Lake Michigan in Chicago, Illinois.

547

The Navy Pier in Chicago is framed in the background by the Sears Tower, 1,450 feet tall (left), and the John Hancock Center (right), nicknamed "Big John."

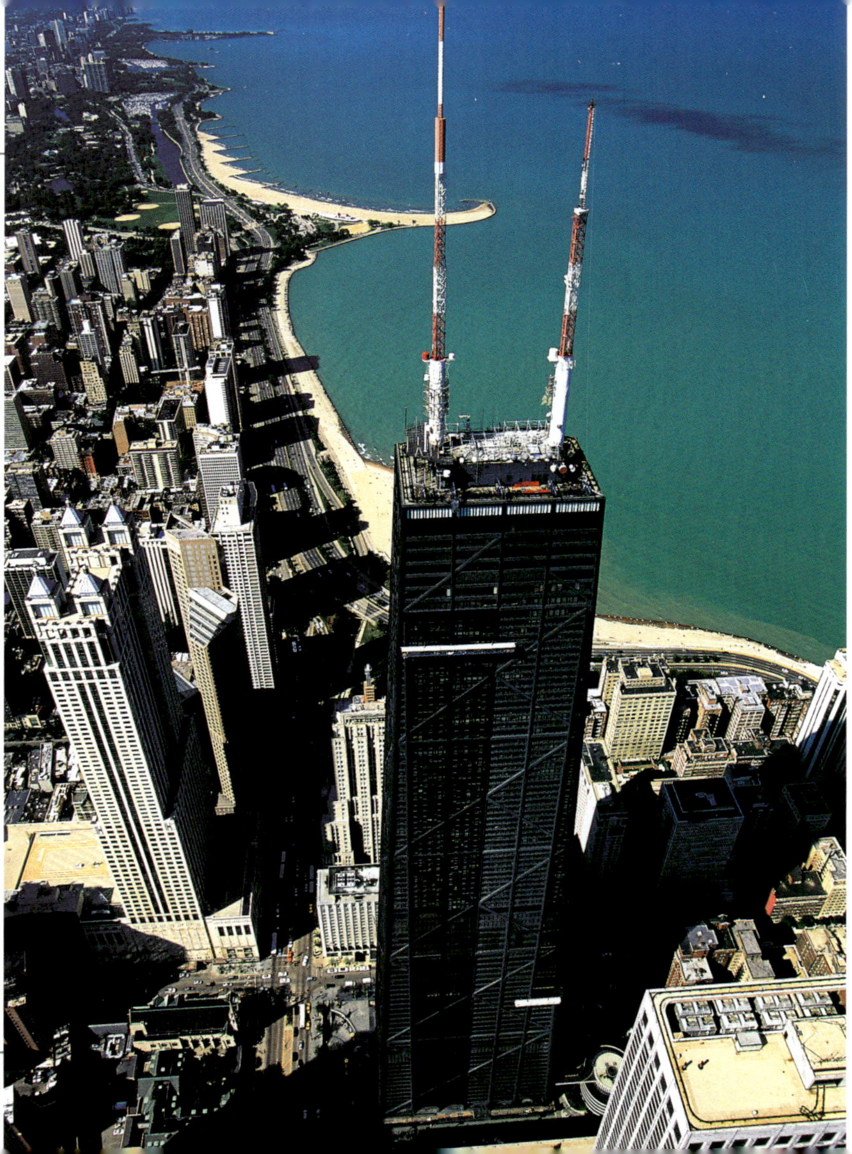

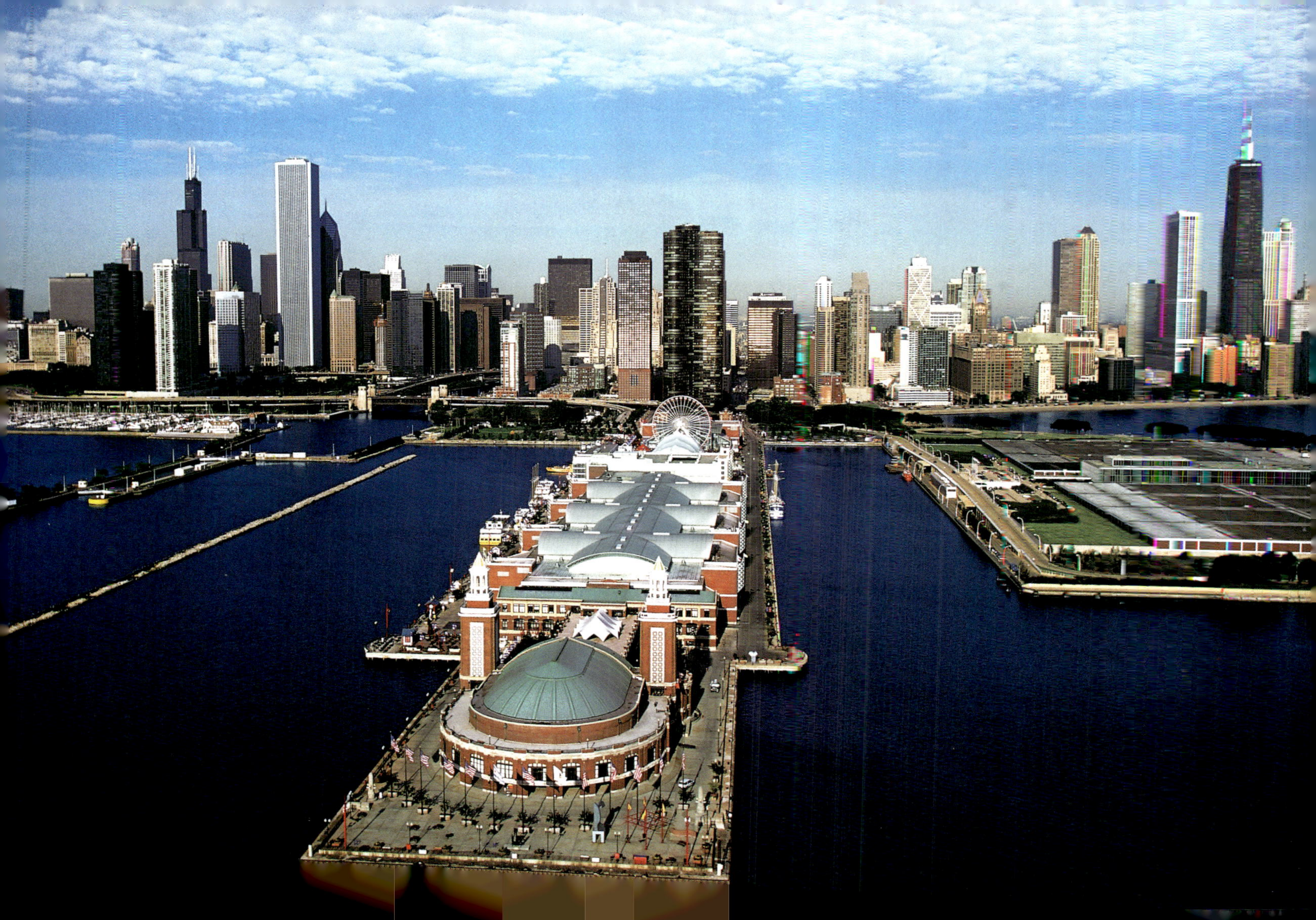

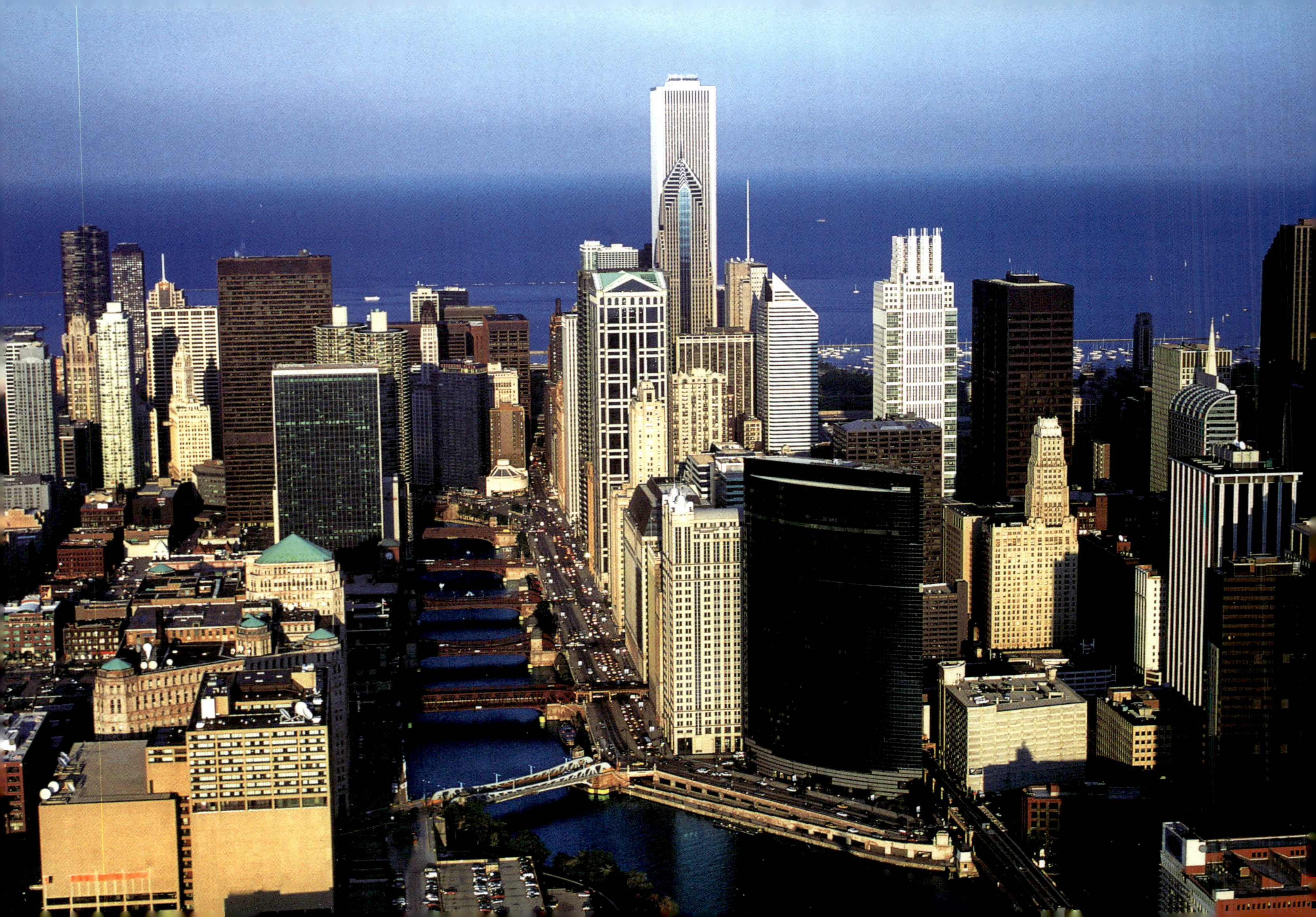

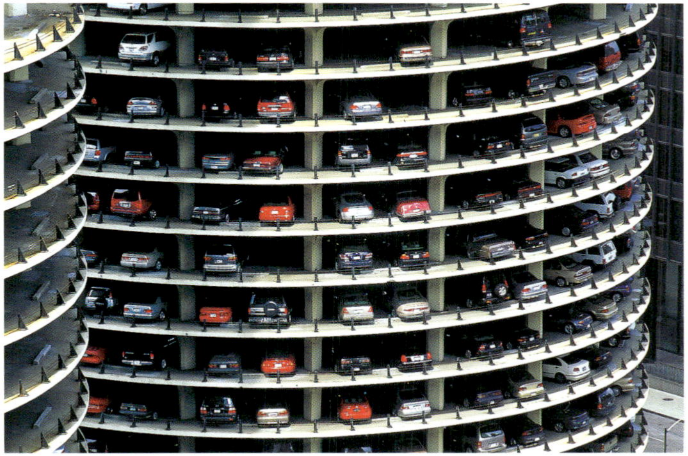

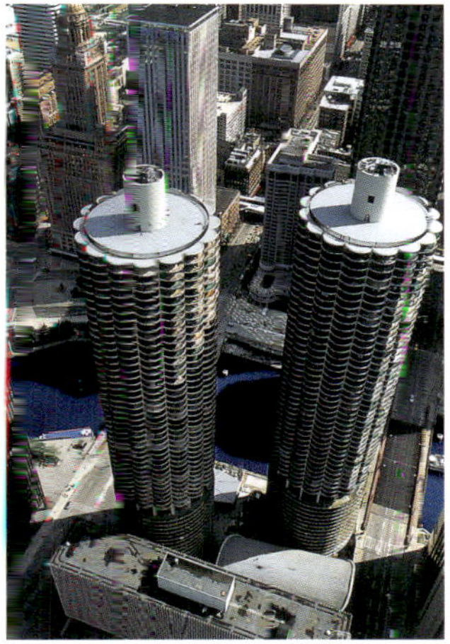

548

The Chicago River and its horizontally pivoted bridges are a feature of the Chicago landscape.

549

The two cylinders of the Marina City Complex have been nicknamed the *Twin Corncobs*; their lower levels have partially solved the ever growing parking problem in Chicago.

Washington DC

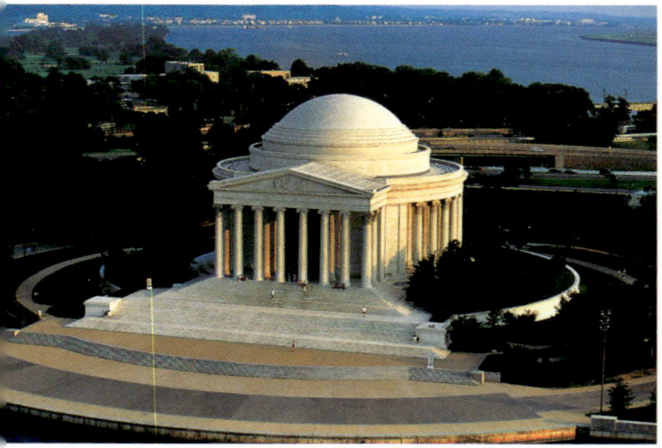

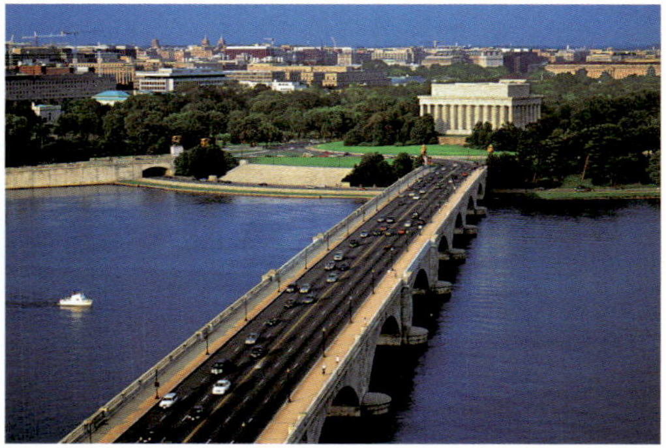

550

Washington, D.C., the capital of the United States, is the place where the country's historical memory is preserved. Monuments featuring classic forms honor the most important presidents, like Thomas Jefferson, whose memorial (left) was inspired by the Pantheon in Rome, and Abraham Lincoln, whose monument (right) imitates a Doric temple.

551

The heart of the nation: the Washington Monument, a 558-foot tall obelisk, stands in line with the dome of the Capitol on the left, across the esplanade of the Mall. In the foreground, the Supreme Court (left) and the Senate are visible.

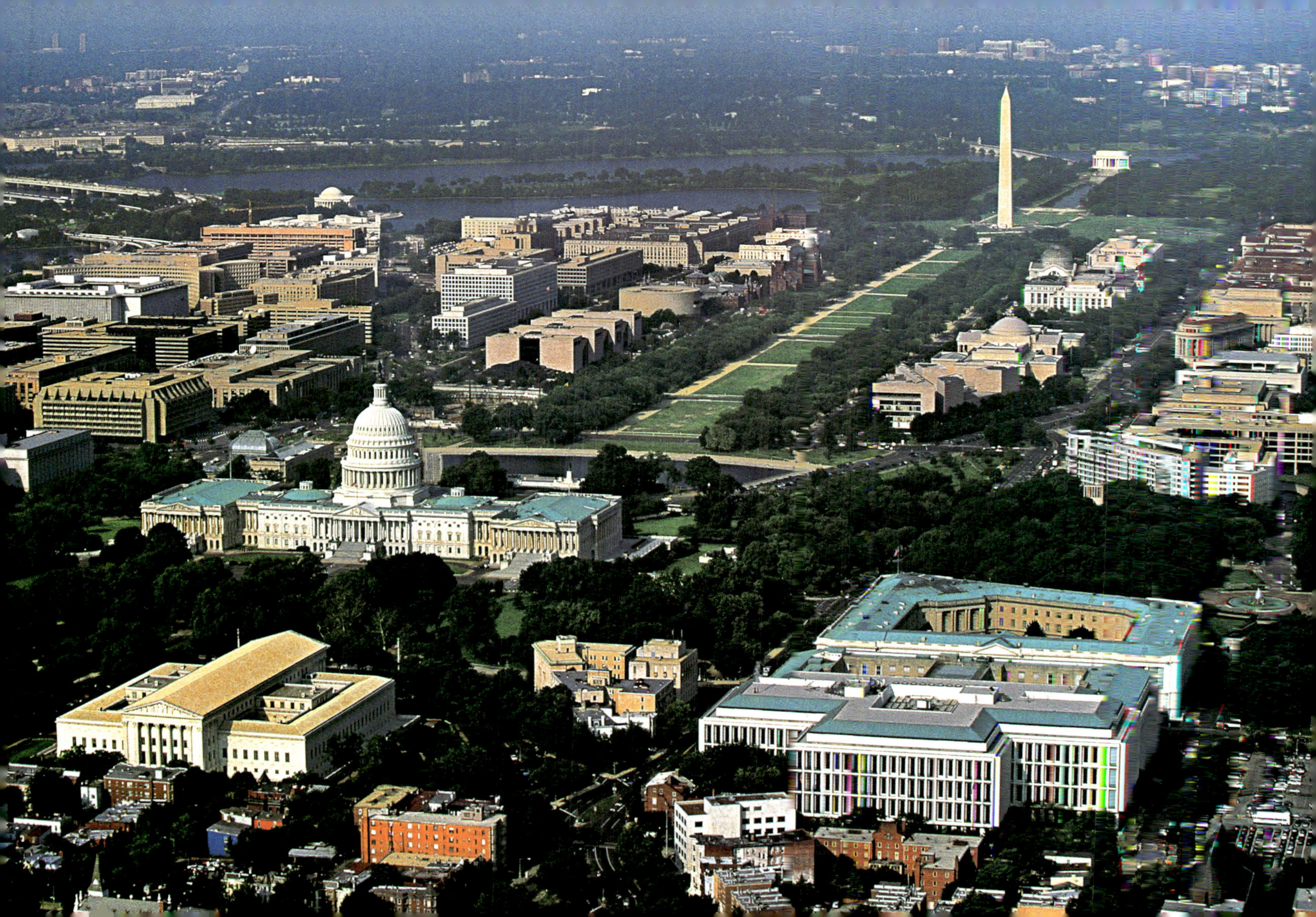

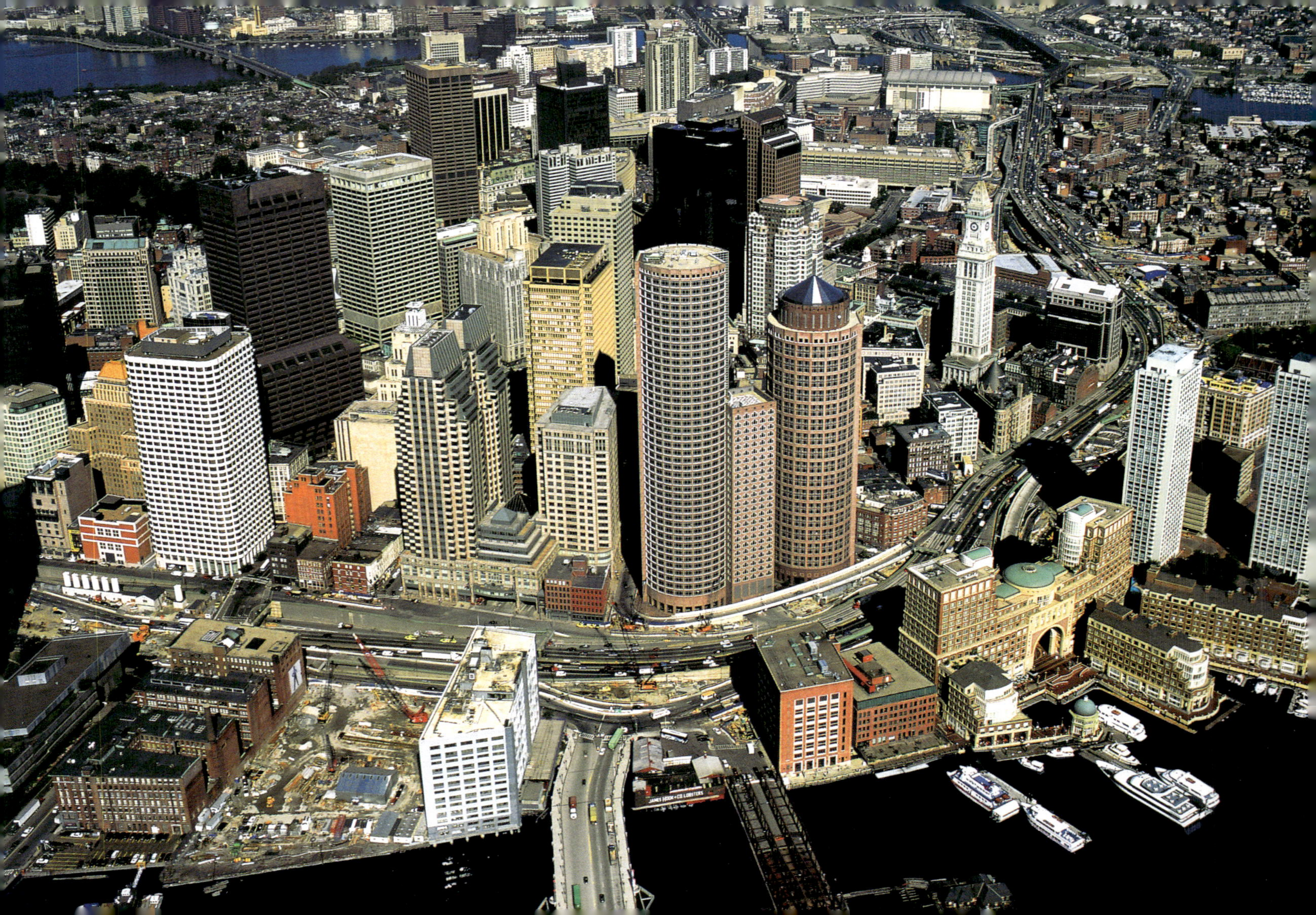

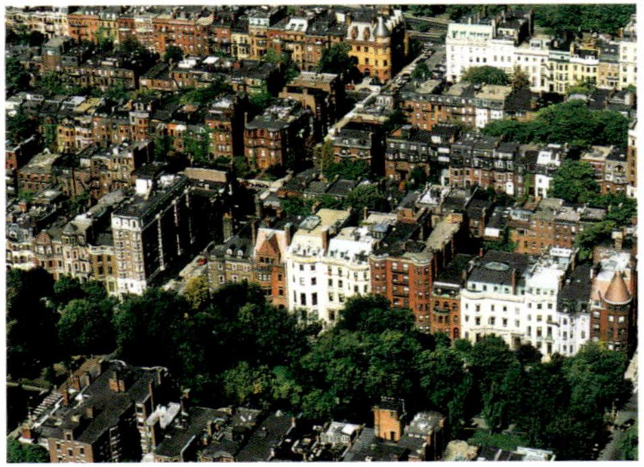

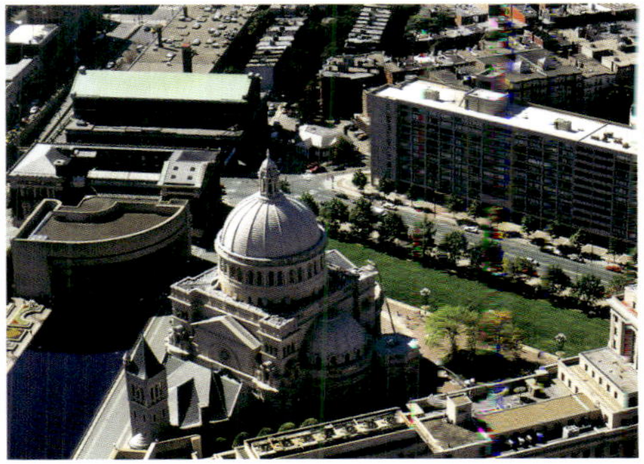

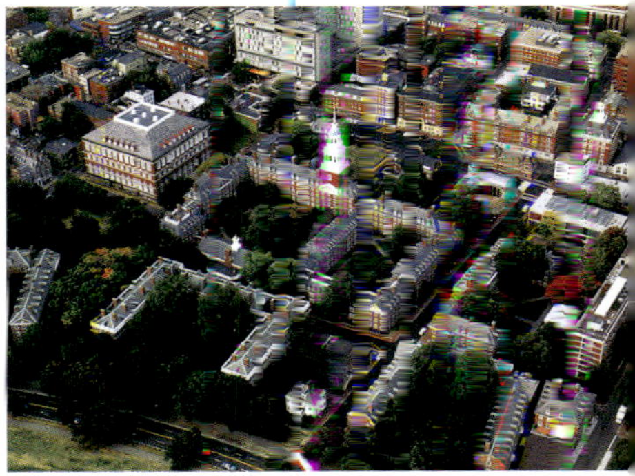

552 and 553 left

Boston, Massachusetts, preserves examples of "period" architecture like the houses of Back Bay alongside the modern buildings of the business district.

553 center and right

Boston's institutions, like the Christian Science Center (in the center, the exuberant architectural style of the Mother Church) and universities like Harvard (on the right, Cambridge, the headquarters of a college like that of the British city of the same name) are steeped in an aura of great prestige.

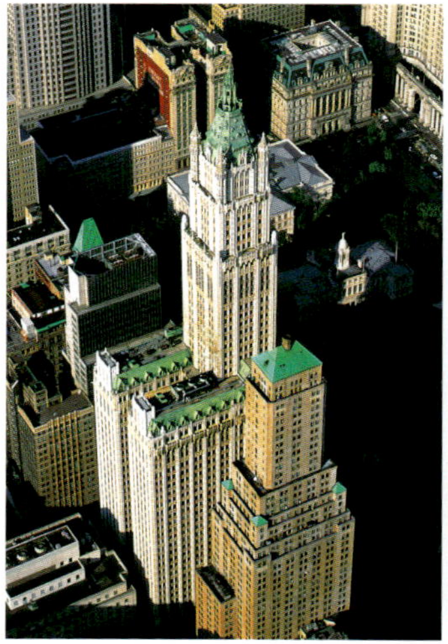

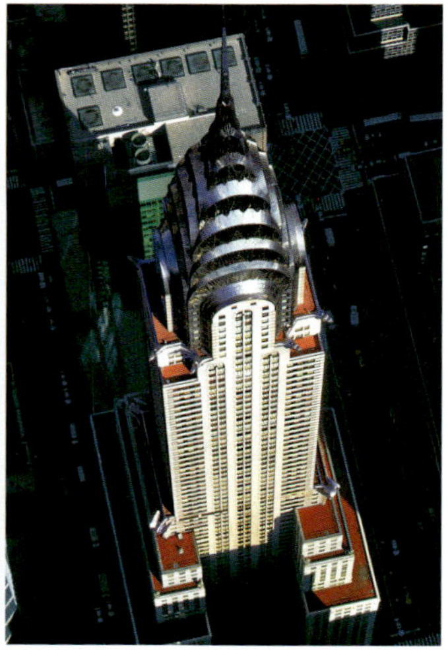

554 left

The Woolworth Building, 791 feet tall, is a triumph of Gothic revival, the same style characterizing some of the most important churches in New York.

554 right

The shiniest spire in Manhattan is definitely that of the Chrysler Building: polished steel sparkles at 1,047 feet in the air.

555

The Hudson River flows into the East River at the southernmost tip of the island of Manhattan: one of the most legendary urban views in the world.

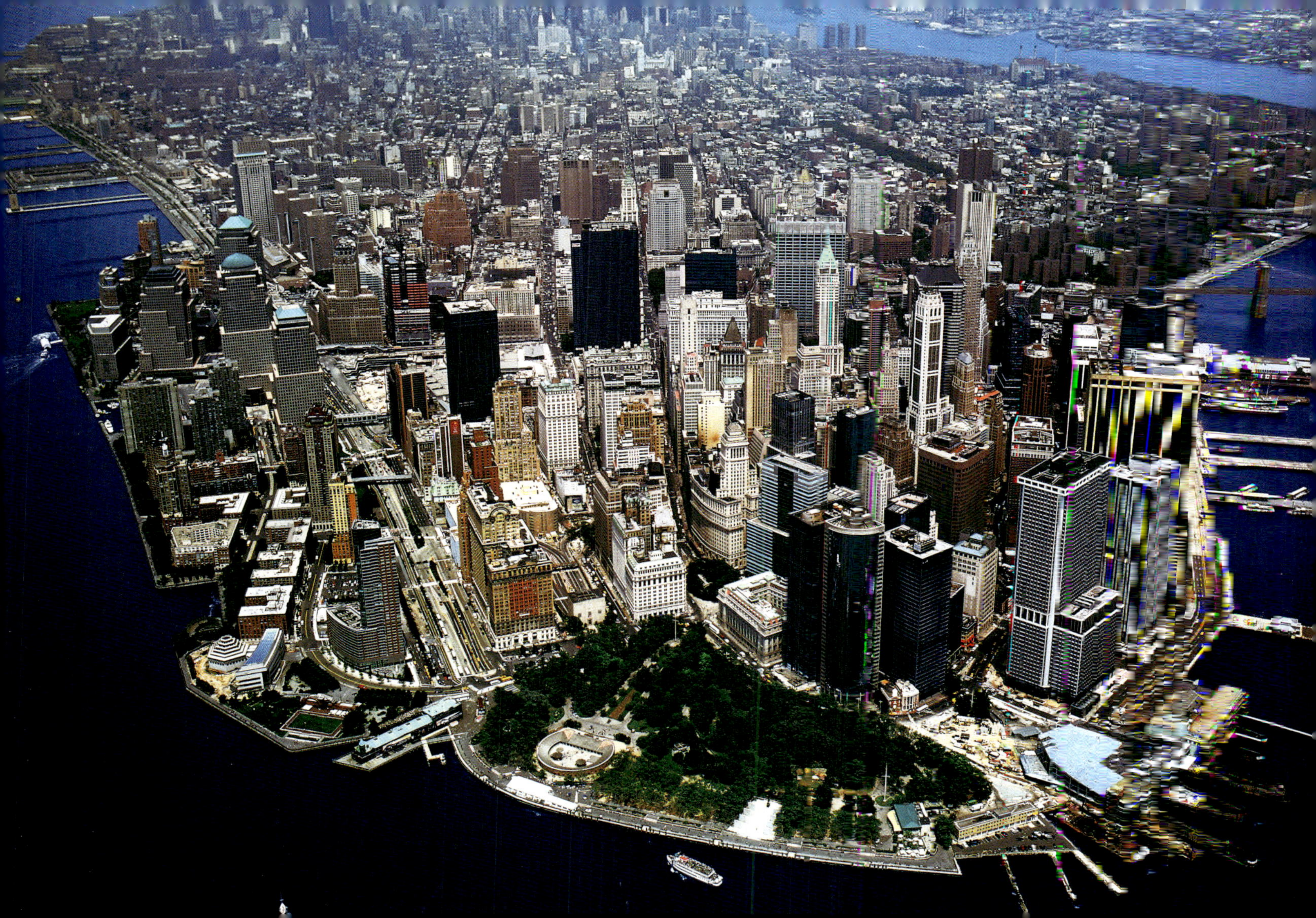

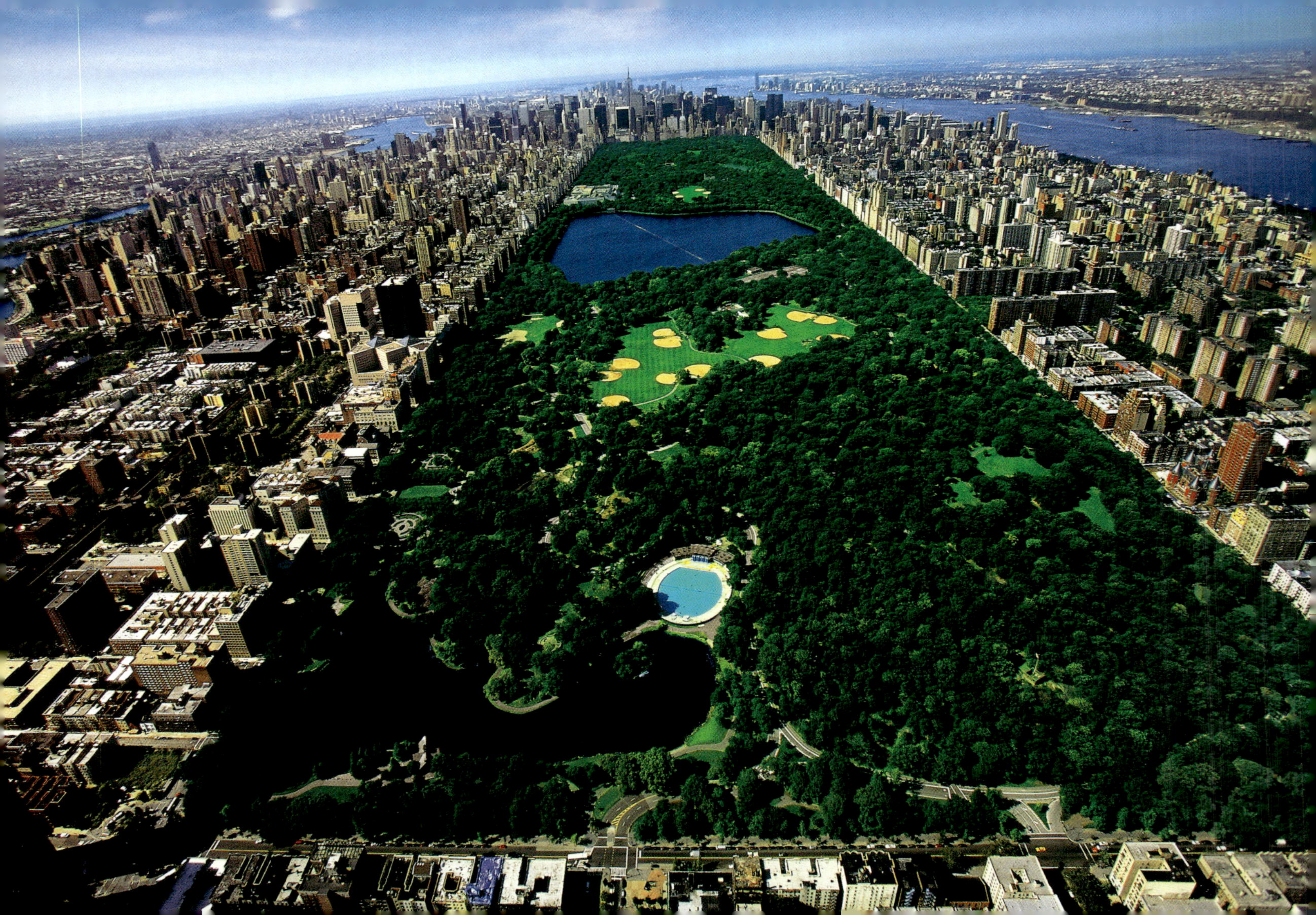

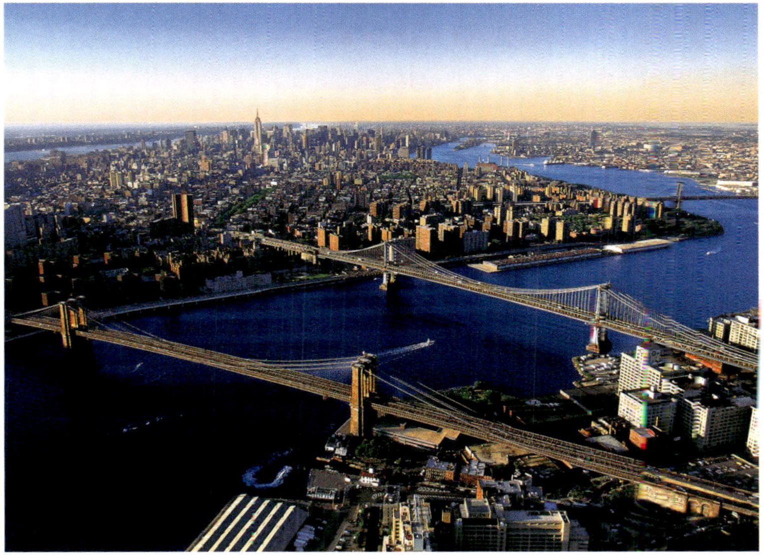

556

Among trees, lakes, ponds, and meadows, the spectacular expanse of Central Park, in New York, opens a sort of "parallel world" right in the middle of Manhattan's endless skyscrapers.

557

Two more New York legends: Brooklyn Bridge, on the left, and Manhattan Bridge ford the East River, linking the two respectively named boroughs.

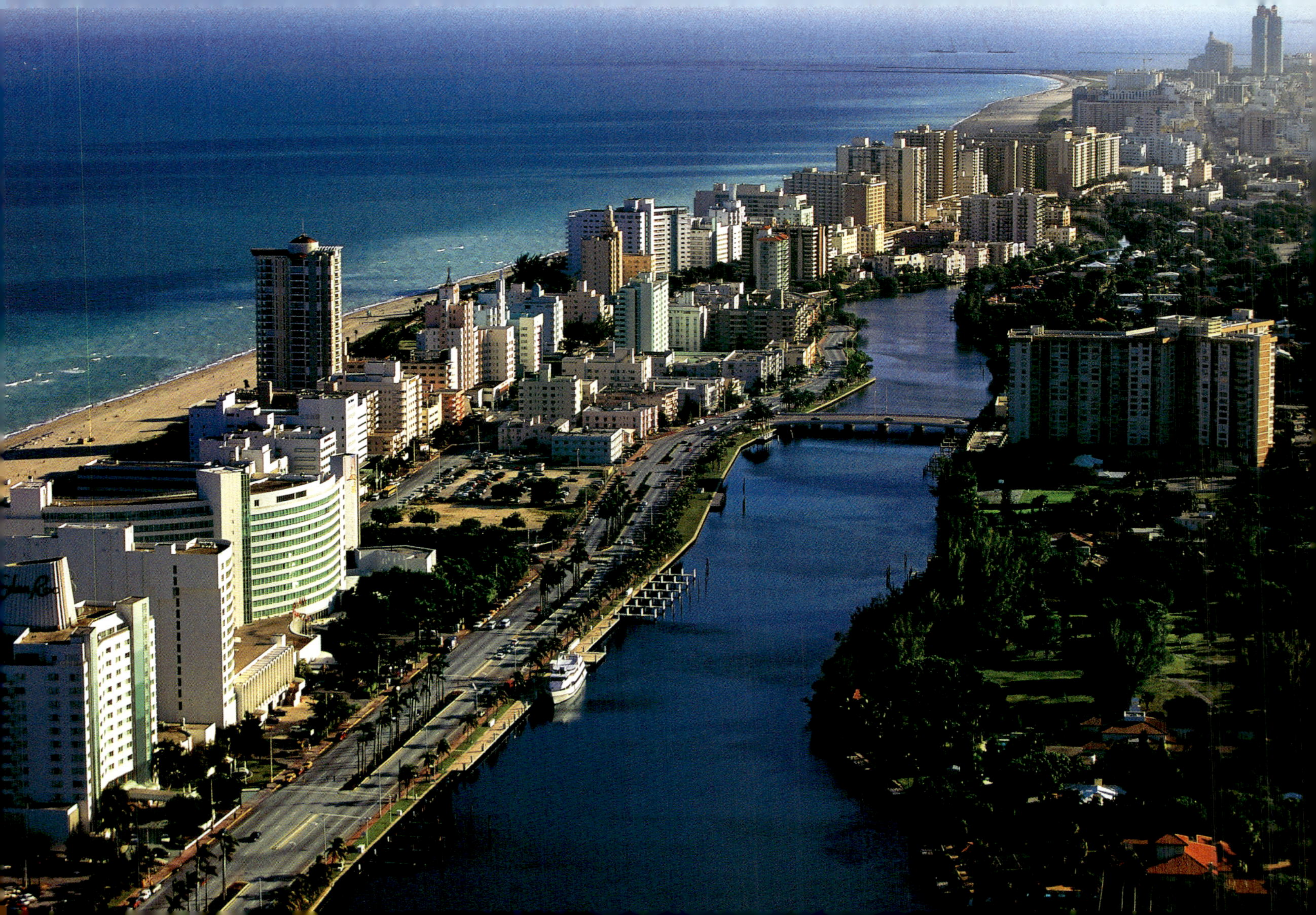

558

Surrounded by water, Miami Beach, in Florida, stands on a long ribbon of land that has been called "the million-dollar strip of sand."

559

Lovely private homes and big luxury hotels compete for space in Miami Beach, among beaches and canals. The territory of southern Florida offers a spectacular combination of sea and mainland.

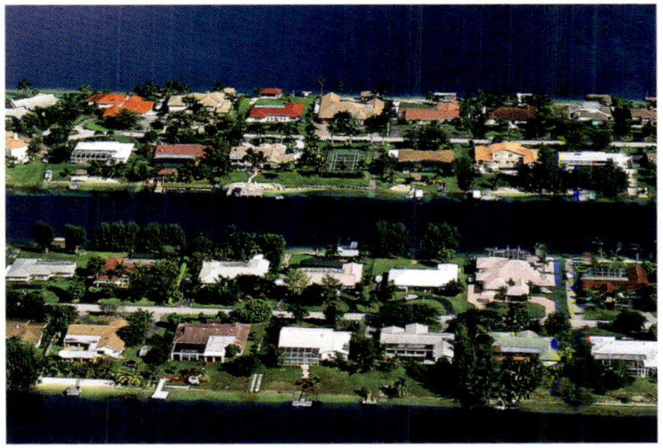

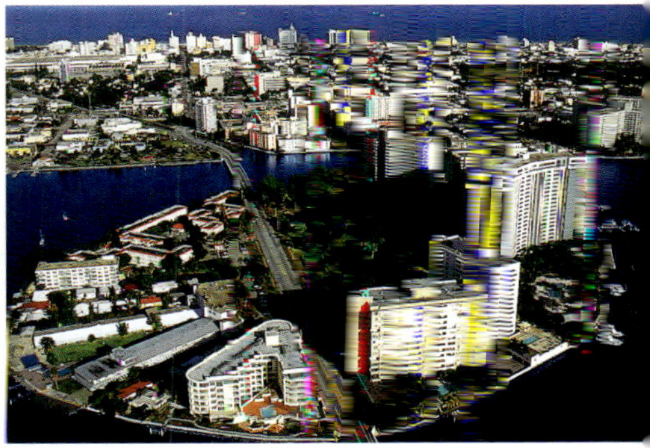

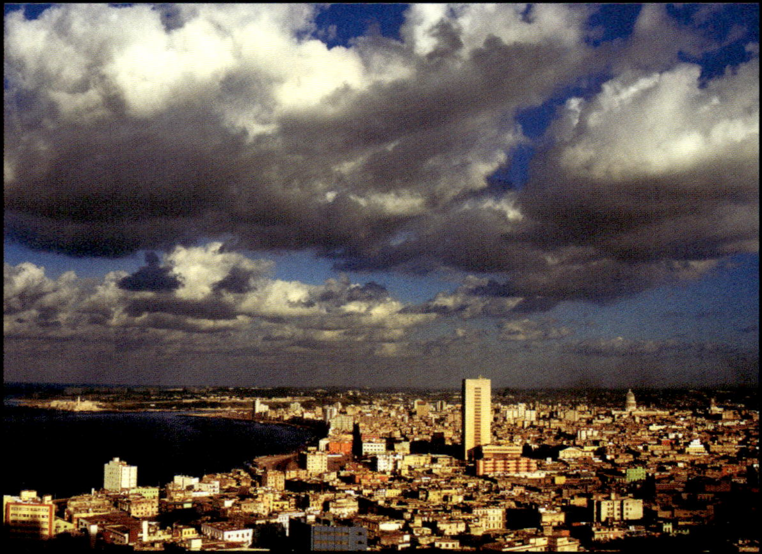

560
The intense and warm light and the ever-changing sky of the Caribbean seem to reflect the spirit of Havana, the capital of Cuba.

561
The Nacional Capitolio of Havana is a copy of the Washington Capitol. Open to the public, today this historical building is the headquarters of the Academy of the Sciences.

Havana

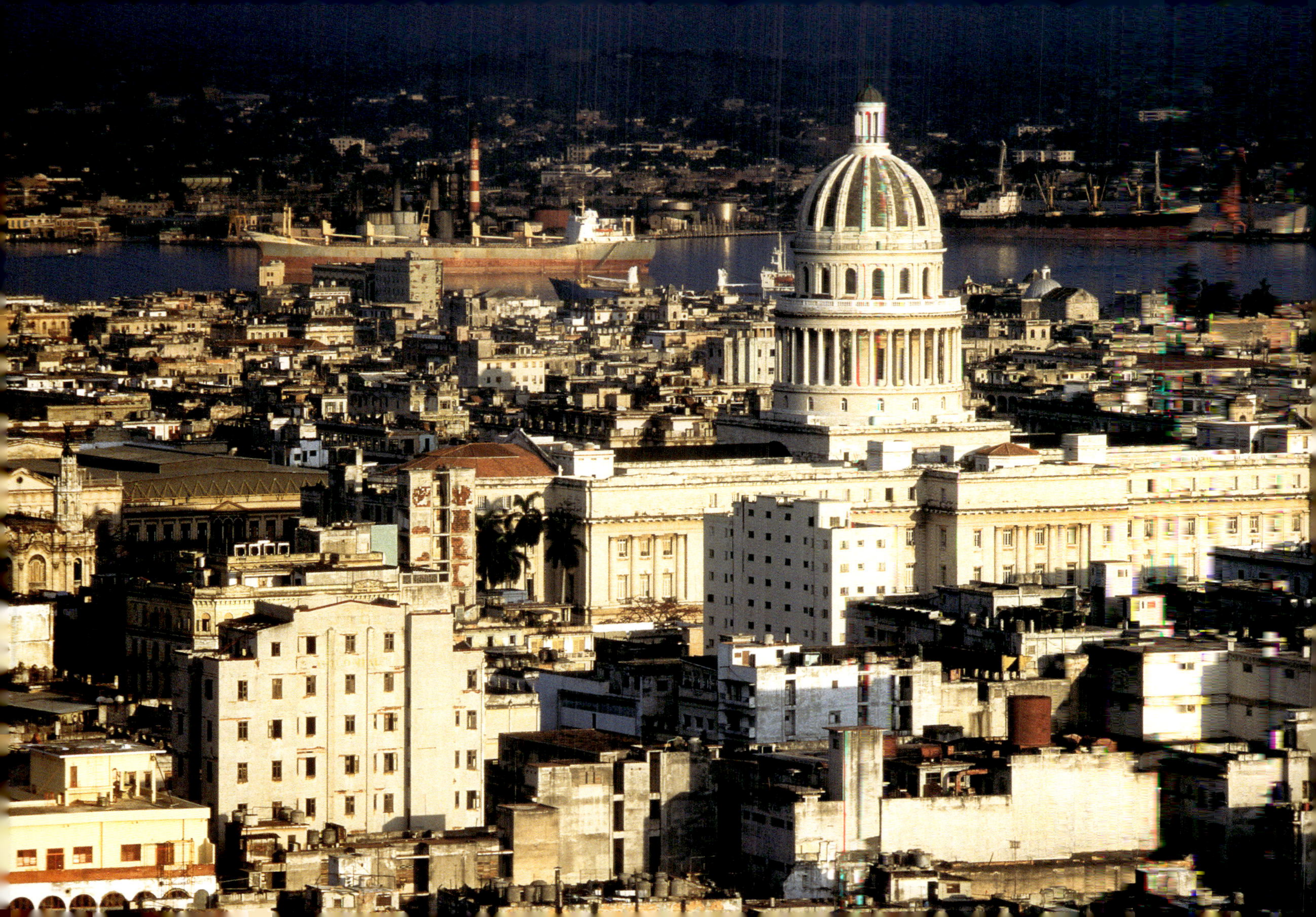

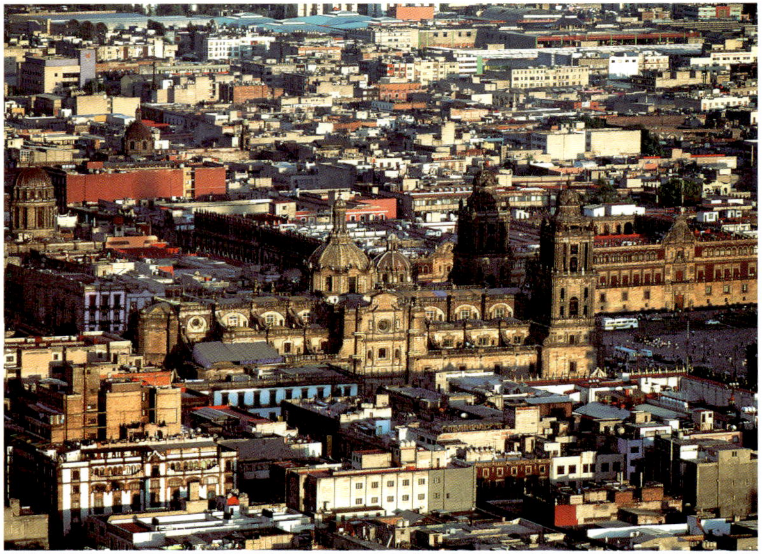

562 and 563

The Metropolitan Cathedral rises from the center of Mexico City. In front of it, the immense "forum" of the Plaza de la Constitution (it is the second biggest square in the world) opens at the exact point where the Templo Major of Montezuma's capital stood.

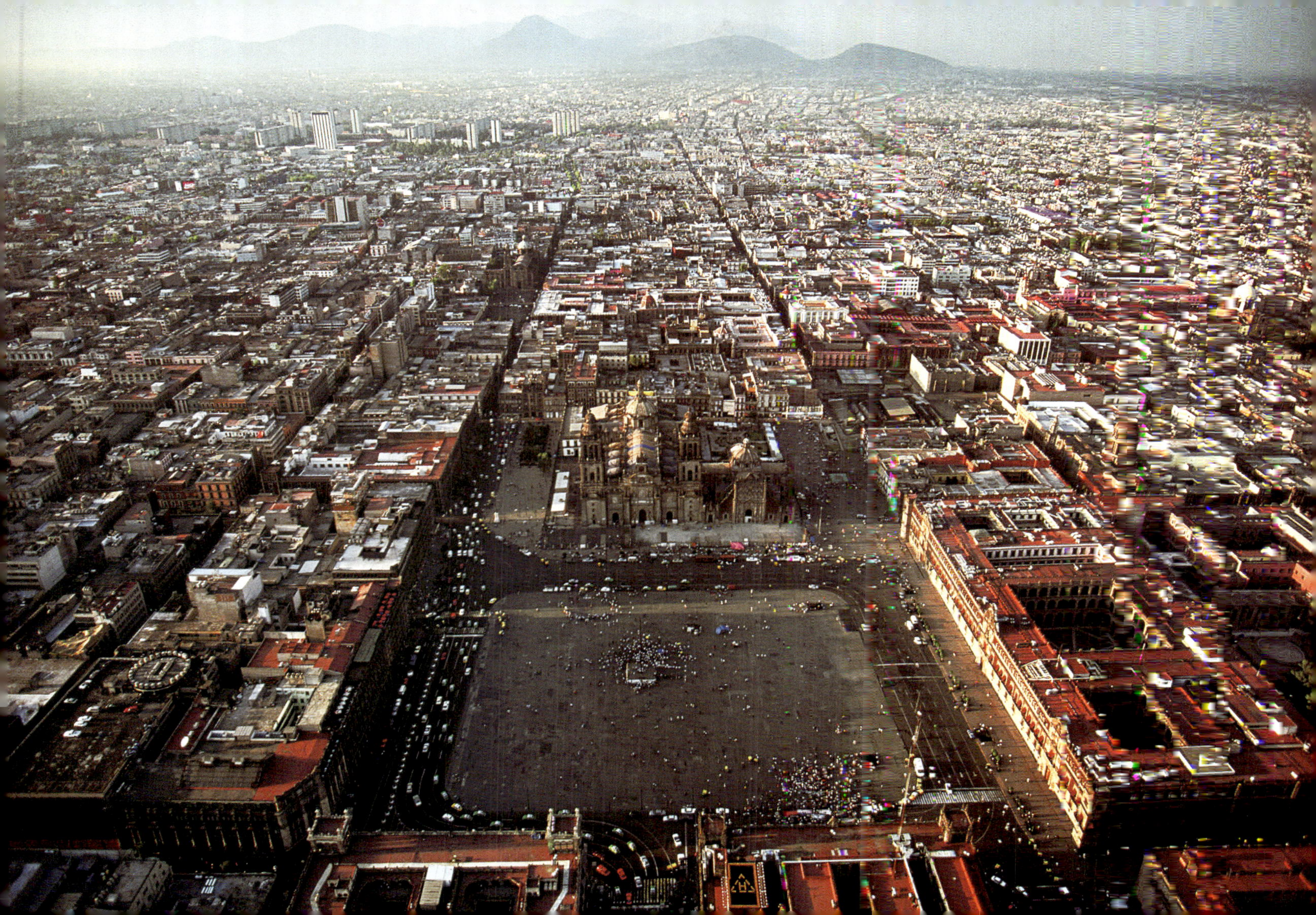

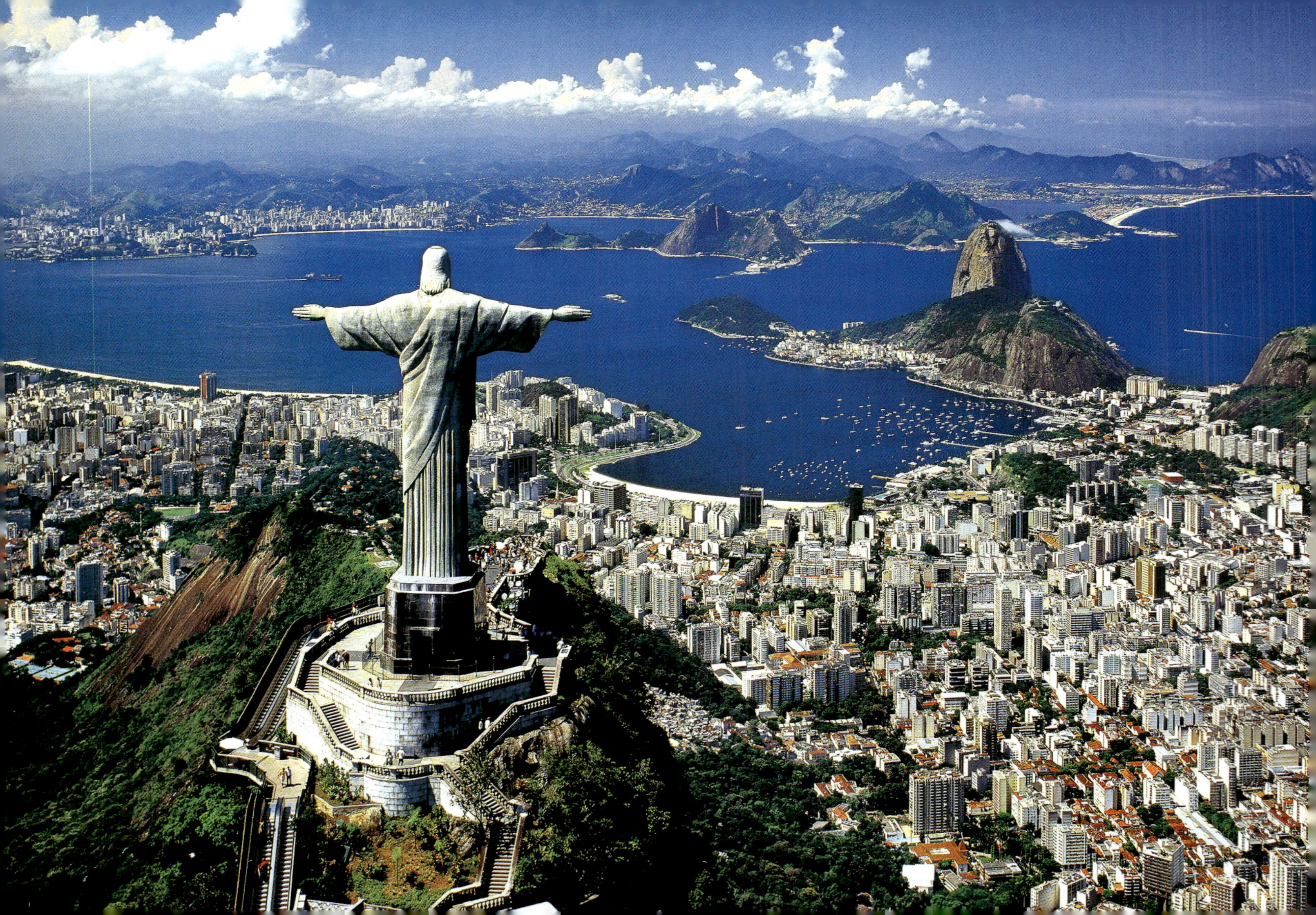

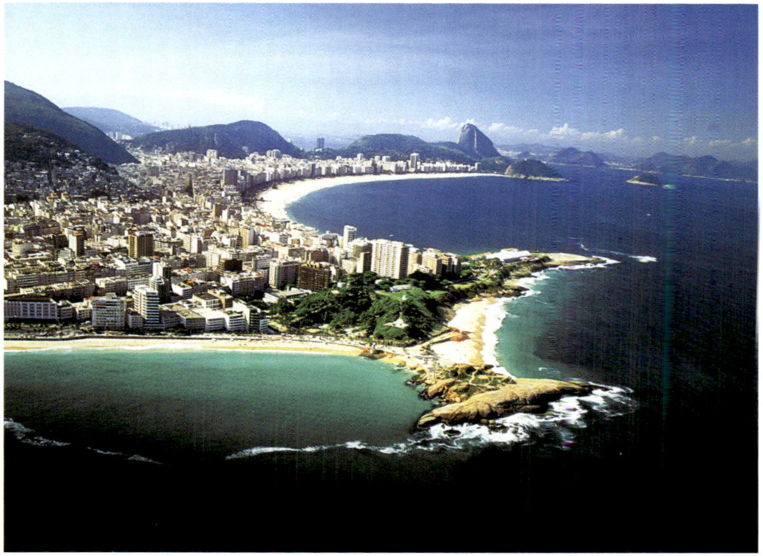

564

The bay of Rio de Janeiro, in Brazil, composes, together with Cristo Redentor, a view among the most spectacular around.

565

Rio de Janeiro has a thousand different faces: every mile of its length offers unparalleled spectacles of the integration of nature and the urban environment.

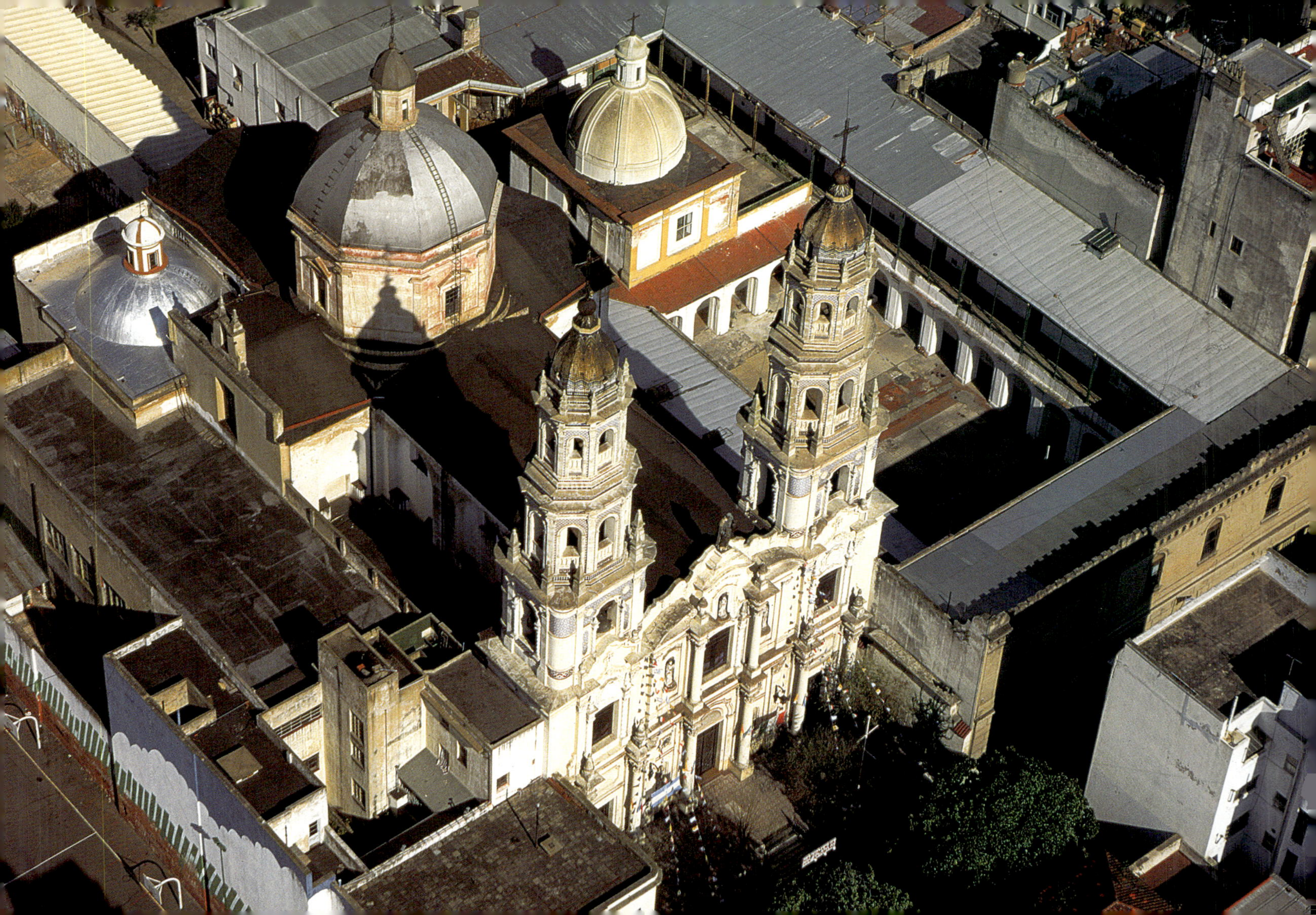

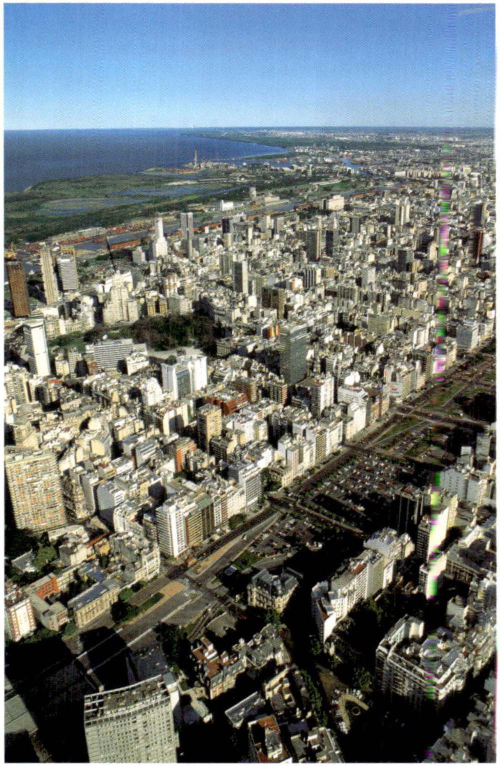

Buenos Aires

566

The church of San Pedro Gonzalez Telmo in Buenos Aires, in Argentina, is one of the 22 neighborhood churches in the capital. Its construction, begun in 1784 by the Jesuits, was finished 22 years later.

567

Avenida 9 de Julio splits the center of Buenos Aires with its incredible width of 3,708 feet (16 lanes).

IN THE FURROWS OF TIME

FLYING HIGH

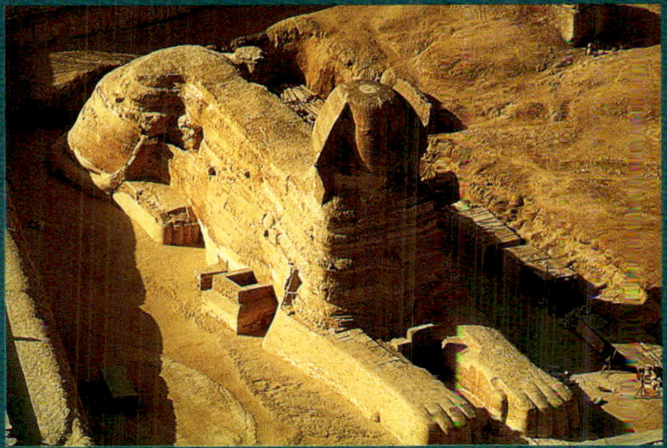

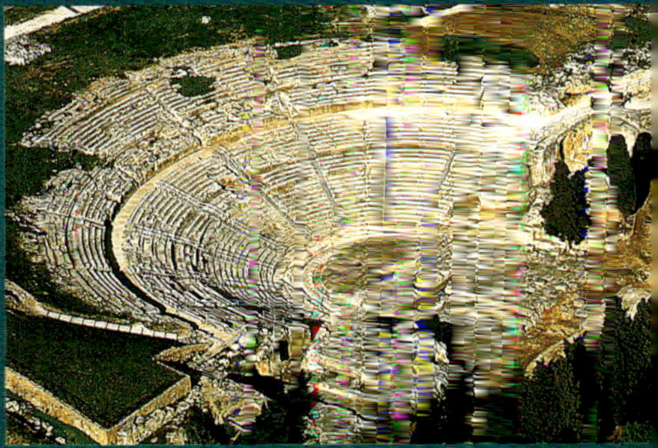

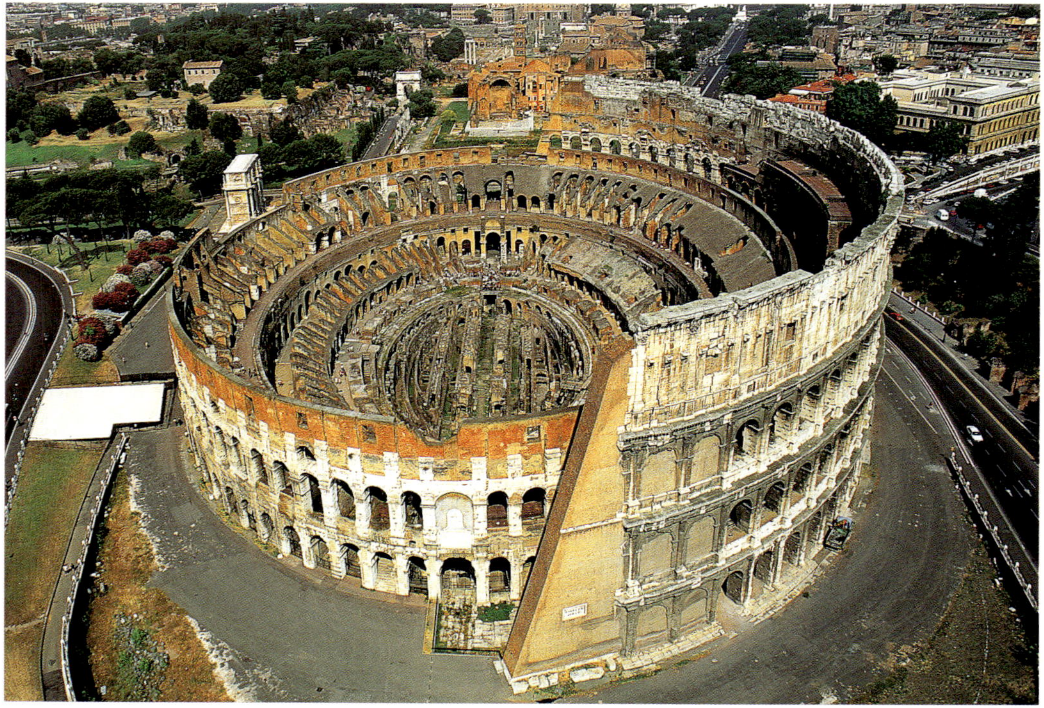

569
The sphinx at Giza, in Egypt (left), and the Greek theater of Segesta, in Italy (right).

Towards the end of the 1700s, something never seen before happened. Hanging from the balloons developed by the Montgolfier brothers, a few fortunate aeronauts were able to contemplate the palace and gardens of Versailles, the gray roofs of the Louvre, the lovely spires of Notre Dame, and the panorama of Paris, thereafter contributing to the scholarly discussions of scientists and academics and the conversations of the common folks about the early impressions of the world from the sky.

Right after, as often happens, the new conquest ended up in the hands of the military, and it was only chance – along with the English canons at Abukir – which destroyed the aerostatic equipment that prevented Napoleon's officers from experiencing the thrill of seeing the pyramids not from their base, at attention in the scorching heat, but from the air, like old gods returned to admired the beloved land of Egypt.

The airways, however, were open, and soon it would be possible to reveal parts of a vanished world, transfigured by time but still better seen from an aerial perspective: ruins of prehistoric villages, walls, towers, palaces, pyramids, temples, tombs, and canals.

Almost all great works really seem, and above all when seen from above, as if ancient man could not help himself but to think and act big when building or creating something, usually in the name of the gods.

Among all the lands, it is Egypt that can boast

570
The Flavian Amphitheater in Rome, Italy, better known as the Colosseum, was commissioned by Emperor Vespasian in A.D. 75 and was inaugurated by Titus five years later.

In the Furrows of Time

the most numerous and evident marks of history. When seen from the sky, the overwhelming monumentality of the pyramids (the few still standing, as many have collapsed and can now be mistaken for naturally eroded little hills) actually looks amplified, also because the original design can be inferred.

The modest eternal abode of the royal officials, all looking "inhabited" in orderly rows of "bench-like" tombs, like modern residential neighborhoods constructed out of nothing, become much more apparent.

Thebes, much further south, features the frighteningly large columns of the temples of Karnak and Luxor, divine dwellings that time could only render more astounding by revealing their stubborn resistance.

Biban el-Moluk, to the west, holds the dark depths of the Valley of the Kings and that of the Queens, dotted by tiny entrances to the royal tombs. At the base of the pyramids of el-Qurn, the sacred Theban Mountain, one of the most spectacular natural amphitheaters in the world opens: the temples of the woman-pharaoh Hatshepsut, of Mentuhotep, and of Thutmosis still comply with their builders' wishes for eternal existence in the embrace of the site, nestled under a cliff that appears to be the vertical continuation of the human work sitting below.

Everywhere in the world man has sought to entrust proof of his greatness, his own accomplishments, and even his limits to erecting monuments. The Great Wall of China and Hadrian's Wall, between Carlisle and Newcastle, are glaring examples. Endless miles of wall push stubbornly along borders that were supposed to endure for the classic 1,000 or even 10,000 years, regardless of the land's nature and conformation.

In fact, their dragon backs follow the profile of the crests with infinite precision, unaffected by slopes and harsh conditions, and proceed from east to west across lands desolate enough to

In the Furrows of Time

make it difficult to imagine that some people, "barbarians" even, could live beyond the borders and threaten the empires that sought to hide behind their backs. In the desolate lands of the north, these works have lost much of their magnificence and yet they are still there, casting to the wind the same warnings they expressed at the time of the great emperors.

However, wise Asia still has much more than just borders to testify to the breadth of its history. Monumental temples have come to us across a sea of centuries, often highly visible now that the forest has been forced to recede. The Khmer temples of Cambodia reveal a perfect weave of thin walls, old roads, and perfectly straight canals, stretched between important points marked by big spires, corn-cob- and bell-shaped reliquaries, and terraces.

The exciting vision of a mandala made of sculpted stones rather than grains of color, as Tibetan monks did, waits in the forest for those who fly over Borobudur, Indonesia, a mountain with a perfect perimeter, cruciform, bristling with chapels that compose designs still not completely understood.

Then, much further north, for those who come by plane, one of the most imposing palaces of the world begins to shape from afar under the golden roofs of the Potala, in Lhasa, along with less famous monasteries, often noticeably built of mud. The thin air of the Roof of the World confers an extraordinary visual power to these monuments in reds, whites and browns still shining in the near total aridness of the landscape.

In Europe, the evidence of the past grows more confusing. Given the thousands of years of continuity of settlements in this westernmost peninsula of Eurasia, and given the small size of the territory, the monuments are laid one over the other, often ending up integrated into the fabric of the city that overwhelms them on all sides, cutting out a small "strip of respect" that allows

In the Furrows of Time

them to show off their magnificence. The Imperial Forum of Rome leaves room to imagine the vast, shining spaces in which the Caesars triumphed like gods descended to earth.

The Colosseum blossoms like a flower of marble in the middle of the city, overwhelmed by the traffic as is Castel Sant'Angelo on the shores of the Tiber. Saint Peter's embraces Christianity with the disarming simplicity of its colonnade designed by Bernini, dominated by a dome offering refuge to "all men of good will," an incredibly majestic "umbrella," as some have defined it.

The splendid bones of the Periclean Acropolis, the Greek Forum, and the Roman Forum bleach in the sun in Athens. In Istanbul, dozens of minarets seem ready to take to the sky, standing tall on gray domes growing green with oxidation. Even here, everything is suffocated by smog yet strangely even more charming in that sort of mist that seems to suggest the heavy veil spread by time.

Not always, however, has Europe imprisoned the vestiges of its past. Because of the abyss of time separating us from the ancients and the spiritual ways and needs that brought ancient peoples to places like Stonehenge and Amesbury in England and Carnac in France have disappeared, leaving these wonders relatively undisturbed in the countryside, where they can continue to "function" to all effects, indicating astral movements, the seasons, and a place of sanctuary, as well as simply creating a play of light and shadow on the grass. Simple, but perhaps magical.

Resistant monuments honor the American lands with the authority of the ancient. Towers and houses of mud bricks, or adobe, crowd the gaps in the sandstone walls of the canyons in the deserts of the United States. Sites like Mesa Verde command respect for those who lived there, so in tune with nature and connected with it to have known how to prosper in such inaccessible

In the Furrows of Time

places. The great Toltec, Aztec, and Mayan ceremonial centers, with their pyramids and altars, were probably never "cities" permanently inhabited as we are used to think of, but rather only visited on the occasion of celebrations and market days. Yet, from the sky, their layout seems familiar: flying over Giza, Saqqara, Angkor Wat, Borobudur, the Forbidden City, and the prehistoric mounds of North America and Britain, we see similarities. They are mountains built by man to be observed by the gods and yet framed in a meticulous order of streets, roads, altars, tombs, and sacred lakes, thus demonstrating the sacrifice inherent to their monumentality and showing an artificial and purely imitation mundus with respect to nature.

Even here, if seen from the sky, the designs conceived by priest-kings are revealed, desperately intent on saving the mundus from chaos at the expense of their most precious possessions, first among them human life.

Macchu Picchu is one of the most impressive marks made by history. The Incas would never have been able to find a stranger place to erect their defensive works, nor more beautiful, suspended as they are on a mountain saddle at almost 6,500 feet high, squeezed between two deep valleys invaded by forest.

To close the circle is one of the most mysterious sites: some have maintained that the wise men of an obscure pre-Columbian people, the Nazca, would only have been able to direct the building of impressive geoglyphs scratched into the surface of the Pampa de Ingenios in Peru, as hard as stone and just as dry, by being aboard some sort of kite or balloon. However, there is no proof to that effect and the explanations can be very uninteresting. The fact remains, nevertheless, that all those animals, flowers, and symbols in exaggerated and silenced proportions, as tight as the strings on a violin, are visible exclusively from the sky.

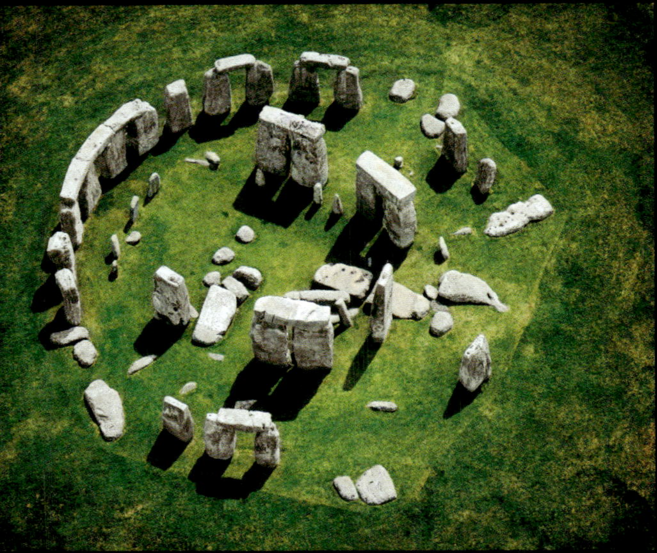

576

The megalithic complex of Stonehenge was built on the Salisbury Plain, in England, in three different phases between 3000 and 1000 B.C.

577

Hadrian's Wall was built in present-day northern England by Emperor Hadrian between 122 and 128 as a defensive barrier against the infiltration of the Celtic tribes of northern Britannia.

Europe

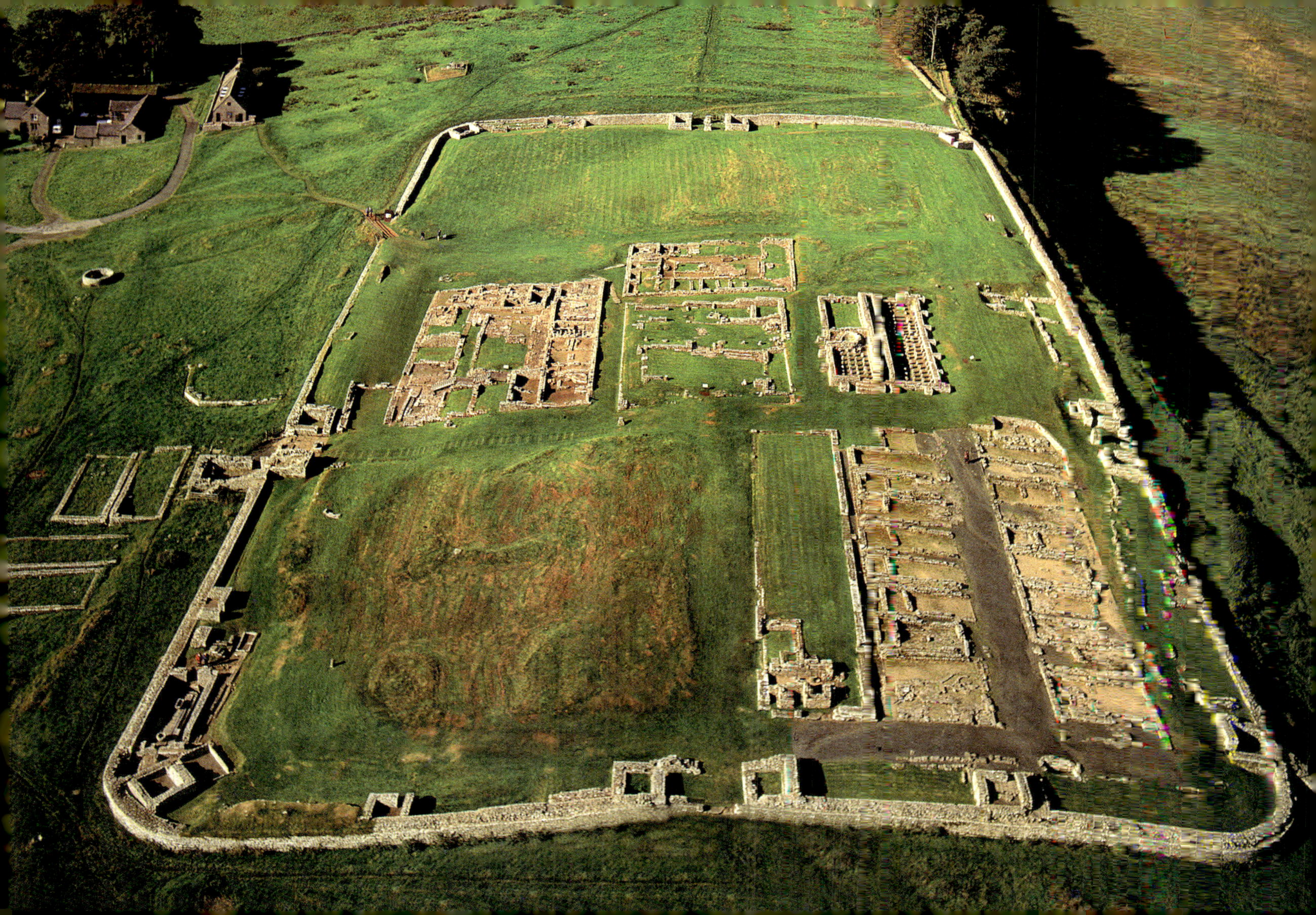

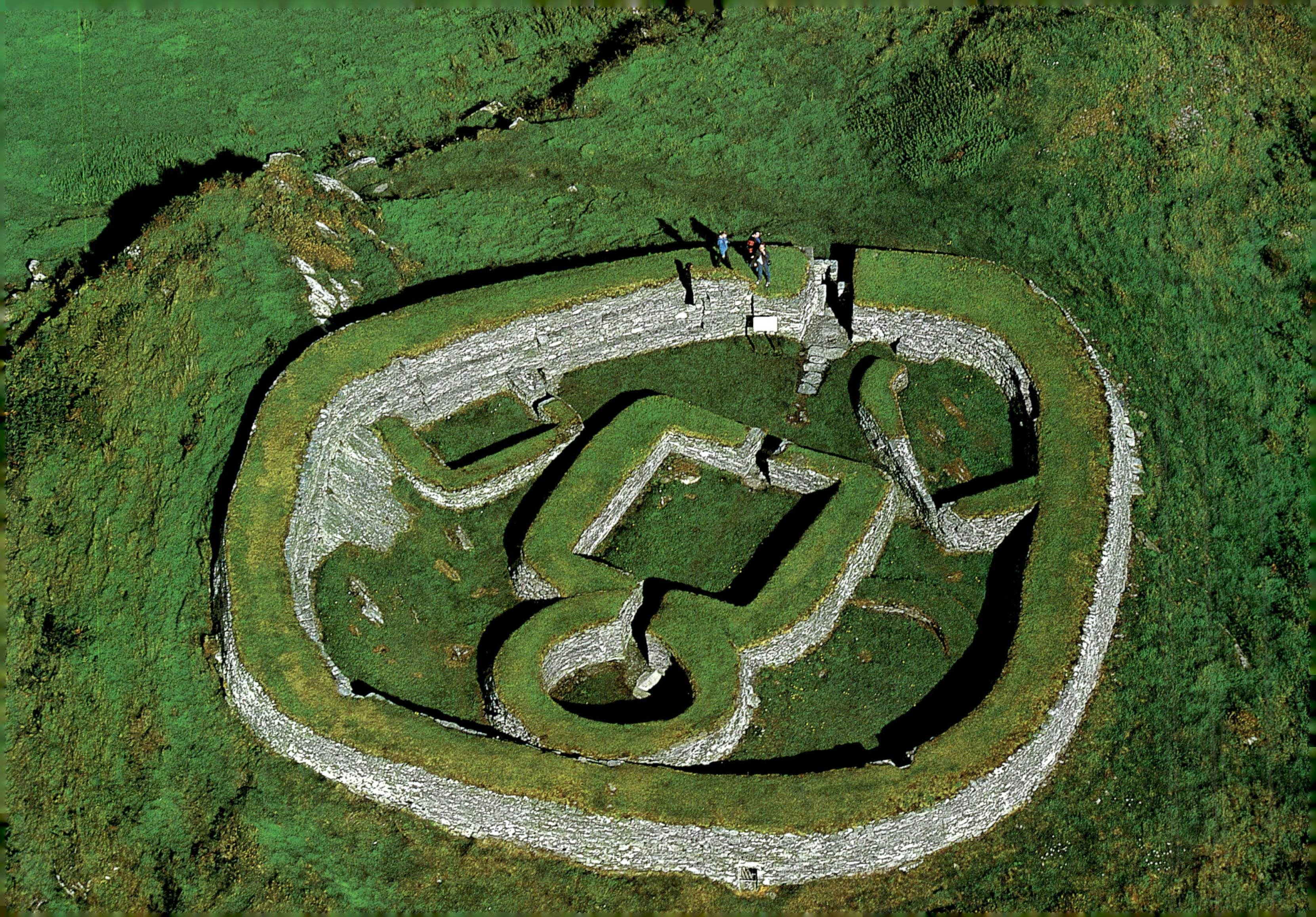

578

Lecanbauile Fort in Ireland has two levels, one on the surface and one underground that is accessed by a corridor.

579 left

The structure of Cahergeal Fort, in the Irish County Kerry, consists of concentric circles.

579 right

The most important prehistoric Irish site is Newgrange, in County Meath, datable to around 3200 B.C.

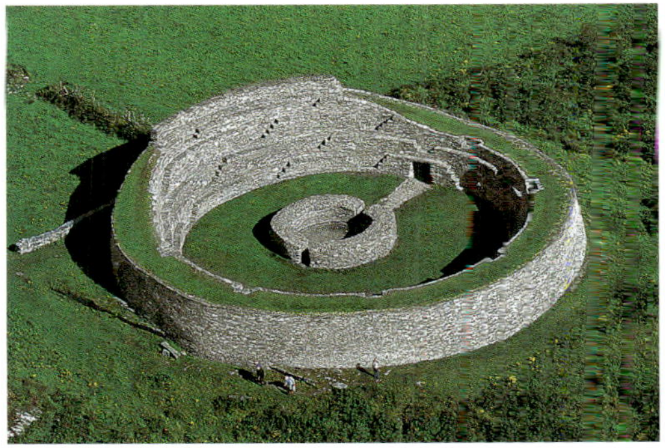

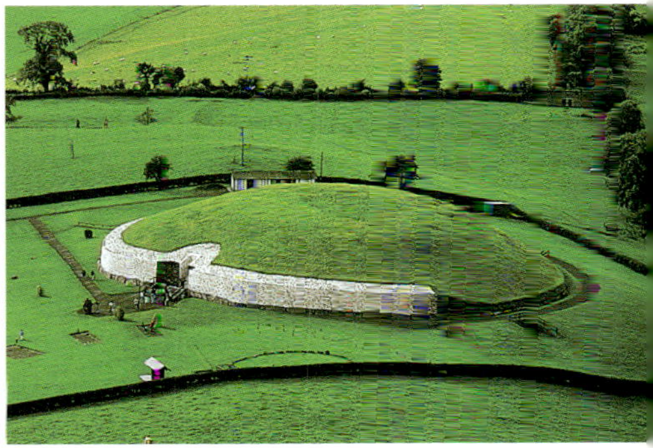

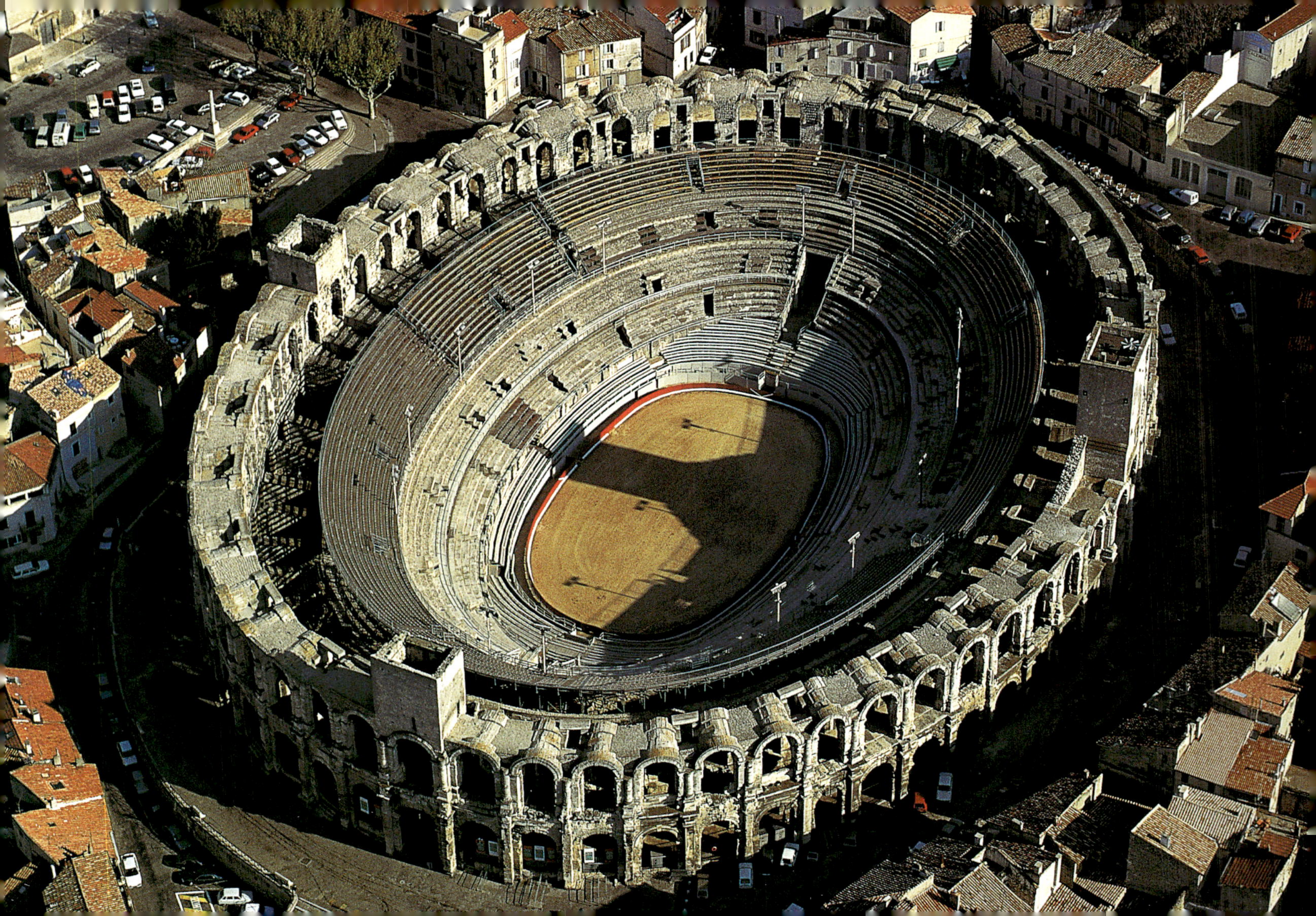

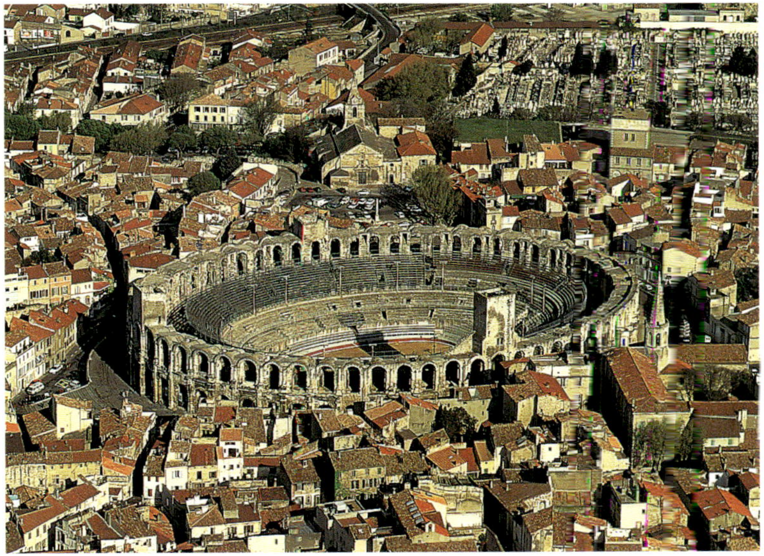

580 and 581

Arles has the biggest amphitheater in France: the building, built at the time of Emperor Hadrian, measures 348 feet by 450 and could hold up to 24,000 spectators.

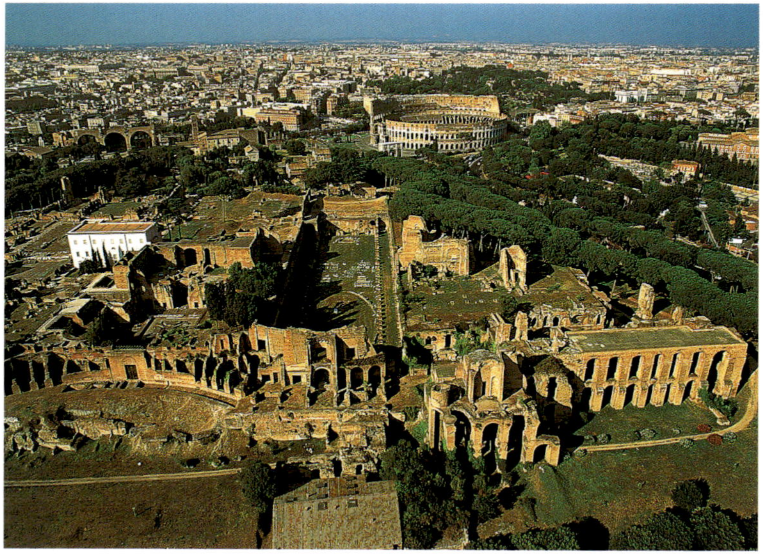

582

The Palatine Hill in Rome, with its abundant archaeological layers, reveals the important political role that Roman civilization played from its origins to the late-ancient period.

583

The Roman Forum, which represented the heart of Ancient Rome's political, commercial, and judiciary life, was subjected to centuries of pillaging, before being safeguarded as one of the city's treasures.

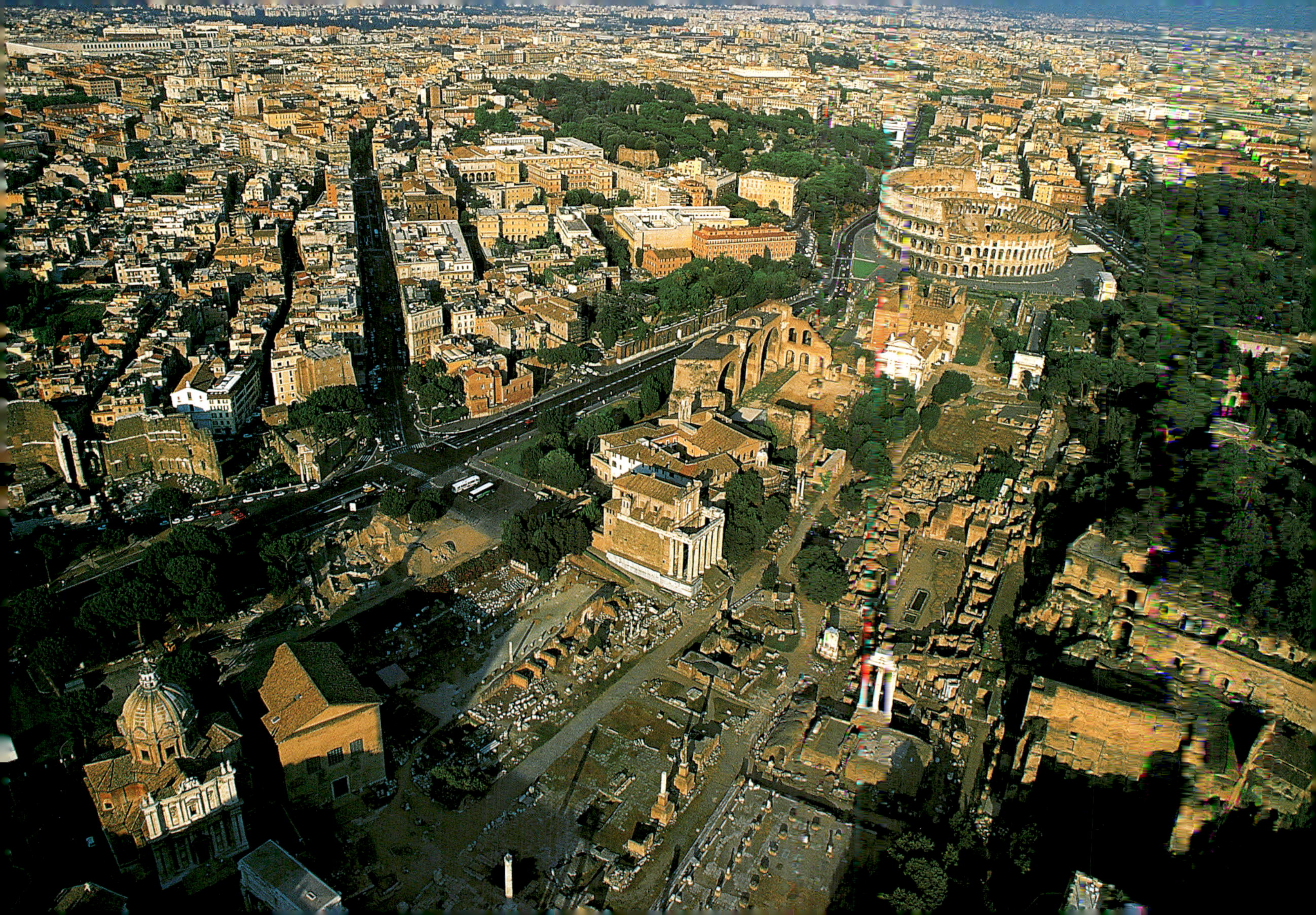

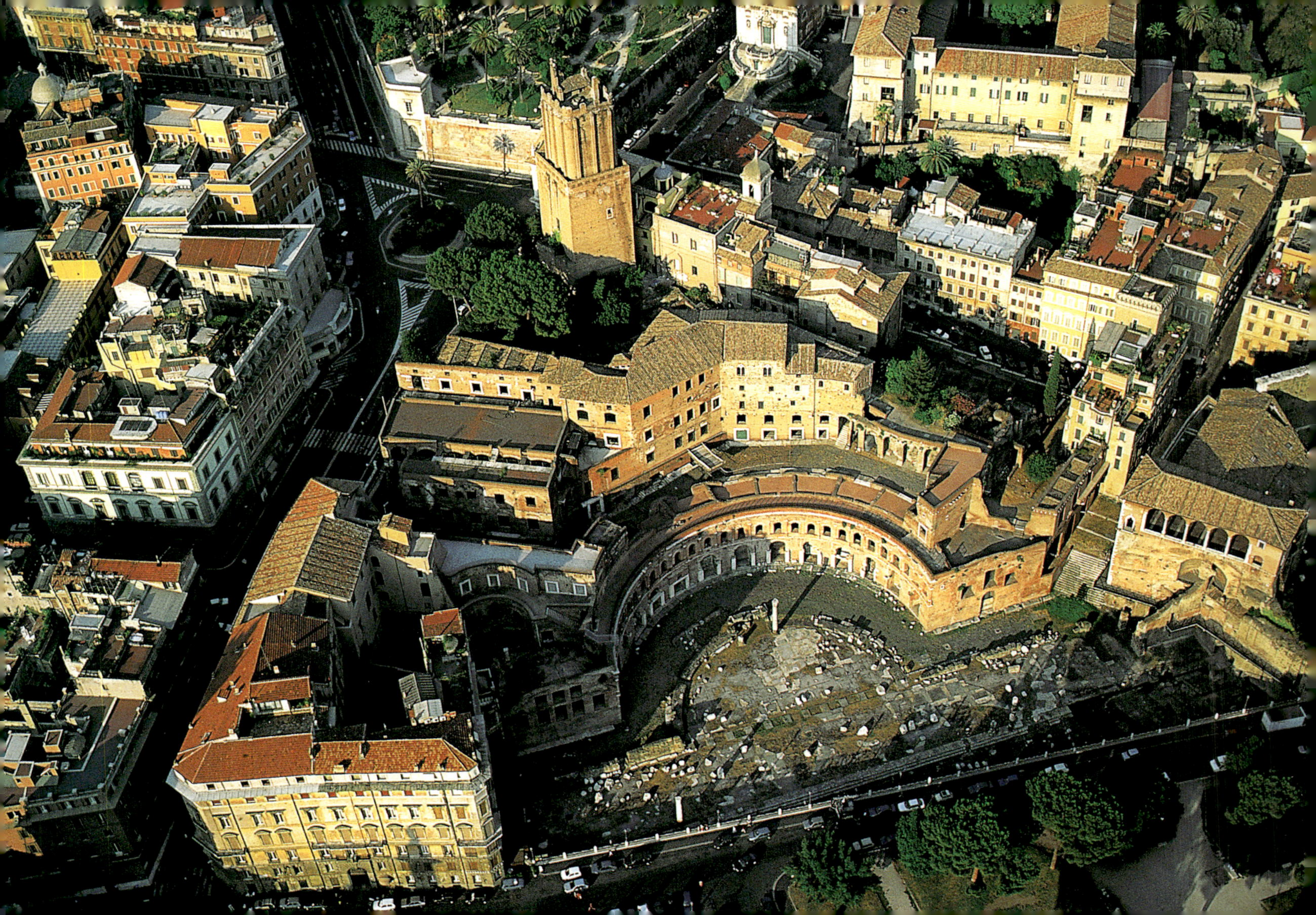

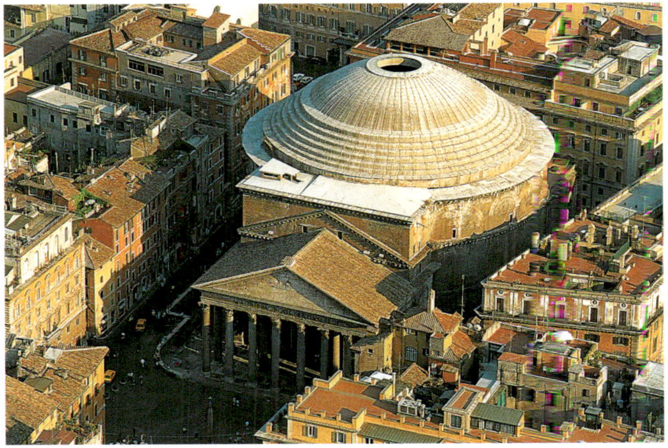

584

Trajan's Markets in Rome are a large complex of brick buildings built in the second century A.D.

585

The Pantheon, commissioned by Hadrian in A.D. 118, is an outstanding example of the conversion of a pagan temple into a Christian church.

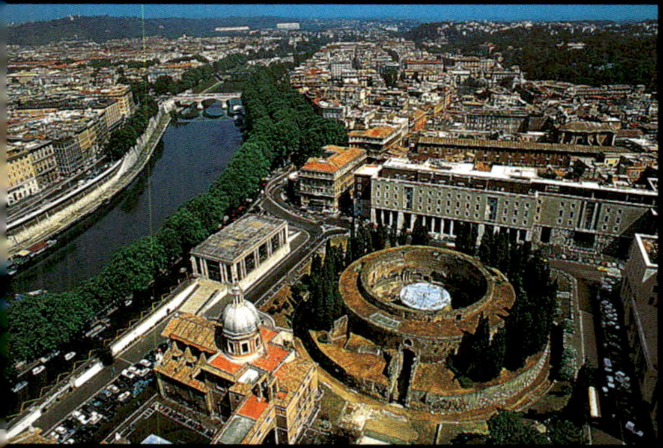

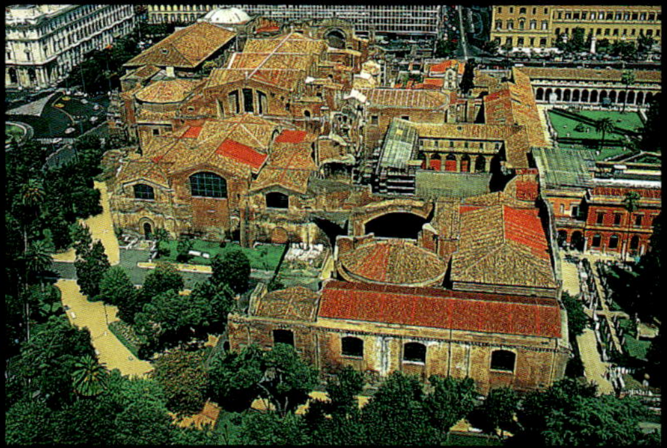

586 left
Augustus' Mausoleum is the burial place that the emperor had built for himself and his descendants in 28 B.C.

586 right
The Diocletian Baths were erected by Maximian in honor of Diocletian on the flatlands between the Viminal and Quirinal hills at the end of the third century A.D.

587
Caracalla's Baths, commissioned in A.D. 216 by Marcus Aurelius Antoninus Bassianus, known as Caracalla, are one of the best-preserved bath complexes from antiquity.

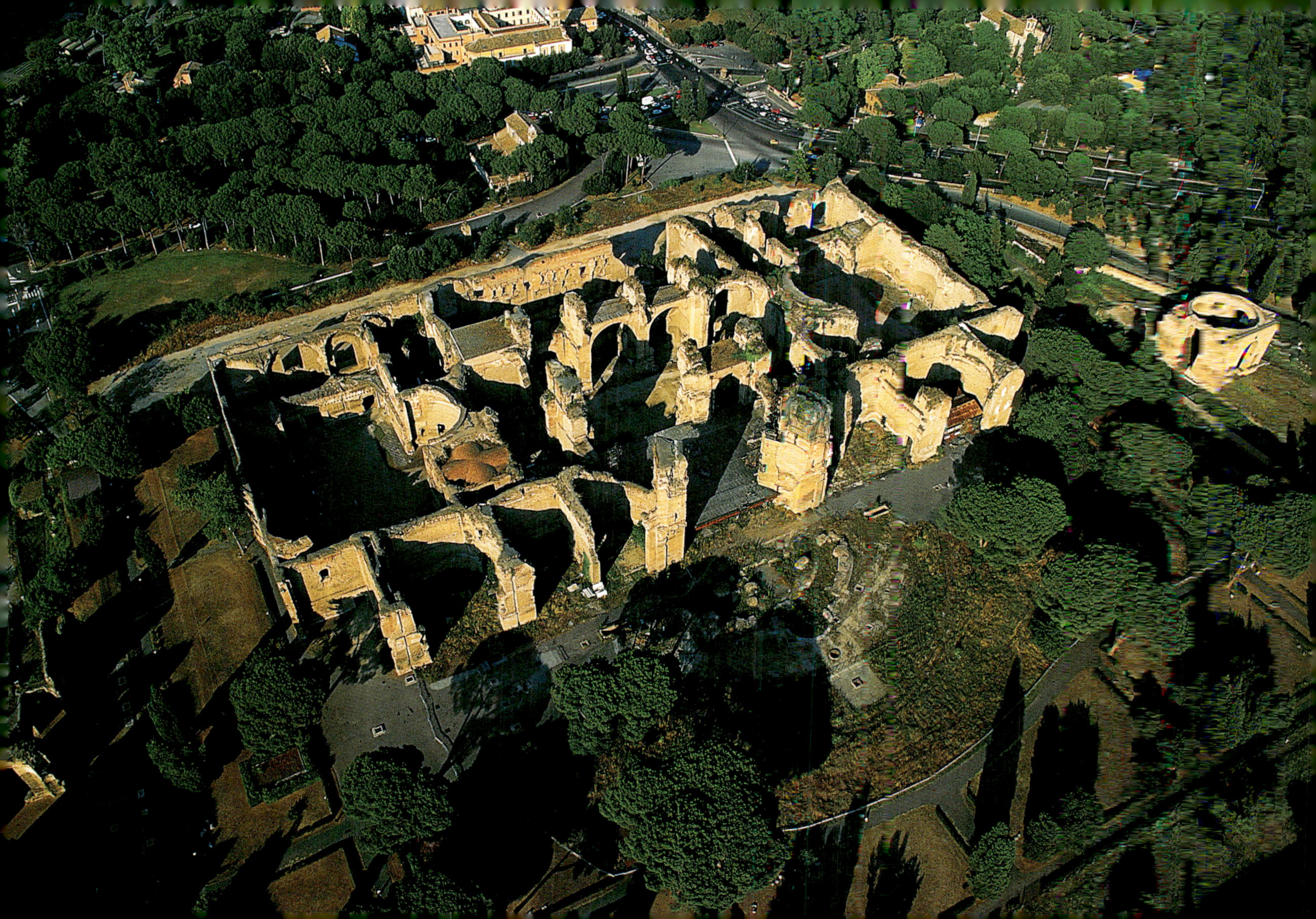

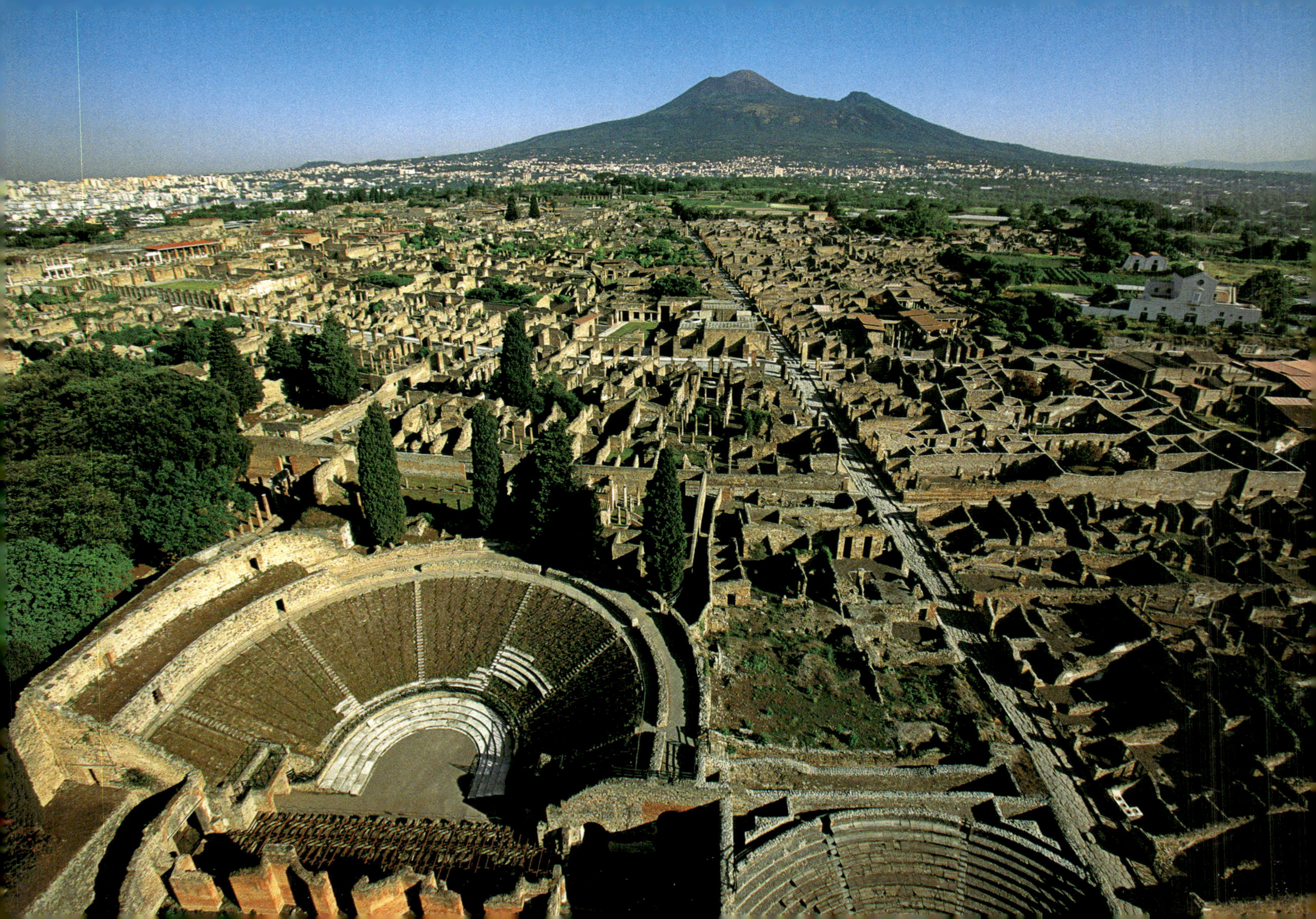

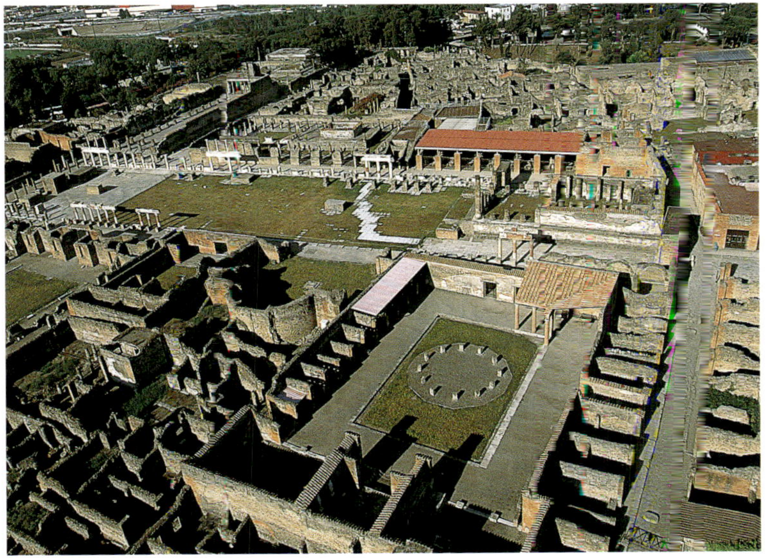

588

The steps of the Big Amphitheater and the Odeion, in ancient Pompeii, are overlooked by Vesuvius from a distance.

589

Inside the forum at Pompeii, the Macellum played a fundamental role, in as much as it was a place responsible for the city's provisioning.

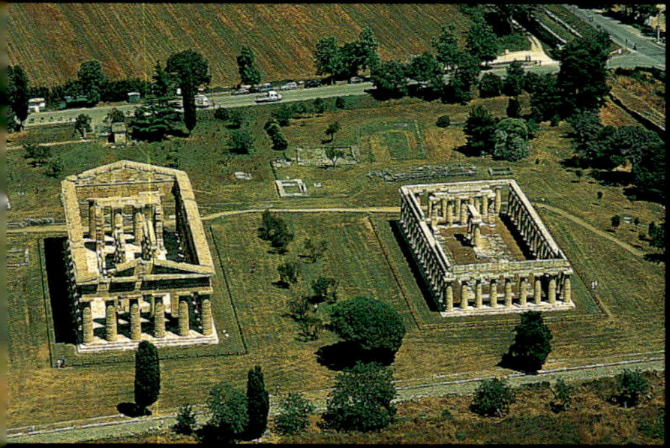

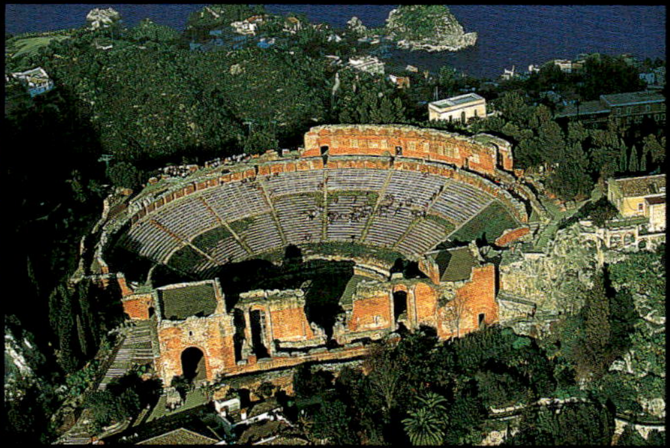

590 left
The Doric temples at Paestum, in Campania, constitute one of the best-preserved architectural complexes of the Greek Empire.

590 right
The ancient amphitheater of Taormina, in Sicily, has uncertain origins: probably built by the Greeks, it underwent renovations in the Roman era.

591
The Valley of the Temples in Agrigento is a hill dominated by Doric-style buildings built during the fifth century B.C. and evidence of the Greek city's prosperity.

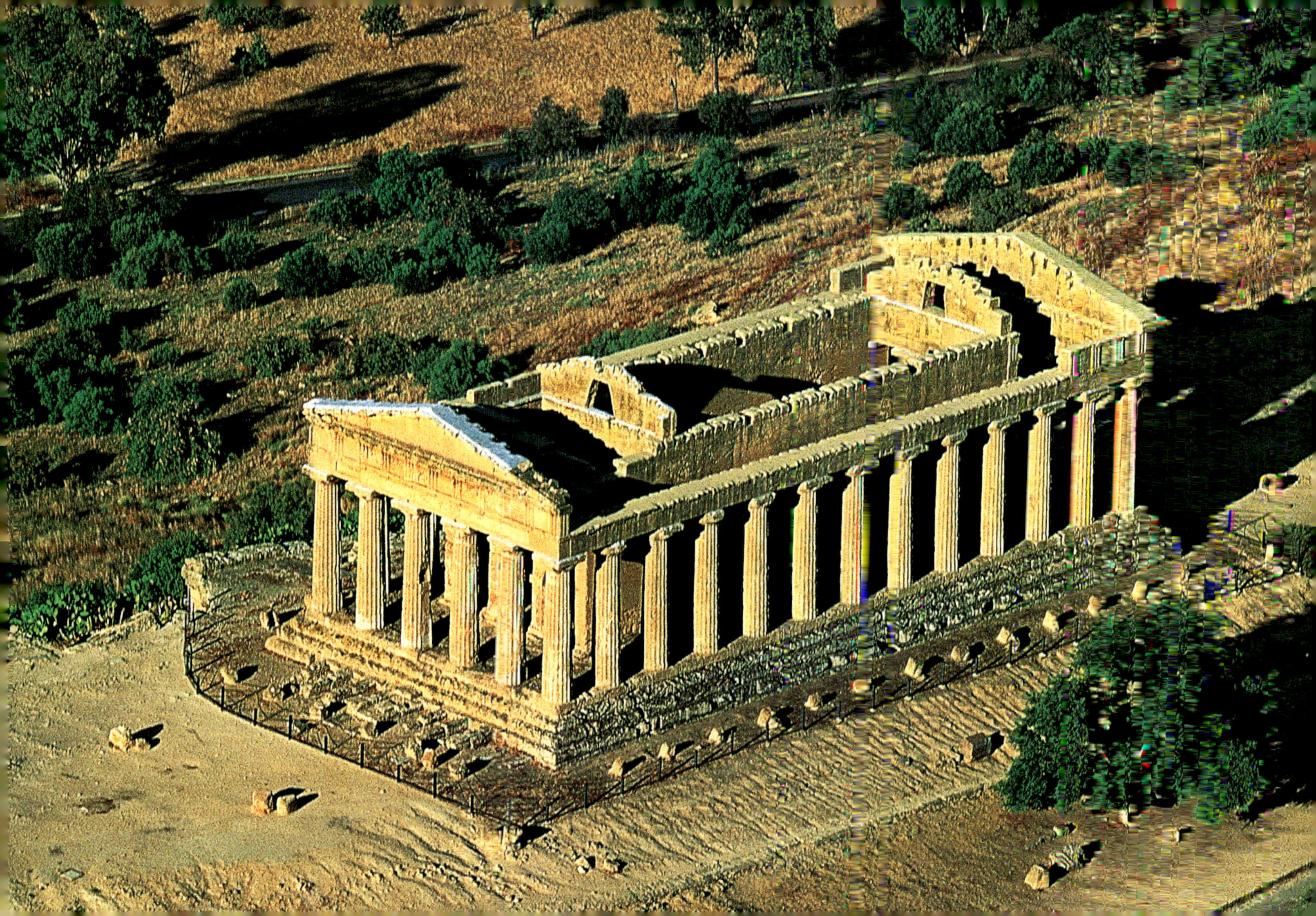

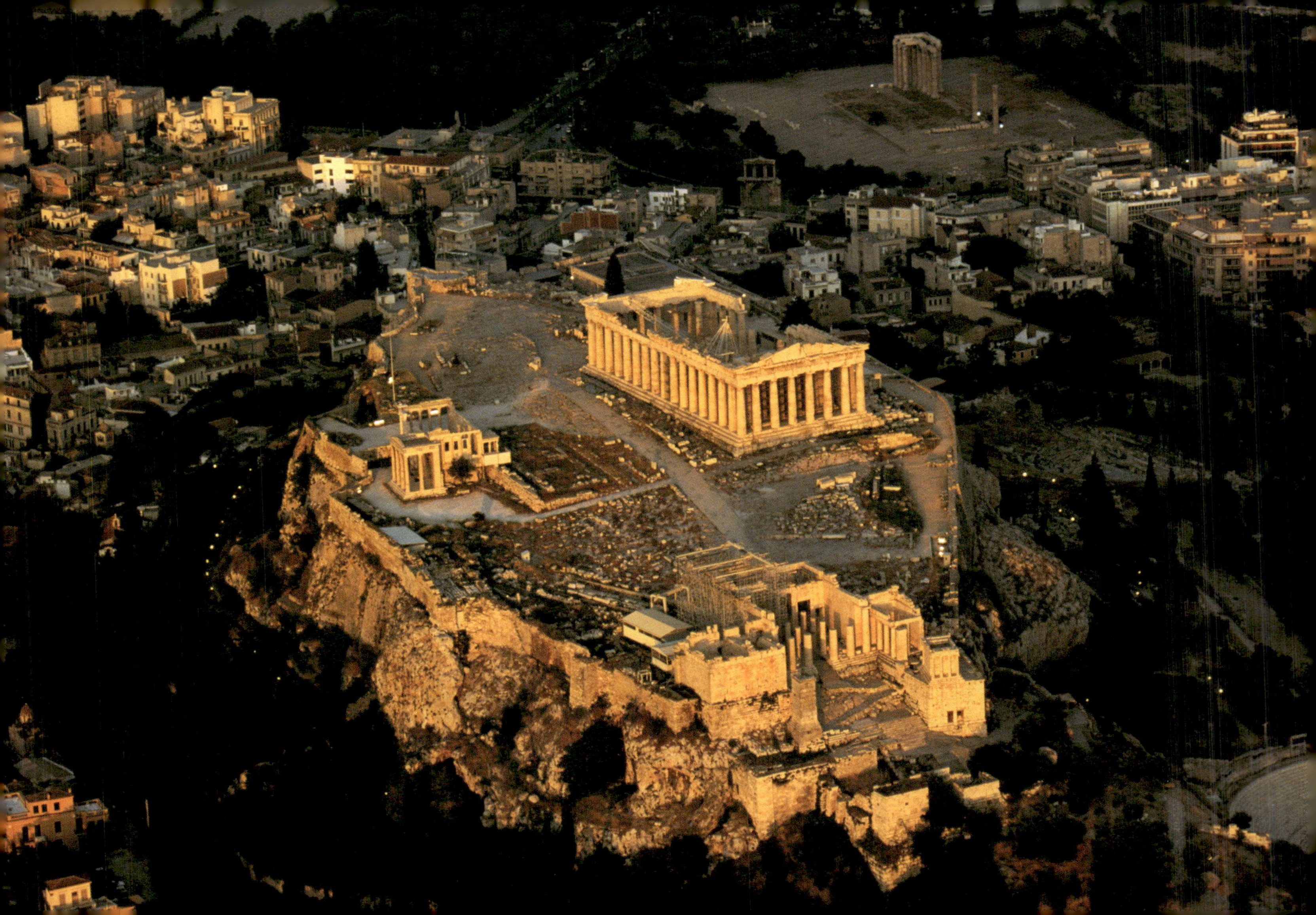

592

The Parthenon, which dominates the Athenian Acropolis in Greece, owes its magnificence to the ingenuity of Phidias, who completed its construction between 447 and 438 B.C.

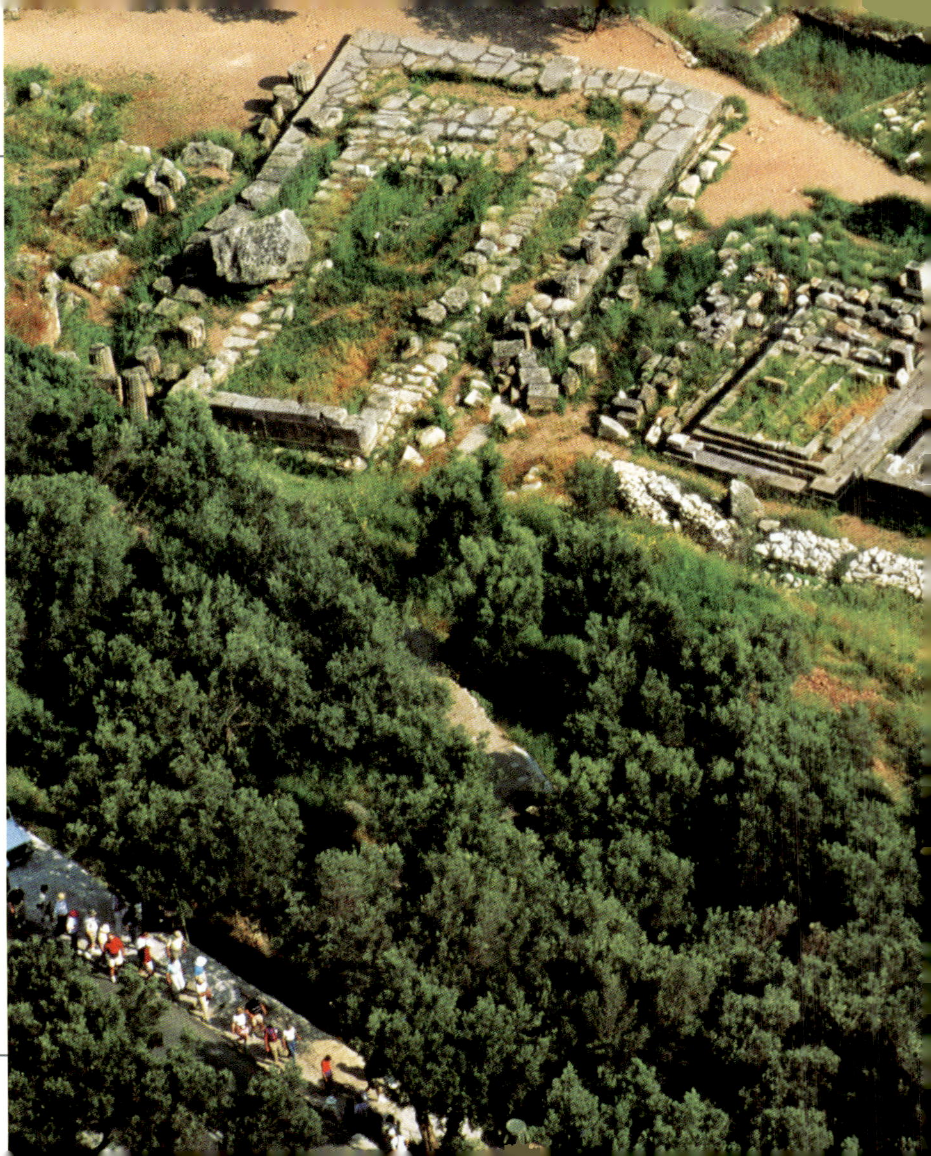

594-595
The archaeological site of Delphi, in Greece, attests to and summarizes the salient chapters in Ancient Greek history, from the intercity battles for hegemony to the military forces united against barbarian attacks.

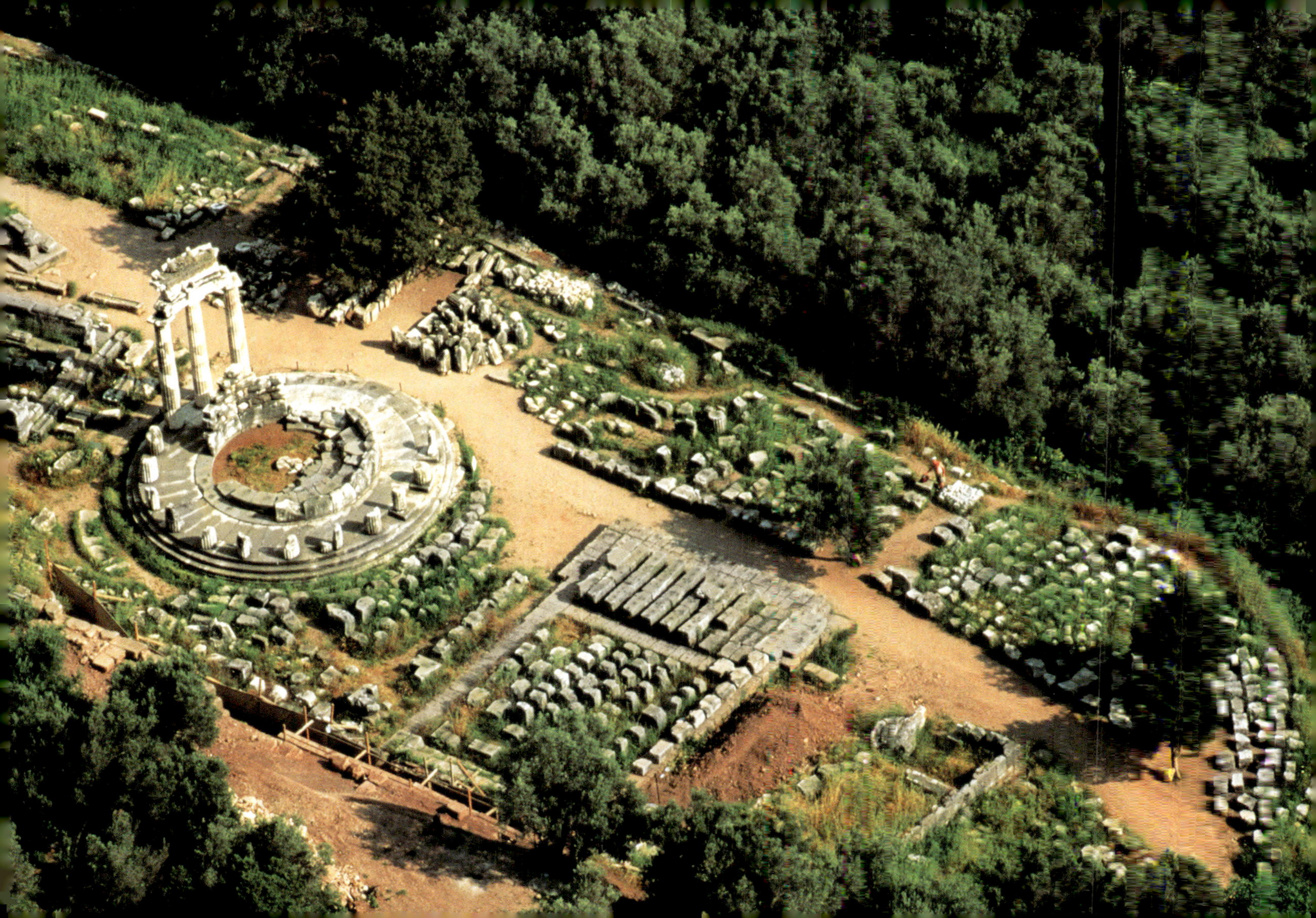

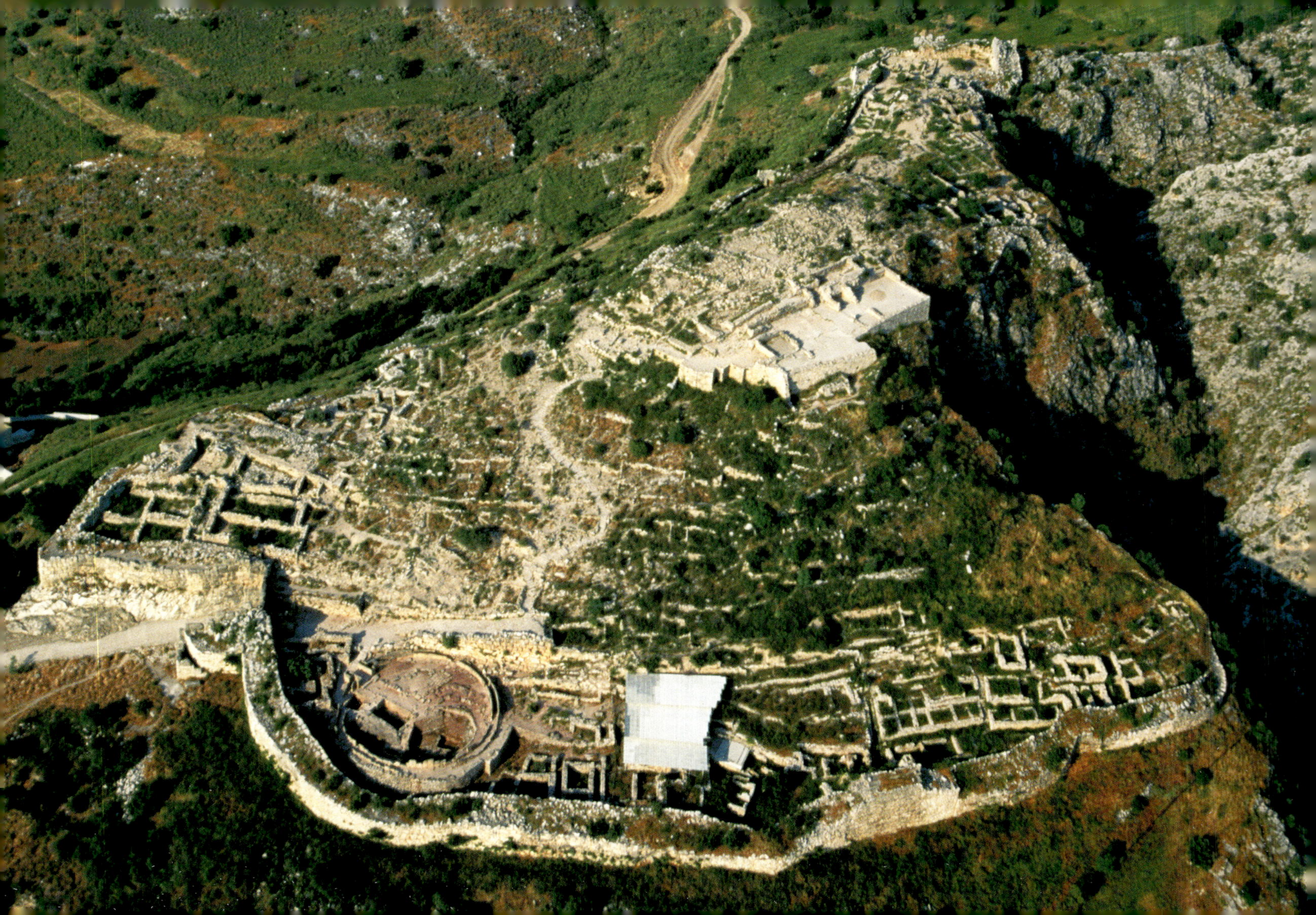

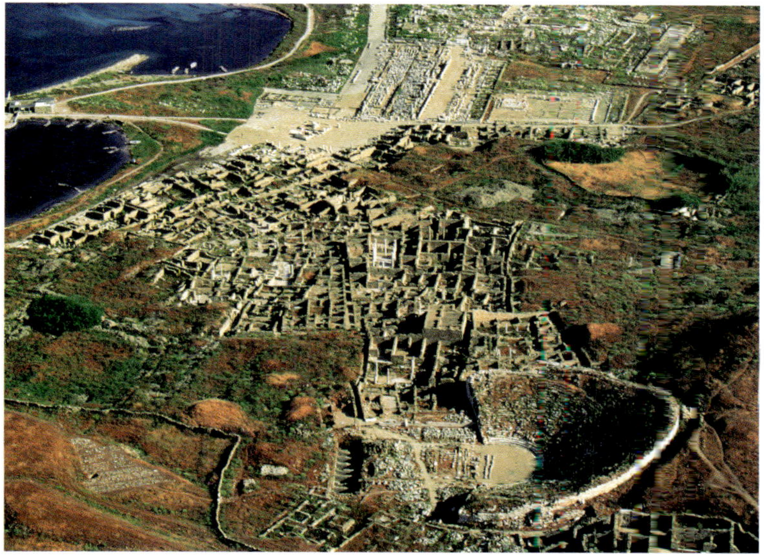

596

In the Argolides, in Greece, stands the citadel of Mycenae, where the most important Bronze-Age Greek civilization, the Myceneean culture developed.

597

The remains of the temples of Delos, one of the Cycladic Islands in Greece, are proof of the Ancient Cycladic civilization, which existed between 3000 and 1000 B.C.

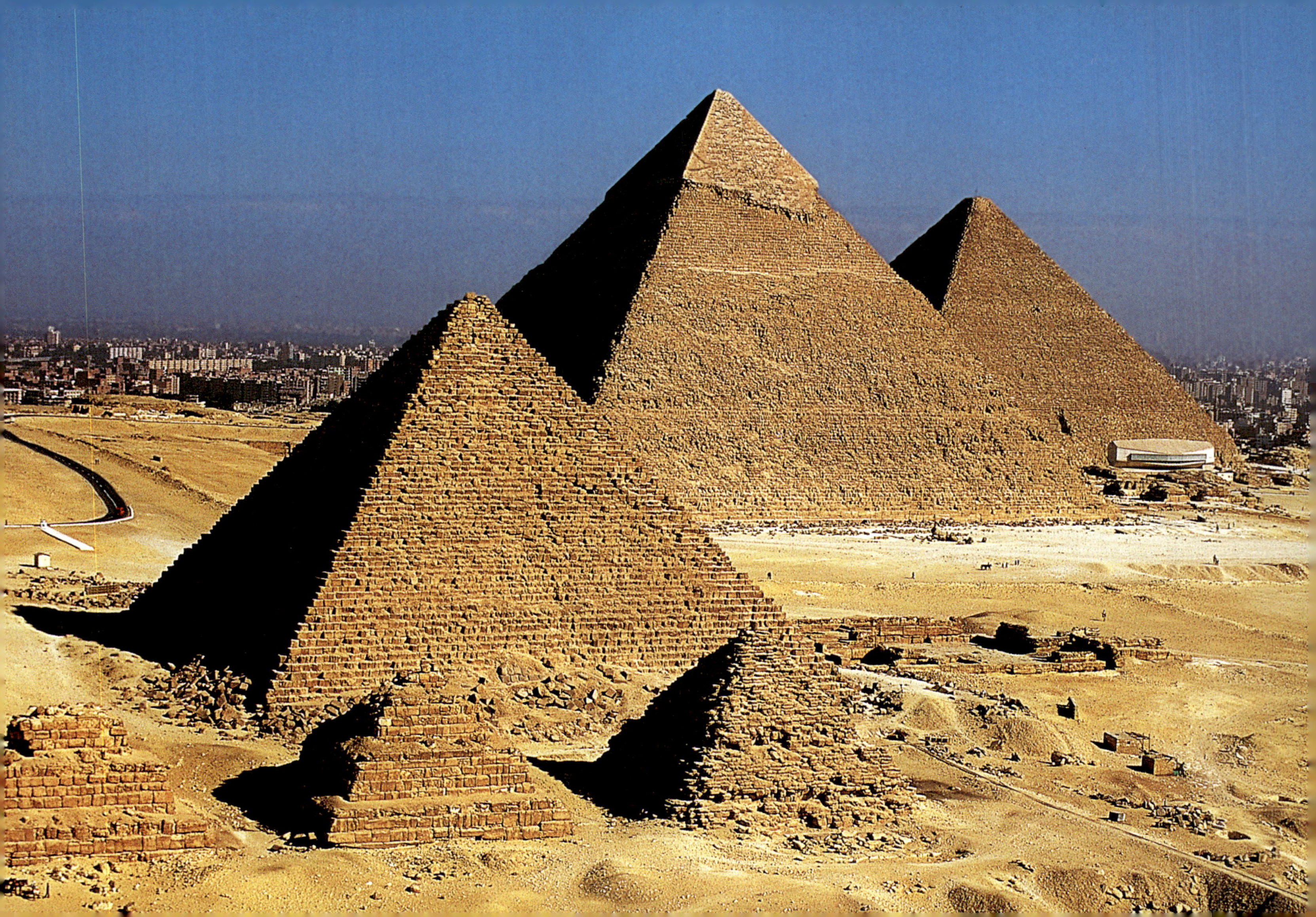

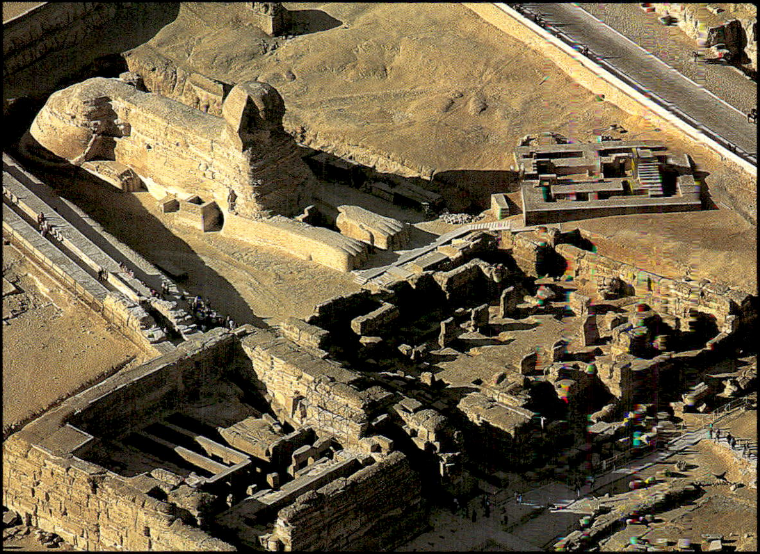

598
The complex of the three pyramids of Giza in Egypt, composed of the three impressive funeral monuments of Khufu, Khefre and Menkaure numbered among the seven ancient wonders of the world.

599
The sphinx of Giza, about 65 feet tall and 187 long, was built according to the wishes of the Pharaoh Khafre.

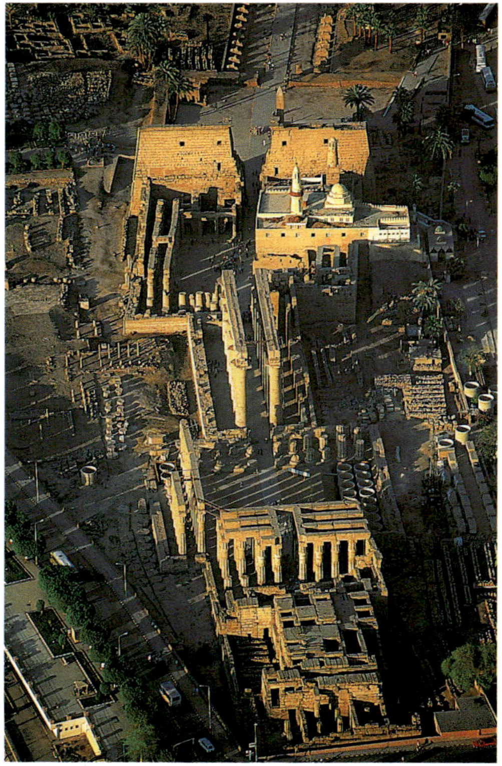

600
The temple of Luxor, on the eastern bank of the Nile, in Egypt, was commissioned by Amenhotep III.

601
The temple of Luxor was connected, by way of a Sphinx-lined avenue, to the immense temple of Karnak.

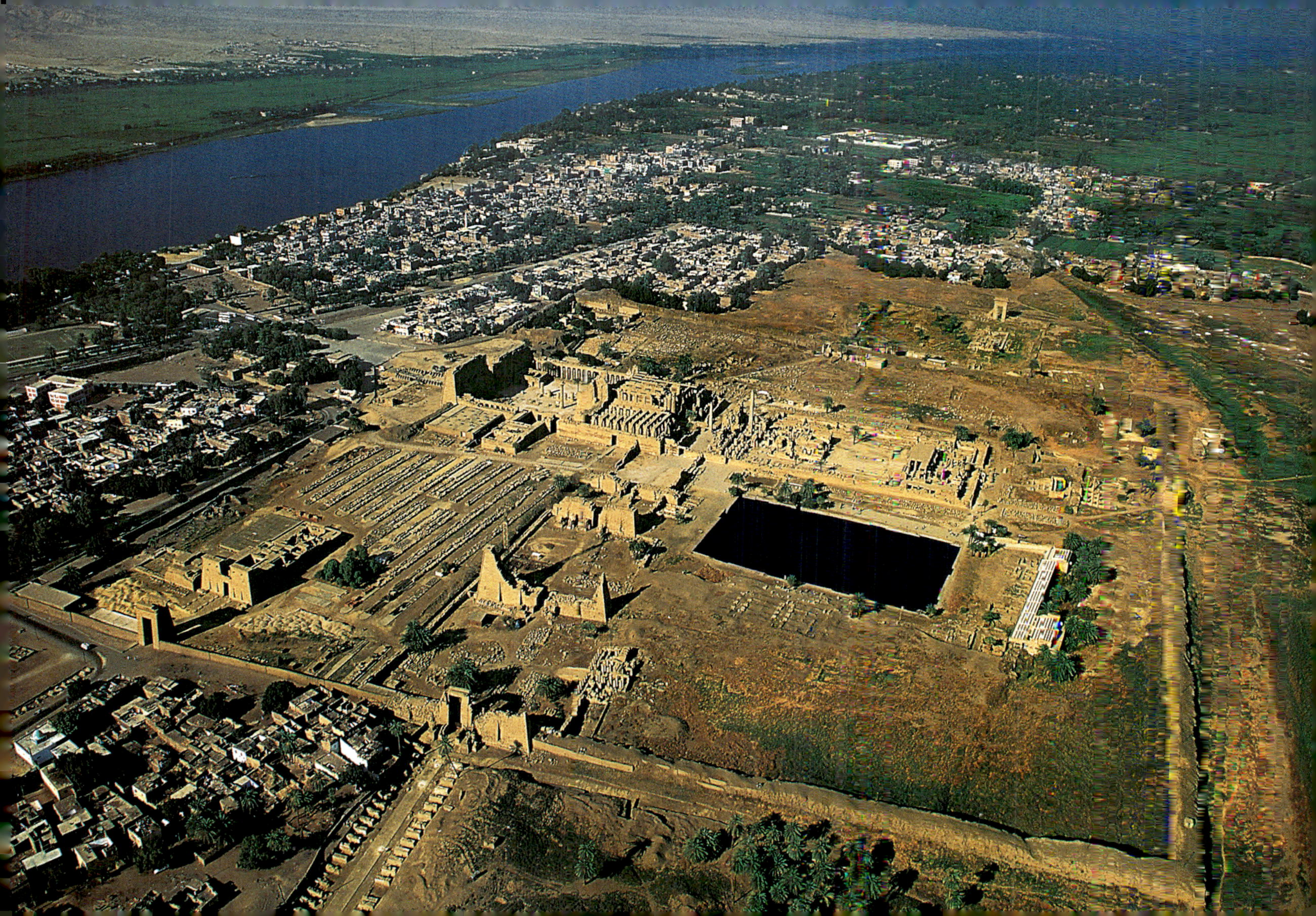

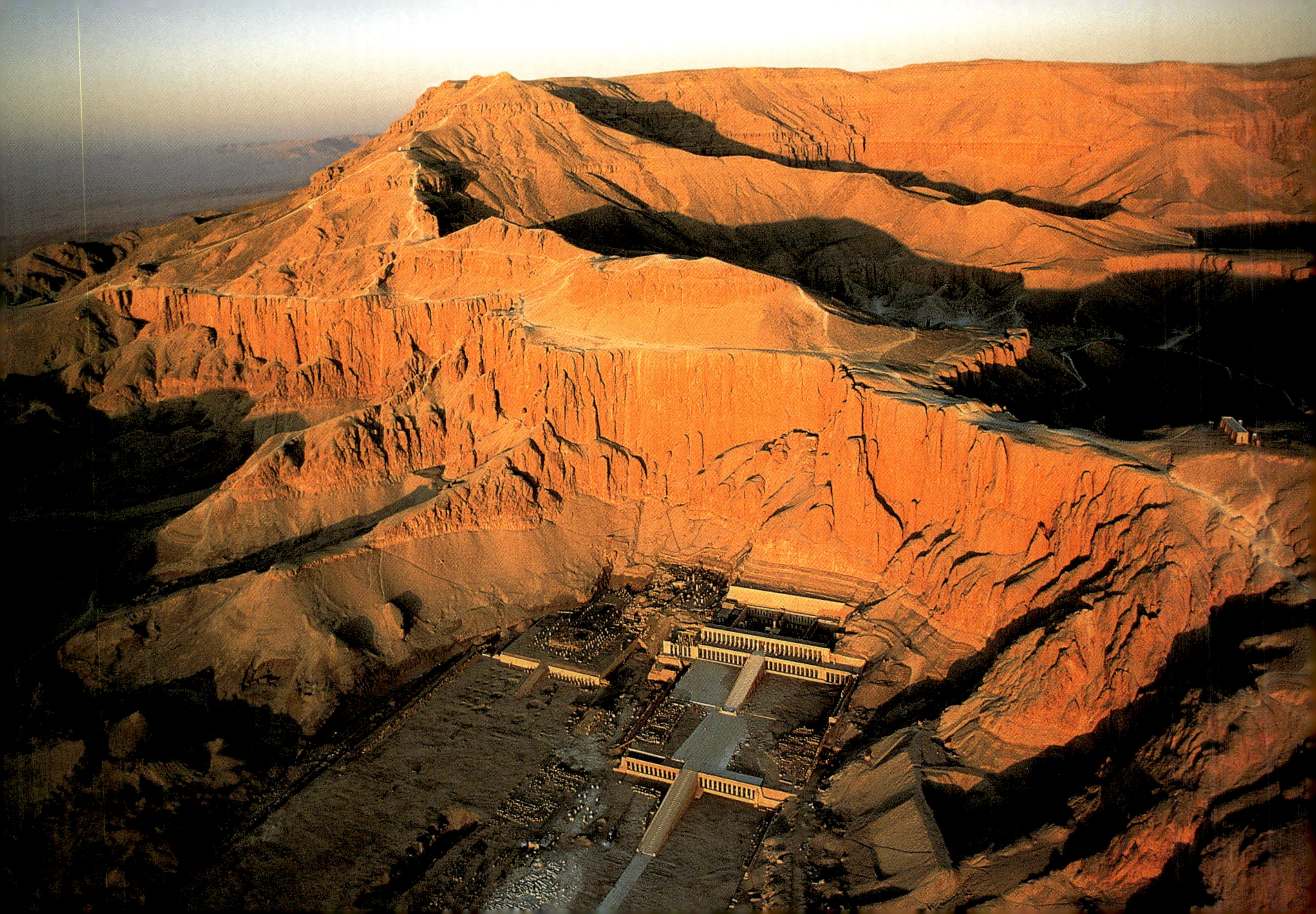

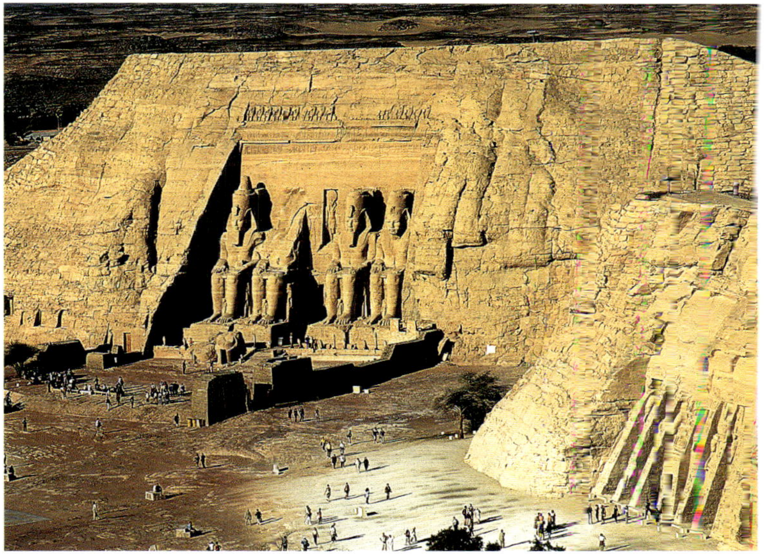

602

The embankment of Deir el-Bahari, in West Thebes in Egypt, encompasses the royal temples of Mentuhotep II, Thutmosis III, and Hatshepsut.

603

The entrance to the Big Temple of Ramesses II at Abu Simbel is flanked by four 66-foot-tall colossi carved into the rock.

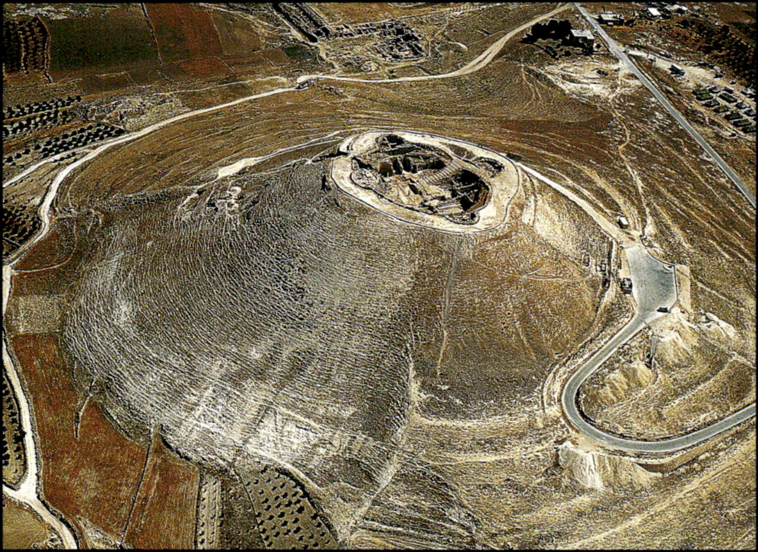

604

On a hill near Bethlehem stand the remains of the Herodion, a circular fortress built by Herod.

605

The fortress of Masada in Israel was ordered built by Herod and was supposed to protect the road to Jerusalem and the area of the Dead Sea.

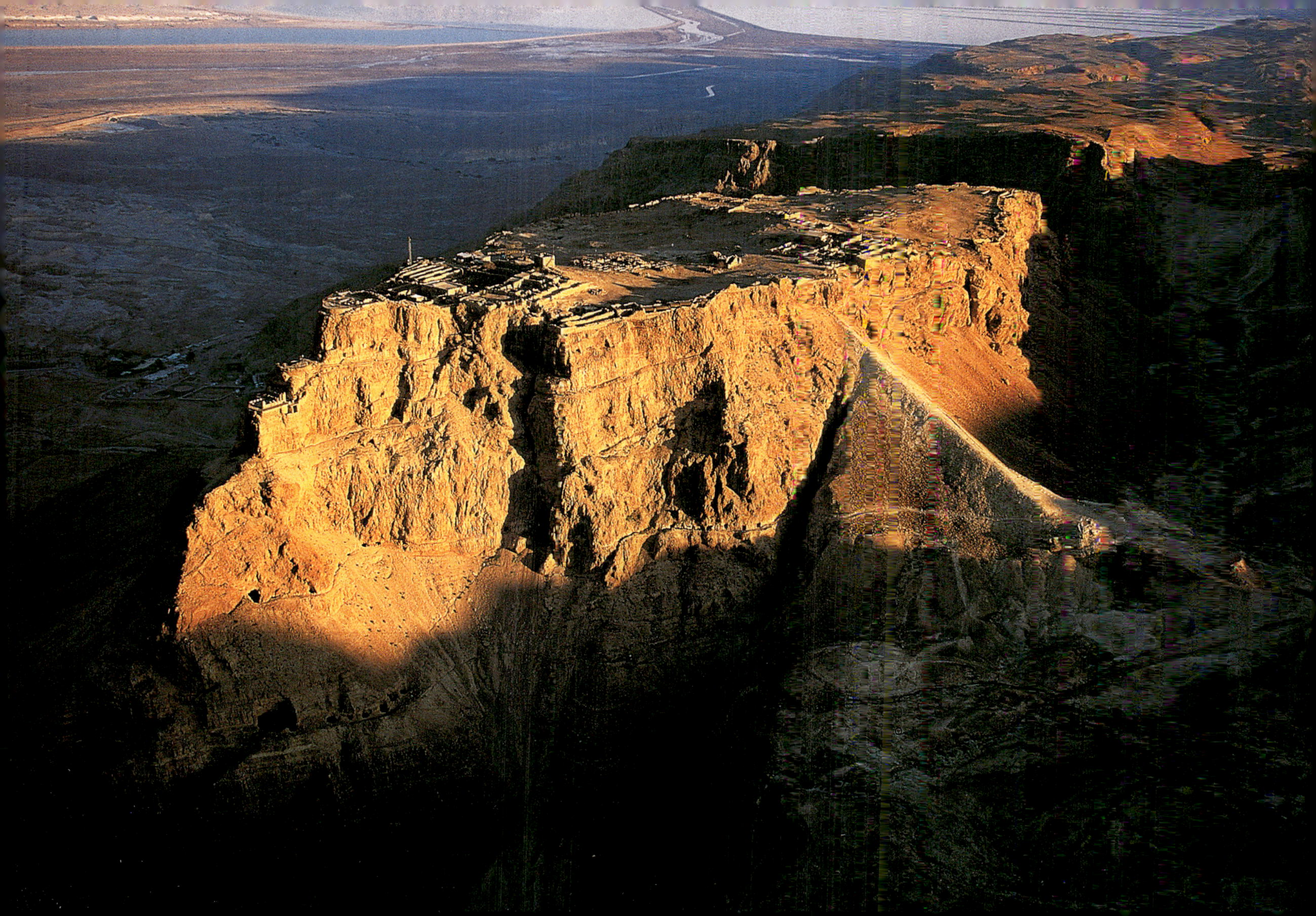

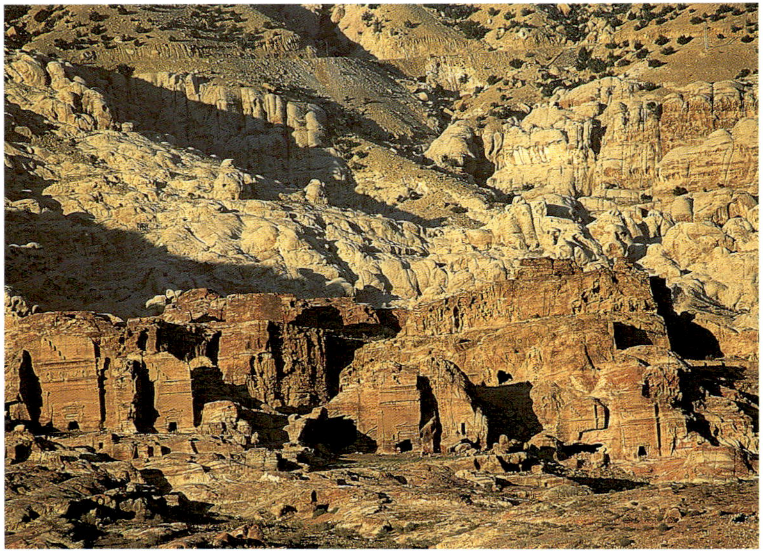

606 and 607

Petra, in Jordan, is an astounding rock city dating back to 1000 B.C. when the Nabatean civilization was flourishing in the territory. In the photo on the left, the Ad-Dayr Monastery can be seen and on the right, a monumental tomb.

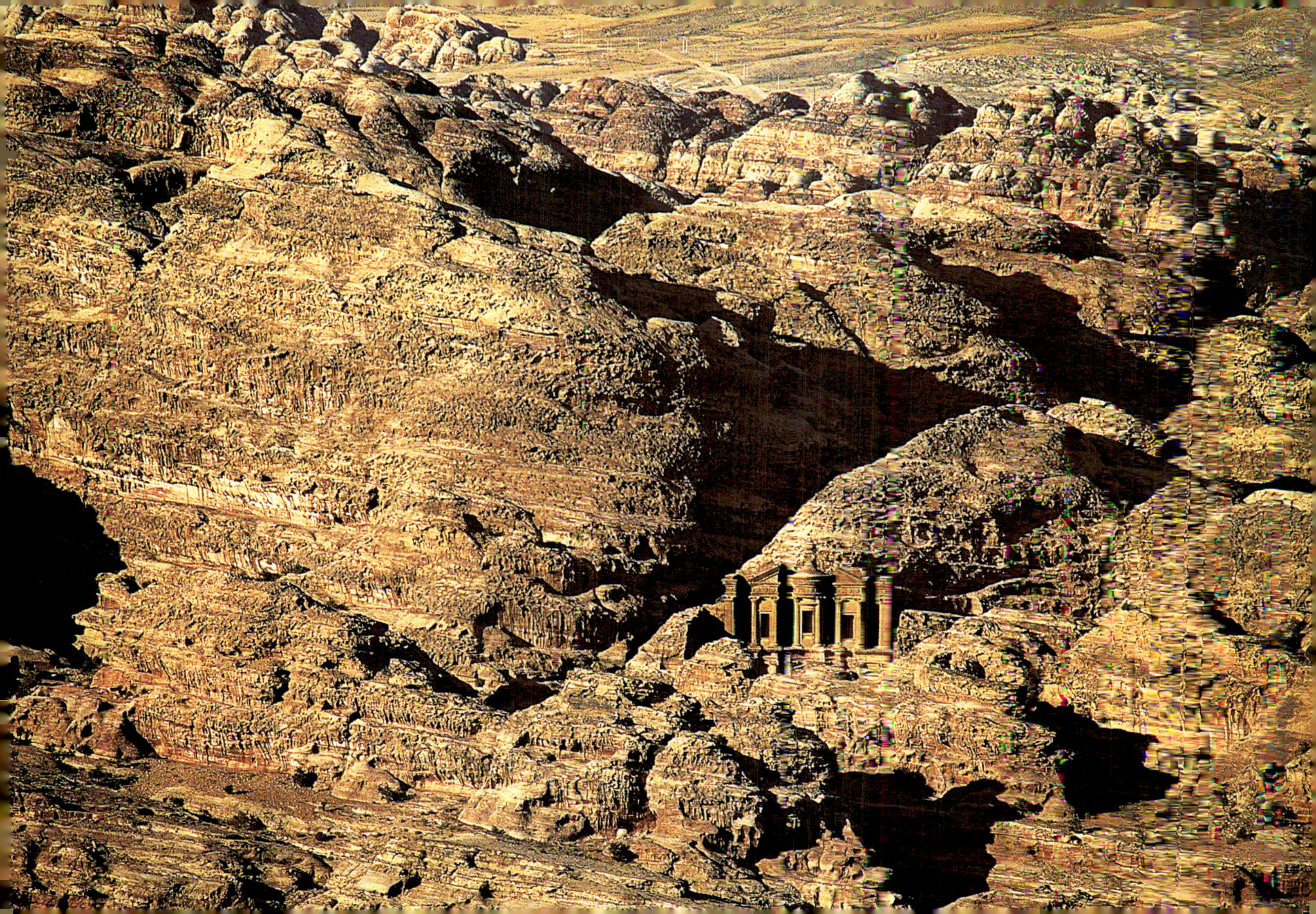

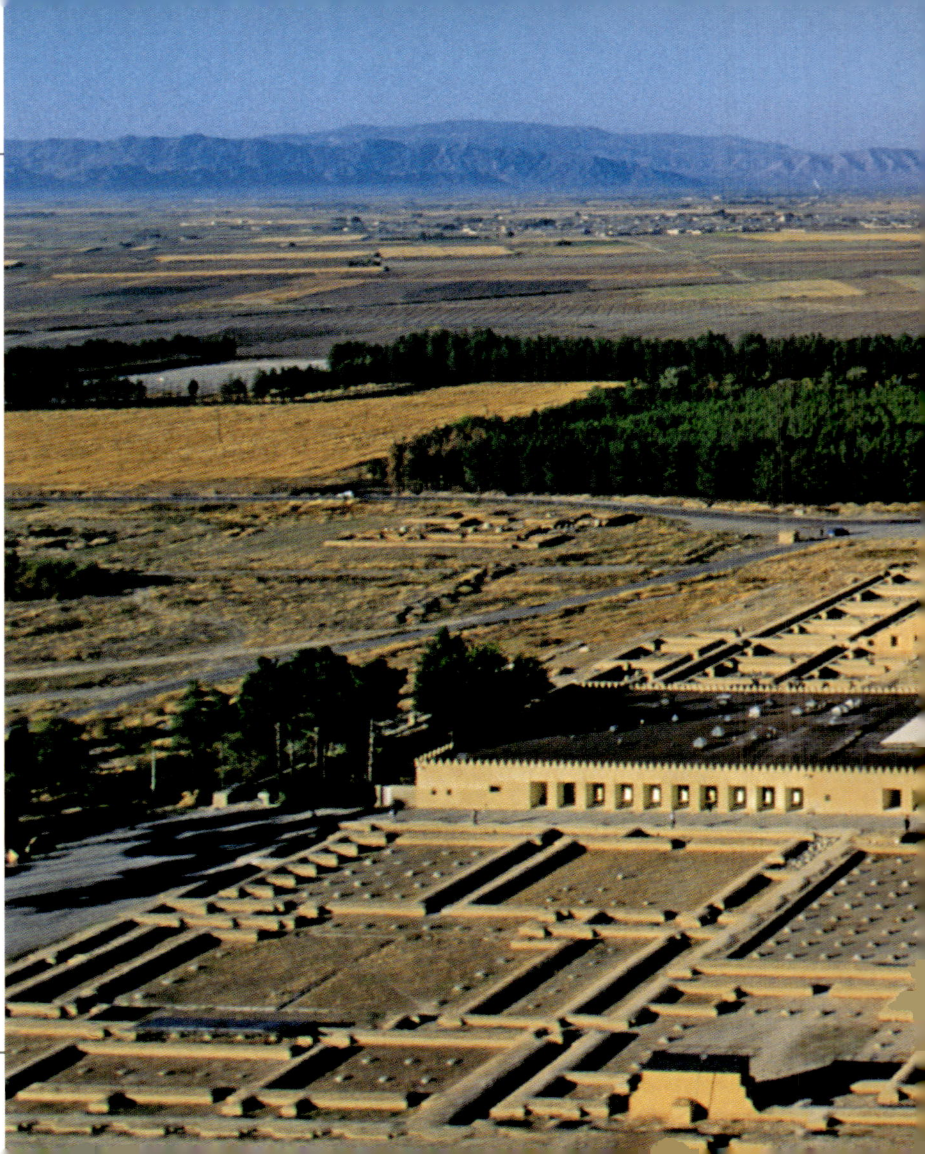

608-609

The ruins of Persepolis, in Iran, are all that remain of a glorious complex of palaces built starting in 512 B.C. and completed only 150 years later. It was burned to the ground during the reign of Alexander the Great in 331 B.C., perhaps in retaliation for the destruction of Athens by Xerxes.

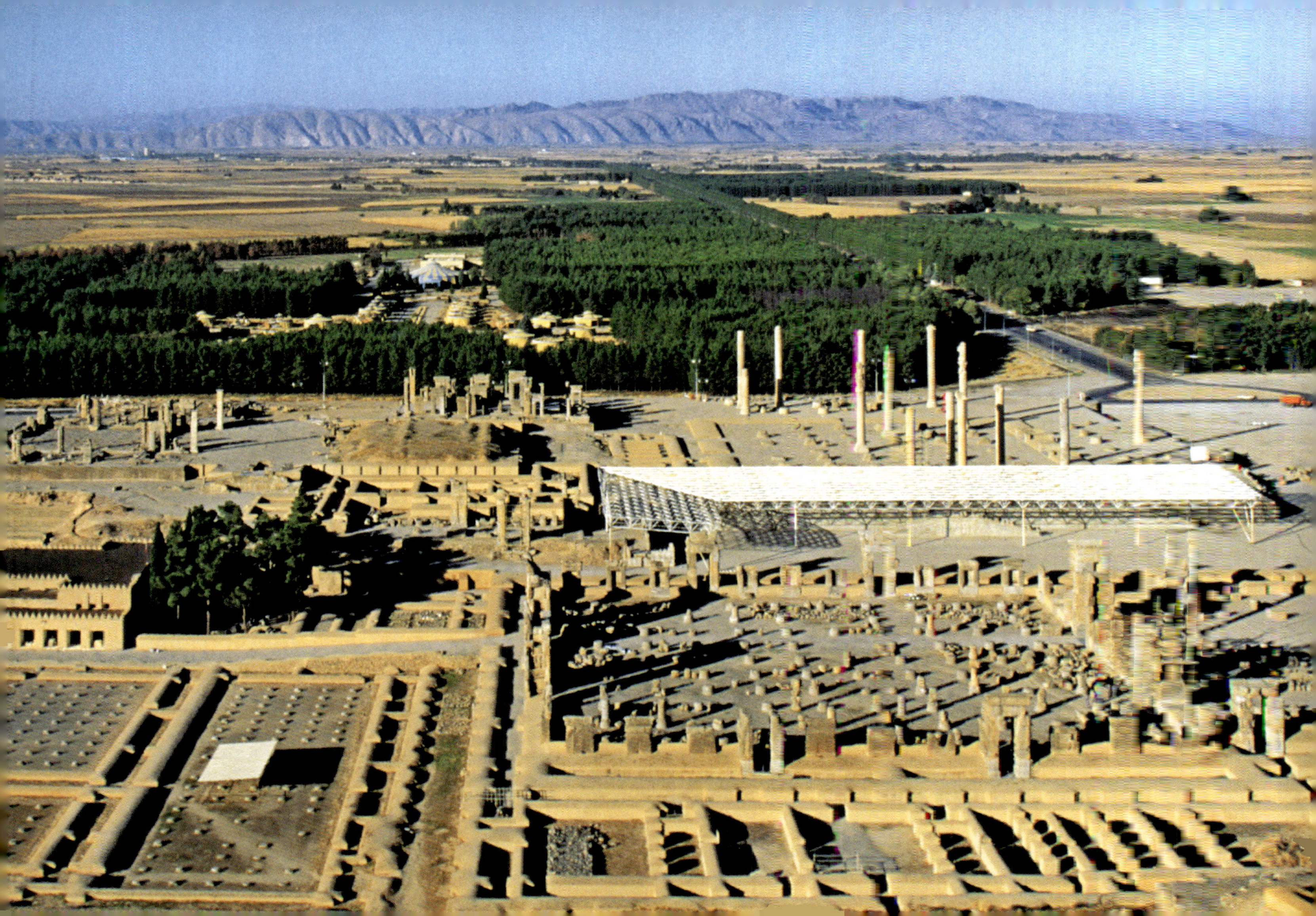

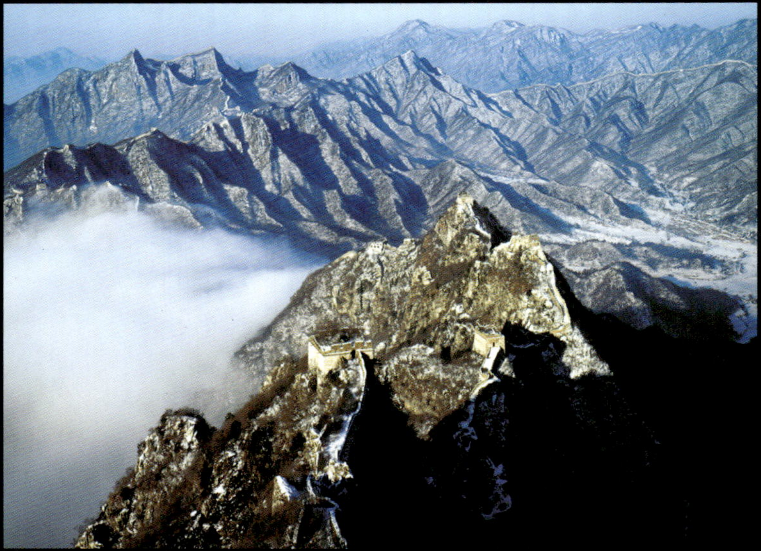

610 and 611

The Great Wall, whose construction was begun in the third century B.C., had the purpose of protecting the northern border of China and linking a series of fortresses.

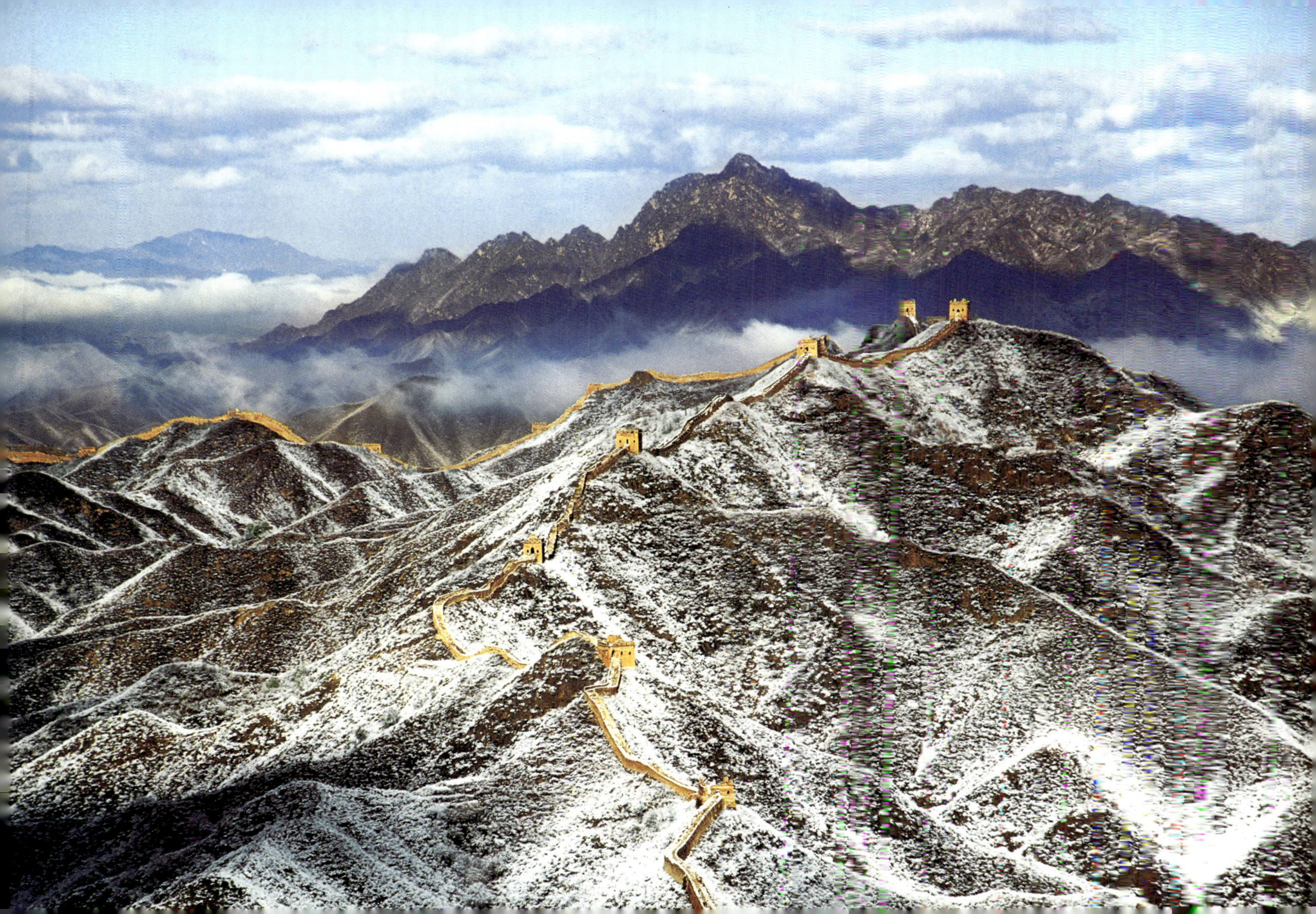

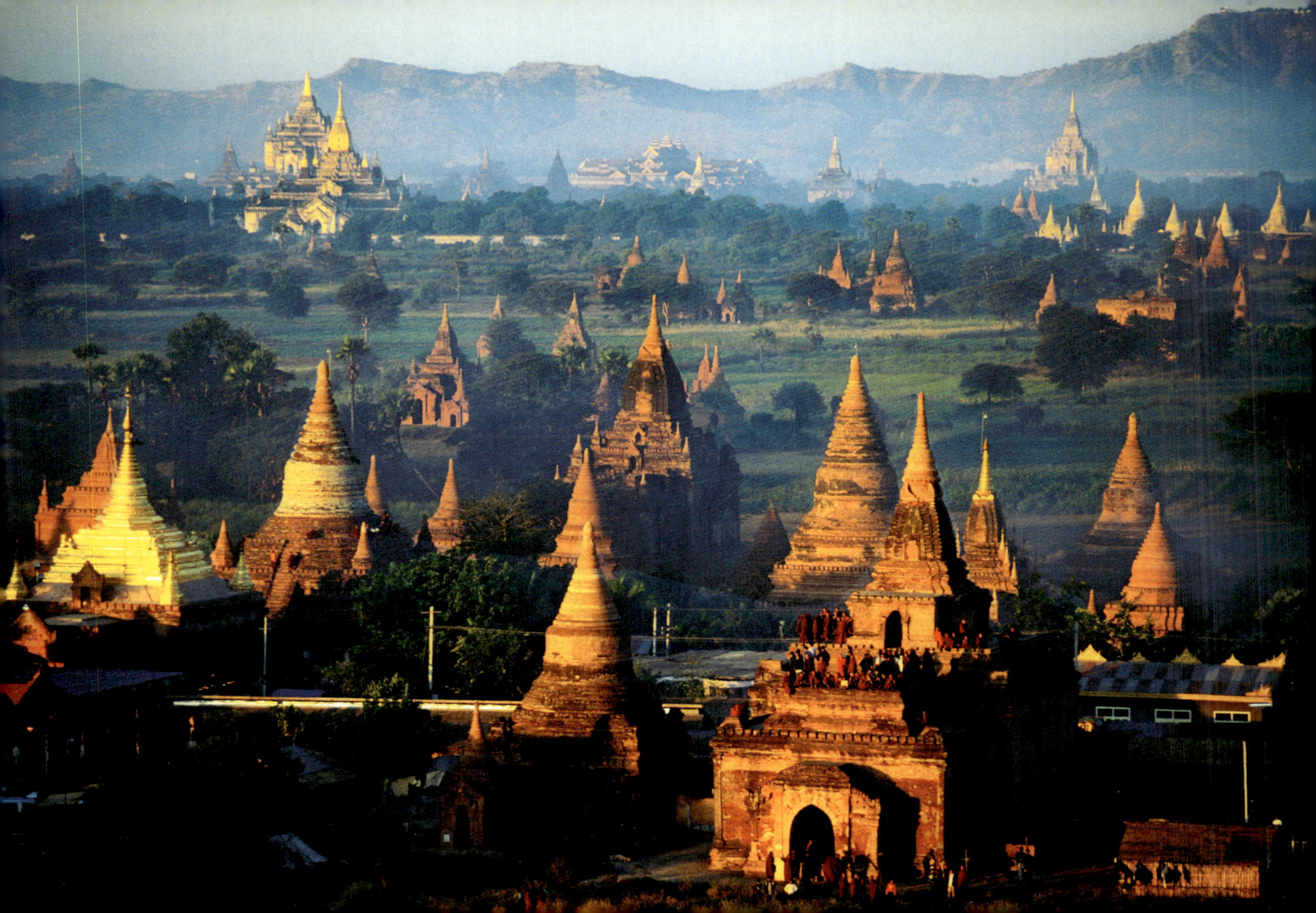

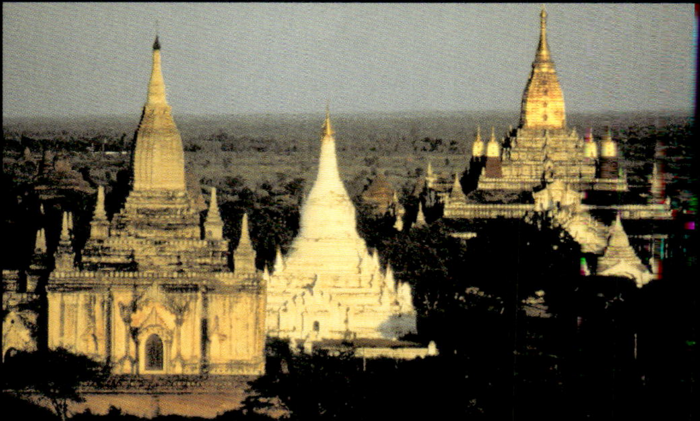

612 and 613

Pagan, in Burma, capital of the kingdom of the same name that flourished between the eleventh and twelfth centuries, is dotted with about 13,000 buildings of a votive nature, like pagodas, temples, and monasteries.

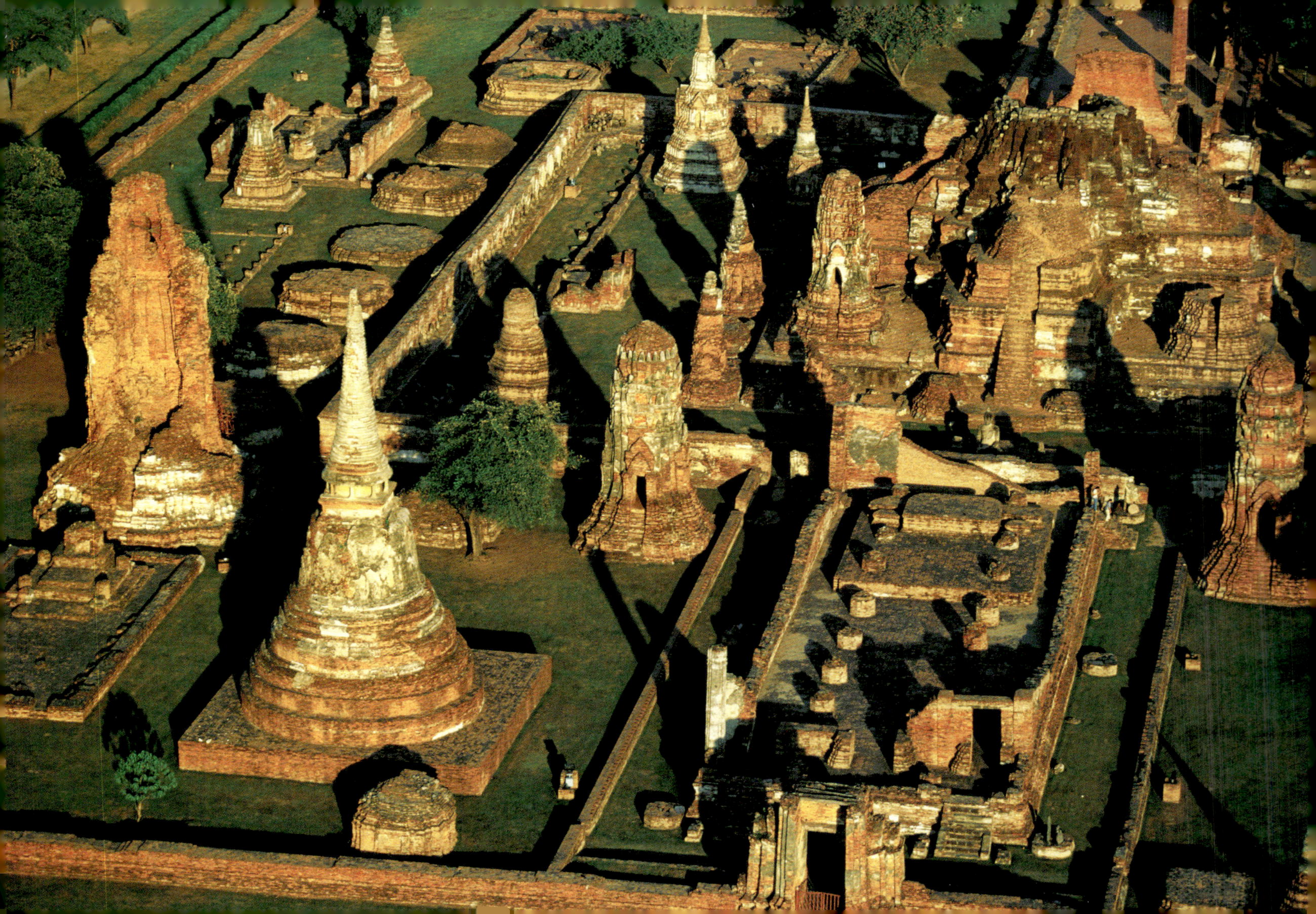

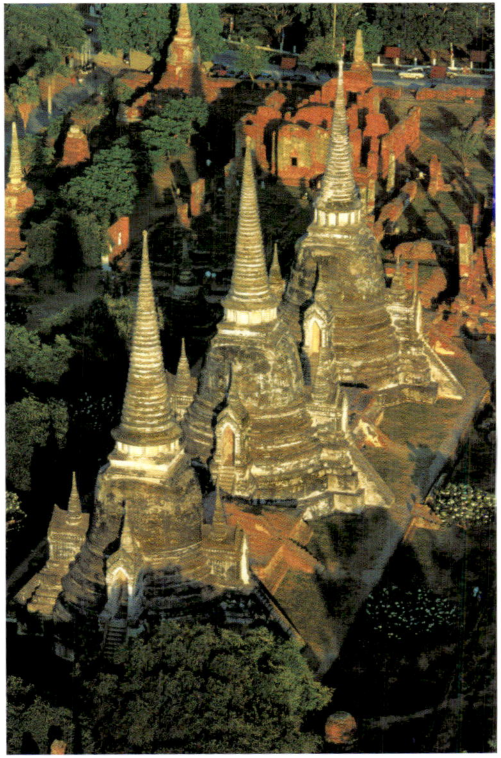

In the Furrows of Time

614 and 615

Ayutthaya, in Thailand, was for four centuries the capital of Siam before being destroyed by the Burmese in 1767; glorious temples were built there, like Wat Mahathat (photo on the left) and Wat Phra Si Sanphet (photo on the right).

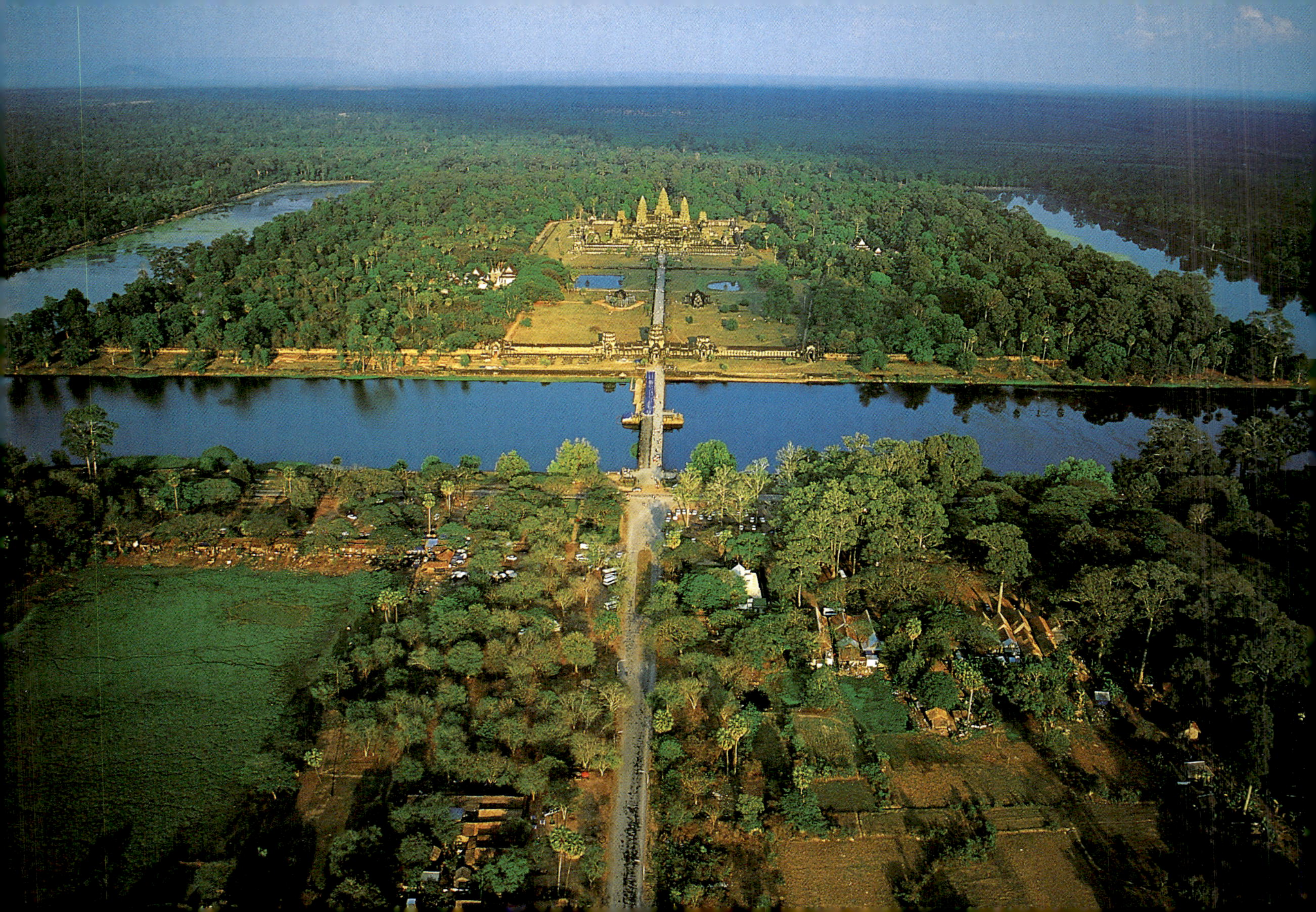

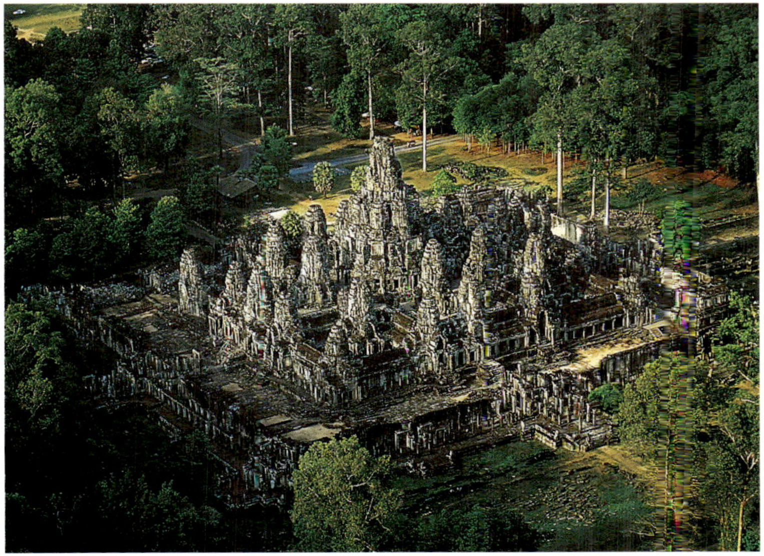

616

The most important monument in the ancient Khmer city of Angkor, built between the ninth and fourteenth centuries in Cambodia, is the temple of Angkor Wat, surrounded by a ditch eight miles by nine miles.

617

Another gem of Angkor is the temple of Bayon, dotted by smiling faces, which, for some, portray Buddha, carved into the 54 towers on the building.

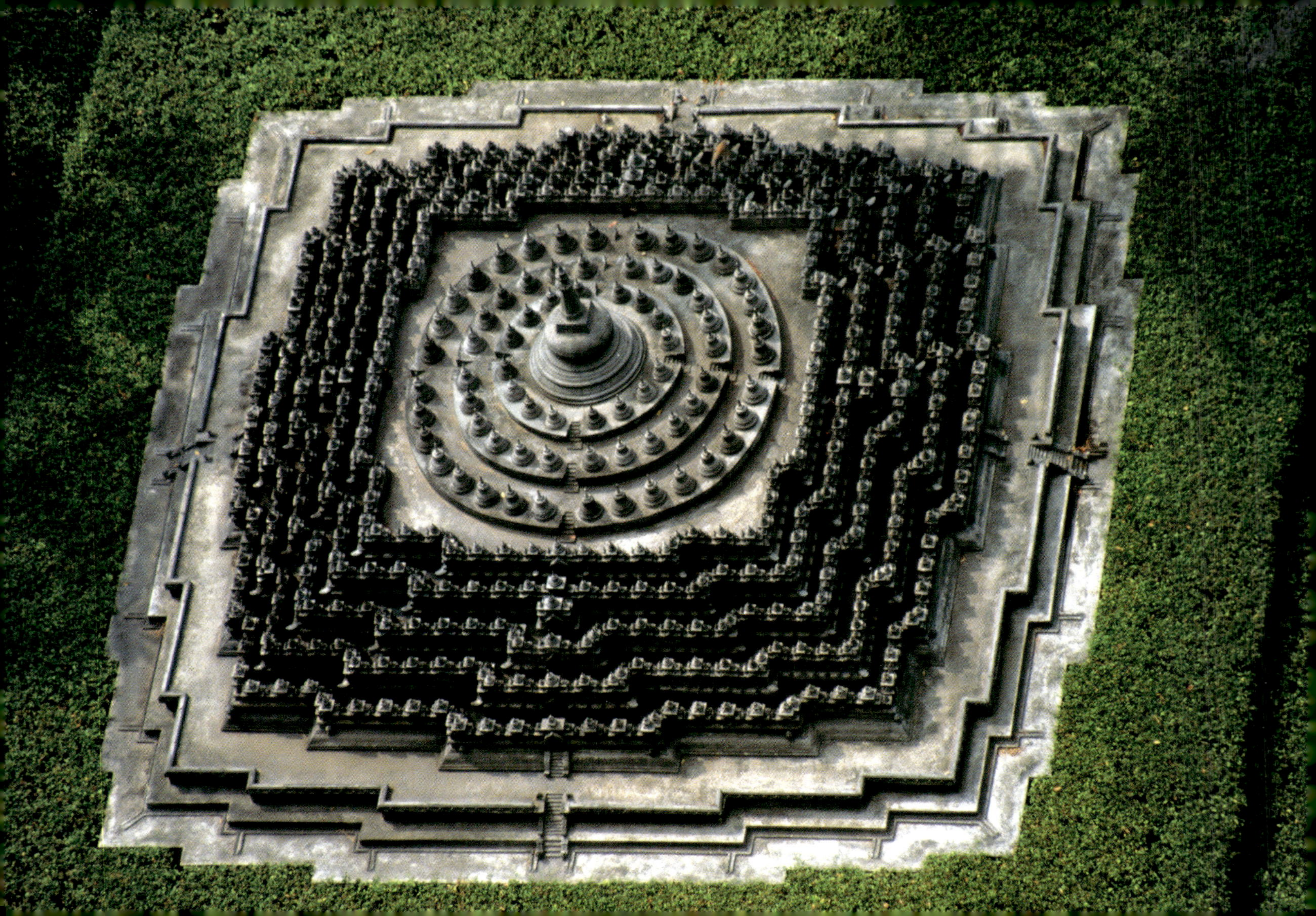

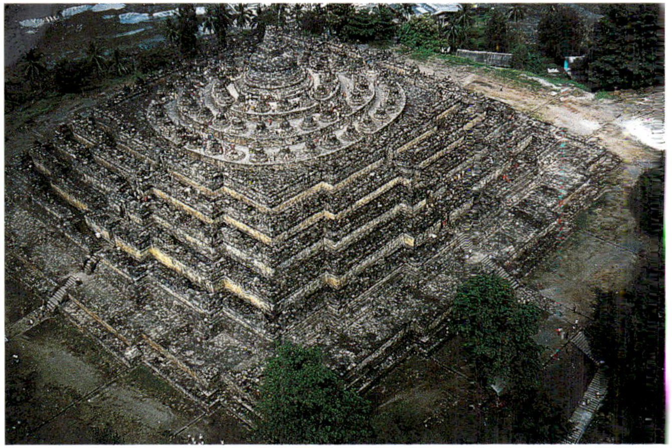

618 and 619

The temple of Borobudur on the island of Java, in Indonesia, was built in the ninth century A.D. and abandoned in the eleventh. Its structure influenced the architectural tastes of many other religious buildings in the area.

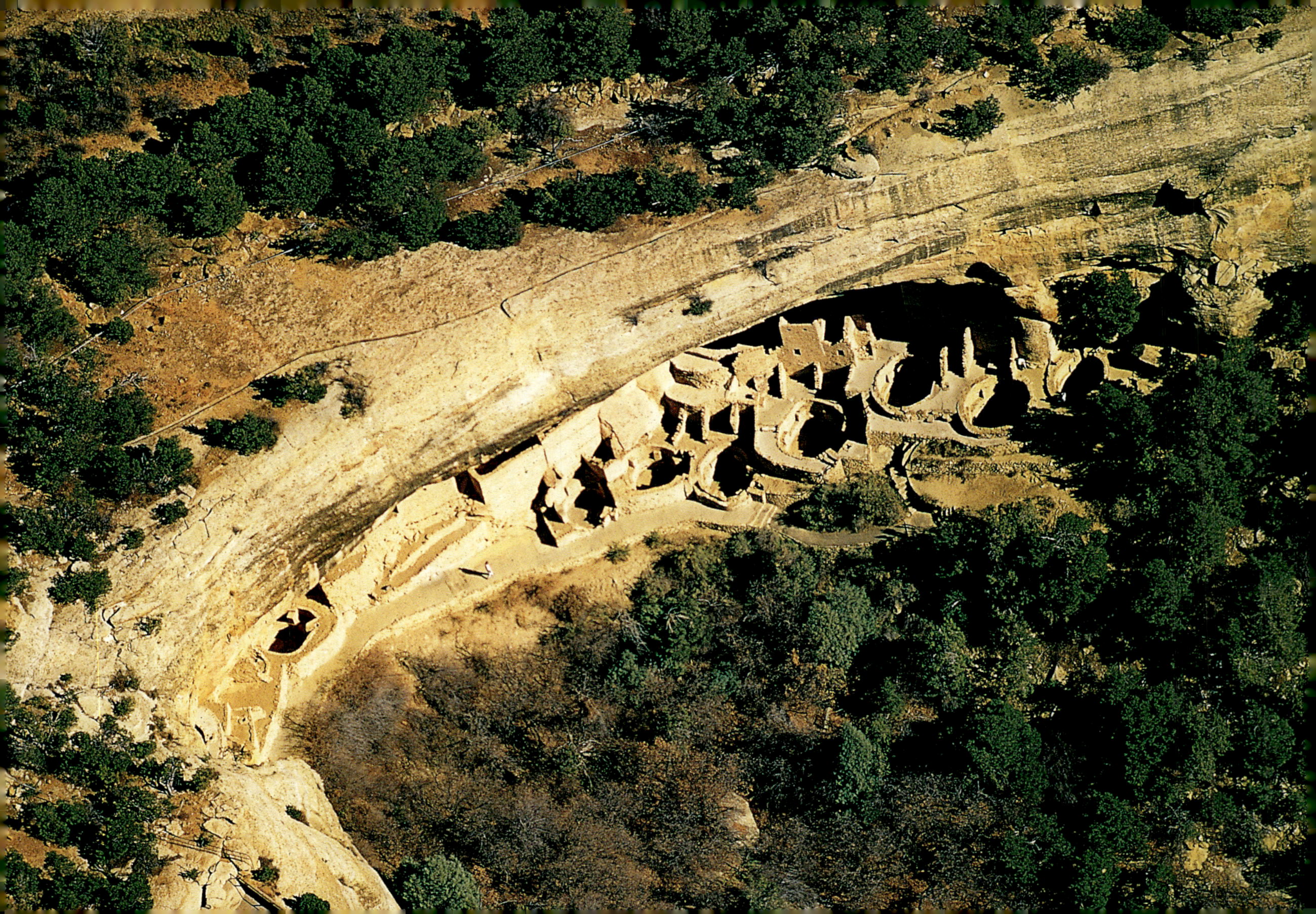

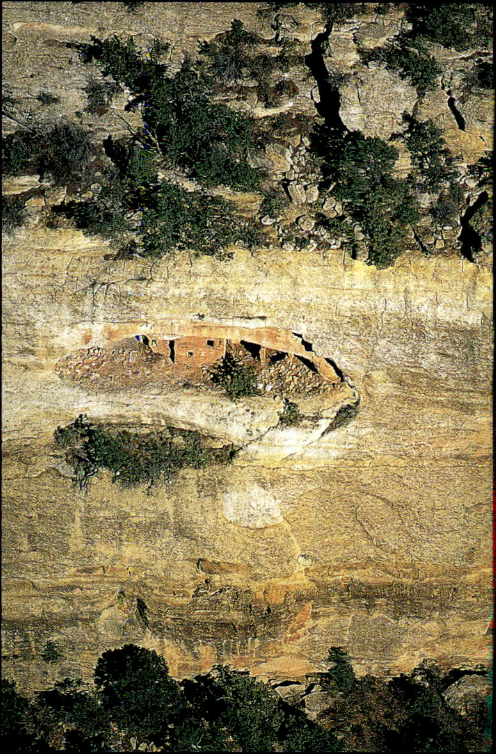

America

620 and 621

Mesa Verde, in Colorado, is a site of both naturalistic and archaeological interest: between the seventh and the fourteenth centuries A.D., a community flourished here that erected elaborate stone villages in the shadow of the canyons.

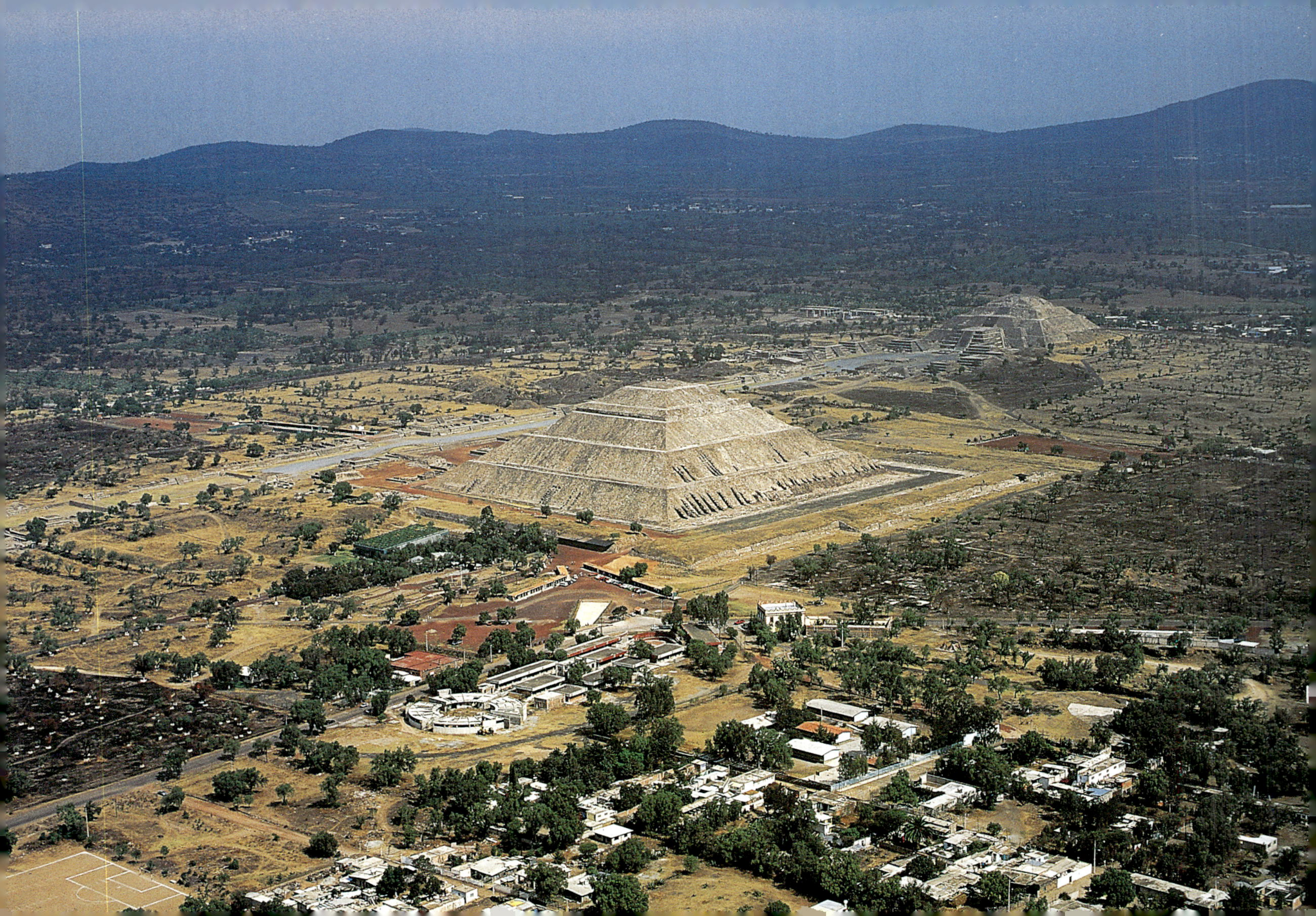

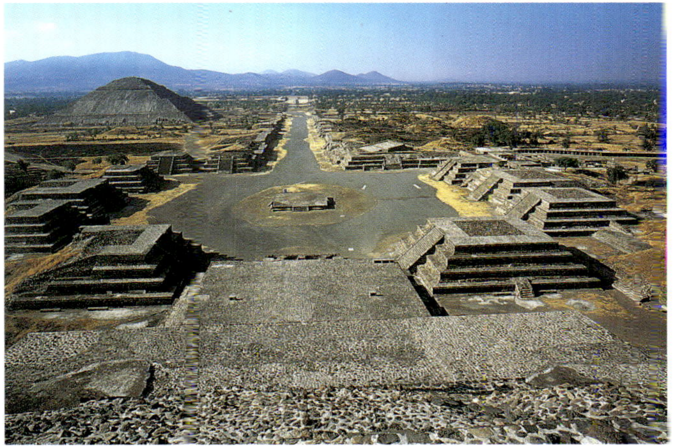

622 and 623

The Avenue of the Dead traces a bisecting line across Teotihuacan, the "City of the Gods," in Mexico. The two most significant monuments are the Pyramid of the Sun, seen on the left in both the views, and the smaller one of the Moon, on the right in the large photo.

624

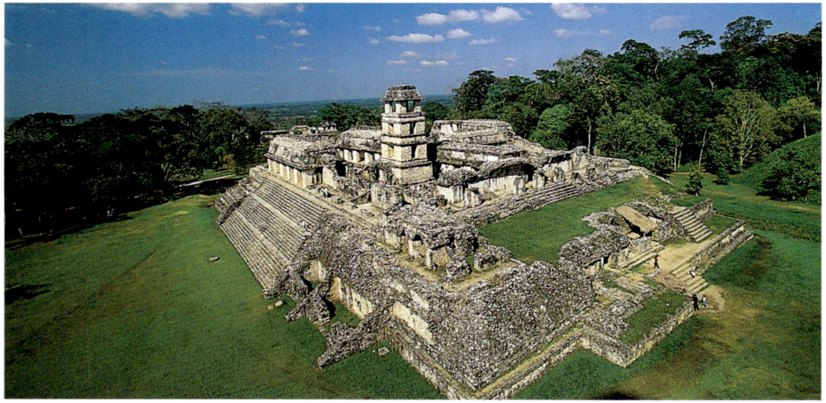

624 and 625

One of the most important archaeological sites in Mexico is that of Palenque, one of the largest religious centers of the classical Mayan era and one of the tourist attractions in the Chiapas region.

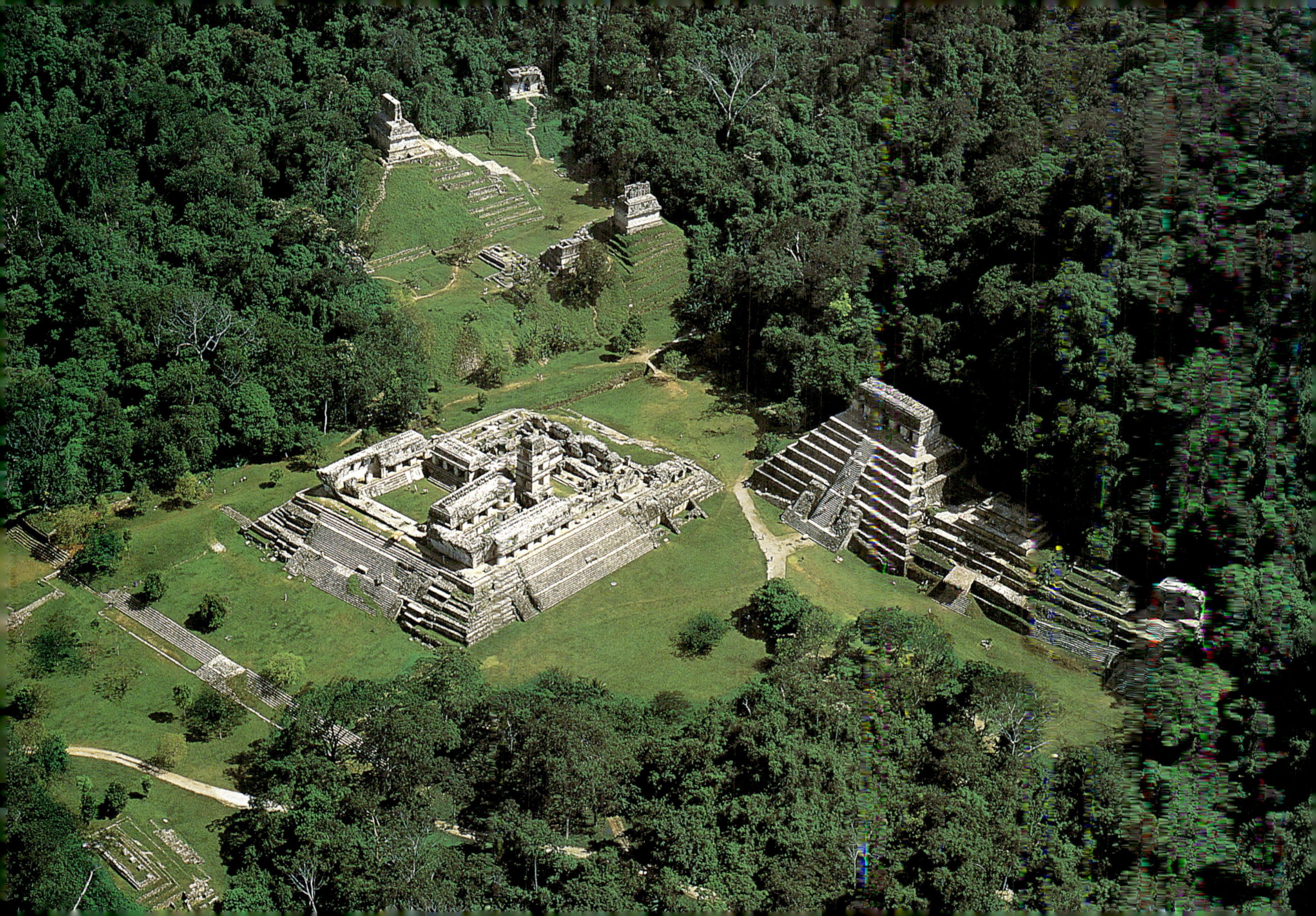

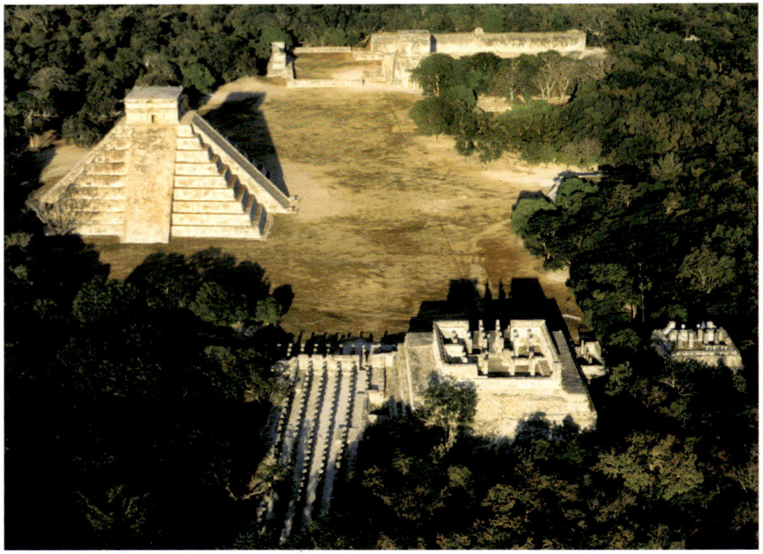

626 and 627

Chichen Itza, on the Yucatan Peninsula in Mexico, was one of the most prestigious towns in the Mayan world. Impressive monuments remain, like the Pyramid of Kukulcan, called *El Castillo* by the Spanish.

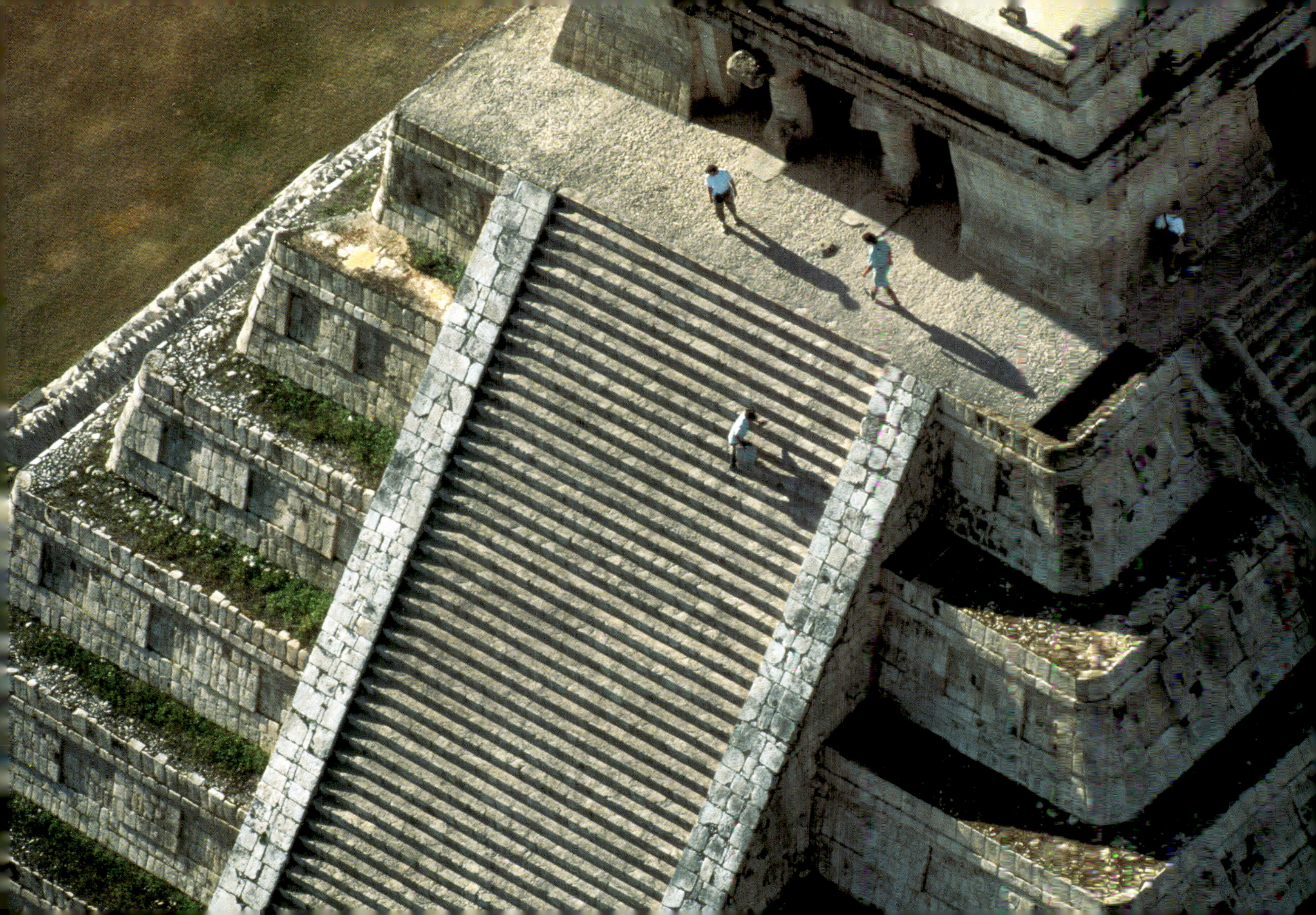

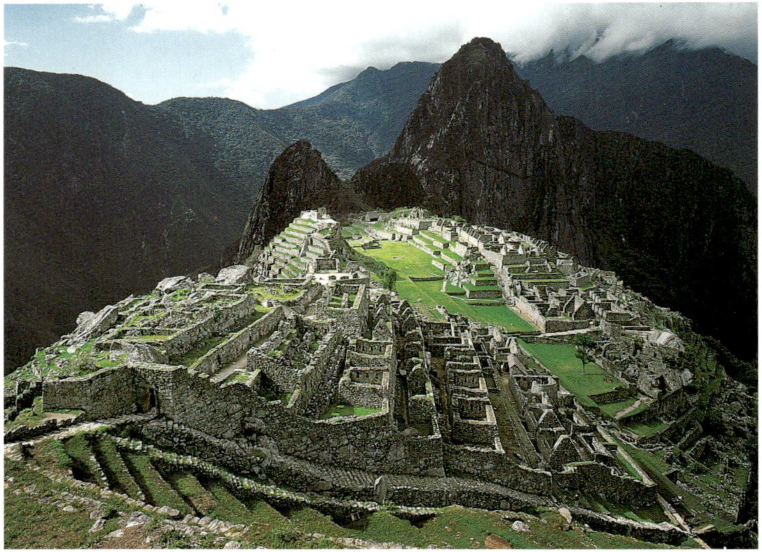

628
Machu Picchu, thanks to its inaccessible position and its extraordinary architecture, is one of the most interesting archaeological sites in the world.

629
The terraces upon which the outskirts of Machu Picchu are spread were probably tied to farming activities.

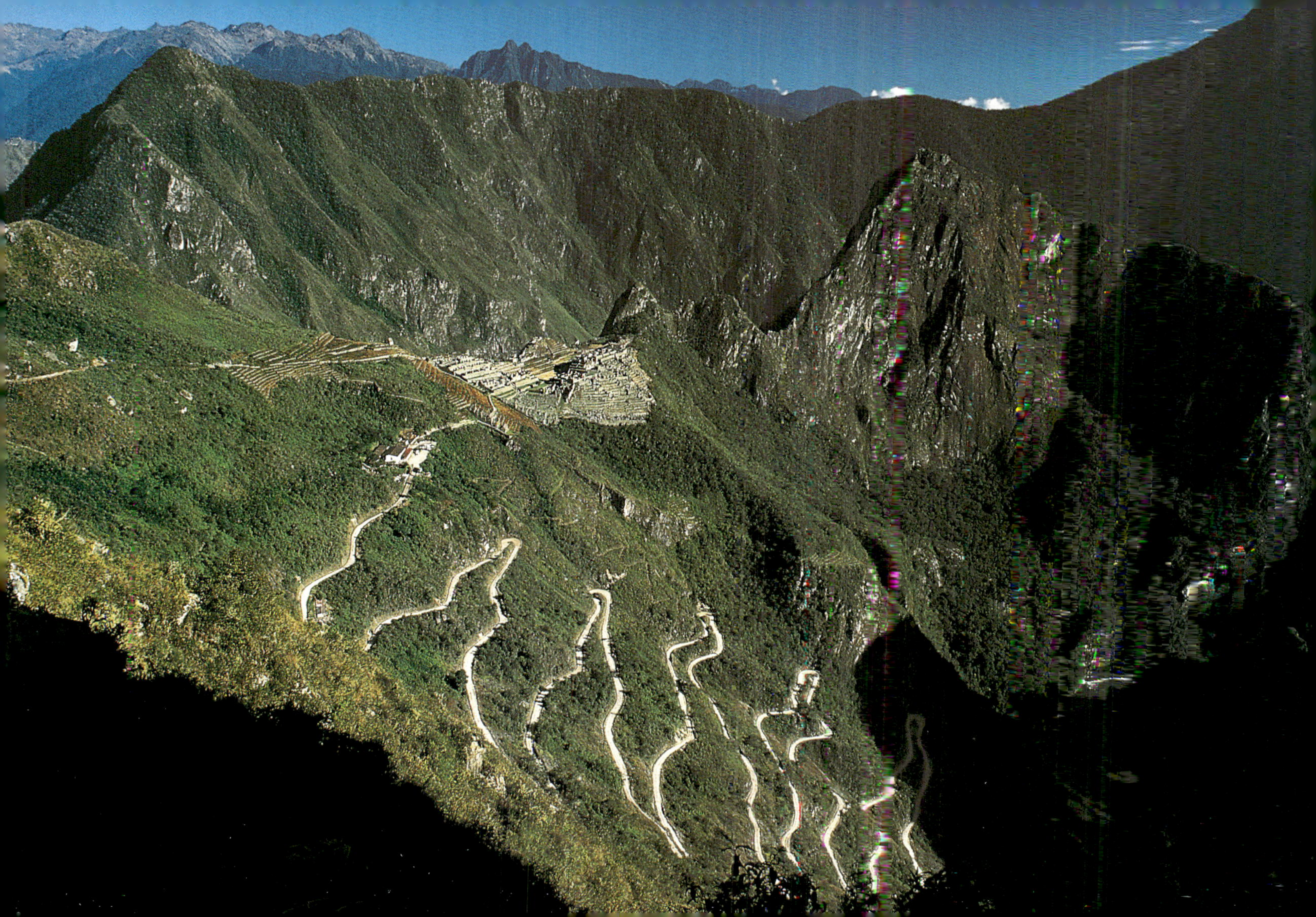

630

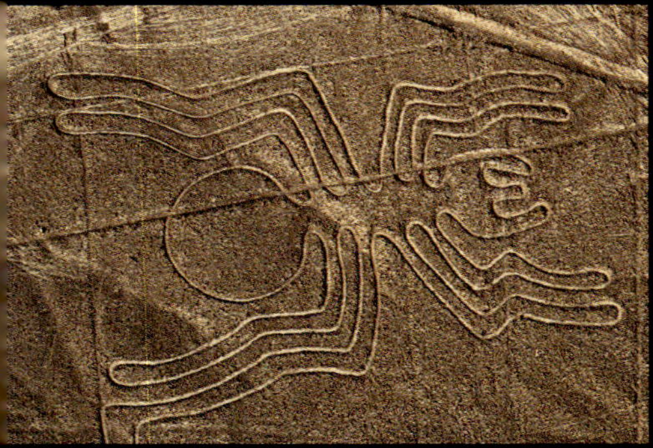

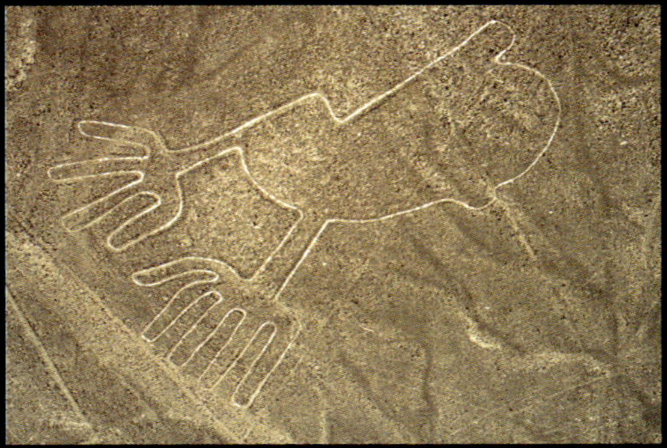

630 and 631
Nazca is a place in the Peruvian Andes linked to the civilization of the same name that developed there between the third and tenth centuries A.D. Hundreds of lines forming enormous geometric designs portraying mostly animal subjects were traced on its approximately 20-square-mile surface area.

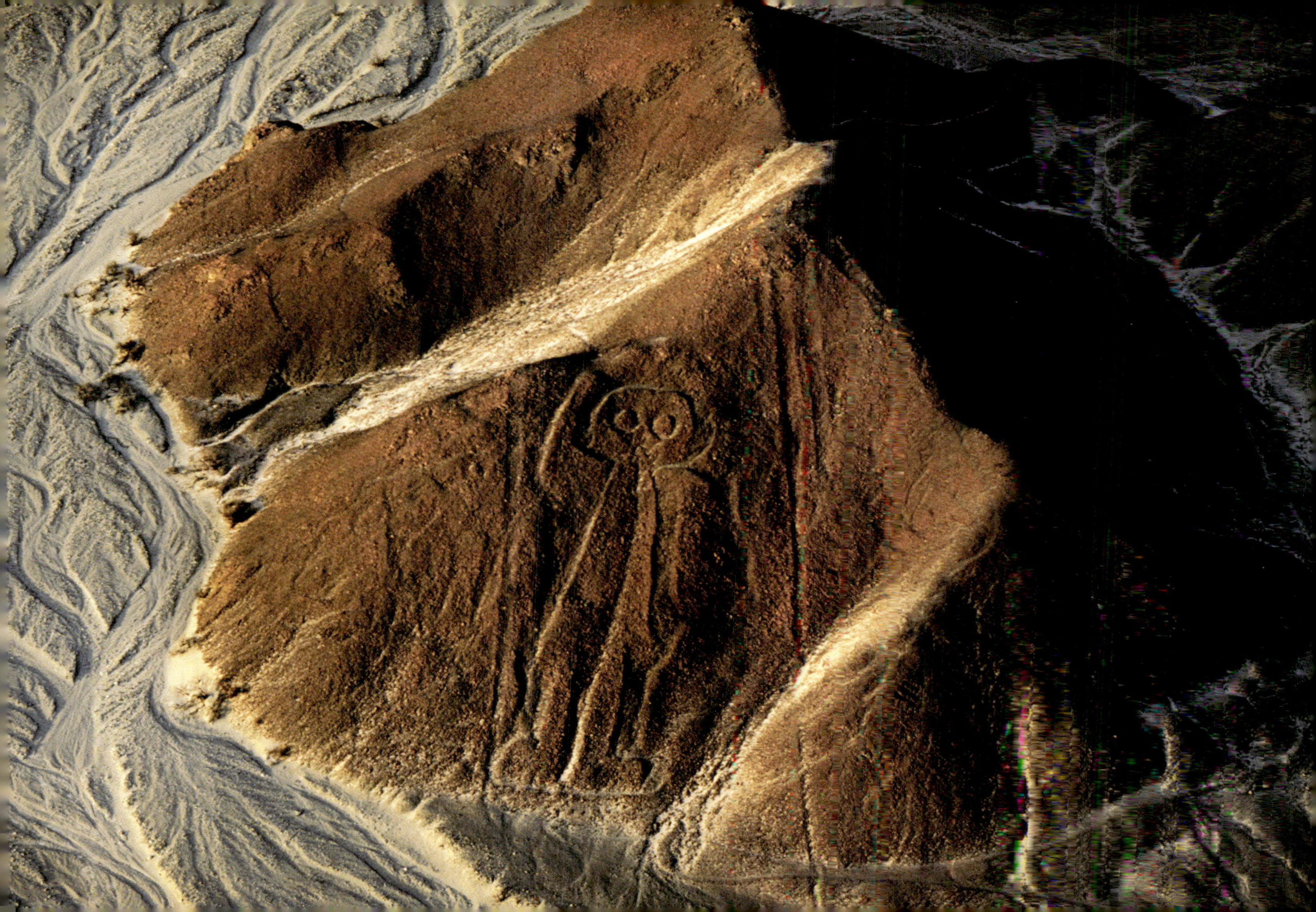

Enrico Lavagno, was born in Turin in 1962. Besides his classical studies, he is also an expert in Oriental cultures. For many years he has worked for White Star publishers, especially in the fields of archaeology, history and art. He has also translated many works on these subjects from English and French into Italian; among these are the unabridged editions of David Roberts's two monumental masterpieces, *The Holy Land and Egypt and Nubia* (White Star, 2000), *Ramses II* by T.G.H. James (White Star 2001), and *The Valley of the Kings* (White Star, 2001), edited and partly written by the archaeologist Kent Weeks. He also translated several books from National Geographic Book Division, and took part in the editorial coordination of the best-selling *Marco Polo, a Photographer's Journey* (White Star, 2002) featuring the three years long assignment on the footsteps of the Venetian traveler by National Geographic Staff photographer Michael Yamashita, succesfully published in several countries around the World. He is co-author of the book *The Holy Land, Guide to the Archaeological Sites of Israel, Sinai and Jordan* (White Star, 2001).

Index

c = caption

Index

Index

Index

Index

Index

Photo credits

Alamy Images: Page 99, 560
Theo Allofs/Corbis/Contrasto: Page 400
Arctic Images: Page 41
Jon Arnold/Danita Delimont: Pages 241 left and right
Yann Arthus–Bertrand/Corbis/Contrasto: Pages 9, 10, 40, 56, 57, 59, 74, 75, 76, 77, 94, 95, 96, 97, 98, 100, 101, 130, 131, 133, 134, 135, 137, 142, 146, 170, 171, 178, 179, 182, 183, 186-187, 189, 202, 203, 284-285, 298, 304, 305, 314, 320, 321, 328, 330, 361, 366, 370, 371, 372, 399 left, 419, 420, 434, 450, 451, 456, 466, 467, 476, 477, 478 left, 478 right, 479, 499, 512, 513, 523 right, 562, 563, 566, 567, 592, 594-595, 596, 597, 614, 615, 627, 630 left, 631
Art Wolfe: Page 234
Art Wolfe/Danita Delimont: Pages 205 left, 242
Antonio Attini/Archivio White Star: Pages 4-5, 12-13, 30-31, 33 left, 42, 43, 44, 45, 64, 65, 70, 71, 110, 111, 112, 113, 127, 144 left, 152, 153, 162, 168-169, 172, 190, 191, 200-201, 313, 323 left, 334, 335, 340, 341, 342 left, 342 right, 343, 344, 345, 374, 375, 382, 383, 384, 385, 386, 387, 389, 404, 442, 443, 444, 445, 455 right, 461, 468 left, 468 right, 469, 470, 471, 492, 493 left, center and right, 530, 531, 536, 537, 538, 539, 540, 544, 546, 547, 548, 549 left, 549 right, 550 left, 550 right, 551, 552, 554 left, 554 right, 556, 557, 558, 559 left, 559 right, 578, 579 left, 579 right, 588, 589, 590 right, 591, 622, 623, 628
AWC Images/Sime Photo/Sie: Page 197
Gianni and Tiziana Baldizzone/Archivio White Star: Page 412
Anthony Bannister/NHPA: Page 360
Bruno Barbey/ Magnum Photos/Contrasto: Page 303
Bruno Barbier/Hemispheres Images: Page 409
Marcello Bertinetti/Archivio White Star: Pages 1, 6-7, 8, 11, 14-15, 26-27, 34, 66 left, 66 right, 67, 68, 69, 78, 79, 80, 81, 82, 83, 84, 85, 102, 103, 104, 105, 106 left, 106 center, 106 right, 107, 132, 140, 145 right, 164, 173, 174, 175, 180, 181, 206, 216, 218, 219, 220, 221, 226, 227, 228, 229, 230, 231, 232, 233, 251, 273 right, 274, 293, 294, 295, 296, 297, 348, 349, 350, 351, 352, 353, 355, 356, 357 left, 357 right, 378, 379, 388, 399 right, 413, 414, 415, 416, 417, 438, 439, 455 left, 488, 489, 490, 491, 494, 495, 496 left, 496 right, 497, 504 left, 504 right, 505, 511, 569 left, 569 right, 570, 582, 583, 584, 585, 586 left, 586 right, 587, 590 left, 598, 599, 600, 601, 602, 603, 604, 619, 629
Walter Bibikow/Agefotostock/Contrasto: Page 485
Massimo Borchi/Archivio White Star: Pages 310, 311, 553 left, 553 center, 553 right, 606, 607, 624, 625
Livio Bourbon/Archivio White Star: Pages 33 right, 92, 93 left, 93 right, 616, 617
Tom Boyden/Lonely Planet Images: Pages 368, 369
Gary Braasch/Corbis/Contrasto: Page 255
Wojtek Buss: Pages 608-609
John Carnemolla/ Australian Picture Library/Corbis/Contrasto: Pages 526-527
Mario Colonel: Page 217
Pablo Corral Vega/Corbis/Contrasto: Page 264
M. Delpho/Blickwnkel: Pages 288, 289
Jay Dickman/Corbis/Contrasto: Page 315
Jean Du Boisberranger/Hemispheres Images: Pages 90, 91, 306, 307
Ric Ergenbright/Corbis/Contrasto: Page 157
ESA/PLI/Corbis/Contrasto: Page 16
Eye Ubiquitous/Corbis/Contrasto: Pages 462 right, 463
Jean Paul Ferrero/Auscape: Pages 436, 437
Kevin Fleming/Corbis/Contrasto: Page 188
Stephane Frances/Hemispheres Images: Pages 408, 506-507
Stuart Franklin/Magnum Photos/Contrasto: Page 522
John Frumm/Hemispheres Images: Pages 86, 410-411
Marc Garanger/Corbis/Contrasto: Pages 446, 447
Bertrand Gardel/Hemispheres Images: Pages 376, 452, 453, 483, 565, 626
Ron Garnett: Pages 117, 195, 244, 245, 250, 377, 532
Alfio Garozzo/Archivio White Star: Pages 396-397
Lowell Georgia/Corbis/Contrasto: Page 141
Gil Giuglio/Hemispheres Images: Page 612
Manfred Gottschalk/Lonely Planet Images: Page 358
Annie Griffiths Belt/Corbis/Contrasto: Pages 270, 428, 429
Itamar Grinberg/Archivio White Star: Pages 180, 426, 427, 510, 605
Christopher Groenhout/Lonely Planet Images: Page 435
David Hannah/ Lonely Planet Images: Page 525
Lynda Harper/ HedgehogHouse: Page 273 left
Hannu Hautala: Pages 280, 281, 282, 283, 332, 333
Jason Hawkes: Pages 286, 287, 364, 465, 472, 473, 475, 498, 514 left, 514 right
Jason Hawkes/Corbis/Contrasto: Page 576
Heuer/Laif/Contrasto: Page 213
Manfred Horvath/ Anzenberger/Contrasto: Page 486
Hans-Peter Huber/Sime/Sie: Page 564

Photo credits

Hervé Hughes/Hemispheres Images: Pages 464, 534, 535
Image 2D: Page 212
ImagineChina/Contrasto: Pages 432, 610
Peter Johnson/Corbis/Contrasto: Pages 421, 422-423
Ed Kashi/Corbis/Contrasto: Page 346
Frank Krahmer: Page 205 right
Kirchner/Laif/Contrasto: Pages 480, 481
Bob Krist/Corbis/Contrasto: Pages 118, 194
Dan Lamont/Corbis/Contrasto: Page 308
Robert Landau/Corbis/Contrasto: Page 542
David Lawrence/Corbis/Contrasto: Pages 524, 529
P. Lavoretti/Panda Photo: Pages 292, 367
Lester Lefkowitz/Corbis/Contrasto: Page 545
Charles & Josette Lenars/Corbis/Contrasto: Page 618
George D.Lepp/Corbis/Contrasto: Page 260
Marcello Libra/Archivio White Star: Pages 176, 354, 484
Liu Liqun/Corbis/Contrasto: Page 611
Yang Liu/Corbis/Contrasto: Page 521
Ian Lockwood/Naturel Picture Library: Page 302
Marka Collection: Page 214
Steve McCurry/Magnum Photos/Contrasto: Page 613
Colin Monteath/Hedgehog House: Pages 235, 240, 271
Kevin R. Morris/Corbis/Contrasto: Page 533
Juan Carlos Munoz/Agefotostock/Contrasto: Pages 394-395
Charles O'Rear/Corbis/Contrasto: Pages 17[illegible], 198, 365
Panorama Stock: Pages [illegible]84-135, 300, 301, 362, 363, 43[illegible], 431, 516, 517 left, 517 right, 518
Daniel Philippe: Pages 501, 502, 503 left, 503 right
Premium/Agefotostock/Marka: Page 482
Raach/Laif/Contrasto: Page 561
José Fuste Raga/Agefotostock/Marka: Page 515
Federico Raiser/K3 Photo: Pages 290-291
Luciano Ramires/Archivio White Star: Pages 580, 581
Steve Raymer/Corbis/Contrasto: Pages 500 left, 500 right
Roberto Rinaldi/Sime/Sie: Page 108
René Robert: Pages 222-223
Tim Rock/Lonely Planet Images: Page 109
Bill Ross/Corbis/Contrasto: Page 257
Guido Alberto Rossi/The Image Bank: Pages 23-23, 52 left, 52 right, 53, 54, 55, 60 left, 60 right, 61, 62, 63, 158, 159, 224, 225, 338, 339, 640
Galen Rowell/Corbis/Contrasto: Pages 237, 261, 262, 263, 265, 266, 267, 268, 269
Royalty-Free/Corbis/Contrasto: Pages 88, 136, 236, 462 left, 543
Dae Sasitorn/lastrefuge.co.uk: Pages 46, 47, 48, 49, 50, 51, 54, 155, 336, 337, 577
Doug Scott/Agefotostock/Contrasto: Page 299
Kevin Schafer/Corbis/Contrasto: Pages 143, 630 right
Giovanni Simeone/ Sime/Sie: Pages 72, 73, 126
Douglas Slone/Corbis/Contrasto: Page 541
Dick & Pip Smith/Hedgehog House: Pages 238-239
Joseph Sohm/ChromoSohm Inc./Corbis/Contrasto: Pages 247, 248, 249
G. Stahlbauer/Blickwinkel: Page 156
Hans Strand: Page 331
Ted Streshinsky/Corbis/Contrasto: Page 199
Oliver Strewe/Lonely Planet Images: Page 160
Studio Murai: Page 523 left
Keren Su/China Span: Page 433
Jim Sugar/Corbis/Contrasto: Page 254
Torleif Svensson/Corbis/Contrasto: Page 359
Pascal Tournaire: Page 2[illegible]3
Sandro Vannini/Corbis/Contrasto: Page 215
Bill Varie/Corbis/Contrasto: Page 2[illegible]6
Giulio Veggi/Archivio White Star: Pages 145 left, 163, 166, 167, 42[illegible]-425, 508, 509
David Wall: Page 528
U.Walz/Blickwinkel: Page 393
Patrick Ward/Corbis/Contrasto: Page [illegible]74
Jim Wark: Pages 2-3, 114, 115, 116, 1[illegible] 120, 121, 122, 123, 124, 125, 179, 192, 193, 19[illegible], 252, 253, 256, 258-259, [illegible] 309, 3[illegible], 324, 379, 380, 381, 440, [illegible] 448, 449, 555, 620, 621
Adrian Warren/lastrefuge.co.uk: Pages 58, 161, 316-317, 390, 391, 392, 4[illegible], 407
Martin Wendler/Nhpa: Pages 313, [illegible]
Phil M Weymouth/Lonely Planet Images: Page 519
Ralph White/Corbis/Contrasto: Pages 138, 139
Pawel Wysocki/Hemispheres Images: Pages 87, 128, 129,
Adam Woolfitt/Corbis/Contrasto: Page 89
Michael S. Yamashita/Corbis/Contrasto: Page 520
Zamut Art/Gamma/Contrasto: Page [illegible]
Jim Zuckerman/Corbis/Contrasto: Page 487
Cover: Marcello Bertinetti/Archivio White Star
Back cover: Antonio Attini/Archivio White Star

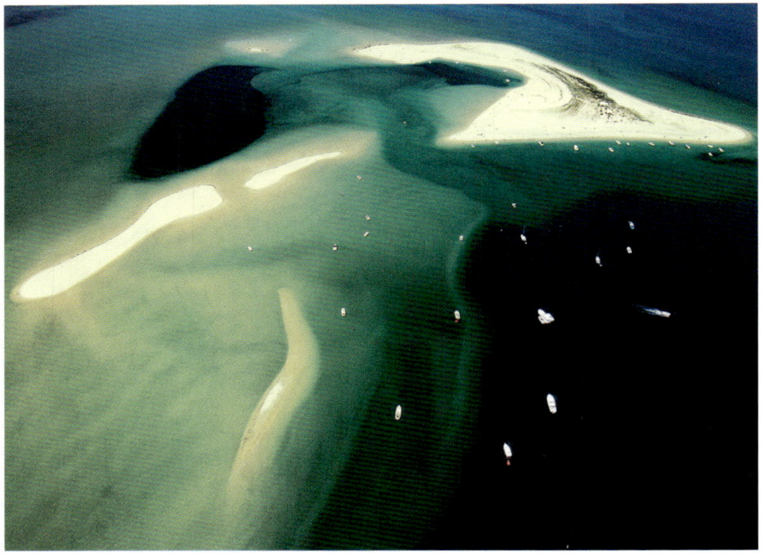

640

The Bassin d'Arcachon, southwest of Bordeaux in France.

FLYING HIGH